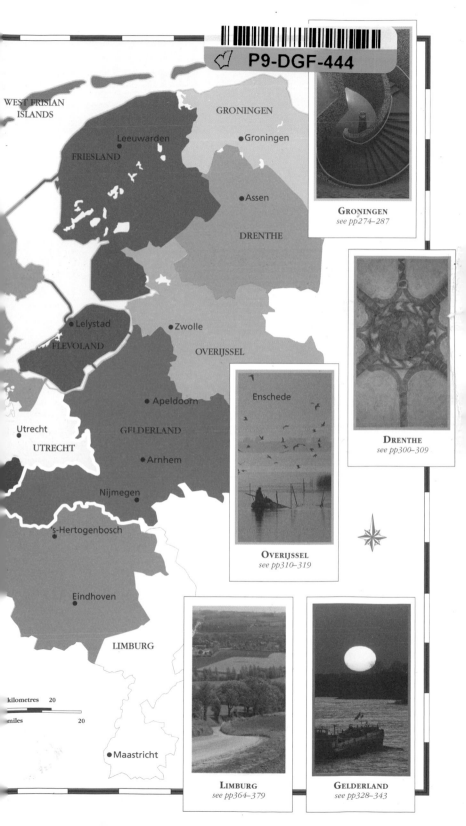

P9-DGF-444

WEST FRISIAN
ISLANDS

GRONINGEN

Leeuwarden
FRIESLAND

● Groningen

● Assen

DRENTHE

GRONINGEN
see pp274–287

● Lelystad

FLEVOLAND

● Zwolle

OVERIJSSEL

DRENTHE
see pp300–309

● Apeldoorn

Enschede

Utrecht

UTRECHT

GELDERLAND

● Arnhem

Nijmegen

's-Hertogenbosch

OVERIJSSEL
see pp310–319

Eindhoven

LIMBURG

kilometres   20

miles   20

● Maastricht

LIMBURG
see pp364–379

GELDERLAND
see pp328–343

EYEWITNESS TRAVEL GUIDES

HOLLAND

EYEWITNESS TRAVEL GUIDES

HOLLAND

Main contributor: GERARD M.L. HARMANS

LONDON, NEW YORK,
MELBOURNE, MUNICH AND DELHI
www.dk.com

Produced by Van Reemst Uitgeverij/Unieboek bv

MAIN CONTRIBUTOR Gerard M.L. Harmans
DESIGN Studio Putto, De Rijp   ART EDITOR Dick Polman
EDITORIAL (DUTCH ORIGINAL) *de Redactie*, boekverzorgers, Amsterdam
PHOTOGRAPHERS Max Alexander, ANWB Audiovisuele Dienst
(Thijs Tuurenhout), George Burggraaff, Jurjen Drenth,
Rubert Horrox, Kim Sayer, Herman Scholten
ILLUSTRATORS Hilbert Bolland, Jan Egas, Gieb van Enckevort,
Nick Gibbard, Mark Jurriëns, Maltings Partnership,
Derrick Stone, Khoobie Verwer, Martin Woodward
CARTOGRAPHY Jane Hanson, Armand Haye, Lovell Johns Limited
(Oxford, UK), Phil Rose, Jennifer Skelley, Peter de Vries
PICTURE RESEARCH Harry Bunk
SENIOR PRODUCTION CONTROLLER Sarah Dodd

ENGLISH-LANGUAGE ADAPTATION PRODUCED BY
International Book Productions Inc.,
25A Morrow Ave, Toronto, Ontario M6R 2H9, Canada
MANAGING EDITOR Barbara Hopkinson   EDITOR Judy Phillips
DTP DESIGNERS Dietmar Kokemohr, Sean Gaherty

Reproduced in Singapore by Colourscan
Printed and bound by Toppan Printing Co. (Shenzhen Ltd)

First American Edition, 2003

05 06 07 08 09 10 9 8 7 6 5 4 3 2 1

Published in the United States by
DK Publishing, Inc., 375 Hudson Street,
New York, New York 10014

Reprinted with revisions 2005

Copyright © 2003, 2005 Dorling Kindersley Limited, London

ISBN 0-7894-9305-5
ISSN 1542-1554

FLOORS ARE REFERRED TO THROUGHOUT IN ACCORDANCE WITH BRITISH USAGE;
IE THE "FIRST FLOOR" IS THE FLOOR ABOVE GROUND LEVEL.

See our complete product line at
www.dk.com

**The information in this
Dorling Kindersley Travel Guide is checked regularly.**
Every effort has been made to ensure that this book is as up-to-date
as possible at the time of going to press. Some details, however,
such as telephone numbers, opening hours, prices, gallery hanging
arrangements and travel information are liable to change. The
publishers cannot accept responsibility for any consequences arising
from the use of this book, nor for any material on third party
websites, and cannot guarantee that any website address in this
book will be a suitable source of travel information. We value the
views and suggestions of our readers very highly. Please write to:
Publisher, DK Eyewitness Travel Guides,
Dorling Kindersley, 80 Strand, London WC2R 0RL, Great Britain.

CONTENTS

HOW TO USE
THIS GUIDE *6*

Zeeland's coat of arms

INTRODUCING
HOLLAND

PUTTING HOLLAND
ON THE MAP *10*

Girl with a Pearl Earring (1665)
by Johannes Vermeer

A PORTRAIT OF
HOLLAND *12*

HOLLAND THROUGH
THE YEAR *32*

THE HISTORY OF
HOLLAND *38*

◁ **A typical Dutch landscape with cows, pastures and windmills – here near the little town of Woudrichem**

The 15th-century Koppelpoort by Amersfoort

Thialf fans *(see p298)*

The imposing Sint Jan
in 's Hertogenbosch

HOW TO USE THIS GUIDE

THIS GUIDE HELPS YOU get the most from your stay in Holland. The first section, *Introducing Holland,* shows where the country is on the map and puts it in its historical and cultural context. Chapters on the provinces and the capital, Amsterdam, describe the most important sights and places of interest. Features cover topics from architecture to tulip growing. They are accompanied by detailed and helpful illustrations. *Travellers' Needs* gives specifics on where to stay and where to eat and drink, while the *Survival Guide* contains practical information on everything from the public telephone system to transport and personal safety.

AMSTERDAM

Amsterdam is divided into five tourist areas. The corresponding chapters all begin with a list of numbered sights and places of interest, which are plotted on the Area Map. The information for each sight follows this numerical order, making sights easy to locate within the chapter.

Sights at a Glance groups the sights by category: historical buildings and monuments, streets, squares and gardens, museums and churches.

All pages about Amsterdam are marked in red.

1 Area Map
This map is numbered to show the most important attractions. They are also given in the Street-by-Street section on pages 148–9.

A locator map places the district in the context of the rest of the city.

A recommended route covers the most interesting streets in the area.

2 Street-by-Street Map
This map gives a detailed summary of the heart of the five main tourist areas of the city.

Stars indicate sights that should not be missed.

3 Detailed Information
All main attractions are described individually, including their addresses, opening hours and other practical information. Keys to the symbols used are on the rear flap of this book.

1 Introduction
The scenery, history and character of each province are outlined here, showing how the area has changed through the centuries, and what it has to offer today's visitor.

THE NETHERLANDS AREA BY AREA

The Netherlands is divided into 12 provinces. Each of these provinces, Amsterdam and the West Frisian Islands are dealt with in separate chapters. The most interesting towns, villages and places are shown on the Pictorial Map.

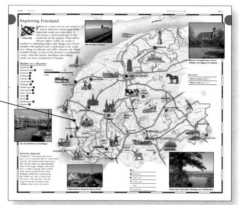

2 Pictorial Map
This map shows the main roads and the main tourist attractions of an area, and also gives useful information about driving and rail travel.

Each province
is colour-coded for easy reference.

3 Detailed Information
Major sights and attractions are described in detail in the order in which they are numbered on the Pictorial Map. Within each entry is detailed information on buildings, parks, museums and other sights.

Story boxes explore specific topics.

The Visitors' Checklist
gives practical information to help you plan your visit.

4 The Top Sights
These sights are described on two or more pages. Cutaway illustrations and floor plans show the most important buildings, museums and other sights.

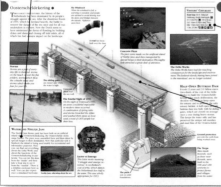

INTRODUCING
HOLLAND

Putting Holland on the Map

THE NETHERLANDS IS SITUATED in Western Europe, bordering Belgium to the south and Germany to the east. To its north and west is the North Sea. The country is popularly known as Holland, although the provinces of North and South Holland form only part of the Netherlands in reality. Since the completion of the Deltawerken (Delta Works), the coastline is some 800 km (500 miles) in length. The country's major waterways and excellent road and rail systems make it an important gateway to the rest of Europe, and to Germany in particular. Approximately one-sixth of its total area is covered with water. The Netherlands has a population of about 16 million.

Satellite photo of the northern part of the western Netherlands with the IJsselmeer

Hull, Harwich

0 kilometres   20

0 miles   20

Peat lake region near Utrecht

WEST FRISIAN ISLANDS

Waddenzee

Den Helder

North Sea

NORTH HOLLAND

Enkhuizen   IJsselmeer

Newcastle

Alkmaar

Markermeer

IJmuiden

AMSTERDAM

FLEV

Schiphol

Amersfoort

Leiden

SOUTH HOLLAND   Utrecht

THE HAGUE   Gouda   UTRECH

Hoek van Holland   Delft   A12

Rotterdam   Lek

Rotterdam   Waal

A15

Dordrecht

Zierikzee   N59   Maas   's-Hertogenbosch

A59   Breda   Tilburg   NOR

ZEELAND   A58   Eindhove

Middelburg   A58   Eindhoven

A67

A21

Antwerp   BELGIUM

N617   Antwerpen   Albertkanaal

N276   A13

Mechelen   Demer

A2

BRUSSELS   Leuven

Zaventem   A3

◁ *View of Delft* (c.1660), a masterpiece by Johannes Vermeer

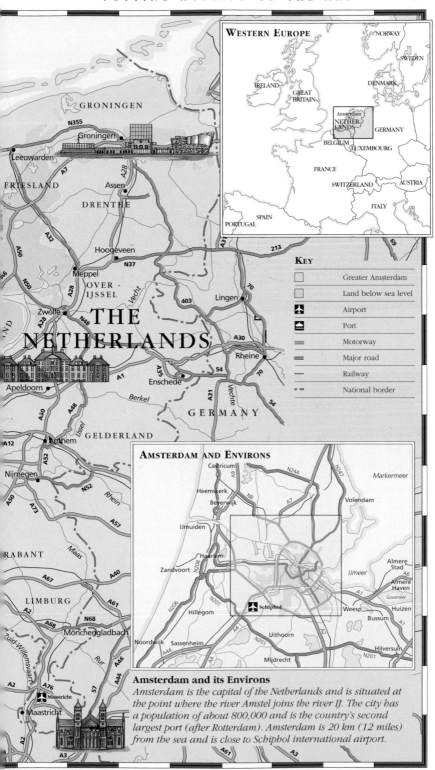

KEY

☐	Greater Amsterdam
☐	Land below sea level
✈	Airport
⚓	Port
═══	Motorway
───	Major road
───	Railway
─ ─ ─	National border

Amsterdam and its Environs

Amsterdam is the capital of the Netherlands and is situated at the point where the river Amstel joins the river IJ. The city has a population of about 800,000 and is the country's second largest port (after Rotterdam). Amsterdam is 20 km (12 miles) from the sea and is close to Schiphol international airport.

A Portrait of Holland

F ROM THE FRISIAN ISLANDS *in the north to Zeeland in the south, the Netherlands is a place of contrasts, with fine sandy beaches, picturesque villages and vibrant towns with multilingual and outward-looking people. The mighty river Rhine bisects the country, bringing trade and prosperity from far and wide.*

The landscape of what is now the Netherlands has changed considerably over the past 2,000 years. Since Roman times, large tracts of land have been swallowed up by the sea in areas such as Zeeland and the former Zuiderzee. Old maps show that during the Middle Ages almost half of today's provinces of North Holland and South Holland were under water. Since then, large parts of this land have been reclaimed. The constant battle with the sea reached its height with the Delta Works. This massive hydraulic engineering achievement *(see pp244–5)* was designed to protect the southwestern part of the country against flooding. The project was started after the disastrous floods of 1953, in which more than 1,800 people died, and has proved to be a huge success.

Typical cottage in Marken

The Netherlands covers an area of 41,547 sq km (16,040 sq miles), about one-tenth the size of California. With some 16 million inhabitants, this means a population density of around 380 per sq km (1,000 per sq mile), making it the third most densely populated country in Europe after Monaco and Malta. However, this is not something that is readily noticeable to visitors outside the main cities, as the flat landscape with its sweeping vistas seems anything but crowded.

Dutch people are friendly and outgoing. They care about social issues and the environment and almost everyone speaks English, many quite fluently. They live in a country that is neat and tidy, where there is excellent public transport and where visitors find it easy to get around.

The pier, the focus of social life on the beach at Scheveningen

◁ **Bulb-grower in his tulip field near Ursem in North Holland**

Holland's dunes, a natural barrier against the sea and an important water catchment area

INTRODUCING HOLLAND

Although the Netherlands is this country's official name, most of the rest of the world call it Holland. However, Holland actually comprises only 2 of the 13 Dutch provinces. North and South Holland contain the country's three main cities of Amsterdam, Rotterdam and Den Haag (The Hague), which together with the cities of Dordrecht, Utrecht, Leiden and Haarlem form a horseshoe-shaped conurbation known as the Randstad, literally, "rim city" *(see pp164–5)*.

When people ask, "What is the capital of the Netherlands?", the smiling Dutch tend to reply: "Our capital is Amsterdam, and the government sits

in The Hague." Amsterdam is the most cosmopolitan of these three cities, as well as the the country's centre for cultural life. Rotterdam, home to the Europoort, one of the world's largest ports, is the Netherlands' industrial centre. The Hague is the seat of government and quarters many prestigious institutions, including the International Court of Justice. With its neighbouring seaside resort of Scheveningen, The Hague is where most of the foreign embassies and consulates are situated.

Holland can be roughly divided into the Protestant north and Catholic south, separated by the great rivers flowing into the North Sea: the Rhine, the Waal and the Maas (Meuse). The people in the north of the country tend to be more sober and matter-of-fact, whereas those of the south tend to be much more flamboyant in their lifestyles.

SOCIETY AND POLITICS

Social life in the Netherlands was for many years based on the idea of *verzuiling,* wherein society lay on four pillars *(zuilen)* on which different sections of society rested their beliefs: Protestantism, Catholicism, liberalism and socialism. At one time, these groups had almost no contact with one another. Catholics would always vote for the *Katholieke Volkspartij,* join

Shoppers at the Albert Cuypmarkt in Amsterdam

Catholic trade unions, base their social lives on Catholic societies and send their children to Catholic schools. The Protestant "pillar", on the other hand, was formed of two main factions: the Dutch Reformed Church and the Calvinist Church. Both had their own political parties, their own trades unions and their own schools and societies. As for socialism and liberalism, the division was less explicit, though the gap between the world of the "workers" and that of the "entrepreneurs" was huge.

View of picturesque Dordrecht marina

A major step towards unity came in 1980, when the three largest religion-based political parties united in the CDA, a Christian Democratic alliance that went on to dominate government coalitions for the next 20 years. The gap between the other parties closed in 1994, when the Labour Party (PvdA) and the small D66 formed a coalition with the conservative Liberal Party (VVD). This resulted in a tripartite "purple" cabinet, which appeared so successful that the coalition was continued in 1998.

A hollow post mill in the polder landscape

The Dutch elections of May 2002 surprised everybody as the country moved to the right of the political spectrum. The assassination, nine days before, of the popular, flamboyant and openly gay Pim Fortuyn had shocked the entire country. With his unyielding views on Muslims and immigration, and his criticism of the establishment, Fortuyn was the antithesis of the Dutch tradition of consensual politics. Formerly the leader of the Livable Netherlands party, and with ambitions to be prime minister, he was ousted for his right-wing views and formed his own party, Lijst Pim Fortuyn (LPF). Despite the loss of their

The de Geul river at Epen in Zuid Limburg

Football fans sporting orange costumes

charismatic leader, LPF became the second largest party in the Lower House; only the Christian Democrats (CDA) did better. The coalition parties of the former government lost 43 seats between them, making this the biggest shake-up in Dutch politics since World War II.

The main challenges facing the Dutch government in the next few years are the social problems brought about by increasing immigration, voters' demands for improvements in both education and health care, and the slowing economy.

LANGUAGE AND CULTURE

Dutch, a Germanic language, is used by more than 20 million people in Holland, Flanders and parts of the former Dutch colonies. Afrikaans, a language of South Africa closely related to Dutch, is regarded as a separate language, as is Frisian, which is spoken by more than 400,000 people in the province of Friesland. Dutch has many dialects, each of which has numerous regional differences. However, these differences are gradually disappearing because of the far-reaching influences of radio and television.

Culturally, Holland has plenty to offer. The country's colourful history is reflected in its many old buildings and large number of valuable museum collections. Exhibits range from those with local themes to world-famous art such as the collections in Amsterdam's Rijksmuseum *(see pp122–5)* and the Mauritshuis in The Hague *(see pp220–21)*. In addition to the major museums of cities such as Amsterdam and Rotterdam, contemporary art can be seen in countless galleries all over the country, as well as in the profusion of works displayed in the streets and at the numerous local markets. As for the performing arts, more variety is available today than ever before. Holland boasts a number of renowned orchestras and is an established name in ballet. Stage and theatre have recently marked a shift from experimental to more conventional performances.

Dutch beer, fresh from the tap

THE DUTCH WAY OF LIFE

The German poet Heinrich Heine (1797–1856) described Holland as a place where "everything happens 50 years later than anywhere else". But today, anyone who reflects on the tolerant Dutch attitude towards drugs, the country's relaxed laws regarding euthanasia and the popular opposition to the deployment of nuclear weapons will come away with a different picture. In fact, the Netherlands was the first country to legalize gay marriages, regulate prostitution, officially sanction euthanasia and tolerate the over-the-counter sale of marijuana. Even the attitude of the Dutch towards their monarchy is modern – they are regarded with an affection more commonly extended to family members than to rulers.

Since the depredations of World War II, much has changed in the way the

A herring stall in Amsterdam

Dutch live their lives. Thrift and moderation, the two traditional virtues of Calvinism, are no longer writ large in society. A measure of flamboyance is slowly but surely making its way into the Dutch lifestyle. Today the Dutch eat out enthusiastically as well as often. Restaurant and cooking columns are now featured in newspapers and magazines, and there are many cookery programmes aired on television.

A Dutch production of *The Three Musketeers*

Dutch drinking habits have also changed. On fine-weather days, people throng the pavement cafés to end the working day with a beer or a glass of wine. They also drink a great deal more wine with meals than once was the case. As well, the renowned Dutch gin, *jenever*, with its various types *(see p426)*, is still popular. Nevertheless, overall per capita alcohol consumption is reasonable.

As soon as they have spare time, Dutch people head outdoors, often on bicycles, which are enormously popu-

lar in Holland. Love of the environment is a strong Dutch characteristic, and the Dutch are great supporters of renewable energy resources.

Outdoors, there are literally hundreds of organized rambling and cycling tours, funfairs and theme parks, as well as a wide assortment of festivals, holiday celebrations and other events held throughout the year *(see pp32–5)*. And wherever you are, you will always find a flea market – with items ranging from flowers to antiques for sale – within a short distance.

The new-found *joie de vivre* of the Dutch reflects the general trend evident in Western European countries. This is the result of a new leisure culture, one which is more "sensory". Less time is devoted to reading and contemplation as food, drink, sport and the arts all take on increasingly prominent roles. Politically, socially and culturally, the Dutch are embracing the 21st century with confidence.

De Waalkade, the promenade of Nijmegen

Holding Back the Water

Recent floods in Holland's river valleys, particularly the one which occurred in 1995, when 200,000 people needed to be evacuated from the area, have shown what a threat water continues to pose to the Netherlands. The only way the sea can be held back is by dams, but in order to contain rivers at high tide, the country is adopting a new approach, that of "controlled flooding".

Flooded farm in Gelderland (1995)

Since the 11th century, increasing areas of land have been reclaimed from the sea. Countless dykes were built over the centuries using elementary tools, such as spades and "burries", a kind of stretcher. The illustration shows a breached dyke being filled.

At the Hook of Holland, the sea is not held back by dunes, as it is along the entire coast of North Holland and South Holland, but by a dyke.

The lowest point in Holland is the Zuidplaspolder at Gouda, 6.74 m (22 ft) below sea level.

At Krimpen, the IJssel discharges into the Nieuwe Maas.

The Krimpenerwaard, between the IJssel and the Lek, consists of high-quality hayfields and pasture.

The River Lek

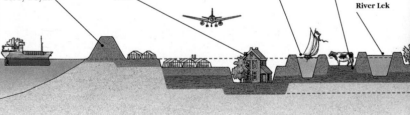

A large part of Holland (blue on the map) is below sea level. These areas have been called "laag-Nederland", or the "low Nether-lands", and have only come into being over the past 10,000 years.

KEY

☐ Above sea level

☐ Below sea level

CROSS-SECTION OF HOLLAND

This cross-section of Holland follows a straight line from the Hook of Holland to Achterhoek (see Locator Map) and shows clearly how low much of the land is. Only some 65 km (40 miles) inland, at Neder-Betuwe, does the ground rise above sea level. The lowest point in Holland is the Zuidplaspolder, which is more than 6.74 m (22 ft) below sea level. Comparatively elevated areas like the Betuwe have nothing to fear from the sea, but this does not mean that they are not at risk of flooding: the Waal River, which runs more or less parallel to this cross-section, may flood at unusually high tides or after a heavy rainfall.

Floods in the river valleys *in 1993 and 1995 led to the implementation of large-scale dyke reinforcement projects, known as the "delta plan for the large rivers". Old flood channels were also repaired as a matter of priority to allow more water to drain off.*

THE STORY OF HANS BRINKER

The tale of the little boy who held his finger in a leak in a dyke to hold back the sea is not a figure from Dutch folklore but probably originated in the book *Hans Brinker, or, The Silver Skates,* by American writer Mary Mapes Dodge (1831–1905). It tells the story of a poverty-stricken boy who helps his ailing father. Hans and the doctor in the book (Boerhaave) are historical figures. The story was published in over 100 editions in Dodge's lifetime.

Statue of Hans Brinker in Spaarndam

Neder-Betuwe is probably Holland's most important fruit-growing region.

Over-Betuwe is an area of fruit orchards, horticulture and cattle farming.

The Pannerdens Canal currently connects the Upper and Lower Rhineland.

Montferland is an important region of lateral moraines. These moraines were formed by the actions of glaciers.

67.1 m (220 ft) above sea level

Merwede Canal

Sea level

6.74 m (22 ft) below sea level

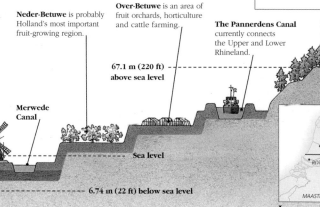

AMSTERDAM
ROTTERDAM
MAASTRICHT

LOCATOR MAP

CROSS-SECTION OF A MODERN RIVER DYKE

Blocks of boulder clay protect the dyke from the wash of the river. The water seeps through the water-resistant clay layer slowly, draining off quickly only once it reaches the sand layer. This way the body of the dyke stays dry and hard.

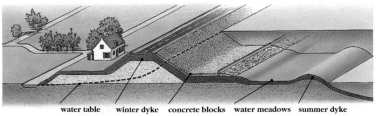

water table   winter dyke   concrete blocks   water meadows   summer dyke

Farmhouses and Windmills

I N THE MAINLY FLAT LANDSCAPE of Holland,
farmhouses always stand in the shelter of trees.
Windmills, on the other hand, needing as much
wind as they can get, usually stand in very
exposed areas. Both are highly valued because
they are so picturesque, and it is easy to forget
that they actually belong in the category of
functional architecture. How a windmill works is
explained on page 177.

*In the farmhouses of North
Holland, the barn, threshing-
floor and house are all under one
pyramidal roof.*

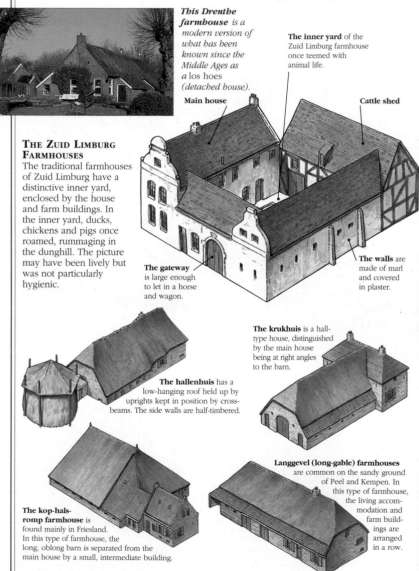

*This Drenthe
farmhouse is a
modern version of
what has been
known since the
Middle Ages as
a* los hoes
(detached house).

The inner yard of the
Zuid Limburg farmhouse
once teemed with
animal life.

Main house

Cattle shed

THE ZUID LIMBURG FARMHOUSES

The traditional farmhouses
of Zuid Limburg have a
distinctive inner yard,
enclosed by the house
and farm buildings. In
the inner yard, ducks,
chickens and pigs once
roamed, rummaging in
the dunghill. The picture
may have been lively but
was not particularly
hygienic.

The gateway
is large enough
to let in a horse
and wagon.

The walls are
made of marl
and covered
in plaster.

The krukhuis is a hall-
type house, distinguished
by the main house
being at right angles
to the barn.

The hallenhuis has a
low-hanging roof held up by
uprights kept in position by cross-
beams. The side walls are half-timbered.

Langgevel (long-gable) farmhouses
are common on the sandy ground
of Peel and Kempen. In
this type of farmhouse,
the living accom-
modation and
farm build-
ings are
arranged
in a row.

**The kop-hals-
romp farmhouse** is
found mainly in Friesland.
In this type of farmhouse, the
long, oblong barn is separated from the
main house by a small, intermediate building.

PALTROK MILLS

Paltrok, or smock, mills were developed for use as sawmills around 1600. They were so called because of their resemblance to the paltrok, a smock that was commonly worn at the time. These windmills were mounted on a circular track, allowing them to rotate in their entirety. Generally, smock mills were used to saw *wagenschot* – entire oak trunks that had been split in two.

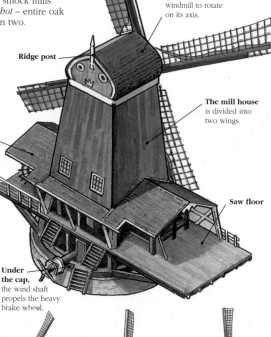

Sail

Wheels allow the windmill to rotate on its axis.

Ridge post

Underneath the porch is a crane for lifting the tree trunks from the water.

The mill house is divided into two wings.

Saw floor

Under the cap, the wind shaft propels the heavy brake wheel.

Belt or berg mills have an extra-high body because of surrounding buildings or trees. A mound (berg) *made at the base of the mill provides access to the sails.*

Stander (post) mills are the oldest type of mill in Holland. The entire wooden body rotates on a central wooden post. Most post mills were used to grind corn.

Wipmolen are a later version of the stander mills and were designed to pump water. The smaller body rotates on a fixed, pyramidal base.

Stellingmolen, like the belt mill, has an extra-tall body. This type was used to produce dye, oil or paper. An encircling platform halfway up the body enables the mill to be rotated and the sails to be reefed on the wings.

Toren mills (tower mills) have a brick cylindrical body and a cap that can be rotated from inside. Only four survive in Holland today. The oldest one can be seen at Achterboek near Zeddam.

The tjasker was used to drain small areas of water. It consisted of a sloping axle with sails at one end and an Archimedes' screw at the other.

Dutch Scientific Breakthroughs

Coster,
Haarlem

The Dutch have put their stamp on many scientific and technical fields, from early book printing (Laurens Janszoon Coster, 1423) to the development of satellites. The country has enjoyed two distinct scientific Golden Ages. The first was in the 17th century, when geniuses such as Simon Stevin, Anthonie van Leeuwenhoek and Christiaan Huygens were acclaimed across Europe. The second period of scientific achievement, from the end of the 1800s, was led by Jacobus Henricus van 't Hoff, Pieter Zeeman, Hendrik Antoon Lorentz and Heike Kamerlingh-Onnes, who were all awarded Nobel Prizes.

Willem Beukelszoon
Around 1380, Willem Beukelszoon discovered how herring could be cured. He showed how the gills, gullet and guts could be removed with a special tool, and the fish preserved in salt while still on board. This allowed the fishing fleet to travel further and brought prosperity to Holland.

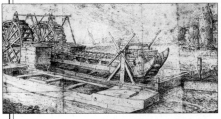

Dredgers
The first dredger was made by the Dutch carpenter Cornelis Dirkzoon Muys around 1600. The dredging industry is based in Sliedrecht (South Holland) and has developed into an international business. Dredging is sometimes needed to deepen water channels, but more commonly is a means of obtaining sand, gravel or other materials.

Adjustment screw

Objective

Lens

Van Leeuwenhoek's Microscope
Zacharias Jansen seems to have made the first microscope around 1595, but it was Anthonie van Leeuwenhoek (1632–1723) who, using lenses he ground himself, made countless scientific discoveries. He was the first to identify bacteria, blood cells and spermatozoa.

17th-century drawing of spermatozoa

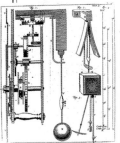

Pendulum Clock
Christiaan Huygens (1629–95), an astronomer, satisfied his need for a very precise way of measuring time by inventing the pendulum clock. Huygens went on to map the rings and moon of Saturn, and wrote the first book on probability theory.

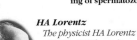

HA Lorentz
The physicist HA Lorentz (1853–1928) made important contributions to a number of fields of study, such as electromagnetism, quantum mechanics, relativity, gravity, radiation and thermodynamics.

Pieter Pauw
(1564–1617)

Dissection table

Anatomical Theatre
The famous anatomical theatre opened by Professor Pieter Pauw in 1593 has been reconstructed in the Museum Boerhaave in Leiden. In Pauw's time, dissections of human corpses were open to the public. Many esteemed professors lectured in the theatre, among them Herman Boerhaave (1668–1738).

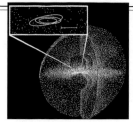

Oort Cloud

Comets can be periodic or non-periodic. The former come from the Kuiper belt, and the latter from the Oort cloud. These "comet reservoirs" were discovered around 1950 by Dutch astronomers GP Kuiper and JH Oort.

Einthoven's Cardiogram

Willem Einthoven (1860–1927) made the first electrocardiogram in 1901, with the help of a sensitive string galvanometer he had constructed himself. In 1906, he even managed to make an electrocardiogram for a patient at the end of a phone line.

JH van 't Hoff

Chemist JH van 't Hoff (1852–1911) was born in Rotterdam. He was the first to imagine molecules as three-dimensional structures, and was therefore the founder of stereochemistry. He was also an early pioneer in physical chemistry. He won a Nobel Prize for his research into thermodynamics and osmotic pressure.

Dutch Nobel Prizewinners

There have been 18 Dutch Nobel laureates since the prizes started in 1901. The very first award for Chemistry went to JH van 't Hoff. And when the Economics prize started, in 1969, it was awarded to Jan Tinbergen, father of macroeconomics.

1901 Jacobus Henricus van 't Hoff (Chemistry)
1902 Hendrik Antoon Lorentz and Pieter Zeeman (Physics)
1910 Johannes Diederik van der Waals (Physics)
1911 Tobias Michaël Carel Asser (Peace)
1913 Heike Kamerlingh-Onnes (Physics)
1924 Willem Einthoven (Medicine)
1929 Christiaan Eijkman (Medicine)
1936 Peter Debeye (Chemistry)
1953 Frits Zernike (Physics)
1969 Jan Tinbergen (Economics)
1973 Nicolaas Tinbergen (Medicine)
1975 Tjalling Koopmans (Economics)
1981 Nicolaas Bloembergen (Physics)
1984 Simon van der Meer (Physics)
1995 Paul Crutzen (Chemistry)
2000 Gerard 't Hooft and Martin Veltman (Physics)

Nicolaas Tinbergen

Tinbergen (1907–88), together with the Austrian Konrad Lorenz, was the founder of ethology, the study of animal behaviour. He taught in Leiden and Oxford and wrote The Study of Instinct, the first ethology textbook.

V-shaped drivebelt

Variomatic System

In 1958, van Doorne's Automobielfabrieken in Eindhoven brought out the DAF 600 passenger car. This was equipped with HJ van Doorne's own gearless automatic transmission system.

Expandable disk, for adjusting the diameter of the drivebelt

The **compact disc** is a Dutch invention, developed by the electronics company Philips and launched in 1982.

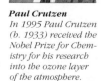

Paul Crutzen

In 1995 Paul Crutzen (b. 1933) received the Nobel Prize for Chemistry for his research into the ozone layer of the atmosphere.

't Hooft and Veltman, winners of the Nobel Physics prize in 2000

The Dutch Masters

THE PROLIFERATION OF PAINTING in the Netherlands during the 17th century – the country's Golden Age – corresponded with the great demand for paintings among newly rich townspeople. The lack of major royal and ecclesiastic patrons meant that there was no official school of painting, which left artists free to specialize in particular fields, such as historical subjects, portraits, landscapes and still life, as well as genre painting.

Willem Heda *(1594–1680) was one of the masters of still life. The painter's simple compositions reflect his signature use of sober colours.*

Frans Hals *(c.1580–1666) left an oeuvre of some 200 portraits and more than 50 genre paintings. He painted not only regents and wealthy townsmen but also peasants, soldiers, fishermen, publicans and drunkards. No sketches for his paintings are known, and it is assumed that he painted* alla prima, *that is, straight onto the canvas without sketches.* The Fool, *shown above, dates from around 1623.*

REMBRANDT VAN RIJN

Rembrandt van Rijn is regarded by many as the greatest Dutch painter of all time. He was born in Leiden in 1606 but lived in Amsterdam from 1632 until his death in 1669. Rembrandt was a master in the use of light and shadow. *The Jewish Bride* (painted around 1665) is regarded as one of the best portraits of his later period.

Jacob van Ruisdael *(1628–82) was an unrivalled landscape painter. In his* View of Haarlem *depicted here, the low horizon is dwarfed by an imposing sky with clouds.*

The silversmith Adam van Vianen (1569–1627) was famous for his ornamental style, which was known as kwabstijl, or "flabby style", and distinguished by flowing ornamentation and the use of various fantasy elements. This gilded silver jug is an example of his style. Much of the silver work from this time has been lost because pieces have been melted down in order to trade in the metal for cash.

Jan Steen (1625–79) was a prolific painter with a variety of works, 800 of which survive today. They include everything from altar pieces to landscape paintings to works with mythological themes. However, Steen is known primarily for his genre painting, which gives a detailed, humorous picture of 17th-century society. The Family Scene, shown above, is a typical "Jan Steen household" – one in disarray. Tavern scenes were another of the artist's favourite subjects.

Gerard van Honthorst (1590–1656) was greatly influenced by the works of Caravaggio. As well as historical scenes and portraits, he painted genre pieces such as The Merry Fiddler (above). His famous nocturnal scenes lit by candle-light led to his being nicknamed "Gherardo delle Notte" in Italy.

Johannes Vermeer (1632–75) spent his entire life in Delft. Only 40 of his works are known today, but even this modest oeuvre plays a prominent role in the history of painting. His balanced compositions appear very modern. Long before the Impressionists, Vermeer succeeded in conveying light through colour. The street depicted in View of Houses in Delft (c.1658), left, has become known as "Vermeer's street".

Pottery and Tiles

WHEN IN 1620 EXPORTS OF PORCELAIN from China to Europe fell because of the troubles in China, Dutch potters seized the opportunity and started to produce their own wares, imitating the Chinese style on a large scale. The quality of the Dutch blue-white porcelain was excellent. The city of Delft became one of the prime centres for the production of this china, which reached its height between 1660 and 1725. During the Art Nouveau and Art Deco periods, Dutch potters regained their international renown. The best known of them was TAC Colenbrander.

Tulip vase

Stylized flowers reflect the Italian majolica tradition.

De Porceleyne Fles is the only Delftware shop which has managed to survive throughout the centuries. The business was bought in 1876 and revived by Joost Thooft, whose initials can still be seen on the workshop's mark. The exquisite painting on the porcelain continues to be done by hand, although the rest of the manufacturing process no longer involves the craft's traditional methods.

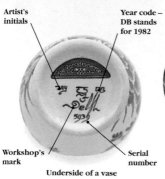

Artist's initials

Year code – DB stands for 1982

Workshop's mark

Serial number

Underside of a vase

DELFTWARE

Although tin-glazed earthenware was also made in other parts of the Netherlands, "Delft" came to describe almost all earthenware made in the Netherlands during this period. Any piece made after 1650 will always have a workshop mark. Later, the glazer's initials, as well as a code denoting the year and a serial number, were added.

This set of four tiles features a pattern of pomegranates, grapes, rosettes and lilies.

The first Dutch porcelain was made in 1759 in the North Holland town of Weesp. At the time, it was second in quality only to Meissen porcelain. However, production was halted after 10 years because of financial difficulties. In 1774, a new factory was opened in Loosdrecht, which was moved to Ouder-Amstel in 1784. This large vase from 1808 is a typical example of the Amstel china that was produced there.

Delft design is used here to decorate a plane tail. The artist Hugo Kaagman decorated the tails of four British Airways' aircraft with blue Delft designs.

TILES

Majolica wall tiles – decorated earthen-ware on a tin-glazed background – were made for the first time in the Netherlands during the 16th century, with production reaching its peak in the 17th century. Until 1625, polychrome decoration predominated, after which the majority of tiles were painted in blue on white. Major centres were Makkum – where in the 17th century the Tichelaar family firm, which operates to this day, was established – as well as Harlingen, Delft, Gouda, Amsterdam, Utrecht and Haarlem. The tiles depicted here are from Haarlem. See also page 425.

The lily often features as a corner motif on Dutch tiles.

TAC COLENBRANDER

One of the biggest names in Art Nouveau pottery is TAC Colenbrander (1841–1930). Originally an architect, he became known for his fanciful floral based designs for the Rozenburg earthenware and porcelain factory in The Hague, where he was chief designer from 1884 to 1889. As celebrated as his designs were, the ceramics had limited commercial success. One reason for this was their expense, a reflection of the labour-intensive production. In 1912–13, Colenbrander worked for the Zuid-Holland pottery in Gouda. In addition to pottery, he designed wallpaper and carpets, and worked as a graphic and interior designer.

The Art Nouveau plate by WP Hartgring was made in 1904, the same year as this master potter won a gold medal at the world exhibition at the St Louis World's Fair. Hartgring worked for 20 years at the Rozenburg factory in The Hague and for 10 years at the Zuid-Holland pottery. His works reflect the Japanese style.

"Day and Night" set by Colenbrander, 1885

Organs and Carillons

HOLLAND BOASTS A LARGE NUMBER of historic church organs. Organ-building flourished from the 15th to 18th centuries. Earlier models of organs were built primarily to meet liturgical requirements, while later models were designed as musical instruments in their own right. The organ chests were often richly decorated. Carillons, too, were very popular. Carillon-making reached its height during the 17th century, with the carillons of the Hemony brothers.

Figure from Elburg organ

Jan Pietersz. Sweelinck, Holland's greatest organ music composer

The organ of the Sint-Bavokerk *in Haarlem (Christian Müller, 1738) is almost 29 m (95 ft) high. The sculptures are by Jan van Logteren. Free organ recitals are held here from May to October.*

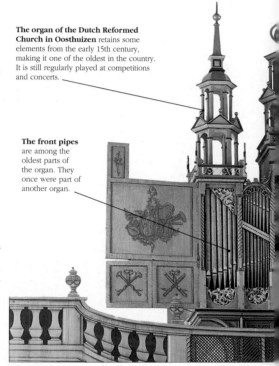

The organ of the Dutch Reformed Church in Oosthuizen retains some elements from the early 15th century, making it one of the oldest in the country. It is still regularly played at competitions and concerts.

The front pipes are among the oldest parts of the organ. They once were part of another organ.

Johann Bätz (1709–70) *built this fine instrument for the Petruskerk in Woerden in 1768. Today it is used for a wide range of organ concerts.*

CHURCH ORGANS

Although there are many concert organs, it is church organs that are most abundant in Holland. Even small towns may have magnificent organs, such as the ones in Abcoude (Roman Catholic Church), Elburg (Grote Kerk), Maassluis (Grote Kerk) and Oosthuizen (Dutch Reformed Church).

Register stops of the Naber organ in St Joriskerk in Amersfoort.

The organ of the Der Aa Kerk *in Groningen was made by Arp Schnitger (1648–1719) in 1702. The organ chest, by Allert Meijer and sculptor Jan de Rijk, was further decorated after 1815 by Mattaeus and Anthonie Walles.*

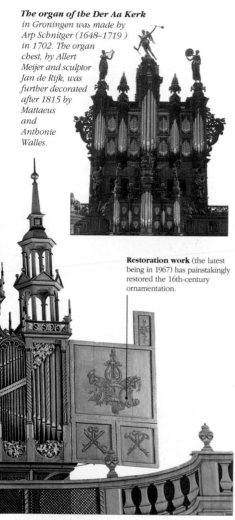

Restoration work (the latest being in 1967) has painstakingly restored the 16th-century ornamentation.

CARILLONS

Carillons sound regularly in Holland from some 150 church towers. Carillons date back to the 14th century, when bells were used to sound the alarm, though the carillon emerged only gradually as a full-fledged musical instrument. Bell-making reached its zenith with the brothers Hemony (François, 1609–67, and Pieter, 1619–80). Of the 51 carillons they made, 29 have survived to this day.

Although carillons are today often played by machines, it is the carillon player who gives the music its individuality. Carillon concerts are hugely popular in Holland, and they often include contemporary as well as classical and folk music. There is a carillon school in Amserfoort, home of a restored 17th-century Hemony carillon, while Asten has a carillon museum.

The organ of Albertus Hinsz *(1704–85) is the pride of the Bovenkerk in Kampen. The latest restoration (completed in 1975) restored it to its state of 1790. The second-level great organ dating from 1790–1866 was also restored. In addition to these two organs, the church has a new choir organ, based on a Reil from the 17th/18th centuries.*

Carillons have at least 30 bells; the carillon player, or carilloneur, strikes the keyboard with his or her fists in order to sound the bells.

Holland in Bloom

THE DUTCH LOVE AFFAIR with flowers began rather unromantically in homes during the 17th century, when flowers were used to keep bad smells at bay. The aesthetic aspect soon developed, and today Holland is one of the world's most important flower-growing countries. It has an unrivalled distribution system, keeping Holland ahead of competition from countries such as Israel, Spain, Colombia, Kenya, Zimbabwe and Zambia. Holland has a 92 per cent share of the world market for flowers.

Orchid

Fields of flowers *are not confined to the west of the country. These rose fields are outside Lottum in the north of the southern province of Limburg, where every year a special rose competition is held.*

Tulips *were introduced to Holland from Turkey in the 17th century. They became the subject of an unparalleled speculative bubble which has become known as "tulip mania". Today the tulip is considered a quintessentially Dutch product, with innumerable varieties.*

The annual flower competition (bloemen corso) *in the bulb-growing region is a grand event (see p32).*

CUT FLOWERS FROM DUTCH NURSERIES

As consumers have become increasingly demanding, the number of flower species and varieties is constantly on the rise. Consumer tastes vary from place to place: in France, gladioli are very popular, whereas in Great Britain, it is lilies and carnations. In Asia, tulips are in great demand. A small sample of the flowers grown commercially in Holland is shown here.

The iris *(Iris)* flower and bulb are in demand.

The chrysanthemum *(Chrysanthemum)* originated in China.

The sandy soil in the high areas behind the dunes of Holland is known as "geest soil" and is very well suited for cultivating bulbs.

Not all daffodil bulbs can survive the winter.

Crocus bulbs should be planted in September.

Hyacinth bulbs range in colour from violet red to white.

Tulip bulbs are highly resistant to disease and pests.

Iris bulbs should be dug up after flowering.

FLOWER SELLERS

Flower sellers are part and parcel of Holland's street scene. They can also be found indoors, in places such as stations or office buildings. In most countries, cut flowers are considered a luxury. In Holland, however, they are practically a daily shopping item. Holland is indeed the land of flowers *par excellence.*

ahlias *Dahlia)* come 20,000 rieties.

The lilac *(Syringa)* is often bought for its fragrance.

The carnation *(Dianthus)* is loved as a spray.

The rose *(Rosa)* is known as "the queen of flowers".

HOLLAND THROUGH THE YEAR

EVERY YEAR, Holland has much to offer in the way of holidays, festivals and other events. However, the choice of cultural events is greatest during the summer months. For example, Amsterdam, Rotterdam, The Hague and Utrecht all host theatre festivals in June. Some festivals, such as the 3-Oktoberfeesten in Leiden, have deep historical roots, whereas

Festival float

others, such as the multicultural Zomercarnaval in Rotterdam, are much more modern. Many of the events are held to honour navigation and fishing, such as Flag Day (Vlaggetjesdag), held each May in Scheveningen. Music, too, plays a prominent role in the country's event calendars. The world-renowned North Sea Jazz festival brings to The Hague the genre's greats.

SPRING

IN MARCH, daffodils and crocuses burst into bloom in the country's towns and villages. From mid-April onwards, when the tulips are in flower, the bulb fields along the Dutch coast are a spectacular sight to see.

MARCH

Foto Biënnale *(mid-Mar to mid-Apr)*, Rotterdam. This biannual international photography exhibition takes place in odd-numbered years.
Meezing Matthäus *(Easter)*, Amsterdam and elsewhere. Concert-goers are welcome to sing along during many

A young street musician on Queen's Day in Amsterdam

performances of Bach's *St Matthew's Passion*.
Keukenhof *(end Mar to mid-May)*, near Lisse. These 32 ha (79 acres) of landscape gardens demonstrate the best of all the flowers Holland has to offer. This open air exhibition was started in 1949, and has become internationally renowned.

Blossoming fruit tree in de Betuwe

APRIL

First of April Celebrations, Brielle. Dressed in 16th-century-style clothing, the inhabitants of Brielle (Den Briel) re-create the 1572 recovery of the city from the Spaniards.
Bloemen Corso *(Flower Competition) (late Apr)*, Bollenstreek. Floats with floral sculptures travel a 40-km (25-mile) route through Haarlem, Hillegom, Lisse and Noordwijk.
Koninginnedag (Queen's Day) *(30 Apr)*. The birthday of the former queen, Juliana, sees festivities throughout the land; the biggest event is held in Amsterdam.

MAY

Nationale Moldendag (National Windmill Day) *(second Sat in May)*. Some 600 of the 1,000 windmills in the country are opened to the public. The day coincides with **Landelijke Fietsdag** (National Cycling Day);

windmills are incorporated into all cycle routes.
Vlaggetjesdag (Flag Day) *(May)*, Scheveningen. The arrival of the first herring catch of the season is celebrated with demonstrations of traditional fishing-related crafts, music and a race.
Aspergerie Primeur (Ascension Day), Venlo. In a festive atmosphere on a re-created old-time village green, visitors can tuck into deliciously cooked asparagus.
Keidagen *(around Ascension Day)*, Lochem. Five days of music, funfairs, street fairs and performances by international artists.

Flag Day, the start of the new herring fishing season

Sloepenrace (Boat Regatta). A regatta from Harlingen to Terschelling.

Jazz in Duketown *(around Whitsun),* 's-Hertogenbosch. Four days of open-air high-quality jazz and blues bands at various venues in town. The beer flows freely.

SUMMER

SUMMER IN THE NETHERLANDS is a time of major cultural events. These include the Holland Festival in Amsterdam, the Theater a/d Werf in Utrecht, the Rotterdam Parade and the Haagse Zomer in The Hague. And if theatre is not your favourite pastime, there are plenty of other activities to keep you entertained.

JUNE

Vliegerfeest (Kite Festival) *(mid-Jun),* Scheveningen. For two days, hundreds of strange creations hover over the beach.

Aaltjesdag (Eel Day) *(second Sat in Jun),* Harderwijk. Major fishing celebration in this former harbour on the Zuider Zee.

Oerol Festival *(mid-Jun),* Terschelling. This alternative cultural festival lasts for ten days, with clowns, street theatre, acrobats, pop concerts and music from around the world.

Poetry International *(mid-Jun),* Rotterdam. Prestigious poetry festival featuring an international programme, in Rotterdam's Doelen district.

Herring-eating by hand

Pasar Malam Besar *(second half of Jun),* The Hague. This festival of Indonesian music and dance, shadow puppets, cooking demonstrations and colourful eastern market takes place at Malieveld in The Hague.

Nationale Vlootdagen (Navy days) *(end Jun/early*

The increasingly popular boat race to Terschelling

Jul), Den Helder. A chance to see frigates, submarines, torpedo boats and mine

Caribbean scenes during the Zomercarnaval in Rotterdam

hunters belonging to the Netherlands Navy, with spectacular shows put on by the Netherlands Marines.

JULY

Oud Limburgs Schuttersfeest (Marksman's Festival) *(first Sun in Jul).* Annual tournament by the marksmen of Limburg is a colourful folk event held in the hometown of the previous year's winner.

North Sea Jazz *(mid-Jul),* The Hague. A three-day spectacle of music at the Congresbouw (Congress Centre) in The Hague, with performances by the biggest names in the jazz world.

Tilburgse kermis (Tilburg Fair) *(end Jul).* One of the biggest and most exuberant fairs in Holland.

Zomercarnaval (Summer Carnival) *(last Sat in Jul),* Rotterdam. A lively Caribbean carnival with exotic music, plenty to eat and drink and a swirling procession.

North Sea Jazz, one of the world's major jazz events

The Nijmegen Fair, a popular tradition dating back centuries

AUGUST

Mosselfeesten (Mussel Festivals) *(third Sat in August),* Yerseke; *(last weekend in August),* Philippine. Harvest festival presenting the new crops of Zeeland.

Ambachtenfestival *(second Sun in August),* Nederweert. Festival where you can see chair-menders, shipwrights and masons at work.

Preuvenemint *(last weekend in August),* Maastricht. Flamboyant festival of food and drink at the historical Vrijthof.

Uitmarkt *(last weekend in August),* Amsterdam. Festive opening of the theatre season with performances and information booths. There is also a book fair, where literary publishers are represented with their own stalls.

An elaborate fruit sculpture at the Tiel Fruitcorso

AUTUMN

A S THE COLD weather starts slowly but surely to set in, indoor events become more prominent. In autumn, the theatres are full in the evenings, and museums are routinely busy. However, open-air events are still held, the golden light of dusk and the magnificent clouds in the sky adding to the atmosphere.

SEPTEMBER

Monumentendag (Monument Day) *(second Sat in Sep).* Private historic buildings are opened to the public.

Fruitcorso *(second weekend in Sep),* Tiel. Spectacular parade of floats with gigantic fruit sculptures.

Jordaanfestival *(second and third weeks in Sep),* Amsterdam. Neighbourhood festivals featuring fairs, street parties, talent contests and live music are held in the southern part of the picturesque former working-class district of Jordaan.

Prinsjesdag *(third Tue in Sep),* The Hague. Accompanied by high-ranking government officials and with a guard of honour, the queen rides in her golden carriage from Noordeinde Palace to the Binnenhof (Parliament Building), where she makes her Royal Speech in the Ridderzaal (Hall of the Knights) in order to open the Dutch Parliament.

Queen Beatrix delivering the Royal Speech on Prinsjesdag

Nijmeegse kermis (Nijmegen fair) *(end Sep/early Oct).* Held every year since the 13th century, the fair stretches ribbon-like through the centre of the city. On Mondays and Tuesdays are the "piekdagen", when children can visit the attractions for the entrance price of 50 eurocents.

OCTOBER

3-Oktoberfeesten, Leiden. A large public festival to commemorate the relief of Leiden from its siege on 3 October 1574.

Permanent fixtures in the festivities are the distribution of herring and white bread to the townspeople, as well as the procession and funfair.

The distribution of white bread in celebration of the relief of Leiden

Eurospoor *(mid- to late Oct)*, Utrecht. Europe's biggest model train show takes place in the Jaarbeues.

NOVEMBER

Sint-Maarten *(11 Nov)*, Western and Northern Netherlands. In the early evening, children equipped with lanterns walk from door to door, singing songs, for which they are given sweets.

Intocht van Sinterklaas (arrival of St Nicholas) *(second or third week in Nov)*. St Nicholas is celebrated in every town and village in Holland. He arrives by ship near St Nicholaskerk *(see p91)* and then rides on his grey horse through town.

The arrival of St Nicholas, attracting a great deal of attention

Until 5 December, children traditionally sing Nicholas carols in the evenings, and every morning find sweets in their shoes.

WINTER

Decorate aside, there are not as many events in the winter calendar as there are for the rest of the year – perhaps to the relief of those who need January to recover from St Nicholas, Christmas and the New Year.

DECEMBER

Sinterklaasavond (St Nicholas' Day) *(5 Dec)*. St Nicholas ends with St Nicholas' Eve on 5 December. Both young and old are brought gifts, more often than not in person by (a hired) Santa Claus. Friends give poems caricaturing each other.

Cirque d'Hiver *(between Christmas and New Year's Eve)*, Roermond. Four days of world-class circus acts in the Oranjerie theatre hotel, in the historic town centre.

New Year's Eve *(31 Dec)*. The Dutch spend the last evening of the old year in festive surroundings at home or with friends. Fritters and apple turnovers are eaten and, in many houses, the champagne corks pop at midnight. Afterwards, people walk the streets to see in the New Year with organized firework displays.

JANUARY

Nieuwjaarsduik (New Year's Dip) *(1 Jan)*, Scheveningen. Every year, at noon on New Year's Day, a starting-gun is fired on the pier in Scheveningen, and hundreds of people in swimsuits run down the beach to take a dip in the ice-cold water.

New Year's fireworks display

Leidse Jazzweek *(mid Jan)*, Leiden. Throughout the week, jazz of all styles is played in the halls and cafés of the old town.

FEBRUARY

Hiswa *(Feb or Mar)*, Amsterdam. Boat show in the RAI *(see p141)*, featuring all types of crafts, from dinghies to yachts.

The latest boats on display at the annual Hiswa

Carnival *(Feb or Mar)*. Officially three, but in practice five, days before Lent, the Catholic south celebrates wildly. There are processions with colourful floats, and costumed people sing and dance in the cafés and in the streets.

The Climate in Holland

HOLLAND HAS A MARITIME CLIMATE, characterized by cool summers and mild winters. In summer, the average maximum temperature is around 20ºC (68ºF), while in winter the average minimum temperature is around 0ºC (32ºF). It is slightly warmer south of the country's big rivers than north of them, and there are slightly more hours of sunshine on the coast than inland. Because of the temperature difference between the land and the sea, there is a constant westerly sea breeze on the coast in summer.

WEST FRISIAN ISLANDS

Leeuwarden

FRIESLAN

NORTH HOLLAND

Lelystad

FLEVOLAND

Haarlem
AMSTERDAM

The Hague

SOUTH HOLLAND

Utrecht

UTRECHT

Rotterdam

Nijmeg

's-Hertogenbosc

NORTH BRABANT

Middelburg
ZEELAND

Eindhoven

DEN HELDER

°C (F)					
		19 (66)	18 (64)		
	14 (57)	14 (57)	13 (55)		
	7 (45)	9 (48)		9 (48)	
5 (41)	2 (36)			5 (41)	
1 (34)					
48 hours	111 hours	227 hours	212 hours	145 hours	50 hours
76 mm	45 mm	32 mm	67 mm	76 mm	79 mm
Month Jan	Mar	May	Jul	Sep	Nov

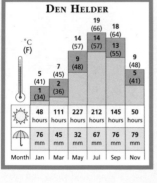

DE BILT

°C (F)					
		21 (70)	19 (66)		
		17 (63)			
	9 (48)	12 (54)	10 (50)	9 (48)	
	7 (45)				
5 (41)	1 (34)			3 (37)	
−1 (30)					
54 hours	118 hours	214 hours	191 hours	143 hours	53 hours
76 mm	44 mm	43 mm	82 mm	73 mm	55 mm
Month Jan	Mar	May	Jul	Sep	Nov

Average maximum temperature

Average minimum temperature

Average hours of sunshine per month

Average rainfall per month

BEEK 22

°C (F)					
		22 (72)	19 (66)		
		18 (64)			
	10 (50)	13 (55)	10 (50)	9 (48)	
	8 (46)				
4 (39)	2 (36)			4 (39)	
−1 (30)					
44 hours	109 hours	202 hours	181 hours	145 hours	53 hours
68 mm	45 mm	62 mm	89 mm	81 mm	62 mm
Month Jan	Mar	May	Jul	Sep	Nov

Ma
tric

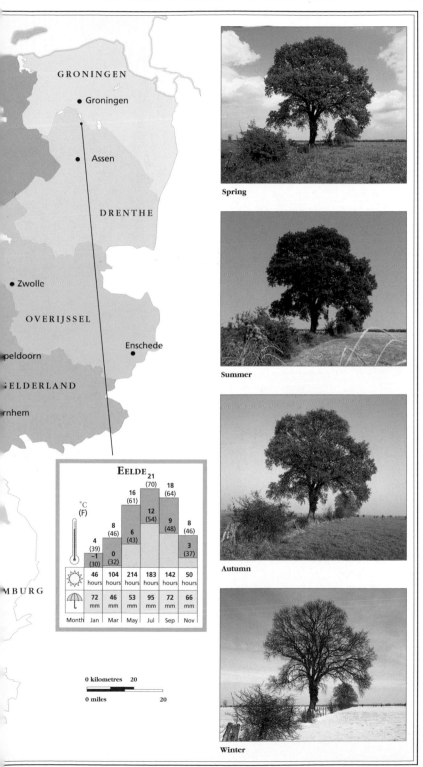

GRONINGEN

● Groningen

● Assen

DRENTHE

● Zwolle

OVERIJSSEL

Enschede
●

peldoorn

GELDERLAND

rnhem

MBURG

Spring

Summer

Autumn

Winter

Eelde

°C (F)					
			21 (70)	18 (64)	
		16 (61)			
	8 (46)	12 (54)		9 (48)	8 (46)
4 (39)	6 (43)				
0 (32)				3 (37)	
−1 (30)					

☀	46 hours	104 hours	214 hours	183 hours	142 hours	50 hours
☂	72 mm	46 mm	53 mm	95 mm	72 mm	66 mm
Month	Jan	Mar	May	Jul	Sep	Nov

0 kilometres   20

0 miles   20

THE HISTORY
OF HOLLAND

IN 12 BC, THE ROMANS conquered southern Holland, and in AD 50 they declared the Rhine the northern border of their empire. The region north of this was conquered by the Frisians. At the end of the 4th century, the Romans withdrew from the Low Countries, which were taken over by the Frisians, Franks and Saxons. In the 8th century, the Franks ruled the region alone. The introduction of Christianity, begun by the missionary Willibrord in 695, was completed under Charlemagne.

Model of a 17th-century merchant ship

After the disintegration of the Frankish Empire, the Netherlands fell under German rule. Actual power was exercized by the vassals, of whom the Bishop of Utrecht was the most powerful – until the Concordat of Worms in 1122, when the German king lost the right to appoint bishops. In the course of the 12th century, the Count of Holland was the most important figure in the region.

In the 14th and 15th centuries, the dispute between the two factions – the Hooks and the Cods – marked, in a certain sense, the end of the feudal age.

When at the end of the 16th century the Northern Netherlands liberated itself from the Habsburg Duke Philip II, it enjoyed a period of unprecedented economic and cultural flowering. By the mid-17th century, it had become the greatest trading nation in the world, a status gradually relinquished during the 18th century.

The different independent regions making up the republic were joined together under Napoleon, with William I becoming king in 1815.

However, unification with Belgium proved unsuccessful and was officially ended in 1839, although it had already ended *de facto* in 1830.

In the 20th century, Holland maintained neutrality during World War I, but suffered greatly during World War II. Invaded by the Germans in May 1940, the country was not liberated entirely until May 1945. It subsequently developed into one of the most prosperous states within the European Union. Today, the country remains a constitutional monarchy, the royal family enjoying great popularity among the Dutch.

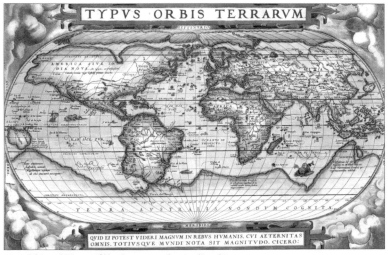

TYPVS ORBIS TERRARVM

QVID EI POTEST VIDERI MAGNVM IN REBVS HVMANIS, CVI AETERNITAS OMNIS, TOTIVSQVE MVNDI NOTA SIT MAGNITVDO. CICERO:

Map of the world from 1564 by the cartographer Ortelius of Antwerp

◁ *The IJ at Amsterdam, Viewed from the Mussel Quay,* painted by Ludolf Backhuysen (1631–1708)

Rulers of the Netherlands

Old coin with image of Queen Beatrix

IN THE MIDDLE AGES, the Netherlands were run by local feudal dukes, as well as by the counts of Holland and the bishops of Utrecht. They were all officially vassals of the German king. In the 15th century, the region came under the rule of the House of Burgundy through marriage alliances, after which it was incorporated into the Habsburg Empire. In 1581, the Northern Netherlands freed itself from the Habsburgs. Since then – with some interruptions – the House of Orange has ruled over parts of what are today called Holland, initially as stadholders, but from 1815 as monarchs.

1417–1433
Jacoba of Bavaria

c. 685–719
Radboud,
King of the
Frisians

1152–1190
Frederik Barbarossa
(German king)

1342–1364
Jan IV van
Arkel, Bishop
of Utrecht

814–840
Louis the
Pious

885–889
Gerulf,
Count
of
Holland

1312–1355
Jan III (Duke of
Brabant and
Limburg)

1203–1222
Willem I,
Count of Holland

1404–1417
Willem VI,
Count of
Holland

700	800	900	1000	1100	1200	1300	1400	

Bu

700	800	900	1000	1100	1200	1300	1400

936–973
Otto I
(German
king)

1371–1402
Willem I,
Duke of Gelre
and Gulik

918–976
Balderik,
Bishop of
Utrecht

1345–1354
Margaretha
of Bavaria

1069–1090
Egbert II,
Count of
Friesland, last
of the
Brunonen

1271–1326
Reinald I,
Count of
Gelre

1433–1467
Philip the Good
(House of Burgundy)

1267–1294
Jan I, Duke of
Brabant (from
1288 also Duke
of Limburg)

1091–1121
Floris II, Count
of Holland

1234–1256
Willem II (Count
of Holland)

1128–1139
Andries van Kuik
(Bishop of Utrecht)

1256–1296
Floris V
(Count of Holland)

768–814
Charlemagne

FLORENT IV XVI Comes Ha

1585–1625
Maurits

1559–1567 and 1572–1584
William of Orange,
"The Silent" (stadholder
of Holland, Zeeland and
Utrecht, under Philip II
until 1581)

1806–1810
Louis Napoleon
(French viceroy,
king of Holland)

1815–1840
William I (king)

1567–1573
Ferdinand, Duke of
Alva (viceroy under
Philip II)

1625–1647
Frederick-Hendrik

1467–1477
Charles the Bold

1647–1650
William II

1477–1482
Maria of Burgundy

1672–1702
William III

1898–1948
Wilhelmina

1687–1711
Johan Willem
Friso, stadholder
of Friesland
(1696), Prince of
Orange (1702)

1890–1898
Emma (regent)

1482–1506
Philip the Handsome
(House of Habsburg)

1500	1600	1700	1800	1900	2000

DY | **HABSBURG** | **HUIS VAN ORANJE**

1500	1600	1700	1800	1900	2000

1849–1890
William III

1840–1849 William II

1795–1806 Batavian Republic

1751–1795
William V

1948–1980
Juliana

1559–1567
Margaretha of Parma
(governor under Philip II)

1506–1555
Charles V

1555–1581
Philip II

1747–1751
William IV

1980–present
Beatrix

HOLLAND AND ITS MONARCHY

The Dutch royal family is extremely
popular. The present queen, Beatrix,
is the fourth queen in a row. When
the crown passes to her son,
Willem Alexander, the country
will have its first king since 1890.

Prehistoric and Roman Times

ABOUT 13,000 YEARS AGO, the Low Countries emerged from under the ice of the last Ice Age. Temperatures gradually rose, turning the tundra into areas of forest and marshes, inhabited by nomadic hunters. In the Early Stone Age (4500–2000 BC), farming communities were established here and there. The megalith builders were the best known of these settled inhabitants. Around 600 BC, Germanic and Celtic tribes settled in the Low Countries. They were here when the Romans conquered the southern part of the region, in the 1st century BC. In AD 50, the Romans finally declared the Rhine as the Roman Empire's northern frontier, establishing Roman settlements in Utrecht and Maastricht.

Roman dagger

THE LOW COUNTRIES (AD 50)

☐ *Germanic peoples*

☐ *Roman territory*

— *Coastline in 3000 BC*

Megaliths
Between 3400 and 3200 BC, the inhabitants of the Drenthe plateau built some 100 megaliths. Of these, 54 have survived into the present (see pp304–5). These impressive tombs were once concealed beneath a mound of sand.

Urns
These urns date from 1150–800 BC.

The dark rings in this picture are of the ditches that originally surrounded the urn-mounds. The rings are interrupted at their southeastern edge, possibly to represent the symbolic entrance to the tomb.

TIMELINE

55,000 BC Small groups of Neanderthal people inhabit the surroundings of Hijken and Hoogersmilde. A few hand axes and two campsites have been found		**4500 BC** Farmers settle on the loess land of Zuid Limburg. They have been referred to as "Bandkeramikers", or the Linear Pottery Culture, after their striped pottery	**1900 BC** Start of the Bronze Age in Low Countries

10,000 BC	7500 BC	5000 BC	2500 BC	2000 BC

11,000 BC Reindeer hunters of the Hamburg Culture inhabit Drenthe	**3400–3200 BC** Farmers of the Beaker Folk build megaliths at Drenthe, Overijssel and Groningen	*Wheel from 2700 BC*

The Simpelveld Sarcophagus
In the 1930s, a Roman burial urn was excavated at Simpelveld near Limburg. The interior of the urn is decorated with reliefs depicting the exterior and the furnishings of a Roman house.

WHERE TO SEE PREHISTORIC AND ROMAN HOLLAND

In addition to the mega-liths of Drenthe and the Someren urnfield, prehis-toric graves have been discovered at Almere, Hilversum, Vaassen, Lunteren, Goirle and Rolde, and at Toterfout/Halfmijl in Brabant, where 16 burial mounds have been restored to their original condition, com-plete with trenches and rings of stakes. The urn-field on the Bosoverheide, a couple of kilometres west of the Weert, was, around 800 BC, one of the largest burial grounds in northwestern Europe. Roman finds can be seen in places like Oudheden in Leiden *(see p215)* and the Valkhof museum in Nijmegen *(see p341)*. The Archeon archaeological theme park in Alphen a/d Rijn *(see p446)* is highly informative and entertaining, for adults and children alike.

THE URNFIELD

In 1991, an urnfield dating from 600 BC was discovered at Someren near Brabant. It had been ploughed under by farmers during the Middle Ages. The dead were cremated in southern Holland from 1500 BC, and in northern Holland from 1000 BC. The burial mounds of Someren were arranged closely together, and each contained its own urn.

Roman Mask
This mask was found near Nijmegen, which was once the camp of a Roman legion.

Farmer with Plough *The plough was used in the Iron Age.*

Glass Flasks
These Roman flasks from the 2nd century AD were excavated at Heerlen.

1500 BC	1000 BC	750 BC	500 BC	250 BC	0

Bronze Age sacrificial dagger

750–400 BC First Iron Age in the Low Countries

450 BC Start of the Second Iron Age, or La Tène Age

55–10 BC Batavians settle in the river area, the Cananefates in the coastal area and the Frisians in the north

Roman temple in Elst

1300 BC The Exloo necklace is made from tin beads from England, Baltic amber and Egyptian pottery beads

300–100 BC The Germans expand southwards across the Rhine, clashing with Celtic tribes

57 BC Caesar conquers the Belgae, who inhabit present-day Belgium

AD 69–70 Batavian Uprising, followed by the re-establishment of Roman rule

Frisians, Franks and Saxons

Frisian cloak pin

WHEN THE ROMANS WITHDREW at the end of the 4th century, the Low Countries, like the rest of Europe, experienced a great migration of peoples. By around 500, the Frisians had spread their territory southwards to the great rivers, while the Saxons lived east of the IJssel and the Franks had settled in the area south of the great rivers. Approximately two centuries later, the Franks took over the whole region as far as the Lauwerszee. With the spread of Christianity and under Charlemagne, the entire area of Holland became Christian. After Charlemagne's death, the region belonged first to the Middle Kingdom of Lothair, and then, from 925, to the German Empire.

THE LOW COUNTRIES (AD 700)

☐ *Frisians*

☐ *Franks*

☐ *Saxons*

THE LIFE OF ST BONIFACE

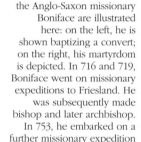

Widukind
In 785, Charlemagne defeated the Saxons led by Widukind. This event led to the east of Holland finally being incorporated into Charlemagne's empire.

Two episodes in the life of the Anglo-Saxon missionary Boniface are illustrated here: on the left, he is shown baptizing a convert; on the right, his martyrdom is depicted. In 716 and 719, Boniface went on missionary expeditions to Friesland. He was subsequently made bishop and later archbishop. In 753, he embarked on a further missionary expedition to Friesland, which resulted in his death the following year.

The staff is one of Boniface's constant possessions. He was reputed to have used it to make a spring well up.

Early Medieval Pottery
For the Frisians, pottery was an important barter good, along with cattle and dye.

A convert being baptized.

Fibula from Dorestad

TIMELINE

295
Constantius Chlorus defeats the Franks at the battle of the Rhine delta, but allows them to remain in the Betuwe, where they are used to defend the frontiers

Relief showing a Roman galley

600–700
Dorestad becomes an important trading settlement

AD 200	400	500	550	600	650

350–400
Romans leave the Low Countries

500
The territory of the Frisians stretches from the Zwin in Zeeland Flanders to the mouth of the Weser in Germany

Frankish denarii

Radboud, King of the Frisians

The Frisian king Radboud was forced to capitulate to the Frankish ruler Pippin II. He later regained the land he had lost, and with his army marched on Cologne. In 734, the Frisians under Count Bubo were again defeated at the de Boorne River, allowing Charles Martel to extend Frankish domain up to the Lauwerszee.

Boniface uses his Bible to protect himself from the sword.

Pagan ceremonial axe

Viking Sword

This sword, dubbed "Adalfriid's sword", was found in the Waal.

DORESTAD

Situated at the confluence of the Lek and the Kromme Rijn (by present-day Wijk bij Duurstede, *see p205*), Dorestad was the most important trading settlement in northern Holland during the Early Middle Ages. It was the centre of Frisian trade in the 7th century and afterwards under the Merovingians and Carolingians. In the 9th century, Dorestad was repeatedly plundered by marauding Vikings, who sailed up the rivers in their longboats in search of booty. The settlement's decline, however, was due to the damming of the Rhine against flooding rather than because of the Viking raids. There is no reference in historical records to Dorestad after 863. During the 10th century, Dorestad's functions were taken over by Tiel, Deventer and Utrecht. In Wijk, the Museum Dorestad (tel. 0343-571448) gives an excellent idea of what life must have been like here during the Early Middle Ages through its various displays of archaeological finds from that period, as well as its informative diorama, complete with models of port houses.

689
Pippin II defeats the Frisian king Radboud at Dorestad and gains the river region and Utrecht

768–814
Rule of Charlemagne. Holland is divided into *pagi* (cantons), each of which is ruled by a count

925
Holland is taken over by the German Empire

1007
Last Viking invasion of the Low Countries

700	750	800	900	1000

695
Willibrord becomes bishop of Frisia and establishes his see in Utrecht

754
Boniface is killed at Dokkum by pagan looters

834–837
Dorestad plundered at various times by Vikings

Viking longboat

The Emergence of Towns

Pilgrim's badge

IN THE 13TH CENTURY, towns started to acquire considerable economic power. At that time, the Low Countries were nominally under the rule of the German king, but in practice local nobles ran things themselves. In the north, the counts of Holland were the most powerful. In the mid-14th century, their territory fell into the hands of the House of Bavaria. Disunity between Margaretha of Bavaria and her son William marked the beginning of the dispute between the Hooks and the Cods, which split towns as well as noble families for one and a half centuries.

THE LOW COUNTRIES (1300)

☐ *German Empire*

☐ *France*

The Fulling Industry
During the 15th century, the cloth industry flourished in Leiden and 's-Hertogenbosch. This painting by IC Swanenburgh shows the fullers and dyers at work. In the background to the right, inspectors are checking the quality of the cloth.

Minting Coins
Minting rights lay not only with the sovereign. Local rulers, both church and secular, were entitled to mint coins.

Pilgrims who had visited Santiago de Compostela, well established as a place of pilgrimage by the 11th century, wore the scallop shell of the apostle St James on their hats.

The sheriff, with his distinctive chain of bells, was the representative of the sovereign. Here he is on the way to pronounce a death sentence, which is shown by the red pole the "rod of justice", carrie by an executioner.

TIMELINE

The coat of arms of 's-Hertogenbosch

c.1050
The first dykes are built

1185
's-Hertogenbosch is granted its town charter

1247
William II of Holland is appointed king of Germany by the pro-Papal party

1000	1050	1100	1150	1200	1250

1076–1122
Investiture dispute between the German king and the Pope on the right to appoint bishops

1165
Frederick Barbarossa places Friesland under the joint rule of the Bishop of Utrecht and the Count of Holland

Cruel Punishment

In the Middle Ages, barbaric punishments were often meted out. This cask on the wall of the waag in Deventer was once used to immerse counterfeiters in boiling oil.

Grain brought by farmers to the towns was inspected by officials. Produce in the meat and fish markets was also inspected daily. An excise tax was charged on the basis of the inspection.

A MEDIEVAL TOWN

Demands of trade and industry meant that towns were given all kinds of privileges from the 13th century onwards. Often important allies for the counts of Holland against local feudal lords, Dutch towns were more powerful than in other countries during this period because of the lack of a powerful central authority.

WHERE TO SEE LATE MEDIEVAL HOLLAND

Famous monuments from this period are the Oude Kerk in Amsterdam (14th century, *see pp76–7*) and the Begijnhof, which has the city's oldest house (1420, *see p87*); the Cathedral Tower (1382) and the Catharijneconvent (15th century) in Utrecht (*see p200*); the Onze-Lieve-Vrouwebasiliek (11th–12th centuries) and the St-Servaasbasiliek (11th–15th centuries) in Maastricht (*see p375*); the 13th-century Ridderzaal and the 14th-century Gevangenpoort in The Hague (*see p218*); the Pieterskerk (15th century) and the town walls of the 12th-century castle in Leiden (*see p215*); the Lange Jan (14th century, *see p247*) and the restored abbey (11th–15th centuries) in Middelburg (*see p248*); the centre of Deventer around the Brink and Bergkerk, including the oldest stone house in Holland (*see p318*); and the Martinitoren in Groningen (1469, *see p278*).

Silver Chalice

As guilds prospered, they attached increasing importance to appearances. This chalice is decorated with a picture of St George defending a maiden against the dragon.

The Guild of St George *(1533)*
This painting by Cornelis Antonisz shows marksmen at a meal. Originally, each guild was responsible for protecting a part of the city walls; later, special guilds were set up.

The Dutch Trading Empire

Brass compass

THE EARLY 17TH CENTURY marked a period of expansion worldwide for northern Holland. Within a few decades, the Levant, the Gulf of Guinea, the Caribbean, North and South America, the East Indies, Persia, Arabia, Japan, India and China were all on the Dutch trading routes. The republic's merchant fleet became the world's largest. The powerful Dutch East India Company (VOC), established in 1602, dominated trade with Asia, with a monopoly on all profits from trade east of the Cape of Good Hope, while the Dutch West India Company, established in 1621, concentrated on the New World and the slave trade.

Dealers on the Stock Exchange
With its market traders and exchange, Amsterdam was the undisputed trading centre of Europe.

Purchase of Manhattan
Pieter Minnewit bought Manhattan Island in 1625 from the Delaware Indians for 60 guilders, 10 guns and a brass cauldron.

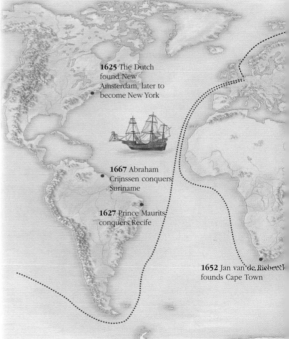

1625 The Dutch found New Amsterdam, later to become New York

1667 Abraham Crijnssen conquers Suriname

1627 Prince Maurits conquers Recife

1652 Jan van de Riebeeck founds Cape Town

The Dutch on Desjima
The Dutch trading office on the island of Desjima was in 1854 the main conduit between Japan and the world.

KEY

·········	**1595–7**	De Houtman and Keyzer
- - - - -	**1596–7**	Barents and Heemskerck
·········	**1616**	le Maire and Schouten
- - - - -	**1642–3**	Tasman

VOC Plaque
The Dutch East India Company (VOC) obtained sole rights to trade for the republic in Asia. It had the authority to make treaties with other powers and even to declare war.

The Silver Fleet
In 1628, Piet Hein captured the Silver Fleet of Spain off the north coast of Cuba.

Surviving the Winter in Novaya Zemlya (1596–97)
During an attempt to find a northern route to the Indies, an expedition led by W Barents and J van Heemskerck ended up on the coast of Novaya Zemlya. The group survived in the Behouden Huys, a hut built from pieces of ships.

THE 80 YEARS WAR

In the second half of the 16th century, Holland officially belonged to the Spanish branch of the House of Habsburg. In 1567, Philip II sent troops to put down Protestant unrest in Flanders and halt the Protestant Reformation sweeping through northern Europe; this led to a revolt against Spanish rule in northern Holland and resulted in years of civil war and religious strife. The 80 Years War ended in 1648 with the Peace of Münster.

Johan van Oldenbarnevelt

Statesman Johan van Oldenbarnevelt and the Count of Nassau, Prince Maurits, were the main Dutch figures in the conflict with Holland's Spanish rulers during the 17th century.

Prince Maurits

1596–1597 The winter camp in Novaya Zemlya

1641 The Dutch establish themselves on Desjima

1624 The Dutch establish themselves on Formosa

1658 The Dutch establish themselves in Ceylon

1619 JP Coen founds Batavia

1606 Willem Jansz discovers Australia

1642 Abel Tasman discovers Tasmania

Three-Master Ship
These top-of-the-line 17th-century Dutch merchant ships required only a small crew.

THE GREAT VOYAGES

While Willem Barents was exploring the Arctic seas, de Houtman and Keyzer set off on the "first voyages" to Java. In 1606, Willem Jansz discovered the north coast of Australia, and in 1616, Jacob le Maire and Willem Schouten were the first to sail around Cape Horn. Abel Tasman discovered Tasmania and New Zealand in 1642–3.

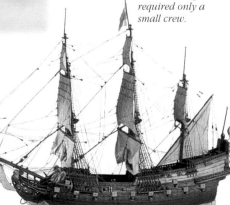

The Golden Age

Baruch de Spinoza

THE 17TH CENTURY was for the north of Holland a time of unprecedented flowering in trade, art *(see pp24–5)* and science *(see pp22–3)*. While elsewhere in Europe economies were in stagnation, the republic's merchant fleet brought great prosperity, particularly to the towns of Amsterdam and Utrecht. The Amsterdam Exchange (Amsterdamse Wisselbank), which was founded in 1609, ensured that Amsterdam became the financial centre of the world. Trade was protected by a powerful navy, which enjoyed significant victories under Michiel de Ruyter.

THE LOW COUNTRIES (1650)

☐ *Republic*

☐ *Spanish possessions*

☐ *Germany*

Johan de Witt

At the time known as the first stadholder-free period (1650–72), the political scene in the republic was dominated by the provincial governor Johan de Witt. This brilliant, impeccable statesman was murdered along with his brother Cornelis by Orange supporters in 1672.

Tapestries and exquisite gilded leather hangings decorated the living rooms.

View of the Weigh House in Haarlem
In the 17th century, Holland became Europe's main commodities market, with strategic logistic and financial advantages. Products from the Baltic Sea, southern Europe, the Levant and Asia were loaded into the holds of merchant ships which came from all over the world.

Oriental carpets were too valuable to put on the floor and so were draped over a table or bench.

Colourful cloths came into fashion in the second half of the 17th century and became a widespread object of study for portrait painters.

TIMELINE

1559 Philip II names Margaretha of Parma the governor of the Netherlands	**1572** The "Beggars of the Sea" take over Den Briel	**1574** The relief of Leiden	Spanish stew-kettle recovered after the relief of Leiden	**1602** Dutch East India Company founded
		1584 Assassination of William of Orange	**1585** Fall of Antwerp	

1550	1565	1580	1595	1610

Caricature painting of the Pope as a pontiff and devil	**1566** Iconoclastic riots	**1581** Northern Holland declares independence from Spain		
	1567 Duke of Alva arrives in Holland		**1588** The States General proclaim the Republic of the Seven United Netherlands	

Antonie van Leeuwenhoek

THE ENLIGHTENMENT

The Enlightenment, or the "Age of Reason", has its roots in the 16th century. In Holland, this emerged in the work of the natural scientists Swammerdam and Van Leeuwenhoek, and the thinker Spinoza. The jurist Hugo de Groot was the first to formulate a rational – as opposed to a theological – basis for what he called "natural law", that is, a universal law applicable to all humans everywhere, which was one of the great themes tackled by thinkers of the Enlightenment.

WHERE TO SEE HOLLAND'S GOLDEN AGE

Good examples of 17th-century architecture are the Trippenhuis in Amsterdam *(see p78)*, the Lakenhal in Leiden *(see p214)* and the Mauritshuis in The Hague *(see pp220–21)*. Vlissingen has the Arsenaal *(see p249)*; Haarlem, the Grote Markt *(see p180)*. Outstanding merchant houses can be seen in the major trading towns of the time, such as Delft *(see pp224–27)* and Utrecht (for example, the Oudegracht, *see p198*).

Wan-Li China Porcelain, also known as egg-shell porcelain, served as a model for blue Delft pottery.

Michiel de Ruyter

The admiral of the Dutch fleet during the Second and Third English-Dutch Naval Wars was a great tactician held in great esteem by his sailors. His nickname "Bestevaer" meant "Grand-father".

INTERIOR OF A PATRICIAN HOME

This painting by Pieter de Hooch, *Portrait of a Family Making Music* (1663), shows the wealth of a patrician residence in the second half of the 17th century. Around 1660, portrait painting shifted in style from sobriety to opulence, a reflection of the flourishing economic prosperity.

The Muider Circle

The artists and scholars who met at the home of the poet PC Hooft at Muiderslot Castle are now known as the members of the "Muiderkring" (Muider Circle).

Prince of Poets

Joost van den Vondel (1587–1679), depicted here by HG Pot as a shepherd, is widely regarded as the greatest Dutch poet and play-wright of the 17th century.

17th-Century Microscope

Antonie van Leeuwenhoek made numerous important discoveries with his home-made microscope.

1625	1640	1655	1670	1685	1700

1642
Rembrandt completes *The Night Watch*

1650–1672
First stadholder-free period starts when the states fail to name a successor after the death of William II

1672–1702
Rule of stadholder William III

1698
Tsar Peter the Great visits Amsterdam and Zaandam

1625
Frederick-Henry becomes stadholder of Holland, Zeeland, Utrecht, Gelderland and Overijssel

1648
The Peace of Münster marks the end of the 80 Years War

1665–1667
The Second English-Dutch Naval War. Michiel Adriaansz. de Ruyter scores legendary victories (Four Days' Battle, The Battle of Chatham)

1689
William III becomes king of England

Calvinism

FROM THE END of the 1500s, Calvinism took hold in Holland as Protestant opposition to Spanish Catholic rule. Amsterdam, which had sided with Spain, switched loyalties in 1578 – an event known as the Alteration – to become the fiercely Protestant capital of an infant Dutch Republic. Reformed Church doctrine was to have a profound influence on Dutch history. Strict living and industriousness became ingrained in the character of Calvinists as well as of Catholics and agnostics and was instrumental in the country's prosperity during the Golden Age.

John Calvin

The Statenbijbel was the translation of the Bible officially recognized by the Synod of Dordrecht (1618–19). The language used in it helped to standardize Dutch. The New Translation (Nieuwe Vertaling) did not appear until 1957.

The iconoclasts use combined efforts to topple a huge religious image from the wall.

Gold and paintings decorated all churches.

Traces of the damage caused by the iconoclasts can still be seen today in some places, such as this retable in Utrecht.

THE ICONOCLASTIC RIOTS

Underground Calvinist preachers goaded troublemakers into the Iconoclastic Riots of 1566, when the decorations of Catholic churches were destroyed with great violence. Invaluable works of religious art were lost in this way.

The interiors of Dutch churches were no longer given the Baroque ornamentation that characterizes churches in the rest of Europe. After all, according to the Ten Commandments in the Bible, "Thou shalt not make graven images" and "Thou shalt not worship nor serve them".

Pieter Saenredam (1597–1665) painted unrivalled pictures of the plain Calvinist churches – this one is Interior of the Sint-Odolphuskerk in Assendelft.

WHERE TO SEE CALVINIST HOLLAND

Strict Calvinism can be found in Holland's "Bible belt" which stretches from Zeeland and south-eastern South Holland via the Veluwe to the cape of Overijssel and Drenthe. The strict Sunday worship, black clothes and head coverings when attending church, as well as absti-nence from modern developments (such as television and vaccina-tions), are gradually disap-pearing. However, when visiting such areas, do remember that photography and driving are still not looked upon kindly in Reformed Church villages. These communities are closed, with strong social controls. Calvinist villages worth visiting are Goede-reede *(see p239)*, in South Holland, and Staphorst *(see p318)*, in Overijssel, as well as the former Zuiderzee island of Urk *(see p324)*, where older people continue to wear traditional dress.

Priceless stained-glass windows are systematically smashed to pieces.

The leaders of the iconoclast riots came from all classes of the population. In addition to fervent Calvinists, there were also paid helpers and all kinds of hangers-on who used the opportunity to do some plundering.

Early to Church **by A. Allebé**

CLANDESTINE CHURCHES

Ons' Lieve Heer op Solder

When, in 1597, the Union of Utrecht proclaimed mandatory Calvinist services throughout Holland and Zeeland, a blind eye – in return for payment – was turned to other confessions. Catholics, Remonstrants and Mennonites held their services in secret churches, which were unrecognizable as such from the outside. They were generally held in town houses, although later they were held in secret churches that were built for the purpose, particularly in Amsterdam, with De Zon and De Rode Hoed. The St Gertrudis-kapel (1645) in Utrecht and Ons' Lieve Heer op Solder (1663, now the Amstelkring Museum) in Amsterdam are the finest surviving early examples of these institutions.

From Republic to Kingdom

THE LOW COUNTRIES IN 1800

☐ *Batavian Republic*

☐ *French territory*

18th-century trader

Aᶠᵀᴱᴿ ᵀᴴᴱ ᴰᴱᴬᵀᴴ of the powerful stadholder William III, the republic no longer played an important role within Europe. Britain took over as most important maritime and trading power. At the end of the 18th century, a long dispute began between the House of Orange and democratically minded patriots, which was resolved in favour of the latter with the founding of the Batavian Republic (1795). After the Napoleonic era, the House of Orange returned to power, this time not as stadholder but as monarch. In 1839, the borders of the present-day Netherlands were finally established.

WILLIAM I
LANDING AT SCHEVENINGEN

In 1813, almost 20 years after the House of Orange had been ousted by the patriots, Prince William returned to the Netherlands. He landed on the shore at Scheveningen, the same place where his father had departed for England. Two days later, he was inaugurated as sovereign. In 1815, he also claimed possession of present-day Belgium and pronounced himself king of the Netherlands.

The British ensign flying on the English warship the *Warrior*, the boat which brought William I back to the Netherlands.

Goejanverwellesluis
In 1785, the patriots took power, and the stadholder William V and his wife Wilhelmina of Prussia fled from The Hague. Wilhelmina attempted to return in 1787 but was stopped at Goejanverwellesluis. It was at this point that the Prussian king decided to send troops to restore the power of the stadholder.

The prince is lowered from the ship in a rowboat, but a farmer's wagon from the beach picks him up to take him ashore through the surf.

TIMELINE

1702–1747 Second stadholder-free period	**1747** William IV "the Frisian" becomes hereditary stadholder of all provinces	**1756–1763** The great powers of Europe become embroiled in the Seven Years War. The republic remains neutral	**1791** Abolition of the Dutch West India Company

1700	1720	1740	1760	1780

| **1713** The Peace of Utrecht marks the end of the republic as a great power | *The city hall of Utrecht, where the Peace of Utrecht was signed* | **1786** The patriots take hold of power in various towns. The rule of stadholder William V is restored in 1787 with the help of Prussia | **1795–1806** The Bataviar Republic |

The Siege of Bergen op Zoom
During the War of Austrian Succession, the French occupied the Southern Netherlands, which had been a possession of Austria. In order to strengthen their hand at the peace negotiations vis-à-vis the republic, in 1747 they also annexed Zeeland Flanders and the fortified town of Bergen.

THE SCHOOLS CONTROVERSY

The 19th-century schools controversy between liberals and denominational supporters was over the inequality between independent education and public education. Under HJAM Schaepman and Abraham Kuyper, Catholics and Protestants joined forces and in 1889 laid the foundations for government subsidies for independent education.

Dr Schaepman   **Dr Kuyper**

The church of the fishing village of Scheveningen is visible in the background.

Child Labour
The Industrial Revolution led to social deprivation in the towns. In 1875, Van Houten's child law was passed, prohibiting children under age 12 from working as paid labourers.

The people of The Hague were overjoyed at the return of the prince. Celebrations were held throughout the town. The times during which the House of Orange had been regarded as a "clique of tyrants" were definitely over.

| 1806 Louis Napoleon, brother of Napoleon I, becomes king of Holland | 1830 The Belgian Revolution. Nine years later, the Netherlands and Belgium separate | 1848 Revision of the constitution and introduction of parliamentary system | *Domela Nieuwenhuis* 1885 Van Gogh paints *The Potato Eaters* | 1888 First socialist, Domela Nieuwenhuis, elected to Parliament |

| 1800 | 1820 | 1840 | 1860 | 1880 | 1900 |

| 1798 Abolition of the Dutch East India Company | 1815 The Northern and Southern Netherlands are united under William I *Steam train* | 1839 Haarlem-Amsterdam railway opens | 1863 Abolition of slavery | 1870 Abolition of the death penalty | 1886 Parliamentary enquiry reveals dire conditions in factories |

Colonialism

DUTCH COLONIAL HISTORY started in the 17th century when trading settlements were established in Asia, Africa and America. Many colonies were lost during the course of time, but the Dutch Indies (Indonesia), Suriname and the Dutch Antilles remained under Dutch rule until far into the 20th century. In the Indonesian archipelago, Dutch power was for a long time limited to Java and the Moluccas. It was only in 1870 that a start was made on subjugating the remaining islands. Indonesia gained independence in 1949 and Suriname in 1975. The Antilles, Aruba and the Netherlands are now equal parts of the Kingdom of the Netherlands.

Tobacco trader

Tortured Slave
Rebellion was cruelly punished.

Jan Pieterszoon Coen
Appointed governor-general in 1618, Jan Pieterszoon Coen devastated the Javanese settlement of Jakarta in 1619, founding in its place the new administrative centre of Batavia. He bolstered the position of the Dutch East India Company on the spice islands (the Moluccas) and is considered one of the founding fathers of Dutch colonialism.

Selling female slaves
half-naked at auctions
was condemned by Holland.

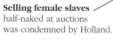

Session of the *Landraad*
This landraad, *or joint court, is presided over by the assistant resident. The* landraad *was the civil and criminal common-law court for native Indonesians and all non-European foreigners in the Dutch Indies. The court could, with government approval, inflict the death penalty.*

SLAVE MARKET IN SURINAME

In total, over 300,000 slaves were shipped to the Dutch colony of Suriname to work the plantations. The slave trade was abolished in 1819, though slavery itself was not abolished until 1863, making Holland the last Western European power to do so.

Batavia During the 17th Century
This painting by Andries Beeckman shows
the fish market with the "Kasteel" in the
background, from which the Dutch ruled
over the strategic Sunda Strait.

Multatuli
The writer Multatuli,
in his novel from 1860
Max Havelaar,
condemned colonial
rule in the Dutch
Indies. In the book's
final chapter, the
author directly
addresses King
William III, in whose
name the people of
the Indies were
being exploited.

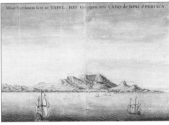

The Establishment of Cape Town
In 1652, Jan van Riebeeck set up a
supply station for ships of the Dutch
East India Company en route to the
Indies. The settlement soon grew into a
Dutch colony, which was settled by
immigrants from the republic, and to
a lesser extent from France (Huguenots)
and Germany. Those who moved
farther inland were later to become
the Boers ("farmers") or Afrikaaners.
In 1806, the Cape Colony was taken
over by the British Empire.

Kris from Java
Many travellers to the
Indies brought back
characteristic items
to Holland. The
Javanese kris was a
favourite souvenir.

The auctioneer sits
taking notes at the table.
The slaves whom he is
selling were delivered by
special traders. Until 1734,
slaves were auctioned
exclusively by the Dutch
West India Company,
which had the monopoly
on the slave trade.

Colonial Wares
From the end of the 19th
century, a number of
Dutch grocers offered for
sale "colonial wares" such
as coffee, tea, rice, sugar
and various exotic eastern
herbs and spices, including
the much-prized pepper-
corns, cloves, nutmeg,
mace and cinnamon.

Modern Holland

Neutrality during World War I meant that Holland survived the first decades of the 20th century relatively unscathed. However, the economic crisis of the 1930s and particularly World War II left deep wounds. In 1957, as the country was rebuilding, it became one of the six founding members of the European Economic Community (EEC). The Dutch welfare state flourished in the 1960s and 1970s, and Amsterdam's tradition of tolerance made it a haven for the hippy culture. Surveys carried out in the 1990s revealed that Holland, along with Iceland, had the most satisfied population in all the countries of Europe.

HOLLAND TODAY

MAANDBLAD VOOR DE MO- DERNE BEELDENDE VAKKEN REDACTIE THEO VAN DOES- BURG MET MEDEWERKING VAN VOORNAME BINNEN- EN BUITENLANDSCHE KUNSTE- NAARS. UITGAVE X. HARMS TIEPEN TE DELFT IN 1917.

1917
The magazine *De Stijl* is set up by figures from the movement of the same name, such as Theo van Doesburg, Piet Mondriaan and JJP Oud

1930–1940
During the economic crisis of the 1930s, hundreds of thousands of Dutch were on the dole

1953
On 1 February, storms cause severe flooding in Zeeland and South Holland, drowning more than 1,800 people

1949
Holland recognizes the independence of its former colony Indonesia

1910	1920	1930	1940	1950

TIMELINE

1910	1920	1930	1940	1950

1918
German kaiser Wilhelm II flees to Holland, where he is given asylum

1926
Road tax introduced. Approximately 10,000 lorries and 30,000 cars are on the roads of Holland

1934
KLM's plane "Uiver", a DC-2, wins the handicap section in the London-Melbourne air race

1948
Willem Drees Sr becomes prime minister of four successive Catholic socialist Drees cabinets and lays the foundations of the Dutch welfare state

1940
On 10 May, German troops enter Holland. Rotterdam capitulates on 14 May. Despite this, the city is bombed

1945
Southern Holland is liberated in 1944 but northern and western Holland have to endure a winter of hunger. The Germans capitulate on 5 May 1945

1958
The first DAF passenger car is launched

1980
The coronation of Queen Beatrix on 30 April is accompanied by heavy battles between police and anti-monarchy demonstrators and youthful rioters

1980
The KVP, ARP and CHU combine to form the CDA, the large Christian Democratic Party

1995
Paul Crutzen is awarded the Nobel Prize for Chemistry for his ground-breaking investigations of the ozone layer

1992
Under Dutch presidency, the European partners sign the draft Maastricht Treaty in 1991. In 1992, the treaty, under which the European Community becomes the European Union, is ratified

1966
"Provos" organize nightly happenings on Amsterdam's Spui

2002
On 2 February Crown Prince Willem-Alexander marries Argentinian Máxima Zorreguieta in Amsterdam's Beurs van Berlage

1960	1970	1980	1990	2000

1960	1970	1980	1990	2000

2002
Politician Pym Fortuyn is assassinated on 6 May

2000
The Dutch team at the Sydney Olympics wins a record 25 medals, including 12 golds

1975
Holland recognizes the independence of its former colony Suriname

1985
A government decision to deploy 48 NATO cruise missiles on Dutch territory causes a storm of opposition. The Komité Kruisraketten Nee (anti-cruise coalition) submits a petition of 3.5 million signatures to Prime Minister Lubbers in October

1962
The release of Jan Vrijman's film *De werekelijkheid van Karel Appel* brings the postwar Dutch painter to the attention of the general public. Karel Appel (b. 1921) caused a sensation with his statement: "I'll just mess something up"

1971
Ajax wins the First Division European Cup at Wembley Stadium in London with star player Johan Cruijff. The club continues as champion in 1972 and 1973

AMSTERDAM

Amsterdam's Best: Canals and Waterways

FROM THE GRACE and elegance of the waterside mansions along the *Grachtengordel* (Canal Ring) to the rows of converted warehouses on Brouwersgracht and the charming houses on Reguliersgracht, the city's canals and waterways embody the very spirit of Amsterdam. They are spanned by many beautiful bridges, including the famous Magere Brug *(see pp114–15)*, a traditionally styled lift bridge. You can also relax at a canalside café or bar and watch an array of boats float by.

Brouwersgracht
The banks of this charming canal are lined with houseboats, cosy cafés and warehouses.

Bloemgracht
There is a great variety of architecture along this lovely, treelined canal in the Jordaan, including a row of houses with step gables.

Canal Ring

Prinsengracht
The best way to see all the beautiful buildings along Amsterdam's longest 17th-century canal is by bicycle.

Museum Quarter

Keizersgracht
A view of this canal can be had from any of its bridges. For an overview of the Canal Ring go to Metz & Co at Leidsestraat 34–36 (see p113).

Leidsegracht
Relax at a pavement café along the exclusive Leidsegracht.

Singel

The Poezenboot, *a boat for stray cats, is just one of the many sights to be found along the Singel, whose distinctive, curved shape established the horseshoe contours of the Canal Ring.*

Entrepotdok

The warehouses on the Entrepotdok (see p134) were redeveloped in the 1980s. The quayside is now lined in summer with lively café terraces that overlook an array of houseboats and pleasure craft.

0 metres	500
0 yards	500

Nieuwe Zijde

Oude Zijde

Plantage

Herengracht

Known as "the twin brothers", these matching neck-gabled houses at Nos. 409–411 are two of the prettiest houses on the city's grandest canal.

Reguliersgracht

Many crooked, brick buildings line this pretty canal, which was cut in 1664. The statue of a stork, located at No. 92, is symbolic of parental responsibility and commemorates a 1571 by-law protecting this bird.

Amstel

This river is still a busy thoroughfare, with barges and, above all, many sightseeing boats.

The Golden Age of Amsterdam

THE 17TH CENTURY was truly a Golden Age for Amsterdam. The population soared; three great canals, bordered by splendid houses, were built in a triple ring round the city; and scores of painters and architects were at work. Fortunes were made and lost, and this early capitalism produced many paupers, who were cared for by charitable institutions – a radical idea for the time. In 1648, an uneasy peace was formalized with Catholic Spain, causing tension between Amsterdam's Calvinist burgomasters and the less-religious House of Orange, which was dominant elsewhere in the country.

Spice Trade
In this old print, a VOC spice trader arrives in Bantam.

Livestock and grain trading

Self-Portrait as the Apostle Paul *(1661)*
Rembrandt (see p78) was one of many artists working in Amsterdam in the mid-17th century.

The new Stadhuis (now the Koninklijk Paleis) was being constructed behind wooden scaffolding.

Nieuwe Kerk, 1395 *(see p86)*

The Love Letter *(1666)*
Genre painting (see p123), such as this calm domestic interior by Jan Vermeer, became popular as society grew more sophisticated. Jan Steen, Honthorst and Terborch were other famous genre painters.

DAM SQUARE IN 1656

Money poured into Amsterdam at this time of civic expansion. Holland was active overseas, colonizing Indonesia, and the spice trade brought enormous wealth. The Dutch East India Company (VOC), the principal trade organization in Holland, prospered – gold seemed almost as common as water. Dutch painter Jan Lingelbach (c.1624–74) depicted the city's Dam square as a busy, thriving and cosmopolitan market, brimming with traders and wealthy merchants.

Delft Tiles
Delicate flower paintings were popular themes on 17th-century Delft tiles (see pp26–7), used as decoration in wealthy households.

Flora's Bandwagon *(1636)*
Many allegories were painted during "tulip mania". This satirical oil by HG Pot symbolizes the idiocy of investors who paid for rare bulbs with their weight in gold, forcing prices up until the market collapsed.

Commodities weighed at the Waag

Ships sailing up the Damrak

Spices

A load of spices was worth a fortune in the 17th century. The VOC traded in a great variety of these costly spices, primarily pepper, nutmeg, cloves, mace and cinnamon. As early as 1611 the VOC was the largest importer of spices.

Cargo unloaded by cranes

Turkish traders

Pepper, nutmeg, cloves, mace, cinnamon

WHERE TO SEE 17TH-CENTURY AMSTERDAM

Many public buildings, such as churches and palaces, sprang up as Amsterdam grew more wealthy. The Westerkerk *(see p110)* was designed by Hendrick de Keyser in 1620; the Lutherse Kerk *(see p90)* by Adriaan Dortsman in 1671. Elias Bouman built the Portugees-Israëlitische Synagoge *(see p80)* in 1675 for members of the city's immigrant Sephardic Jewish community.

Apollo *(c.1648) Artus Quellien's statue is in the South Gallery of the Koninklijk Paleis (see pp88–9). Construction of the place, a masterwork by Jacob van Capenwhich, began in 1648.*

VOC

In the Scheepvaart Museum (see pp132–3), an entire room is dedicated to the Dutch East India Company.

Giving the Bread
This painting by Willem van Valckert shows the city's needy receiving alms. A rudimentary welfare system was introduced in the 1640s.

Rembrandthuis *(1606) Jacob van Campen added the pediment in 1633 (see p78).*

Amsterdam's Best: Museums

For a fairly small city, Amsterdam has a surprisingly large number of museums and galleries. The quality and variety of the collections are impressive, covering everything from bibles and beer to shipbuilding and space travel. Many are housed in buildings of historical or architectural interest. The Rijksmuseum, with its Gothic façade, is a city landmark, and Rembrandt's work is exhibited in his original home.

Anne Frankhuis
Anne Frank's photo is exhibited in the house where she hid during World War II.

Amsterdams Historisch Museum
A wealth of historical information is on display here. Once an orphanage for boys, it is depicted in Governesses at the Burgher Orphanage *(1683) by Adriaen Backer.*

Rijksmuseum
An extensive collection of paintings by Dutch masters can be seen in the country's largest national museum. Jan van Huysum's Still Life with Fruit and Flowers, *dating from about 1730, is a fine example (see pp122–5).*

Canal Ring

Museum Quarter

Stedelijk Museum
Gerrit Rietveld's simple Steltman chair (1963) is one of many exhibits at this modern art museum (see pp128–9).

Van Gogh Museum
Van Gogh's Self-portrait with Straw Hat (1870) hangs in this large, stark building, built in 1973 to house the bulk of his work.

Koninklijk Paleis
The royal palace on the Dam, a former town hall designed in 1648 by Jacob van Campen, is still regularly used today by the queen on official occasions (see pp88–9).

NEMO
This amazing building, designed in the form of a ship and overhanging the water by 30 m (99 ft), houses a museum of science and technology (see pp136–7).

Nederlands Scheepvaart Museum
This maritime museum is decorated with reliefs relating to the city's maritime history. Moored alongside is a replica of the East Indiaman, Amsterdam, *which is open to the public.*

0 metres		500
0 yards		500

Joods Historisch Museum
Four adjoining synagogues are linked to form this museum.

Verzetsmuseum
Located in the Plantage, this museum documents and commemorates the activities of Dutch Resistance workers in World War II (see p141).

Amsterdam's Best: Cafés

Amsterdam is a city of cafés and bars, about 1,500 in all. Each area has something to offer, from friendly and relaxed brown cafés – a traditional Dutch local pub characterized by dark wooden panelling and furniture, low ceilings, dim lighting and a fog of tobacco smoke – to lively and crowded designer bars. Each café and bar has some special attraction: a large range of beers, live music, canalside terraces, art exhibitions, board games and pool tables or simply a brand of *gezelligheid*, the unique Dutch concept of "cosiness".

Karpershoek
This lively café (the oldest café in Amsterdam) is close to the Centraal Station and is frequented by travellers looking for a cup of coffee.

Café Chris
This brown café in the Jordaan is patronized by regular customers (artists and students).

Odeon
This popular disco is on three floors; in the bar, look up at the beautifully painted ceiling.

Canal Ring

Vertigo
The café terrace of the Nederlands Filmmuseum in the Vondelpark is very busy on warm summer days.

Museum Quarter

Hoppe
The dark wooden interior and tang of cigar smoke in the air are the essence of this classic brown café, situated on the lively Spui.

De Drie Fleschjes
In one of the oldest pubs (1650) of Amsterdam, you can choose from a wide variety of gins.

Kapitein Zeppos
This café, frequented by trendy Amsterdammers, often hosts live concerts on Sunday afternoons.

Oude Zijde

Nieuwe Zijde

Plantage

De Jaren
Popular with students, this trendy two-storey café has a superb view of the Amstel and a wide selection of newspapers.

Sportcafé Soccerworld
In the café of the arena you can admire the football shirts of the famous Ajax team.

| 0 metres | 500 |
| 0 yards | 500 |

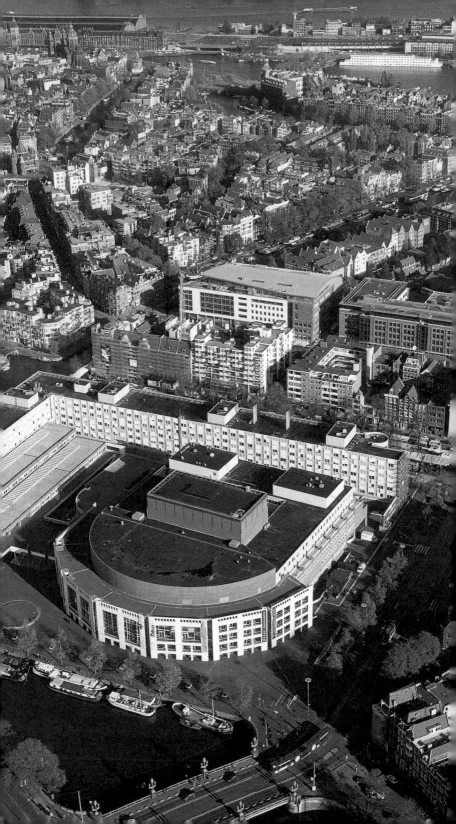

OUDE ZIJDE

THE EASTERN HALF of Amsterdam became known as the Oude Zijde (Old Side). Originally it occupied a narrow strip on the east bank of the Amstel river, running between Damrak and the Oudezijds Voorburgwal. At its heart was built the Oude Kerk, the oldest church in the city. In the early 15th century the Oude Zijde began an eastward expansion that continued into the 1600s. This growth was fuelled by an influx of Jewish refugees from Portugal. The oldest of the four synagogues, now containing the Joods Historisch Museum, dates from this period. These were central to Jewish life in the city for centuries. During the Golden Age *(see pp50–51)*, the Oude Zijde was an important commercial centre. Boats could sail up the Geldersekade to Nieuwmarkt, where goods were weighed at the Waag before being sold at the market.

Aäron from Mozes en Aäronkerk

SIGHTS AT A GLANCE

Historic Buildings and Monuments
Agnietenkapel ❺
Montelbaanstoren ⓱
Oost-Indisch Huis ❼
Oudemanhuispoort ❻
Pintohuis ⓰
Scheepvaarthuis ⓲
Schreierstoren ⓳
Trippenhuis ❽
Waag ❷

Opera Houses
Stadhuis-Muziektheater ⓫

Museums
Hash Marihuana Hemp
  Museum ❹
Joods Historisch Museum ⓮
Rembrandthuis ❿

Churches and Synagogues
Mozes en Aäronkerk ⓭
Oude Kerk pp76–7 ㉑
Portugees-Israëlitische
  Synagoge ⓯
Zuiderkerk ❾

Streets and Markets
Nieuwmarkt ❸
Red Light District ❶
Waterlooplein ⓬
Zeedijk ⓴

GETTING THERE
The best way to reach the Oude Zijde is to get a tram to the Dam (trams 1, 2, 4, 5, 9, 13, 14, 16, 17, 24 and 25) and then walk along Damstraat. Alternatively, take tram 9 or 14 directly to Waterlooplein, or the metro to Nieuwmarkt.

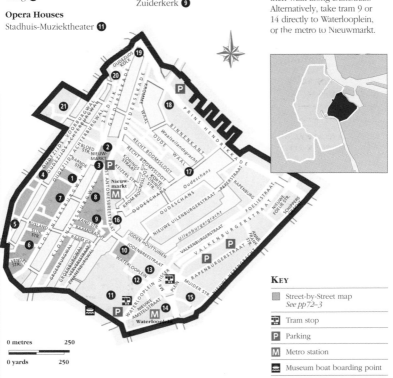

KEY
🔲 Street-by-Street map
See pp72–3

🚊 Tram stop

🅿 Parking

Ⓜ Metro station

🚤 Museum boat boarding point

0 metres   250
0 yards   250

◁ **The enormous town hall/opera house, an unusual combination in the old part of town**

Street-by-Street: University District

THE UNIVERSITY OF AMSTERDAM, founded in 1877, is predominantly located in the peaceful, southwestern part of the Oude Zijde. The university's roots lie in the former Athenaeum Illustre, which was founded in 1632 in the Agnieten-kapel. Beyond Damstraat, the bustling Red Light District meets the Nieuw-markt, where the 15th-century Waag evokes a medieval air. South of the Nieuwmarkt, Museum Het Rembrandt-huis gives a fascinating insight into the life of the city's most famous artist.

★ Red Light District
The sex industry brings billions of euros to Amsterdam every year ❶

Hash Marihuana Hemp Museum
This museum showcases marijuana through the ages ❹

Agnietenkapel
Like many buildings in this area, the cloisters, which house a museum, belong to the University of Amsterdam ❺

House (1610), unusually facing three canals

Oudemanhuispoort
The spectacles carved on the gateway into this 18th-century almshouse for elderly men symbolize old age ❻

VOORBURGWAL
ACHTERBURGWAL
OUDE ZIJDS
OUDEZIJDS
RUSLAND

Lift bridge over Groenburgwal

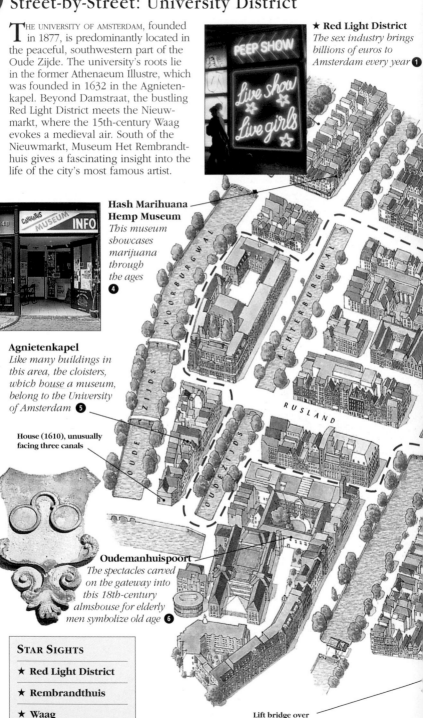

STAR SIGHTS

★ **Red Light District**

★ **Rembrandthuis**

★ **Waag**

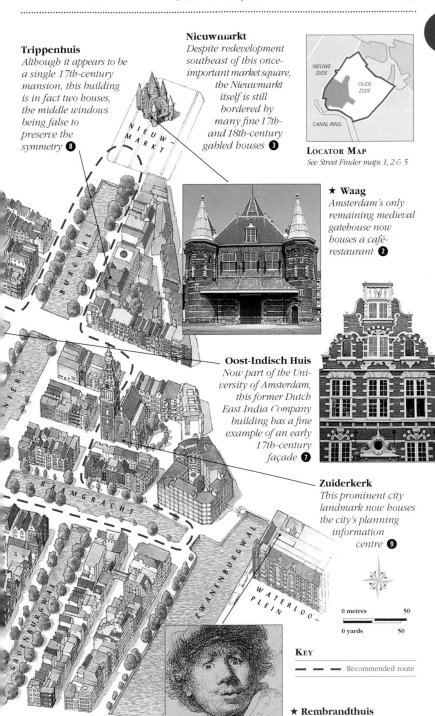

Trippenhuis
Although it appears to be a single 17th-century mansion, this building is in fact two houses, the middle windows being false to preserve the symmetry **8**

Nicuwmarkt
Despite redevelopment southeast of this once-important market square, the Nieuwmarkt itself is still bordered by many fine 17th- and 18th-century gabled houses **3**

LOCATOR MAP
See Street Finder maps 1, 2 & 5

★ **Waag**
Amsterdam's only remaining medieval gatehouse now houses a café-restaurant **2**

Oost-Indisch Huis
Now part of the University of Amsterdam, this former Dutch East India Company building has a fine example of an early 17th-century façade **7**

Zuiderkerk
This prominent city landmark now houses the city's planning information centre **9**

0 metres   50
0 yards   50

KEY

– – – Recommended route

★ **Rembrandthuis**
Hundreds of Rembrandt's etchings, including many self-portraits, are on display in the artist's former home **10**

Red Light District ❶

Map 5 A1. 🚋 *4, 9, 16, 24, 25.*

BARELY CLAD prostitutes bathed in a red neon glow and touting for business at their windows is one of the defining images of modern Amsterdam. The city's Red Light District, referred to locally as de Walletjes (the little walls), is concentrated on the Oude Kerk *(see pp76–7)*, although it extends as far as Warmoesstraat to the west, the Zeedijk to the north, the Kloveniersburgwal to the east and then along the line of Damstraat to the south.

Prostitution in Amsterdam dates back to the city's emergence as a port in the 13th century. By 1478, prostitution had become so widespread, with increasing numbers of sea-weary sailors flooding into the city, that attempts were made to contain it. Prostitutes straying outside their designated area were marched back to the sound of pipe and drum.

A century later, following the Alteration, the Calvinists *(see pp52–3)* tried to outlaw prostitution altogether. Their attempts were half-hearted, and by the mid-17th century prostitution was openly tolerated. In 1850, Amsterdam had a

Entrance to one of the clubs in the Red Light District

population of 200,000, and more than 200 brothels. The most famous of these, like the luxurious Madame Traese's, catered for rich clients.

Today, the whole area is criss-crossed by a network of narrow lanes, dominated by garish sex shops and seedy clubs, and peppered with junkies, dealers and pickpockets. At night, the little alleys assume a somewhat sinister aspect, and it is unwise to wander away from the main streets. But by day, hordes of visitors crowding in generate a festive buzz, and among the sleaze there are interesting cafés, bars, restaurants and beautiful canalside houses to be discovered.

Waag ❷

Nieuwmarkt 4. **Map** 2 E5. 🚋 *9, 14.* **M** *Nieuwmarkt.* ⬤ *to public.*

THE MULTI-TURRETED Waag is Amsterdam's oldest surviving gatehouse. Built in 1488, it was then, and often still is, called St Antoniespoort. Public executions were held here, and condemned prisoners awaited their fate in the "little gallows room". In 1617, the building became the public weigh house *(waaggebouw)*. Peasants had their produce weighed here and paid tax accordingly. Various guilds moved into the upper rooms of each tower. From 1619 the Guild of Surgeons had their meeting room and anatomy theatre here. They added the central octagonal tower in 1691. Rembrandt's *Anatomy Lesson of Dr Nicholaes Tulp,* now in the Mauritshuis *(see pp220–21)*, and *The Anatomy Lesson of Dr Jan Deijman,* in the Amsterdams Historisch Museum *(see pp92–3)*, were commissioned by guild members and then hung here.

The weigh house closed in the early 19th century and the Waag has since served as a fire station and two city museums. It is now home to the restaurant In de Waag.

The 15th-century Waag dominating the Nieuwmarkt, with an antique market on the right

Part of the commemorative photo display in Nieuwmarkt metro

Nieuwmarkt ❸

Map 2 E5. 🚋 9, 14. Ⓜ Nieuwmarkt.
Antiques market ◻ May–Sep:
9am–5pm Sun.

A̶N OPEN, PAVED square, the Nieuwmarkt is flanked to the west by the Red Light District. With the top end of the Geldersekade, it forms Amsterdam's Chinatown. The Waag dominates the square, and construction of this gateway led to the site's development in the 15th century as a marketplace. When the city expanded in the 17th century (see pp64–5), the square took on its present dimensions and was called the Nieuwmarkt. It retains an array of 17th- and 18th-century gabled houses. True to tradition, an antiques market is held on Sundays during the summer.

The old Jewish Quarter leads off the square down St Antoniesbreestraat. In the 1970s, many houses in this area were demolished to make way for the new metro, sparking off clashes between protesters and police. The action of conservationists persuaded the city council to adopt a policy of renovating rather than redeveloping old buildings. In tribute to them, photographs of their protests decorate the metro.

Hash Marihuana Hemp Museum ❹

Oudezijds Achterburgwal 148.
Map 2 D5. 🕻 020-6235961. 🚋 4, 9, 14, 16, 24, 25. Ⓜ Nieuwmarkt.
◻ 11am–11pm. 🗺 🄾 🕭 🄱

T̶HIS MUSEUM is the only one in Europe to chart the history of hemp (marijuana). Exhibits refer back 8,000 years to early Asiatic civilizations,

which used the plant for medicines and clothing. It was first used in the Netherlands, according to a herbal manual of 1554, as a cure for earache.

Until the late 19th century, however, hemp was the main source of fibre for rope, and was therefore important in the Dutch shipping industry. Other exhibits relate to the psychoactive properties of this plant. They include an intriguing array of pipes and bongs (smoking devices), along with displays that explain smuggling methods. The museum also has a small cultivation area where plants are grown under artificial light. Police sometimes raid and take away exhibits, so there may be occasional gaps in displays.

Agnietenkapel ❺

Oudezijds Voorburgwal 231.
Map 2 D5. 🕻 020-5253339. 🚋 4, 9, 14, 16, 24, 25. ◻ 9am–5pm Mon–Fri. ● public hols. 🗺 🄾

N̶OW HOME to the University Museum, the Agnieten-kapel was part of the convent of St Agnes until 1578 when it was closed after the Alter-ation. In 1632, the Athenaeum Illustre, the precursor of the University of Amsterdam, took over the building and by the mid-17th century it was a centre of scientific learning. It also housed the municipal library until the 1830s. While the museum focuses on the history of the University of Amsterdam, the main attrac-tion is the Agnietenkapel itself, dating from 1470. It is one of the few Gothic chapels to have survived the Alteration. During rest-oration from 1919 to 1921, elements of the Amsterdam School architecture were introduced (see pp142–3). Despite these changes and long periods of secular use, the building still has the feel of a Franciscan chapel. The large auditorium on the first

floor is the oldest in the city and is today used for lectures at the university. It has a lovely ceiling, painted with Renaiss-ance motifs and a portrait of Minerva, the Roman goddess of wisdom and the arts. The walls are hung with 40 por-traits of European humanist scholars, including one of Erasmus (1466–1536).

Entrance to Agnietenkapel, home to the University Museum

Oudemanhuis-poort ❻

Between Oudezijds Achterburgwal and Kloveniersburgwal. **Map** 2 D5. 🚋 4, 9, 14, 16, 24, 25. **Book market** ◻ 10am–6pm Mon–Sat.

T̶HE OUDEMANHUISPOORT was once the entrance to old people's almshouses (Oude-mannenhuis), built in 1754. Today the building is part of the University of Amsterdam. The pediment over the gateway in the Oudezijds Achterburgwal features a pair of spectacles, a symbol of old age. Trading inside this covered walkway dates from 1757 and today there is a market for second-hand books. Although the building is closed to the public, visitors may enter the 18th-century courtyard via the arcade.

Crest of Amsterdam, Oudemanhuispoort

Oude Kerk ㉑

THE ORIGINS of the Oude Kerk date from the early 13th century, when a wooden church was built in a burial ground on a sand bank. The present Gothic structure is 14th century and has grown from a single-aisled church into a basilica. As it expanded, the building became a gathering place for traders and a refuge for the poor. The church's paintings and statuary were destroyed after the Alteration in 1578, but the gilded ceiling and stained-glass windows were undamaged. The Great Organ was added in 1724, and the stark interior has changed little since.

Carving on 15th-century choir misericord

The spire of the bell tower was built by Joost Bilhamer in 1565. François Hemony added the 47-bell carillon in 1658 *(see p29)*.

Tomb of Saskia, first wife of Rembrandt *(see p78)*

The Oude Kerk Today
The old church, surrounded by shops, cafés and houses, remains a calm and peaceful haven at the heart of the frenetic Red Light District.

Christening chapel

Tomb of Admiral Abraham van der Hulst (1619–66)

★ **Great Organ** *(1724)*
Jan Westerman's oak-encased organ has eight bellows and 54 gilded pipes. Marbled-wood statues of biblical figures surround it.

TIMELINE

	1300	1400	1500	1600	1700	1800	1900

1412 North transept completed

1330 Church consecrated to St Nicholas

1462 First side chapel demolished to build south transept

1552 Lady Chapel added

1658 Carillon installed

1724 Great Organ installed

1979 Church re-opens to public

1951 Church closes

1500 Side chapels added

1340 Church enlarged

1566 Spire added to 13th-century tower

1300 Small stone church built

1578 Calvinists triumph in the Alteration

Stained-glass coats of arms in Lady Chapel

1912–14 Partial restoration of northwest corner

1955–99 Restoration of church

★ **Gilded Ceiling**
The delicate 15th-century vault paintings have a gilded background. They were hidden with layers of blue paint in 1755 and not revealed until 1955.

VISITORS' CHECKLIST

Oudekerksplein 23. **Map** 2 D4.
☎ 020-6258284. 🚊 4, 9, 16, 24, 25.
Church ◯ 11am–5pm Mon–Sat, 1–5pm Sun. ✝ 11am Sun. 📷
📷 ♿ **Tower** 📷 phone 020-6126865 to arrange. ● 1 Jan, 25 Dec. 🌐 www.oudekerk.nl

Tomb of Admiral Jacob van Heemskerk (1567–1607)

★ **Lady Chapel** *(1552)*
The Death of the Virgin Mary *by Dirk Crabeth is one of three restored stained-glass windows in the Lady Chapel.*

Brocaded Pillars
Decorative pillars originally formed niches holding a series of statues of the Apostles, all destroyed by the iconoclasts in 1578.

17th- and 18th-century houses

Former sacristy

The Red Door
The inscription on the lintel above the door into the former sacristy warns those about to enter: "Marry in haste, repent at leisure".

STAR FEATURES

★ **Gilded Ceiling**

★ **Great Organ**

★ **Lady Chapel**

Oost-Indisch Huis 🌀

Oude Hoogstraat 24. **Map** 2 D5.
🚋 *4, 9, 14, 16, 24, 25.*
Ⓜ *Nieuwmarkt.* ⚫ *to the public.*

THE AUSTERE Oost-Indisch
Huis, former headquarters
of the Dutch East India Company *(see pp48–9),* is part of
the University of Amsterdam.
Built in 1605 and attributed to
Hendrick de Keyser, it was expanded several times to house
spices, silk and porcelain from
the East Indies. Restyling in
the 1890s destroyed
much of the inte-
rior decoration,
but the façade
has remained
largely intact.

**Ornate balustrade of
the Oost-Indisch Huis**

Trippenhuis 🌀

Kloveniersburgwal 29. **Map** 2 E5.
🚋 *4, 9, 14, 16, 24, 25.*
Ⓜ *Nieuwmarkt.* ⚫ *to the public.*

JUSTUS VINGBOONS designed this
ornate Classical mansion,
completed in 1662. It appears
to be one house: it is in fact
two. The façade, outlined by
eight Corinthian columns, features false middle windows.
The house was designed for
arms merchants Lodewijk and
Hendrick Trip; the chimneys
look like cannons. The city's
art collection was housed here
1817–85, when it moved to the
Rijksmuseum *(see pp122–5).*
Trippenhuis now houses the
Dutch Academy. Opposite at
No. 26 is the Kleine Trippenhuis (1698). Only 2.5 m (7 ft)
wide, it has detailed cornicing,
including two carved sphinxes.

Zuiderkerk 🌀

Zuiderkerkhof 72. **Map** 2 E5.
📞 *020-5527987.* 🚋 *9, 14.*
Ⓜ *Nieuwmarkt.* ⏱ *11am–4pm
Mon, 9am–4pm Tue, Wed & Fri,
9am–8pm Thu.* 📷 ♿ **Tower**
🎦 📸 *Jun–Sep: 2pm & 4pm.*
🆆 *www.zuiderkerk.amsterdam.nl*

DESIGNED BY Hendrick de
Keyser in 1603 in the
Renaissance style, the
Zuiderkerk was the first
Calvinist church to open
in Amsterdam after the

The spire of the Zuiderkerk, a prominent city landmark

Alteration. The spire has
columns, decorative clocks
and an onion dome.
   The Zuiderkerk ceased to
function as a church in 1929.
Restored in 1988, it is now
a public housing exhibition
centre. The surrounding community housing includes the
"Pentagon" by Theo Bosch.

Rembrandthuis 🌀

Jodenbreestraat 4-6. **Map** 2 E5.
📞 *020-5200400.* 🚋 *9, 14.*
Ⓜ *Nieuwmarkt.* ⏱ *10am–5pm
Mon–Sat, 1–5pm Sun & public hols.*
⚫ *1 Jan.* 🎦 📷 📁 📚 📸
🆆 *www.rembrandthuis.nl*

REMBRANDT worked and
taught in this house from
1639 until 1660. He lived in
the ground-floor rooms with
his wife, Saskia, who died here
in 1642, leaving the artist with
a baby son, Titus.
   Many of Rembrandt's most
famous paintings were created

in the first-floor studio. Lessons
were conducted in the attic. A
fine collection of Rembrandt's
etchings and drawings includes
various self-portraits. There
are also landscapes, nude
studies, religious and crowd
scenes and sketches of the
artist with his wife. The house
has recently undergone historically accurate restoration
and a further wing has been
opened to the public.

**Self-portrait by Rembrandt with
his wife, Saskia (1636)**

Stadhuis-Muziektheater ⓫

Waterlooplein 22. **Map** 5 B2. 🚊 4, 9,
14. Ⓜ Waterlooplein. **Stadhuis** 🚻
020-5529111. ⏱ 8:30am–3:30pm
Mon–Fri, 8:30am–3:30pm & 5–7pm
Thu, 3pm Sat (free concerts Sep–May:
6:30pm Tue). **Muziek–theater** 🚻
020-6255455. See **Entertainment**
pp146–7. 🅰 🅾
ⓦ www.hetmuziektheater.nl

F EW BUILDINGS in Amsterdam
caused as much controversy
as the new Stadhuis (city hall)
and Muziektheater (opera
house). Nicknamed the "Stopera" by protesters, the plan
required the destruction of
dozens of medieval houses,
which were virtually all that
remained of the original Jewish quarter. This led to running battles between squatters
and the police.

The building, completed in
1988, is a huge confection of
red brick, marble and glass. A
mural illustrating the Normaal
Amsterdams Peil is shown on
the arcade linking the two parts
of the complex. The complex
has the largest auditorium in
the country, and it is home
to the Netherlands' national
opera and ballet companies.

Waterlooplein ⓬

Map 5 B2. 🚊 9, 14. Ⓜ Waterlooplein. **Holland Experience** 🚻 020-
4222233. ⏱ 10am–6:30pm daily.
🎪 **Market** ⏱ 9am–5pm Mon–Fri,
8:30am–5pm Sat.

T HE WATERLOOPLEIN dates from
1882, when two canals
were filled in to create a market square. The site was originally known as Vlooyenburg,
an artificial island built in the
17th century to house Jewish
settlers. It is now the setting
for Holland Experience, a
spectacular multi-media show.

At the northern end of the
Waterlooplein is a lively market that sells anything from
bric-a-brac and army-surplus
clothing to Balinese carvings.

Mozes en Aäronkerk ⓭

Waterlooplein 205. **Map** 5 B2.
🚻 020-6247597. 🚊 9, 14.
Ⓜ Waterlooplein. ⚫ to the
public except for exhibitions.

D ESIGNED BY Flemish architect
T Suys the Elder in 1841,
Mozes en Aäronkerk was built
on the site of a clandestine
Catholic church. The later

church took its name from the
Old Testament figures depicted on the gable stones of the
original building. These are
now set into the rear wall.

The church was restored in
1990, its twin wooden towers
painted to look like sandstone.
It is now used for exhibitions,
public meetings and concerts.

**The central hall in the Grote
Synagoge, which opened in 1671**

Joods Historisch Museum ⓮

Jonas Daniel Meijerplein 2–4. **Map**
5 B2. 🚻 020-6269945. 🚊 9, 14.
🚋 Muziektheater. Ⓜ Waterlooplein.
🎪 📷 🅰 🍴 🅾 on request, incl.
for the visually handicapped. 🅰 🅾
ⓦ www.jhm.nl

T HIS COMPLEX of four synagogues was built by Ash-
kenazi Jews in the 17th and
18th centuries and opened as
a museum in 1987. The synagogues were central to Jewish
life in Amsterdam, until the
devastation of World War II
left them empty. Restored in
the 1980s, they are connected
by internal walkways. Displays
of art and religious artefacts
depict Jewish culture and the
history of Judaism in the
Netherlands. For children,
there is an exhibit on Jewish
culture. Temporary exhibitions are also held here.

Highlights include the Grote
Synagoge, its hall lined with
galleries; and the Holy Ark
(1791) from Enkhuizen (see
p176) which dominates the
Nieuwe Synagoge and holds
two 18th-century silver Torah
shields and three velvet man-
tles. Also not to be missed is
the 1734 Haggadah illuminated
manuscript, containing the
Passover order of service.

Eclectic goods on offer at the Waterlooplein market

Portugees-Israëlitische Synagoge ⑮

Mr Visserplein 3. **Map** 5 B2.
📞 *020-6245351.* 🚊 *9, 14.*
Ⓜ *Waterlooplein.* ◯◯
10am–4pm Sun–Thu, 10am–3pm Fri.
◯ *Jewish hols.* 🖼 📷 ♿ 🏠

E LIAS BOUMAN'S design for the Portugees-Israëlitische Synagoge is said to be inspired by the architecture of the Temple of Solomon in Jerusalem. Built for the influential and wealthy Portuguese Sephardic community of Amsterdam and inaugurated in 1675, the huge brick building has a rectangular ground plan with the Holy Ark in the southeast corner facing towards Jerusalem, and the *tebah* (the podium from which the service is led) at the opposite end.

The wooden, barrel-vaulted ceiling is supported by four Ionic columns. The interior of the synagogue, with its pews made of mahogany, is illuminated by more than 1,000 candles and 72 windows.

Italianate façade of the 17th-century Pintohuis

Pintohuis ⑯

Sint Antoniesbreestraat 69. **Map** 2 E5.
📞 *020-6243184.* 🚊 *9, 14.* Ⓜ
Nieuwmarkt. **Library** ◯ *2–8pm Mon & Wed, 2–5pm Fri, 11am–2pm Sat (except summer hols).* ◯ *public hols.*

I SAAC DE PINTO, a wealthy Portuguese merchant, bought the Pintohuis in 1651 for the then enormous sum of 30,000

guilders. He had it remodelled over the next decades to a design by Elias Bouman, and it is one of the few private residences in Amsterdam to follow an Italianate style. The exterior design was reworked from 1675 to 1680. Six imposing pilasters break up the severe, cream façade into five recessed sections, and the cornice is topped by a blind balustrade concealing the roof.

In the 1970s, the house was scheduled for demolition because it stood in the way of a newly planned main road. Concerted protest saved the building, which now houses a public library. Visitors can still admire the original painted ceiling, which is decorated with birds and cherubs.

Montelbaanstoren ⑰

Oude Waal /Oudeschans 2. **Map** 5 B1.
🚊 *9, 14.* Ⓜ *Nieuwmarkt.* ◯ *to the public.*

T HE LOWER PORTION of the Montelbaanstoren was built in 1512 and formed part of Amsterdam's medieval fortifications. It lay just beyond the city wall, protecting the city's wharves on the newly built St Antoniesdijk (now the Oudeschans) from the neighbouring Gelderlanders.

The octagonal structure and open-work timber steeple were both added by Hendrick de Keyser in 1606. His decorative addition bears a close resemblance to the spire of the Oude Kerk, designed by Joost Bilhamer, which was built 40 years earlier *(see pp76–7)*. In 1611, the tower began to list, prompting Amsterdammers to attach ropes to the top and pull it right again.

Sailors from the Dutch East India Company would gather at the Montelbaanstoren before being ferried in small boats down the IJ to the massive East Indies-bound sailing ships, anchored further out in deep water to the north.

The building appears in a number of etchings by Rembrandt, and is still a popular subject for artists. It now houses the offices of the Amsterdam water authority.

One of many stone carvings on the Scheepvaarthuis façade

Scheepvaarthuis ⑱

Prins Hendrikkade 108. **Map** 2 E4.
🚊 *1, 2, 4, 5, 9, 11, 13, 16, 17, 24, 25.*
Ⓜ *Centraal Station.* ◯ *to the public.*
🖋 *call Archivisie (tel. 020-6258908).*

B UILT AS AN OFFICE complex in 1916, the Scheepvaarthuis (shipping house) is regarded as the first true example of Amsterdam School architecture *(see p142–3)*. It was designed by Piet Kramer (1881–1961), Johan van der May (1878–1949) and Michel de Klerk (1884–1923) for a group of shipping companies which no longer wanted to conduct business on the quay.

The imposing triangular building has a prow-like front and is crowned by a statue of Neptune, his wife and four female figures representing the

The medieval Montelbaanstoren, with its decorative timber steeple

four points of the compass. No expense was spared on the construction and internal decoration of the building, and local dock workers came to regard the building as a symbol of capitalism. The doors, stairs, window frames and interior walls are festooned with nautical images, such as sea horses, dolphins and anchors. Beautiful stained-glass skylights are also decorated with images of sailing ships, maps and compasses.

The Scheepvaarthuis is closed to the public; but may re-open one day as a hotel.

Schreierstoren ⑲

Prins Hendrikkade 94–95.
Map 2 E4. 🚊 *1, 2, 4, 5, 9, 11, 13, 16, 17, 24, 25.* Ⓜ *Centraal Station.*
Ⓦ *www.schreierstoren.nl*

T HE SCHREIERSTOREN (weepers' tower) was a defensive structure forming part of the medieval city walls, dating from 1480. It was one of the few fortifications not to be demolished as the city expanded beyond its medieval boundaries in the 17th century. The building is now used for occasional private parties.

Popular legend states that the tower derived its name from the weeping (*schreien* in the original Dutch) of women who came here to wave their men off to sea. It is more likely, however, that the title has a less romantic origin and comes from the tower's position on a sharp (*screye* or *scherpe*), 90-degree bend in the old town walls. The earliest of four wall plaques, dated 1569, adds considerably to the confusion by depicting a weeping woman alongside the inscription *scrayer hovck,* which means sharp corner.

In 1609, Henry Hudson set sail from here in an attempt to discover a new and faster trading route to the East Indies. Instead, he unintentionally "discovered" the river in North America which still bears his name. A bronze plaque, laid in 1927, commemorates his voyage.

The Schreierstoren, part of the original city fortifications

Zeedijk ⑳

Map 2 E4. 🚊 *1, 2, 4, 5, 9, 11, 13, 16, 17, 24, 25.* Ⓜ *Centraal Station.*

A LONG WITH the Nieuwendijk and the Haarlemmerdijk, the Zeedijk (sea dyke) formed part of Amsterdam's original fortifications. Built in the early 1300s, some 30 years after Amsterdam had been granted its city charter, these defences took the form of a canal moat with piled-earth ramparts reinforced by wooden palisades. As the city grew in prosperity and its boundaries expanded, canals were filled in and the dykes became obsolete. The paths that ran alongside them became the streets and alleys which bear their names today.

One of the two remaining wooden-fronted houses in the city is at No. 1. It was built in the mid-1500s as a hostel for sailors and is much restored. Opposite is St Olofskapel, built in 1445 and named after the first Christian king of Norway and Denmark. By the 1600s, the Zeedijk had be- come a slum. The area is on the edge of the city's Red Light District, and in the 1960s and 1970s it became notorious as a centre for drug-dealing and street crime. However, following an extensive clean-up campaign in the 1980s, the Zeedijk is much improved. Architect Fred Greves has built a Chinese Buddhist temple, Fo Kuang Shan.

Plaques on the gables of some of the street's cafés reveal their former use – the red boot at No. 17 indicates that it was once a cobbler's.

The Zeedijk, today a lively street with plenty of restaurants

Nieuwe Zijde

"The calf" emblem on a house in the Begijnhof

THE WESTERN SIDE of medieval Amsterdam was known as the Nieuwe Zijde (New Side). Together with the Oude Zijde it formed the heart of the early maritime settlement. Nieuwendijk, today a busy shopping street, was originally one of the earliest sea defences. As Amsterdam grew, it expanded eastwards, leaving large sections of the Nieuwe Zijde, to the west, neglected and in decline. With its many wooden houses, the city was prone to fires and in 1452 much of the area was burned down. During rebuilding, a broad moat, the Singel, was cut, along which warehouses, rich merchants' homes and fine quays sprang up. The interesting Amsterdams Historisch Museum, which is now housed in a splendid former orphanage, has scores of maps and paintings charting the growth of the city from these times to the present day. One room is devoted to the Miracle of Amsterdam, which made the city a place of pilgrimage, and brought commerce to the Nieuwe Zijde. Nearby lies Kalverstraat, Amsterdam's main shopping street, and also the secluded Begijnhof. This pretty courtyard is mostly fringed by narrow 17th-century houses, but it also contains the city's oldest surviving wooden house.

Sights at a Glance

Historic Buildings, Monuments and Bridges
Beurs van Berlage ⑮
Centraal Station ⑫
Koninklijk Paleis pp88–9 ❷
Magna Plaza ⑩
Nationaal Monument ❹
Torensluis ❾

Streets and Squares
Begijnhof ❼
Nes ❺

Churches
Lutherse Kerk ⑪
Nieuwe Kerk ❶
St Nicolaaskerk ⑬

Museums
Allard Pierson Museum ❽
Amsterdams Historisch Museum pp92–3 ❻
Madame Tussaud's Scenerama ❸
Museum Amstelkring ⑭

Getting There

The Nieuwe Zijde is easily accessible by public transport. Most tram routes terminate at Centraal Station (1, 2, 4, 5, 9, 13, 16, 17, 24 and 25), as does the metro. Or take a tram (4, 9, 14, 16, 24 and 25) to the Dam. Or 1, 2, 5, 13 or 17 to Magna Plaza.

```
0 metres    250
0 yards     250
```

Key

	Street-by-Street map See pp84–5
	Tram stop
	Parking
	Metro station
	Train station
	Museum boat boarding point

◁ **The Fatal Fall of Icarus**, one of the many Classical sculptures in the Koninklijk Paleis

Street-by-Street: Nieuwe Zijde

ALTHOUGH MUCH of the medieval Nieuwe Zijde has disappeared, the area is still rich in buildings that relate to the city's past. The Dam, dominated by the Koninklijk Paleis and Nieuwe Kerk, provides examples of architecture from the 15th to the 20th centuries. Around Kalverstraat, narrow streets and alleys follow the course of some of the earliest dykes and footpaths. Here, most of the traditional gabled houses have been turned into bustling shops and cafés. Streets such as Rokin and Nes are now home to financial institutions, attracted by the nearby stock and options exchanges. Nes is also well known for its venues which feature alternative theatre.

★ Amsterdams Historisch Museum
Wall plaques and maps showing the walled medieval city are on display in this converted orphanage that dates from the 16th century **❻**

Kalverstraat
This busy tourist shopping area took its name from the livestock market which was regularly held here during the 15th century.

A pillar marks the site of the Miracle of Amsterdam *(see p87).*

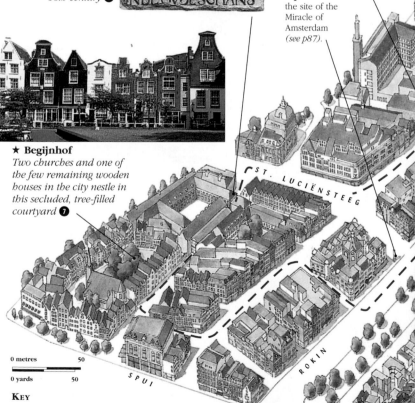

★ Begijnhof
Two churches and one of the few remaining wooden houses in the city nestle in this secluded, tree-filled courtyard **❼**

ST. LUCIËNSTEEG

ROKIN

SPUI

| 0 metres | 50 |
| 0 yards | 50 |

KEY

— — — Recommended route

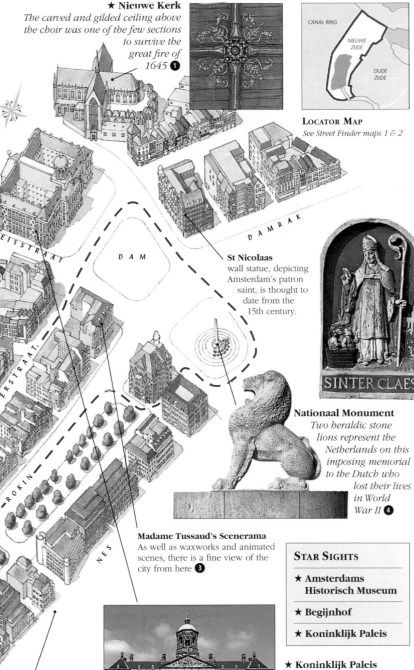

★ **Nieuwe Kerk**
The carved and gilded ceiling above the choir was one of the few sections to survive the great fire of 1645 ❶

LOCATOR MAP
See Street Finder maps 1 & 2

CANAL RING

NIEUWE ZIJDE

OUDE ZIJDE

DAMRAK

DAM

EISSTRAAT

VERSTRAAT.

ROKIN

NES

St Nicolaas
wall statue, depicting Amsterdam's patron saint, is thought to date from the 15th century.

SINTER CLAES

Nationaal Monument
Two heraldic stone lions represent the Netherlands on this imposing memorial to the Dutch who lost their lives in World War II ❹

Madame Tussaud's Scenerama
As well as waxworks and animated scenes, there is a fine view of the city from here ❸

STAR SIGHTS

★ **Amsterdams Historisch Museum**

★ **Begijnhof**

★ **Koninklijk Paleis**

Nes
This street is one of Amsterdam's oldest and has been a centre for theatre for 150 years ❺

★ **Koninklijk Paleis**
Built as the town hall, the building's Classical façade and fine sculptures were intended to glorify the city and its government ❷

Nieuwe Kerk ❶

Dam. **Map** 1 C4. 📞 *020-6386909.*
🚋 *1, 2, 4, 5, 9, 13, 14, 16, 17, 24,
25.* ⬛ *during exhibitions only (phone
to check).* ⬛ *30 Apr.* 🖼 🅾 ♿ ⬛

Dating from the late 14th
century, Amsterdam's sec-
ond parish church was built
as the population outgrew
the Oude Kerk *(see pp76–7)*.
During its turbulent history,
the church has been destroyed
several times by fire, rebuilt
and then stripped of its finery
after the Alteration. It eventually reached its present size
in the 1650s.

The pulpit, not the altar, is
the focal point of the interior,
reflecting the Protestant belief
that the sermon is central to
worship. The carved central
pulpit, unusually flamboyant
for a Dutch Protestant church,
was finished in 1664 and took
Albert Vinckenbrink 15 years
to carve. Above the transept
crossing, grimacing gilded
cherubs struggle to support the
corners of the wooden barrel
vault. Magnificent three-tiered
brass candelabra were hung
from the ceilings of the nave
and transepts during restoration work following the fire
of 1645. The colourful arched
window in the south transept
was designed by Otto Mengel-
berg in 1898. It depicts Queen
Wilhelmina surrounded by
courtiers at her coronation. In
the apse is Rombout Verhulst's
memorial to Admiral De Ruyter
(1607–76), who died at sea in
battle against the French.

Stained-glass window, Nieuwe Kerk

Koninklijk Paleis ❷

See pp88–9.

Scene by Vermeer, in Madame Tussaud's Scenerama

Madame Tussaud's Scenerama ❸

Gebouw Peek & Cloppenburg, Dam 20.
Map 2 D5. 📞 *020-5221010.* 🚋 *4,
9, 14, 16, 24, 25.* ⬛ *Sep–Jun: 10am–
5:30pm daily; Jul–Aug: 9:30am–
6:30pm daily.* ⬛ *30 Apr.* 🖼 🅾
♿ 🔳 www.madametussauds.com

Madame tussaud's offers an
audio-visual tour of Am-
sterdam's history, plus project-
ed future developments. Some
of the displays, such as the
animated 5-m (16-ft) figure
of "Amsterdam Man", are
bizarre, but the wax models
of 17th-century people give
an insight into life in the
city's Golden Age.

Nationaal Monument ❹

Dam. **Map** 2 D5.
🚋 *4, 9, 14, 16, 24, 25.*

Sculpted by John Raedecker
and designed by architect
JJP Oud, the 22-m (70-ft) obelisk in the Dam commemorates
Dutch World War II casualties.
It was unveiled in 1956 and is
fronted by two lions, heraldic
symbols of the Netherlands.
Embedded in the wall behind
are urns containing earth
from all the Dutch provinces
as well as from the former
Dutch colonies of Indonesia,
the Antilles and Suriname.

Nes ❺

Map 2 D5. 🚋 *4, 9, 14, 16, 24, 25.*

This quiet, narrow street is
home to several theatres.
In 1614, Amsterdam's first
pawnshop opened at Nes No.
57. A wall plaque marks the
site, and pawned goods
continue to clutter the shop
window. At night, Nes can
prove to be dangerous for
the unguarded visitor.

Amsterdams Historisch Museum ❻

See pp92–3.

Begijnhof **7**

Spui. **Map** 1 C5. 🚊 *1, 2, 5, 9, 14, 16, 24, 25.* ☎ *020-6233565.*
🕐 *8–11am daily.*

THE BEGIJNHOF was originally built in 1346 as a sanctuary for the Begijntjes, a lay Catholic sisterhood who lived like nuns, although they took no monastic vows. In return for lodgings within the complex, these women undertook to educate the poor and look after the sick. Nothing survives of the earliest dwellings, but the Begijnhof, cut off from traffic noise, retains a sanctified atmosphere. Among the houses that overlook its well-kept green is the city's oldest surviving house at No. 34. On the adjoining wall there is a fascinating collection of wall plaques taken from the houses. In keeping with the Begijntjes' religious outlook, the plaques have a biblical theme.

The southern fringe of the square is dominated by the Engelse Kerk (English Church), dating from the 15th century.

Directly west stands the Begijnhof Chapel, a clandestine church in which the Begijntjes and other Catholics worshipped in secret until religious tolerance was restored in 1795. Stained-glass windows and paintings depict scenes of the Miracle of Amsterdam. Occupants are trying to close public access to the Begijnhof, and public tours are not allowed. It may close in the future.

Plaque on the Engelse Kerk

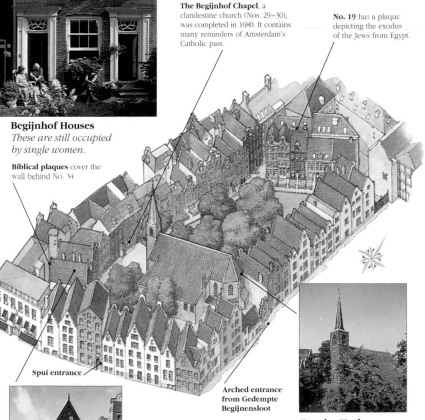

The Begijnhof Chapel, a clandestine church (Nos. 29–30), was completed in 1680. It contains many reminders of Amsterdam's Catholic past.

No. 19 has a plaque depicting the exodus of the Jews from Egypt.

Begijnhof Houses
These are still occupied by single women.

Biblical plaques cover the wall behind No. 34

Spui entrance

Arched entrance from Gedempte Begijnensloot

Houten House
No. 34 is Amsterdam's oldest house, dating from around 1420. It is one of the city's two wooden-fronted houses; timber houses were banned in 1521 after a series of catastrophic fires. Most of the Begijnhof houses were built after the 16th century.

Engelse Kerk
This church was built around 1419 for the Begijntjes. It was confiscated after the Alteration and rented to a group of English and Scottish Presbyterians in 1607. The Pilgrim Fathers may have worshipped here.

Koninklijk Paleis ❷

FORMERLY THE TOWN HALL, the Koninklijk Paleis is still regularly used by the Dutch royal family on official occasions. Construction of the sandstone building began in 1648, at the end of the 80 Years War *(see p49)*. More than 13,600 piles were used for the foundations of this enormous building. The Neo-Classical design of Jacob van Campen (1595–1657) reflected Amsterdam's new-found self-confidence after the victory against the Spanish.

★ Burgerzaal
The Burgerzaal (citizens' hall) has an inlaid marble floor depicting the two hemispheres (western and eastern).

★ Sculptures
The palace is decorated with a large number of sculptures of mainly allegorical figures.

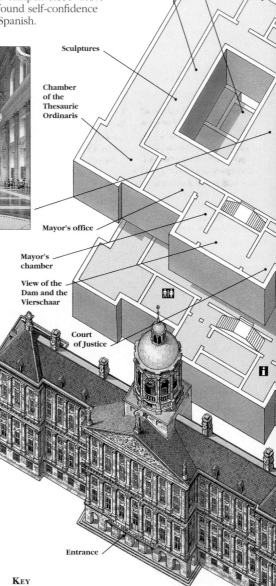

Chamber of the commissioners of small affairs

Courtyard

South gallery

Sculptures

Chamber of the Thesaurie Ordinaris

Mayor's office

Mayor's chamber

View of the Dam and the Vierschaar

Court of Justice

Entrance

STAR SIGHTS

★ Burgerzaal

★ Sculptures

★ Vroedschapszaal

KEY

▢ Ground floor

▢ First floor

Alderman's hall

Courtyard

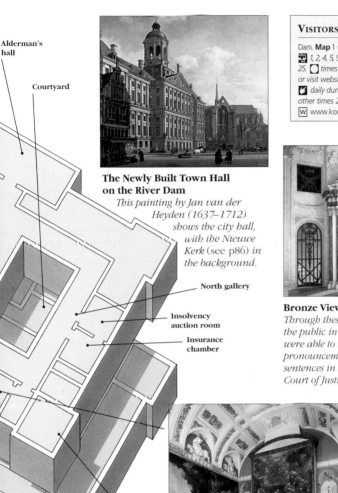

The Newly Built Town Hall on the River Dam
This painting by Jan van der Heyden (1637–1712) shows the city hall, with the Nieuwe Kerk (see p86) in the background.

North gallery

Insolvency auction room

Insurance chamber

Institution managing property of orphans

Bronze Viewing Screens
Through these bronze screens, the public in the 17th century were able to watch the official pronouncement of death sentences in the palace's Court of Justice.

★ **Vroedschapszaal**
This hall of the city fathers has two fine fireplaces with mantelpieces by Govert Flinck and Han van Bronckhorst. The grisailles from 1738 are the work of Jacob de Wit.

TIMELINE

1648	1665	1720	1810
Construction begins under Jacob van Campen	Building completed	Interior decoration completed	Complete refurbishment of the palace, with galleries divided up into rooms with wood partitions; the rooms are furnished in Empire style

1600		1700	1800	1900	2000

1655	1808	1960	2002
Ceremonial inauguration of the building	Louis Napoleon converts the town hall into a palace	Thorough restoration work throughout the 20th century undoes the building work of Louis Napoleon	Crown Prince Willem-Alexander kisses his bride, Maxima, on the palace balcony

Allard Pierson Museum  ❽

Oude Turfmarkt 127. **Map** 5 A2.
📞 *020-5252556.* 🚃 *4, 9, 14, 16, 24, 25.* ⏱ *10am–5pm Tue–Fri, 1–5pm Sat, Sun & public hols.* ⬤ *1 Jan, Easter Sun, 30 Apr, 1 May, Whitsun, 25 Dec.* 🎦 📷 ♿ 🎫 🆆 *www.uba.uva.nl/apm*

AMSTERDAM'S only specialist archaeological collection is named after Allard Pierson (1831–96), a humanist and scholar. The collection was moved into this handsome Neo-Classical building in 1976.

The museum contains Cypriot, Greek, Egyptian, Roman, Etruscan and Coptic artefacts.

Allard Pierson Museum's Neo-Classical façade of Bremer and Bentheimer stone

Torensluis ❾

Singel, between Torensteeg and Oude Leliestraat. **Map** 1 C4. 🚃 *1, 2, 5, 13, 14, 17.*

THE TORENSLUIS is one of the widest bridges in Amsterdam. Built on the site of a 17th-century sluice gate, it took its name from two towers that stood here on each side of the Singel until demolished in 1829. A lock-up jail was built in its foundations.

In summer, café tables on the bridge offer pleasant views down the Singel.

Magna Plaza ❿

Nieuwezijds Voorburgwal 182. **Map** 1 C4. 📞 *020-6269199.* 🚃 *1, 2, 5, 13, 14, 17.* ⏱ *noon–7pm Sun, 11am–7pm Mon, 10am–7pm Tue, Wed, Fri & Sat, 10am–9pm Thu.* ⬤ *public hols. See* **Shopping** *p144.* 📷 ♿

A POST OFFICE building has been sited here since 1748. The present building was completed in 1899; CP Peters, the architect, was ridiculed for the extravagance of its Neo-Gothic design. Redeveloped but well preserved, in 1990 it opened as the city's first shopping mall.

Lutherse Kerk ⓫

Kattengat 2. **Map** 2 D3. 📞 *020-6212223.* 🚃 *1, 2, 5, 13, 17.* ⏱ *concerts only.* 📷 ♿ *with assistance.*

THE LUTHERSE KERK was designed by Adriaan Dortsman (1625–82) and opened in 1671. It is the first Dutch Reformed church to feature a circular ground plan and two upper galleries, giving the whole congregation a clear view of the pulpit.

In 1882 a fire destroyed everything but the exterior walls. When the interior and entrance were rebuilt in 1883, they were made squarer and more ornate. A vaulted copper dome replaced the earlier ribbed version. Falling attendance led to the closure of the church in 1935. The building is now used by Renaissance Amsterdam Hotel (see p391) as a business centre. Concerts are sometimes held here.

Centraal Station ⓬

Stationsplein. **Map** 2 E3. 📞 *0900-9292.* 🚃 *1, 2, 4, 5, 9, 13, 16, 17, 24, 25.* Ⓜ *Centraal Station.* **Information** ⏱ *Inland: 24 hrs daily. International: 6:30am–10:30pm.* 📷 ♿

WHEN THE Centraal Station opened in 1889, it replaced the old harbour as the symbolic focal point of the city and effectively curtained Amsterdam off from the sea. The Neo-Gothic red-brick railway terminus was designed by PJH Cuypers and AL van Gendt. Three artificial islands were created, 8,600 wooden piles supporting the structure. The twin towers and central

An outdoor café on the Torensluis bridge overlooking the Singel canal

section have architectural echoes of a triumphal arch. The imposing façade's decorations show allegories of maritime trade, a tribute to the city's past. It is now a transport hub: 1,400 trains operate daily, and buses and trams terminate here.

Neo-Renaissance façade of the Sint-Nicolaaskerk

Sint-Nicolaaskerk ⓭

Prins Hendrikkade 73. **Map** 2 E4. 020-6248749. 1, 2, 4, 5, 9, 13, 16, 17, 24, 25. Centraal Station. Easter–mid Oct: 11am–4pm daily; mid Oct–Easter 1–4pm daily. 5:40pm Tue & Thu, 10:30am, 1pm (Spanish), 5pm Sun.

SINT NICOLAAS was the patron saint of seafarers, and so was an important icon in Amsterdam. Many Dutch churches are named after him, and the Netherlands' principal day for the giving of presents, 5 December, is known as Sinterklaasavond (see p35).

Completed in 1887, Sint-Nicolaaskerk was designed by AC Bleys (1842–1912). It replaced some clandestine Catholic churches set up in the city when Amsterdam was officially Protestant.

The exterior is forbidding, its twin towers dominating the skyline. The monumental interior has squared pillars and coffered ceiling arches.

Ons' Lieve Heer op Solder

Museum Amstelkring ⓮

Oudezijds Voorburgwal 40. **Map** 2 E4. 020-6246604. 4, 9, 16, 24, 25. 10am–5pm Mon–Sat, 1–5pm Sun & public hols. 1 Jan, 30 Apr.

TUCKED AWAY on the edge of the Red Light District is a restored 17th-century canal house, with two smaller houses to the rear. The combined upper storeys conceal a secret Catholic church, known as Ons' Lieve Heer op Solder (Our Dear Lord in the Attic), built in 1663. Following the Alteration, when Amsterdam officially became Protestant,

many such clandestine churches were built in the city.

The lower floors of the building became a museum in 1888 and today contain elegantly refurbished and decorated rooms, as well as a fine collection of church silver, religious artefacts and paintings.

Restored to its former opulence, the drawing room is an unusually fine example of a living room decorated and furnished in the Dutch Classical style of the 17th century, and is a highlight of the museum.

Beurs van Berlage ⓯

Damrak 243. **Map** 2 D4. (box office) 020-5217575. 4, 9, 16, 24, 25. 11am–5pm Tue–Sun. 1 Jan. www.beursvanberlage.nl

THE CLEAN, FUNCTIONAL appearance of Hendrik Berlage's 1903 stock exchange marked a departure from late 19th-century revivalist architecture. Many of its design features were adopted by the Amsterdam School. An impressive frieze shows the evolution of man from Adam to stockbroker. Now used for concerts and shows, it is home to the Nederlands Philharmonic Orchestra. The Beurs houses changing exhibitions.

Decorative brickwork on the façade of the Beurs van Berlage

Amsterdams Historisch Museum ❻

THE CONVENT OF ST LUCIEN was turned into a civic orphanage two years after the Alteration of 1578. The original red brick convent has been enlarged over the years; new wings were added in the 17th century by Hendrick de Keyser and Jacob van Campen. The present building is largely as it was in the 18th century. Since 1975 the complex has housed the city's historical museum, charting Amsterdam's development.

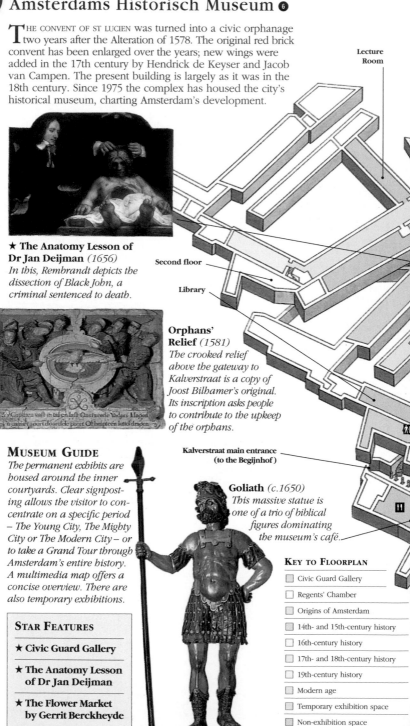

★ **The Anatomy Lesson of Dr Jan Deijman** *(1656)*
In this, Rembrandt depicts the dissection of Black John, a criminal sentenced to death.

Lecture Room

Second floor

Library

Orphans' Relief *(1581)*
The crooked relief above the gateway to Kalverstraat is a copy of Joost Bilhamer's original. Its inscription asks people to contribute to the upkeep of the orphans.

MUSEUM GUIDE

The permanent exhibits are housed around the inner courtyards. Clear signposting allows the visitor to concentrate on a specific period – The Young City, The Mighty City or The Modern City – or to take a Grand Tour through Amsterdam's entire history. A multimedia map offers a concise overview. There are also temporary exhibitions.

Kalverstraat main entrance
(to the Begijnhof)

Goliath *(c.1650)*
This massive statue is one of a trio of biblical figures dominating the museum's café.

STAR FEATURES

★ **Civic Guard Gallery**

★ **The Anatomy Lesson of Dr Jan Deijman**

★ **The Flower Market by Gerrit Berckheyde**

KEY TO FLOORPLAN

- Civic Guard Gallery
- Regents' Chamber
- Origins of Amsterdam
- 14th- and 15th-century history
- 16th-century history
- 17th- and 18th-century history
- 19th-century history
- Modern age
- Temporary exhibition space
- Non-exhibition space

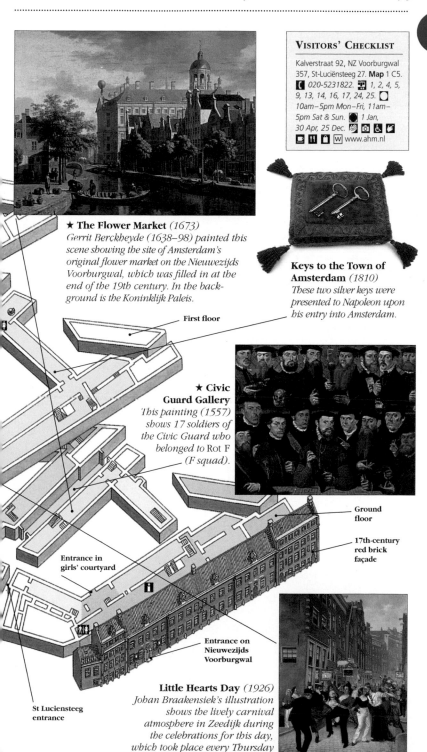

★ **The Flower Market** *(1673)*
Gerrit Berckheyde (1638–98) painted this scene showing the site of Amsterdam's original flower market on the Nieuwezijds Voorburgwal, which was filled in at the end of the 19th century. In the background is the Koninklijk Paleis.

VISITORS' CHECKLIST

Kalverstraat 92, NZ Voorburgwal 357, St-Luciënsteeg 27. **Map** 1 C5.
(020-5231822. ⛟ 1, 2, 4, 5, 9, 13, 14, 16, 17, 24, 25. ◯ 10am–5pm Mon–Fri, 11am–5pm Sat & Sun. ⬤ 1 Jan, 30 Apr, 25 Dec. ▨ ◎ ◔ ✓ ▢ 🍴 ⓗ ⓦ www.ahm.nl

Keys to the Town of Amsterdam *(1810)*
These two silver keys were presented to Napoleon upon his entry into Amsterdam.

First floor

★ **Civic Guard Gallery**
This painting (1557) shows 17 soldiers of the Civic Guard who belonged to Rot F (F squad).

Ground floor

17th-century red brick façade

Entrance in girls' courtyard

Entrance on Nieuwezijds Voorburgwal

St Luciensteeg entrance

Little Hearts Day *(1926)*
Johan Braakensiek's illustration shows the lively carnival atmosphere in Zeedijk during the celebrations for this day, which took place every Thursday throughout August.

GETTING THERE

It is a 15-minute walk from the Dam to Leidseplein, or take tram 1, 2 or 5; Nos. 6, 7 and 10 also cross the square going east. It is a 5-minute walk from the Dam to the Jordaan. Trams 13, 14 and 17 go to Rozengracht; 3 and 10 to Haarlemmerpoort. Frederik-splein (Nos. 4, 6, 7, 10) and Muntplein (Nos. 4, 9, 14, 16, 24, 25) are good starting points for exploring the eastern canal ring, a short walk from the Dam.

SIGHTS AT A GLANCE

Historic Buildings and Monuments
American Hotel ⑩
Haarlemmerpoort ⑥
Huis met de Hoofden ④
Magere Brug ⑱
Metz & Co ⑮
Munttoren ㉑

Museums
Anne Frankhuis see pp108–9 ①
Bijbels Museum ⑬
Museum Van Loon ⑲
Museum Willet-Holthuysen ⑰
Theatermuseum ②

Churches
De Krijtberg ⑫
Noorderkerk ⑤
Westerkerk ③

Markets
Looier Kunst en
   Antiekcentrum ⑭
Noordermarkt ⑤

Theatres
Stadsschouwburg ⑪
Tuschinski Theater ⑳

Canals and Squares
Brouwersgracht ⑦
Leidseplein ⑨
Rembrandtplein ⑯
Western Islands ⑧

◁ **Cyclist crossing a bridge on Leidse**

CANAL RING

I**N THE EARLY** 1600s, construction of the *Grach-tengordel* (canal ring) began and the marshy area beyond these fashionable canals, later called Jordaan, was laid out for workers whose industries were pro-

Pillar decoration on the Felix Meritis Building

hibited in the centre. Immigrants fleeing religious persecution also settled here. Historically a poor area, it now has a bohemian air. Extension of Amsterdam's major canals continued as merchant

classes bought land along the new extensions to the Herengracht, Keizersgracht and Prinsengracht to escape the city's squalor. In the 1660s, the wealthiest built houses on a stretch known today as the Golden Bend. Many of these grand buildings are now owned by institutions. The canal ring was also extended east towards the Amstel. Houses here, like the Van Loon, convey a sense of life in the Golden Age.

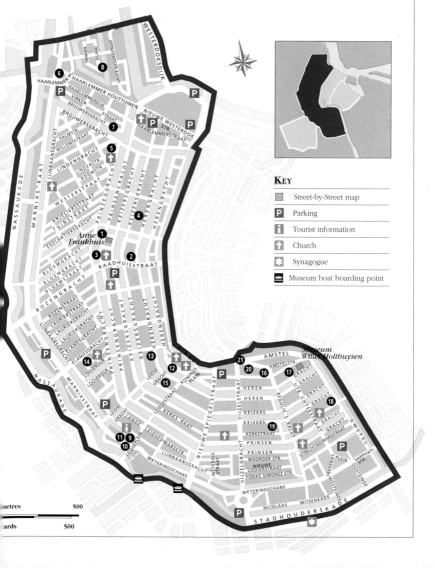

KEY

	Street-by-Street map
P	Parking
i	Tourist information
	Church
	Synagogue
	Museum boat boarding point

metres 500

yards 500

A Guide to Canal House Architecture

AMSTERDAM HAS BEEN CALLED a city of "well-mannered" architecture because its charms lie in intimate details rather than in grand effects. From the 15th century on, planning laws, plot sizes and the instability of the topsoil dictated that façades were largely uniform in size and built of lightweight brick or sandstone, with large windows to reduce the weight. Canal house owners stamped their own individuality on the buildings, mainly through the use of decorative gables and cornices, ornate doorcases and varying window shapes.

Broken pediment and vase

"Broken handle" window surrounds

Pediment carvings symbolize the arts and sciences.

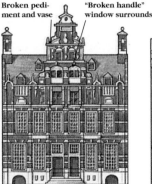

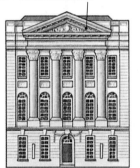

Bartolotti House (1617)
The contrasting brick and stone, flamboyant step gable, with its marble obelisk and scrolls, is typical of the Dutch Renaissance style of Hendrick de Keyser (see p110).

Felix Meritis Building (1778)
The Corinthian columns and triangular pediment are influenced by Classical architecture. This marks the building by Jacob Otten Husly as Dutch Classical in style.

Ground Plans
Taxes were levied according to width of façade, so canal houses were often long and narrow, with a achterhuis (back annexe) used for offices and storage.

CORNICES

Decorative top mouldings, called cornices, became popular from 1690 onwards when the fashion for gables declined. By the 19th century, they had become unadorned.

Louis XV-style with rococo balustrade (1739)

19th-century cornice with mansard roof

19th-century dentil (tooth-shaped) cornice

GABLES

The term "gable" refers to the front apex of a roof. It disguised the steepness of the roof under which goods were stored. In time, gables became decorated with scrolls, crests, and even with coats of arms.

Simple triangular gable

Warehouse-style spout gable

Dutch Renaissance style

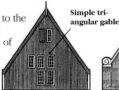

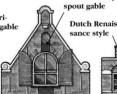

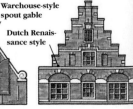

No. 34 Begijnhof (c.1420) is one of the few remaining timber houses.

The style of gable on No. 213 Leliegracht (c.1620) was used for warehouses.

Step gables like the one on No. 2 Brouwersgracht were in vogue between 1600–65.

Leaning Façades

Canal houses were often built with a deliberate tilt, allowing goods to be winched up to the attic without crashing against the windows. A law dating from 1565 restricted this lean to 1:25, to limit the risk of buildings collapsing into the streets.

GOLDEN BEND

The stretch of the Herengracht between Leidenstraat and Vijzelstraat was first called the Golden Bend in the 17th century, because of the great wealth of the ship-builders, merchants and politicians who originally lived here. The majority of the buildings along this stretch are faced with imported sandstone, which was more expensive than brick. An excellent example is house No. 412, which was designed by Philips Vingboons in 1664. He was also responsible for the design of the Witte Huis at Herengracht No. 168 as well as Bijbels Museum at Herengracht 366. Building continued into the 18th century, with the Louis XIV style predominating. The house at No. 475, with its ornate window decoration, is typical of this trend. Built in 1730, it is often called the jewel of canal houses. Two sculpted female figures over the front door adorn its monumental sandstone façade.

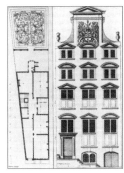

Ground plan and façade of the building at Herengracht 168

Dutch *Hofjes*

Almshouses (hofjes) *were built throughout the Netherlands by rich benefactors in the 17th and 18th centuries. By providing accommodation for the elderly and infirm, the* hofjes *marked the beginning of the Dutch welfare system.*

Sign of a sailors' hostel

Noah's Ark – a refuge for the poor

Symbol of a dairy producer

WALL PLAQUES

Carved and painted stones were used to identify houses before street numbering was introduced in the 19th century. Many reflect the owner's occupation.

Shell motif · **Dolphin ornament** · **Unadorned bell gable** · **Stonework with cornucopia decoration**

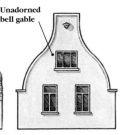
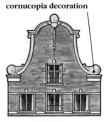

No. 419 Singel has a neck gable, a common feature from 1640 to around 1840.

No. 119 Oudezijds Voorburgwal has an ornate 17th-century neck gable.

No. 57 Leliegracht has a plain bell gable, popular from the late 17th century.

No. 298 Oudezijds Voorburgwal has a bell gable dating from the 18th century.

Dam Square to Herengracht 487

THE WALK along Amsterdam's finest canals begins in Dam square *(see p84–5)*. Following the grey dots on the map, leave the square past the Koninklijk Paleis *(see pp88–9)*, cross Nieuwezijds Voorburgwal and Spuistraat down Paleisstraat, and turn left along the left bank of Singel, marked by purple dots. Further directions are incorporated into the route below.

LOCATOR MAP

SINGEL •

No. 239 Singel
AL Van Gendt designed this massive stone office block for trader Julius Carle Bunge. Known as the Bungehuis, it was completed in 1934.

The double-fronted 17th-century canal house at No. 265 Singel has been rebuilt several times since it was first constructed.

The step gable at No. 279 Singel dates from the 19th century – most along this canal were built between 1600–65.

The three neck gables on Nos. 353–7 Keizersgracht date from the early 18th century.

Huidenstra

No. 345a Keizersgracht is a narrow house sharing a cornice with its neighbour.

In 1708, No. 333 Keizersgracht was rebuilt for tax collector Jacob de Wilde. It has recently been converted into apartments.

The Sower at Arles *(1888 In March 1878, Vincent va Gogh (see pp126–7) visited his uncle, who ran a book-shop and art dealership at No. 453 Keizersgracht.*

The unusual office block at No. 313 Keizersgracht was built in 1914 by CN van Goor.

No. 319 Keizersgracht was built by the architect Philips Vingboons (1608–78) in 1639. It has a rare, highly decorated façade covered with scrolls, vases and garlands.

Peter the Great *(1716)*
The Russian tsar sailed up Keizersgracht to No. 317, the home of his friend Christoffel Brants. Legend says the tsar got drunk and kept the mayor waiting while at a civic reception.

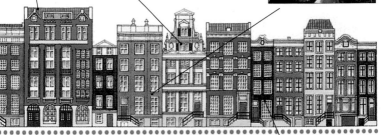

The Louis XIV-style house at No. 323 Keizersgracht was built in 1728. It has a raised cornice embellished with two hoisting beams, one functional and the other to provide symmetry.

Leidsegracht
This canal marked the end of Daniel Stalpaert's city expansion plan of 1664. It has a mixture of fine 17th- and 18th-century canal houses.

No. 475 Herengracht
Art patron Jan Gilde-mester bought this house in 1792. Attributed to Jacob Otten Husly, it has a stuccoed entrance hall.

Jan Corver
Burgomaster of Amsterdam 19 times, Corver built No. 479 Herengracht in 1665.

Turn over to continue walk at top of page 102

Herengracht 489 to the Amstel

THE SECOND HALF of the walk takes you along Herengracht, winding past grand, wide-fronted mansions. It then follows Reguliersgracht and Prinsengracht down to the Amstel. Many of the fine houses have recently been converted into banks, offices and exclusive apartment blocks.

LOCATOR MAP

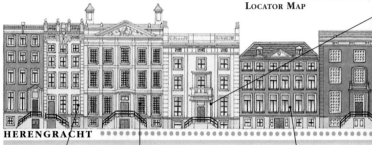

HERENGRACHT ●●●●●●●●●●●●●●●●●●●●●●●●●●●●●●●●●●●●●

The house at No. 491 Herengracht was built in 1671. The façade, rebuilt in the 18th century, is decorated with scrolls, vases and coats of arms.

No. 493 Herengracht
This 17th-century house was given a Louis XV-style façade in 1767 by Anthony van Hemert.

The Kattenkabinet at No. 497 Herengracht was created by financier B Meijer in 1984. It is devoted to exhibits featuring the cat in art.

DIRECTIONS TO REGULIERSGRACHT

At Thorbeckeplein, take the bridge to the right, which marks the beginning of Reguliersgracht. Follow the left bank.

REGULIERSGRACHT ●●●●●●●●●●●●●●●●●●●●●●●●●●●●●

Amstelveld in the 17th Century
This etching shows the construction of a wooden church at Amstelveld, with sheep grazing in front of it.

Café Moko
The Amstelkerk (Amstel Church) now houses a restaurant and offices, while the square is a popular playground for children from the surrounding area.

DIRECTIONS TO PRINSENGRACHT

Turn left by the church, take the left bank of Prinsengracht and walk to the Amstel river.

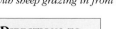

PRINSENGRACHT ●●●●●●●●●●●●●●●●●●●●●●●●●●●

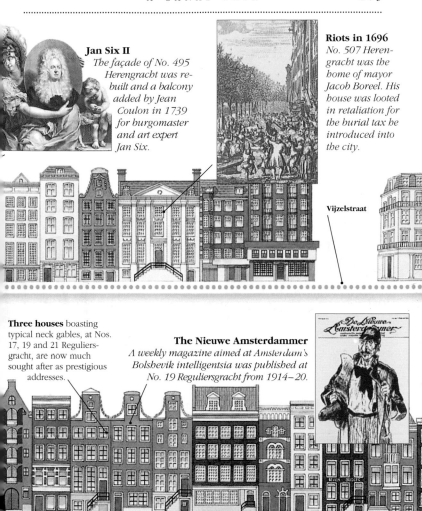

Jan Six II
The façade of No. 495 Herengracht was re-built and a balcony added by Jean Coulon in 1739 for burgomaster and art expert Jan Six.

Riots in 1696
No. 507 Herengracht was the home of mayor Jacob Boreel. His house was looted in retaliation for the burial tax he introduced into the city.

Vijzelstraat

Three houses boasting typical neck gables, at Nos. 17, 19 and 21 Reguliers-gracht, are now much sought after as prestigious addresses.

The Nieuwe Amsterdammer
A weekly magazine aimed at Amsterdam's Bolshevik intelligentsia was published at No. 19 Reguliersgracht from 1914–20.

The spout-gabled *(see pp96–7)* 16th-century ware-houses at Nos. 11 and 13 Reguliersgracht are called the Sun and the Moon.

Café Marcella, at No. 1047a Prinsengracht, is a typical local bar which has seating outside in summer.

Houseboats on Prinsengracht
All registered houseboats have postal addresses and are con-nected to the electricity mains.

Utrechtsestraat

Keizersgracht

This photograph of the "emperor's canal" is taken at dusk, from the corner of Leidsegracht. The Westerkerk (see p110) is in the distance.

Behind the contrasting 18th-century façades at Nos. 317 and 319 Singel are two second-hand bookshops, which are well worth browsing through.

Directions to Keizersgracht

At Raamsteeg, cross the bridge, take the Oude Spiegelstraat, cross Herengracht and walk along Wolvenstraat to the left bank of Keizersgracht.

KEIZERSGRACH

No. 399 Keizersgracht dates from 1665, but the façade was rebuilt in the 18th century. Its *achterhuis (see p96)* has been perfectly preserved.

No. 409 Keizersgracht
Built in 1671 on a triangular piece of land, this house contains a newly discovered, highly decorated wooden ceiling.

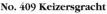

The wall plaque on No. 401 Keizersgracht shows a bird's-eye view of the port of Marseilles.

No. 469 Herengracht
The modern office block by KL Sijmons replaced the original 18th-century houses in 1971.

The plain, spout-g building *(see pp96–* No. 403 Keizersgrac originally a warehou rarity in this predom residential area.

Nos. 289–293 Singel
These houses stand on an alley once called Schoorsteenvegersteeg (chimney sweeps' lane), home to immigrant chimney sweeps.

Yab Yum Brothel
The huge lantern is the only sign that this famous brothel operates at No. 295 Singel.

No. 365 Keizersgracht
The doorway was taken from an almshouse on Oudezijds Voorburgwal in the 19th century.

Jacob de Wit
The artist (see p115) bought Nos. 383 and 385 Keizersgracht, living in No. 385 until his death in 1754.

Metz & Co is an elegant department store at No. 34–6 Leidsestraat on the corner with Keizersgracht *(see p113)*.

Gerrit Rietveld
Rietveld (see p113) designed the glass façade on Metz & Co, and a line of plain, inexpensive furniture for the store.

De Vergulde Ster
(gilded star), at No. 387 Keizersgracht, was built in 1668 by the municipal stonemasons' yard. It has an elongated neck gable *(see pp96–7)* and narrow windows.

DIRECTIONS TO HERENGRACHT

Turn left on to Leidsestraat, and walk to Koningsplein, then take the left bank of the Herengracht eastwards towards Thorbeckeplein.

HERENGRACHT

Tsar Peter *(see p101)* stayed at No. 527 Herengracht, home of the Russian ambassador, after a night of drunken revelry at No. 317 Keizersgracht in 1716.

Herengracht *(1790)*
A delicate watercolour by J Prins shows the "gentlemen's canal" from Koningsplein.

The asymmetrical building at Nos. 533–7 Herengracht was built in 1910 on the site of four former houses. From 1968–88 it was the Registry of Births, Marriages and Deaths.

The façades of Nos. 37 and 39 Reguliersgracht lean towards the water, showing the danger caused by subsidence when building on marshland.

Reguliersgracht Bridges
Seven arched stone bridges cross the ca[nal] which was original[ly] designed to be a str[eet]

Keizersgracht

Nos. 1059 and 1061 Prinsengracht have tiny basement entrances, rare amid the splendour of the Canal Ring, where the height of the steps was considered an indication of wealth.

The sober spout-gabled building at No. 1075 Prinsengracht was built as a warehouse in 1690.

My Domestic Companions
Society portraitist Thérèse van Duyl Schwartze painted this picture in 1916. She owned Nos. 1087, 1089 and 1091 Prinsengracht, a handsome row of houses where she lived with her extended family.

Herengracht *(c.1670)*
GA Berckheyde's etching shows one side of the canal bare of trees. Elms were later planted, binding the topsoil, to strengthen the buildings' foundations.

No. 543 Herengracht was built in 1743 under the supervision of owner Sibout Bollard. It has a double-fronted façade with an ornate balustrade and decorated balcony.

The small houses at the corner of Herengracht and Thorbeckeplein contrast with the grand neighbouring buildings.

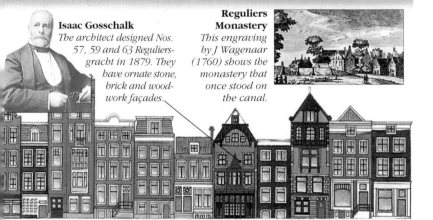

Isaac Gosschalk
The architect designed Nos. 57, 59 and 63 Reguliers-gracht in 1879. They have ornate stone, brick and wood-work façades.

Reguliers Monastery
This engraving by J Wagenaar (1760) shows the monastery that once stood on the canal.

The Amstel
Turn left and follow the road sweep of the Amstel river, up past the Magere Brug on up Rokin and back to the Dam, where the walk began.

Street-by-Street: Around the Jordaan

W EST OF THE *Grachtengordel*, the Jordaan still retains a network of narrow, characterful streets and delightful canals. Among the 17th-century workers' houses are dozens of quirky shops, which are well worth a browse, selling anything from designer clothes to old sinks, and lively brown cafés and bars, which spill onto the pavements in summer. A stroll along the *Grachtengordel* provides a glimpse into some of the city's grandest canal houses, including the Bartolotti House.

Egelantiersgracht is a charming tree-lined Jordaan canal over-looked by an interesting mixture of old and new architecture. Its numerous bridges provide pretty views.

The quiet Bloemgracht canal was once a centre for makers of paint and dye.

EGELANTIERSGRACHT

BLOEMGRACHT

PRINSENGRACHT

★ Westerkerk
Hendrick de Keyser's church is the site of Rembrandt's unmarked grave and was the setting for the wedding of Queen Beatrix and Prince Claus in 1966 ❸

★ Anne Frankhuis
For two years, the Frank family and four others lived in a small upstairs apartment that was hidden behind a revolving book-case (see pp108–9) ❶

Huis met de Hoofden
*The name "House with the Heads"
refers to the six Classical busts at
the entrance, depicting Apollo,
Ceres, Mars, Minerva,
Bacchus and Diana* ❹

LOCATOR MAP
See Street Finder map 1

| 0 metres | 75 |
| 0 yards | 75 |

★ **Theatermuseum**
*The Bartolotti House, now
home of the Theatermuseum,
was built by Hendrick de
Keyser in 1617 for wealthy
banker Guillelmo Bartolotti,
formerly a brewer* ❷

KEY

━ ━ ━ Recommended route

The Greenpeace
building, at the corner
of Kaizersgracht and
Leliegracht, is a
rare example of Dutch
Art Nouveau, designed
by Gerrit van Arkel in
1905. It is now home to
the environmental group.

STAR SIGHTS

★ **Anne Frankhuis**

★ **Theatermuseum**

★ **Westerkerk**

Anne Frankhuis ❶

Star of David

O N 6 JULY 1942, to avoid their German persecutors, the Jewish Frank family moved from Merwedeplein to the rear annexe of the house at Prinsengracht 263. Anne; her mother, Edith; her father, Otto; and her older sister, Margot, lived here, along with the Van Pels family and dentist Fritz Pfeffer. It was here that Anne wrote her famous diary. On 4 August 1944, the annexe was raided by the Gestapo. All those hiding here were arrested and taken to German concentration camps.

The Secret Entrance
Behind the hinged bookcase was a small suite of rooms where the eight hideaways lived.

Anne in May 1942
This photograph was taken in 1942, when Anne started writing in the now-famous diary that she had been given on 12 June 1942, her 13th birthday. Less than one month later, the Frank family went into hiding.

Attic

Van Pels family's room

The annexe

Bathroom

Frank family bedroom

Anne's bedroom

View of the Annexe
The rear annexe of the house adjoined the main building, which housed the offices of Otto Frank's herb and spice business.

VISITORS' CHECKLIST

Prinsengracht 267. **Map** 1 B4.
020-5567100. 13, 17.
Apr–Aug: 9am–9pm daily;
Sep–Mar: 9am–7pm daily.
Yom Kippur.
W www.annefrank.nl

The Helpers
*The people in hiding were
wholly dependent on their
helpers, all of whom
were close colleagues
of Anne's father, Otto
Frank. From left to
right: Miep Gies,
Johannes Kleiman,
Otto Frank,
Victor Kugler
and Bep Voskuijl.*

Anne and Margot's Bedroom
*Anne and Margot slept on the first
floor of the annexe. On the bedroom
walls were photos of film stars,
which Anne collected. Anne
wrote most of her diary at
the table here.*

**Façade of
Prinsengracht 263**

**Main building
housing offices**

MUSEUM GUIDE
*The rear annexe is accessible via the reconstructed
offices of Otto Frank. Only a limited number of
people are admitted each day. The new building
beside Anne Frankhuis holds various exhibitions.*

THE DIARY OF ANNE FRANK

Otto Frank returned to Amsterdam in 1945 to
discover that his entire family had perished: his
wife, Edith, in Auschwitz and his daughters, Anne
and Margot, in Bergen-Belsen. Miep Gies, one of
the family's helpers while they were in hiding, had
kept Anne's diary. First published in 1947, it has
since been translated into 55 languages, with some
20 million copies sold. For many, Anne symbolizes
the six million Jews murdered by the Nazis in
World War II. The diary is a moving portrait of a
little girl growing up in times of oppression.

Theatermuseum interior, with 18th-century staircase and stuccowork

Theatermuseum ➋

Herengracht 168. **Map** 1 C4.
📞 020-5513300. 🚊 13, 14, 17.
🚋 Prinsengracht. 🕐 11am–5pm
Mon–Fri, 1–5pm Sat & Sun. ⬤ 1 Jan,
30 Apr, 25 Dec. 📷 🚫 🔲 🔽 🔲

TWO FINE BUILDINGS house
the theatre museum, which
contains costumes, sets and
memorabilia. You can even
play with antique sound effects
and create your own storm.
The museum entrance is in
the White House, No. 168, a
Neo-Classical house designed
by Philips Vingboons (see p97)
in 1638. The interior was re-
styled in about 1730, and has

a magnificent spiral staircase,
stuccowork by Van Logteren
and rich ceiling paintings by
Jacob de Wit.

The museum extends into
Bartolotti House (Nos. 170–
172). Built by Hendrick de
Keyser (1565–1621) in 1617,
its elaborate Renaissance
façade contrasts sharply with
the austerity of the White
House. Its interior decoration
was carried out by Jacob de
Wit and Isaac de Moucheron.

Westerkerk ➌

Prinsengracht 281. **Map** 1 B4.
📞 020-6247766. 🚊 13, 14,
17. 🕐 Apr–Sep: 11am–3pm
Mon–Fri. 📷 **Tower** 📷 🔲
Apr–Sep: hourly 10am–5pm
Mon–Sat. Oct–Mar: phone
020-6892565 to arrange.

BUILT AS PART of the
development of the
Canal Ring, this church
has the tallest tower
in the city at 85 m
(279 ft), and the
largest nave of any
Dutch Protestant
church. It was designed by
Hendrick de Keyser, who
died in 1621, a year after
work began.
Rembrandt was
buried here but his

grave has never been found.
The organ shutters (1686) were
painted by Gerard de Lairesse,
with lively scenes showing
King David, the Queen of
Sheba and the Evangelists.
The tower carries the crown
bestowed on Amsterdam
in 1489 by Maximilian, the
Hapsburg emperor. The stunning views justify the climb.

Huis met de Hoofden ➍

Keizersgracht 123. **Map** 1 C4.
📞 020-5524888. 🚊 13, 14, 17.
⬤ to the public.

BUILT IN 1622, the
Huis met de Hoof-
den (house with the
heads) is one of the
largest double houses
of the period. It has a
fine step gable and
takes its name from
the six heads placed
on pilasters along
the façade. Legend
has it that they com-
memorate a house-
maid who, when alone
in the house, surprised six
burglars and cut off their
heads. The sculptures
are in fact portrayals
of six Classical deities

**Head of Apollo on
the Huis met de
Hoofden**

The Westerkerk in the 18th century, a view by Jan Ekels

(from left to right): Apollo, Ceres, Mars, Minerva, Bacchus and Diana. The design of the building is sometimes attributed to Pieter de Keyser (1595–1676), son of Hendrick de Keyser. It is now home to the Bureau Monumenten en Archeologie, an organization that since 1953 has supervised care of Amsterdam's officially recognized public monuments.

Stone plaque on the *hofje* founded in 1616 by the merchant Anslo

Noorderkerk and Noordermarkt ❺

Noordermarkt 44–48. **Map** 1 C3.
📞 020-6266436. 🚊 *3, 10, 13, 14, 17.* 🕐 *11am–1pm Mon & Sat.* 🕐 *10am & 7pm Sun.* **General market** 🕐 *9am–1pm Mon;* **Boerenmarkt** 🕐 *9am–5pm Sat.*

BUILT FOR poor settlers in the Jordaan, the recently renovated North Church was the first in Amsterdam to be constructed in the shape of a Greek cross. Its layout around a central pulpit allowed everyone in the encircling pews to see and hear well.

The church, designed by Hendrick de Keyser, was completed in 1623, in time to hold its inaugural service at Easter. It is still well attended by a Calvinist congregation. By the entrance is a sculpture of three bound figures, inscribed: "Unity is Strength". It commemorates the Jordaan Riot of 1934. On the south façade, a plaque recalls the 1941 February Strike, protesting the Nazis' deportation of Jews.

Since 1627, the square that surrounds the Noorderkerk has been a market site. At that time, it sold pots and pans and *vodden* (old clothes), a tradition that continues today with a flea market. Since the 18th century, the area has been a centre for bed shops. Bedding, curtains and fabrics are still sold on Monday morning along the Westerstraat; yet you can buy anything from net curtain material to buttons. On Saturday mornings, the *vogeltjes* (small birds) market sells chickens, pigeons, small birds and rabbits. At 10am, the *boerenmarkt* takes over, selling health foods, ethnic crafts and candles.

Haarlemmer-poort ❻

Haarlemmerplein 50. **Map** 1 B1. 🚊 *3.* 🚌 *to the public.*

ORIGINALLY a defended gateway into Amsterdam, the Haarlemmerpoort marked the beginning of the busy route to Haarlem. The present gateway, dating from 1840, was built for King William II's triumphal entry into the city and named Willemspoort. However, as the third gateway to be built on or close to this site, it is still called the Haarlemmerpoort by Amsterdammers.

Designed by Cornelis Alewijn (1788–1839), the Neo-Classical gatehouse was used as tax offices in the 19th century and was made into flats in 1986. Traffic no longer goes through the gate, since a bridge has been built over the adjoining Westerkanaal.

Brouwersgracht ❼

Map 1 B2. 🚊 *3.*

BROUWERSGRACHT (brewers' canal) was named after the breweries established here in the 17th and 18th centuries. Leather, spices, coffee and sugar were also processed and stored here. Today, most of the warehouses, with their spout gables and shutters, are residences that look out on moored houseboats.

Western Islands ❽

Map 1 C1. 🚊 *3.*

THIS DISTRICT comprises three islands built on the IJ in the early 1600s to quarter warehouses and shipyards. Some of these are still in use and many period houses have survived.

Merchant and developer Jan Bicker bought Bickerseiland in 1631. Today, the island is a mix of colourful apartment blocks and a jumble of houseboats.

Realeneiland has the pretty waterside street of Zandhoek. A row of 17th-century houses built by the island's founder, Jacobsz Reaal, overlooks the moored sailboats.

Prinseneiland is dominated by characterful warehouses, many now apartments.

DUTCH HOFJES

The "house with the writing hand" (c.1630) in Claes Claeszhofje

Before the Alteration, the Catholic Church often provided subsidized housing for the poor and elderly, particularly women. During the 17th and 18th centuries, rich merchants and Protestant organizations took on this charitable role and built hundreds of almshouse complexes, which were planned around courtyards and known as *hofjes*. Behind their street façades lie pretty houses and serene gardens. Visitors are admitted to some but asked to respect the residents' privacy. Many *hofjes* are found in the Jordaan and some still serve their original purpose.

De Melkweg's star-lit façade

Leidseplein 🄈

Map 4 E2. 🚋 *1, 2, 5, 6, 7, 10.*

Amsterdam's liveliest square, Leidseplein is also a busy tram intersection and centre of night-time transport.

The square developed in the 17th century as a wagon park on the outskirts of the city – farmers and peasants would leave their carts here before entering the centre. It takes its name from the Leidsepoort, the massive city gate demolished in 1862, which marked the beginning of the route out to Leiden.

During the day, the square is buzzing with fire-eaters, buskers and other street performers playing to café audiences. It is also popular with pickpockets. At night, it is the focal point for the city's youth, who hang out in the many bars, cafés, restaurants, nightclubs and cinemas in and around the square.

American Hotel 🄉

Leidsekade 97. **Map** 4 E2.
📞 *020-5563000.* 🚋 *1, 2, 5, 6, 7, 10.*
🖥 See **Where to Stay** *p392.*

Leidseplein was fast becoming a fashionable entertainment area when the American Hotel was built overlooking it in 1882. The hotel got its name because its architect, W Steinigeweg, studied hotel design in the United States, and adorned his Neo-Gothic creation with a bronze eagle, wooden figures of native Indians and murals of American landscapes. Within 20 years it was deemed *passé* and the hotel was demolished. The present building is by Willem Kromhout (1864–1940) and was completed in 1902.

His design marked a radical departure, interpreting the Art Nouveau style in an angular Dutch fashion. The building's turreted exterior and elaborate brickwork anticipated the progressive Amsterdam School *(see pp142–3).*

The Art Deco-style Café Americain is one of the most elegant in Amsterdam. It retains its period furnishings and stained-glass windows. The rest of the hotel was redecorated in the 1980s. Samples of the original furnishings are in the Rijksmuseum *(see pp122–5).*

Stadsschouwburg 🄋

Leidseplein 26. **Map** 4 E2. 📞 *020-6242311.* 🚋 *1, 2, 5, 6, 7, 10.* **Box office** 🕐 *10am–6pm Mon–Sat.* See **Entertainment** *p428.* 🅿 🚻 ♿ 🆆 www.stadsschouwburgamsterdam.nl

This neo-renaissance building is the most recent of the city's three successive municipal theatres, its predecessors having burned down. The theatre was designed by Jan Springer, whose other credits include the Frascati building on Oxford Street in London, and AL van Gendt, who was responsible for the Concertgebouw *(see p120)* and for part of the Centraal Station *(see p90).* The planned ornamentation of the theatre's redbrick exterior was never carried out because of budget cuts. This, combined with a hostile public reaction to his theatre, forced a disillusioned Springer into virtual retirement. Public disgust was due, however, to the management's policy of restricting use of the front door to patrons who had bought expensive tickets.

The former home of the Dutch national ballet and opera companies, the theatre today stages plays by local drama groups such as the resident Toneelgroep, as well as international companies, including many English-language productions.

The American Hotel seen from Singelgracht

De Krijtberg

Singel 448. **Map** 4 F1.
☎ 020-6231923. ▓ 1, 2, 5.
○ 1:30–5pm Tue–Thu, Sun.
✝ 12:30pm, 5:45pm Mon–Fri;
12:30pm, 5:15pm Sat; 9:30am,
11am, 12:30pm, 5:15pm Sun. &

AN IMPRESSIVE Neo-Gothic church, the Krijtberg (or chalk hill) replaced a clandestine Jesuit chapel in 1884. It is officially known as Franciscus Xaveriuskerk, after St Francis Xavier, one of the founding Jesuit monks.

Designed by Alfred Tepe, the church was built on the site of three houses; the presbytery beside the church is on the site of two other houses, one of which had belonged to a chalk merchant – hence the church's nickname. The back of the church is wider than the front, extending into the space once occupied by the original gardens. The narrowness of the façade is redeemed by its two magnificent, soaring, steepled towers.

The ornate interior of the building contains some good examples of Neo-Gothic design. The stained-glass windows, walls painted in bright colours and liberal use of gold are in striking contrast to the city's austere Protestant churches. A statue of St Francis Xavier stands in front and to the left of the high altar; one of St Ignatius, founder of the Jesuits, stands to the right.

Near the pulpit is an 18th-century wooden statue of the Immaculate Conception, which shows Mary trampling the serpent. It used to be housed in the original hidden chapel.

Bijbels Museum ⓭

Herengracht 366–368. **Map** 4 E1.
☎ 020-6242436. ▓ 1, 2, 5. ▒
Herengracht/Leidsegracht. ○ 10am–
5pm Mon–Sat, 11am–5pm Sun &
public hols. ● 1 Jan, 30 Apr. ▓
▣ & Ⓦ www.bijbelsmuseum.nl

REVEREND Leendert Schouten founded the Bible museum in 1860, when he put his private artefact collection on public display. In 1975, the museum moved to its present site, two 17th-century houses designed by Philips Vingboons. The artefacts attempt to give weight to Bible stories. Displays feature models of historic sites and archaeological finds from Egypt and the Middle East. Highlights are a copy of the Book of Isaiah from the Dead Sea Scrolls and the Delft Bible (1477).

Looier Kunst en Antiekcentrum ⓮

Elandsgracht 109. **Map** 4 D1. ☎ 020-
6249038. ▓ 7, 10, 13, 14, 17. ○
11am–5pm Sat–Thu. ● public hols.
∅ & **Rommelmarkt** Looiersgracht 38.
○ 11am–5pm daily. ● public hols.

THE LOOIER ANTIQUES CENTRE, a vast network of rooms in a block of houses, is named after its location near the Looiersgracht (tanners' canal). With the largest collection of art and antiques in Holland, its 100 stalls sell everything from glassware to dolls. On the Looiersgracht, a door opens into the Rommelmarkt (rummage market), a corridor lined with old toys, records and bric-a-brac. One may even find a genuine antique here.

Metz & Co ⓯

Leidsestraat 34–36. **Map** 4 E1.
☎ 020-5207020. ▓ 1, 2, 5.
○ 11am–6pm Mon, 9:30am–6pm
Tue, Wed, Fri & Sat, 9:30am–9pm
Thu, noon–5pm Sun. ● public hols.

ON ITS COMPLETION in 1891, this was the tallest commercial building in the city, measuring 26 m (85 ft). Designed by J van Looy, it was built for the New York Life Insurance Company. Since 1908, it has housed the luxury store Metz & Co. In 1933, a glass cupola by Gerrit Rietveld *(see p99)* was added. Liberty of London, which bought Metz & Co in 1973, renovated the building. The sixth-floor café, designed by Cees Dam, offers superb city views.

The 1933 cupola of Metz & Co

ON THE CANALS

Though Amsterdam's canals were built for moving goods, today they provide a marvellous means of viewing the city's sights and its everyday life. There are many operators in the city offering canal tours with foreign-language commentaries; boats depart from an embarkation point, mainly from opposite Centraal Station, along Prins Hendrikkade, the Damrak and along the Rokin. Other canal-sightseeing options include the popular canalbus and the Museum Boat. The former runs along three routes, with 11 stops near the major museums, shopping areas and other attractions, while the Museum Boat takes in and stops near all the major city sights. If you feel energetic, try a canal bike, which is really a two- or four-seater pedal-boat that can be picked up and left at any of the canal-bike moorings in the city centre.

Rembrandtplein ⑯

Map 5 A2. 🚊 *4, 9, 14.*

FORMERLY CALLED the Botermarkt, after the butter
market held here until the
mid-19th century, this square
acquired its present name
when the statue of Rembrandt
was erected in 1876.

Soon afterwards, Rembrandtplein developed into a centre
for nightlife with the opening
of various hotels and cafés.
The Mast (renamed the Mille
Colonnes Hotel) dates from
1889, and the Schiller Karena
hotel and the Café Schiller
both opened in 1892. De
Kroon, which epitomizes a
typical grand café, dates from
1898. The popularity of Rembrandtplein has endured,
and the café terraces are
packed during summer with
people enjoying a pleasant
drink and watching the
world go by.

Museum Willet-Holthuysen ⑰

Herengracht 605. **Map** 5 A2.
📞 *020-5231822.* 🚊 *4, 9, 14.*
🕐 *10am–5pm Mon–Fri, 11am–5pm
Sat & Sun.* ⬤ *1 Jan, 30 Apr, 25 Dec.*
📷 🎥 📹 🔒 W www.ahm.nl

NAMED AFTER the building's
last residents, the muse-
um now housed here allows
visitors a glimpse into the
lives of the merchant class
who lived in luxury along the
Grachtengordel (Canal Ring).
The house was built in 1685
and became the property
of coal magnate Pieter Holt-
huysen (1788–1858) in 1855.

Interior of Willet-Holthuysen

Two of the many outdoor cafés on Rembrandtplein

It passed to his daughter Sandrina and her art-connoisseur
husband, Abraham Willet –
both fervent collectors of paintings, glass, silver and ceramics.
When Sandrina died childless
in 1895, the house and its
many treasures were left to the
city. Some of the rooms remain
unchanged, while others, such
as the kitchen and Garden
Room, have been restored in
the style of the 18th century.

The Blue Room, hung with
heavy blue damask and boasting a chimney piece by Jacob
de Wit, was the exclusive preserve of the men of the house.

The wallpaper in the dining
room today is a careful copy
of the 18th-century silk original. The elaborate 275-piece
Meissen dinner service provided up to 24 places.

The 18th-century kitchen
has been restored using items
salvaged from similar houses,
including the sink and pump.

On the second floor is a full-
length portrait of Willet.

Magere Brug ⑱

Amstel. **Map** 5 B3. 🚊 *4.*

OF AMSTERDAM'S 1,400 or so
bridges, Magere Brug
(skinny bridge) is the best-
known. The original draw-
bridge was built in about 1670.
According to legend, it was
named after two sisters called
Mager, who lived either side of
the Amstel. It is more likely
that the name comes from its
narrow *(mager)* design.

Magere Brug, a traditional double-leaf Dutch drawbridge

The present drawbridge was put up in 1969 and, though wider than the original, it still conforms to the traditional double-leaf style. Constructed from African azobe wood, it was intended to last 50 years. Every 20 minutes, the bridge master has to let boats through. He then jumps on his bicycle and opens up the Amstelsluizen and Hoge Sluis.

Museum Van Loon ⑲

Keizersgracht 672. **Map** 5 A3. 020-6245255. *16, 24, 25.* *11am–5pm Fri–Mon.* *public hols.* *www.museumvanloon.nl*

THE VAN LOONS were one of Amsterdam's most prestigious families in the 17th century. They did not move into this house on the Keizersgracht, however, until 1884. Designed by Adriaan Dortsman, No. 672 is one of a pair of symmetrical houses built in 1672 for Flemish merchant Jeremias van Raey. In 1752, Dr Abraham van Hagen and his wife, Catharina Elisabeth Trip, moved in.

In 1974, after 11 years of restoration, it opened as a museum, retaining the house's original character. Its collection of Van Loon family portraits stretches back to the early 1600s. The period rooms have fine pieces of furniture, porcelain and sculpture. The sumptuous wall paintings are known as *witjes* after their famous creator, Jacob de Wit (1695–1754).

Tuschinski Theater ⑳

Reguliersbreestraat 26–28. **Map** 5 A2. 020-6262633. *4, 9, 14.* **Box office** *noon–10pm.* *Jul–Aug: 10:30am Sun & Mon.*

ABRAHAM TUSCHINSKI'S cinema and variety theatre caused a sensation when it opened in 1921. Until then, Amsterdam's cinemas had been sombre places; this was an exotic blend of Art Deco and Amsterdam School architecture (*see pp142–3*). Built in a slum area known as Devil's Corner, it was designed by Heyman Louis de Jong and decorated by Chris Bartels, Jaap Gidding and Pieter de Besten. In its heyday, Marlene Dietrich and Judy Garland performed here.

Now a six-screen cinema, the building has been meticulously restored, inside and out. The best way to appreciate its opulence is to see a film. For a few extra euros, you can take a seat in one of the exotic boxes that make up the back row of the huge semi-circular auditorium.

View of the medieval Munttoren at the base of Muntplein

Munttoren ㉑

Muntplein. **Map** 4 F1. *4, 9, 14, 16, 24, 25.* **Munttoren** *to public.* **Gift shop** *10am–6pm Mon–Sat.*

THE POLYGONAL BASE of the Munttoren (mint tower) formed part of the gate in Amsterdam's medieval wall. Fire destroyed the gate in 1618, but the base survived. In 1619, Hendrick de Keyser added the clock tower; François Hemony, the set of bells in 1699. During the 1673 French occupation, the city mint was housed here.

How the Magere Brug Works

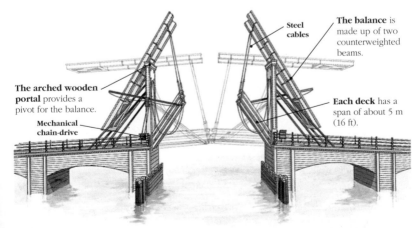

Steel cables

The balance is made up of two counterweighted beams.

The arched wooden portal provides a pivot for the balance.

Mechanical chain-drive

Each deck has a span of about 5 m (16 ft).

MUSEUM QUARTER

NTIL THE LATE 1800s, the Museum Quarter was little more than an area of farms and small-holdings. At this time, the city council designated it an area of art and culture and plans were conceived for constructing Amsterdam's great cultural monuments: the Rijksmuseum, the Stedelijk Museum and the Concertgebouw. The Van Gogh Museum followed in 1973, its striking extension being added in 1999. The Museumplein has two memorials to the victims of World War II. The *plein* is still used today as a site for political demonstrations. To the north and south are late 19th-and early 20th-century houses, where the streets are named after artists and intellectuals, such as the 17th-century Dutch poet Roemer Visscher. To the west, the Vondelpark offers a pleasant, fresh-air break from all the museums.

"Russia" gablestone in Roemer Visscherstraat

SIGHTS AT A GLANCE

Museums and Workshops
Coster Diamonds ❷
Nederlands Filmmuseum ❾
Rijksmuseum pp122–5 ❶
Stedelijk Museum pp128–9 ❹
Van Gogh Museum pp126–7 ❸

Concert Halls
Concertgebouw ❺

Historic Buildings
Hollandse Manege ❼
Vondelkerk ❽

Parks
Vondelpark ❻

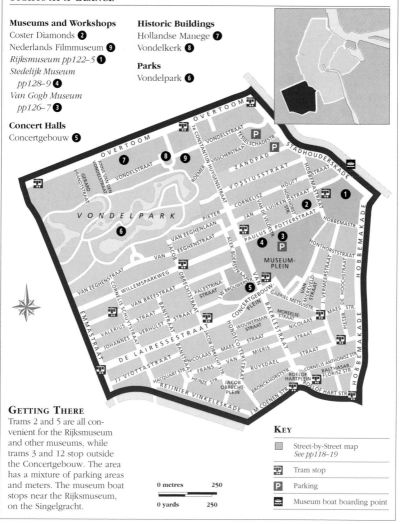

GETTING THERE
Trams 2 and 5 are all convenient for the Rijksmuseum and other museums, while trams 3 and 12 stop outside the Concertgebouw. The area has a mixture of parking areas and meters. The museum boat stops near the Rijksmuseum, on the Singelgracht.

0 metres 250
0 yards 250

KEY

	Street-by-Street map *See pp118–19*
	Tram stop
	Parking
	Museum boat boarding point

◁ Statue of the sculptor Thomas de Keyser (1596–1667) on the façade of the Stedelijk Museum

Street-by-Street: Museum Quarter

T HE GREEN EXPANSE of Museumplein was once bisected by a busy main road known locally as the "shortest motorway in Europe". But dramatic renovation between 1996 and 1999 has transformed it into a stately park, fringed by Amsterdam's major cultural centres. The district is one of the

Statue on façade of Stedelijk wealthiest in the city, with wide streets lined with grand houses.

After the heady delights of the museums, it is possible to window-shop at the many up-market boutiques along the exclusive PC Hooftstraat and Van Baerlestraat, or watch the diamond polishers at work in Coster Diamonds.

★ **Van Gogh Museum**
The new wing of the museum, an elegant oval shape, was designed by Kisho Kurokawa and opened in 1999. It is dedicated to temporary exhibitions of 19th-century art ❸

Van Baerlestraat
contains exclusive
clothing shops
(see p144).

★ **Stedelijk Museum**
Housing the civic collection of modern art, this museum also stages controversial contemporary art exhibitions. A sculpture garden is behind the building ❹

Concertgebouw
Designed by AL van Gendt, the building has a Classical façade and a concert hall with near-perfect acoustics ❺

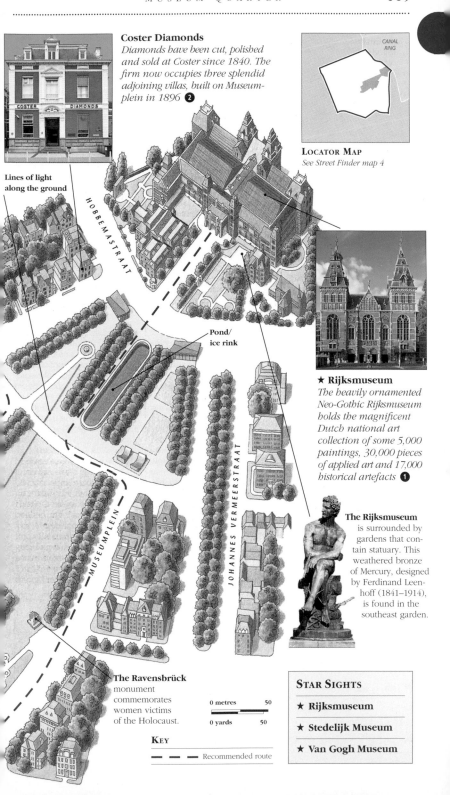

Coster Diamonds
Diamonds have been cut, polished and sold at Coster since 1840. The firm now occupies three splendid adjoining villas, built on Museum-plein in 1896 ❷

CANAL RING

LOCATOR MAP
See Street Finder map 4

Lines of light along the ground

HOBBEMASTRAAT

Pond/ ice rink

★ **Rijksmuseum**
The heavily ornamented Neo-Gothic Rijksmuseum holds the magnificent Dutch national art collection of some 5,000 paintings, 30,000 pieces of applied art and 17,000 historical artefacts ❶

JOHANNES VERMEERSTRAAT

MUSEUMPLEIN

The Rijksmuseum
is surrounded by gardens that contain statuary. This weathered bronze of Mercury, designed by Ferdinand Leenhoff (1841–1914), is found in the southeast garden.

The Ravensbrück
monument commemorates women victims of the Holocaust.

0 metres   50

0 yards   50

KEY

– – – – Recommended route

STAR SIGHTS

★ **Rijksmuseum**

★ **Stedelijk Museum**

★ **Van Gogh Museum**

Rijksmuseum ❶

See pp122–5.

Coster Diamonds ❷

Paulus Potterstraat 2–8. **Map** 4 E3.
☎ *020-3055555.* 🚋 *2, 5.* ⏰ *9am–5pm daily.* ⬤ *1 Jan, 25 & 26 Dec.*
📷 ✏ 🖥 🅦 costerdiamonds.com

ONE OF AMSTERDAM's oldest diamond factories, Coster was founded in 1840. Twelve years later, Queen Victoria's consort, Prince Albert, honoured the company by giving them the task of repolishing the enormous *Koh-i-Noor* (mountain of light) diamond. This blue-white stone is one of the treasures of the British crown jewels and weighs in at 108.8 carats. A replica of the coronation crown, which incorporates a copy of the fabulous stone, is found in Coster's spacious entrance hall.

More than 1,000 people visit the factory each day to witness the processes of grading, cutting and polishing the stones. The goldsmiths and diamond-cutters work together in the factory to produce customized items of jewellery, in a range of styles, which are available over the counter. For serious diamond-buyers, such as the jewellers who come to Amsterdam from all over the world, there are private sales rooms where discretion is assured.

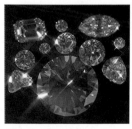

**Glistening diamonds
at Coster Diamonds**

Van Gogh Museum ❸

See pp126–7.

Stedelijk Museum ❹

See pp128–9.

Façade of the award-winning Concertgebouw (1881) by AL van Gendt

Concertgebouw ❺

Concertgebouwplein 2–6. **Map** 4 D4.
☎ *020-6754411 or 020-6718345.* 🚋
2, 3, 5, 12, 16. **Box office** ⏰ *10am–7pm daily.* 🎧 ✏ ♿ *by arrangement.* 🅦 www.concertgebouw.nl

FOLLOWING an open architectural competition held in 1881, AL van Gendt (1835–1901) was chosen to design a vast new concert hall for Amsterdam. The resulting Neo-Renaissance building boasts an elaborate pediment and colonnaded façade, and houses two concert halls. Despite Van Gendt's lack of musical knowledge, he managed to produce near-perfect acoustics in the Grote Zaal (main concert hall), which is renowned the world over.

The inaugural concert at the Concertgebouw was held on 11 April 1888, complete with an orchestra of 120 musicians and a choir of 600. A resident orchestra was established at the hall seven months later.

The building has been renovated several times over the years, most recently in 1983, when some serious subsidence threatened the building's entire foundation. To remedy this, the whole superstructure had to be lifted up off the ground while the original supporting piles, which rested on sand 13 m (43 ft) underground, were removed and replaced by concrete piles sunk into the ground to a depth of 18 m (59 ft). A glass extension and new entrance were added by Pi de Bruijn in 1988. The original entrance was relocated round to the side of the building. Though primarily designed to hold concerts, the Concertgebouw has become a multifunctional building. It has played host to business meetings, exhibitions, conferences, political meetings and occasional boxing matches.

Bandstand in Vondelpark

Vondelpark ❻

Stadhouderskade. **Map** 4 E2. 🚋 *1, 2, 3, 5, 6, 12.* **Park** ⏰ *24hrs daily.*
Open-air theatre ⏰ *Jun–last week Aug: Wed–Sun.*

IN 1864, A GROUP consisting of prominent Amsterdammers formed a committee with the aim of founding a public park, and they raised enough money to buy 8 ha (20 acres) of land. JD and LP Zocher, a father-and-son team of landscape architects, were then commissioned to design the park in typical English landscape style. They used vistas, pathways and ponds to create the illusion of a large natural area, which was opened to the public on 15 June 1865, as the Nieuwe Park. The park's present name was adopted in 1867, when a statue of Dutch poet Joost van den Vondel

(1587–1679) was erected on the grounds. The committee soon began to raise money to enlarge the park, and by June 1877 it had reached its current dimensions of 45 ha (110 acres). The park now supports around 100 plant species and 127 types of tree. Squirrels, hedgehogs, ducks and garden birds mix with a huge colony of greedy, bright green parakeets, which gather in front of the pavilion every morning to be fed. Herds of cows, sheep, goats and even a lone llama graze in the pastures.

Vondelpark welcomes about 8 million visitors a year, and is popular with the locals for dog-walking, jogging, or just for the view. Free concerts are given at the *openluchttheater* (open-air theatre) or at the bandstand during summer.

Façade of the Hollandse Manege, the Dutch riding school

Hollandse Manege ❼

Vondelstraat 140. **Map** 3 C2. ☎ 020-6180942. 🚊 1, 6. 🕐 2pm–midnight Mon, 9am–midnight Tue–Fri, 9am–5pm Sat & Sun. 📷 🖥

THE DUTCH RIDING SCHOOL was originally situated on the Leidsegracht, but in 1882 a new building was opened, designed by AL van Gendt and based on the Spanish Riding School in Vienna. The riding school was threatened with demolition in the 1980s, but was saved after a public outcry. Reopened in 1986 by Prince Bernhard, it has been restored to its former glory. The Neo-Classical indoor arena boasts gilded mirrors and moulded horses' heads on its elaborate plasterwork walls. Some of the wrought-iron stalls remain and sound is muffled by sawdust. At the top of the staircase, one door leads to a balcony overlooking the arena, another to the café.

Vondelkerk ❽

Vondelstraat 120. **Map** 3 C2. 🚊 1, 3, 6, 12. 🕐 to the public.

THE VONDELKERK was the largest church designed by PJH Cuypers, architect of the Centraal Station. Work began on the building in 1872, but funds ran out by the following year. Money gathered from public donations and lotteries allowed the building to be completed by 1880. When fire broke out in November 1904, firefighters saved the nave of the church by forcing the burning tower to fall away into Vondelpark. A new tower was added later by the architect's son, JT Cuypers. The church was deconsecrated in 1979 and converted into offices in 1985.

Nederlands Filmmuseum ❾

Vondelpark 3. **Map** 4 D2. 🕿 020-5891400. 🚊 1, 3, 6, 12. **Library** 🕐 call for opening times. 🔴 July & Aug. **Box office** 🕐 9am–10pm Mon–Fri, 6–10pm Sat, 1–10pm Sun. **Screenings**: from 7pm daily; plus 3pm Sun. 🎞 for cinema. 🚫 🖥 🚻 🗺 www.filmmuseum.nl

VONDELPARK'S pavilion was designed by the architects PJ Hamer (1812–87) and his son W Hamer (1843–1913), and opened on 4 May 1881 as a café and restaurant. After World War II, it was restored and then reopened in 1947 as an international cultural centre.

In 1991, the pavilion was renovated once more. The complete Art Deco interior of the Cinema Parisien, Amsterdam's first cinema, built in 1910, was moved into one of the rooms. It is now an important national film museum, showing more than 1,000 films a year. The museum also owns a film poster collection, runs a public film library at Nos. 69–71 Vondelstraat and holds free outdoor film screenings during the summer.

The terrace of Café Vertigo at the Filmmuseum

Rijksmuseum ❶

THE RIJKSMUSEUM, an Amsterdam landmark, possesses an unrivalled collection of Dutch art, begun in the early 19th century. The huge museum opened in 1885 to bitter criticism from Amsterdam's Protestant community for its Neo-Gothic style. The main building is closed until mid-2008 for a major renovation. However, a selection of the best works can be viewed in the Philips Wing and in other temporary venues.

First floor

Winter Landscape with Skaters *(1608)*
Painter Hendrick Avercamp specialized in intricate icy winter scenes.

The Gothic façade
of Cuypers' building is red brick with elaborate decoration, including coloured tiles.

★ The Kitchen Maid *(1658)*
The light falling through the window and the stillness of this domestic scene are typical of Jan Vermeer.

Key to Floorplan

- ☐ Dutch history
- ☐ Foreign works
- ☐ 17th-century painting
- ☐ 18th- and 19th-century painting
- ☐ Hague School of Impressionism
- ☐ Sculpture and applied art
- ☐ Prints and drawings
- ☐ Asiatic art
- ☐ Non-exhibition space

Entrance

Star Paintings

- ★ St Elizabeth's Day Flood
- ★ The Kitchen Maid by Vermeer
- ★ The Night Watch by Rembrandt

★ St Elizabeth's Day Flood *(1500)*
An unknown artist painted this altarpiece, showing a disastrous flood in 1421. The dykes protecting Dordrecht were breached, and 22 villages were swept away by the flood water.

Entrance

Study collections

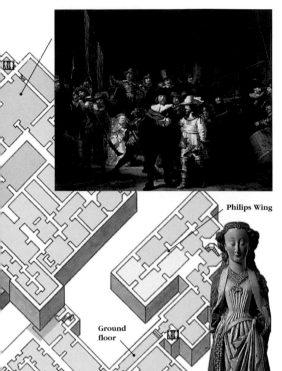

Visitors' Checklist

Stadhouderskade 42. **Map** 4 E3.
020-6747047. 2, 3, 5, 6,
7, 10, 12. Stadhouderskade.
10am–5pm daily. 1 Jan.

w www.rijksmuseum.nl

★ **The Night Watch** *(1642)*
*The showpiece of Dutch
17th-century art, this vast
canvas was commissioned
as a group portrait of an
Amsterdam militia company.*

Gallery Guide

*There are entrances on either
side of the driveway under the
building – the left leads into the
Dutch history section, the right
to prints and drawings, sculpture and applied art, and then
continues on up the stairs. On
the first floor is a huge antechamber, with an information
desk and shop. The entrance on
the left starts with 16th- to 19th-
century painting. The museum
is undergoing renovation
from October 2003, and all
the highlights are on show
throughout the Philips Wing.*

Philips Wing

**Ground
floor**

St Catherine *(c.1465)*
*This sculpture by the Master of
Koudewater shows the saint stamping on Emperor Maxentius, who
allegedly killed her with his sword.*

Genre Painting

For the contemporaries of
Jan Steen (1625–79), this
cosy everyday scene was full
of symbols that are obscure
to the modern viewer. The
dog on the pillow may represent fidelity, and the red
stockings, the woman's
sexuality; she is probably a
prostitute. Such genre paintings were often raunchy, but
most had a moral twist *(see
p221)* – domestic scenes by
artists such as Terborch and
Honthorst were symbolic of
brothels, while other works
illustrated proverbs. Symbols
such as candles or skulls
indicated mortality.

Jan Steen's *Woman at Her Toilet* was
painted in about 1660

Basement

Exploring the Rijksmuseum

THE RIJKSMUSEUM is almost too vast to be seen in a single visit. It is famous for owning probably the best collection of Dutch art in the world, from early religious works to the masterpieces of the Golden Age. However, the applied art and sculpture sections, and the Asiatic artefacts, are equally wonderful. Due to renovation, only a selection of works can be seen now in the Philips Wing. The selected pieces demonstrate the enormous prosperity of Holland's Golden Age in the 17th century. Rembrandt's *The Night Watch* is one of the masterpieces still on display.

Feeding the Hungry from a series of panels by the Master of Alkmaar

DUTCH HISTORY

THE TURBULENT HISTORY of the Netherlands is encapsulated in this section. In the opening room is the medieval altar painting of *St Elizabeth's Day Flood (see p122)*. The central room has 17th-century ship models, artefacts salvaged from shipwrecks and paintings of factories and townscapes from the days of the Dutch Empire. Later displays recall battles in naval history; exhibits from the 18th century deal with the impact of revolutionary France on Amsterdam, ending in 1815 after the Napoleonic Wars.

EARLY PAINTING AND FOREIGN SCHOOLS

ALONGSIDE a small collection of Flemish and Italian art, including portraits by Piero di Cosimo (1462–1521), are the first specifically "Dutch" paintings. These works are mostly religious, such as *The Seven Works of Charity* (1504) by the Master of Alkmaar, Jan van Scorel's quasi-Mannerist *Mary Magdalene* (1528) and Lucas van Leyden's triptych, *Adoration of the Golden Calf* (1530). As the 16th century progressed, religious themes were superseded by pastoral subjects; by 1552, paintings like Pieter Aertsen's *The Egg Dance* were full of realism, by then the keystone of much Dutch art.

17TH-CENTURY PAINTING

BY THE ALTERATION in 1578, Dutch art had moved away completely from religious to secular themes. Artists turned to realistic portraiture, landscapes, still lifes, seascapes, domestic interiors, including genre work *(see p123)*, and animal portraits. Rembrandt

(see p78) is the most famous of many artists who lived and worked around Amsterdam at this time. Examples of his work hanging in the Rijksmuseum include *Portrait of Titus in a Monk's Habit* (1660), *Self-Portrait as the Apostle Paul* (1661), *The Jewish Bride (see pp24–5),* as well as *The Night Watch (see p123)*. Look out too for the work of his many pupils, who included, among others, Nicolaes Maes and Ferdinand Bol.

Don't miss Jan Vermeer's (1632–75) serenely light-filled interiors including *The Kitchen Maid (see p122)* and *The Woman Reading a Letter* (1662). Of several portraits by Frans Hals *(see pp184–5)*, the best known are *The Wedding Portrait* and *The Merry Drinker* (1630). *The Windmill at Wijk* by Jacob van Ruisdael (1628–82) is a great landscape by an artist at the very height of his power. Other artists whose works contribute to this unforgettable collection include Pieter Saenredam *(see p53)*, Jan van de Capelle, Jan Steen *(see p123)* and Gerard Terborch.

18TH- AND 19TH-CENTURY PAINTING

IN MANY WAYS, 18th-century Dutch painting merely continued the themes and quality of 17th-century work. This is

The Wedding Portrait (c. 1622) by Frans Hals

particularly true of portraiture and still lifes, with the evocative *Still Life with Flowers and Fruit* by Jan van Huysum (1682–1749) standing out. A trend developed later for elegant "conversation pieces" by artists such as Adriaan van der Werff (1659–1722) and Cornelis Troost (1696–1750). Most had satirical undertones, like *The Art Gallery of Jan Gildemeester Jansz* (1794) by Adriaan de Lelie (1755–1820), showing an 18th-century salon whose walls are crowded with 17th-century masterpieces.

HAGUE SCHOOL AND THE IMPRESSIONISTS

THE SO-CALLED Hague School was made up of a group of Dutch artists who came together around 1870 in The Hague. Their landscape work, which earned them the alternative title the "Grey School" for their overcast skies, captures the atmospheric quality of subdued Dutch sunlight. One of the prizes of the Rijksmuseum's 19th-century collection is *Morning Ride on the Beach* (1876) by Anton Mauve (1838–88), painted in soft pearly colours. Alongside hangs the beautiful polder landscape *View near the Geestbrug* by Hendrik Weissenbruch (1824–1903). In contrast, the Dutch Impressionists, closely linked to the French Impressionists, preferred active subjects such as *The Bridge over the Singel at Paleisstraat, Amsterdam* (1890) by George Hendrik Breitner (1857–1923).

SCULPTURE AND APPLIED ARTS

BEGINNING WITH religious medieval sculpture, this section moves on to the splendour of Renaissance furniture and decoration. Highlights that capture the wealth of the Golden Age include the exquisite collections of glassware and Delftware *(see pp26–7)*, and diamond jewellery. A late 17th-century, 12-leaf Chinese screen incorporates European figures on one side, a phoenix on the other; and two dolls'

Still Life with Flowers and Fruit (c.1730) by artist Jan van Huysum (1682–1740), one of many still lifes exhibited in the Rijksmuseum

houses are modelled on contemporary town houses. Some outstanding 18th-century Meissen porcelain and Art Nouveau glass complete the collection.

PRINTS AND DRAWINGS

THE RIJKSMUSEUM owns about a million prints and drawings. Although the emphasis is on Dutch works (most of Rembrandt's etchings as well as rare works by Hercules Seghers (c.1589–1637) are here), there are prints by major European artists, including Dürer, Tiepolo, Goya, Watteau and Toulouse-Lautrec, as well as a set of coloured Japanese woodcuts. Small exhibitions are held on the ground floor of the museum, but particular prints can be viewed with special permission from the Study Collection in the basement.

ASIATIC ART

REWARDS OF the Dutch imperial trading past are on show in this department, which has a separate entrance at the rear of the museum. Some of the earliest artefacts are the most unusual: tiny bronze Tang dynasty figurines from 7th-century China and gritty, granite rock carvings from Java (c.8th century). Later exhibits include a lovely – and extremely explicit – Hindu statue entitled *Heavenly Beauty*, luscious Chinese parchment paintings of tigers, inlaid Korean boxes and Vietnamese dishes painted with curly-tailed fish. This is a veritable hoard of delights and, above all, a monument to the sophistication and skill of craftsmen and artists in early Eastern cultures.

Late 7th-century Cambodian *Head of Buddha*

Van Gogh Museum ❸

THE VAN GOGH MUSEUM is based on a design by De Stijl architect Gerrit Rietveld *(see pp202–3)* and opened in 1973. A new, freestanding wing, designed by Kisho Kurokawa, was added in 1999. When Van Gogh died in 1890, he was on the verge of being acclaimed. His younger brother Theo, an art dealer, amassed a collection of 200 of his paintings and 500 drawings. These, combined with around 850 letters by Van Gogh to Theo, and selected works by his friends and contemporaries, form the core of the museum's outstanding collection.

★ **Vincent's Bedroom in Arles** *(1888)*
One of Van Gogh's best-known works, this was painted to celebrate his achievement of domestic stability at the Yellow House in Arles. He was so delighted with the colourful painting that he did it twice.

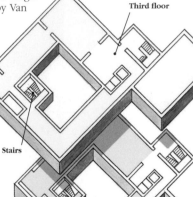

Third floor

Stairs

Second floor (study collection)

First floor

★ **Sunflowers** *(1889)*
The vivid yellows and greens in this version of Van Gogh's Sunflowers *have been enriched by broad streaks of bright mauve and red.*

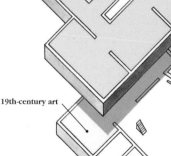

19th-century art

MUSEUM GUIDE
Paintings from Van Gogh's Dutch period and from his time in Paris and Provence are on the first floor. The study collection, occasional exhibits of Van Gogh's drawings and other temporary exhibitions are on the second floor. Works by other 19th-century artists are on the third floor and the ground floor, where there is also a bookshop and café. The new wing houses temporary exhibitions.

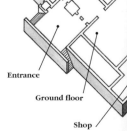

Entrance

Ground floor

Shop

STAR PAINTINGS

★ **The Bedroom at Arles**

★ **Sunflowers**

★ **Wheatfield and Crows**

An Artist's Life

Vincent van Gogh (1853–90), born in Zundert, began painting in 1880. He worked in the Netherlands for five years before moving to Paris, later settling at Arles in the south of France. After a fierce argument with Gauguin, he cut off part of his own ear; his mental instability forced him into an asylum in Saint-Remy. He sought help in Auvers, where he shot himself, dying two days later.

Van Gogh in 1871

Visitors' Checklist

Paulus Potterstraat 7. **Map** 4 E3.
020-5705200. 1, 2, 3, 5, 12. ◯ 10am–6pm daily, 10am–10pm Fri. ● 1 Jan.
Ø ⌂ & ▭ ▯ ▮ ▯
W www.vangoghmuseum.nl

Pietà (after Delacroix) *(1889)*
Van Gogh painted this work while in the asylum at Saint-Rémy. The figure of Christ is thought to be a self-portrait.

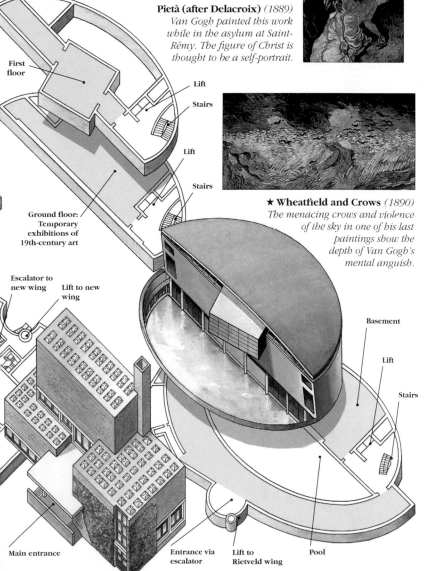

First floor

Lift

Stairs

Lift

Stairs

Ground floor: Temporary exhibitions of 19th-century art

★ Wheatfield and Crows *(1890)*
The menacing crows and violence of the sky in one of his last paintings show the depth of Van Gogh's mental anguish.

Escalator to new wing

Lift to new wing

Basement

Lift

Stairs

Main entrance

Entrance via escalator

Lift to Rietveld wing

Pool

Stedelijk Museum ❹

THE STEDELIJK MUSEUM was built to house a personal collection bequeathed to the city in 1890 by art connoisseur Sophia de Bruyn. In 1938, the museum became the national museum of modern art, displaying works by artists such as Picasso, Matisse, Mondriaan, Cézanne and Monet. The museum is now closed for an estimated three-year renovation. During this time, part of its collection will be lent out for exhibitions at other galleries.

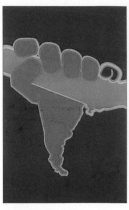

Portrait of the Artist with Seven Fingers *(1912)*
Marc Chagall's self-portrait is heavily autobiographical; the seven fingers of the title allude to the seven days of Creation and the artist's Jewish origins. Paris and Rome, the cities Chagall lived in, are inscribed in Hebrew above his head.

Solidaridad con America Latina *(1970)*
The Stedelijk's collection of rare posters comprises some 17,000 works, including this graphic image by the Cuban human rights campaigner Asela Perez.

THE MUSEUM BUILDING

The Neo-Renaissance building was designed by AW Weissman (1858–1923) in 1895. The façade is adorned with turrets and gables and with niches containing statues of artists and architects. Inside, it is ultra-modern. The museum is undergoing renovation in 2003.

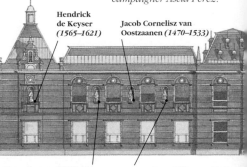

Hendrick de Keyser *(1565–1621)*

Jacob Cornelisz van Oostzaanen *(1470–1533)*

Pieter Aertsen *(1509–75)*

Joost Jansz Bilhamer *(1541–90)*

DE STIJL MOVEMENT

The Dutch artistic movement known as De Stijl (The Style) produced startlingly simple designs which have become icons of 20th-century abstract art. These include Gerrit Rietveld's famous *Red Blue Chair* and Piet Mondriaan's *Composition in Red, Black, Blue, Yellow and Grey* (1920). The movement was formed in 1917 by a group of artists who espoused clarity in their work, which embraced the mediums of painting, architecture, sculpture, poetry and furniture design. Many De Stijl artists, like Theo van Doesburg, split from the founding group in the 1920s; their legacy can be seen in the work of the Bauhaus and Modernist schools which followed (see pp202–3).

Gerrit Rietveld's *Red Blue Chair* (1918)

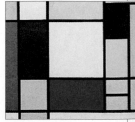

Composition in Red, Black, Blue, Yellow and Grey by Mondriaan

Dancing Woman (1911)
Ernst Ludwig Kirchner (1880–1938) was inspired by the primitive art of African and Asian cultures, and by the natural qualities of the materials he worked with.

Elaborate bell tower

Man and Animals (1949)
Karel Appel (b. 1921) was a member of the short-lived experimental Cobra movement (see p187). The human figure, dog fish and mythical creature are painted in the naive style of a child.

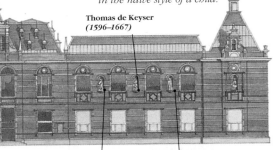

Thomas de Keyser
(1596–1667)

Jan van der Heyden
(1637–1712)

Jacob van Campen
(1595–1657)

Untitled (1965)
Jasper Johns (b. 1930) believed viewers should draw their own conclusions from his work. This huge canvas, with its bold rainbow (red, blue and yellow streaks and slabs), invites the viewer to think about the symbolism of colour.

VISITORS' CHECKLIST

Paulus Potterstraat 13. **Map** 4 D3.
020-5732911. 2, 3, 5, 12.
11am–5pm daily. until 2007. Call
020-5732737 for more details.
www.stedelijk.nl

★ KAZIMIR MALEVICH (1878–1935)

The Russian visual artist Kazimir Malevich can be counted, along with Piet Mondriaan, as one of the founders of abstract art. As well as paintings, Malevich created posters, sculptures, furniture, interior decoration and costumes.

After studying Futurism and Cubism in Moscow, he formulated a new art form called Suprematism, an abstract movement known for its experimentation with colour. Suprematism's central element is the theory of unlimited pre-eminence of free invention in the artistic process. Up until his 20s, Malevich painted abstract geometric forms. The square was his "supreme element". The Stedelijk Museum owns the largest part of the paintings and sketches from Malevich's Suprematist period. One of the most important works, *Suprematisme 1920–1927*, was defaced by a visitor to the museum in 1997.

In 1999, a conflict arose between the Malevich estate and the Stedelijk Museum over the ownership of the dozens of Suprematist works from the Stedelijk's collection.

Self-portrait by Malevich

OUTSIDE THE CENTRE

GREAT ARCHITECTURE and good town planning are not confined to central Amsterdam. Parts of the Nieuw Zuid (New South) bear testament to the imagination of the innovative Amsterdam School architects *(see pp142–3)*. Many fine buildings can be found in De Dageraad Housing complex and the streets around the Olympic Quarter. The area known as the Plantation was once green parkland beyond the city wall, where 17th-century Amsterdammers spent their leisure time. From about 1848, it became one of Amsterdam's first suburbs. The tree-lined streets around Artis and Hortus Botanicus are still popular places to live. From the Werf 't Kromhout, once a thriving shipyard, there is a fine view of De Gooyer Windmill, one of the few in Amsterdam to survive. The national maritime collection is kept at Scheepvaart Museum, a former naval store-house. NEMO, an educational science centre, is nearby. Fine parks are just a short tram ride from the city centre and offer a host of leisure activities.

Sculpture on the fountain at Frankendael

SIGHTS AT A GLANCE

Historic Buildings and Structures

Amstelsluizen ⑧
Amsterdam RAI ⑰
De Gooyer Windmill ⑤
Entrepotdok ②
Frankendael ⑪
Heineken Experience ⑭
Huizenblok de Dageraad ⑮
Java-eiland and KNSM-eiland ③
Koninklijk Theater Carré ⑦
Muiderpoort ④

Markets

Albert Cuypmarkt ⑱

Museums and Zoos

Gemeentearchief Amsterdam ⑬
Natura Artis Magistra pp138–9 ⑩
Nederlands Scheepvaart Museum pp132–3 ①
NEMO pp136–7 ⑨
Tropenmuseum ⑫
Verzetsmuseum ⑯
Werfmuseum 't Kromhout ⑥

SYMBOLEN

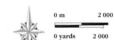

Oude Zijde
Nieuwe Zijde
Canal Ring
Museum Quarter
Outside the Centre

0 m ⎯⎯⎯ 2 000
0 yards ⎯⎯⎯ 2 000

OUTSIDE THE CENTRE

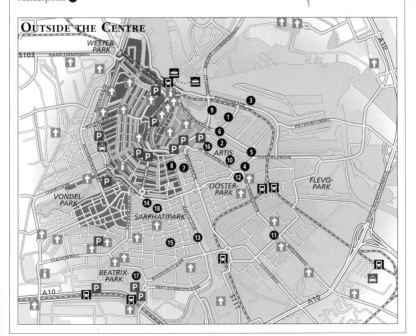

◁ **Replica of the *Amsterdam*, an East Indiaman, moored alongside the Scheepvaart Museum**

Nederlands Scheepvaart Museum ❶

O NCE THE ARSENAL of the Dutch Navy, this vast Classical sandstone building was built by Daniel Stalpaert in 1656. It was constructed round a massive courtyard and supported by 18,000 piles driven into the bed of the Oosterdok. The navy stayed in residence until 1973, when the building was converted into the Netherlands Maritime Museum, holding one of the world's largest maritime collections. Displays of boats, models and maps give a survey of Dutch naval history.

Ornate 17th-century brass sextant

★ The Blaeu Atlas
During the 17th century, the city was at the forefront in the area of cartography. The family Blaeu published an atlas in nine parts.

First floor

Ajax
This figurehead is from a ship built in 1832. It portrays Ajax, a hero of the Trojan War, who killed himself in despair when Achilles' armour was given to Odysseus.

MUSEUM GUIDE
The museum is arranged chronologically. The first floor covers the early maritime history of the Netherlands. The second floor spans merchant shipping from the 19th century to date, including technical developments. A cinema is on the first floor, and a full-size replica of the East Indiaman Amsterdam, *which can now be visited, is docked at the quayside.*

STAR EXHIBITS
★ **Royal Barge**

★ **The *Amsterdam***

★ **The Blaeu Atlas**

Classical sandstone façade

Map of the World
This map of Asia forms part of a series of five published in the Netherlands in 1780. Too inaccurate for navigation, they were used as wall decorations.

Main entrance

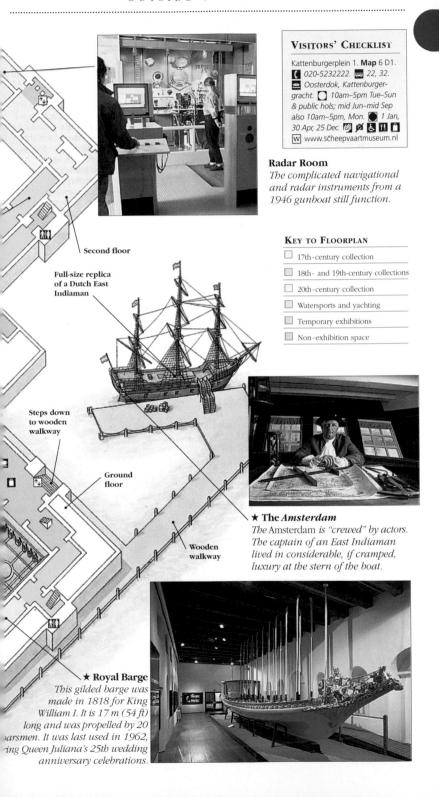

VISITORS' CHECKLIST

Kattenburgerplein 1. **Map** 6 D1.
📞 020-5232222. 🚌 22, 32.
🚊 Oosterdok, Kattenburgergracht. ⏰ 10am–5pm Tue–Sun
& public hols; mid Jun–mid Sep
also 10am–5pm, Mon. ⏺ 1 Jan,
30 Apr, 25 Dec. 📷 🚫 ♿ 🍴 🎁
Ⓦ www.scheepvaartmuseum.nl

Radar Room
*The complicated navigational
and radar instruments from a
1946 gunboat still function.*

Second floor

KEY TO FLOORPLAN

- 17th-century collection
- 18th- and 19th-century collections
- 20th-century collection
- Watersports and yachting
- Temporary exhibitions
- Non-exhibition space

**Full-size replica
of a Dutch East
Indiaman**

**Steps down
to wooden
walkway**

**Ground
floor**

★ **The *Amsterdam***
The Amsterdam *is "crewed" by actors.
The captain of an East Indiaman
lived in considerable, if cramped,
luxury at the stern of the boat.*

**Wooden
walkway**

★ **Royal Barge**
*This gilded barge was
made in 1818 for King
William I. It is 17 m (54 ft)
long and was propelled by 20
oarsmen. It was last used in 1962,
during Queen Juliana's 25th wedding
anniversary celebrations.*

Entrepotdok ❷

Map 6 D2. 🚃 6, 9, 14, 20. 🚌 22, 32.

THE REDEVELOPMENT of the old VOC warehouses at Entrepotdok has revitalized this dockland area. During the mid-19th century, it was the greatest warehouse area in Europe, being a customs-free zone for goods in transit. The quayside buildings are now a lively complex of homes, offices and eating places. Some of the original façades of the warehouses have been preserved, unlike the interiors, which have been opened up to provide an attractive inner courtyard. Café tables are often set out alongside the canal. On the other side, brightly coloured houseboats are moored.

Java-eiland and KNSM-eiland ❸

Map 6 D2. *Java-eiland* 🚌 59, *KNSM-eiland* 🚌 32.

SITUATED SIDE BY SIDE in the eastern docklands of the city are the islands of Java-eiland, which is long and narrow, and the broader KNSM-eiland. Java-eiland, designed by Sjoerd Soeters during the 1990s, demonstrates a wide variety of architectural styles. By combining these styles with a number of canals across the island, the architect succeeded in creating a very credible

The 18th-century De Gooyer windmill, with its renovated balcony

Amsterdam canal atmosphere. This is compounded by the many shops and small cafés. KNSM-eiland is slightly broader, giving architect Jo Coenen the space to create a central avenue flanked on either side by tower blocks.

Muiderpoort ❹

Alexanderplein. **Map** 6 E3. 🚃 7, 9, 10, 14. 🚫 *to the public.*

FORMERLY A CITY GATE, the Muiderpoort was designed by Cornelis Rauws (1732–72) in about 1770. The central

archway of this Classical structure is topped with a dome and clock tower. Napoleon entered the city through this gate in 1811 and, according to legend, forced the citizens to feed and house his ragged troops.

De Gooyer Windmill ❺

Funenkade 5. **Map** 6 F2. 🚃 7, 10. 🚫 *to the public.*

OF THE SIX remaining windmills within the city's boundaries, De Gooyer, also known as the Funenmolen, is the most central. Dominating the view down the Nieuwevaart, the mill, built around 1725, was the first corn mill in the Netherlands to use streamlined sails.

It first stood to the west of its present site, but the Oranje Nassau barracks, built in 1814, acted as a windbreak, and the mill was then moved piece by piece to the Funenkade. The octagonal wooden structure was rebuilt on the stone foot of an earlier water-pumping mill, demolished in 1812.

By 1925, De Gooyer was in a very poor state of repair and was bought by the city council, which fully restored it. Since then, the lower part of the mill, with its neat thatched roof and tiny windows, has been a private

Spout-gable façades of former warehouses along Entrepotdok

KNSM-eiland: a thriving modern city district

home, though its massive sails still creak into action sometimes. Next to the mill is the IJ brewery, with its own tasting room (www.brouwerijhetij.nl).

Werfmuseum 't Kromhout ❻

Hoogte Kadijk 147. **Map** 6 E2. [020-6276777. 🚋 6, 9, 10, 14. 🚢 22, 32. 🚤 Oosterdok or Kattenburgergracht. 🕐 10am–3pm Tue and by appointment. ● public hol. 📷 🅾 ♿ 🎫 W www.machinekamer.nl/museum

THE WERFMUSEUM 't Kromhout is one of the oldest working shipyards in Amsterdam and is also a museum. Ships were being built here as early as 1757. In the second half of the 19th century, production changed from sailing ships to steamships. As ocean-going ships got bigger, the yard, due to its relatively small size, turned to building lighter craft for inland waterways. It is now used only for restoration and repair work.

In 1967, the Prince Bernhard Fund bought the site, saving it from demolition.

The Amsterdam Monuments Fund later became involved to safeguard the shipyard's future as a historical site and helped turn it into a museum.

The museum is largely dedicated to the history of marine engineering, concentrating on work carried out at the shipyard, with steam engines, maritime photographs and ephemera. Another point of interest is the shipyard's forge featuring a variety of interesting tools and equipment. Some impressive historical ships are moored at the quayside. The museum's eastern hall is sometimes used for receptions and dinners.

The Werfmuseum 't Kromhout

Koninklijk Theater Carré ❼

Amstel 115–125. **Map** 5 B3. [0900-2525255. 🚋 4, 6, 7, 9, 10, 14, 20. M Weesperplein. **Box office** ◯ 9am–9pm daily. See **Entertainment** p147. 📷 🎫 3pm Wed & Sat (phone in advance). 📶 ♿ ▦ W www.theatercarre.nl

DURING the 19th century, the annual visit of the Carré Circus was a popular event. In 1868, Oscar Carré built wooden premises for the circus on the banks of the Amstel river. The city council considered the structure a fire hazard, so Carré persuaded them to accept a permanent building modelled on his other circus in Cologne. Built in 1887, the new structure included both a circus ring and a stage. The Classical façade is richly decorated with sculpted heads of dancers, jesters and clowns.

The Christmas circus is still one of the annual highlights at the theatre, but for much of the year the recently enlarged stage is taken over by concerts and blockbuster musicals.

Pillar decoration on Theater Carré

Amstelsluizen ❽

Map 5 B3. 🚋 4, 6, 7, 9, 10, 14. M Weesperplein.

THE AMSTELSLUIZEN, a row of sturdy wooden sluice gates spanning the Amstel river, form part of a complex system of sluices and pumping stations that ensure Amsterdam's canals do not stagnate. Four times a week in summer and twice a week in winter, the sluices are closed while fresh water from large lakes north of the city is allowed to flow into Amsterdam's canals. Sluices to the west of the city are left open, allowing the old water to flow, or be pumped, into the sea.

The Amstelsluizen date from 1673, and were operated manually until 1994, when they were mechanized.

NEMO ⑨

NEMO, AN EDUCATIONAL CENTRE for science and technology, is housed in a striking modern building by the Italian architect Renzo Piano. Designed in the form of a ship, it overhangs the water by 30 m (99 ft): the view from the roof is breathtaking. In the centre's thematic zones, young and old alike can learn through interactive experiments and hands-on displays, games, demonstrations and workshops.

Tanker Traffic
This mock-up of a tanker port gives an idea of the complexity of tanker traffic.

The motorway approach to the tunnel under the IJ is beneath the building.

★ Magic Metal
Experiment with the properties of metals and discover what electromagnetism is.

The Machine Park focuses on technology.

★ Ball Manufacture
This ingenious ball manufacture shows that technology is nothing more than an extension of the human body.

STAR SIGHTS
★ Ball Manufacture
★ Magic Metal
★ View from the Roof

Bubble-blowing
Museum-goers can blow gigantic bubbles using a ring and vats of soapy water.

Nemo: The Philosophy

The word "nemo", Latin for "no one", is used as the name of Holland's national science centre in order to imply the journey of discovery visitors will make at the centre. The name has been used by a number of important writers over the centuries to describe events and people who find themselves on the thin line between reality and fantasy. For example, Nemo turns up in the Latin translation of Homer's *Odyssey*, when the protagonist Ulysses adopts the name to deceive the Cyclops. And Jules Verne, in his 1870 novel *20,000 Leagues Under the Sea*, enlists Nemo as the mystical captain of the underwater *Nautilus*, which journeys in the shadowy world between reality and fantasy. He crops up again in 1905, when American cartoonist Winsor McCay creates *Little Nemo*, a young boy whose dreamland adventures once again suggest a mingling of fact and fiction.

Visitors' Checklist

Oosterdok 2. **Map** 5 C1.
📞 0900-9191100 (groups
0900-9191200). 🚋 1, 2, 4, 5, 9,
13, 14, 17, 24, 25. 🚌 22, 32.
⭘ 10am–5pm Tue–Sun; during
school holidays: 10am–5pm daily.
⭘ 1 Jan, 30 Apr, 25 Dec. 🅿 ♿
🖵 🍴 📷 🆆 www.e-NEMO.nl

Waterpower
At the waterfall, children have to channel the fast-flowing water and build dams in the basins using sandbags. The water is also used to drive a turbine.

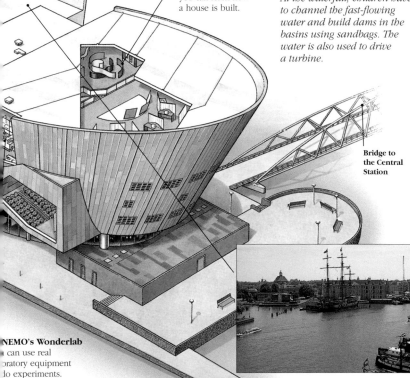

In Little NEMO's Bamboo House you can learn how a house is built.

Bridge to the Central Station

NEMO's Wonderlab
 can use real
oratory equipment
do experiments.

★ View from the Roof
The view from the building's roof, which is accessible only to the museum's visitors, provides a stunning vista of the port and city. In summer, part of the roof becomes a beach.

Museum Guide

Level 1 (the first floor) is devoted to the Zany World of Science, with sections dealing with light, sound and electricity. On Levels 2, 3 and 4 you will find areas such as Machine Park, Magic Metal, Perpetuum Mobile and NEMO's Wonderlab. Exhibitions here change regularly.

Natura Artis Magistra ❿

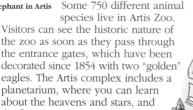

Elephant in Artis

Amsterdam's Artis Zoo (Natura Artis Magistra) is in Plantage, an elegant Amsterdam neighbourhood of broad tree-lined streets with elegant painted sandstone houses. Some 750 different animal species live in Artis Zoo. Visitors can see the historic nature of the zoo as soon as they pass through the entrance gates, which have been decorated since 1854 with two "golden" eagles. The Artis complex includes a planetarium, where you can learn about the heavens and stars, and the fine Neo-Classical aquarium, containing a wide variety of marine life, from tropical fish and sharks to huge moray eels.

Tiger Python
The female specimen in Ar can bear young simply by cloning herself.

★ Planetarium
The planetarium explores the relationship between humans and the stars. The night sky is recreated on the dome, and interactive exhibitions show the positions of the planets. Model spacecraft are on display in the hall around the auditorium. The interesting slide show is specially designed for youngsters.

Parrots
These birds are the first creatures you will see when you enter the zoo in summer and pass through the Parrot Lane. In winter, they join the other birds in the birdhouse.

The Playground
Based on a zoo theme, the playground, with its giraffe slide, is always popular with children.

STAR FEATURES

★ African Savannah

★ Aquarium

★ Planetarium

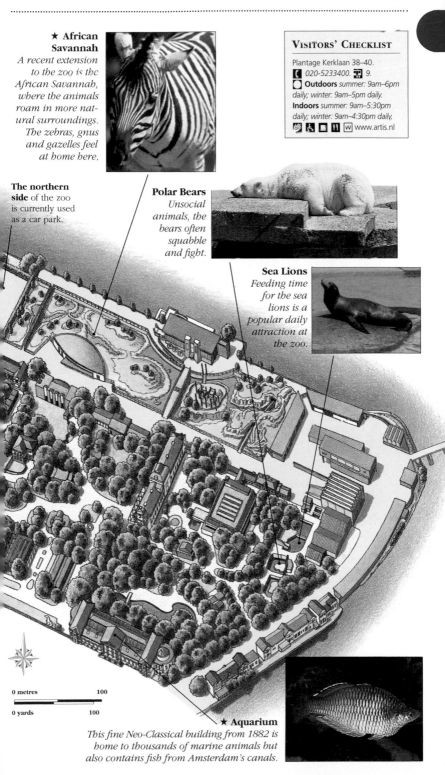

★ **African Savannah**

A recent extension to the zoo is the African Savannah, where the animals roam in more natural surroundings. The zebras, gnus and gazelles feel at home here.

VISITORS' CHECKLIST

Plantage Kerklaan 38–40.
📞 020-5233400. 🚊 9.
⭕ **Outdoors** summer: 9am–6pm daily; winter: 9am–5pm daily.
Indoors summer: 9am–5:30pm daily; winter: 9am–4:30pm daily.
🖼 ♿ 🏧 🍴 🚻 www.artis.nl

The northern side of the zoo is currently used as a car park.

Polar Bears
Unsocial animals, the bears often squabble and fight.

Sea Lions
Feeding time for the sea lions is a popular daily attraction at the zoo.

0 metres 100
0 yards 100

★ **Aquarium**
This fine Neo-Classical building from 1882 is home to thousands of marine animals but also contains fish from Amsterdam's canals.

Frankendael ⓫

Middenweg 72. **Map** *6 F5.* 🚋 *9.*
🚌 *59, 120, 126, 136.* **Gardens**
📞 *020-5687811.* ○ *dawn–dusk.*

Dᴜʀɪɴɢ ᴛʜᴇ early part of the
18th century, many of
Amsterdam's wealthier citizens
built country retreats south of
Plantage Middenlaan on reclaimed land called the Watergraafsmeer. The elegant Louis
XIV-style Frankendael is the
last survivor. The house is
closed to the public; the best
views of the ornamented
façade are from Middenweg.
This is also the best place to
view the fountain made in
1714 by Ignatius van Logteren
(1685–1732), a sculptor who,
along with his son, played a
central role in the development of Amsterdam's Louis
XIV style. The fountain, in the
front garden, is complete with
reclining river gods.
　The rear gardens are open to
the public, and offer a peaceful, if unkempt, refuge where
overgrown shrubs and ancient
trees line the footpaths. Visitors
are free to wander into the
large nurseries.

The late-19th-century façade of the Gemeentearchief Amsterdam

**Ignatius van Logteren's fountain
on the grounds of the Frankendael**

Tropenmuseum ⓬

Linnaeusstraat 2. **Map** *6 E3.* **Tropen-**
museum 📞 *020-5688215.* ○
*10am–5pm daily, 10am–3pm 5 Dec,
24 Dec, 31 Dec.* ● *1 Jan, 30 Apr, 5
May, 25 Dec.* 🖳 *www.tropenmuseum.nl*
Kindermuseum 📞 *020-5688233.*
○ *for special programmes in Dutch
language only (phone or see website).*
● *As Tropenmuseum.* 🚋 *6, 9, 10,
14.* 🎫 📷 🚻 ♿ 🎁 🍴 🛍 🏪
🖳 *www.kindermuseum.nl*

Bᴜɪʟᴛ ᴛᴏ ʜᴏᴜsᴇ the Dutch
Colonial Institute, this
vast complex was finished in
1926 by architects MA and

J Nieukerken. The exterior is
decorated with symbols of
imperialism, such as stone
friezes of peasants planting
rice. Upon completion of
the building's renovation
in 1978, the Royal Tropical
Institute opened a muse-
um, with a huge central
hall and three levels of
galleries. The institute's
aims are to study and to
help improve the lives of
the indigenous populations
of the tropics. The displays
focus on development issues
regarding daily life, education
and colonization.

**Balinese tiger protector mask and
model at the Tropenmuseum**

The impressive mask collection includes feathered fertility
masks from Zaire and carved
wooden masks from Central
America. Gerrit Schouten's
1819 diorama made of papier-
mâché and painted wood
depicts life in Suriname.

Gemeentearchief
Amsterdam ⓭

Amsteldijk 67. **Map** *5 B5.* 📞 *020-
5720202.* 🚋 *3, 4.* ○ *10am–5pm
Mon–Sat.* ● *public hols; Jul–Aug:
Sat.* 🚫 ♿

Tʜɪs ᴇʟᴀʙᴏʀᴀᴛᴇ 19th-century
building, with its ornate
Neo-Renaissance façade, used
to be the town hall of Nieuwer
Amstel, a small community
partly annexed by Amsterdam
in 1869. It has been home to
the city's municipal archives
since 1914, though these may
move to Vijzelstraat in 2004/5.
　The oldest document in the
archives is the Toll of Privilege
of 1275, by which Floris V
granted freedom from tolls "to
the people living near the Dam
in the river Amstel". The city

records include a register of baptisms, marriages and burials dating back to 1550.

Heineken Experience ⓮

Stadhouderskade 78. **C** 020-523 9666. **Ⓣ** 16, 25. **O** 10am–6pm Tue–Sun. **Ⓖ Ⓑ Ⓘ** Under 18s admitted only with parents.

Tₕᵢₛ ʜɪꜱᴛᴏʀɪᴄ 1867 building once housed the Heineken brewery. Now it offers an exhibition of how beer is made, culminating in a tasting room where you can have a drink.

Huizenblok De Dageraad ⓯

Pieter Lodewijk Takstraat. **Ⓣ** 4, 12, 25. **●** to the public.

Oₙₑ ᴏꜰ ᴛʜₑ best examples of Amsterdam School architecture (see pp142–3), De Dageraad (the Dawn) housing project was developed for poorer families following the Housing Act of 1901, by which the city council condemned slums and rethought housing policy. Architect HP Berlage drew up plans for the suburbs, aiming to integrate rich and poor by juxtaposing their housing. After Berlage's death, Piet Kramer and Michel de Klerk of the Amsterdam School adopted his ideas. From 1918–23, they designed this complex for the De Dageraad housing association.

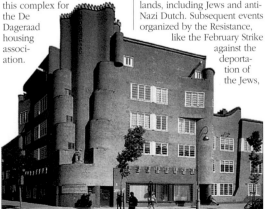

Imposing corner block of De Dageraad public housing

Interior of Amsterdam RAI with a trade fair in progress

Verzetsmuseum ⓰

Plantage Kerklaan 61. **C** 020-6202535. **Ⓣ** 6, 9, 14. **O** 10am–5pm Tue–Fri, noon–5pm Sat & Mon. **●** 1 Jan, 30 Apr, 25 Dec. **Ⓖ Ⓞ Ⓑ Ⓕ Ⓓ** **Ⓗ Ⓦ** www.verzetsmuseum.org

Pʀₑᵥᵢₒᵤₛₗʏ based in a former synagogue in Nieuw Zuid (New South), now at a site in the Plantage, the Resistance Museum holds a fascinating collection of memorabilia recording the activities of Dutch Resistance workers in World War II. It is run by former members of the Resistance and focuses on the courage of the 25,000 people actively involved in the movement. False documents, weaponry, film clips, photographs and equipment are on display.

By 1945 there were 300,000 people in hiding in the Netherlands, including Jews and anti-Nazi Dutch. Subsequent events organized by the Resistance, like the February Strike against the deportation of the Jews, are brought to life by exhibits showing where the refugees hid and how food for them was smuggled in.

Amsterdam RAI ⓱

Europaplein. **C** 020-5491212. **Ⓣ** 4. **Ⓜ Ⓡ** RAI. **Ⓔ** 15, 66, 169. **O** depending on exhibition. **Office & enquiries:** 8am–6pm Mon–Fri. **Ⓖ Ⓞ** **Ⓑ** with assistance. **Ⓦ** www.rai.nl

Aₘₛᴛₑʀᴅₐₘ ʀₐᵢ is one of the largest exhibition and conference centres in the country. It hosts over 1,000 events annually, from cabaret to horse shows and trade fairs. The first Amsterdam trade fair was a bicycle exhibition in 1893. Subsequent shows included cars and became an annual event known as the "RAI" (Rijwiel Automobiel Industrie). The present complex opened in 1961. It has since undergone several extensions.

Albert Cuypmarkt ⓲

Albert Cuypstraat. **Map** 5 A5. **Ⓣ** 4, 16, 24, 25. **O** 9:30am–5pm Mon–Sat.

Tₕₑ ₐₗᵦₑʀᴛ ᴄᵤʏₚₘₐʀₖᴛ began trading in 1904. Described by the stallholders as "the best-known market in Europe", it attracts some 20,000 visitors on weekdays and often twice as many on Saturdays. Goods on sale at the 325 stalls range from fish, poultry, cheese, fruit and vegetables to clothes; prices are among the cheapest in the city.

The Amsterdam School

THE INDUSTRIAL REVOLUTION at the end of the 19th century led to a boom in the growth of towns. New districts grew around Amsterdam to accommodate the growing number of factory workers. The architects of these districts, who sought new elements for decorating building façades, became known collectively as the Amsterdam School. Their designs were characterized by exotic rooflines, ornamental brickwork, cornices, window frames and corner formations which gave the façades "movement".

Curves *and serpentines on façades are typical features of the Amsterdam School.*

The Scheepvaarthuis was erected on the spot where in 1595 Cornelis Houtman set off on his first voyage to the East Indies.

The Betondorp *(Concrete Village), officially known as Tuindorp Watergraafsmeer, was the first place where experimental concrete-work was used. It also features many brick buildings in the Amsterdam School style.*

HP BERLAGE (1856–1934)

Berlage studied at the technical college of Zurich from 1875 to 1878, where he came into contact with architects such as Semper and Viollet-le-Duc. Inspired by their ideas, he developed his own style, which incorporated traditional Dutch materials. It later evolved into the Amsterdam School style of architecture. Berlage designed not only buildings but also interiors, furniture and graphics. In 1896, he was appointed to design the Beurs, the new stock exchange in Amsterdam *(see p91).* Completed in 1903, it is an austere building whose structure is clearly visible. Berlage was also active as a town planner. His design of Amsterdam-Zuid ("Plan Zuid") consists of monumental residential blocks. At its centre stands JF Staal's *Wolkenkrabber* (skyscraper).

Detail of a set of windows on the Zaanstraat

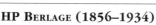

Het Schip, *built by Michel de Klerk, is a former post office which now provides a home for the Museum voor de Volkshuisvesting (museum of public housing).*

Interiors and exteriors are characterized by an excess of expressionist glass ornamentation and details.

*An astonishing variety of **decoration** could be achieved with this kind of brickwork.*

Sculptures

Amsterdam School lettering

THE ARCHITECTURE OF THE AMSTERDAM SCHOOL

From 1911 to 1923, the members of the Amsterdam School built a large number of office and residential complexes. One of the greatest examples of this is the Scheepvaarthuis (1913–16 and 1926–8), which is today the head office of the Gemeente Vervoerbedrijf (municipal traffic directorate). It is the first building to be completed entirely in the Amsterdam School style. It was designed by the Van Gendt brothers and JM van der Meij. Michel de Klerk, who later designed Het Schip, was also involved in the project.

Michel de Klerk (1884–1923)

Street furniture was among the repertoire of the Amsterdam School architects. In the Spaarndammerbuurt in particular, many examples can still be seen, including fire alarms, cable boxes and post boxes.

SHOPPING IN AMSTERDAM

AMSTERDAM HAS a huge range of shops and markets. Most of the large clothing and department stores are to be found in the Nieuwe Zijde, especially along Kalverstraat, but there are many other shopping areas to discover. The narrow streets crossing the Canal Ring, such as Herenstraat and Hartenstraat, contain a diverse

Traditional wooden clogs

array of specialist shops selling everything from ethnic fabrics and beads to unusual games and handmade dolls. The best luxury fashion is to be found on PC Hooftstraat and Van Baerlestraat. However, if you are looking for a bargain, take time to explore the street markets and numerous second-hand shops.

The northern end of the Waterlooplein, home to the famous flea market

OPENING HOURS

SHOPS ARE usually open from 9am to 6pm Tuesday to Saturday, from 1pm to 6pm Mondays. Many are open Sundays. In the city centre, shops stay open until 9pm on Thursdays.

HOW TO PAY

CASH IS the most popular method of payment. If you intend to use a credit card, ask first if it is accepted. Cards are becoming more widely accepted, but department stores may require purchases to be paid for at a special till, and smaller shops may accept them only for non-sale items and goods costing more than 45 euros. Most shops accept travellers' cheques. Some tourist shops take foreign currency but usually offer a poor rate of exchange.

VAT EXEMPTION

MOST DUTCH GOODS are subject to value added tax (BTW) of 19 per cent for clothes and other goods, and

6 per cent for books. Non-EU residents may be entitled to a refund. Shops that stock the relevant customs forms post a "Tax free for tourists" sign.

SALES

SALES OCCUR mainly in January and July but smaller shops and boutiques may offer discounts at any time. *Uitverkoop* describes anything from a closing-down sale to a clearance sale; *korting* merely indicates that discounts are offered. Towards the end of a sale, further discounts are often calculated at the till. Beware of

clothes rails marked, for example, *VA 40* or *Vanaf 40*, as this sign means "From 40", not exactly 40 euros.

DEPARTMENT STORES AND MALLS

AMSTERDAM's best-known department store is **De Bijenkorf**. It has a huge perfumery and stocks a wide range of clothing. **Maison de Bonneterie** and **Metz & Co** are more exclusive. Among the less expensive stores, **Hema** is popular for household goods, children's clothes and underwear. Also popular for basic items is **Vroom & Dreesman**. The only shopping malls in central Amsterdam

A shop selling kitchen gadgets

are the Kalvertoren (Kalverstraat, near Singel) and **Magna Plaza** *(see p90)*, containing upmarket boutiques and shops.

Trendy clothing for women and men in "De Negen Straatjes"

MARKETS

A MSTERDAMMERS' love of street trading is best illustrated on Koninginnedag *(see p32)*, when the city centre becomes the world's biggest flea market as locals sell off their unwanted junk.

Each district in Amsterdam has its own market. The best-known is the Albert Cuypmarkt *(see p141)*. There are also many specialist markets. Visitors and residents alike are drawn to the array of seasonal flowers at the Bloemenmarkt. Another market popular with tourists is Waterlooplein flea market *(see p79)*, where bargains can be found among the bric-à-brac; new and second-hand clothes are also for sale.

Browsers will be fascinated by the dozens of stalls at the **Looier Kunst en Antiekcentrum** *(see p113)*, selling anything from antique dolls to egg cups. Wednesdays and Saturdays on Nieuwezijds Voorburgwal there is a stamp and coin market. Gourmets

Jenever of Amsterdam

should head for the **Noordermarkt** *(see p111)*, for the Saturday organic food market. The best prices, however, are to be found about 25 km (16 miles) northwest of Amsterdam at the Saturday **Beverwijkse Bazar**, one of Europe's largest indoor flea markets. Next door you will find Oriental merchandise.

SPECIALIST SHOPS

S PECIALIST SHOPS are dotted throughout the city. The unusual **Condomerie Het Gulden Vlies**, located in a former squat, sells condoms from all over the world. **Christmas World** sells festive adornments year round, and **Party House** has a vast collection of paper decorations. **Capsicum Natuurstoffen** has a huge selection of silks and linens, while **Coppenhagen 1001 Kralen** offers over 1,000 types of beads. It is also worth exploring **Joe's Vliegerwinkel** for kites, **Simon Levelt** for tea and coffee and **Jacob Hooy & Co.** for herbs.

BOOKS AND NEWSPAPERS

E NGLISH-LANGUAGE BOOKS are easily available, particularly at **The American Book Center** and **Waterstone's**. They can also be picked up cheaply at second-hand shops, such as **De Slegte**. Comics collectors should not miss **Lambiek**. Amsterdam does not have its own English-language newspaper, but many newsagents stock foreign papers. *Het Financieel Dagblad* has a daily business update in English and a weekly English-language edition.

Organic foods for sale at the Noordermarkt

DIRECTORY

DEPARTMENT STORES AND MALLS

De Bijenkorf
Dam 1. **Map** 2 D5.
☎ 020-6218080.

Hema
Kalvertoren, Kalverstraat.
Map 4 F1.
☎ 020-4228988.
Nieuwendijk 174–176.
Map 2 D4.
☎ 020-6234176.

Magna Plaza
Nieuwezijds Voorburgwal 182. **Map** 2 D4.
☎ 020-6269199.

Maison de Bonneterie
Rokin 140–142. **Map** 4 F1.
☎ 020-5313400.

Metz & Co
Leidsestraat 34–36.
Map 4 E1.
☎ 020-5207020.

Vroom & Dreesman
Kalverstraat 201. **Map** 4 F1.
☎ 020-6220171.

MARKETS

De Beverwijkse Bazar
Montageweg 35, Beverwijk.

Looier Kunst en Antiekcentrum
Elandsgracht 109.
Map 4 D1. 🚊 7, 10, 17.
⬜ 11am–5pm Sat & Sun.

Noordermarkt
Noordermarkt. **Map** 1 C3.
🚊 3, 10, 13, 14, 17.

Boerenmarkt
⬜ summer: 9am–4pm
Sat; winter: 9am–3pm Sat.

SPECIALIST SHOPS

Capsicum Natuurstoffen
Oude Hoogstraat 1.

Map 2 D5.
☎ 020-6231016.

Christmas World
Damrak 33.
Map 2 D5.
☎ 020-4202838.

Condomerie Het Gulden Vlies
Warmoesstraat 141.
Map 2 D5.
☎ 020-6274174.

Coppenhagen 1001 Kralen
Rozengracht 54.
Map 1 B4.
☎ 020-6243681.

Jacob Hooy & Co
Kloveniersburgwal 12.
Map 2 E5.
☎ 020-6243041.

Party House
Rozengracht 93a/b.
Map 1 B4.
☎ 020-6247851.

Simon Levelt
Prinsengracht 180.

Map 1 B4.
☎ 020-6240823.

Joe's Vliegerwinkel
Nieuwe Hoogstraat 19.
Map 2 E5.
☎ 020-6250139.

BOOKS AND NEWSPAPERS

The American Book Center
Kalverstraat 185. **Map** 4 F1.
☎ 020-6255537.

Lambiek
Kerkstraat 78. **Map** 4 E1.
☎ 020-6267543.

De Slegte
Kalverstraat 48–52.
Map 2 D5.
☎ 020-6225933.

Waterstone's Premier English Bookseller
Kalverstraat 152.
Map 4 F1.
☎ 020-6383821.

ENTERTAINMENT IN AMSTERDAM

Amsterdam offers a large and diverse array of world-class entertainment. Various performances are staged in hundreds of venues throughout the city, ranging from the century-old Concertgebouw *(see p120)* to the 17th-century IJsbreker café on the Amstel. The Dutch people's passion for American jazz draws international greats like BB King, Pharoah Sanders and expatriate Nina Simone to annual

Relief showing three counts

events such as the Blues Festival and Drum Rhythm Festival. The city's most popular events take place during the summer and include the Holland Festival as well as the Amsterdam Roots Festival. There is a huge choice of multilingual plays and films throughout the year. There is also plenty of free entertainment from the multitude of street performers and live bands showcased in late-night bars and cafés.

ENTERTAINMENT INFORMATION

ONE OF THE CITY's most useful sources of entertainment information is *Uitkrant,* a free listings magazine. It is published monthly and available, as are a variety of other Dutch-language listings, from theatres, cafés and bars, as well as libraries and tourist offices. Although written in Dutch, it is easy to follow and offers the most comprehensive daily listings of what's going on in the city.

VVV (Amsterdam Tourist Board) publishes an English-language listings magazine every two weeks called *Day by Day*. It can be picked up for a nominal price at tourist board offices and some newsagents, or free issues can be found in selected hotels and restaurants. For music listings look out for the *Pop & Jazz*

Uitlijst published by the **AUB Ticketshop** (Amsterdam Uitburo). Daily newspapers including *De Volkskrant, Het Parool, NRC Handelsblad* and *De Telegraaf* publish a selection of listings on Thursdays, although they are mainly excerpts from *Uitkrant.*

BOOKING TICKETS

AMSTERDAM'S MAJOR classical music, opera and dance performances, such as those by the Dutch National Ballet, tend to sell out weeks in advance. Book tickets for these shows ahead of time to ensure you get the day, time and seats of your choice. For most other events, it is usually fine to purchase tickets on the day of the performance. The main reservations office for enter-

Outdoor café in the Rembrandtplein

tainment and all cultural activities is the AUB Ticketshop. You can make reservations, pick up tickets in advance (a booking fee is charged) and obtain information. You can also make bookings at the venue itself, or through tourist board offices.

Tickets to major rock concerts can be obtained at the tourist board, AUB and at some of the large record shops in the city centre. Although some of the most popular club dates

The Stopera complex, home to the Dutch national opera and ballet companies

need to be booked in advance, entrance to nightclubs like the Paradiso and De Melkweg can usually be bought at the door. The **Heineken Music Hall** is also good for music, while less-known bands perform at **Hotel Arena** or **More**.

Going to the cinema is popular with Amsterdammers, so it is advisable to book tickets in the afternoon for evening performances during a film's opening week. Most multi-screen cinemas provide a Dutch-speaking automated booking service. All booking offices are usually open from Monday to Saturday, between 9am and 6pm or later. Credit cards are generally not accepted and it is important to collect reserved tickets at least an

hour before the show starts or the tickets may be resold. The largest cinemas can be booked via a central reservation system, Belbios (tel: 0900-9363).

REDUCED-PRICE TICKETS

ENTRY TO SOME performances can be obtained at bargain prices for holders of the CJP, the Cultureel Jongeren Passport. Valid for one year, it is available to anyone under the age of 26 for 11 euros. Some hotels include reduced-price entry to certain events as part of their package deals – check details with your travel agent. Cinemas usually offer a 30 per cent discount from Monday to Wednesday. Several of the city's venues, including the

The Art Deco Tuschinski Theatre

Concertgebouw *(see p120)* and the Westerkerk *(see p110)*, hold free lunch-time concerts throughout the year.

FACILITIES FOR TRAVELLERS WITH DISABILITIES

NEARLY ALL OF Amsterdam's major theatres, cinemas and concert halls have unrestricted wheelchair access and assistance is always available. A number of the city's smaller venues, however, are housed in old buildings not designed with the disabled in mind. Venues like the IJsbreker will make special arrangements if they are notified beforehand. Cinemas also provide facilities for the hard of hearing and visually impaired. Always telephone the box office a couple of days before your visit and specify what you require.

Disco in the Heineken Music Hall

DIRECTORY			
AUB Ticketshop Leidseplein 26. **Map** 4 E2. 📞 0900-0191. 🅦 www. amsterdam.uitlijn.nl **VVV** Stationsplein 10. **Map** 2 E3. Leidseplein 1. **Map** 4 E2. 📞 0900-4004040. @ info@amsterdam tourist.nl **THEATRE AND CABARET** **De Brakke Grond** Vlaams Cultureel Centrum, Nes 45.	**Map** 2 D5. 📞 020-6266866. **Koninklijk Theater Carré** Amstel 115–125. **Map** 5 B3. 📞 0900-2525255. **Stadsschouwburg** Leidseplein 25. **Map** 4 E2. 📞 020-6242311. 🅦 www.stadsschouw burgamsterdam.nl **Theater De Kleine Komedie** Amstel 56–58. **Map** 5 B3. 📞 020-6240534. 🅦 www.dekleine komedie.nl	**ORCHESTRAL, CHAMBER AND CHORAL MUSIC** **Beurs van Berlage** Damrak 243. **Map** 2 D4. 📞 020-5304141. **Concertgebouw** Concertgebouwplein 2–6. **Map** 4 D4. 📞 020-6718345. **OPERA, MUSIC AND DANCE** **Muziektheater (Stopera)** Amstel 3. **Map** 5 B2. 📞 020-6255455. 🅦 www.muziektheater.nl	**CLUBS AND DISCO** **Heineken Music Hall** Arena Boulevard, Amsterdam Zuid-Oost. 📞 0900-3001250. 🅦 www.heineken musichall.nl **Hotel Arena** 's-Gravensandestraat 51. **Map** 6 D4. 📞 020-6947444. 🅦 www.hotelarena.nl **More** Rozengracht 133. **Map** 1 B4. 📞 020-5287451.

STREET FINDER

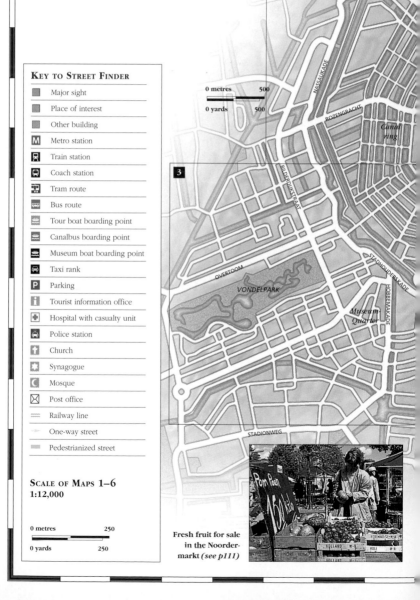

THE PAGE GRID superimposed on the *Area by Area* map below shows which parts of Amsterdam are covered in this *Street Finder*. Map references given for all sights, hotels, restaurants, shopping and entertainment venues described in this guide refer to the maps in this section (the *road map* is to be found on the book's inside back cover). An index of street names and places of interest marked on the maps is on pages 156–7. The key below indicates the maps' scale and other features marked on them, including transport terminals, emergency services and information centres. All major sights are clearly marked.

KEY TO STREET FINDER

▪	Major sight
▪	Place of interest
▪	Other building
M	Metro station
🚊	Train station
🚌	Coach station
🚋	Tram route
🚍	Bus route
⛴	Tour boat boarding point
⛴	Canalbus boarding point
⛴	Museum boat boarding point
🚕	Taxi rank
P	Parking
ℹ	Tourist information office
✚	Hospital with casualty unit
🚓	Police station
✝	Church
✡	Synagogue
☪	Mosque
⊠	Post office
=	Railway line
→	One-way street
▬	Pedestrianized street

SCALE OF MAPS 1–6
1:12,000

0 metres	250
0 yards	250

0 metres	500
0 yards	500

Fresh fruit for sale in the Noorder-markt *(see p111)*

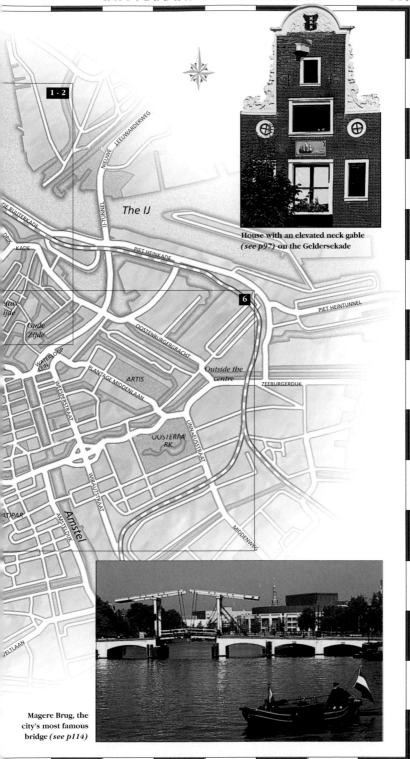

1 - 2

The IJ

PIET HEINTUNNEL

6

OOSTENBURGERGRACHT

Outside the centre

ZEEBURGERDIJK

PLANTAGE MIDDENLAAN

ARTIS

OOSTERPARK

LINN EUSSTRAAT

WIBAUTSTRAAT

MIDDENWEG

WATERLOOPLEIN

WEESPERSTRAAT

Amstel

AMSTELDIJK

DE RUITERKADE

KADE

PIET HEINKADE

uwe zijde

Oude Zijde

NIEUWE LEEUWARDERWEG

IJ-TUNNEL

ATIPAR

ELTLAAN

House with an elevated neck gable
(see p97) on the Geldersekade

Magere Brug, the
city's most famous
bridge *(see p114)*

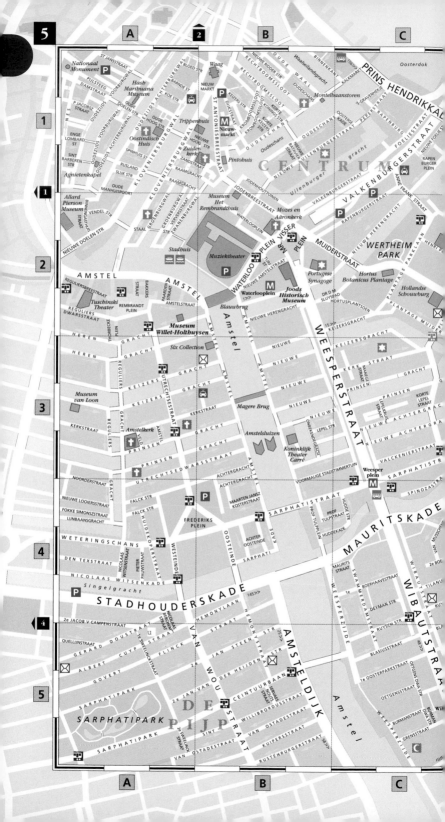

Street Finder Index

A

Achter Oosteinde	5 B4
Achtergracht	5 B3
Admiralengracht	3 A1
Admiraliteitstraat	6 E2
Akoleienstraat	1 A4
Alberdingk Thijmstraat	4 D2
Albert Cuypstraat	4 F4
Alexander Boersstraat	4 D3
Alexanderkade	6 E3
Alexanderplein	6 E3
Amstel	5 A2
Amsteldijk	5 B5
Amstelstraat	5 A2
Amstelveenseweg	3 A4
Amstelveld	5 A3
Andreas Bonnstraat	5 C4
Anjeliersdwarsstraat, 1e	1 B3
Anjeliersdwarsstraat, 2e	1 B3
Anjeliersstraat	1 B3
Anna Spenglerstraat	3 C2
Anna van den Vondelstraat	3 C2
Anne Frankstraat	2 F5
Apollolaan	3 B5
Arie Biemondstraat	3 B2
Assendelftstraat	1 B1

B

Bachstraat	4 D5
Baerlestraat, Van	4 D3
Bakkersstraat	5 A2
Balthasar Floriszstraat	4 F4
Banstraat	3 C4
Barentszstraat	1 C1
Barndesteeg	2 E5
Beethovenstraat	4 D5
Begijnhof	1 C5
Beijersweg	6 F5
Berenstraat	1 B5
Bergstraat	1 C4
Beukenplein	6 D4
Beukenweg	6 D4
Beulingstraat	4 F1
Beursplein	2 D4
Beursstraat	2 D4
Bickersgracht	1 C2
Bijltjespad	6 D1
Bilderdijkstraat	3 C1
Binnen Dommersstraat	1 B2
Binnengasthuisstraat	5 A2
Binnenkant	2 E4
Binnen Oranjestraat	1 C2
Blankenstraat	6 F2
Blauwburgwal	1 C4
Bloedstraat	2 E5
Bloemdwarsstraat, 1e	1 B4
Bloemdwarsstraat, 2e	1 B4
Bloemgracht	1 A4
Bloemstraat	1 A4
Blokmakerstraat	1 C2
Boerenwetering	4 E5
Boerhaaveplein	6 D4
Boerhaavestraat, 1e	5 C4
Boerhaavestraat, 2e	5 C4
Bonairestraat	3 A3
Boomdwarsstraat, 1e	1 B3
Boomdwarsstraat, 2e	1 B3
Boomstraat	1 B3
Borgerstraat	3 A2
Bosboom Toussaintstraat	4 D1
Boulevardpad	6 E2
Breestraat, Van	3 C4
Breitnerstraat	3 C5
Brouwersgracht	1 B2

C

Camperstraat	6 D4
Ceintuurbaan	4 F5
Claes Claeszhofje	1 B3
Coehoornstraat, 1e	6 F2
Commelinstraat	6 E3
Compagniestraat	6 E2
Concertgebouwplein	4 D4
Constantijn Huygensstraat, 1e	3 C1
Constantijn Huygensstraat, 2e	3 C2
Cornelis Anthoniszstraat	4 E4
Cornelis Krusemanstraat	3 A5
Cornelis Schuytstraat	3 C4
Costakade, Da	1 A5
Costaplein, Da	1 A5
Costastraat, Da	1 A5
Cremerplein, JJ	3 A3
Cruquiuskade	6 F2
Cruquiusstraat	6 F2
Czaar Peterstraat	6 F2

D

Dam	2 D3
Damrak	2 D4
Damstraat	2 D5
Daniël de Langestraat	4 E5
Daniël Stalpaertstraat	4 F4
Dapperplein	6 F3
Dapperstraat	6 F3
Den Texstraat	5 A4
Deymanstraat	5 C4
Dijkstraat	2 E5
Dirk v. Hasseltssteeg	2 D4
Domselaerstraat	6 F4
Driehoekstraat	1 B2
Driekoningenstraat	1 C4
Droogbak	2 D3
Dufaystraat	3 B4

E

Eeghenlaan, Van	4 D3
Eeghenstraat, Van	3 C4
Egelantiersgracht	1 B4
Egelantiersstraat	1 B4
Eggertstraat	2 D4
Eikenplein	6 E4
Eikenweg	6 E4
Eilandsgracht	1 C2
Elandsgracht	1 B5
Elandsstraat	1 A5
Emmalaan	3 B4
Emmaplein	3 B4
Emmastraat	3 C4
Enge Lombardsteeg	2 D5
Entrepotdok	6 D2

F

Falckstraat	5 A4
Ferdinand Bolstraat	4 F5
Foeliestraat	2 F5
Fokke Simonszstraat	5 A4
Frans Halsstraat	4 F4
Frans van Mierisstraat	4 D4
Frederik Hendrikstraat	1 A4
Frederiksplein	5 A4
Frederiksstraat	3 A3
Funenkade	6 F2

G

Gabriel Metsustraat	4 E4
Galgenstraat	1 C1
Gedempte Begijnensloot	1 C5
Geldersekade	2 E4
Genestetstraat, De	4 D1
Gerard Brandtstraat	3 B2
Gerard Doustraat	4 F4
Gerard Terborgstraat	4 E5
Gerrit van der Veenstraat	3 C5
Gieterstraat	1 B3
Gijsbrecht v. Aemstelstraat	5 C5
Goudsbloemstraat	1 B3
Govert Flinckstraat	4 F4

H

Gravenstraat	2 D4
Gravesandestraat, 's-	6 D4
Gravesandeplein, 's-	6 D4
Grensstraat	5 C5
Groenburgwal	5 A2
Groenmarktkade	1 A5
Grote Bickersstraat	1 C2
Grote Wittenburgerstraat	6 E1
Haarlemmerdijk	1 B2
Haarlemmerhouttuinen	1 C2
Haarlemmerplein	1 B2
Haarlemmerstraat	1 C3
Hacquartstraat	3 C4
Handboogstraat	4 F1
Hartenstraat	1 C5
Hasebroekstraat	3 B1
Hazenstraat	1 B5
Heiligeweg	4 F1
Heintje Hoeksteeg	2 E4
Heinzestraat	4 D4
Hekelveld	2 D3
Helmersstraat, 1e	3 A3
Helmersstraat, 2e	4 D2
Helmersstraat, 3e	4 D2
Hemonylaan	5 B4
Hemonystraat	5 B4
Henri Polaklaan	5 C2
Herengracht	1 C3
Herenmarkt	2 D3
Herenstraat	1 C3
Hobbemakade	4 E5
Hobbemastraat	4 E3
Hondecoeterstraat	4 D4
Honthorststraat	4 E3
Hoogte Kadijk	6 D1
Hortusplantsoen	5 C2
Houtmankade	1 B1
Houtmanstraat	1 B1
Huddekade	5 B4
Huddestraat	5 C4
Hugo de Grootkade	1 A4
Hugo de Grootstraat, 1e	1 A4
Hugo de Grootstraat, 2e	1 A4
Huidekoperstraat	5 A4
Huidenstraat	4 E1

I

IJplein	2 F2
Ite Boeremastraat	3 C2

J

Jacob Obrechtplein	4 D4
Jacob Obrechtstraat	3 C3
Jacob v. Campenstraat, 1e	4 F3
Jacob v. Campenstraat, 2e	5 A4
Jan Hanzenstraat	3 B1
Jan Luijkenstraat	4 D3
Jan Pieter Heijestraat	3 B2
Jan Steenstraat, 1e	4 F4
Jan Steenstraat, 2e	5 B5
Jan van der Heijdenstraat, 1e	4 F4
Jan van der Heijdenstraat, 2e	5 A5
Jan van Goyenkade	3 B5
Jan Willem Brouwersstraat	4 D4
Jodenbreestraat	2 E5
Jodenhouttuinen	2 E5
Johannes Verhulststraat	3 B4
Johannes Vermeerstraat	4 E4

K

Kadijksplein	6 D1
Kalkmarkt	2 F5

(unlabeled)

Kalverstraat	1 C5
Karthuizersdwarsstraat	1 B3
Karthuizersplantsoen	1 B3
Karthuizersstraat	1 B3
Kastanjeplein	6 E4
Kastanjeweg	6 E4
Kattenburgergracht	6 D1
Kattenburgerkade	6 D1
Kattenburgerkruisstraat	6 E1
Kattenburgerstraat	6 D1
Kattenburgervaart	6 E1
Kattengat	2 D3
Kattenlaan	3 B3
Kazernestraat	6 E3
Keizersgracht	1 C3
Keizersstraat	2 E5
Kerkstraat	4 E1
Kleine Gartmanplantsoen	4 E2
Kleine Wittenburgerstraat	6 E1
Kloveniersburgwal	2 D5
Koestraat	2 E5
Konijnenstraat	1 B5
Koninginneweg	3 A5
Koningslaan	3 A4
Koningsplein	4 F1
Korte Keizersstraat	2 E5
Korte Koningsstraat	2 E5
Korte Leidsedwarsstraat	4 E2
Korte Lepelstraat	5 C3
Korte Marnixkade	1 B2
Korte Niezel	2 E4
Kromboomssloot	2 E5

L

Laagte Kadijk	6 D1
Lairessestraat, De	3 B5
Lange Leidsedwarsstraat	4 E2
Lange Niezel	2 E4
Langestraat	1 C4
Lassusstraat	3 B4
Laurierdwarsstraat, 1e	1 B5
Laurierdwarsstraat, 2e	1 B5
Lauriergracht	1 A5
Laurierstraat	1 A5
Leeghwaterstraat, 1e	6 F1
Leeghwaterstraat, 2e	6 F1
Leidsegracht	4 E1
Leidsekade	4 D1
Leidsekruisstraat	4 E2
Leidseplein	4 E2
Leidsestraat	4 E1
Leliedwarsstraat, 1e	1 B4
Leliedwarsstraat, 2e	1 B4
Leliedwarsstraat, 3e	1 A4
Leliegracht	1 B4
Lepelkruisstraat	5 C3
Lepelstraat	5 B3
Lijnbaansgracht	1 A5
Lijnbaansstraat	1 A5
Lindengracht	1 B3
Lindenstraat	1 B3
Lindendwarsstraat, 1e	1 B3
Lindendwarsstraat, 2e	1 B3
Linnaeusplantsoen	6 F4
Linnaeusstraat	6 E3
Lomanstraat	3 A5
Looiersdwarsstraat, 3e	4 D1
Looiersgracht	4 D1
Louise Wentstraat	6 E3

M

Maarten Jansz. Kosterstraat	5 B4
Madelievenstraat	1 B4
Manegestraat	5 C3
Marnixkade	1 A2
Marnixplantsoen, 1e	1 B2
Marnixstraat	1 A4
Martelaarsgracht	2 D3
Martin Vlaarkade	1 B1
Mary Zeldenruststraat	6 D4

WESTERN
NETHERLANDS

Exploring Western Netherlands

THE LANDSCAPE OF THE WESTERN NETHERLANDS is strongly influenced by the old ports and commercial towns, which claim a prosperous past. During the 20th century, the most important ones have grown together to form the Randstad *(see pp164–5)*. But you can still find plenty of quiet outside the cities – in Europe's biggest coastal dune area, boasting its distinct flora and fauna; along the Vecht, with its pretty country houses; and along rivers such as the Vlist and the Linge. Main watersports areas are Zeeland, on the IJsselmeer and the lakes in the peat region.

0 kilometres   20

0 miles

The gothic Sint Bavo Church in Haarlem (see p182), known colloquially as Grote Kerk, was built between 1400 and 1550. This gigantic building dominates the Grote Markt. The Sint Bavo has one of the finest organs in Europe, built by Christiaan Müller.

The Mauritshuis at The Hague (see pp220–21) was built by Pieter Post in 1644 as instructed by Johan Maurits van Nassau, in the style of North Netherlands Neo-Classicism. Since 1821 it has been the home of the royal painting collection. This compact collection includes a number of first-rate works by old masters, including Rembrandt, Jan Steen and Johannes Vermeer.

The Hague

Construction of the Oosterscheldekering (Oosterschelde barrier) (see pp244–5) was prompted by the disastrous floods of 1953. In an effort to combat the water while also preserving the unique mud-flat bed of the Oosterschelde, a half-open multiple buttress dam with 62 sliding gates was built.

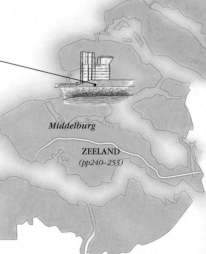

Middelburg

ZEELAND
(pp240–253)

◁ **Distinctive Marken, once an island in the Zuiderzee, now a popular fishing village on the IJsselmeer**

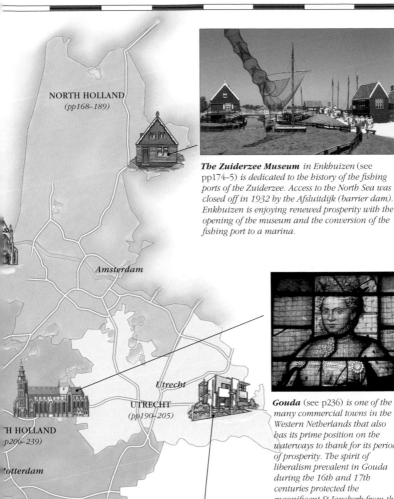

NORTH HOLLAND
(pp168–189)

Amsterdam

Utrecht

UTRECHT
(pp190–205)

'H HOLLAND
p206–239)

otterdam

The Zuiderzee Museum *in Enkhuizen (see pp174–5) is dedicated to the history of the fishing ports of the Zuiderzee. Access to the North Sea was closed off in 1932 by the Afsluitdijk (barrier dam). Enkhuizen is enjoying renewed prosperity with the opening of the museum and the conversion of the fishing port to a marina.*

Gouda *(see p236) is one of the many commercial towns in the Western Netherlands that also has its prime position on the waterways to thank for its period of prosperity. The spirit of liberalism prevalent in Gouda during the 16th and 17th centuries protected the magnificent St Janskerk from the Iconoclasm, meaning that the Gouda stained glass is still here to be enjoyed today.*

The Rietveld Schröder-Huis *in Utrecht (see pp202–3) is a famous example of "nieuwe bouwen" (new building). It was Rietveld's first complete architectural work and reveals his background as a furniture maker. At the time it was considered to be radically modern. Visitors nowadays are struck by the modesty and human proportions of the house.*

Reclaimed Land

HOLLAND IS CONTINUALLY increasing in size. Various methods of reclaiming land have been employed as far back as the 11th century. One fairly simple method was to build a dyke around a marshy area. Later, deep lakes were drained with the help of windmills. The far-reaching IJsselmeer polders – fertile farmlands – were created after the Zuiderzee was closed off using ingenious reclamation methods. Even now, huge efforts are being made to extend areas of reclaimed land – hence the new Amsterdam residential area of IJburg, which has sprung up from the IJmeer.

***To create a polder**,
a ditch was first dredged.
The dredgings were used
to build up the dyke.*

GRADUAL DRAINAGE

To overcome the height difference between the polder and the ring canal, which is sometimes large, the water is continually raised metre by metre by three windmills placed in a row, known as a *driegang* or row of three.

Because a polder lies some metres below sea level, the ground water level is always very high and has to be continually drained.

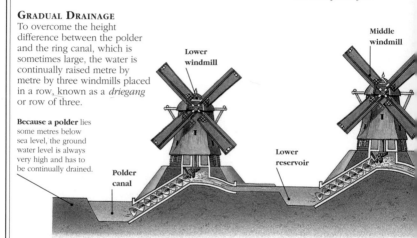

Lower windmill

Middle windmill

Lower reservoir

Polder canal

LAND RECLAMATION

About 3,000 years ago, houses were built on mounds so that they would not be flooded when the water rose. As far back as the 4th to 8th centuries, dykes were built around the houses and land. Land reclamation was carried out on a large scale from the 11th century, when the population increased sharply. In the 17th and 18th centuries, deeper lakes were drained with the help of rows of windmills. The steam engine meant a new phase of land reclamation: it was finally possible to control the Haarlemmermeer. It is thought that, in Leeghwater's time *(see p163)*, at least 160 windmills were necessary for this. In 1891, the engineer C Lely put forward a plan to close off the treacherous Zuiderzee. This only actually happened in 1932, when the Afsluitdijk (barrier dam) was completed. Construction of the IJsselmeer polders then got underway.

***Many dyke houses** are facing a
threat to their continued existence
because of the raising of the river dy*

***An artificial island** in the North Sea
is being considered for the site of a new
airport, as Schiphol airport proves to be
both inconvenient and with limited
opportunities for expansion. Technical
and financial problems, however, are
delaying construction plans.*

The old port of Schokland *(see p324)* now
lies firmly on the mainland

This view is of the oldest polder in North Holland (anonymous, c.1600). The West Friesland Omringdijk, which runs around Het Grootslag, is 126 km (78 miles) long and was completed as far back as 1250. North Holland ceased to exist to the north of the dyke.

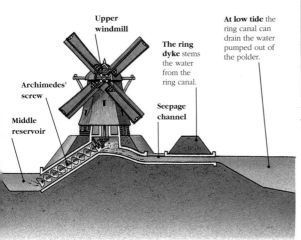

Upper windmill

The ring dyke stems the water from the ring canal.

At low tide the ring canal can drain the water pumped out of the polder.

Archimedes' screw

Middle reservoir

Seepage channel

In the 16th century, Jan Adriaansz. Leeghwater invented a system that used windmills to drain a lake after a ring canal had been constructed around it. This meant that it became relatively easy to pump dry deeper and larger lakes, giving rise to the first pieces of reclaimed land.

CONQUERING THE SEA

God created the earth – except Holland, for the Dutch did that. This statement by the French poet Voltaire comes close to the truth. This is because since the 14th century, the surface area of the Netherlands has increased by approximately 10 per cent, thanks to land reclamation. Land continues to be extended today, with the construction, for example, of IJburg, a new area of Amsterdam, which was built on an island in the IJmeer.

1860 Land could be drained only by using windmills. Limited areas were reclaimed.

1900 Thanks to the steam engine, increasingly lower-lying polders, such as the Zuidplaspolder, at -6.74 m (22 ft), could be drained.

2000 The new Amsterdam district of IJburg is built in the IJmeer using the most modern methods available.

The Randstad

IT APPEARS THAT the term Randstad (literally, "rim city") was introduced by Albert Plesman, managing director of Dutch airline KLM, which was established in 1919. Apparently he pointed out to the passengers on one of his airplanes the horseshoe-shaped band of towns formed by Utrecht, Amsterdam, Haarlem, Leiden, The Hague, Rotterdam and Dordrecht. The relatively undeveloped area in the middle was quickly named the Groene Hart ("green heart").

By 2015, 500,000 new houses are to be built in the Randstad.

GROENE HART

The Groene Hart is a man-made landscape formed from an association with water that has lasted for centuries. It is characterized by elongated pieces of reclaimed land, peat lakes and river landscape with marshes and pools. The most important agrarian activity is dairy-cattle breeding; the cheese produced here is world-famous. Environmental organizations are dedicated to developing and protecting natural resources and historical landscapes. In de Venen, which surrounds the Nieuwkoopse and Vinkeveense lakes, a project is underway to combine extensive arable farming, natural development of the environment, and recreation facilities. It is hoped that this type of project will provide a balance to urbanization.

Hiking and cycling paths *have been erected throughout the Groene Hart. They pass dairy farms, windmills and old villages. Visit the local VVV (tourist board) for more information on recreational paths.*

Congestion *is a major problem. During rush hour periods, the Randstad is clogged by traffic jams. The government is trying to reduce congestion on the roads by improving public transport and introducing other measures, such as road pricing. Up until now, this has not met with much success. The number of cars in the Randstad is constantly increasing. Transferiums, or park-and-rides, are meant to free up the town centres, which often still have old infrastructure and are not geared to a lot of traffic.*

Car-pooling *is another way of reducing the number of cars. Over 750,000 people have car-pooled in the last few years.*

IJburg is a new district, built on the IJmeer to the east of Amsterdam. Another plan for municipal expansion into the water is Nieuw Holland, a long, narrow piece of land in front of the coast between Scheveningen and Hoek van Holland.

GROWTH OF THE RANDSTAD

As far back as the end of the 15th century, the Western Netherlands was one of the most urbanized regions of Europe. It was only during the 20th century that the borders between the towns became blurred and what is now known as the Randstad emerged. At present 6.5 million people live here.

Randstad around 1900

Randstad around 1950

Randstad around 2000

In contrast, the Groene Hart has only 600,000 inhabitants. Earnings in the Randstad account for half of the gross national product. The main product is provision of services, with Amsterdam as the financial centre, The Hague as the administrative centre, Hilversum as the focus of the audio-visual media and Rotterdam-Rijnmond and Schiphol as an important port and airport respectively.

Schiphol was, in the last decade, the fastest-growing airport in Europe. It benefits from a central location – close to many of Holland's major cities – and good rail and road connections. Expansion of the airport was halted by the objections of residents and environmental groups, but after considering other locations, such as an artificial island in the North Sea, Schiphol will indeed expand into adjacent areas.

Dunes

THE DUTCH COAST IS FAMOUS for its dunes. These natural sea walls, with a vegetation of their own, were used in earlier times as common ground for cattle grazing (the *oerol, see p272*) in the absence of sufficient grassland. They now play an important role in the purification of water. The dunes are also a particularly popular recreational area – many of the protected dune areas are open to ramblers and cyclists.

A catamaran on the beach

Marram grass *is a sturdy plant whose root system holds new dunes together. It plays an important role in the formation and protection of Holland's dunes.*

Water collection *is done by way of the dunes, which retain the fresh water that falls inside them in the form of precipitation. Drinking water has been collected since the 19th century from the dunes of North and South Holland (such as at Meyendel, near Wassenaar, pictured above), helping to eliminate diseases like cholera from densely populated cities.*

The sea supplies the sand from which the dunes are built.

On the beach, the dry, white sand drifts and piles up.

A sea inlet is form when the sea brea through the row of

NATURE RESERVES

The dunes are being used less and less as areas for water collection, meaning that the groundwater level is rising again and the damp dunes can once again be established. Protected against such environmentally damaging influences as industry and land development, they are becoming important nature reserves where there is a great deal for hikers and cyclists to enjoy. Vegetation includes gorse, spindle trees, creeping willow and hawthorn. Resident and migratory birds, such as curlews, tawny pipits and sometimes ospreys, inhabit the dunes. During World War II, anti-tank trenches with steep banks were built in the Midden-Heeren dunes (in Nationaal Park Zuid-Kennemerland). Today, even the rare kingfisher feels at home there.

The Dutch coast seriously damaged by storms

Rabbits may look cute, but they have been known to seriously undermine the dunes with their intricate network of burrows.

ORIGINS

Dunes are created by a process which can be seen time and time again during a stormy day on the country's long, flat beaches. The sand carried by the sea dries on the surface of the beach and is then dragged by the wind like a white shroud over the beach. Held back by any obstacles in its way, the sand starts to accumulate. If the obstacle is a plant, a dune begins to form. Plants involved in forming dunes are called pioneer plants. They must be able to tolerate being buried by the sand and also be able to grow back through the sand. Sand couch grass (*Elymus farctus*) is renowned for being one such plant.

Sea holly and bee

After the initial dune formation, marram grass often begins to stabilize the new dune with its enormous root system. Dunes along the coast of the Netherlands can become as high as 10 m (33 ft). The dunes here – new dunes – were formed after 1200. When the sea breaks through dunes which have collapsed or have been cut through, it creates a sea inlet, or channel, around which an entire vegetation system develops, attracting all types of birds.

Common sea buckthorn

The first row of dunes, golden in colour because of the overgrowth, has higher summits.

The dune valleys have their own particular vegetation.

The sea inlet surface is home to many types of bird.

The dune overgrowth becomes richer as it moves inland, as limestone is replaced by humus.

Bulb fields are evidence that the bulbs thrive in the sandy dune soil. The blooms' vivid colours are a pretty contrast to the yellowish-grey colour of the dunes.

The beachcomber gazes out to sea near the North Holland Camperduin, at the start of the Hondsbossche sea wall. The wall was constructed in the 19th century when the sea broke through the dunes. The lessons learned from this were used when building North Holland's Noorder-kwartier (north district).

NORTH HOLLAND

ALTHOUGH NORTH HOLLAND'S *landscape is mainly flat, it is by no means featureless. Low-lying polders, with windmills and grazing cows, give way to market gardens and colourful bulb fields. Around Amsterdam the land is more built-up, with lively towns and picturesque villages almost cheek by jowl.*

North Holland has always been one of the most important areas of the Netherlands economically, due to its industry, fishing and commerce. The Zuiderzee ports played a major part in the voyages of the Dutch East India Company *(see p48)* and their merchants became wealthy from the trade in exotic imports. They built splendid houses and filled them with expensive furniture and fine art, much of which has found its way into the province's leading museums.

This part of the country has learned to live with and profit from water. The province has it on three sides, with the unpredictable North Sea to the west and the vast IJsselmeer (formerly the Zuiderzee) to the east. The flat land in between is bisected by two major canals; one connects Zaandam to Den Helder in the north, while the other, the important North Sea Canal, gives Amsterdam's busy port access to the North Sea at IJmuiden. Land reclamation, in which the Dutch excel, has been going on since the 14th century, and many historical island communities are now surrounded by dry land.

Tourism is a major industry in North Holland, with Schiphol, the country's major airport, at its heart. The North Sea coast has a string of delightful resorts and sea-front hotels among the dunes, while in the communities on the IJsselmeer such as Edam, famous for its cheese, and picturesque Volendam, you can still find villagers wearing traditional costume and the famous Dutch wooden clogs.

...akhuizen, a fine historical fishing town on the IJsselmeer

...e Afsluitdijk, a dyke which turned the Zuiderzee into the IJsselmeer

Exploring North Holland

THE LANDSCAPE OF NORTH HOLLAND is varied and the province has many old buildings and fine museums. The whole province can be easily explored on day trips from Amsterdam but areas such as West Friesland and Het Gooi, a woodland east of Amsterdam, are worth a longer visit. You can also alternate sightseeing with more relaxing activities such as walking in the beautiful nature reserve de Kennemerduinen (Kennemer dunes), sailing on the IJsselmeer or sunbathing on one of the many beaches. Round trips through towns or on rivers are also good ways of exploring the province.

The working windmills on the Zaanse Schans

GETTING AROUND
During rush hour, roads around the large towns in the southern part of the province are fairly congested. Parking is also difficult to find in most of the larger towns and as bus and train connections in the area are good, it's often better to leave the car behind. The northern part of North Holland is also easily reached by public transport or by car on the A7 and A9 motorways. The natural landscape of North Holland lends itself to countless footpaths and cycle routes, each with different characteristics. Bicycles can be hired from most of the region's train stations.

SIGHTS AT A GLANCE

Aalsmeer **22**
Alkmaar **14**
Amstelveen **23**
Cruquius **20**
De Beemster **7**
Den Helder **12**
Edam **4**
Egmond **16**
Enkhuizen **9**
's-Graveland **26**
Haarlem **15**
Heemskerk **17**
Hilversum **27**
Hoorn **10**
Jisp **5**
Laren **29**

Marken **1**
Medemblik **11**
Monnickendam **2**
Muiden **24**
Naarden **25**
Naardermeer **28**
Ouderkerk aan de Amstel **21**
Velsen/IJmuiden **18**
Volendam **3**
Zaanse Schans **6**
Zandvoort **19**
Zuiderzee Museum
pp174–5 **8**

Tour
West Friesland **13**

ALKMA

EGMOND **16**

Alkma

HEEMSKERK **17**

A22

VELSEN
IJMUIDEN   ASSENDE
18

Voor

15

ZANDVOORT **19**   HAAR

A205

N201   CRUQUIUS

20   N201

A4

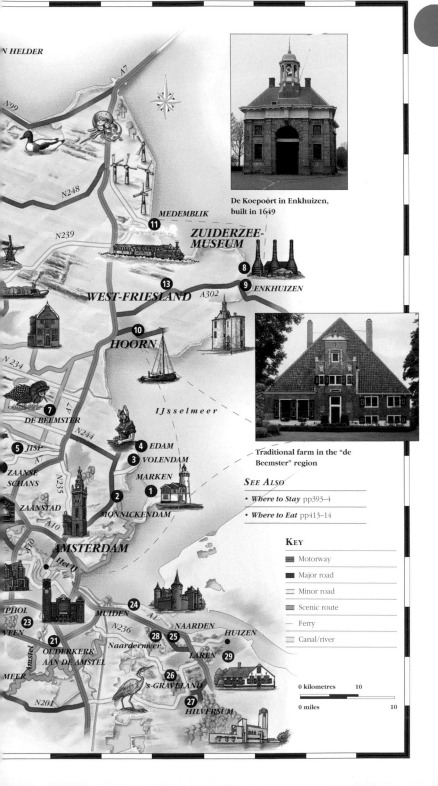

De Koepoort in Enkhuizen, built in 1649

N HELDER

N99

N248

N239

MEDEMBLIK

11

ZUIDERZEE-MUSEUM

8

9 **ENKHUIZEN**

WEST-FRIESLAND A302

13

10

HOORN

IJsselmeer

N234

7

DE BEEMSTER

N244

5 JISP

A7

ZAANSE SCHANS

4 EDAM

3 VOLENDAM

MARKEN

N235

2

1

ZAANSTAD

A10

MONNICKENDAM

A8

AMSTERDAM

Het IJ

PHOL

23

VEEN

21

OUDERKERK AAN DE AMSTEL

MEER

N201

24

MUIDEN

A1

N236

NAARDEN

28 **25**

HUIZEN

Naardermeer

LAREN

29

26

's-GRAVELAND

27

HILVERSUM

Traditional farm in the "de Beemster" region

SEE ALSO

- **Where to Stay** pp393–4
- **Where to Eat** pp413–14

KEY

Motorway

Major road

Minor road

Scenic route

Ferry

Canal/river

0 kilometres   10

0 miles   10

Marken ❶

Road map C3. 🏠 *1,900*. 🚌
📞 *0299–651998*.

For almost eight centuries, Marken was a fishing community that saw little change. The construction of a causeway link to the mainland in 1957 put an end to its isolation. The island, however, has kept its original atmosphere, retaining its wooden houses built on mounds and piles to guard against flooding. **Het Paard Lighthouse** is a famous landmark. **Marker Museum**, located in four smokehouses, gives a flavour of past and present life in Marken. There is also a cheese factory and clog-making workshop.

🏛 **Marker Museum**
Kerkbuurt 44–47. 📞 *0299–601904*.
🗓 *Apr–Oct: daily.* 🎫 ♿

Monnickendam ❷

Road map C3. 🏠 *10,000*. 🚌 🚹
Nieuwpoortslaan 15 (0299–651998).
🚢 *Sat*.

This old town on the Gouwzee, founded by monks, has many buildings dating back to the 17th and 18th centuries, including the Stadhuis, or town hall, and the Waag, or weigh house. The **Museum de Speeltoren** explains Monnickendam's

Traditional dress, today worn as costume at Volendam's fishery

local history. It is located in the Stadhuis clock tower, with its ornate 15th-century carillon. Every hour, a procession of clockwork horsemen parade around the tower's exterior.

🏛 **Museum de Speeltoren**
Noordeinde 4. 📞 *0299–652203*.
🗓 *May–Sep: 11am–5pm Tue–Sat, 1–5pm Sun.* 🎫

Volendam ❸

Road map C3. 🏠 *19,000*. 🚌 🚹
Zeestraat 37 (0299–363747). 🚢 *Sat*.

This old fishing village on the IJsselmeer is world-famous, attracting a huge number of tourists. The village is built along a dyke; at its small harbour, you can still buy all sorts of fish.

Traditional costume is one of this town's biggest attractions: the women wear tight bodices, lace caps and brightly striped skirts; the men, loose trousers and jackets. You too can dress up and have your photo taken. On the other side of the dyke is a different Volendam: an ancient maze of narrow streets, wooden houses and little canals where you can take your time and soak up the past.

Edam ❹

Road map C3. 🏠 *8,000*. 🚌 🚹
Damplein 1 (0299–315125). 🚢 *Sat*.

Edam is known worldwide for the rounds of cheeses covered with red wax it exports. (Yellow wax is used if for local consumption.) Visit the **kaasmarkt** (cheese market) in July and August to see how they are sold. Founded in the 12th century, the town has many historical buildings, including the brightly painted **Waag** (weigh house). The 17th-century stained-glass windows in the **Grote Kerk** are considered some of the finest in Holland.

The **Edams Museum** is located in a 16th-century merchant's house which has lost none of its atmosphere. Here you can see 17th-century portraits of famous Edammers, such as Trijntje Kever, who was supposedly 2.8 m (9 ft) tall.

🏛 **Edams Museum**
Damplein 8. 📞 *0299-372644*.
🗓 *Apr–Oct: Tue–Sun.* 🎫

Distinctive 17th-century wooden houses at Marken

Typical Dutch windmill on the Zaanse Schans

able to see the windmills working. The products (oil, paint, mustard) are for sale. All the houses are built from timber, as stone houses would sink at once into the soft peat earth. Also, at the time they were built, wood was readily available from local sawmills.

A visit to Zaanse Schans will also reveal **Albert Heijn's** first shop from 1887, a baking museum and a cheese factory. The **Zaans Museum** showcases the history of the region. Beside the mustard mills, you will see the pleasure boats which offer trips on the Zaan.

🏛 Zaans Museum

Schansend 7, Zaandam.
📞 075–6162862. 🕐 Tue–Sun.
🔵 1 Jan, 30 Apr, 25 Dec. 🎟 ♿

Environs: At the **Molenmuseum** (windmill museum) at Koog on the Zaan, you will learn everything you ever wanted to know about the windmills of the Zaan region. It is located in an 18th-century wooden house.

Haaldersbroek, opposite the Zaanse Schans, was once a boating village with narrow locks, brick paths and typical Zaan houses and farmhouses. Here, you'll feel as though you've gone back in time.

🏛 Molenmuseum

Museumlaan 18, Koog a/d Zaan.
📞 075–6288968. 🕐 Tue–Sun.
🔵 1 Jan, Easter Sun, Whitsun. 🎟

Jisp ❺

Road map B3. 🏘 760. 🚌
📞 075–6162221.

The old whaling village of Jisp, on one of the many former Zuiderzee islands, has a 17th-century feel. The *stadhuis* (town hall) and *dorpskerk* (village church) are worth a visit. The village lies in the middle of the **Jisperveld**, a nature reserve which is home to many different birds, such as lapwings, black-tailed godwits, redshanks, ruffs and spoonbills. This is a lovely spot to cycle, row, fish or, in

the summer, visit on an excursion. The tourist office, VVV, has information about the various excursions offered.

Zaanse Schans ❻

Schansend 1. **Road map** C3.
🏘 25. 🚌 📞 075–6162221.
Museum 🕐 Apr–Nov.
🌐 www.zaanseschans.nl

The zaanse schans is the tourist heart of the Zaan region. This neighbourhood has typical Zaan houses, windmills and buildings. When it's windy, you will be

De Beemster ❼

Road map B3. 🚌 ℹ *Middenbeemster (0299–6684019).*

The beemster was once a lake that was drained in 1612 by **Jan Adriaans Leeghwater** *(see p163)*. This unusual region has hardly changed since the 17th century, and in 1999 it was named a World Heritage Site by UNESCO. You can see historic objects and period rooms in the **Museum Betje Wolf**.

🏛 Museum Betje Wolf

Middenweg 178, Middenbeemster.
📞 0299–681968. 🕐 May–Sep:
Tue–Sun; Oct–Apr: Sun. 🎟

CZAAR-PETERHUISJE (TSAR PETER'S HOUSE)

In 1697, the Russian Peter the Great visited the shipyards of Zaandam in order to learn how the local people built ships. He lodged with Gerrit Kist, a tradesman whom he had

Peter the Great, who stayed in Zaandam twice

employed in St Petersburg. The tsar paid another visit to the town in 1717. The first mention of "Tsar Peter's house" in an official document was in 1780. This led to the tiny wooden house being supplied with a stone casing and foundations for protection. Every year, this humble house attracts a great number of tourists. (Krimp 23, Zaandam, tel. 075-6160390. Open Apr–Oct: 1–5pm Tue–Sun; Nov–Mar: 1–5pm Sat & Sun.)

Zuiderzee Museum ❽

ENKHUIZEN WAS ONE OF THE TOWNS whose economy was based on fishing and which was devastated when its access to the North Sea was blocked in 1932 by the construction of a barrier dam, the Afsluitdijk (see p162). Enkhuizen is today enjoying renewed prosperity with the opening of the Zuiderzee museum complex and the restructuring of the fishing port into a marina. Seven centuries of Zuiderzee history is depicted at the Binnenmuseum (indoor museum). The Buitenmuseum (open-air museum) is a reconstruction of an old Zuiderzee town.

★ Houses from Urk
Houses from the former island of Urk (see p324) have been rebuilt here. Actors portray life at the beginning of the 20th century.

Monnickendam smoke-houses

Entrance to Buitenmuseum

Reconstruction of Marken harbour

Children's Island

★ Schepenhal
The Schepenhal (marine hall) at the Binnen-museum (indoor museum) features an exhibition of 14 historic ships in full regalia. Children can listen to an exciting audio play while sitting in a boat.

Sailmaker's Workshop
At the beginning of the 20th century, most ships and fishing boats had sails. The traditional craft of sailmaking is kept alive in this workshop.

Ferries take visitors from the station to the Buitenmuseum (open-air museum).

Entrance to Buitenmuseum

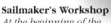

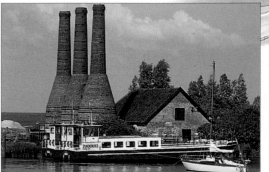

Lime Kilns
Shells dredged from the sea bed were burned in bottle-shaped lime kilns. The resulting quicklime was then used as an ingredient in mortar for brickwork. These ovens come from Akersloot in North Holland.

★ **Apothecaries' Gapers**

De Grote Gaper *apothecary, with its wonderful Art Nouveau shopfront, has a collection of "gapers"– brightly painted heads which were used as shop signs for chemists' shops in the 19th century.*

Shipbuilding and repairs

Fish Smoking

The Zuiderzee fishing industry relied mainly on herrings and anchovies, which were often salted or smoked. Here, herrings are smoked above smouldering wood chips.

A working windmill shows how polder drainage works *(see pp162–3).*

Houses from the Zuiderzee island of Urk

The houses in this area come from Zoutkamp, a fishing village on what was once the Lauwerszee.

0 metres	50
0 yards	50

The Church

The builders of this late-19th-century church, from the island of Wieringen, hid the organ in a cupboard to avoid the tax levied on church organs at that time.

STAR SIGHTS

★ **Apothecaries' Gapers**

★ **Houses from Urk**

★ **Schepenhal**

Hoorn harbour

Enkhuizen ⑨

Road map C2. 🏠 *16,500.* 🚉 🚌
ℹ️ *Tussen twee havens 1 (0228–313164).* 🛒 *Wed.*

ENKHUIZEN IS STILL one of Holland's major ports. Its many fine buildings are evidence of the wealth of the Golden Age. The most famous building is the **Drommedaris**, dating back to 1540, used to keep watch over the entrance to the old port. The city walls also date back to the 16th century. Enkhuizen has two splendid churches, the **Westerkerk** and the **Zuiderkerk**. The Flessenscheepjes (ships in bottles) Museum located in the 17th-century sluice house is also unusual. Summer boat trips to Medemblik, Stavoren, and Urk are especially pleasant.

Hoorn ⑩

Road map C3. 🏠 *63,500.* 🚉 🚌
ℹ️ *Veemarkt 4 (0900–4031055).*

HOORN'S RICH PAST, as the capital of the ancient province of West Friesland and one of the great seafaring towns of the Golden Age *(see pp50–51)*, has produced many beautiful buildings. The late gothic **Oosterkerk** has a marvellous Renaissance façade, just like the St Jans Gasthuis. Hoorn's historic past is set out in the **Westfries Museum**. In the summer, an old **steam tram** runs between Hoorn and Medemblik.

🏛 **Westfries Museum**
Rode Steen 1. ☎ *0229–280028.*
⭕ *daily.* ⚫ *1 Jan, 30 Apr, 3rd Mon in Aug, 25 Dec.*

Medemblik ⑪

Road map C2. 🏠 *7,500.* 🚌
ℹ️ *Dam 2 (0227–542852).* 🛒 *Mon.*

MANY PRETTY 17th-century houses are still to be found in Medemblik. Also worth a look at are the Reformed Church, the weigh

house and the orphanage. **Kasteel Radboud**, built in 1288 by Count Floris V, houses a museum.

Kasteel Radboud in Medemblik

Den Helder ⑫

Road map B2. 🏠 *60,000.* 🚉 🚌
ℹ️ *Bernhardplein 18 (0223–625544).*
🛒 *Jul–Aug: Tue.*

THIS TOWN, the base for the Dutch Royal Navy, has a **Marinemuseum** that displays marine history from 1488. The Marine Rescue Museum Dorus Rijkers has original rescue boats; at the North Sea Aquarium at Fort Kijkduin, a glass tunnel weaves among the fish.

🏛 **Marinemuseum**
Hoofdgracht 3. ☎ *0223-657534.*
⭕ *daily.* ⚫ *1 Jan, 25 Dec.* ♿

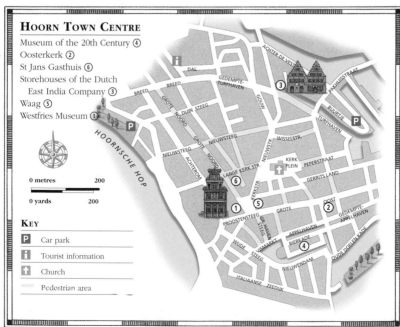

HOORN TOWN CENTRE

Museum of the 20th Century ④
Oosterkerk ②
St Jans Gasthuis ⑥
Storehouses of the Dutch
  East India Company ③
Waag ⑤
Westfries Museum ①

0 metres   200
0 yards   200

KEY

🅿️ Car park
ℹ️ Tourist information
✝️ Church
▬ Pedestrian area

Windmills

Dutch miller

SINCE THE 13TH CENTURY, windmills have been an inseparable part of the landscape of Holland. They have been used for a variety of purposes, including milling corn, extracting oil and sawing wood. One of their most important uses was to pump away excess water from the polders *(see pp162–3)*. Windmills consist of a fixed tower and a cap which carries the sails. The cap can be turned so that the sails face the wind. The sails can be very dangerous when they are turning – hence the Dutch saying, *"Een klap van de molenwiek hebben"* ("To be struck by a windmill"), that is, to have a screw loose. The Netherlands had thousands of windmills in earlier times, but since the arrival of modern machines, their number has dropped to just over 1,000. Many of these windmills are still working and are open for visits. See also *pp20–21*.

Watermill in the Schermer polder

Lattice and canvas sail

Polder mills *for draining became common during the 17th century. Standing in groups, they were each responsible for part of the pumping, through the use of an Archimedes' screw.*

Drive shaft

Archimedes' screw

Upper reservoir

Modern wind turbines *are common in Holland. They supply electricity without the pollution caused by burning oil or coal.*

The cogs *are turned by the sails. A rotating spindle makes a cog move, causing the water pump to start working.*

Rolled-up canvas

The upper section could be turned on its axis in the wind.

Main spindle

Grain was ground by two millstones.

The sails were covered with canvas to catch more wind.

Wooden sails

Flour was poured into bags through chutes.

FLOUR MILLS

Flour mills were covered with reeds and looked like enormous pepper mills. The millstones were linked to the sails by the spindle and gearwheels and milled wheat, barley and oats.

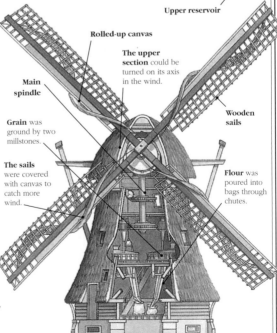

West Friesland ⑬

DURING HOLLAND'S GOLDEN AGE, West Friesland played a major part in the Dutch economy as an important centre for trade and shipping. Nowadays the main inland activity is farming. Watersports bring in the most money on the IJsselmeer coast. If you take the route in spring, you will travel alongside blooming bulb fields and orchards. There is a pleasant bustle along the IJsselmeer in the summer, and part of the route is great for cycling.

TIPS FOR DRIVERS

Length: 80 km (50 miles)
Places to stop: Cafés and restaurants in any of the villages and towns along the way.
Roads: The roads in West Friesland are good. Along the IJsselmeer you will travel over a narrow, winding dyke where you will certainly encounter many cyclists and walkers.

Twisk ⑤
This long village has pretty farmhouses, many of which can often be reached only by little bridges.

't Regthuis, Abbekerk ④
This museum has collections of West Friesland clothing, curiosities and – most important for the children – toys.

Stoommachinemuseum (Steam Engine Museum) ③
The old steam pumping station "Vier Noorder Koggen" near Medemblik has a unique collection of steam-operated machinery.

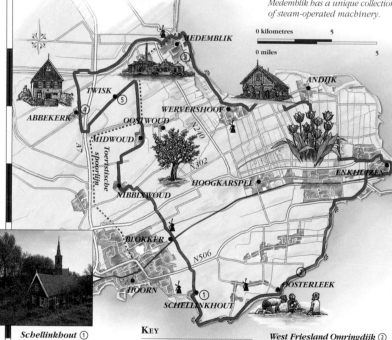

0 kilometres 5
0 miles 5

Schellinkhout ①
This attractive village just a stone's throw from Hoorn has been inhabited since prehistoric times. It once had an old sandy cove of the Zuiderzee.

KEY

━━ Suggested route
━━ Other road
— Railway line
∙∙∙ Tourist railway
❂ Good viewing point
🏠 Windmill

West Friesland Omringdijk ②
In the 13th century, a ring dyke to protect against flooding was built around West Friesland. Through land reclamation, a large proportion of the dyke now lies inland. Two wiels, or pools, by the IJsselmeer are reminders of when water broke through the dyke.

Porters carrying cheese on sledges at Alkmaar's traditional cheese market

Stedelijk Museum (municipal museum) depicts the history of the town.

🏛 Stedelijk Museum

Canadaplein 1. 📞 072-5110737.
🕐 10am–5pm Tue–Fri, 1–5pm Sat & Sun. 🖼 ♿
🌐 www.stedelijkmuseumalkmaar.nl
This museum tells the history of the town through paintings, videos and models. It also has a collection of paintings from the Bergen School.

🏛 Waaggebouw

Waagplein 2. 📞 072-5114284.
🕐 Apr–mid Oct: Mon–Sat. 🖼 ♿
The public weigh house was originally a chapel; it was converted in 1582. The **Kaasmuseum** (cheese museum) now located here shows both modern and traditional methods of dairy farming.

🔒 Grote Kerk

Koorstraat 2. 📞 072-5140707.
🕐 Jul–mid Sep: Tue–Sun.

The Renaissance façade of the weigh house

The 15th-century cruciform church contains the tomb of Count Floris V and the oldest church organ in the Netherlands.

Alkmaar ⑭

Road map B3. 🏠 92,900. 🚌 🚉
ℹ️ Waagplein 2 (072-5114284).
🛒 Tue, Wed, Sat.

Alkmaar is famous for its traditional **kaasmarkt** (cheese market), which is held every Friday morning from early April to early September. Porters sporting colourful hats carry the cheeses off on sledges to the **waaggebouw** (public weigh house) for weighing.

This old town has at least 400 monuments. The street layout has barely changed over the centuries. Along the canals, old merchants' houses and small courtyards can still be seen. The

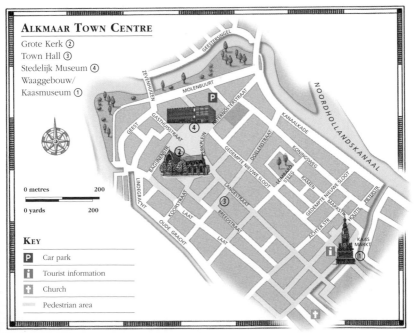

ALKMAAR TOWN CENTRE

Grote Kerk ②
Town Hall ③
Stedelijk Museum ④
Waaggebouw/
Kaasmuseum ①

```
0 metres     200
0 yards      200
```

KEY

🅿️ Car park
ℹ️ Tourist information
✝️ Church
▬ Pedestrian area

Street-by-Street: Haarlem ⑮

Misericord in the Grote Kerk

H AARLEM IS the commercial capital of North Holland province and the eighth largest city in the Netherlands. It is the centre of the Dutch printing, pharmaceutical and bulb-growing industries, but there is little sign of this in the delightful pedestrianized streets of the historic heart of the city. Most of the sights of interest are within easy walking distance of the Grote Markt, a lively square packed with ancient buildings, cafés and restaurants. Old bookshops, antique dealers and traditional food shops are all to be discovered in nearby streets.

Statue of Laurens Coster
According to local legend, Haarlem-born Laurens Jansz Coster (1370–1440) invented printing in 1423, 16 years before Gutenberg. The 19th-century statue in the Grote Markt celebrates the claim.

The Hoofd-wacht is a 17th-century former guard house.

Stadhuis
Lieven de Key's allegorical figure of Justice *(1622) stands above the main entrance. She carries a sword and the scales of justice.*

GROTE MARKT

★ **Vleeshal** *(1603)*
The old meat market is part of the Frans Hals Museum (see pp184–5).

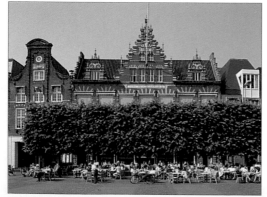

Grote Markt
The tree-lined market square is bordered with busy pavement restaurants and cafés. It has been the meeting point for the townspeople for centuries.

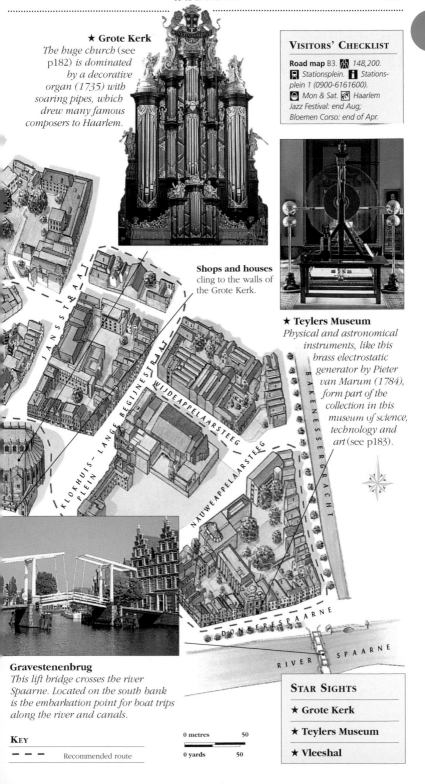

★ **Grote Kerk**
The huge church (see p182) is dominated by a decorative organ (1735) with soaring pipes, which drew many famous composers to Haarlem.

VISITORS' CHECKLIST

Road map B3. 148,200.
Stationsplein. Stationsplein 1 (0900-6161600).
Mon & Sat. Haarlem Jazz Festival: end Aug; Bloemen Corso: end of Apr.

Shops and houses cling to the walls of the Grote Kerk.

★ **Teylers Museum**
Physical and astronomical instruments, like this brass electrostatic generator by Pieter van Marum (1784), form part of the collection in this museum of science, technology and art (see p183).

Gravestenenbrug
This lift bridge crosses the river Spaarne. Located on the south bank is the embarkation point for boat trips along the river and canals.

KEY

– – – Recommended route

0 metres 50
0 yards 50

STAR SIGHTS

★ **Grote Kerk**

★ **Teylers Museum**

★ **Vleeshal**

Exploring Haarlem

H AARLEM BECAME A CITY IN 1245, and had grown into a thriving clothmaking centre by the 15th century. But in the Spanish siege of 1572–3, the city was sacked, and a series of fires wreaked further destruction in 1576. The town's fortunes changed in the 17th century, when industrial expansion ushered in a period of prosperity lasting throughout the Golden Age. The centre was largely rebuilt by Lieven de Key (1560–1627) and still retains much of its character. The Grote Kerk continues to overlook the city's *hofjes* (almshouses), and the brick-paved lanes around the Grote Markt are little changed.

Grote Markt, Haarlem (c.1668) by Berckheyde, showing the Grote Kerk

🏛 Frans Hals Museum
See pp184–5.

⛪ Grote Kerk
Oude Groenmarkt 23.
📞 023-5532040. ⭕ Mon–Sat.
🖼 ♿ 📷

The enormous Gothic edifice of Sint Bavo's great church, often referred to simply as the Grote Kerk, was a favourite subject of the 17th-century Haarlem School artists Pieter Saenredam (1597–1665) and Gerrit Berckheyde (1639–98). Built between 1400 and 1550, the church and its ornate bell tower dominate the market square. Clinging on to the exterior of the south wall is a jumble of 17th-century shops and houses. The rents raised from these ramshackle, untidy buildings contributed to the maintenance of the church.

Today, the entrance to the Grote Kerk is through one of the surviving shops, a tiny antechamber that leads straight into the enormous nave. The church has a high, delicately patterned, vaulted cedarwood ceiling, white upper walls and 28 supporting columns painted in greens, reds and golds. The intricate choir screen, like the magnificent brass lectern in the shape of a preening eagle, was made by master metal worker Jan Fyerens in about 1510. The choirstalls (1575) are painted with coats of arms, and the armrests and misericords are carved with caricatures of animals and human heads. Not far away is the simple stone slab covering the grave of Haarlem's most famous artist, Frans Hals.

The Grote Kerk boasts one of Europe's finest and most flamboyant organs, built in 1735 by Christiaan Müller *(see pp28–9).* In 1738 Handel tried the organ and pronounced it excellent. It also found favour with the infant prodigy Mozart, who shouted for joy when he gave a recital on it in 1766. The organ is still often used for concerts, recordings and teaching.

🏛 Stadhuis
Grote Markt 2. 📞 023-5113000.
⭕ by appt only or go to reception. ♿

Haarlem's Stadhuis (town hall) has grown rather haphazardly over the centuries and is an odd mixture of architectural styles dating from 1250. The oldest part of the building is the beamed medieval banqueting hall of the counts of Holland, originally known as the Gravenzaal. Much of this was destroyed in two great fires in 1347 and 1351, but the 15th-century panel portraits of the counts of Holland can still be seen.

The wing of the town hall bordering the Grote Markt was designed by Lieven de Key in 1622. It is typical of Dutch Renaissance architecture, combining elaborate gables, ornate painted detail and Classical features, such as pediments over the windows.

In a niche above the main entrance is a plump allegorical figure of Justice, bearing a sword in one hand and scales in the other as she smiles benignly upon the pavement cafés in the market below. To the left, in Koningstraat, an archway leads to the university buildings behind the Stadhuis, where there is a 13th-century cloister and library.

🏛 Verweyhal and Vleeshal
Grote Markt 16. 📞 023-5115775.
⭕ daily. ● 1 Jan, 25 Dec. 🖼

The Verweyhal (museum for modern art) and the Vleeshal (exhibition space), both in the Grote Markt, are part of the Frans Hals Museum *(see pp184–5).* The more recent Verweyhal accommodates exhibitions of Dutch Expressionism, the Cobra School *(see p187),* Impressionism and contemporary works. It is named after the painter Kees Verwey, whose Impressionist still lifes are an important feature of the collection. The heavily ornamented Vleeshal (meat market) is situated just to the west of the church and houses temporary

Detail on Vleeshal façade by Lieven de Key

The west gate of the Amsterdamse Poort (1355)

exhibitions of modern art. It was built in 1602 by the city surveyor, Lieven de Key, and has a steep step gable which disguises the roof line. The extravagantly over-decorated miniature gables above each dormer window bristle with pinnacles. A giant painted ox's head on the façade signifies an earlier function of the building.

🏛 Amsterdamse Poort
Amsterdamsevaart. ● *to public.*
The imposing medieval gateway that once helped protect Haarlem lies close to the west bank of the river Spaarne. The Amsterdamse Poort was one of a complex of 12 gates guarding strategic transport routes in and out of Haarlem. The gate was built in 1355, though much of the elaborate

brickwork and tiled gables date from the late 15th century.

The city defences were severely tested in 1573, when the Spanish, led by Frederick of Toledo, besieged Haarlem for seven months during the Dutch Revolt. The city fathers agreed to surrender the town on terms that included a general amnesty for all its citizens. The Spanish appeared to accept the terms, but once the city gates were opened, they marched in and treacherously slaughtered nearly 2,000 people – almost the entire population of the city.

🏛 Teylers Museum
Spaarne 16. 📞 *023-5319010.*
◐ *Tue–Sun.* ● *1 Jan, 25 Dec.* 🏷 ♿
🌐 *www.teylersmuseum.nl*
This was the first major public museum to be founded in the Netherlands. It was established in 1778 by the silk merchant Pieter Teyler van der Hulst to encourage the study of science and art. The museum's eccentric collection of fossils, drawings and scientific paraphernalia is displayed in Neo-Classical splendour in a series of 18th-century rooms.

Tiles in Haarlem Station

The two-storey Oval Hall was added in 1779 and contains bizarre glass cabinets full of minerals and cases of intimidating medical instruments. A significant collection of sketches by Dutch and Italian masters, including Rembrandt and Michelangelo, is shown a few at a time.

🏛 St Elisabeth's Gasthuis Historisch Museum Kennemerland
Groot Heiligland 47. 📞 *023-5422427.*
◐ *Tue–Sun.* ● *1 Jan, 25 Dec.*
Haarlem is well known for its *hofjes* (almshouses), set up to minister to the poor and sick *(see p111).* They first appeared in the 16th century and were run by rich guild members, who took over the role traditionally filled by the monasteries until the 1578 Alteration.

St Elisabeth's Gasthuis was built in 1610 around a courtyard opposite what is now the Frans Hals Museum. A 1612 plaque above the main doorway depicts an invalid being carried off to hospital. After restoration, the almshouse was opened in 1995 as Haarlem's principal historical museum.

🚉 Haarlem Station
Stationsplein.
The first railway line in the Netherlands opened in 1839 and ran between Haarlem and Amsterdam. The original station, built in 1842, was refurbished in Art Nouveau style between 1905 and 1908. It is a grandiose brick building with an arched façade and rectangular towers. The green and beige interior is decorated with brightly coloured tiles depicting various modes of transport. Other highlights are the woodwork of the ticket offices and the highly decorative wrought ironwork, particularly on the station's staircases.

17th- and 18th-century gabled houses along the river Spaarne in Haarlem

Frans Hals Museum

CELEBRATED AS THE FIRST "modern" artist, Frans Hals (1580–1666) introduced a new realism into painting. Although his contemporaries strove for perfect likenesses, Hals knew how to capture his models' characters by using an impressionistic technique. Even at the age of 80, he still painted impressive portraits, such as *De regentessen van het Oude Mannenhuis in Haarlem* (Regentesses of the Old Men's Home in Haarlem) (1664). The Oude Mannenhuis (old men's home) became the Frans Hals Museum in 1913. It also has on show paintings by other Dutch artists.

★ **Stilleven (Still Life)** *(1613)*
Floris Claeszoon van Dyck (1575–1651) was famous for his minute attention to detail and texture.

Courtyard

KEY TO FLOORPLAN

☐ Works by Frans Hals
☐ Renaissance Gallery
☐ Old Masters
☐ History of 17th-century Haarlem
☐ Temporary exhibitions
☐ Non-exhibition space

Paintings of huntsmen by Hals

★ **Officieren van de St-Jorisdoelen (Officers of the Civic Guard of St George)** *(1616)*
The features of each of the archers and the luxury of their banquet room are beautifully portrayed in this group portrait by Frans Hals.

STAR PAINTINGS

★ **Mercurius by Hendrick Goltzius**

★ **Officieren van de St-Jorisdoelen**

★ **Stilleven by Floris Claesz. van Dyck**

Moeder en Kind (Mother and Child)
After the Reformation (see pp52–3), artists such as Pieter de Grebber (1600–53) painted secular versions of religious themes. This work of a mother feeding her child (1622) is reminiscent of Mary with Jesus.

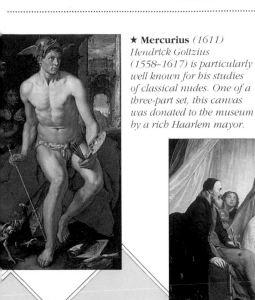

★ Mercurius *(1611)*
Hendrick Goltzius
(1558–1617) is particularly
well known for his studies
of classical nudes. One of a
three-part set, this canvas
was donated to the museum
by a rich Haarlem mayor.

VISITORS' CHECKLIST

Groot Heiligland 62, Haarlem.
📞 023-5115775. ⏰ 11am–
5pm Tue–Sat, noon–5pm Sun &
public hols. ⚫ 1 Jan, 25 Dec.
🎨 📷 ♿ 🍴 🛍 🚻 Sun.
🌐 www.franshalsmuseum.com

De Wapenvermeerdering
(1630) Pieter de Grebber.
The German Kaiser
supposedly allowed the city
of Haarlem to add a sword
to its coat of arms for heroic
action in the capture of
Damietta (Egypt).

Main
entrance

De Amsterdamse Poort, *Isaak Ouwater*
(1750–93). The only town gateway not to be
demolished dates from the 14th century. The
canal boats departed from here for Amsterdam.

**Delft
Plate** *(1662)*
The Grote
Markt and Grote
Kerk in Haarlem (see
p182) are depicted on this
earthenware plate by M Eems.

MUSEUM GUIDE
The best direction to take through the
museum is counter-clockwise, as exhibitions
of the works of Frans Hals, other portraits,
still lifes and pieces of genre paintings are
displayed in roughly chronological order.
In the Verweyhal (see p182) you will find
modern art, and in the Vleeshal (see p182)
temporary exhibitions are held.

Egmond lighthouse, a welcoming beacon for ships at sea

Egmond 🔞

Road map B3. 🏠 *11,300.* 🚌
ℹ️ *Voorstraat 82a, Egmond aan Zee (072-5061362).* 🛒 *Thu.*

Egmond is divided into three parts: Egmond aan de Hoef, Egmond-Binnen and the seaside resort of Egmond aan Zee. The counts of Egmond once lived in Egmond aan de Hoef. Only the foundations remain of the **kasteel** (castle), which is open to visitors.

The **Egmond abbey**, which is in Egmond-Binnen, is the oldest abbey in Holland and Zeeland. This 10th-century structure was destroyed, however, by Sonoy, chief of the Beggars of the Sea *(see p239)*. It was not until 1934 that a new abbey was built; Benedictine monks still live here today. The small **Abdij-museum** (abbey museum) can be visited by appointment (tel. 072-5061415).

Heemskerk 🔞

Road map B3. 🏠 *35,700.* 🚌
ℹ️ *0900-6161600.*

An obelisk in honour of Dutch artist Maarten van Heemskerck stands in the cemetery of the 17th-century **Hervormde Kerk** (Reformed church). **Slot Assumburg** (Assumburg castle), dating from the 15th century, was built on the site of a 13th-century fortified house. **Slot Marquette** is just as old but acquired its present form only two centuries ago. **Fort Veldhuis** is part of the **Stelling van Amsterdam**, a 135-km (84-mile) defensive line which encircles Amsterdam. It is now a museum dealing with the air force during World War II.

🏛 Fort Veldhuis
Genieweg 1. 🎫 *0251-230670.*
🕐 *May–Sep: Sun.* 🖼 🚻

Velsen/IJmuiden 🔞

Road map B3. 🏠 *66,000.* 🚉 🚌
ℹ️ *Plein 1945 105, IJmuiden (0255-515611).* 🛒 *Thu.*

Holland's largest fishing port is IJmuiden. This can easily be guessed from the penetrating smell of fish and the many wonderful restaurants in the port. The **Noordersluis** (north lock), which forms part of the North Sea canal lock system, is one of the biggest locks in the world. As you come across you will pass by the Hoogovens (blast-furnaces), where you can take a round trip on a steam train.

From the **pier** you can see the huge ocean liners arriving.

The area around Velsen was already inhabited in Roman times; archaeological findings are exhibited in the **Ruïne van Brederode**, a 13th-century fortress. You will also feel you are going back in time in the Romanesque **Engelmunduskerk**. **Slot Beeckestein**, now a museum with gardens, is one of the many houses built on the coast in the 17th and 18th centuries by rich Amsterdammers.

🏰 Ruïne van Brederode
Velserenderlaan 2, Santpoort. 🎫 *023-5378763.* 🕐 *Mar–Nov: Sun–Fri.* 🖼

🏛 Slot Beeckestein
Rijksweg 136. 🎫 *0255-512091.*
🕐 *Wed–Sun.* ● *1 Jan.* 🖼

Zandvoort 🔞

Road map B3. 🏠 *15,500.* 🚉 🚌
ℹ️ *Schoolplein 1 (023-5717947).* 🛒 *Wed.*

Once a fishing village, Zandvoort is now a modern seaside resort where in the summer half the population of Amsterdam relaxes on the beach or saunters down the busy main street. The centre of the village still has old fishermen's houses. Zandvoort is famous for its motor racing circuit, where Formula 1 races were once held. Recently restored, it is attempting to achieve its former status. To escape the crowds, take a ramble through the **Amsterdamse Waterleidingduinen**.

🏁 Circuit Zandvoort
Burg. van Alphenstraat t/o 63.
🎫 *023-5740750 (24hr info line).*
🕐 *daily.* 🖼 *during meets.*

Stoomgemaal De Cruquius 🔞

Cruquiusdijk 27. **Road map** B3. 🚌
🎫 *023-5285704.* 🕐 *Mar–Oct: daily.* 🖼 🚻

The stoomgemaal (steam-driven pumping station) at De Cruquius is one of the three steam-driven pumping stations used to drain the **Haarlemmermeer**. It has not been in use since 1933 and is

Slot Assumburg in Heemskerk, a youth hostel since 1933

The Cruquius steam pump

now a museum. The original steam engine is in the machine hall, which has eight pumps moved by beams. An exhibition gives a comprehensive overview of water management in the Netherlands.

Ouderkerk aan de Amstel ㉑

Road map B3. 🏘 *8,000.*
🚌 *Amstelveen (023-4415545).*

THIS PRETTY VILLAGE at the junction of the Amstel and the Bullewijk rivers has been a favourite with Amsterdammers since the Middle Ages. They had no church of their own until 1330, and worshippers had to travel to the 11th-century Ouderkerk that gave the village its name. The Old Church was destroyed in a tremendous storm in 1674, and a fine 18th-century church now stands on its site. Today Ouderkerk aan de Amstel is popular with cyclists who come to enjoy its waterfront cafés and restaurants.

Aalsmeer ㉒

Road map B3. 🏘 *22,500.* 🚌
🚋 *Drie Kolommenplein 1 (0297-325374).* 🛍 *Tue.*

AALSMEER IS FAMOUS as the centre for floriculture in the Netherlands (*see pp30–31*). It also holds the biggest **bloemenveiling** (flower auction) in the world; you can take part in the auction from a special gallery.

Many greenhouses are to be seen around Aalsmeer. One important activity here is the development of new varieties and colours of flower. Many modern heroes have a "new" flower named after them.

Electric tram

🌷 Bloemenveiling
Legmeerdijk 313. 📞 *0297-392185.*
🕐 *7:30–11am Mon–Fri.* 🎫 📷

Amstelveen ㉓

Road map B3. 🏘 *77,700.* 🚌
🚋 *Th. Cookstraat 1 (020-4415545).*
🛍 *Fri.*

AMSTELVEEN IS home to many interesting modern art museums, such as **Museum van der Togt**, with its unique collection of glass objects. The **Electrische Museumtramlijn** (electric museum tramline) (tel. 020-6737538) keeps the past alive. On Sundays from April to October you can take a return trip from Amsterdam to Amstelveen on a historic tram. The **Amsterdamse Bos** (Amsterdam forest) is lovely for rambling, picnicking or playing sport. The interesting **Bosmuseum** is dedicated to the origins of the forest.

The **Cobra Museum voor Moderne Kunst** (Cobra museum of modern art) concentrates on the work of the Cobra group, established in 1948 by Danish, Belgian and Dutch artists. During its brief existence, Cobra abandoned dreary postwar art and introduced modern art definitively to the Netherlands.

🏛 Museum Van der Togt
Dorpsstraat 50. 📞 *020-6415754.*
🕐 *Thu–Sun.* ⬤ *1 Jan, 25 Dec.* 🎫
🏛 Cobra Museum voor Moderne Kunst
Sandbergplein 1–3. 📞 *020-5475050.*
🕐 *Tue–Sun.* ⬤ *1 Jan, 25 Dec.*
🎫 ♿ 🌐 *www.cobra-museum.nl*

Women, Children, Animals (1951) by Karel Appel in the Cobra Museum

The Muiderslot, built in 1280, a site of many legends

Muiden ㉔

Road map C3. 🏘 *6,700.*
🚌 ℹ️ *035-6942836.*

IN THE MIDDLE AGES, the pretty town of Muiden was an outpost for Utrecht but later became part of the defence system of the **Stelling van Amsterdam** *(see p186)*, together with **forteiland Pampus**. The town is mainly known for its castle, the **Muiderslot**, which is more than 700 years old and was built by Floris V. After his death it was demolished and rebuilt. The most famous inhabitant was the 17th-century poet PC Hooft, who formed the *Muiderkring* (Muiden circle), a circle of friends occupied with literature and music. Most of the castle rooms are furnished in 17th- and 18th-century style. The garden and orchard also retain their former glory. Boats once left from the castle jetty for the fortified island of Pampus.

Knight in armour

♟ Muiderslot
Herengracht 1. ☎ *0294-261325.*
🕐 *Apr–Oct: daily; Nov–Mar: Sat & Sun.* 🎫 🔲 www.muiderslot.nl

Naarden ㉕

Road map C3. 🏘 *16,900.* 🚌 🚉
ℹ️ *Adriaan Dortsmanplein 1b (035-6942836).* 🏳 *Sat.*

THE FORTIFIED town of Naarden lies behind a double ring of canals and walls. The original town is thought to have been founded in the 10th century, then later destroyed and rebuilt around 1350. In the 15th and 16th centuries, it was occupied in turn by the Spanish and the French. The first thing you notice on arrival is the tower of the 14th-century **Grote Kerk**. The church dome has been beautifully decorated with pictures from the Old and New Testament. Around 400 years ago, Czech freedom fighter Komensky Comenius fled to the Netherlands, and now lies buried in the 15th-century **Waalse kapel** (Walloon chapel). The Spaanse Huis (Spanish house), which was converted into the Waag (weigh house), is now home to the **Comenius-museum**, which explores the lives and ideas of Holland's greatest scholars. The **Nederlands Vestingmuseum** (fortress museum) is in one of the six bastions of the fortress and has an exhibition of the Hollandse Waterlinie, a strip of land flooded as a defence line in Holland, and of Naarden's eventful past. Costumed gunners regularly demonstrate the ancient artillery. There is a nice walk around the town along the footpaths on the walls.

🏛 Comenius museum
Kloosterstraat 33. ☎ *035-6943045.*
🕐 *Wed–Sun.* ● *1 Jan, 25 Dec, 31 Dec.* 🎫 🔲

🏛 Nederlands Vestingmuseum
Westwalstraat 6. ☎ *035-6945459.*
🕐 *Mar–Oct: Tue–Sun; mid Jun–Aug: also Mon; Nov–Feb: Sun & Christmas hols.* ● *1 Jan, 25 Dec, 31 Dec.*
🎫 ♿ 🔲

's-Graveland ㉖

Road map C3. 🏘 *9,200.* 🚌
(035-6241751).

'S-GRAVELAND IS a special place in Het Gooi *(see p170)*. In the 17th century, nine country estates were built here for rich Amsterdammers. Just across from these lie the modest houses that belonged to the labourers. Businesses now use the country houses, as the upkeep is too expensive for individuals. Five parks are owned by the Vereniging Natuurmonumenten and are open to visitors. You can learn more at the **Bezoekers-centrum** (visitors' centre).

🚏 Bezoekerscentrum 's-Graveland
Noordereinde 54b. ☎ *035-6563080.* 🕐 *Tue–Sun.*

Aerial view of the fortress of Naarden's star formation

Hilversum town hall, finished in yellow brick

Hilversum ❷

Road map C3. 🏛 *83,000.* 🚌 🚉
🛈 *Noordse Bosje 1 (035-6241751).*
🛒 *Wed, Sat.*

T HIS DYNAMIC CENTRE in Het
Gooi *(see p170)* is known
as the media centre of the
Netherlands, because of the
large number of broadcasting
companies established here.

Hilversum boasts a busy
shopping centre and attractive
residential areas with a lot of
greenery. Here and there you
will see houses and buildings
designed by architect Willem
Dudok (1884–1974), a representative of the Nieuwe
Bouwen. One of his most
famous creations is the 1931
Raadhuis (town hall), with
its towers and beautiful
interior (tours are given on
Sundays). Its basement holds
an exhibition on Dudok
and temporary architectural
exhibitions. The **Museum
Hilversum**, a new museum
that combines the Goois
Museum and the Dudok
Centrum, illuminates the past
of Het Gooi and features an
archaeological collection. The
Neo-Gothic **Sint-Vituskerk**,
designed by PJH Cuypers
(*see p90*), with its 98-m
(322-ft) tower, dates from
1892 and is worth a visit.

🏛 **Museum Hilversum**
Kerkbrink 6.
📞 *035-6292826.*
🕐 *call ahead for opening hours.*

Naardermeer ❷

Road map C3. 🛈 *Natuurmonumenten (035-6559933).* 🅿 ♿

T HE NAARDERMEER is an area
of lakes and marshland
with lush vegetation and is
renowned for its breeding
colonies for cormorants and
purple herons. Several other
birds, such as the marsh
harrier, the bittern, the reed
warbler and the spoonbill,
can also be observed here.
Unusual orchids, rare mosses
and fungi grow here. It is
Natuurmonument (nature
reserve association) property
and accessible only via a boat
excursion organized by the
association (spring and summer, also for non-members;
tel 035-6951315). The excursion includes a visit to a
Vogelobservatiehut (bird-
watching cabin). Natuur-
monumenten members
can also follow a pleasant
rambling route here.

Laren ❷

Road map C3. 🏛 *11,700.*
🚌 📞 *035-6241751.* 🛒 *Fri.*

A LONGSIDE PRETTY VILLAS and
country houses, Laren
has many converted old farmhouses, a reminder of the
time when it was a farming
village. During the 19th and
at the beginning of the 20th
century, Laren and its surroundings was the inspiration
for many landscape and interior painters, such as Mauve,
Israëls and the American W
Singer. The **Singer Museum**
has been set up in his old
house. Here you can see
his work and that of other
19th- and 20th-century artists.
There is also a sculpture garden. **Sint-Jansbasiliek** (1925)
towers above the Brink and
its charming restaurants.

🏛 **Singer Museum**
Oude Drift 1. 📞 *035-5315656.* 🕐
Tue–Sun. ● *1 Jan, 25 Dec.* 🎨 ♿

THE ERFGOOIERS

During the Middle Ages, the farmers of Het Gooi *(see p170)*
joined together in a group to regulate the use of the heathland and meadows. Since 1404, their rights were held in
plough share notes. Members of the group were known
as *erfgooiers*, men living in Het Gooi who were descen-
dants of these medieval farmers. The right of use was later
converted into common property. The *erfgooiers* had
to constantly fight for their rights. From the 19th century
onwards, the government strived to disband the group. In
1932, the heathland was sold, as were the meadows after
1965. The Association of *Erfgooiers* was disbanded in 1971.

De Erfgooiers (1907) by F Hart Nibbrig

UTRECHT

THE PROVINCE OF UTRECHT, *with the lively university city of the same name at its heart, has a vast range of attractions for visitors, including farmhouses, mansions, museums and castles, all set in a varied and attractive wooded landscape, and with a fascinating history dating back to Roman times.*

The city of Utrecht has its origins in AD 47, when the Romans built a camp by a ford *(trecht)* at the river Rhine, which followed a different course in those days. In 695, Bishop Willibrord established himself here to promote the spread of Christianity. From the 11th century, the church authorities enjoyed not only spiritual but also secular power in this region, which has seen much conflict: over the centuries the counts of Holland, the dukes of Burgundy, the Spaniards, the French and the Germans have all tried to make their mark here.

The region's proximity to Amsterdam has meant that it has been able to share in the capital's prosperity as wealthy merchants and landowners built their mansions and estates along the river Vecht *(see p196)*. In more recent times, the University of Utrecht has been a great source of economic and artistic development, and the city is home to a modern manufacturing industry and major Dutch corporations.

Visitors will enjoy the pretty countryside – ideal for car or cycle touring – the country houses and historic buildings, the street markets and a great variety of attractions ranging from eclectic furniture and old steam locomotives to barrel-organs and Australian Aboriginal art. But in this eco-conscious country, with its awareness of the need for conservation, it may be the outdoors, with its sparkling lakes and possibilities for leisurely country walks, that will appeal the most.

De Haar castle in Haarzuilens, a Neo-Gothic construction (1892) built by Pierre Cuypers

◁ IJsselstein flour mill, still worked in the traditional manner

Exploring Utrecht

THE CITY OF UTRECHT is the central point of
the province and is therefore the ideal base
for sightseeing in the surrounding area. The
Vinkeveense Plassen (Vinkeveense Lakes) are
popular for watersports, and nature lovers will
appreciate the woodland area of the Utrecht
Heuvelrug. There are castles in Amerongen
and Wijk bij Duurstede and numerous imposing
country houses along the Vecht. Windmills and
working farms can be spotted here and there in
the countryside. Many defence points, such as in
Woerden, serve as reminders of the turbulent
past of this province, which has been at stake
during fierce battles more than once.

**The Vinkeveense Plassen, formed by
excavations**

Sights at a Glance

Amerongen **16**	Oudewater **5**
Amersfoort **13**	Rhenen **17**
Baarn/Soest **8**	Slot Zuylen **3**
Bunschoten-Spakenburg **11**	Soestdijk **9**
Country Estates on	*Utrecht pp198–203* **12**
the Vecht **7**	Vinkeveense Plassen **1**
Doorn **14**	Wijk bij Duurstede **15**
Lage Vuursche **10**	Woerden **4**
Loenen **2**	
Nieuwe Hollandse Waterlinie **6**	

**The *heksenwaag* (witches'
scales) in Oudewater**

Getting There

Larger towns have railway stations; smaller ones
can be reached easily by bus. Utrecht, the capital
of the province, is the biggest railway junction in
the Netherlands and so train connections from this
town are excellent. There is also a regional bus station. Utrecht has a highly developed road network
and is served by important main roads such as the
A2 (north-south) and the A12 (east-west), but there
is also a large number of minor roads, tourist routes
and cycle paths in the area.

Key

▬	Motorway
▬	Main road
═	Minor road
▬	Scenic route
═	Canal/river

Paleis Soestdijk, its park designed by landscape gardener Zocher

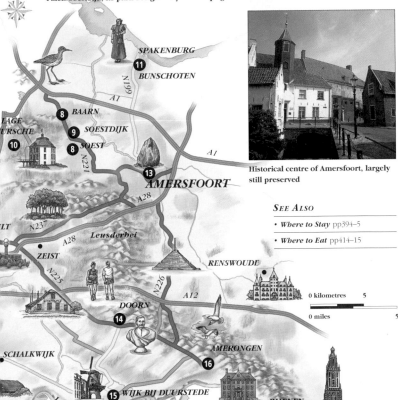

SPAKENBURG

11 BUNSCHOTEN

N199

A1

8 BAARN

9 SOESTDIJK

LAGE

URSCHE

10

8 SOEST

N221

A1

13

AMERSFOORT

A28

N237

A28 Leusderhei

ILT

ZEIST

N225

RENSWOUDE

N26

DOORN

14

A12

AMERONGEN

SCHALKWIJK

16

15 WIJK BIJ DUURSTEDE

RHENEN

17

Lek

Historical centre of Amersfoort, largely
still preserved

SEE ALSO

• **Where to Stay** pp394–5

• **Where to Eat** pp414–15

0 kilometres 5

0 miles 5

The Windmill at Wijk by Jacob
van Ruisdael *(see p124)*

View of Rhenen, with its characteristic Cuneratoren

Vinkeveense Plassen ❶

Road map C3. 🚗 ⛵ **ℹ** *Herenweg 144, Vinkeveen (0297-214231).*

D E VINKEVEENSE Plassen (Vinkeveense Lakes) came about through human intervention – this site was once marsh. The thick peat layers have been excavated over the centuries. The large towns in the surrounding area needed peat; sales of this fuel meant that the people here started to earn a decent living. The peat was therefore dug up more and more extensively, eventually leading to a large area of lakes.

Today, the Vinkeveense Lakes attract many watersports lovers, as well as cyclists and walkers. When it's not the breeding season, you can take a rowing boat through the nature reserve of **Botshol**, which is home to marsh and grassland birds.

Loenen ❷

Road map C3. 🏰 *8,350.* 🚗 **ℹ** *VVV Loosdrecht, Oud-Loosdrecht-sedijk 198 (035-5823958).* 🛒 *Tue.*

I N THE 10TH CENTURY, this place was called Lona, meaning "water" or "mud". Loenen fell under two different jurisdictions and has, therefore, two courts dating from the beginning of the 18th century. Loenen on the Vecht is famous for its rural atmosphere as well as for its castles and country estates complete with coach houses, summerhouses and boathouses, built over the centuries by wealthy citizens. It is now a protected village.

Kasteel Loenersloot, built on the bank of the Angstel, is one of the oldest country estates. The building dates back to the 13th century, though only the round defence tower remains; the rest dates from the 17th and 18th centuries. The castle is not open to the public.

Stately Slot Zuylen, where Belle van Zuylen lived in the 18th century

Slot Zuylen ❸

Road map C3. 🚗 **ℹ** *VVV Utrecht, Vredenburg 90 (0900-4141414).* **Castle** *Tournooiveld 1, Oud-Zuilen.* **☎** *030-2440255.* ⏰ *15 Mar–15 May & 15 Sep–15 Nov: Sat & Sun; groups by appointment.* 🖌

T HE ORIGINAL U-shaped castle was built around 1520 on the remains of a medieval residential tower. At the beginning of the 16th century, a new castle was built on the foundations of the old house and the gateway was added. Up to the 18th century, extensive rebuilding brought the castle into line with contemporary architectural style.

The author Belle van Zuylen (1740–1805) was one of the castle's most famous inhabitants. She was famous for her correspondence at home and abroad, which she cleverly used to show her modern attitude. Several rooms are furnished as they were when she resided here.

The serpentine wall that runs alongside the castle is interesting because its unique shape provides so much protection that even in this cool sea climate, subtropical fruits such as peaches and grapes can flourish here.

Loenen on the Vecht still has an aristocratic appearance

Woerden ❹

Road map C4. 🏃 47,500. 🚉 🚌
ℹ️ Molenstraat 40 (0348-414474).
🗓️ Wed.

W OERDEN CAME INTO being on the dykes along the Rhine and Lange Linschoten. Granted its town charter in 1372, it has been besieged many times but always managed to hold out. Between 1575 and 1576, during the 30 Years War, the Spaniards tried to conquer Woerden, as did the French in 1672, but neither invader succeeded in capturing the town. Impenetrable **kasteel van Woerden** (Woerden castle), built between 1405 and 1415, was extensively restored around 1990.

In the 18th century, the **Oude Hollandse Waterlinie** (old Holland waterline) – a strip of land flooded as a defence line – was extended, thereby strengthening Woerden.

Oudewater ❺

Road map C4. 🏃 10,000. 🚌
ℹ️ Kapellestraat 2 (0348-564636).
🗓️ Wed.

T HIS LITTLE TOWN, thanks to its favourable position on the IJssel and the Linschoten, became a prosperous town early on and, by 1265, had been granted its city charter.

Nesting storks in Oudewater

The counts of Holland and the bishops of Utrecht fought fiercely for Oudewater, which was converted into a border stronghold by Floris V. In 1349, Oudewater was captured by Jan van Arkel, the Bishop of Utrecht. In 1572, Oudewater sided with the Prince of Orange and, as a result, the town was seized in 1575 by the Spanish. They exacted a bloody revenge by burning the town to the ground. Oudewater flourished again during Holland's Golden Age.

The town's most famous attraction is the scales, dating from the 16th century, better known as the *heksenwaag* (witches' scales). Women who were suspected of witchcraft came here to be weighed. If their weight and their outward appearance tallied, they were given a certificate as proof of their innocence. Oudewater was the only place where "witches" could be legally weighed in public.

🏛️ **Heksenwaag**
Leeuweringerstraat 2. 📞 0348-563400. 🕙 10am–5pm Tue–Sat, noon–5pm Sun. ⬤ 1 Oct–31 Mar.
🈺 ♿

Nieuwe Hollandse Waterlinie ❻

Road map C3–C4.

T HE NIEUWE Hollandse Waterlinie (New Dutch Inundation Line), laid out from 1815 to 1940, is comprised of 68 forts and public works, from Muiden and Naarden in North Holland to Werkendam in North Brabant. Utrecht has 27 installations, more than any other province. The Waterlinie was intended as a defence against invading armies; a wide strip of land would simply be flooded. Utrecht's installations are now being protected, and have been put forward for UNESCO's World Heritage Site register. The original reconnaissance positions and unimpeded lines of fire will hopefully be preserved. The best installations are at Rijnauwen, Groenekan en Tull en 't Waal.

"Bombproof" barracks of the Nieuwe Hollandse Waterlinie (Fort Rijnauwen, Bunnik)

Country Estates along the Vecht ❼

Plaque with coat of arms

COUNTRY ESTATE HOUSES, with their summerhouses, magnificent railings and extensive gardens, can be seen threaded along the Vecht, especially between Maarssen and Loenen. They were built in the 17th and 18th centuries by wealthy Amsterdam inhabitants who wanted to escape the noise and stench of the city in the summer. The estates were status symbols, places where city-dwellers could devote themselves to hobbies such as tree cultivation, hunting and still-life painting.

VISITORS' CHECKLIST

Road map C4. **Museum Maarssen** Diependaalsedijk 19, Maarssen. 📞 0346-554440. ⏰ 1–4pm Wed, Sat, Sun. 📷 📷 ♿ in places.

GOUDESTEIN IN MAARSSEN

One of the first country estates in the Vecht region, Goudestein was built in 1628 by Joan Huijdecoper. The present building, which dates from 1775, is now used for local government offices. The former coach house is now a museum.

The chimneys were considered to be decorative elements.

Nijenrode
A university has now been set up in this castle formerly belonging to the Lords of Nijenrode.

The coat of arms of the Huijdecoper family decorates the façade.

The entrance has an impressive flight of stone steps.

The house contains grand staircase and rooms furnished with decorative drapes. One of the rooms is used for wedding ceremonies.

Between Breukelen and Loenen *the Vecht resembles an architectural museum. The country estates (Vechtvliet is shown here) are surrounded by established parks and ornamental outbuildings.*

Baarn/Soest ❽

Roadmap C4. 🚗 🚌 👥 69,000.
🛈 *Stationsplein 7, Baarn (035-5413226).* 🛒 *Baarn Tue, Soest Thu.*

Dᴜʀɪɴɢ ʜᴏʟʟᴀɴᴅ's Golden Age, regents and wealthy merchants had splendid summer residences built in Baarn and its environs. This place has retained its leafy, elegant appearance. The **Kasteel Groeneveld** (1710) lies in the middle of a magnificent park. Soest's past is pre-9th century, and the old centre remains largely in its original state. The church dates from 1400. The surrounding area is beautiful and offers a wealth of leisure activities.

🏛 **Kasteel Groeneveld**
Groeneveld 2. 📞 *035-5420446.*
🕐 *10am–5pm Tue–Fri, noon–5pm Sat & Sun.* ⬤ *Mon.* ♿

Soestdijk ❾

Roadmap C3. 🛈 *Stationsplein 7, Baarn (035-5413226).*

Jᴜꜱᴛ ᴏᴜᴛꜱɪᴅᴇ ʙᴀᴀʀɴ lies **Paleis Soestdijk**. It was built in 1674 as a place for Viceroy William III to hunt. In 1815, it came into the hands of the crown prince, who later became King William II. The two wings of the palace were added in 1816 and the park was designed by landscape gardener Zocher. The **Naald van Waterloo** (Waterloo needle) stands opposite, erected in honour of William Frederick, Prince of Orange, for his services during the Battle of Waterloo.

Lage Vuursche ❿

Roadmap C3. 👥 250. 🚌
🛈 *Stationsplein 7, Baarn (035-5413226).*

Tʜᴇ ɴᴀᴍᴇ "ꜰᴜʀꜱ" for Lage Vuursche has been around since 1200, though the village itself has existed only since the 17th century. The village, surrounded by woodland, is very popular with ramblers.

Before her accession to the throne in 1980, the former

Bunschoten-Spakenburg, once home to an important fishing industry

Crown Princess Beatrice lived in the small octagonal castle **Drakenstein**, which dates back to 1640–43.

Bunschoten-Spakenburg ⓫

Roadmap C3. 👥 19,000. 🚌
🛈 *Oude Schans 90 (033-2581310).*
🛒 *Sat.*

Oᴠᴇʀ ᴛʜᴇ ʏᴇᴀʀꜱ, the towns of Bunschoten and Spakenburg have merged into one another. Livestock farming was the traditional livelihood in Bunschoten, and there are still some pretty farms to see here. Bunschoten is older than Spakenburg, having

been granted its town charter as early as 1383.

Spakenburg came into being in the 15th century. It was once an important fishing town; its smoke-houses, fishermen's houses and historic shipbuilding yard are now reminders of this time. When the Zuiderzee was closed in 1932 because of partial land reclamation, the inhabitants had to look for other work.

Some of the women in the town still wear traditional dress. **Museum 't Vurhuus** brings the fishing activities of the past back to life.

🏛 **Museum 't Vurhuus**
Oude Schans 47–56. 📞 *033-2983319.* 🕐 *10am–5pm Mon–Sat.*
⬤ *Nov–Apr.* 📷 ♿

Outdoor cafés in Lage Vuursche offering respite after a walk in the woods

Street-by-Street: Utrecht ⑫

Museum van Speelklok tot Pierement

THE AREA TO THE SOUTH of the centre gives one a good idea of how people once lived in Utrecht. Rich citizens lived in the stately houses on the Nieuwegracht, with its typical Utrecht wharves, and built almshouses for their less fortunate neighbours. No doubt because of the great number of museums in this area, it came to be called Museumkwartier (museum district). The old city walls gave way to a magnificent park which was designed by landscape gardener Zocher.

★ Oudegracht
The Oudegracht represented a vital transport route for the economy of Utrecht in the 13th century. When the water level fell, cellars were built along the wharves. These were used as warehouses or workshops. Today, some of them house cafés and restaurants.

0 metres		100
0 yards		100

STAR SIGHTS

- **★ Catharijneconvent**
- **★ Centraal Museum**
- **★ Oudegracht**

★ Centraal Museum
The rich and varied contents include works by the 16th-century artist Jan van Scorel, as well as the largest collection of Rietveld furniture in the world.

Almshouses
The Pallaeskameren (Pallaes rooms) are 12 little almshouses built on the instructions of Mari van Pallaes in 1651. Th inhabitants had free accommodation and a certain amount of food and drink annually.

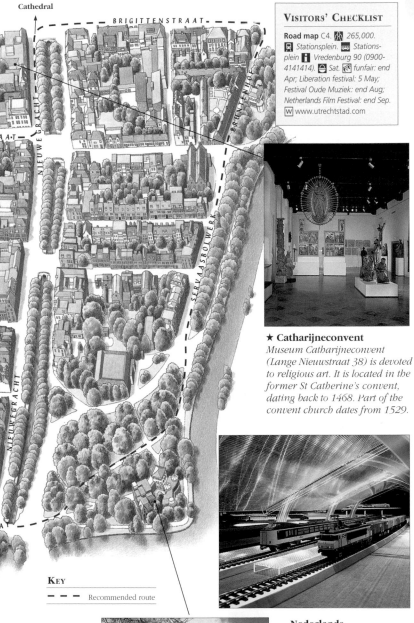

Cathedral

BRIGITTENSTRAAT

NIEUWEGRACHT

BRUNTENH

A·A·T

SERVAASBOLWERK

NIEUWEGRACHT

A·T

VISITORS' CHECKLIST

Road map C4. 🏘 265,000.
🚊 Stationsplein. 🚌 Stations-
plein 🛈 Vredenburg 90 (0900-
4141414). 🛒 Sat. 🎡 funfair: end
Apr; Liberation festival: 5 May;
Festival Oude Muziek: end Aug;
Netherlands Film Festival: end Sep.
🌐 www.utrechtstad.com

★ Catharijneconvent
*Museum Catharijneconvent
(Lange Nieuwstraat 38) is devoted
to religious art. It is located in the
former St Catherine's convent,
dating back to 1468. Part of the
convent church dates from 1529.*

Nederlands Spoorwegmuseum (Dutch railway museum)
*Old carriages and steam
locomotives can be seen in
the former Maliebaan
Station, dating back to the
19th century. The exhibi-
tion room features the history of the Dutch railways.*

KEY

- - - Recommended route

Sonnenborgh
*The 19th-century
observatory, now
home to the Royal
Dutch Meteorological
Institute, was estab-
lished on one of the
four bulwarks along
the Singel.*

Exploring Utrecht

A euro coin from the Mint

U TRECHT, FOUNDED BY THE ROMANS in AD 47, has been a bishopric and university town for centuries. It has grown into a lively city, thanks to its central position. Utrecht was very prosperous during the 16th and 17th centuries, when many of the magnificent canalside houses were built. These houses are a characteristic feature of the town centre, as are the medieval churches and monasteries. The city centre is compact so is very suitable for exploring on foot.

The 112-m (367-ft) Domtoren

♛ Domtoren

Domplein. 🚌 🛈 030-2333036.
◯ 10am–4pm Mon–Sat, noon–4pm
Sun. ● 1 Jan, 25 Dec. 🎨 📷
🎥 obligatory.
The first thing you will see from the distance is the Domtoren (cathedral tower) rising above the town. The Dom (cathedral) has become the symbol of the town, which could almost be called Domstad (cathedral town). Utrecht came into being on the Domplein (cathedral square), where the Romans had a settlement in the 1st century AD. In 695, Bishop Willibrord established himself here. In 1040, Bishop Bernold ordered a "cross of churches" to be built, which meant four churches with the later Domkerk as the central point. Work began on building the Domkerk in 1254 and in 1321 on the imposing tower. Due to a severe lack of funds, the Gothic tower was not finished until 1382.

Collegiate churches usually have two towers, but the Domkerk has only one. The nave of the church was connected to the tower by an arch, allowing the bishop to move safely to and from the church. The tower was left open underneath, as the Salvator chapter had the right of free access. In 1674, the nave was destroyed by a hurricane. The tower has stood on its own since then. The interior of the church, with its impressive stained-glass windows, Neo-Gothic organ (1831) and magnificent chancel, is worth a visit.

♛ Aboriginal Art Museum

Oudegracht 176. 🚌 🛈 030-2380100.
◯ 11am–5pm Tue–Sun. ● 1 Jan,
30 Apr, 25 Dec. 🎨 🚻 📷 🛈
This museum, the only one of its kind in Europe, is devoted to the many different styles of Aboriginal art. There are around 500 paintings and sculptures on display here. The emphasis is on traditional art being produced in the Australian co-operatives.

♛ Museum Catharijneconvent

Lange Nieuwstraat 38. 🚌 🛈 030-2317296. ◯ 10am–5pm Sat, 11am–5pm
Sun & hols. ● 1 Jan, 30 Apr. 🎨 🚻 📷
The Museum Catharijneconvent is split between a canalside house and a 15th-century former convent. The collection of this fascinating museum provides a good overview of the troubled history of Christianity in the Netherlands. It includes paintings by, among others, Rembrandt van Rijn, ancient manuscripts and richly decorated books, vestments, altarpieces and much more. The museum also houses numerous visiting exhibitions. From the museum you can enter into the Catharijnekerk (1551).

♛ Centraal Museum

Nicolaaskerkhof 10. 🚌 🛈 030-2362362. ◯ 11am–5pm Tue–Sun.
● 1 Jan, 30 Apr, 25 Dec. 🎨 🚻
🎥 📺 Ⓦ www.centraalmuseum.nl
Centraal Museum, the oldest municipal museum in the Netherlands, has a large and extremely varied collection, the oldest pieces of which date from the Middle Ages. Extensive rebuilding and renovations were carried out in 1999, giving rise to an interesting combination of old and new. The museum has the largest collection of Gerrit Rietveld furniture in the world.

Painting by Surrealist JH Moesman in the Centraal Museum

Crowded terraces along the Oudegracht on a fine day

Works by Utrecht artists such as Van Scorel and Bloemaert, as well as 20th-century artists such as Pyke Koch and Dick Bruna *(Nijntje/Miffy)* are also showcased. The varied exhibitions range from traditional art to fashion and historical costumes, to modern art and applied art and design, to the local history of Utrecht.

🏛 Nederlands Spoorwegmuseum

Maliebaanstation. 🚃 📞 030-2306206. ⬜ 10am–5pm Tue–Fri, 11:30am–5pm Sat, Sun & public hols. ● 1 Jan, Easter Day, Whitsun, 25 Dec. 📷♿📷💻

The superb Dutch railway museum is very appropriately situated in a former railway station dating from 1874 which was used as such until 1939. Magnificent old locomotives, carriages and trains line the platforms. In some cases you can even see with your own eyes how people travelled 100 years ago. Children can ride over the museum grounds on a miniature railway and will find lots of interesting things in the attractive museum shop. Adults and children alike

will enjoy the exhibition inside, which covers a variety of subjects, from old advertising posters and model trains to engines and a stagecoach.

🏛 Nationaal Museum van Speelklok tot Pierement

Buurkerkhof 10. 🚃 📞 030-2312789. ⬜ 10am–5pm Tue–Sat, noon–5pm Sun & hols. ● 1 Jan, 30 Apr, 25 Dec. 📷♿📷💻

This museum is inside the 13th-century Buurkerk – Utrecht's oldest church in an enclosed square in the heart of the city centre. The museum's collection displays the history of mechanical musical instruments. The showpiece is a rare 15th-century musical clock. You will also see – and hear – *pierementen,* the large organs pushed through the town by the organ-grinder, music boxes, fairground organs and dance organs, and chiming clocks, as well as countless smaller instruments with built-in chiming mechanisms. Many of the instruments are demonstrated on the guided tour. The paintings on walls and pillars serve as a reminder that the museum is housed in a church building.

🏛 Universiteitsmuseum

Lange Nieuwstraat 106. 🚃 📞 030-2538008. ⬜ 11am–5pm Tue-Sun. ● 1 Jan, 30 Apr, 25 Dec. 📷♿📷

The Universiteitsmuseum is in a new, purpose-built building close to the Centraal Museum. The collection here covers education since the university was established in 1636 and includes weighing and measuring instruments, anatomical material and a "collection of curiosities". Behind the museum is the University of Utrecht's Old Botanical Garden (1723), which is open to the public. Numerous interesting plants and trees grow in this lovely enclosed garden. There is also an ancient medicinal herb garden here.

🖼 Markets

Whoever likes browsing in markets will not have far to look in Utrecht. The Vredenburg holds a large general market twice a week, on Wednesdays and Saturdays. On Fridays it holds a market for agricultural produce (selling only ecologically genuine products). On Saturdays, the Janskerkhof hosts a large flower and plant market – the flower-filled stalls are a sight for sore eyes. On the same day, you will find magnificent bouquets of flowers for sale along the Oudegracht, the old canal. The Breedstraat market, also held on Saturdays, is the venue of the Stoffenmarkt, or cloth market, also known as the Lapjesmarkt.

The Domkerk quadrangle

Rietveld Schröder-Huis

Gerrit Rietveld and his employees

WHEN DESIGNING THIS HOUSE, architect Gerrit Rietveld worked closely with his client, Mrs Schröder, who lived here from 1924 until her death in 1985. The house was to epitomize all that was "modern" and broke with many of the architectural standards of the time. This can be seen in the design of the top floor, which may be divided in different ways by sliding partitions, according to the requirements of the inhabitants. The house was declared a World Heritage Site by UNESCO in 2001.

★ **Sliding Partitions**
Using sliding partitions, the top floor could be divided into separate rooms for Mrs Schröder's children.

Telephone Seat
The house was to reflect the modern times in which it was designed, and so functional items like the telephone and fuse box were given a prominent location.

STAR SIGHTS

★ **Disappearing Corner**

★ **Rietveld Furniture**

★ **Sliding Partitions**

DE STIJL

This Dutch artistic movement, founded in 1917, aimed to integrate art further into everyday life. Proponents wanted to bring painting and architecture closer together in a new way. The use of colour in the Rietveld Schröder-huis is one expression of this idea. Rietveld was a member of De Stijl from 1919, though he disagreed with certain ideas held by others in the group *(see p128)*.

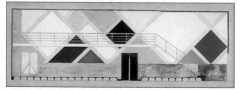

De Stijl member Theo van Doesburg was mainly interested in straight lines and primary colours. The geometric surfaces of this painting do not depict reality but offer a glimpse of universality.

BOODSCHAPPEN
EERST BELLEN BIJ GEEN GEHOOR SPREEKBUIS

Intercom
The Schröder's intercom sign instructed visitors to "First ring. If no answer use mouthpiece"

The Hanging Lamp
Rietveld designed this unusual lamp in around 1922.

Gerrit Rietveld
The architect always used scale models when designing houses but could also draw excellent floor plans, contrary to what was often said.

VISITORS' CHECKLIST

Road map C4. Prins Hendrik-laan 50, Utrecht. **C** 030-2362310. 11am–3:30pm Wed–Sun, call for appt. 1 Jan, 30 Apr, 25 Dec.

The skylight in the roof above the stairs allows additional light to reach the top floor.

★ Rietveld Furniture
In 1918, Rietveld made his first red-blue chair. He designed his furniture so that it could be partly manufactured by machine, in contrast to many of his colleagues, who prided themselves on handmade articles.

★ Disappearing Corner
The dining corner has a spectacular feature: when the windows are opened, the corner disappears. Formerly the view from here was panoramic but in 1939, much to Rietveld's consternation, a road was built just next to the house.

Amersfoort ⑬

Road map C4. 🏙 *130,000.* 🚍
🚌 ℹ *Stationsplein 9–11 (0900-
1122364).* 🏪 *Fri & Sat.*

T HE OLD TOWN CENTRE of
Amersfoort contrasts
sharply with the districts that
surround it, which resound
with the hum of building
activity. The character of
the town within the ring is
defined by small streets with
old houses and gardens. The
Muurhuizen (wall houses)
were built on the site of the
old defence ring. The **Onze**

The 15th-century Koppelpoort, one of Amersfoort's three surviving gates

Die Leiter **by Armando (1990)**

Lieve Vrouwetoren (Tower
of Our Lady), also known as
Lange Jan, is difficult to miss.
The contours of this old chapel
can still be seen in the stones
of the pavement. In 1787, the
chapel, which was used to
store gunpowder at that time,
was blown up.

The **Amersfoortse kei** boulder appeared in the town in
1661, when a nobleman bet
he could drag the stone from
the Leusderheide. Ever since,
Amersfoort has held the annual Keistadfeest (Keistad festival)
in celebration of the event.

The **Museum Flehite** gives
an overview of the history of

Amersfoort from the Middle
Ages. The **Armandomuseum**
showcases the work of this ver-
satile artist, whose disciplines
include painting, sculpture,
film, and poetry, strongly influenced by what he saw during
World War II at Kamp Amersfoort, a Nazi prisoner-transit
camp just outside the town.

🏛 **Museum Flehite**
Westsingel 50. 📞 *033-4619987.*
⏰ *11am–5pm Tue–Fri, 1–5pm Sat &
Sun.* ● *Mon & public hols.* 🎫
🏛 **Armandomuseum**
Langegracht 36. 📞 *033-4614088.*
⏰ *11am–5pm Tue–Fri, noon–5pm
Sat, Sun & hols.* ● *1 Jan.* 🎫

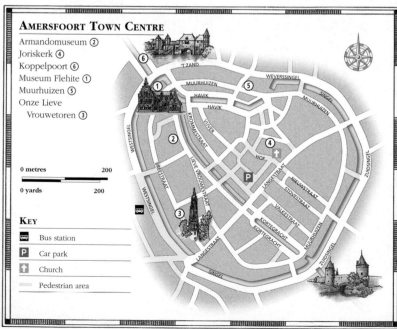

AMERSFOORT TOWN CENTRE

Armandomuseum ②
Joriskerk ④
Koppelpoort ⑥
Museum Flehite ①
Muurhuizen ⑤
Onze Lieve
  Vrouwetoren ③

0 metres   200
0 yards   200

KEY

🚌 Bus station
🅿 Car park
✝ Church
▒ Pedestrian area

Doorn  ⑭

Road map C4. 👥 *10,000.* 🚌
ℹ️ *Dorpsstraat 4 (0343-412015).*
🔵 *Thu.*

DOORN, ORIGINALLY called Thorheim (home of Thor, god of thunder), is a pretty village in wooded surroundings. The greatest tourist attraction here is **Huis Doorn**, where between 1920 and 1941 the German Kaiser, Wilhelm II, lived with his retinue. (He fled his country after World War I.) The kaiser lies buried in a mausoleum to be found in the castle gardens. Deer and birds of prey live in the **Kaapse Bossen**, woods situated to the east of Doorn.

♠ Huis Doorn
Langbroekerweg 10. 📞 *0343-421020.* ⏰ *10am–5pm Tue–Sat, 1–5pm Sun (1 Nov–mid Mar: 1–5pm Tue–Sun.* 🎟️ *mandatory.* 🚻 ♿

Wijk bij Duurstede ⑮

Road map C4. 👥 *23,000.* 🚌
ℹ️ *Markt 24 (0343-575995).* 🔵 *Wed.*

DORESTAD WAS an important trade centre in Carolingian times. Plundering Vikings and a shift in the river basin of the Rhine led to its decline. Then soon after, in the 13th century, Wijk (near Dorestad) emerged and became the home of the Utrecht bishops around 1450. They brought prosperity and influence to the town until, in 1528, the bishop lost his

Castle tower in Wijk bij Duurstede

secular power. The impressive **Kasteel Wijk bij Duurstede** dates from as far back as the 13th century, when it was originally built as a donjon, the castle's fortified inner tower. This was extended in 1500, and bishops lived here until 1580. The castle's park was laid out in 1850 by Jan David Zocher.

♣ Kasteelpark Duurstede
Langs de Wal 7. ⏰ *daily.*

Amerongen ⑯

Road map C4. 👥 *7,000.* 🚌 ℹ️
Drostestraat 14 (0343-452020). 🔵 *Wed.*

AMERONGEN IS situated on the bank of the lower Rhine, which can be crossed by ferry. It lay originally on the Via Regia, the "royal route" from Utrecht to Cologne. From the 17th to 19th centuries, tobacco

was grown in this area, as is evident by the drying sheds which are still standing. You can have a proper look at an old drying shed in **Amerongs Historisch Museum**. In 1672, the town's castle, **Kasteel Amerongen**, was destroyed by the French. It has since been rebuilt in the Dutch Classical style.

🏛 Amerongs Historisch Museum
Burg. Jhr H van de Boschstraat 46
📞 *0343-456500.* ⏰ *Tue–Sun pm.*

♠ Kasteel Amerongen
Drostestraat 20. 📞 *0343-454212.*
⏰ *1 Apr–1 Nov: 10am–5pm Tue–Fri, 1–5pm Sat, Sun & public hols.* 🎟️ 🎟️

Rhenen ⑰

Road map C4. 👥 *17,700.* 🚉 🚌
ℹ️ *Markt 20 (0317-612333).* 🔵 *Thu.*

RHENEN LIES ON the north bank of the Rhine, at the border between the flat Betuwe and the Utrecht Heuvelrug. This area was inhabited as far back as the Iron Age. Many of the town's historic buildings were destroyed during World War II, but the Late Gothic **Cuneratoren** (Cunera tower), built between 1492 and 1531, escaped the bombs. The **Raadhuis** (town hall) dates from the Middle Ages. May 1940 saw a fierce battle on the 53-m (174-ft) **Grebbeberg**, a long-time strategic point in the surrounding area. The victims lie buried in the military cemetery.

One of numerous country houses set amidst the large parks surrounding Wijk bij Duurstede

SOUTH HOLLAND

OR TOURISTS, SOUTH HOLLAND *is pure delight. Although densely populated, the province still has plenty of open space and offers a remarkable range of attractions for visitors of all kinds. The landscape is typically Dutch, with large areas of reclaimed land dotted with windmills and grazing cattle.*

From Roman times on, South Holland was principally a low-lying swampy delta as the various courses of the river Rhine reached the sea. The influence of the counts of Holland (9th–13th centuries), who took up residence in The Hague, attracted trade with Flanders, Germany and England, and settlements became towns. Leiden's university, the oldest in the country, was founded as long ago as 1565. Peat extraction for fuel created lakes, reclaimed land *(see pp18–19)* was turned into productive farmland, and the Dutch dairy industry flourished. Other products in international demand included beer and textiles and, in more recent times, year-round flowers and the famous Dutch bulbs. Overseeing all this activity is the port of Rotterdam, one of the largest in the world, and The Hague, home of the Dutch government, the royal family, and the International Court of Justice.

Delft is famous for its exquisite hand-painted porcelain and china, while Gouda is renowned for its cheese. The North Sea coast has charming resorts, from busy Scheveningen, with its attractive pier, to the smaller seaside towns of Katwijk and Noordwijk, with long sandy beaches. It is an ideal region for family holidays and for children of all ages.

Visitors in spring are in for a treat when they tour the north of the province. Bulb fields erupt in a riot of colour, and the Keukenhof's flower gardens are simply unforgettable.

The queen arriving in her Golden Coach to open Parliament on the third Tuesday of September (Prinsjesdag)

◁ One of numerous windmills that once drained the land in the Alblasserwaard

Exploring South Holland

IN THE NORTH of the province of South Holland are the colourful bulb fields and the Keukenhof, while to the south in a semi-circle lie the old university town of Leiden, bustling The Hague, cosy Delft and the modern port city of Rotterdam. The islands of South Holland bear witness to the country's military history in Hellevoetsluis and Brielle. Ramblers will find all they wish for in the dunes by Wassenaar or in the river countryside at Leerdam, which is best known for its glass-blowing industry. From Gorinchem you can take a passenger ferry to the 14th-century castle of Slot Loevestein, which played a key role in the history of Holland.

The 14th-century Huis Dever by Lisse

The Panorama Mesdag in The Hague

SEE ALSO

- *Where to Stay* pp395–6
- *Where to Eat* pp415–16

Greenhouses in the Westland

SCHEVENINGEN **6**

5 THE HAG

Westland **DELFT**

● HOEK VAN HOLLAND

Nieuwe Waterweg A20

8 MAASSLUIS

BRIELLE **18**

A15

19 HELLEVOETSLUIS

GOEDEREEDE **21**

Haringvliet

MIDDELHARNIS **20**

Goeree Overflakkee

Grevelingenmeer

Hoeks Waar

OUDE TONGE ●   N59

GETTING AROUND

South Holland has a comprehensive system of roads, and both big cities and small towns can be reached equally quickly. However, during the morning and afternoon rush hours you should watch out for traffic jams. In the centres of the big cities it is best to leave your car in a car park, as finding an on-street parking space can often be a problem. Trains are a fast way of getting from A to B. As a rule you will find a train for your particular destination departing every quarter or half hour. Lisse and the bulbfields, Nieuwpoort and the towns on South Holland's islands can be reached only by local bus. VVV and ANWB tourist information offices provide information on cycling routes.

KEY

- ▬ Motorway
- ▬ Major road
- ▬ Minor road
- ▬ Scenic route
- ▬ Canal/river

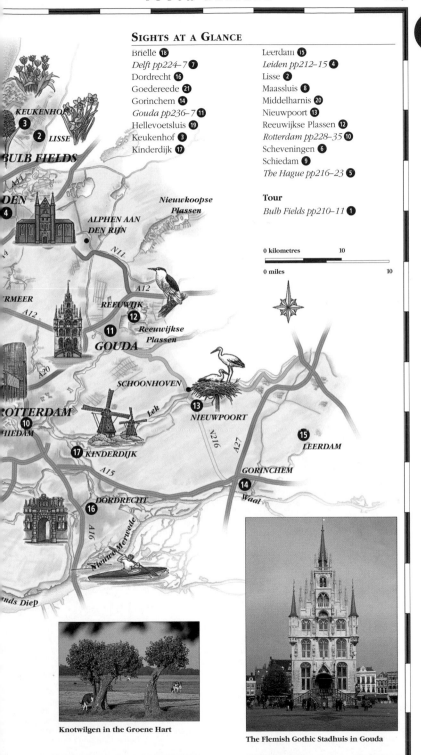

Sights at a Glance

KEUKENHOF

③

② LISSE

BULB FIELDS

DEN

④

Nieuwkoopse
Plassen

ALPHEN AAN
DEN RIJN

N11

A12

RMEER

A12

REEUWIJK

⑫

⑪

Reeuwijkse
Plassen

GOUDA

A20

SCHOONHOVEN

Lek

⑬

NIEUWPOORT

⑮

LEERDAM

ROTTERDAM

⑩

HIEDAM

⑰ KINDERDIJK

A15

GORINCHEM

⑭

Waal

DORDRECHT

⑯

A16

Nieuwe Merwede

nds Diep

0 kilometres   10

0 miles   10

Knotwilgen in the Groene Hart

The Flemish Gothic Stadhuis in Gouda

Bulb Fields ❶

THE BOLLENSTREEK, a 30-km (19-mile) stretch
between Haarlem and Leiden, is Holland's
primary bulb-growing area. From March, the
polders are aglow with glorious colours – the
crocuses are the first to flower and the season
culminates around mid-April with the majestic tulips.
The lilies then follow at the end of May. Visitors
without cars can obtain information about cycle
routes from the tourist information office, the VVV,
at Lisse *(see p211)*. Bikes can be hired at
railway stations in Haarlem and
Heemstede-Aerdenhout.

TIPS FOR DRIVERS

Starting point: Haarlem.
Distance: approximately 30 km
(19 miles).
Stopping-off points: along with
the places discussed below, where
various cafés and restaurants are
to be found, Noordwijk aan Zee
is worth a short detour. This lively
coastal town, with its wonderful
beach and dunes, makes an ideal
place for a stopover.

The dunes of North Holland

Keukenhof ③
*Visitors are greeted by the
intoxicating aroma and
vivid colours of millions
of flowering bulbs.*

Sassenheim ⑤
*To the west of the town
lie the ruins of Burcht
Teylingen, the 11th-
century castle where
Jacoba of Bavaria,
countess of
Holland, died
in 1436.*

North Sea

Cruquiusmuseum ①
*In this former steam-
driven pumping stati
you can see how the
people of Hollan
managed to keep
the water in check
(see pp186–7).*

Linnaeushof ②
*This huge park, named after
the famous 18th-century
botanist, has one of the bigge
recreation grounds in Europe*

Lisse ④
*Lisse's museum showcases the
bulb-growing industry; you ca
also take a boat trip on the lakes*

HAARLEM

ZANDVOORT

AMSTERDAM

A5

N208

N201

N201

AALSMEER

Amsterdamse
Waterleiding-
duinen

HILLEGOM

N206

N208

Haarlemmermeerpolder

NOORDWIJK
AAN ZEE

N206

N208

Ringvaart van de

AALSMEER

A44

Kager-
plassen

RIJNSBURG

LEIDEN/
THE HAGUE

0 kilometres   4

0 miles   4

KEY

▬▬ Route

═══ Roads

❁ Good viewing point

Katwijk ⑦
*An unusual early 17th-
century lighthouse stands
to the north of this coastal
town, which lies on the
estuary of the Oude Rijn.*

Voorhout ⑥
*Panorama Tulip Land is a
panoramic painting of the
Bollenstreek. Its dimensions are
enormous: 63 m (207 ft) wide
and 4 m (13 ft) tall.*

A tulip field in the Bollenstreek

FLOWERING BULBS

Flowers such as gladioli, lilies, narcissi, hyacinths, irises, crocuses and dahlias are mainly grown in the Bollenstreek. By far the most important, though, is the tulip, which originally came from Turkey and was cultivated by Carolus Clusius in 1593 for the first time in the Netherlands.

'Aladdin' tulips

'China Pink' tulips

'Tahiti' narcissi

'Minnow' narcissi

'Blue Jacket' hyacinths

Colourful flowering bulbs in the shady Keukenhof

Lisse ➋

Map B3. 🏘 20,000. 🚌 50 & 51 (from Leiden & Haarlem) & 52 (from Noordwijk). 🚶 Grachtweg 53 (0252-414262).

THE BEST TIME to see Lisse is at the end of April, when the colourful **Bloemen Corso** (flower parade) takes place (see p32). A vibrant procession of floats passes from Noordwijk to Haarlem, where they are brightly illuminated at night and can still be seen the next day. On the two days before the parade, you can see close-up how the floats are decorated in the *Hobabo* halls in Lisse.

The **Museum De Zwarte Tulp** (black tulip museum) covers the history of bulb growing and illustrates the life cycle of bulbs. It also touches upon the "tulipomania" from 1620–37 (see pp30–31), when investors pushed up the demand for rare tulip bulbs to such an extent that they were worth their weight in gold.

📇 Bloemen Corso
📞 0252-428237 (Stichting Bloemen corso Bollenstreek).

🏛 Museum De Zwarte Tulp
Grachtweg 2a. 📞 0252-417900. ⭘ Tue–Sun 1–5pm. ⬤ public hols. 🎦 ♿ ▯

ENVIRONS: Just outside Lisse is **Huis Dever**, a fortified residential tower which dates from the second half of the 14th century. The permanent exhibition at the tower illustrates the lives of the families who lived here.

🏰 Huis Dever
Heereweg 349a. 📞 0252-411430. ⭘ Tue–Sun 2–5pm. ⬤ public hols. 🎫 by arrangement.

Keukenhof ➌

Map B3. 🚌 54 (from Leiden). 📞 0252-465555. ⭘ daily 21 Mar–end May 8am–6pm (ticket office). 🎦 ♿ 🍴

LYING IN A WOODED PARK of 32 ha (79 acres) close to Lisse, the Keukenhof is one of the most spectacular public gardens in the world. It was set up in 1949 as a showcase for bulb-growers and currently has around 6 million bulbs planted in it. Fields are full of dazzling narcissi, hyacinths and tulips in bloom from the end of March to the end of May. You can also see the white blossom of the Japanese cherry tree in the park early in the season and, later in the year, the bright flowers of the azaleas and rhododendrons.

Street-by-Street: Leiden 4

L EIDEN IS A THRIVING university town which dates from Roman times. The town developed because of its position on a branch of the Rhine and is still an important trade centre. Some excellent museums chart Leiden's eventful past, including the Golden Age, when the town was a centre for world trade (see pp48–9). Rembrandt van Rijn (see pp24–5) was born here in June 1606 – a plaque on the façade of a Weddesteeg house marks his birthplace. During term time, the streets of Leiden are busy with students cycling between lectures or frequenting the cafés and bookshops.

Statue of Justice on Stadhuis wall

★ **Rijksmuseum van Oudheden**
This squat statue of a kneeling treasury scribe is just one of the many impressive Egyptian artefacts on display in this fascinating museum of antiquities.

★ **Hortus Botanicus**
The botanical gardens belonging to the University of Leiden (see p214) were started in 1590 "for the teaching of every body who studies in the medicinal sciences".

Façades
Aristocrats, professors and textile families all contributed to the face of the Leiden canals.

Dutch Classicism can be seen in the university buildings on Rapenburg.

Het Gravensteen
Part of the law faculty is now accommodated in this former count's prison, built between the 13th and 17th centuries.

VISITORS' CHECKLIST

Wegenkaart B3. 117,000.
Stationsplein. Stationsweg
2d (0900-2222333). Wed &
Sat. Zomerfestival: early Jul;
Relief of Leiden Celebrations: 2 &
3 Oct. W www.leidenpromotie.nl

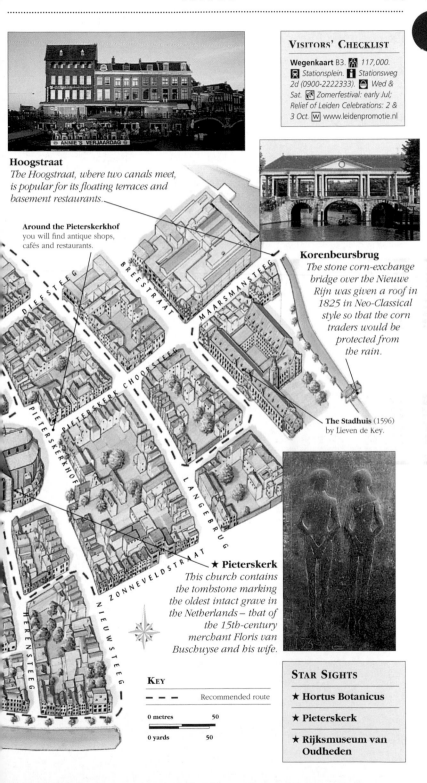

Hoogstraat
*The Hoogstraat, where two canals meet,
is popular for its floating terraces and
basement restaurants.*

Around the Pieterskerkhof
you will find antique shops,
cafés and restaurants.

Korenbeursbrug
*The stone corn-exchange
bridge over the Nieuwe
Rijn was given a roof in
1825 in Neo-Classical
style so that the corn
traders would be
protected from
the rain.*

The Stadhuis (1596)
by Lieven de Key.

★ Pieterskerk
*This church contains
the tombstone marking
the oldest intact grave in
the Netherlands – that of
the 15th-century
merchant Floris van
Buschuyse and his wife.*

DIEFSTEEG
BREESTRAAT
MAARSMANSTEEG
PIETERSKERK CHOORSTEEG
PIETERSKERKHOF
LANGEBRUG
ZONNEVELDSTRAAT
HERENSTEEG
NIEUWSTEEG

KEY

- - - Recommended route

0 metres   50

0 yards   50

STAR SIGHTS

★ **Hortus Botanicus**

★ **Pieterskerk**

★ **Rijksmuseum van
Oudheden**

Exploring Leiden

L EIDEN IS FAMOUS FOR ITS UNIVERSITY, which is the oldest
in the country. It was founded in 1575, one year
after the Beggars of the Sea *(see p239)* freed the town
from a protracted siege by the Spanish *(see p49)*. As a
reward for their endurance, William of Orange offered
the people of Leiden the choice between a university
and the abolition of taxes. The people made a shrewd
choice and the town went on to become a centre of
intellectual progress and religious freedom. English
Puritan dissidents, victims of persecution in their
homeland, were able to settle here in the 17th century
before undertaking their journey to the New World.

One of the 35 almshouses in Leiden

🏛 Stedelijk Museum de Lakenhal

Oude Singel 28–32. **(** *071-5165360.*
○ *10am–5pm Tue–Fri, noon–5pm
Sat, Sun & hols.* **●** *1 Jan, 25 Dec.*
🖼 🛉 🛗 🖂

In the 17th century, the
lakenhal (cloth merchants'
hall) was the centre of the
Leiden textile industry. Arent
van 's Gravesande designed
the building in 1640 in Dutch
Classical style. The municipal
museum has been here since
1874. The showpiece of the
collection, which was rescued
from the Pieterskerk (St Peter's
Church) during the religious
disputes of 1566 *(see pp52–3)*
is *The Last Judgment* (1526–7),
a triptych in Renaissance style
by Lucas van Leyden. Other
Leiden artists, from
Rembrandt to Theo
van Doesburg,
are also featured.
The museum
has displays of
silver, glass,
tin and tiles

and explores the history of
Leiden. Not to be missed is
the large bronze cooking pot
said to have been left by the
Spaniards during the relief of
Leiden in 1574. The spicy
casserole it contained is the
forerunner to the stew which
is now cooked every year on
3 October to commemorate
Dutch victory over the Spanish.

🌿 Hortus Botanicus Leiden

Rapenburg 73. **(** *071-5277249.*
○ *summer: 10am–6pm daily;
winter: 10am–4pm daily (Clusiustuin:
Mon–Fri).* **●** *8 Feb am, 3 Oct.*
🖼 🖼 🛉 *(partial).*

The botanical garden of Leiden
was founded in 1590 as part
of the university. A number
of its trees and shrubs are

particularly old, such as a
laburnum dating from 1601.
In 1593, Carolus Clusius, who
introduced the tulip to Holland
(see pp30–31), became the first
professor of botany at the University of Leiden. The Hortus
Botanicus features a reconstruction of this botanist's
walled garden, the Clusiustuin
(Clusius garden). Also worth
a look are the tropical greenhouses, the fragrant rose garden and the Von Siebold
Japanese memorial garden.

🏛 Museum Boerhaave

Lange St Agnietenstraat 10. **(** *071-
5214224.* **○** *10am–5pm Tue–Sat (Mon
on school hols), noon–5pm Sun & public
hols.* **●** *1 Jan, 3 Oct.* 🖼 🖼 🛉 🖂
W *www.museumboerhaave.nl*

The Leiden physician
Hermanus
Boerhaave
(1668–1738)
wrote the defin-
itive medical
reference book
Institutiones

**Lucas van Leyden's triptych of *The Last Judgment*,
in the Stedelijk Museum de Lakenhal**

Medicae. The museum named after him is devoted to the development of science and medicine in the Netherlands. Alongside practical inventions such as electrostatic generators and pendulum clocks by Christiaan Huygens (1629–95), who discovered the rings of Saturn, you can see the bizarre Anatomisch Theater, dating from around 1600.

🏛 Rijksmuseum voor Volkenkunde
Steenstraat 1. 📞 *071-5168800.*
⏰ *10am–5pm Tue–Sun & public hols.*
⬤ *1 Jan, 23 Oct, 25 Dec.* 🎫 ♿ ▣
ᵂ *www.rmv.nl*
This excellent ethnological museum, founded in 1837, has collections which feature non-Western cultures, such as ethnographic items brought by the German explorer Philipp von Siebold from Japan in the 19th century. The vast collection focuses on the interaction between various cultures and their links with the Netherlands; hence Indonesia has a considerable amount of floor space. The museum covers practically the whole world, from the Arctic to Oceania.

Heraldic lion at De Burcht

🏛 Naturalis
Darwinweg. 📞 *071-5687600.* ⏰ *10am–6pm Tue–Sun; school & public hols: 10am–6pm daily.* ⬤ *1 Jan, 25 Dec.* 🎫 ♿ ▣ ▣ ▣
As soon as it opened (1998), the national natural history museum attracted a record number of visitors. It has succeeded in providing a truly fascinating insight into the evolution of the earth and its inhabitants with displays of fossils more than a million years old, and lifelike replicas of animals, stones and minerals. Special exhibitions for children are also held.

⛪ Pieterskerk
Pieterskerkhof 1a. 📞 *071-5124319.*
⏰ *1:30–4pm daily.* ⬤ *3 Oct & when the church is hired out.* ♿
This impressive Gothic cruciform church, built mainly in

THE PILGRIM FATHERS

In the 17th century, the Netherlands was a refuge for English Puritans. Minister John Robinson (1575–1625) founded a church in Leiden in 1609, where he inspired his congregation with his dream of the New World. The Pilgrim Fathers set out in 1620 from Delfshaven aboard the *Speedwell*, but the ship proved to be unseaworthy. They then crossed the Atlantic from Plymouth, England, on the *Mayflower*, but Robinson stayed behind, too ill to travel. He died in Leiden in 1625.

The *Mayflower* crossing the Atlantic Ocean

---

the 15th century, stands in the middle of a shady square that seems to be from a different age. It is worth a visit for its austere interior and the recently restored Van Hagerbeer organ (1639–43), one of the few meantone-tuned organs *(see pp28–9).* The floor of the nave is covered with worn stones which mark the graves of famous 17th-century intellectuals such as Puritan leader John Robinson, physician Hermanus Boerhaave and Golden Age artist Jan Steen.

♟ De Burcht
Burgsteeg. ⏰ *daily.*
The Burcht is a 12th-century fortress which features a still-intact circular wall and crenellated battlements. At the foot of the 12-m (39-ft) artificial mound is a wrought-iron gate

covered in heraldic symbols. There is a marvellous view of Leiden's historic centre from the gallery.

🏛 Rijksmuseum van Oudheden
Rapenburg 28. 📞 *071-5163163.*
⏰ *10am–5pm Tue–Fri, noon–5pm Sat, Sun & public hols.* ⬤ *1 Jan, 3 Oct, 25 Dec.* 🎫 ♿ ▣ ▣ ▣
ᵂ *www.rmo.nl*
This museum has one of the top seven Egyptian collections in the world, the centrepiece of which is the 2,000-year-old Taffeh Temple. Other civilizations from the Near East and from Classical Antiquity are also represented. The section on archaeology of the Netherlands gives visitors an idea of what the Low Countries were like from prehistoric times to the Middle Ages. Mummies, textiles and shoes, musical instruments and fragments of Roman mosaics and frescoes form just a part of the museum's impressive holdings.

A drawbridge across the Oude Rijn in Leiden

Street-by-Street: The Hague ❺

THE VILLAGE OF DIE HAGHE ("the hedge") grew around the Binnenhof (inner courtyard), which has been an important political centre since the 13th century. The princes of Orange, the upper classes and an extensive diplomatic corps gave instructions for palaces and mansion houses to be built, and a stroll across the Voorhout or along the Hofvijver will still evoke its aristocratic charm.

The Hague today is represented by the new Spuikwartier (Spui district), with the city hall by Richard Meier and the Lucent Danstheater by Rem Koolhaas. To the west, the dunes and many parks and woods are still reminiscent of the country estate it once was.

Jantje

★ Escher in Het Paleis
A permanent exhibition of the graphic artist Maurits Cornelis Escher can be visited in the Paleis Lange Voorhout, where Queen Emma and Queen Wilhelmina once lived.

Gevangenpoort
The Dutch lion adorns the façade of the Gevangenpoort (prison gate), originally the main gate of the 14th-century castle of the counts of Holland. From the 1400s, it was used as a prison.

KEY

━ ━ ━ Recommended route

STAR SIGHTS

★ **Binnenhof**

★ **Escher in Het Paleis**

★ **Mauritshuis**

0 metres 50

0 yards 50

Prince William V's Picture Gallery
This was the first public art gallery in the Netherlands.

Jantje, famous from a Dutch nursery rhyme, points to the Binnenhof.

Haags Historisch Museum

Featured is the history of The Hague, from the Middle Ages to the present day.

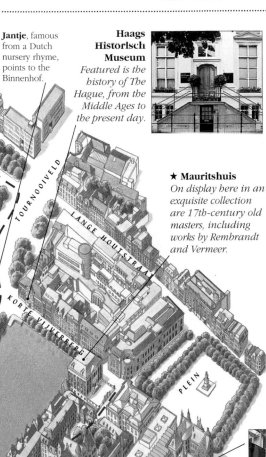

★ Mauritshuis

On display here in an exquisite collection are 17th-century old masters, including works by Rembrandt and Vermeer.

The Tweede Kamer

The new accommodation for the Tweede Kamer, the Dutch Lower House, was designed by Pi de Bruijn and has been in use since 1992. The building blends tastefully with the older buildings surrounding it. Plenary sessions are held in the Grote Vergaderzaal (great assembly hall) behind the circular extension.

"The Hague, you tap it and it sings" wrote Dutch poet Gerrit Achterberg in "Passage". The elegant covered arcade of shops in Neo-Renaissance style on the Hofweg is a famous feature of the town centre.

★ Binnenhof

This ancient structure comprises the parliament and government buildings and was originally the 13th-century hunting lodge of the counts of Holland.

Exploring The Hague

Cartoon character Haagse Harry

THE HAGUE HAS NUMEROUS attractions and museums, of which the Mauritshuis *(see pp220–21)* and the Gemeentemuseum (municipal museum) *(see p222)* are the most famous. There are many bookshops, antique shops and cafés on and around the Denneweg, which comes out onto the Lange Voorhout, as well as luxury boutiques on the promenade beginning at Paleis Noordeinde *(see p219)*. Behind the Mauritskade lies the stately late 19th-century Willemspark, which is still almost completely intact, with the Panorama Mesdag *(see p222)*. You can admire the peaceful Japanese garden in Park Clingendael *(see p222)*. The old fishing village of Scheveningen has expanded to become a lively seaside resort but the dunes all around still offer peace and quiet.

🏛 Binnenhof met Ridderzaal

Binnenhof. ☎ 070-3646144. 🖥 🔲 ◻ *10am–3:45pm Mon–Sat.* ⬤ *Sun, public hols, 3rd Tue in Sep.* ◰ ✔ *Booking recommended.*

The historic Binnenhof is a series of buildings erected around the hunting lodge of the counts of Holland. In 1247, William II was proclaimed Holy Roman Emperor; he later had the gothic Ridderzaal (Hall of the Knights) built as a banqueting hall. The Binnenhof has since then been the residence of stadholders, princes and governments. The court of Holland has administered justice since 1511 in the Rolzaal (roll court). The northern provinces of the Netherlands broke free from Spanish rule in 1581 with the *Plakkaat van*

Verlatinge ("Decree of Abandonment"); they held a huge feast for William of Orange in the Ridderzaal. The Binnenhof was one of the most important European centres of diplomacy in the Golden Age. The magnificently ornate meeting hall dates from this period and is where the Upper House currently sits. The Lower House met in William V's old ballroom until 1992, when it was moved to a new location. Tours of the building begin in the medieval cellars and pass through the Ridderzaal and debating chambers of the Upper or Lower House.

🏛 Museum De Gevangenpoort

Buitenhof 33. ☎ 070-3460861. 🖥 🖳 ◻ *11am–5pm Tue–Sun (from noon Sat & Sun).* ⬤ *1 Jan, 25 Dec.* ◰ ✔ *obligatory; last guided tour 4pm.*

The prison gate museum, in a 14th-century gatehouse, contains an old prison that is still largely in its original state. Cornelis de Witt was kept here on suspicion of conspiracy against Prince Maurice. In 1672, as he and his brother Johan left the prison, they were murdered by a provoked mob, under the watchful eye of the civic guard. The museum has a unique collection of horrific torture instruments.

🏛 Galerij Prins Willem V

Buitenhof 35. ☎ 070-3624444. 🖥 🖳 ◻ *11am–4pm Tue–Sun.* ⬤ *1 Jan, 25 Dec.* ◰

Prince William V was an enthusiastic collector of 17th-century art. In 1774, his private collection was put on show for the public in this former inn, which the prince had converted into his office. The treasures in this gallery include paintings by Rembrandt, Jan Steen and Paulus Potter (1625–54).

Porcelain from the Museum Bredius collection

🏛 Museum Bredius

Lange Vijverberg 14. ☎ 070-362 0729. 🖥 🖳 ◻ *noon–5pm Tue–Sun.* ⬤ *1 Jan, 5 May, 25 Dec.* ◰

Art historian and art collector Abraham Bredius was also director of the Mauritshuis *(see pp220–21)* from 1895 to 1922. On his death in 1946 he bequeathed his collection of 17th- and 18th-century art, including paintings by Rembrandt and Jan Steen, to the city of The Hague. The elegant 18th-century mansion on the north side of the Hofvijver which houses the museum also has fine antique furniture and porcelain and beautifully engraved silver.

🏛 Escher in de Paleis

Lange Voorhout 74. ☎ 070-427 7730. 🖥 🖳 ◻ *11am–5pm Tue–Sun.* ⬤ *1 Jan, 25 Dec.* ◰
🖳 www.escherinhetpaleis.nl

***Landscape by Fading Light* by Albert Cuyp (Museum Bredius)**

A large proportion of MC Escher's (1898–1972) work is displayed in the Paleis Lange Voorhout, including well-known works such as *Day and Night*, *Rising and Falling* and *Belvédère*. In addition to graphic works, there are sketches, personal documents and photographs. The museum also features multimedia installations such as the Escher Experience, a virtual journey through his world.

🏛 Paleis Noordeinde

Noordeinde. ☐ *Only the Paleistuin (palace garden) is open to the public, from sunrise to sunset.*

In 1640, Stadholder Frederik Hendrik had his mother's house converted into a palace in the classical style. The property of the Princes of Orange since William V (1748–1806), this is where Queen Beatrix concentrates on her work. On Prinsjesdag (state opening of parliament), the queen drives from here to the Binnenhof in a golden coach.

🏛 Vredespaleis

Carnegieplein 2. 🚋 *4 and 13.* 🚌 *7, 8.* ☎ *070-3024137.* ☐ *Mon–Fri a few guided tours daily.* 🎧 *obligatory.* ⬤ *Public hols and when court is in session.* 📷 ♿ ∅

In 1899, The Hague hosted the first international peace conference. Contributions from the court's members decorate the interior of the mock-Gothic Vredespaleis (peace palace), designed by the French architect Louis Cordonnier and completed in 1913. The International Court of the United Nations, formed in 1946, is now based here. It has the largest international law library in the world.

🏛 Passage

Between the Spuistraat, Hofweg and Buitenhof. 🚋 🚌

The Peace Palace (Vredespaleis), home to the International Court of Justice

A visit to The Hague would not be complete without a stroll along the elegant Passage, the only covered arcade remaining from the 19th century in the Netherlands. Unusual specialist shops can be found here, such as the umbrella and fountain pen shop. The arcade wing that leads to the Hofweg was added in 1928–9. The shops in the Passage and the town centre of The Hague are open all year, including Sundays.

The Classical-style Paleis Noordeinde, where Queen Beatrix has her administrative offices

Mauritshuis

AFTER HE WAS RECALLED as captain general of Brazil, Johan Maurits of Nassau gave instructions for this house to be built. It was completed in 1644 by Pieter Post in the North Dutch Classical style with influences from the Italian Renaissance and has a marvellous view of the Hofvijver. After the death of Maurits in 1679, the house passed into state hands and, in 1822, became the home of the royal painting collection. Though the collection is not large, it contains almost exclusively superior works by old masters. This, combined with the imaginative presentation in elegant period rooms, makes Mauritshuis one of the country's finest museums.

★ **The Anatomy Lesson of Dr Nicolaes Tulp** *(1632)*
Rembrandt's painting of doctors examining a corpse reflects the burgeoning contemporary interest in anatomy and science.

MUSEUM GUIDE

The three floors of this little museum are hung with paintings from top to bottom. To feature all aspects of the collection, the exhibited artwork is constantly changing. The masterpieces are always on view, although not always hanging in the same location. Presentation is pleasantly haphazard and many of the paintings have no commentary. If you have any questions, you can ask for help at the information desk located in the museum's golden room.

Bordello Scene
(1658) This typical 17th-century genre painting of a brothel scene by Frans van Mieris de Oude (1635–81) has an unmistakable erotic undertone.

Ground floor

Offices and secretariat

Vase with Flowers *(1618)*
Ambrosius Bosschaert captured the beauty of summer flowers but added the flies to remind us of our mortality.

Basement

Main staircase

The Goldfinch *(1654)*
This small, elegant painting is by Carel Fabritius (1622–54), a pupil of Rembrandt.

First floor

KEY TO FLOORPLAN

- ☐ Portrait gallery
- ☐ 15th- and early 16th-century works
- ☐ Late 16th- and 17th-century works
- ☐ Golden room
- ☐ 17th-century art
- ☐ 17th-century Flemish artists
- ☐ Early 17th-century collection
- ☐ Non-exhibition space

The Way You Hear It Is the Way You Sing It *(1663)*
This moralistic genre painting by Jan Steen (see p123) probably shows what is meant by a "huishouden van Jan Steen" – keeping one's house like a pigsty.

★ The Louse Hunt *(1653)*
Gerard ter Borch's painting depicts a domestic tableau and reflects the Dutch preoccupation with order and cleanliness during the 17th century.

Main entrance

★ Girl with a Pearl Earring *(1665)*
At the mid-point of his career, Johannes Vermeer painted this haunting portrait of a girl wearing a pearl earring. His daughter Maria may have been the model.

STAR PAINTINGS

- ★ **Girl with a Pearl Earring**
- ★ **The Anatomy Lesson of Dr Nicolaes Tulp**
- ★ **The Louse Hunt**

The Hague's municipal museum, one of HP Berlage's most handsome designs

🏛 Panorama Mesdag

Zeestraat 65. 🚋 *4, 5.* 🚆 *8, 17.*
📞 *070-3644544.* ⏱ *10am–5pm*
Mon–Sat, noon–5pm Sun & public
hols. ● *25 Dec.* 📷 🎫 *By request.*

Panorama Mesdag is one of
the best remaining panoramic
paintings of the 19th century.
The circular canvas, with an
impressive circumference of
120 m (395 ft), depicts the old
fishing village of Scheveningen.
It is a breathtaking moment
when, after climbing the
creaking stairs leading up to
the panorama, you suddenly
emerge into daylight, to
be surrounded by the
dunes and the sea.
The illusion is
strengthened by
genuine sand and
pieces of wreckage
laid at the foot of the
painting. The painting
was done in 1881 by
members of the Haag
School, led by HW
Mesdag (1831–1915) and
his wife Sientje (1834–1909).
George Hendrik Breitner
(1857–1923) painted the
cavalrymen on the sand.

Victory Boogie Woogie

🏛 Gemeentemuseum Den Haag en Fotomuseum

Stadhouderslaan 41. 🚋 *4.* 🚆 *7, 10.*
📞 *070-3381111.* ⏱ *11am–5pm*
Tue–Sun. ● *1 Jan, 25 Dec.* 📷 ♿
📷 🖥 *www.gemeentemuseum.nl*

The Gemeentemuseum (muni-
cipal museum) was the last
piece of work to be carried
out by HP Berlage, founder of
the Amsterdam School. The
museum was completed in
1935, one year after his death,
and now contains the largest
collection of paintings by
Mondriaan in the world, with
works from all his various
periods. One of the high points
of the collection is *Victory
Boogie Woogie* (1943). Other
works exhibited here include
paintings by JH Weissenbruch
and brothers Maris and Josef
Israëls, all of whom were
representatives of the Haag
School, which was profoundly
inspired by the coastal landscape. The main feature of
the applied art section is the
antique Delftware and oriental porcelain. An ex-
hibit of clothing from
the 18th century
onwards is dis-
played in an annex
to the main building.
Another major attraction
at the museum is the
stunning collection of
musical instruments
dating from the 15th
to the 19th centuries. The
Schamhart Wing opened in
2002, and the photography
museum, which stages tem-
porary exhibitions of Dutch
photography, is now open.

〰 Omniversum

President Kennedylaan 5. 🚋 *4.*
🚆 *7, 10.* 📞 *0900-6664837.*
⏱ *hours depends on programme,*
phone for details. 📷 ♿ 🖥

The Omniversum (next to
the Gemeentemuseum) is
a cross between a planetarium and a high-tech cinema.
It puts on an amazing programme of exciting films
of space flights, volcanic
eruptions and ocean life.

🍂 Park Clingendael

Entrance from Alkemadelaan or the
Ruychrocklaan. 🚋 *18, 23.* 🖥
Japanese Gardens
Park Clingendael. ⏱ *end of Apr–mid*
Jun: from sunrise to sunset daily.

This country estate already
existed in the 16th century,
when it had a large, formal
French-style garden. In 1830
it was converted into a pretty
landscaped park. It contains
a Dutch garden, a rose garden, grazing land for animals,
rhododendron woods and
an ancient beech tree.

Overgrown bunkers in the
wood are a sombre reminder
of World War II, when the
Netherlands was occupied

The picturesque Japanese garden in Park Clingendael

and the most senior German authorities took up quarters in Huis Clingendael. At the centre of the park lies the famous Japanese garden, which was laid out in 1903 on the instructions of Baroness Marguérite Mary after a trip to Japan. The tea house and all the stones and ornaments in the garden were brought over from Japan by boat at the time.

🏛 Madurodam

George Maduroplein 1. 🚋 22.
📞 1. ☎ 070-4162400.
🕐 Sep–Mar: 9am–6pm; Apr–Jun: 9am–8pm; Jul–Aug: 9am–10pm. 🅿
♿ 🍴 ⓦ www.madurodam.nl

Madurodam depicts the Netherlands in miniature – it consists of replicas of historically significant buildings like the Binnenhof in The Hague *(see p218)*, canalside houses in Amsterdam and the Euromast tower in Rotterdam *(see p230)*, built to a scale of 1:25. Other models here include Schiphol Airport, windmills, polders, bulb fields and some intriguing examples of the country's modern architecture. At night time the streets and buildings are illuminated by 50,000 tiny lamps.

Madurodam was opened in 1952 by Queen Juliana. JML Maduro designed the town in memory of his son George, who died at Dachau concentration camp in 1945. Profits go to children's charities.

The model city of Madurodam

Scheveningen ❻

Road map B4. 🏠 *18,000.* 🚋 *22.*
📞 *1, 9.* ℹ *Gevers Deynootweg 1134 (0900-3403505).* ⛵ *Thu.*

THE PLEASANT SEASIDE resort of Scheveningen can be easily reached by tram from the centre of Den Haag in just 15 minutes. Like so many of the North Sea beach resorts, Scheveningen had its heyday in the 19th century. Nowadays it is a mixture of faded charm and modern garishness, though it remains a popular holiday resort because of its long sandy beach and the **Pier**. There are many places to eat, including good seafood restaurants.

The impressive **Kurhaus**, designed in the Empire style and now a luxurious hotel, was built in 1885, when Scheveningen was still a major spa town. Not far from the Kurhaus is **Sea Life Scheveningen**, where you can look through transparent tunnels at stingrays, sharks and many other fascinating sea creatures.

Museum Scheveningen is devoted to the history of the fishing village and the spa resort. Tours of Scheveningen lighthouse can also be booked.

Designed by Wim Quist, **Museum Beelden aan Zee** (seaside sculpture museum) can be found on the boulevard, half hidden by a sand dune. Contemporary sculptures on the theme of the human figure are shown in the light, airy rooms, on the terraces outside and in the museum's garden.

Although the seaside resort has all but swallowed up the original fishing village, there is still a harbour and a large fish market. Fishing boat trips can be booked on the southern side of the harbour – a fun outing for the afternoon.

🐟 Sea Life Scheveningen

Strandweg 13. ☎ 070-3542100.
🕐 10am–6pm; to 8pm Jul & Aug. ● 25 Dec. 🅿 ♿ 📷
🖥 ⓦ www.sealife.nl

🏛 Museum Scheveningen

Neptunusstraat 92. ☎ 070-3500830
🕐 11am–5pm Tue–Sat, 1–5pm Sun.
● public holidays. 🅿 📷

🏛 Museum Beelden aan Zee

Harteveltstraat 1. ☎ 070-3585857.
🕐 11am–5pm Tue–Sun. 🅿 🖥

Thsuki-no-hikari (Light of the Moon) by Igor Mitoraj in the dunes of the Museum Beelden aan Zee

Street-by-Street: Delft ❼

19th-century Delftware

DELFT DATES BACK to 1075, its prosperity based on the weaving and brewing industries. In October 1654, however, an enormous explosion at the national arsenal destroyed much of the medieval town. The centre was rebuilt at the end of the 17th century and has remained relatively unchanged since then – houses in Gothic and Renaissance styles still stand along the tree-lined canals. Town life is concentrated on the Markt, which has the town hall at one end and the Nieuwe Kerk at the other. Visitors can dip into the scores of shops selling expensive, hand-painted Delftware or take a tour of local factories, the shops of which are often reasonably priced.

★ **Stedelijk Museum Het Prinsenhof**
William of Orange was killed on this staircase in 1584, the bullet holes still visible.

0 metres   50
0 yards   50

★ **Oude Kerk**
The 13th-century Oude Kerk contains the graves of prominent citizens such as that of the inventor of the micro-scope, Antonie van Leeuwenhoek (see p22).

The Oude Delft
is lined with canalside houses in Renaissance style.

Sint-Hippolytuskapel
This austere red-brick chapel (1396) was used as an arsenal during the Reformation (see pp52–3).

STAR SIGHTS

★ **Nieuwe Kerk**

★ **Oude Kerk**

★ **Stedelijk Museum Het Prinsenhof**

KEY

− − − Recommended route

View of Delft *(c.1660)*
Johannes Vermeer's painting captures Delft on a cloudy summer afternoon. The original tower of the Nieuwe Kerk can be seen in the distance.

Stadhuis *(1618)*
The Renaissance-style town hall was designed by Hendrick de Keyser. The building is erected around a 13th-century Gothic tower.

★ Nieuwe Kerk
The church was built in several phases spread over many years. This statue of William of Orange stands in the middle of his opulent mausoleum.

Koornbeurs *(1650)*
The façade of the old meat hall is decorated with animal heads. After 1871, the building was used as a corn exchange.

Exploring Delft

ATTRACTIVE DELFT is world-famous for its blue-and-white pottery and is renowned in Holland as being the resting place of William of Orange (1533–84), the "father of the Netherlands". William led the resistance against Spanish rule in the 80 Years War *(see p49)* from his Delft headquarters; his victory meant religious freedom and independence for the Dutch. Delft was the Republic's main arsenal in the 17th century; an explosion of gunpowder destroyed a large part of the town in 1654. Artist Johannes Vermeer (1632–75) was born and lived in Delft.

The impressive Renaissance-style pulpit (1548) in the Oude Kerk

🔒 Oude Kerk
Heilige Geestkerkhof 25. 📞 *015-2123015.* 🕐 *Apr–Oct: 9am–6pm Mon–Sat; Nov–Mar: 11am–4pm Mon–Sat.* 🈲 ♿

The original 13th-century church on this site has been extended many times. The beautifully carved clock tower, with its eye-catching steeple, dates from the 14th century. The Gothic north transept was added at the beginning of the 16th century by architect Anthonis Keldermans from Brabant. Inside the church, the most striking feature is the wooden pulpit with canopy. The floor is studded with 17th-century gravestones, many of which are beautifully decorated, including those for Johannes Vermeer and admiral Piet Hein (1577–1629).

🔒 Nieuwe Kerk
Markt 80. 📞 *015-2123025.* 🕐 *Apr–Oct: 9am–6pm Mon–Sat; Nov–Mar: 11am–4pm Mon–Sat.* 🈲 ♿

The Nieuwe Kerk was built between 1383 and 1510 but needed large-scale restoration after the damaging fire of 1536 and again after the massive explosion of 1654 in the arsenal. In 1872, PJH Cuypers *(see p369)* added the 100-m (328-ft) tower to the Gothic façade. The most noticeable feature of the church's interior is William of Orange's imposing mausoleum, designed in 1614 by Hendrick de Keyser. In the middle stands a statue of William, impressive in his battledress. Not far from him is the lonely figure of his dog, which died a few days after his master. The tombs of the royal family lie in the crypt.

🏛 Stedelijk Museum Het Prinsenhof
St-Agathaplein 1. 📞 *015-2602358.* 🕐 *10am–5pm Tue–Sat, 1–5pm Sun & hols.* ⬤ *1 Jan, 25 Dec.* 🈲

This peaceful Gothic building, formerly a convent, was the scene of William of Orange's assassination. It now houses Delft's history museum, with displays of pottery, tapestries, and portraits of royalty. In 1572, during the uprising against the Spanish, William commandeered the convent for use as his headquarters. A fanatical Catholic, Balthasar Geraerts, shot and killed him in 1584 on the instructions of Philip II of Spain.

The Nieuwe Kerk overlooking Delft market

DELFTWARE

Delftware *(see pp26–7)* stems from majolica, introduced to the Netherlands in the 16th century by Italian immigrants who had settled around Delft and Haarlem and begun producing wall tiles with Dutch designs, such as birds and flowers. By the next century, however, Dutch traders had started to deal in delicate Chinese porcelain; this eventually led to the collapse of the market for the less refined Dutch earthenware. Towards 1650, though, the Chinese example was adopted in the Netherlands and craftsmen designed plates, vases and bowls with pictures of Dutch landscapes, biblical tableaux and scenes from everyday life. De Porceleyne Fles factory, which dates from 1652, is one of the several Delftware potteries open to the public for tours.

17th-century hand-painted Delft tiles

🏛 Legermuseum Delft

Korte Geer 1. 📞 *015-2150500.*
⏰ *10am–5pm, Mon–Fri, noon–5pm Sat & Sun.* ● *1 Jan, 25 Dec.* 🎫

The Legermuseum (army museum) is located in the *armamentarium*, the former arsenal for the old provinces of Western Friesland and Holland. The rather unattractive armoury was built in 1692 and still contains a large number of weapons, which are now exhibited alongside uniforms, scale models of battlefields and army vehicles. The exhibition shows the history of the Dutch army from the Middle Ages to the present day.

Coat of arms on the façade of the Legermuseum

Maassluis ❽

Road map B4. 🏙 *33,000.* 🚉
🚌 *Goudsteen 4 (010-75903354).*
🚆 *Tue, Fri.*

THE SETTLEMENT of Maassluis grew up around the locks, which date from 1367; the herring trade brought prosperity to the town. The historic town centre is adorned with 17th-century buildings, such as the **Grote Kerk**, with its famous organ *(see pp28–9)* and the **Stadhuis**, from 1650. The town's fine steam tug still goes out to sea. Many of Maarten 't Hart's novels are set in the Maassluis of his youth.

Schiedam ❾

Road map B4. 🏙 *75,000.*
🚉 🚌 *Buitenhavenweg 9 (010-4733000).* 🚆 *Fri.*

SCHIEDAM WAS granted its city charter in 1275 and soon after expanded into a centre for trade and fishing. It became the centre of the genever (Dutch gin) industry. The production of genever is still important to the town, as evidenced by the **five tallest windmills in the world** and the old warehouses and distilleries. In the bar of the **Gedistilleerd Museum De Gekroonde Brandersketel** (national distillery museum), you can familiarize yourself with the enormous range of Dutch genevers and liqueurs.

The **Stedelijk Museum** (municipal museum), with exhibits of contemporary art and on modern history, is in the former St-Jacobs Gasthuis. Its main attraction is the collection of artwork by the group known as COBRA (consisting of painters from COpenhagen, BRussels and Amsterdam).

🏛 Gedistilleerd Museum De Gekroonde Brandersketel

Lange Haven 74. 📞 *010-4261291.*
⏰ *11am–5pm Tue–Sat, from 12:30pm Sun.* ● *1 Jan, 25 Dec.* ♿

🏛 Stedelijk Museum

Hoogstraat 112. 📞 *010-2463666.*
⏰ *11am–5pm Tue–Sat, 12:30–5pm Sun & public hols.* ● *1 Jan, 25 Dec.* ♿

Genever and corn brandy, products of the Genever capital of Schiedam

Street-by-Street: Rotterdam ⓾

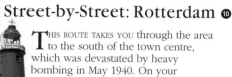

THIS ROUTE TAKES YOU through the area to the south of the town centre, which was devastated by heavy bombing in May 1940. On your way you will see the Witte Huis (white house), one of the few buildings spared by the bombs. Further on you will pass by some unusual modern architecture, such as the cube-shaped apartments, "Het Potlood" ("the pencil"), and the maritime museum, devoted to the history of shipping. In front of this museum is a monument by Ossip Zadkine, which is one of the symbols of Rotterdam. The undeveloped area around Station Blaak was completely built up before the bombing.

Museumhaven lighthouse

★ **Schielandhuis**, *Rotterdam's history museum, holds exhibitions of paintings and textiles and serves as a solemn reminder of World War II bombing.*

BLAAK

★ **De Verwoeste Stad**
The statue De Verwoeste Stad (The Devastated City) *by Ossip Zadkine, located in front of the maritime museum, commemorates the bombing of May 1940. It is considered one of the most famous statues in the country.*

De Buffel
The old armoured vessel De Buffel, *now open for visitors, was for many years a training ship.*

GLASHAVEN

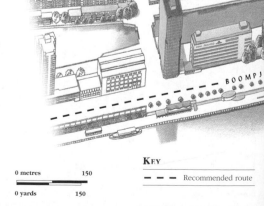

BOOMPJ

STAR SIGHTS

★ **De Verwoeste Stad by Ossip Zadkine**

★ **Kubus-Paalwoningen**

★ **Schielandhuis**

0 metres	150
0 yards	150

KEY

– – – Recommended route

Erasmusbrug (Erasmus Bridge)
The glittering Erasmusbrug is now one of the symbols of Rotterdam.

VISITORS' CHECKLIST

Road map B4. 🏠 598,500. 🚉
Stationsplein. 🚏 *Stationsplein.*
ℹ️ *Coolsingel 67 (0900-4034065).*
🗓️ *Sat.* 🎬 *Film festival: Jan;
Dunya festival: May; Metropolis
festival (pop concerts): Jul; Zomer-
carnaval: Jul; Wereldhavendagen:
Sep.* 🌐 *www.vvvrotterdam.nl*

Station Blaak is an unusual metro and railway station, designed by architect HCH Reijnders.

Het Potlood (the pencil), an unusually shaped apartment block near Station Blaak, was designed by P Blom.

★ Kubus-Paalwoningen
A bizarre creation (1978–84) by architect P Blom, the cube-shaped apartments are among the most striking buildings of modern Rotterdam.

VERLENGDE WILLEMSBRUG

Witte Huis (White House)
This is one of the few buildings to survive the World War II bombing raids. For a long time, the 45-m (148-ft) building was one of the tallest office blocks in Europe.

Willemswerf
Willemswerf is one of Rotterdam's highest and most impressive office blocks. The building, which is completely white, was completed in 1989 and is a design by architect WG Quist.

Exploring Rotterdam

ROTTERDAM IS NOT ONLY a symbol of post-war economic recovery – it has more to offer than endless stretches of thriving docklands and industrial areas. Rotterdam has increasingly become one of the most important cultural centres of the Netherlands. Although the city was a wasteland immediately after World War II, it quickly recovered and now boasts one of the country's largest universities, a park containing a number of interesting museums and a large zoo.

Bram Ladage sculpture

Gorilla and her young at Blijdorp

🏃 Blijdorp

Blijdorplaan 8. 🚋 3. 🚌 32, 33, 44. 📞 010-4431431. ◯ winter: 9am–5pm daily; summer & school hols: 9am–6pm daily. 🖼 🅿 ♿ 🍴 🌐 www.rotterdamzoo.nl

Rotterdam Zoo, often called *Diergaarde Blijdorp*, is in many ways a unique zoo. Its predecessor, De Rotterdamsche Diergaarde (Rotterdam zoo), was built in 1857 in the town centre. In 1937, the zoo was moved to Blijdorp polder, a location outside the centre. The architect Van Ravesteyn was commissioned to design the new zoo and Blijdorp became one of the first zoos in the world to be designed entirely by one single architect.

Blijdorp is also one of the few European zoos to have its own research department. This department plays an important part in the breeding programmes involving rare and endangered species, including the black-footed penguin.

For the last few years, attempts have been made to convert Blijdorp to the type of zoo which tries to present the animals in the most natural habitat possible. This means that animals from Asia can now be admired in imitation Asian surroundings. Another recent addition at the zoo is the gorilla island. The huge, extremely popular, Oceanium is a theme park showcasing a large variety of sea creatures, including sharks.

🏛 Delfshaven

Informatiecentrum Historisch Delfshaven, Voorhaven 3. 🚋 4.

Delfshaven, which is outside the town centre and is mainly famous for being the birthplace of national naval hero Piet Hein, looks very different from the rest of Rotterdam. This oasis of both history and culture within the modern, commercial city consists of a few streets with historic buildings and a little harbour with old sailing boats. The former warehouses are now shops selling antiques, paintings and antiquarian books. Alongside these are interesting museums,

Canalside houses in a peaceful corner of Delfshaven

an old-fashioned brewery and numerous restaurants. The 17th-century porters' house with a tin-smelting workshop is also worth a visit.

It was from Delfshaven that the Dutch Pilgrim Fathers left for America in 1620.

🌸 Euromast

Parkhaven 20. 🚋 8. Ⓜ Dijkzicht. 📞 010-4364811. ◯ Apr–Sep: 10am–7pm daily; Oct–Mar: 10am–5pm daily; Jul–Aug: until 10:30pm Tue–Sat. 🖼 🅿 🍴 🌸 🌐 www.euromast.nl

One of the most famous symbols of Rotterdam, Euromast is the tallest building in the town. Before its construction began, in 1960, the mayor at the time, Van Walsum, complained that there was only enough money to build a 50-m (165-ft) tower. This caused

The Rotterdam Beurstraverse, or "Koopgoot", a bustling shopping mall

Peter Struycken's masterpiece of light effects under the Nederlands Architectuur Instituut

an uproar, because the mast was meant to be higher than the Utrecht Domtoren (cathedral tower), which was, at 112 m (367 ft), the highest building in the country. That same evening, the mayor was called by rich Rotterdam port barons wanting to contribute money to the construction of the building. These donations in part enabled the tower to reach 110 m (361 ft). A space tower was later added to the top of the building for the Communicatie-'70 show in 1970, bringing the tower to a total height of 185 m (607 ft).

🏛 Kunsthal

Westzeedijk 341, Museumpark. 🚃 8.
🕻 010-4400301. ◯ 10am–5pm Tue–Sat, 11am–5pm Sun & public hols. ● 1 Jan, 30 Apr, 25 Dec.
🅿 🚻 🆆 www.kunsthal.nl
The Kunsthal, with its very austere style, is used as a hall for temporary exhibitions. The Kunsthal offers museums the opportunity to show those parts of their collections which would normally be in storage because of lack of exhibition space. This gives refreshing insight into the possessions of Dutch museums and means that the Kunsthal has a unique and respected position in the art-life of the country.

Designed by the avant-garde architects OMA, the building is considered to be revolutionary and has ramps instead of stairs.

🏛 Kinderkunsthal Villa Zebra

Museumpark 30.
🕻 010-2411717. 🚃 4, 5.
◯ call ahead for opening hours.
🅿 🚻 🆆 www.villazebra.nl
This is an arts centre specifically created for children. They can become familiar with the

The Euromast with space tower

art of other people and express themselves through poetry, theatre and the visual arts.

🏛 NAI

Museumpark 25. 🕻 010-4401200.
🚃 4. ◯ 10am–5pm Tue–Sat, 11am–5pm Sun & public hols.
● 1 Jan, Good Friday, Easter, 30 Apr, 25 & 26 Dec; also Sat Jul–Aug. 🅿 🚻 🆆 www.nai.nl
After being bombed in 1940 and then ravaged by fire, the old city centre was a wasteland. Because of large-scale rebuilding after the war, Rotterdam now has more modern architecture than any other town in the Netherlands. This includes famous structures such as the *paalwoningen* (cube-shaped apartments) and the tallest office block in the country, the Nationale Nederlanden. Outside the town centre are some examples of the pre-war *nieuwe bouwen* (new building), such as the Van-Nelle factory and Huis Sonneveld, now a museum. It is appropriate that Nederlands Architectuur Instituut (the Netherlands Architectural Institute), housing Holland's architectural archives, should be in Rotterdam, in a building that is itself an architectural phenomenon. Temporary exhibits are held at the institute.

Museum Boijmans Van Beuningen

THE MUSEUM IS NAMED AFTER two art experts, FJO Boijmans and DG van Beuningen, who presented their own private collections to the town. The museum thus ended up with one of the finest collections in the Netherlands. Originally housed in the Schielandhuis, the pictures were transferred to their present location in 1935. Although it is particularly renowned for its unique collection of old masters, the museum represents all aspects of Dutch art, from medieval works by Jan van Eyck to rare glasswork and modern art using laser techniques.

I am too sad to tell you *(1970) is a film by the Dutch artist Bas Jan Ader.*

★ **Surrealists**
The work of Salvador Dalí is well represented in the museum. He was commissioned by art collector Edward James to paint the triptych Landscape with Girl Jumping Rope.

Cloakroom/ticket desk

Library

Digitaal Depot
You can explore the museum's collection just by touching the interactive screen.

Courtyard

Art lab

Shop

Entrance

Lyrical *(1911) This is one of the most important works by the Russian avant-garde artist Wassily Kandinsky.*

STAR PAINTINGS

★ **Le Modèle Rouge**

★ **Surrealists**

★ **The Tower of Babel**

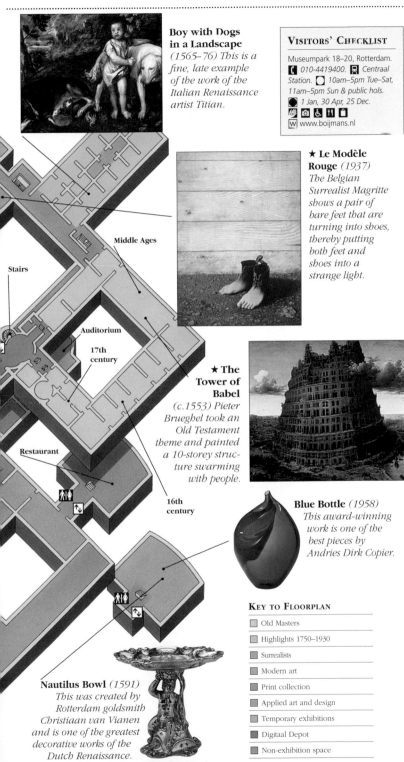

Boy with Dogs in a Landscape *(1565–76)* This is a fine, late example of the work of the Italian Renaissance artist Titian.

VISITORS' CHECKLIST

Museumpark 18–20, Rotterdam.
☎ 010-4419400. 🚉 Centraal Station. ◯ 10am–5pm Tue–Sat, 11am–5pm Sun & public hols. ● 1 Jan, 30 Apr, 25 Dec.
🚫 📷 ♿ 🏪 🎞 🛗
ⓦ www.boijmans.nl

★ Le Modèle Rouge *(1937)* The Belgian Surrealist Magritte shows a pair of bare feet that are turning into shoes, thereby putting both feet and shoes into a strange light.

Middle Ages

Stairs

Auditorium

17th century

Restaurant

★ The Tower of Babel *(c.1553)* Pieter Brueghel took an Old Testament theme and painted a 10-storey structure swarming with people.

16th century

Blue Bottle *(1958)* This award-winning work is one of the best pieces by Andries Dirk Copier.

Nautilus Bowl *(1591)* This was created by Rotterdam goldsmith Christiaan van Vianen and is one of the greatest decorative works of the Dutch Renaissance.

KEY TO FLOORPLAN

☐ Old Masters
☐ Highlights 1750–1930
☐ Surrealists
☐ Modern art
☐ Print collection
☐ Applied art and design
☐ Temporary exhibitions
☐ Digitaal Depot
☐ Non-exhibition space

Rotterdam, City of Water

ONE OF ROTTERDAM's biggest and busiest attractions is its port, one of the largest ports in the world. Various operators organize daily tours around the port area, where you will see container ports, shipyards and dry docks. The sheer scale of the port **Sailor** and related industrial areas, which have a turnover of billions of euros, is quite staggering. The world's largest container port, the Europoort alone stretches for 37 km (23 miles) along the river banks.

Rotterdam
The port sees approximately 30,000 vessels docking each year. Germany's Ruhr district is the main destination for the transported goods.

THE PORT OF ROTTERDAM

Rotterdam Port, of which only a fraction is shown by this map, stretches from the town centre to the North Sea coast and is divided into nine areas. These are, from east to west, the Stadhavens, the Vierhavens, Merwehaven, Waalhaven, Eemhaven, Vondelingenplat, Botlek, Europoort and the Maasvlakte. The port is still expanding and will soon run out of available space. Land reclamation from the North Sea is considered the most appropriate solution.

Pernis
The biggest refinery in the world, Pernis operates day and night refining crude oil, which is used to make hundreds of products. Lit up at night, it looks like something out of a science fiction story.

Old Delfshav

Dry docks

World Port Days
There are many types of ships to be admired on the World Port Days, which are held in early September and attract thousands of visitors.

Spido Tour
Various tours around the port of Rotterdam are available. Those lasting an hour and a half visit the town centre ports (see map below), whereas the day-long tours travel as far as the Maasvlakte.

Euromast

Maashaven

Zuiderpark

Maastunnel
filtration plant

Hotel New York
This hotel has been set up in the early 20th-century head office of the former Holland-America Line. The nearby arrival halls are also of architectural significance.

EUROPOORT

A total of 29,092 ocean-going vessels and 133,000 inland vessels put in at Rotterdam Port during 2002. This makes it the busiest port in the world. The name "Europoort" says it all – Rotterdam is Europe's port. Rotterdam Port is one of the major employers of the Netherlands, with more than 300,000 people working for it either directly or indirectly. Total added value of the port is more than 24.5 billion euros, approximately 10 per cent of the country's gross domestic product.

Bustling Rotterdam port, loading and unloading many millions of containers every year

0 kilometres   3

0 miles   3

KEY

━━ Road

━━ Railway

St Janskerk, Gouda

THIS FORMER CATHOLIC CHURCH dating from 1485 was rebuilt in the Gothic style after it was struck by fire in 1552. The church received a number of unusual stained-glass windows from rich Catholic benefactors, such as Philip II of Spain, between 1555 and 1571. After the Reformation *(see pp52–3)*, the church became Protestant, but even the fanatical Iconoclasts did not have the heart to destroy the windows. Prominent Protestants, including Rotterdam aldermen, donated stained-glass windows to the church up to 1604. The stained-glass windows are heavily symbolic of the politics of the time – Bible stories had to be covered after the conflict between the Catholics and Protestants, which led to the 30 Years War between Spain and the Netherlands.

Benefactor's coat of arms (1601)

The Nave
At 123 m (404 ft), this nave is the longest in Holland. The floor is inset with memorial stones.

The Adulteress *(1601)*
Dressed as a Franciscan monk, Jesus appeals to the people in the temple to forgive the adulteress, who is being guarded by Spanish soldiers.

Baptism of Jesus

North aisle

Visitors' entrance

The Purification of the Temple

South aisle

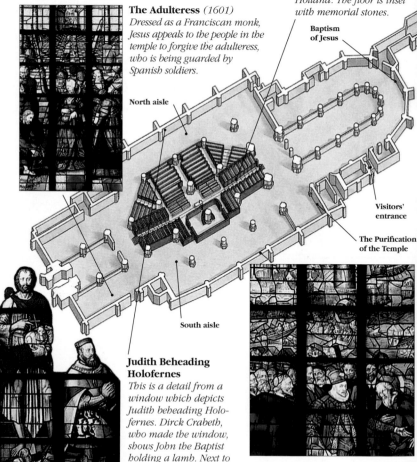

Judith Beheading Holofernes
This is a detail from a window which depicts Judith beheading Holofernes. Dirck Crabeth, who made the window, shows John the Baptist holding a lamb. Next to him kneels Jan de Ligne, the count of Arenberg, who commissioned the window.

The Relief of Leiden *(1603)*
William of Orange as leader of the resistance of the people of Leiden against the Spanish siege of 1574.

The Purification of the Temple
William of Orange donated this window, symbolizing the Netherlands' longing to drive out the Spaniards, in 1567. Traders watch angrily as Jesus drives moneylenders from the temple.

Baptism of Jesus *(1555)*
John the Baptist baptizes Jesus in the Jordan River. The window was a gift from the Bishop of Utrecht.

Nieuwpoort town hall, built over the canal in 1696

Gouda ⓫

Road map B4. 72,000.
Markt 27 (0900-4683288).
Cheese & crafts market mid Jun–end Aug: 10am–12:30pm Thu; general market Thu am & Sat.

IN 1272, FLORIS V granted Gouda its city charter. Thanks to its strategic position on the Hollandse IJssel and the Gouwe, the town developed into a flourishing centre for beer brewing and the textile industry in the 15th century. However, Gouda became economically and politically isolated during the 30 Years War. The town recovered in the 17th and beginning of the 18th century due to its trade in cheese, candles and pipes.

Gouda is still famous today for its **cheese** and **cheese markets**. The markets are held on an enormous three-sided square around the **Stadhuis**, which dates from 1450 and is one of the oldest in the Netherlands. With its many pinnacles and turrets, the building gives the impression of being in the Flemish Gothic style.

The **Stedelijk Museum** (municipal museum) is in the former **Catharina Gasthuis** (St Catherine's hospital), which dates from the 14th century and later. The museum features paintings from the Hague School and unusual 16th-century altar pieces.

Stadhuis

Markt 1. 0182-588758. 10am–noon & 2–6pm Mon–Fri, 11am–3pm Sat. public hols. by appt.

Stedelijk Museum Catharina Gasthuis

Oosthaven 9–10. 0182-588441.
10am/noon–5pm daily.
1 Jan, 25 Dec. over 18s.

Reeuwijkse Plassen ⓬

Road map B4. VVV by Gouda.

THE REEUWIJK LAKE district was formed through peat excavation. Narrow roads pass through the rectangular lakes, which owe their shape to former parcels of land. The small village of **Sluipwijk** seems almost to fade away into the water. The best way to explore this area is by bicycle or on foot. In the summer months you can also take a boat trip through this typically Dutch lakeland scenery.

Nieuwpoort ⓭

Road map C4. 1,600. from the Rabobank at the Binnenhaven. 154 from Utrecht or Rotterdam.

THE WHOLE OF this magnificent fortified town, which obtained its city charter in 1283, has been declared a listed area. The 17th-century street layout is practically intact. The city walls, which are also intact, were originally built to ward off attacks from the French but served mainly to protect the town against flooding. The town hall, built over the inundation lock, dates from 1696, while the arsenal dates from 1781.

Gorinchem ⓮

Road map C4. 🏠 *35,000.* 🚉
ℹ️ *Grote Markt 17 (0183-631525).*
📧 *Mon.*

GORINCHEM, situated on the Linge and the Waal, was the property of the Lords van Arkel in the 13th century. They were driven out by Count William VI and the town was then absorbed into Holland. Fortifications built at the end of the 16th century are still partially intact and offer marvellous views over the water meadows and the Waal. Of the four town gateways, only the **Dalempoort** remains. The Linge harbour, in the heart of the town, is still mostly authentic, especially the narrow part. The impressive **St-Janstoren** (early 16th century) sank and started to lean while being built and so has a kink in it.

ENVIRONS: On the other side of the Waal is the 14th-century **Slot Loevestein**. It has a very eventful history as a toll castle, a defence point along the Hollandse Waterlinie (a strip of land flooded as a defence line) and a state prison in the 17th century. A ferry for foot passengers runs between Gorinchem and the castle between May and September.

🏰 **Slot Loevestein**
🔔 *0183-447171.* ⏰ *call ahead for opening hours.* 🎫 🅿️ ♿

Glass blower in Leerdam

Leerdam ⓯

Road map C4. 🏠 *20,000.* 🚉
ℹ️ *Kerkstraat 18 (0345-613057).*
📧 *Tue am.*

LEERDAM IS RENOWNED for its glass industry. The Royal Dutch Glass Factory became world famous for its glass designs by Berlage, Copier and other artists. These can be admired in the **Nationaal Glasmuseum** (national glass museum). Traditional crystal production can be observed at Royal Leerdam Kristal. **Fort Asperen**, on the Linge, is one of the best-preserved defence points remaining along the Nieuwe Hollandse Waterlinie.

🏛 **Nationaal Glasmuseum**
Lingedijk 28. 🔔 *0345-612714.*
⏰ *10am–5pm Tue–Fri, 1–5pm Sat & Sun.* ⚫ *public hols.* 🎫

Dordrecht ⓰

Road map B4. 🏠 *120,000.* 🚉
ℹ️ *Stationsweg 1 (0900-4636888).*
📧 *Fri am & Sat.*

THE OLDEST TOWN in Holland, Dordrecht received its city charter in 1220 and was the most important harbour and commercial town of the region until the 1500s. Even after being outstripped by Rotterdam, Dordrecht remained an important inland port. In the old port area, mansions, warehouses and almshouses are reminders of the past. The **Grote Kerk** (13th to 17th century), in the Brabant Gothic style, has an ornate interior with attractive choir stalls. **Museum Simon van Gijn**, in the period rooms of an 18th-century mansion house, has a varied collection of old prints, clothes and toys. There is a great view over the Oude Maas and the Merwede from the **Groothoofdspoort** (main gate), dating from 1325. The shady Hof (court of justice) (1512) contains the **Statenzaal** (state room), where the States of Holland met.

🏰 **Grote Kerk**
Lange Geldersekade 2. 🔔 *078-614 4660.* ⏰ *Apr–Oct: 10:30am–4:30pm Tue–Sat, noon–4pm Sun.* 🎫 *2:15pm Thu & Sat.*
🏰 **Statenzaal**
Hof 12. 🔔 *078-6134626.* ⏰ *Apr–Oct: 1–5pm Tue–Sat.*

A group of windmills at Kinderdijk, for centuries draining water from the Alblasserwaard

Kinderdijk ⓱

Road map B4. 🚌 *154 from Rotterdam Zuidplein.* 🚉

THE FAMOUS **19 windmills** which were used to drain the Alblasserwaard in the past are situated where the Noord and the Lek converge. New *boezems* (drainage pools) and windmills, however, were needed time and time again in order to span the height differences as the land settled. The group of windmills has been declared a UNESCO World Heritage Site.

Middelharnis Lane (c.1689) by Meindert Hobbema

Brielle ⓲

Road map B4. 👥 *16,000.* 🚌 *103.* 🛈 *Markt 1 (0181-475475).* 🔄 *Mon.*

THE MAGNIFICENT PORT and fortified town of Brielle is a protected town. The 18th-century fortifications are still mostly intact. The town, birthplace of Admiral van Tromp, held a strategic position until the 1872 opening of the *Nieuwe Waterweg* (new waterway). The **Historisch Museum Den Briel** (historic museum of Brielle) depicts this and the famous Beggars of the Sea invasion in 1572 *(see box).* The imposing 15th-century **St.-Catharijnekerk**, in Brabant Gothic style, rises from the middle of surrounding monuments.

🏛 **Historisch Museum Den Briel**
Markt 1. 📞 *0181-475477.* ⏰ *call ahead for opening hours.* ● *Mon, public hols, Nov–Mar: Sun.* 📷 ♿

Hellevoetsluis ⓳

Road map B4. 👥 *37,000.* 🚌 *metro Rotterdam CS to Spijkenisse, then 102, 104.* 🛈 *Oostzanddijk 26 (0181-312318).* 🔄 *Sat.*

AT THE END OF the 16th century, this was the naval port for the States of Holland. Fleets led by van Tromp, de Ruyter and Piet Hein left from Hellevoetsluis for their naval battles in the 1600s. Within the old fortifications, visitors are reminded of the town's naval

past by the **Prinsehuis**, the 17th-century lodgings of the Admiralty of the Maze, the dry dock and **Fort Haerlem** from the 19th century.

You can learn all about fire and fire-fighting in the local **National Brandweermuseum** (fire service museum).

🏛 **National Brandweermuseum**
Industriehaven 8. 📞 *0181-314479.* ⏰ *Apr–Oct: 10am–4pm Mon–Sat, 11am–4pm Sun.* ♿ 🅿

Middelharnis ⓴

Road map B4. 👥 *10,000.* 🚌 *136 from Rotterdam Zuidplein.* 🛈 *Vingeeling 3 (0187-484870).* 🔄 *Wed.*

DURING THE 16TH century, Middelharnis became the regional port, outstripping Goedereede. Until the end of

the 19th century, fishing remained the most important source of income.

The Late Gothic cruciform church (15th century) stands at the heart of the village. Outside the town hall (1639) hang the wooden blocks that women branded as gossips had to carry through the town.

Goedereede ㉑

Road map A4. 👥 *1,900.* 🚌 *metro R'dam CS to Spijkenisse, then 104.* 🛈 *Bosweg 2, Ouddorp (0187-681789).* 🔄 *Thu.*

GOEDEREEDE WAS an important port in the 14th and 15th centuries. This town, where Pope Adrianus VI was born, began to decline when it began to silt up. The early harbour houses are reminiscent of the livelier days of old.

THE BEGGARS OF THE SEA

The Beggars of the Sea were a pirate fleet which consisted of minor Dutch and Flemish nobles who had fled at the beginning of the Inquisition and sailed across the North Sea. They plundered other ships and caused trouble in English and German ports. They were forced to leave England, where some of their ships were berthed, in spring 1572. Without any clear plan, they entered Den Briel on 1 April under the command of van Lumey, which they then held "for the Prince". Other towns joined the Beggars of the Sea or were forcibly occupied by them. Their pursuits represented the first steps towards Dutch independence from Spain and the creation of Dutch sea power.

Van Lumey

ZEELAND

THE TINY PROVINCE OF ZEELAND, *as its name implies, is inextricably linked with water and the sea. From earliest times, the power of the North Sea and the flooding deltas of the Maas and Schelde rivers have shaped the landscape, encouraging resilience in the inhabitants and the desire to control the elements.*

From earliest times, storms and floods have taken their toll here. In the last century, the devastation of two world wars was followed by the disastrous floods and storm surges of 1953. Although there are a number of fine churches and public buildings dating as far back as the 14th century, in places near the coast there are very few houses more than 50 years old. As a result, determination to keep the waters at bay has spawned massive construction and canal building, with giant dams and land reclamation schemes offering a level of security that has changed the landscape forever.

The storms were not all bad news. Traces of Roman settlements were uncovered, and lakes and inland waterways have become a haven for wildlife and a playground for lovers of watersports. Towns such as Middelburg, Zierikzee and Veere and villages such as Nisse, St Anna-ter-Muiden and Dreischor have lots of old buildings, some of which have been restored to their 17th-century grandeur, with attractive features such as bell towers and frescoes.

The close relationship with water and the sea is well documented in a variety of small museums. The tangible benefits are perhaps twofold: an abundance of seafood for the province's restaurants, and marvellous opportunities for watersports. Few regions in Europe offer as much scope for sailing, windsurfing, water skiing and diving as does little Zeeland.

The 15th-century Stadhuis (town hall) dominating the historic town of Veere

◁ **Groynes covered with cockles, a characteristic feature of the beaches along the Zeeland coast**

Exploring Zeeland

Memorial plaque

Touring around Zeeland, one cannot ignore the sea. The journey becomes a small adventure as you encounter bridges, dams and ferry docks. Sometimes you will travel along a straight ribbon of a road, sometimes a windy lane. The ever-present and often turbulent water is never the same colour for long: it can quickly change from a grey green reflecting the vivid blue sky to the white of wave crests beneath leaden skies. Passing over one of the many dams, you will reach the next island, with its own special character. Tholen, for example, is quiet – almost morose and withdrawn – whereas Walcheren is full of surprises and has a wonderful atmosphere. Travelling through Zeeland is a real journey of discovery.

GETTING AROUND

The best way to visit all the islands of Zeeland is by car. The roads here are excellent – the A58, A29 or the N57 will quickly bring you to the centre of the province, where you can choose one of the smaller roads to take you to your destination. The through train will take you from Amsterdam to Middelburg and Vlissingen in just two and a half hours. If you want to explore other islands, you will need to continue on a regional bus – though this can be quite time-consuming. There are many cycle paths and it is great fun cycling over the dykes.

SIGHTS AT A GLANCE

Tilting at the ring – a Zeeland sport

KEY

▬	Motorway
▬	Main road
▬	Minor road
▬	Scenic route
—	Foot/cycle ferry
—	Canal/river
∷	Tunnel

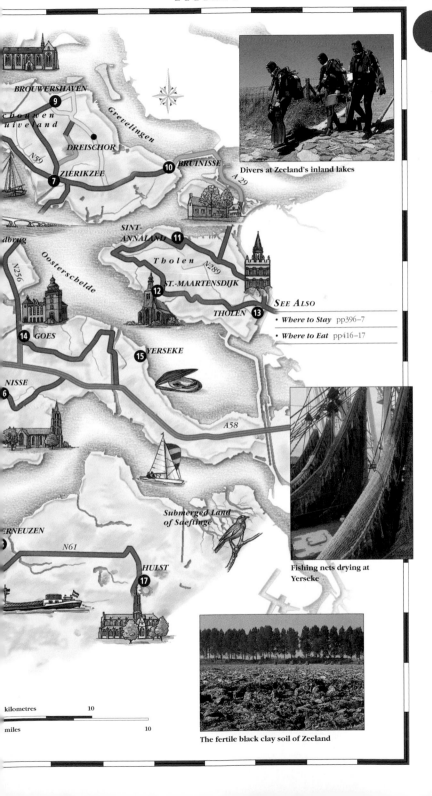

BROUWERSHAVEN 9

Schouwen Duiveland

N59

DREISCHOR

ZIERIKZEE 7

Grevelingen

10 **BRUINISSE**

A 29

Divers at Zeeland's inland lakes

dbrug

SINT-ANNALAND 11

Oosterschelde

Tholen

N256

N289

ST.-MAARTENSDIJK

12

THOLEN 13

SEE ALSO

• *Where to Stay* pp396–7

• *Where to Eat* pp416–17

14 **GOES**

15 **YERSEKE**

NISSE

6

A58

Submerged Land of Saeftinge

Fishing nets drying at Yerseke

RNEUZEN

N61

HULST

17

kilometres   10

miles   10

The fertile black clay soil of Zeeland

Oosterscheldekering ❶

THROUGHOUT THE CENTURIES, the history of the Netherlands has been dominated by its people's struggle against the sea. After the disastrous floods of 1953, which hit Zeeland heavily, the battle to remove the danger of the sea once and for all was undertaken in earnest. Now the Dutch seem to have minimized the threat of flooding by building dykes and dams and closing off tidal inlets, all of which has had a major impact on the landscape.

The Windsock
When the windsock is full, a warning is sounded, and people are advised to avoid driving over the dams and bridges between the islands. Vigilance saves lives.

A road has been built over the da

Storms
Storms are a part of every-day life in Zeeland: storms on the beach or over the flat polders, storms which blow the cobwebs away and storms which make you fear for your life.

The sliding gates
are closed only when the water is high.

Concrete piers bear the sea wall.

The Fateful Night of 1953
On the night of 31 January 1953, an event considered impossible in modern times occurred. A combination of spring tides and storms breached the dykes and washed them away as loose sand. A total of 1,835 people lost their lives.

WATERLAND NEELTJE JANS

The Neeltje Jans theme park has been built on an artificial island of the Oosterscheldekering, the Oosterschelde storm surge barrier. The piers were assembled here and then taken by special barges to their destination. Now that particular task is finished, the island is being used mainly for recreational and informative purposes. Here you can find out everything about the Delta Works and about the functions of the Oosterscheldekering in particular. You can see the dam from the "inside" and then take a boat trip to see it from the "outside". There is a dolphin enclosure here as well. You can also experience a simulated hurricane.

Neeltje Jans, educating about the sea

Luctor et Emergo
This Latin motto meaning "I struggle and emerge victorious" is on Zeeland's coat of arms, which depicts the Netherlands lion half in the water. This was wholly appropriate for 1953.

Concrete Piers
The piers were made on the artificial island of Neeltje Jans and then transported by special barges to their destination. This mighty task attracted a great deal of attention.

VISITORS' CHECKLIST

Road map A4–5. Dijkgraaf Gelukweg, Burgh-Haamstede. 0111-652702. 104. Apr–Oct: 10am–5:30pm daily; Nov–Mar: 10am–5pm Wed–Sun. 1 Jan, 25 Dec.

The Delta Works
The Delta Works have had far-reaching consequences for the landscape and environment. The Zeeland islands, having been joined to the mainland, are no longer isolated.

HALF-OPEN BUTTRESS DAM

It took 13 years and 3.6 billion euros (two-thirds of the cost of the Delta Works) to build the Oosterschelde-kering. After much deliberation, the decision was made to keep open the estuary and to preserve the salty estuary habitat. A half-open multiple buttress dam was built, with 62 sliding gates, which are closed on average once a year during heavy storms. This keeps the water salty and has preserved the unique salt marshes and mud flats of the Oosterschelde.

Ground protection prevents the earth from being washed away.

The Terps
Man-made mounds, such as these near Borssele, were built in the 11th and 12th centuries to protect farms and villages from the water.

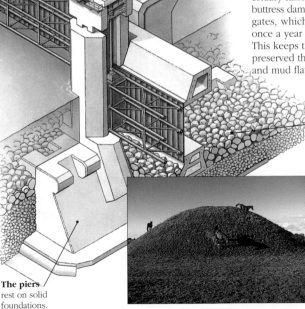

The piers rest on solid foundations.

Street-by-Street: Middelburg

Detail from Middelburg's Stadhuis

MIDDELBURG SUFFERED HEAVY German bombing in 1940. A lot of what is to be seen in the town today has been rebuilt, including the Stadhuis (town hall) and the abbey. The town is still redolent with the atmosphere of the Golden Age, an era during which the Dutch East India Company thrived in the port area along the quay. Middelburg is a pretty town and there is plenty to be seen on a walk around the centre. Children will be kept busy by Miniatuur-Walcheren.

★ St-Jorisdoelen
This doelen, *the guardsmen's guild building, was built in 1582 and destroyed in 1940; the façade was rebuilt in 1969.*

Zeeuws Archief, the archives of the province, are now housed in a historic monument, the van de Perre House on the Hofplen, which has been given a spectacular new wing.

KEY

– – – Recommended route

★ Stadhuis
The 15th-century town hall was completely destroyed by fire in 1940 and has been partially rebuilt. A 20th-century extension can be seen on the northern side.

| 0 metres | | 50 |
| 0 yards | | 50 |

STAR SIGHTS

★ Abbey

★ St-Jorisdoelen

★ Stadhuis

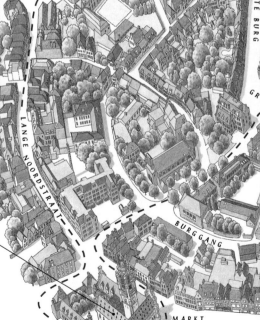

The fish market
already existed in 1559. The passageway, with its Tuscan pillars, dates from 1830.

Miniatuur-Walcheren
This miniature town started in 1954 now contains more than 350 buildings.

VISITORS' CHECKLIST

Road map A5. ⓘ Nieuwe Burg 40. 📞 0118–659900. 🚶 38,200. 🚌 🚂 🚢 Thu. **Stadhuis** Markt. 📷 Apr–Oct: Mon–Fri **Abbey** (see p248). **Miniatuur-Walcheren** Koepoortlaan 1. 📞 0118-612525. ◯ Apr–Jun, Sep–Oct: 10am–6pm daily; Jul & Aug: 9:30am–7pm. ♿ ♿

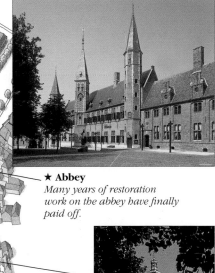

★ Abbey
Many years of restoration work on the abbey have finally paid off.

Lange Jan
The 91-m (300-ft) tower called the tall Jan belongs to the Nieuwe Kerk in the abbey complex. It has an octagonal plan and dates from the 14th century.

London Quay
The names of the quays reflect the goods that were being exported from and imported to the Netherlands during the Golden Age (see pp50–51).

Zeeuws Abbey Museum

Bronze armband from 50 BC

MIDDELBURG ABBEY dates back to 1100, when it was inhabited by Norbertine monks from the monastery of St Michiel of Antwerp. These very powerful monks were driven away in 1574 by William of Orange, after which the abbey was secularized. In the abbey's *Historama* you can discover everything about the eventful past of this group of buildings, whose journey through the centuries has not been easy. The Zeeland museum, situated in the wing of the building that was once the monks' quarters, exhibits a much more ancient past.

VISITORS' CHECKLIST

Zeeuws Abbey Museum. **Road map** A5. 0118-653000. 10am–5pm Mon–Sat, noon–5pm Sun. Historama Abdij Middelburg, Abdij 9. 0118-626655. **Historama**: Apr–Oct; **Abbey**: limited opening times; **Museum**: closed until 2005. W www.zeeuwsmuseum.nl

Folklore room/regional costumes

Changing exhibition

18th-century period room

17th-century period room

Tapestry room

Film about Zeeland tapestries

Royal quarters

Zeeland around 1900

Changing exhibition

Film room

Gallery

Changing exhibition

Rarities

Entrance

The Romans in Zeeland

MUSEUM GUIDE

The Zeeland Museum is accommodated in one of the oldest wings of the abbey. It is a provincial museum with various different sections, the most important being devoted to the altars to the Roman goddess Nehalennia, first exposed by storms in 1647 at Domburg. The museum also exhibits rarities, traditional costume and art.

Archaeology

Shop

Altar of Nehalennia
The altars found near Domburg in the 17th century were consecrated to the indigenous goddess Nehalennia, who was worshipped by the Romans.

Traditional Costume
The folklore room of the Zeeland Museum pays tribute to costumes from the recent past, which until not too long ago were a frequent sight on the streets of the region.

Veere ❸

Road map A5. 👥 *1,500.* 🚌 ℹ️
Oudestraat 28 (0900-2020280).

PAST AND PRESENT merge in Veere. Modern pleasure boats moor along the quay opposite the Gothic façades of **Het Lammetje** (the lamb) (1539) and **De Struijs** (the ostrich) (1561). These **Schotse Huizen** (Scottish houses) serve as a reminder of the time that the port was important for its trade in precious Scottish wool. Other monuments to Veere's illustrious past are the **stadhuis** (1474), the **Campveerse Toren**, a tower dating to around 1500, and the **OL-Vrouwekerk** (Church of Our Lady), dating from the 15th–16th centuries. This enormous church, once almost demolished, is now used as a venue for contemporary music concerts.

Domburg ❹

Road map A5. 👥 *1,600.* 🚌 ℹ️
Schuitvlotstraat 32 (0900-2020280).

DOMBURG WAS one of the first seaside resorts in the Netherlands. In the 19th century, this little town on Walcheren was popular among prominent Europeans, who came here to relax and recuperate in the chic seaside hotels in the dunes. It has now given way to mass tourism.

ENVIRONS: An inland lake lies hidden between dunes, woods and the Oostkapelle polder. The pretty nature reserve **De Manteling** is worth visiting, as is **Westhove** castle, which was the Abbot of Middelburg's country house until the 16th century. **Zeeuws Biologisch Museum** (Zeeland biology museum) is now situated in the former orangery.

🏛 **Zeeuws Biologisch Museum**
Duinvlietweg 6. 📞 *0118-582620.*
🕐 *May–Oct: noon–5pm daily; Nov–Apr: noon–5pm Wed–Sun.*

Pleasure boats moored at the marina in Vlissingen

Vlissingen ❺

Road map A5. 👥 *43,200.* 🚌 🚉
ℹ️ *Oude Markt 3 (0118-422190).*
🛒 *Fri.*

VLISSINGEN IS a bustling town. The main thrust behind the economy of this, the largest town in Zeeland, are the ports in Vlissingen itself, as well as those of the industrial area Vlissingen-Oost and the famous **scheepswerf De Schelde** (De Schelde shipyard). Vlissingen has always been of great military significance. The wartime activity this attracted meant that the town could not escape the consequences. One of the few remaining buildings from the time of Michiel de Ruyter to have withstood the ravages of time is the **Arsenaal**, dating from 1649. A second arsenal dating from 1823 is now the **Maritiem Attractie-centrum Het Arsenaal** *(see*

Michiel de Ruyter

The chic Badhôtel in Domburg

p446), which is especially interesting for children. The reptiles and insects showcased at **Reptielenzoo Iguana**, which is housed in two adjoining 18th-century mansions, offer a completely different type of attraction.

🏛 **Maritiem Attractie-centrum Het Arsenaal**
Arsenaalplein 1. 📞 *0118-415400.*
🕐 *Jul & Aug: 10am–8pm daily; Sep–Jun: 10am–7pm daily.*
🚫 *Jan, 25 Dec., 31 Dec.* ♿
🏛 **Reptielenzoo Iguana**
Bellamypark 35. 📞 *0118-417219.*
🕐 *2–5:30pm daily; Jun–Sep: 10am–12:30pm & 2–5:30pm Tue–Sun.* 🚫 *1 Jan, 25 Dec.*

Westkapelle ❻

Road map A5. 👥 *2,800.* 🚌 ℹ️
Zuidstraat 134 (0900-2020280). 🛒 *Fri.*

THE MOST IMPRESSIVE SIGHT in Westkapelle is its sea wall, the history of which is fascinating. In former times, this town lay securely behind the dunes, but these were washed away in the 15th century. This meant that the access route to the island shifted. A dyke was built, which was completed in 1458. The lighthouse also dates from this time; it was once a church tower, until the demolition of the church in 1831. In 1944, the dyke was bombed by the Allies in order to flood Walcheren so it could be liberated. In 1987 the dyke was built to the height of the delta.

The medieval Zuidhavenpoort in Zierikzee

Zierikzee ⑦

Road map A4. 🏛 *9,900.* 🚌 🚇
Meelstraat 4 (0111-450524). 🚢 *Thu.*

WITH 558 LISTED HOUSES, Zierikzee ranks eighth in the list of Dutch historic towns. The impressive city gateways – Nobelpoort, Noordhavenpoort and Zuidhavenpoort – can be seen from afar. The many terraces on the Havenplein offer a marvellous view of the two harbour entrances and ornate mansion houses on Oude Haven (old harbour), and the trickle of the **Gouwe**, the creek that brought trading prosperity to Zierikzee. The Gothic **Gravensteen** (1524–6), once the residence of the Count of Holland and his bailiffs, is now the **Maritiem Museum** (maritime museum).

The Zierikzee skyline shows the still unfinished **Dikke Toren** (great tower), construction of which began in 1454. At 130 m (425 ft), it must have been the highest point of the colossal 12th-century **St-Lievenskerk**, which burnt to the ground in 1832.

By strolling through the narrow streets along the new and old harbours, such as the Meelstraat or the Poststraat, you will chance upon passageways that offer glimpses of old façades, such as of the 14th-century De Haene house, or the former Stadhuis (1550–54), now the **Stadhuismuseum**.

One of the most famous historic events in Holland,

the revolt of Zierikzee in 1472 against Charles the Stout, is re-enacted each summer with a historical pageant.

🏛 **Maritiem Museum**
Mol 25. 📞 *0111-454493.*
🕐 *1 Apr–31 Oct: 10am–5pm.* 📷
🏛 **Stadhuismuseum**
Meelstraat 6. 📞 *0111-454409.* 🕐
May–Oct: 10am–5pm Mon–Sat. 📷

ENVIRONS: A new museum in Ouwerkerk is devoted to the devastating floods of February 1953.
🏛 **Museum Watersnood 1953**
Weg van de buitenlandse pers 5.
📞 *0111-644382.* 🕐 *Apr–Oct: 1–5pm Tue–Sun.* 📷

Haamstede ⑧

Road map A4. 🏛 *3,800.* 🚌 🚇
Noordstraat 45a (0111-651513). 🚢 *Thu.*

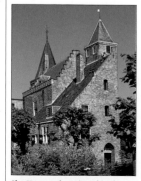

Slot Haamstede, painstakingly restored in the 1960s

HAAMSTEDE IS a peaceful town built around a church. The nearby **Slot Haamstede**, a castle dating from the 13th century, is surrounded by a park with pleasant walks.

♣ **Slot Haamstede**
Haamstede, near church. 🕐 *mid Jun–Sep: Wed aft; Jul & Aug: also Tue eve.*

ENVIRONS: Westerschouwen, 5 km (3 miles) southwest of Haamstede, has an impressive landscape and illustrious past. The dunes lie on the western edge, sometimes barren with a scattering of marram grass and gorse, sometimes covered with coniferous forest.

You can climb to the top of **Plompetoren**, the tower of the now-submerged Koudekerke, which rises from the salt marshes. On the edge of the dunes is **Slot Moermond**.

🏛 **Plompetoren**
Corner of Plompetorenweg & Koudekerkseweg.
🕐 *10am–4:30pm Tue–Sun.*

Isolated Plompetoren of the now-submerged Koudekerke

Brouwershaven ⑨

Road map A4. 🏛 *1,400.* 🚌
🚇 *see Zierikzee.* 🚢 *Mon.*

QUIET BROUWERSHAVEN combines a historic centre with a modern port. The Havenkanaal to the marina and the Stadhuis date from 1599. The 14th-century **St-Nicolaaskerk** (Church of St Nicholas) is a monument to past glory. The town prospered a second time acting as an outport to Rotterdam until the Nieuwer Waterweg (new waterway) was built in 1870.

🏛 **Brouws Museum**
Haven Zuidzijde 14–15. 📞 *0111-691342.* 🕐 *11am–5pm Tue–Sun.*

Brouwershaven, now a focus for water recreation

Bruinisse ⑩

Road map B4. 🏛 *3,000.* 🚌
ℹ️ *see Zierikzee.* 🛒 *Wed.*

Bruinisse is now mainly a centre for watersports. The modern bungalow park **Aqua Delta** is situated outside the old village directly next to the marina.

Environs: To get an idea of what the surrounding countryside looked like in earlier times, visit the *ringdorp* (circle-shaped village) **Dreischor**, 10 km (6 miles) west of Bruinisse. It has a typical village church and town hall. On the edge of the village is **Goemanszorg**, an agricultural museum devoted to farming past and present.

🏛 Goemanszorg
Molenweg 3, Dreischor.
📞 *0111-402303.* ⭕ *Easter–Oct: 10am–5pm Tue–Sat, noon–5pm Sun; Jul & Aug: also 10am–5pm Mon.* 🖼 ♿

St.Annaland ⑪

Road map B5. 🏛 *3,000.* 🚌 ℹ️
see St Maartensdijk.

Tholen is the least well-known island of Zeeland. Here there is a constantly changing scenery of poplars and pollard willows, fields and quiet towns, such as St Annaland, with its picturesque harbour on the Krabbenkreek. **Streekmuseum De Meestoof** (regional madder museum) is

an interesting reminder of Zeeland's industrial past. The cultivation of the madder plant and processing of its root into a red dye was, until the 19th century, one of the main livelihoods of the region. It was brought to an end in 1868 by the invention of artificial dyes.

🏛 Streekmuseum De Meestoof
Bierensstraat 6–8. 📞 *06-22826192.* ⭕ *Apr–Oct: 2–5pm Tue–Sat.* 🖼

St Maartensdijk ⑫

Road map B5. 🏛 *3,300.* 🚌
ℹ️ *Haven 10 (0900-681666).*

St Maartensdijk has been the "capital" of Tholen since 1971. This town has much to remind us of its patrons, the powerful Lords van Borssele. The remains of the tomb of Floris van Borssele (who died in 1422) and his wife are still to be seen in a burial chapel of the slender 14th- to 15th-century church. Much of the original carving and fragments of the old painting have been preserved. The foundations and moat of the van Borssele castle, which was demolished in 1820, can still be found outside the town.

The most impressive part of the town itself is the Markt, with its 16th-century houses and elegant Stadhuis.

Tholen ⑬

Road map B5. 🏛 *6,100.* 🚌
ℹ️ *see St Maartensdijk.*

Tholen is a Zeeland town with a Brabant flavour. Two buildings dominate the town – the marvellous Stadhuis (1452) with its robust battlements and the ornate **OL-Vrouwekerk** (Church of Our Lady), dating from the 14th to 16th centuries. The **kapel van het St-Laurensgasthuis** (St Laurensgasthuis chapel), which has been rebuilt into a residential home, stands opposite the church. Even though Tholen became a fortified town in the 16th century, it has retained its old character. Gothic façades are everywhere to remind us of its former prosperity.

Pumping station in a rural setting in the neighbourhood of Tholen

Goes 🔟

Road map A5. 👥 *24,000.* 🚌 🚉
ℹ️ *Stationsplein 3 (0900-1681666).*
🛍️ *Fri.*

SOME OF THE historical towns of Zeeland are charming but sleepy, but Goes is wide-awake. Every Friday there is an old-fashioned market featuring fabrics and groceries which takes place on a square full of Brabant atmosphere, the Grote Markt. The Raadhuis (town hall), dating from 1463 (rebuilt between 1771 and 1775), stands at the front of the square, representing the magistrates' power with all its bulk and loftiness. The rococo interior with its grisailles and stucco ceiling is particularly attractive. The majestic St-Maria-Magdalenakerk (Church of Mary Magdalen) (15th to 16th century) rises up behind the town hall. The cruciform basilica has been restored.

Yerseke 🔟

Road map A5. 👥 *6,100.* 🚌 🚉
ℹ️ *Kerkplein 1 (0900-1681666).*
🛍️ *Fri.*

AS THEY SAY in Zuid-Beveland, *"De een zijn dood de ander zijn brood"* ("One man's meat is another man's poison"). Yerseke came to be situated on the Oosterschelde following the St-Felixstormvloed

Imposing heraldic ornament on Goes Raadhuis

(St Felix storm flood) of 1530. So began a tradition of oyster farming and mussel fishing that has continued until the present day.

The nature reserve Yerseke Moer to the west of the village shows how the island used to look: a desolate patchwork of inlets, hamlets, rough pasture

A fishing boat in Yerseke bringing home the catch

lands, coves, castles, peat moors and water holes. To the east of Yerseke lies the submerged land of Zuid-Beveland, lost in 1530 along with Reimerswaal, at the time the third largest Zeeland town.

Nisse 🔟

Road map A5. 👥 *580.* 🚌
ℹ️ *see Goes.*

NISSE IS A TYPICAL Beveland village with square, ford and church. The church is worth a visit; though it does not look like much from the outside, inside you will be surprised by unique, 15th-century frescoes depicting the saints, scenes from the life of Mary and the coats of arms of the Lords van Borssele. Carvings on the choir vault and stalls are also from the 15th century.

🏛️ Hervormde kerk
Key available from church secretary, Dorpsplein 36 (0113-649399).

ENVIRONS: The **Zak van Zuid-Beveland**, south of the railway line to Middelburg, is characteristic for its balance between nature and culture. The landscape is a succession of polders, divided by luxuriant dykes covered with flowers or flocks of sheep grazing.

Hulst 🔟

Road map B5. 👥 *9,900.* 🚌 ℹ️ *Grote Markt 19 (0114-389299).* 🛍️ *Mon.*

CROSS OVER the Westerschelde and you are at the same time in Flanders and in the Netherlands. **St-Willibrordus-basiliek** (St Willibrordus basilica) towers above the town

---

OYSTER FARMING

Oysters apparently have all sorts of beneficial side effects, improved virility being the most well known. Whether this is true or not, this slippery delicacy makes any meal seem festive. Oyster farming began in 1870 when suitable parts of the river bed were no longer available for free fishing and were transferred to private use. Oyster farming flourished along the Oosterschelde, particularly in Yerseke, but the oysters were vulnerable to disease and harsh winters. Concern

Oysters, a tasty delicacy

that oyster farming would be impossible when the Grevelingen was changed from an open estuary to a lake after the completion of the Delta Works *(see pp244–5)* has so far proved unfounded – the oysters already are less prone to disease.

from the distance. Generations of Keldermans, a Mechelen building family, have worked on this church. One unusual feature in Hulst is the trio of hostels, once safe houses for the monks from the Flemish abbeys Ten Duinen, Baudelo and Cambron.

Nearby is the former village of Hulsterloo, famous from the medieval epic Reynard the fox.

Terneuzen ⓲

Road map A5. 👥 24,500. 🚌 ℹ️
Markt 11–13 (0115-695976). 🛒 *Wed.*

Tᴇʀɴᴇᴜᴢᴇɴ ʜᴀꜱ an important port. The mighty sea locks in the **Kanaal van Gent naar Terneuzen** (Gent-Terneuzen canal), built between 1825 and 1827, are also impressive. The town is surrounded by industrial areas to the north and by nature reserves to the west (de Braakman) and the east (Otheense Kreek).

Sluis ⓳

Road map A5. 👥 2,100. 🚌 ℹ️ *St Annastraat 15 (0117-461700).* 🛒 *Fri.*

Tʜᴇ ᴢᴇᴇʟᴀɴᴅ-ꜰʟᴀɴᴅᴇʀꜱ landscape is scarred by the effects of floods and the dykes built to deal with them. Both polders and inner dykes bear witness to the constant struggle with the sea. The liberation of Zeeland-Flanders in 1944 was also hard fought and led to the complete devastation of towns and villages, one of which was Sluis. The 14th-century **Stadhuis**, with its belfry, the only one existing in the Netherlands, was restored in its former style after 1945, including the bell tower with the statue which has the nickname Jantje van Sluis.

Eɴᴠɪʀᴏɴꜱ: 2 km (1.5 miles) to the west lies **St-Anna-ter-Muiden**, a village beloved by artists. Once a prosperous town on the Zwin, the town now boasts just a few houses around the square, with a village pump and the stump of a tower. To the south is the oldest town in Zeeland: **Aardenburg**. The Romans

Gentse Poort, the gateway to the Flemish-tinged town of Hulst

built a fort here in the 2nd century in order to ward off Saxon pirates. Aardenburg later became one of the most powerful towns in Flanders. This can still be seen from **St-Baafskerk**, a flawless 13th-century example of the Scheldt Gothic style famous for its painted sarcophagi.

The **Gemeentelijk Archeologisch Museum Aardenburg** (Aardenburg municipal archaeological museum) deals solely with the Romans.

🏛 **Gemeentelijk Archeologisch Museum Aardenburg**
Marktstraat 18. 📞 *0117-492888.* ⭕
May–Sep: 1:30–5pm Tue–Sun. 🈲 📷

Cadzand ⓴

Road map A5. 👥 800.
ℹ️ *Boulevard de Wielingen 44d (0117-391298).* 🛒 *Mon.*

Mᴏᴅᴇʀɴ ꜱᴇᴀꜱɪᴅᴇ resort Cadzand is particularly popular for its wide stretch of sand. A popular pursuit here is to search for fossilized sharks' teeth. Along the dunes are dignified seaside hotels reminiscent of those of Domburg. A little way past Cadzand is the nature reserve the Zwin, which extends as far as Knokke in Belgium. The resort Nieuwvliet lies to the east of Cadzand.

The broad sandy beaches of Cadzand, always popular in summer

NORTHERN
AND EASTERN
NETHERLANDS

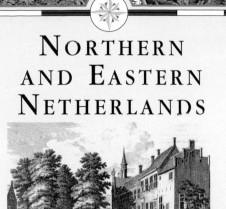

Exploring the Northern and Eastern Netherland

THE NORTHERN AND EASTERN Netherlands are comparatively sparsely populated. They encompass the
West Frisian Islands (Waddeneilanden) and
the provinces of Groningen, Friesland,
Drenthe, Overijssel, Flevoland and
Gelderland. Agriculture has
always played a predominant
role here. This part of Holland
has many natural and recreation areas, such as the
Waddenzee mud flats, Frisian
coast, coastal Lauwersmeerge-
bied, Hondsrug, Nationaal Park
De Hoge Veluwe, Sallandse
Heuvelrug and the
Oostvaardersplassen.

WEST FRISIAN ISLANDS
(see pp262–273)

Leeuwe

FRIESLAND
(see pp288–29

De Elfstedentocht (see pp292–3) *has been
held 15 times during the last century. Over
16,000 skaters have skated the Tocht der
Tochten, a 200-km (124-mile) stretch.*

The waddengebied (see p276)
*provides a habitat for many species
of birds. It is an important area for
annual and migrating birds. The
worms, molluscs and crustaceans
are an ideal source of food for
ducks, seagulls and wading birds.*

Lelystad

FLEVOLAND
(see pp320–327)

The Batavia (see
p325) *was owned by
the Dutch East India
Company. This three-
master was 45 m
(148 ft) long and had
room for 350 men. A
replica of the Batavia
was built between
1985 and 1995 at the
Batavia-Werf
(Batavia wharf) in
Lelystad, which is now
working on a replica
of Michiel de Ruyter's
17th-century flagship,
De Zeven Provinciën.*

| 0 kilometres | 20 |
| 0 miles | 20 |

◁ **Punting in one of the many canals in the region of Giethoorn, Overijssel**

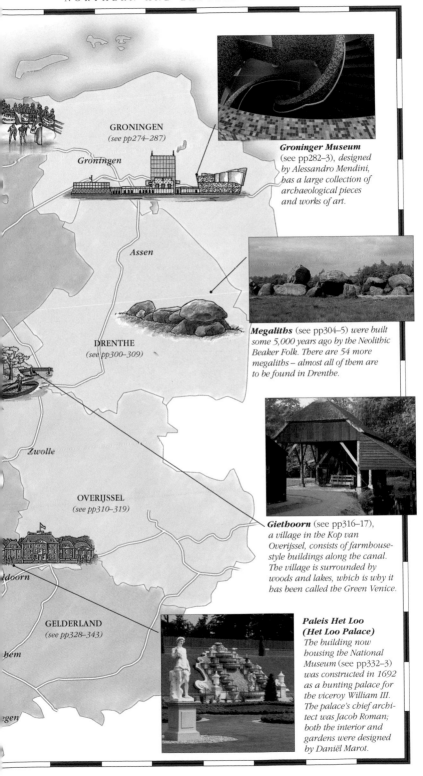

GRONINGEN
(see pp274–287)

Groningen

Groninger Museum
(see pp282–3), *designed by Alessandro Mendini, has a large collection of archaeological pieces and works of art.*

Assen

DRENTHE
(see pp300–309)

Megaliths (see pp304–5) *were built some 5,000 years ago by the Neolithic Beaker Folk. There are 54 more megaliths – almost all of them are to be found in Drenthe.*

Zwolle

OVERIJSSEL
(see pp310–319)

Giethoorn (see pp316–17), *a village in the Kop van Overijssel, consists of farmhouse-style buildings along the canal. The village is surrounded by woods and lakes, which is why it has been called the Green Venice.*

doorn

GELDERLAND
(see pp328–343)

hem

***Paleis Het Loo
(Het Loo Palace)***
The building now housing the National Museum (see pp332–3) was constructed in 1692 as a hunting palace for the viceroy William III. The palace's chief architect was Jacob Roman; both the interior and gardens were designed by Daniël Marot.

egen

Environmental Policy

I N THE 1990s, THE DUTCH GOVERNMENT drew up the Natuurbeleidsplan, a programme designed to make nature reserves accessible to the public. This is of great importance to the northern and eastern Netherlands, with their many lakes, woods and polders. The region's ecosystem has been divided into core areas, development areas and connecting zones in an attempt to give permanence to the natural environment. The connecting zones join the areas together. When the policy is fully implemented, it will aid in the survival of many plant and animal species.

The ermine

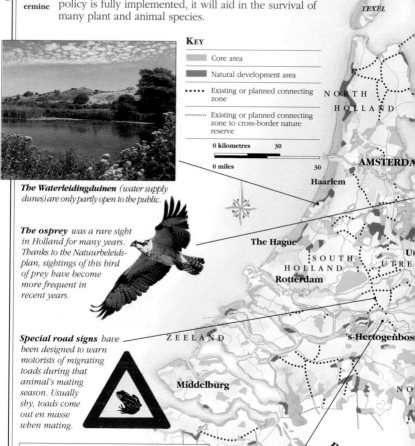

KEY

Core area

Natural development area

•••• Existing or planned connecting zone

·········· Existing or planned connecting zone to cross-border nature reserve

0 kilometres   30

0 miles   30

WEST
ISLA
VLIELA
TEXEL
NORTH
HOLLAND
AMSTERDA
Haarlem
The Hague
SOUTH
HOLLAND
U
UTRE
Rotterdam
's-Hertogenbos
ZEELAND
Middelburg
NO
Antwerp
BELG

The Waterleidingduinen (water supply dunes) are only partly open to the public.

The osprey was a rare sight in Holland for many years. Thanks to the Natuurbeleidsplan, sightings of this bird of prey have become more frequent in recent years.

Special road signs have been designed to warn motorists of migrating toads during that animal's mating season. Usually shy, toads come out en masse when mating.

READ THE SIGNS!

Most natural areas (or parts of them) in the northern and eastern Netherlands are freely accessible. However, some parts are open only from sunrise *(zonsopkomst)* to sunset *(zonsondergang)*, and it is therefore important to read the signs. It goes without saying that you should not make excessive noise, cause damage or leave litter in the area. Further information is available at VVV offices, the ANWB and the Vereniging Natuurmonumenten (tel. 035-6559933).

The adder is the only venomous snake in Holland and is very rare here. However, this small, distinctive snake can still be found in sandy regions and peat moors. In order to feed properly, adders require an extensive habitat.

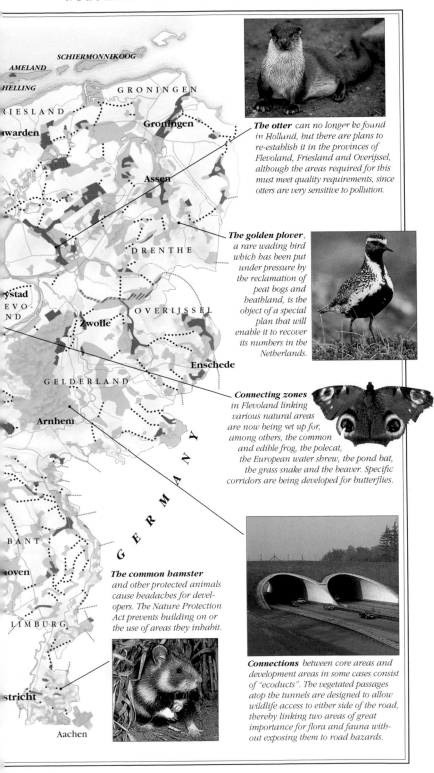

AMELAND
SCHIERMONNIKOOG
HELLING
RIESLAND
GRONINGEN
warden
Groningen
Assen
DRENTHE
ystad
EVO-
ND
OVERIJSSEL
Zwolle
Enschede
GELDERLAND
Arnhem
G E R M A N Y
BANT
oven
LIMBURG
stricht
Aachen

The otter *can no longer be found in Holland, but there are plans to re-establish it in the provinces of Flevoland, Friesland and Overijssel, although the areas required for this must meet quality requirements, since otters are very sensitive to pollution.*

The golden plover, *a rare wading bird which has been put under pressure by the reclamation of peat bogs and heathland, is the object of a special plan that will enable it to recover its numbers in the Netherlands.*

Connecting zones *in Flevoland linking various natural areas are now being set up for, among others, the common and edible frog, the polecat, the European water shrew, the pond bat, the grass snake and the beaver. Specific corridors are being developed for butterflies.*

The common hamster *and other protected animals cause headaches for developers. The Nature Protection Act prevents building on or the use of areas they inhabit.*

Connections *between core areas and development areas in some cases consist of "ecoducts". The vegetated passages atop the tunnels are designed to allow wildlife access to either side of the road, thereby linking two areas of great importance for flora and fauna without exposing them to road hazards.*

Distinctive Landscapes

THE NORTHEAST OF THE NETHERLANDS has a number of distinctive landscape types, such as the unique mud flats, or Waddenzee, where the sand and clay is exposed at low tide; the peat moors in southeast Groningen; the enchanting heathland of Drenthe; the endless polder landscape of Flevoland; the splendid forests of Gelderland (Hoge Veluwe and Posbank) and the magnificent riverscapes and seascapes in the northeast of Overijssel.

Heath spotted-orchid

The Oostvaardersplassen (lakes), between Lelystad and Almere, make up a unique natural landscape. It is a breeding ground and feeding area for hundreds of species of birds.

Glasswort is a wild plant which grows in mud flats and on silt deposits. It is a prized culinary delicacy.

Water crowfoot occurs in both flowing and standing water.

WEST FRISIAN ISLANDS

The Waddenzee *(see pp268–9)* is an area of mud flats which is largely dry at low tide. It attracts many species of birds that come here to forage and to feed. The island of Texel features the peat walls of the Hoge Berg.

Rapeseed plantations are used for land improvements in new polders. The yellow fields seem to stretch endlessly to the horizon.

Bulrushes were once common in the region. The "cigars" grow only by fresh water and are now protected.

POLDER LANDSCAPE

Forests (het Knarbos), lakes (the Oostvaardersplassen) and coastal lakes (the Veluwemeer) distinguish the flat polder landscape of the "new" province of Flevoland *(see pp320–27).*

Common polypody *occurs in juniper brush and in woodlands on poor sandy soil.*

Boletus edulis *is a delicious edible mushroom. Picking it, however, is no longer allowed.*

Bracken fern *grows in sparse woodland on lime and nutrient-poor sand and loamy ground, and on dried peat moors.*

Mosses *thrive in humid environments such as forest floors. Shady areas with acidic soil are ideal for sphagnum moss.*

The cran-berry *grows in sphagnum moss on peat moors and in fens.*

FORESTS

One of the best-known and largest forest areas in Holland is at Hoge Veluwe in the province of Gelderland *(see pp328–43)*, where a variety of animals, such as wild boar and red deer, are to be found.

Common sundew, *an insect-eating plant, grows on heathland and in the fenland of Groningen and Drenthe.*

Cross-leaved heath *thrives on nutrient-poor, dry, sandy soil and in the troughs of dunes.*

HEATHLAND

The northeastern Netherlands abounds with delightful heathland. Some of the most picturesque heathland can be found at Drenthe *(see pp300–309)*; herds of sheep still graze in the region of Ellertsveld.

Heather *occurs mainly in sand and peat bogs, typically poor in nutrients*

THE WEST FRISIAN ISLANDS

PERHAPS THE LEAST KNOWN PART *of the Netherlands despite their natural beauty, the West Frisian Islands form a barrier protecting the north of the country from the worst of the North Sea. Comprising five main islands and a few sandbanks, they are among Europe's last areas of wilderness.*

The West Frisian Islands are the remaining fragments of an ancient sandbank that once stretched from Cap Gris Nez in France to Esbjerg in Denmark, a remnant of the last Ice Age. Since Roman times the sea has been eroding this sandbank, creating the shallow Waddenzee behind and washing away much of the peat soil that lay beyond the dunes. The islands of Griend and Rottumeroog were threatened to such an extent that they were abandoned. Rottumerplatt, too, is uninhabited.

Monks established the first settlements as far back as the 8th century; islanders made a living from farming, fishing and collecting shellfish. On Texel and Terschelling, the two largest islands, churches dating from the 15th century still stand. Later, the islands prospered from links with the Dutch East India Company and, in the 19th century, from whaling. Vlieland and Ameland are quieter islands, good for bird-watching. Schiermonnikoog is the most isolated, with rare plant life.

Nowadays the islands, reached by ferries from the mainland, have much to offer the visitor in search of peace and quiet, with nature rambles over dunes and salt marsh, and seal- and bird-watching, especially in summer. The islands' quaint museums are strong on ecology and conservation. The best way to get around is by bicycle and visitors will find a wide range of hotels and guesthouses, excellent seafood restaurants, and some of the best sunsets anywhere.

Former captain's house *(commandeurhuisje)* **on Ameland**

◁ **Aerial view of the head of Texel island, with its lighthouse**

Exploring the West Frisian Islands

THE HISTORY OF the West Frisian Islands (Waddeneilanden) has been shaped by the wind and the sea. It was not until the 17th century that the larger islands were stabilized by dykes. Den Burg on Texel, the largest village on the islands, is a historic fortification with a pleasant old centre. Nearby is Hoge Berg, with its characteristic peat walls; in the west, the distinctive tower of Den Hoorn can be seen. To the north is the unique natural area of De Slufter. The crown of the Frisian Islands, Vlieland, has the prettiest village of the islands. Terschelling, Ameland and Schiermonnikoog are typical Frisian islands, with wide beaches, partly forested dunes, villages and polders or mud flats on the Waddenzee side.

Cranberry liqueur

Shrimp fishermen sorting their catch

Bird-watching in the Mookbai, Texel

SIGHTS AT A GLANCE

Ameland ❾	Rottumeroog ⓬
De Koog ❸	Rottumerplaat ⓫
Den Burg ❷	Schiermonnikoog ❿
Den Hoorn ❺	Terschelling ❽
De Slufter ❹	Vlieland ❻
Griend ❼	
Noorderhaaks ❶	

0 kilometres   10

0 miles   10

TERSCHELLING
OOSTEREND
HOORN
MIDSLAND
WEST-TERSCHELLING

Vliestroom

OOST-VLIELAND

Richel

Waddeneilanden

❻ **VLIELAND**

❼ **GRIEND**

Eijerlandse Gat

Harlingen

DE COCKSDORP

❹ **DE SLUFTER**

TEXEL

DE KOOG
❸
OOSTEREND
● **DE WAAL**

DEN BURG ❷

❺
DEN HOORN

● **OUDESCHILD**

...DER

Rescued seals being returned to the wild by members of EcoMare, Texel (see p447)

De Wadden – the mud flats are ideal for beach walks

GETTING AROUND

The West Frisian Islands are reached by ferries from the mainland. **Texel** is served by TESO (tel. 0222-369600); no cars allowed, no reservations. Foot passengers can take a bus to De Koog or De Cocksdorp via Den Burg, or order a taxi-bus when buying their ticket. **Vlieland** is served by Rederij Doeksen (tel. 0900-3635736); cars not permitted. On arrival, a bus takes passengers to Posthuis, where there are taxis. **Terschelling** is served by Rederij Doeksen (0900-3635736); reservations recommended for cars. There is a bus service on the island, and taxis are available on arrival. **Ameland** is served by Rederij Wagenborg (tel. 0519-546111); reservations recommended. There are bus services to all villages. **Schiermonnikoog** is served by Rederij Wagenborg (tel. 0519-349050); foot passengers only. Bus service and taxi-buses connect the dock and village. Bicycles can be hired easily.

ROTTUMERPLAAT ROTTUMEROOG

11 **12**

SCHIERMONNIKOOG **10**

AMELAND **9**

NES

UM

HOLWERD

LAUWERSOOG

The Koegelwieck seacat (West Terschelling)

SEE ALSO

- *Where to Stay* p397
- *Where to Eat* p417

KEY

▬	Main road
═	Minor road
▬	Scenic route
—	Ferry

The splendid coastline of Vlieland

Birds of the Waddenzee

THE EXTENSIVE WETLANDS of the Waddenzee are an important area for breeding and migratory birds. The North Sea coasts of the islands are sandy, with little animal life; the Waddenzee coasts of the islands, however, consist of fine sand and clay which are rich in minerals and nutrients. The innumerable worms, molluscs and crustaceans that live here are an ideal source of food for a huge variety of ducks, seagulls and wading birds. At the peak of the migratory season (August), the number of birds here runs into millions.

Black-headed gull

Curlew
This is the largest European wading bird and is easily recognizable by its long, curved beak.

Bird-watching Hide
There are many hides for bird-watchers on the mud flats of the Waddenzee, allowing the birds to be observed without disturbance.

BIRD CATCHERS
Bird catchers, whose interests in Holland have gone far beyond mere hunting, have become an important pressure group for the protection of birds and the natural environment. Their organization is Vogelbescherming Nederland, based in Zeist.

BEAK SHAPES

People are often surprised at the many varieties of birds that feed on the mud flats. The different species, however, have managed to avoid competing with one another. The various shapes and lengths of their beaks are suitable for the assorted types of food that can be found in the water and in the sand. Ducks get their food from the surface or dive for it, whereas wading birds get their food from underground – what prey at which depth underground depends on the shape of the beak. Other birds catch fish (spoonbills, cormorants or terns), shellfish (eider ducks) or even other seabirds (the white-tailed eagle), or steal their food from other birds.

The ringed plover feeds from the surface.

The lapwing feeds on small crabs in the mud.

The silver plover catches small sea-worms.

The oystercatcher pulls shellfish out of the sand.

The black-tailed godwit feeds on worms living underground.

The curlew, with its curved sharp beak, can reach invertebrates living deep in the sand.

Arctic Tern
This extremely rare bird, which breeds in the West Frisian Islands, spends the winter in the Antarctic. This gives it the longest migratory path of all birds.

Sandwich Tern
This bird has its largest breeding colony in Holland on Griend. Its dwindling numbers mean it requires careful protection.

Oystercatcher
The oystercatcher is characteristic of the Waddenzee. It forages for cockles and mussels.

BIRD SPECIES
The wealth of bird species – including diving birds, petrels, cormorants, spoonbills, ducks, birds of prey, waders, scavengers, seagulls, terns, razorbills and songbirds – that occur in the Waddenzee is a good reason to ensure that the area is carefully protected. For many of the birds, these are the only breeding grounds in Holland, as they are the only wetlands remaining in the Netherlands. Various parts are closed to visitors, and it is important to observe the regulations in order to help preserve the bird population.

Avocet
This magnificent wading bird has an upward-curving bill and black and white plumage.

Black-Tailed Godwit
This wading bird, with fiery red-brown plumage, is a bird of passage but spends the winters and summers in the Waddenzee.

Large numbers of oyster-catchers can be seen both in winter and in summer.

Ringed Plover
This is an active bird that rarely breeds here but passes through in large numbers.

Eider Duck
The eider duck has breeding colonies on Texel, Vlieland and Terschelling. The male is far more impressive in appearance than the brown-coloured female.

Herring Gull
The herring gull is just one of the many varieties of gull that occur here. At more than half a metre (1.5 ft) long, it is an impressive bird.

Red Knot
This bird of passage stops over sometimes in summer and sometimes in winter. It is a robust bird, one that is always on the move.

The Waddenzee

THE WADDENZEE is a tidal area whose sand or mud flats *(wadden)* are mainly exposed at low tide and disappear at high tide. Together with the West Frisian Islands, the Waddenzee forms the last extensive wild part of Holland. The entire area has an extremely rich ecosystem because of the large sources of nourishment. It is a feeding and breeding ground for many species of birds. Two species of seal, 30 species of fish, shrimps and crabs live in the Waddenzee or come here to breed.

Cockle

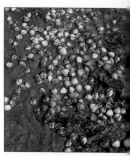

Cockles (Cardium edule), *which form the diet for many bird species, are intensively harvested using mechanical methods. The catch is exported.*

The VVVs *(tourist offices) on the West Frisian Islands offer all kinds of sailing trips around the islands, including romantic luxury cruises on a three-master. Rederij Zoutkamp (tel. 0595-401052) arranges sailing trips on local boats.*

Sea Lavender (Limonium vulgare), *along with sea purslane and sea aster, grows in the higher parts of the salt marshes. Fields of blue-violet sea lavender flowers make a very pretty sight.*

Exposed Sections of the Mud Flats
Much of the Waddenzee mud flats is exposed during low tide. This leaves places like the marina pictured below high and dry. Mooring places that are inaccessible at low tide are increasingly being dredged as marinas.

Low tide

High tide

FLORA IN THE WADDENZEE

Because of the diversity of the Waddenzee landscape, with its changing environment (salt water and fresh water, lime-rich soil and lime-poor soil, wet land and dry land, clay ground and sandy ground), almost 900 plant species grow here. Many of them grow on the island-side of the old dunes in the dune valleys. Amongst the flowers to be found here are autumn gentian and creeping willow, as well as grasses and weeds such as black bog-rush, fragrant orchid and grass of Parnassus. Lavender is among the plants which grow on the higher ground.

Lavender (Salicornia europaea) *is one of the first plants to colonize the mud flats and the low-lying parts of the salt marshes. When the land has silted up completely, the salt marsh grass establishes itself.*

Cracks in the dried silt provide a good foothold for lavender, as well as for other plants.

THREATS TO THE WADDENZEE

According to the Dutch oil company NAM, there are between 70 and 170 billion cubic metres (2,500 and 6,000 billion cubic feet) of natural gas beneath the Waddenzee. The value of this gas runs into many billions of euros. The Waddenzee Society is completely opposed to any gas drilling in the Waddenzee on several grounds: first, because there is no social need for it and second, because the environmental effects of drilling – in particular, the consequences the falling ground level would have on life in the Waddenzee – have not been properly investigated. For the time being, therefore, drilling on the Waddenzee is banned, pending further environmental impact studies. But the Waddenzee is also threatened by the harvesting of mussels and cockles. Since 1992, the Dutch government has scaled this back, and is considering closing the area to the shellfish industry.

WADLOPEN (WALKING THE MUD FLATS)

A walk on the Waddenzee takes you through salt marshes and past the *wantij,* a place below an island where two tidal flows meet. Since the mid-1970s, walking on the mud flats has been a popular hobby. There are now six major mud-flat walking societies: De Fryske Waedrinners (Leeuwarden, tel. 058-2153040; Dijkstra's Wadlooptochten (Pieterburen, tel. 0595-526345); Lammert Kwant (Ezinge, tel. 0594-622029); Stichting Uithuizer Wad (only for Rottumeroog; tel. 050-5792414), Stichting Wadloopcentrum Friesland (Holwerd, tel. 0519-561656) and Stichting Wadloopcentrum Pieterburen (tel. 0595-528300).

Cockle harvesting

Noorderhaaks, above sea level at high tide for some decades now

Noorderhaaks ❶

Road map B2. 🚶 none. ℹ️ *district Den Helder (0223-671333).*

Noorderhaaks, also known as Razende Bol (raging ball), is a fairly bleak sandbank west of Den Helder, 2.5 km (1.5 miles) offshore. The sea currents cause the island to shift eastwards towards Texel, after which another "raging ball" appears at the same point off Den Helder. The Dutch air force occasionally uses the island for target practice, but it is not off-limits for visitors. Rowing and swimming here are risky because of the powerful currents. Adventure-seekers regularly visit Noorderhaaks by boat or by helicopter, unable to resist this piece of total wilderness, where mirages are common.

Den Burg ❷

Road map B2. 🚶 *6,000.* ⛴ 🚌 ℹ️ *Emmalaan 66 (0222-314741).* 🛒 *Wed.*

Den Burg is the main town of Texel and situated right in its centre. Around 1300, the village was fortified by a circular rampart with a moat, which are now marked by the Burgwal and Parkstraat Streets. A sheep market was once held in April and May at the Groeneplats, Den Burg's main square with the present-day town hall. Today, a sheep day is held on the first Monday of September. Further on, by the Binnenburg, or inner castle, stands the 15th-century

Late Gothic **Hervormde kerk** (Protestant church). The Kogerstraat runs the length of the Binnenburg. Located here is the **Oudheidkamer**, an antiquities museum set up in a picturesque 16th-century building, which used to be a doss-house. Today it contains period rooms, a display of artefacts and works of art in the attic, and a herb garden on the grounds.

Along and around the town wall are several interesting shopping streets, such as the Weverstraat. A number of excellent restaurants are to be found on the Warmoesstraat.

🏛 Oudheidkamer

Kogerstraat 1, Den Burg. 📞 *0222-313135.* 🕐 *2 Apr–2 Nov: 10am–12:30pm & 1:30–3:30pm Mon–Fri.* 📷

Environs: South of Den Burg is sloping landscape with the 15 m (50 ft) **Hoge Berg** (high mountain), which offers a

wonderful view of the island. For a good walk, follow the Skillepaadje from the tomb of the Georgiers (resistance fighters who died fighting the Germans in 1945) to the fishing village of Oudeschild, past the distinctive peat walls and sheep pens.

Beachcomber on Texel

De Koog ❸

Road map B2. 🚶 *825.* ⛴ 🚌 ℹ️ *Emmalaan 66, Den Burg (0222–314741).* 🛒 *Tue.*

In 1900, the former fishing settlement of De Koog consisted of a church (built in 1415) and a few houses and farms. The first tourist facility was the Badhotel, later the Hotel Prinses Juliana, with a garden overlooking the sea. Today, Den Koog has accommodation for 20,000 visitors in hotels, pensions and camp sites. The centre of De Koog is the Dorpsstraat, which has cafés, snack bars and discos. De Koog's attractions for visitors are the Calluna waterpark and EcoMare, an information centre for the Waddenzee and the North Sea *(see p447).*

The Nederlands-Hervormde church in Den Burg (1481)

De Slufter ❹

Road map B2. 🚶 none. 🚌 🚐
⭕ all year, northern part closed
1 Mar–1 Sep. ℹ️ Emmalaan 66,
Den Burg (0222-314741).

T HE UNIQUE natural area of
De Slufter, consisting of
salt marshes covering 450 ha
(1,100 acres), is covered with
salt-loving plants such as sea
thrift and sea lavender, and is
an important breeding and
feeding ground for many different bird species. De Slufter,
and the neighbouring **De Muy**,
where spoonbills breed, are
magnificent rambling areas.

Den Hoorn ❺

Road map B2. 🚶 450. 🚌 🚐
ℹ️ Emmalaan 66, Den Burg (0222-
314741). 🚐 Thu.

L IKE DEN BURG, Den Hoorn
stands on boulder clay. It
has a distinctive **Hervormde
kerk** (Protestant church) with
a pointed steeple and churchyard dating from 1425. This
exquisitely restored village has
been given protected status.

Vlieland ❻

Road map C1. 🚶 1,150. 🚌
ℹ️ Havenweg 10 (0562-451111).

V LIELAND IS THE smallest of
the Waddenzee Islands. In
some places, less than one
kilometre (half a mile) sepa-
rates the Waddenzee and the
North Sea. Unlike the other

Salt-loving plants thriving at the water's edge, De Slufter

islands, Vlieland consists only
of dunes, covered with a purple haze of heather, marram
grass and sea buckthorn. In
the east, the woods planted
just after 1900 provide a bit of
variety in the landscape.

In the south is the only village, **Oost-Vlieland,** where
the boat from Harlingen
docks. Many old buildings
line the main street. One of
them, the **Tromp's Huys**
(1576), used to belong to the
Amsterdam Admiralty. Today
it houses a museum with

19th-century paintings. The
houses are separated by alleys
known as "gloppen". There is
no room for cars here, not
even for those of the islanders

The best way to explore
Vlieland is by bicycle; the
island can be covered in one
day. From Oost-Vlieland, you
can cycle westwards along
tracks through the dunes or
along the Waddenzee shore-
line to the **Posthuys** (post
house), where in the 17th
century the overseas mail was
brought from Amsterdam to
be loaded onto ships waiting
to sail. Further westwards is
de Vliehors, an area of natural interest which can be
explored if no military exer-
cises are taking place here.
Beware, though: you run the
risk of getting stuck in the
soft drifting sand. This is also
where the wealthy village of
West-Vlieland once stood. It
was consumed by the waves
after the last inhabitants
abandoned it in 1736.

🏛 **Tromp's Huys**
Dorpsstraat 99, Vlieland. 📞 0562-
451600. ⭕ May–Sep: 10am–noon
& 2–5pm Mon–Sat; Nov–Mar: 2–5pm
Wed & Sat. 🖼

The village hall in Oost-Vlieland

The Oerol Festival on Terschelling

Griend ❼

Road map C1. 🏠 none. 🚌 *very limited.* ℹ️ *Vereniging Natuurmonumenten (035-6559933).*

HALF-WAY THROUGH the boat trip from Harlingen to Terschelling or Vlieland, one will come across Griend. The island was abandoned by its inhabitants after the St Lucia Flood of 1287. For centuries it seemed about to disappear beneath the waves. In 1988, the Natuurmonumenten trust, which has leased Griend since 1916, had a dam built to prevent further erosion. At high tide, the highest part of the island is just 1 m (3 ft) above the water. Access to Griend is forbidden, save for a handful of bird wardens and biology students. This is Holland's largest breeding ground for great tern.

Tombstone from Striep

Terschelling ❽

Road map C1. 🏠 5,000. 🚌 🚐 ℹ️ *Willem Barentszkade 19a, West-Terschelling (0562-443000).*

TERSCHELLING IS the second largest of the West Frisian Islands. The north of the island consists of dunes, where in the olden days cattle were let out to graze everywhere ("oerol"). This is where the Oerol Festival, held each year in June, gets its name.

In Formerum, West, and Hoorn, the dunes have been planted with coniferous and deciduous woods. In the south are polders, and beyond the dykes are the salt marshes. There is a nature reserve at either end of the island: the Noordvaarder in the west, and the Boschplaat in the east. If you happen to be sailing over from Harlingen at low tide on a sunny day, you may see seals basking in the sun on the de Richel and Jacobs Ruggen sandbanks.

West is a real mud-flat village, with old houses and a famous lighthouse, **Brandaris**, dating from 1594. It is closed to visitors, but the same view can be enjoyed from the high dune known as the Seinpaalduin behind the village. **Het Behouden Huys** is a local history museum dedicated to famous islanders such as Willem Barentsz; there is also the educational **Centrum voor Natuur en Landschap**, where you can learn about the ecology of the mud flats.

The two largest villages in the west are Midsland and Hoorn. Midsland is surrounded by small hamlets with intriguing names such as Hee, Horp and Kaart, which date back to when the Frisians settled on the islands. The hamlet with the **kerkhof van Striep** cemetery is where the first church on the island was built, in the 10th century. Its outline is still visible. Further eastwards is Hoorn, with 13th-century Gothic-Romanesque St Janskerk standing on the site of the original church.

🏛 **Museum 't Behouden Huys**
Commandeurstraat 32, West-Terschelling. 📞 0562-442389. ⏱ *1 Apr–31 Oct: 10am–5pm Mon–Fri, 1–5pm Sat; 15 Jun–30 Sep: also 10am–5pm Sun.* ⬤ *Nov–Mar (except for school holidays).* 🖼

🏛 **Centrum voor Natuur en Landschap**
Burg. Reedekerstraat 11, West-Terschelling. 📞 0562-442390. ⏱ *Apr–Oct: 9am–5pm Mon–Fri, 2–5pm Sat & Sun.* 🖼 ♿

Ameland ❾

Road map C/D1. 🏠 3,200. 🚌 🚐 ℹ️ *Rixt van Doniastraat 2, Nes (0519-546546).*

THE DUNES IN the north of this island are dry, with the exception of **Het Oerd**, a wet valley in the east which is a bird reserve. The region is best explored by bicycle; there is a cycle track to a scenic spot on a 24-m (79-ft) dune. In the mud flats in the south there are four villages. The largest of these is **Nes**, where the boat from Holwerd calls. **Commandeurshuizen** (commodores' houses) in the old centre recall the days when many islanders made their living from whaling.

Het Oerd – the edge of the mud flats on Ameland

A horse-drawn lifeboat, the pride of Ameland

If you want to see the real Ameland, you must visit Hollum. The Zuiderlaan and Oosterlaan are steeped in the atmosphere of past times. At the southern end of the village is the church, surrounded by an oval cemetery with tombstones where the deeply pious inscriptions are overgrown with lichen.

Beyond Hollum lies the **Reddingsmuseum Abraham Fock**, a museum dedicated to life-saving, where the pride of Ameland, a lifeboat launched by horses, is kept operational.

🏛 **Reddingsmuseum Abraham Fock**
Oranjeweg 18, Hollum. 📞 0519-554243. 🕐 Apr–Nov: 10am–noon & 1:30–5pm daily. 📷 ♿

Schiermonnikoog ⑩

Road map D1. 🏠 1,000. 🚆 🚌
🚌 Reeweg 5, Schiermonnikoog (0519-531233/531900).

SCHIERMONNIKOOG, or Lytje Pole (small land), was a farm belonging to Cistercian monks during the Middle Ages. The village of Schiermonnikoog, which is named after them, has many exquisitely restored houses. The island as a whole is a national park and under the protection of Natuurmonumenten. The beach of Schier is one of the widest in Europe. The eastern side of the island (Het Balg, Kobbeduinen and the salt marshes) in particular make for wonderful walking areas, with their varied flora (including many orchids) and bird life. No cars at all are allowed on the island.

Rottumerplaat ⑪

Road map D1. 🏠 none.
🚌 Staatsbosbeheer (050-5207247).

NATURE HAS BEEN LEFT to her own devices with the 900 ha (2,225 acre) uninhabited island of Rottumerplaat. This protected nature reserve is jointly managed by the Ministry of Agriculture, Waterways and Planning, and the Friends of Rottumeroog and Rottumerplaat Society (SVRR). Outsiders are rarely admitted to the island. This has had a good effect on Rottumeroog as well as on Rottumerplaat, which has been expanding quickly. Dunes many metres in height and an impressive salt marsh are its characteristic features. The island also belongs to the seals and birds.

Rottumeroog ⑫

Road map D1. 🏠 none. 🚗 very limited. 🚌 Staatsbosbeheer (050-5207247).

THIS MOST EASTERN of the West Frisian Islands is due to disappear into the mouth of the Ems soon. Since 1991 it has been left in the hands of nature. Attempts over many years to prevent it from drifting eastwards were unsuccessful. In 1998, the northern dunes collapsed, after which the last traces of human settlement were removed by the state forestry commission. The island is now less than 300 ha (740 acres) in size and shrinks with each storm. Walkers are prohibited in the area.

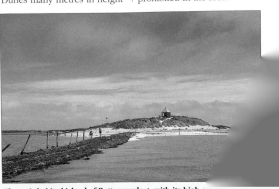

The uninhabited island of Rottumerplaat, with its high

GRONINGEN

H OLLAND'S NORTHERNMOST PROVINCE *is distinguished by its rich cultural history and unusual landscape, where you often see* terps *or small areas of elevated land. To the north and west it is bounded by the shallow Waddenzee and to the east by the Ems river estuary and the border with Germany.*

The *terps* originated centuries ago, when the inhabitants of this region needed to protect themselves from high water levels. The elevated land is sometimes crowned by a solitary Romanesque church, visible for miles across the fens. Elsewhere in the province you will see straight roads and canals, often evidence of reclaimed land. The region grew rich during the Middle Ages from agriculture and peat extraction, and the medieval port of Appingedam, nowadays a little town inland from the port of Delfzijl, was once a member of the powerful Hanseatic League.

Groningen province is also noted for its windmills, castles and moated manor houses and, in the east, for its restored fortified towns, such as picturesque Bourtange, which is right on the border with Germany. Conservation areas abound. Close to Lauwersoog, where you can catch a ferry to Schiermonnikoog, one of the West Frisian Islands *(see p273)*, a vast nature reserve has been established. Nearby Pieterburen has a seal sanctuary.

Groningen, the provincial capital, is proud of its glorious past and boasts a wealth of world-class museums, historic buildings and other attractions. A number of Dutch corporations have their headquarters in this thriving university city, and a further boost to the economy arrived in the 1960s after the discovery in nearby Slochteren of some of the world's largest natural gas deposits.

Hay bales in Westerwolde near the old fortified town of Bourtange

◁ **Monumental spiral staircase in the Groninger Museum designed by Alessandro Mendini**

Exploring Groningen

SOME OF THE MOST attractive and historically interesting castles, or *borgs,* are in the Groningen region: the medieval Fraeylemaborg in Slochteren, Menkemaborg in Uithuizen and the charming Verhildersum in Leens. The natural area around the Lauwersmeer is particularly suitable for rambling. Not far from here, in Pieterburen, is a famous refuge for seals. Ter Apel, which is on the province's eastern boundary, is a magnificent medieval monastery. Groningen itself *(see pp278–83)* has much to offer, including the peaceful Prinsenhof, with its beautiful gardens, and the ultra-modern Groninger Museum *(see pp282–3),* which houses collections that range from archaeology to oriental porcelain to modern art.

Wensum, one of the prett villages in Groningen

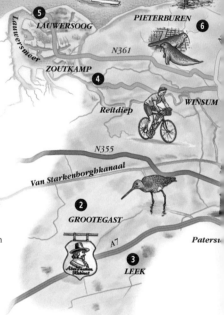

The Lauwersmeer nature reserve, created through the draining of the Lauwerszee

GETTING AROUND

Groningen can be reached from the south along the A28 motorway; the A7 crosses the province from Friesland in the west to Germany in the east. The best way to see the town of Groningen is on foot. From Groningen there are rail links to Roodeschool in the north, Delfzijl in the northeast and to Nieuweschans in the east. Most of the countryside is accessible by regional *(interlokal)* or local *(buurt)* buses. The Groningen region is well suited for cycling and rambling, especially the area around the Lauwersmeer, the mud-flat region *(waddengebied)* and Westerwolde, in the south.

SEE ALSO

* **Where to Stay** p398

* **Where to Eat** p417

SIGHTS AT A GLANCE

Recreation possibilities on the Paterswoldse Meer, south of Groningen

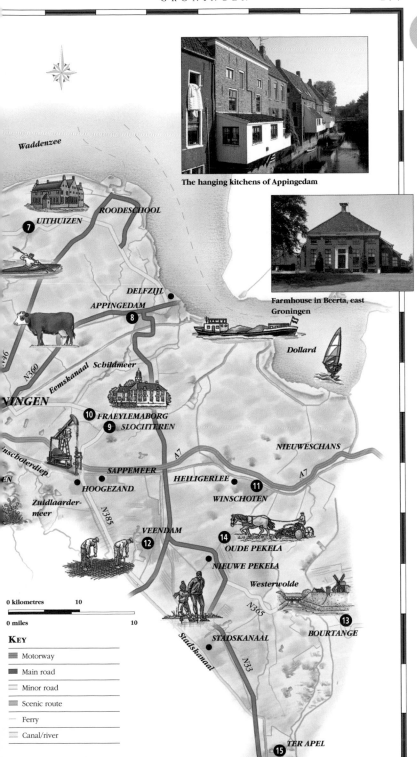

The hanging kitchens of Appingedam

Farmhouse in Beerta, east Groningen

Waddenzee

ROODESCHOOL

UITHUIZEN ⑦

DELFZIJL

APPINGEDAM ⑧

Schildmeer

Eemskanaal

N360

N46

VINGEN

⑩ FRAEYLEMABORG
⑨ SLOCHTEREN

nschoterdiep

EN

SAPPEMEER

HOOGEZAND

Zuidlaarder-
meer

A7

NIEUWESCHANS

A7

HEILIGERLEE ⑪

WINSCHOTEN

N385

VEENDAM ⑫

⑭

OUDE PEKELA

NIEUWE PEKELA

Westerwolde

N365

⑬

BOURTANGE

Dollard

0 kilometres 10

0 miles 10

STADSKANAAL

Stadskanaal

N33

TER APEL ⑮

KEY

Motorway

Main road

Minor road

Scenic route

Ferry

Canal/river

Street-by-Street: Groningen ❶

THE TOWN OF GRONINGEN has for centuries been the cultural and historical capital of the province. Its glory was at its height in the 15th century, when the town was freed from the jurisdiction of the Bishop of Utrecht and was able to extend its influence into the present-day province of Friesland. In 1614, the Groninger Academie was founded, which was the precursor of the Rijksuniversiteit. Thus, in addition to being a centre of trade and government, the town also became an academic centre.

TURFSINGEL

SINT WALBURGSTR.

MARTINIKERKHOF

★ **Prinsenhof**
In the gardens of the Prinsenhof, where in 1568 the first Bishop of Groningen, and later the stadholder, resided, stands a magnificent sundial from 1730. The garden is laid out as it was in the 18th century.

★ **Martinitoren**
The 97-m (318-ft) Martinitoren (St Martin tower) dating from 1496 is called The Old Grey by the locals because of the colour of the Bentheim sandstone.

The Martinikerk
(St Martin's Church) dates back to the 13th century, though only parts of that basilica are preserved. The Romanesque church which followed was refurbished in Gothic style in the 1400s.

Stadhuis
The Stadhuis on the Grote Markt is a monumental Neo-Classical building, completed in 1810.

Goudkantoor
This 1635 Renaissance building on the Waagplein was known as the "Goudkantoor" (gold depository) in the 19th century, when it functioned as a treasury. It now houses an inn.

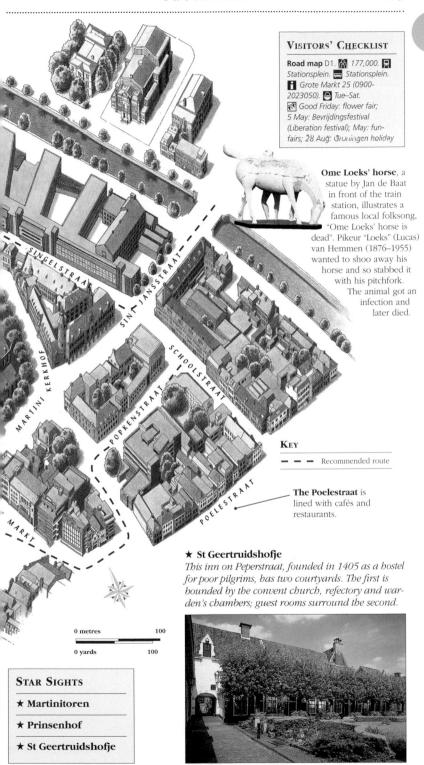

VISITORS' CHECKLIST

Road map D1. 👥 *177,000.* 🚉
Stationsplein. 🚌 *Stationsplein.*
ℹ *Grote Markt 25 (0900-*
2023050). 🛒 *Tue–Sat.*
🎪 *Good Friday: flower fair;*
5 May: Bevrijdingsfestival
(Liberation festival); May: fun-
fairs; 28 Aug: Groningen holiday

Ome Loeks' horse, a
statue by Jan de Baat
in front of the train
station, illustrates a
famous local folksong,
"Ome Loeks' horse is
dead". Pikeur "Loeks" (Lucas)
van Hemmen (1876–1955)
wanted to shoo away his
horse and so stabbed it
with his pitchfork.
The animal got an
infection and
later died.

SINGELSTRAAT

SINT JANSSTRAAT

MARTINI KERKHOF

SCHOOLSTRAAT

POPKENSTRAAT

KEY

- - - Recommended route

POELESTRAAT

The Poelestraat is
lined with cafés and
restaurants.

MARKT

★ St Geertruidshofje
This inn on Peperstraat, founded in 1405 as a hostel
for poor pilgrims, has two courtyards. The first is
bounded by the convent church, refectory and war-
den's chambers; guest rooms surround the second.

0 metres   100

0 yards   100

STAR SIGHTS

★ Martinitoren

★ Prinsenhof

★ St Geertruidshofje

Exploring Groningen

THE CITY OF GRONINGEN has a number of interesting buildings and museums, among them the Noordelijk Scheepvaartmuseum (northern maritime museum) which illustrates the history of navigation. The Groninger Museum (see pp282–3) possesses an art collection of international stature. A visit to one of the gardens of Groningen will provide peace in the middle of the bustling university city.

The distinctive Gasunie building, known locally as the "monkey cliff"

🏛 Martinikerk and Martinitoren

Grote Markt. 🔔 050-3111277. ⭕ Jun–Aug: noon–5pm Tue–Sat. **Martinitoren** Grote Markt. 🔔 050-3135713. ⭕ Apr–Sep: noon–4:30pm Mon–Sun; Jan–Mar & Oct–Dec: noon–4:30pm Sat & Sun. ● 1 Jan, 25 Dec. 🈳

The Grote Markt is the old city centre. A large number of the buildings standing on the square were badly damaged by air raids towards the end of World War II. When it was rebuilt, the market was enlarged on the northern and eastern sides, and new buildings of a modern character were constructed.

The famous Martinitoren (St Martin tower) was also damaged but still standing, and it was possible to rebuild it. The carillon of d'Olle Grieze ("The Old Grey"), whose bells were cast by the Hemony brothers, has since been enlarged and now has four octaves and 49 bells. The Martinikerk (St Martin's

Church), dating from the 13th century, still retains traces of the original building: both the northern and southern façades of the transept and the ornamental brickwork of the windows and window niches of the northern side are recognizably 13th century. During the 15th century, when the city was at the height of its development, the church was extended in Gothic style. The choir, which features sumptuous murals from 1530 illustrating the life of Christ, had been completed before 1425. The central part of the church became a hall-type church. East of the Grote Markt is the Poelestraat, which on fine days comes to life with its many outdoor cafés and restaurants.

🏛 Gebouw van de Gasunie

Concourslaan 17. 🔔 050-5219111. ● to the public.

The main office of the Dutch Gasunie (gas board) was designed by the Alberts and Van Huur architects on the principles of "organic" architecture, the inspiration of which lies with natural forms. The "organic" nature of the building can be seen at every turn, even in the specially designed furniture. The locals' nickname for the building is the "apenrots" (monkey cliff).

🌿 St Geertruidshofje

Peperstraat 22. 🔔 050-3124082.
Groningen has a number of pretty *hofjes*, or gardens, often belonging to inns. They were once charitable institutions whose aim was to help the poor. The finest of these is the garden of the 13th-century Heilige Geest-gasthuis, or Pelstergasthuis (in the Pelsterstraat), and St Geertruidshofje (see p279), whose Pepergasthuis inn was established in 1405. It later became a senior citizens' home. The pump in the courtyard dates from 1829.

The Poelestraat: a favourite haunt for the students of Groningen

🏛 Noordelijk Scheepvaart-
en Tabaksmuseum

Brugstraat 24–26. ☎ *050-3122202.*
⏰ *10am–5pm Tue–Sat, 1–5pm Sun*
& hols. ⏰ *public holidays.* 🖼

This maritime museum,
arranged over two restored
medieval houses, deals with
the history of navigation in
the northern provinces from
1650 to the present. Exhibits
are arranged in chronological
order, from the Utrecht ships,
Hanseatic cogs, West Indies
merchantmen, peat barges
and Baltic merchant ships to
Groningen coasters from the
20th century. A number of historical workshops, such as a
carpenter's shop and a smithy,
are held in the attic of the
museum. In the same building,
the Tobacco Museum covers
the use of the weed in
western Europe from
1500 up to today.

🍃 Prinsenhof
and Prinsen-
hoftuin

Martinikerkhof 23.
☎ *050-3183688.*
⏰ *Apr–15 Oct.*

Theeschenkerij

(tea room) ⏰ *Mon & Tue.*
The Prinsenhof originally
housed the monastic order of
the Broeders des Gemenen
Levens. It later became the
seat of the first Bishop of
Groningen, Johann Knijff,
who had the entire complex
converted into a magnificent
bishop's palace. Until late
into the 18th century, the
building served as the residence of the stadholder. The
Prinsenhoftuin (Prinsenhof
Gardens) is truly an oasis in
the midst of the busy city.

The magnificent Prinsenhof, formerly the stadholder's residence

Its highlights include a herb
garden and a rose garden.
There is also a flowerbed that
is arranged into two coats of
arms, one with the letter W
(for William Frederick, the
stadholder of Friesland),
the other with a letter
A (for Albertine Agnes,
William's wife).
At the side of the
entrance is a
fine sundial
(see p278)
which dates
back to 1730.
The course of
the old city

**Decorative element from the
Provinciehuis of Groningen**

walls of Groningen is still
clearly discernible in the
Prinsenhoftuin.

🏛 Hortus Haren

Kerklaan 34, Haren. ☎ *050-5370053.*
⏰ *9:30am–5pm daily.* 🖼 ♿
Immediately south of the city
is the fashionable town of
Haren, where an extensive
park, Hortus Haren, is situated. The park was set up in
1642 by Henricus Munting.
Its 20 ha (50 acres) include
a large hothouse complex
comprising a number of

different greenhouses dedicated to a wide array of climatic
zones. There is a tropical
rainforest with a great variety
of exotic flowers. A sub-
tropical hothouse numbers
orange trees among its plants.
The various climatic areas
continue with a desert section.
Here, gigantic cacti are showcased. Another greenhouse
featuring a monsoon climate
contains unusual carnivorous
plants. In the tropical culture
greenhouse, you can admire
a traditional Indonesian
sawah (ricefield).

The Chinese garden ("Het
verborgen rijk van Ming", or
"The hidden Ming Empire")
is well worth a visit. It is a
faithful reconstruction of a
real garden owned by a 16th-
century high Chinese official
of the Ming Dynasty (1368–
1644). It features original
Chinese pagodas, which have
been painstakingly restored
by Chinese craftsmen in
fine pavilions and then beautifully decorated with carvings
of lions and dragons. Het
verborgen rijk van Ming also
has a waterfall and a tea
house where visitors can
enjoy Chinese refreshments.

Another interesting theme
garden is the Ogham Gardens,
a Celtic garden whose main
attractions is the Horoscope
of Trees, consisting of an earth-
and-stone circular wall, which
is a replica of the enclosures
the ancient Celts built to live
within. Inside the circle is a
labyrinth representing life;
at its centre is a small garden
and the Well of Wisdom.

In summer, a variety of
exhibitions and events are
held on the grounds, attracting locals and tourists alike.

The fascinating Hortus Haren, with its innumerable attractions

Groninger Museum

Mirror by Jeff Koons

BETWEEN THE CENTRAL station and the inner city lies the Groninger Museum, standing on an island in the 19th-century Verbindingskanaal. Designed by internationally renowned Italian architect Alessandro Mendini and opened in 1994, the museum showcases archaeology and history, applied arts (including a remarkable collection of Chinese and Japanese porcelain), early art and cutting-edge modern art.

★ Spiral Staircase
The spiral staircase which visitors have to climb to see the exhibits is the museum's main meeting point and a work of art in itself.

★ Geldermalsen Collection
The stunning Geldermalsen porcelain collection consists of 18th-century China porcelain salvaged from the wreck of a Dutch East India Company ship.

Curtains
The applied arts section, which includes oriental porcelain, is divided by winding curtains.

A cycle and pedestrian bridge
connects the museum with the station square. There is also a direct connection with the station and the town centre.

The museum café features furniture by various designers and was set up as an addition to the museum collection.

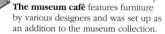

The museum shop
sells reproductions of the exhibits and books about the artists who are represented in the museum.

STAR SIGHTS

★ De Ploeg

★ Geldermalsen Collection

★ Spiral Staircase

Rembrandt
This ink drawing of Saskia in Bed *by Rembrandt can be seen in the spectacular Mendini Pavilion.*

VISITORS' CHECKLIST

Museumeiland 1. ▐ 0900-821
2132. ☐ 10am–5pm Tue–Sun.
● Mon, 1 Jan, 5 May, 25 Dec.
▨ **Café** ☐ 9.30am–6pm Tue–
Sun. ● same as above.

★ De Ploeg
The Groningen art collective De Ploeg has its own pavilion. In addition to works by the group, the section also displays works by other expressionists from northern Europe. The picture Rotating Door of the Post Office *is by De Ploeg painter HN Werkman.*

The Mendini Pavilion is easily distinguished by its apparent haphazardness and chaos, and is a good example of deconstructivism.

MUSEUM GUIDE

Groninger Museum was designed by Alessandro Mendini (1931). He based the design around the collections of the museum, which consisted of archaeology, applied arts and early and modern pictorial arts. The focus of the building is the 30-m (98-ft) tower in the middle, housing the museum shop.

Bridge to the Coop Himmelb(l)au Pavilion

A large concrete staircase in the Mendini Pavilion leads to the upper pavilion, where some of the collection of early pictorial art is on display.

This wing of the museum was designed by Wolfgang Prix and Helmut Swiczinsky.

Grootegast ❷

Road map D1. 👥 *11,500*. 🚌 *39*.
🛈 *Tolbertstraat 39, Leek (0594-512100)*. 🅰 *Fri*.

THE LITTLE TOWN of Lutjegast, close to Grootegast, is the birthplace of the 17th-century explorer Abel Tasman *(see box)*. The **Abel Tasmankabinet** houses an interesting exhibition about his life. The fascinating collection it contains includes old sea charts and books.

🏛 **Abel Tasmankabinet**
Kompasstraat 1. 📞 *0594-612431*.
⭕ *8:30am–noon, 1–5pm Mon–Sat*.

Leek ❸

Road map D2. 👥 *18,000*.
🚌 *100, 180*. 🛈 *Tolbertstraat 39 (0594-512100)*. 🅰 *Thu*.

IN THE SMALL TOWN of Leek stands the castle of Nienoord, built in approximately 1524 by Wigbold van Ewsum. During the 19th century, things at the castle

Landgoed Nienoord

seemed to be taking a turn for the worse. In 1846, the then owner, Ferdinand Folef Kniphausen, nicknamed "the mad squire", burned all the family portraits in a drunken fit. Later, the orangery and part of the upper floor were destroyed by fire. In 1950, the municipality bought the castle. Eight years later, the **Nationaal Rijtuigmuseum**, featuring horse-drawn vehicles, was established here. It contains a unique collection of royal coaches, gigs, mail coaches and hackney carriages.

🏛 **Nationaal Rijtuigmuseum**
Nienoord 1. 📞 *0594-512260*.
⭕ *Apr–Oct: 10am–5pm Tue–Sat, 1–5pm Sun*. ⬤ *Mon*. 📷 ♿

The harbour of the delightful fishing village of Zoutkamp

Zoutkamp ❹

Road map D1.
👥 *1,200*. 🚌 *63, 65, 165*.
🛈 *Reitdiepskade 11 (0595-401957)*.

THE SMALL FISHING village of Zoutkamp changed its character dramatically after the damming of the Lauwerszee in 1969. By the waterside (Reitdiepskade) there are still a number of fisherman's cottages retaining the erstwhile charm of the village.

Lauwersoog ❺

Road map D1. 👥 *350*.
🚌 *63*. 🛈 *Expo-zee, Strandweg 1 (0519-349133)*.

AT LAUWERSOOG, from where the ferry leaves for Schiermonnikoog *(see p273)*, is the Lauwersmeer, a 2,000-ha (4,940-acre) nature reserve. When the Lauwerszee was drained, the land was designated for four purposes: agriculture, recreation, a nature reserve and an army training area.

ENVIRONS: Lauwersoog is a good base from which to explore the tuff churches that, in the middle ages, were built in villages such as Doezum, Bedum and Zuidwolde. They can be recognized by their grey or green porous stone.

ABEL TASMAN (1603–59)

Abel Janszoon Tasman was born in Lutjegast in 1603 but lived in Amsterdam from an early age. In 1633, as a navigating officer for the Dutch East India Company *(see pp48–9)*, he travelled to Asia. In 1642, he sailed on the yacht *De Heemskerck* and then with the cargo ship *Zeehaen* in search of the legendary southern continent. Tasman charted some of the coast and later reached New Zealand's South Island. On 13 June 1643, he arrived in Batavia (now Jakarta), which he called home until his death 16 years later. From 1644 to 1648, he sat on the Batavian council of justice; during this time he also joined trading missions to Sumatra (1646) and Siam (1647). Tasman died on 10 October 1659, having bequeathed his money to the poor of Lutjegast.

Pieterburen

Road map D1. 🏛 *500.* 🚌 *68, 69.*
ℹ️ *Waddencentrum, Hoofdstraat 83
(0595-528522).*

O NE OF THE best-known
places in Groningen is
Pieterburen, home to the
Zeehondencrèche. This
seal nursery was founded by
Lenie 't Hart and others as a
reception centre for sick and
disabled seals from the nearby Waddenzee, where some
1,750 seals live. Half of these
owe their lives to the care
they received at the centre.

The **Waddencentrum**, also
located here, is an exhibition
centre dedicated to the mud
flats of the Waddenzee. It also
provides useful information for
people wishing to walk there.

🦭 Zeehondencrèche Pieterburen
Hoofdstraat 94a. 📞 *0595-526526.*
🕐 *9am–6pm daily.*

🦭 Het Waddencentrum
Hoofdstraat 83. 📞 *0595-528522.*
🕐 *Apr–Nov: 1–5pm Tue–Sun;
Nov–Mar: 1–5pm Sat & Sun.*

ENVIRONS: In Leens, 10 km
(6 miles) to the southwest of
Pieterburen is the stunning
14th-century *borg* (moated
manor house) Verhildersum,
which contains 19th-century
furnishings. The castle is surrounded by a wide moat. Its

gardens include an arbour and
sculptures. The castle's coach
house is regularly used as a
venue for exhibitions, while
the Schathuis (treasury) is now
a lively café and restaurant.

🏰 Borg Verhildersum
Wierde 40, Leens.
📞 *0595-571430.* 🕐 *Apr–Oct:
10:30am–5pm Tue–Sun.* 🅿️

Uithuizen ⑦

Road map E1. 🏛 *5,300.* 🚌 *61.*
ℹ️ *Mennonietenkerkstraat 13 (0595-
434051).* 🛍 *Sat.*

T HE EXCEPTIONALLY pretty
castle of Menkemaborg in
Uithuizen dates back to the

14th century. It acquired its
present-day form around 1700.
The bedroom features a ceremonial bedstead dating from
the early 18th century, when
King William III stayed here.
The kitchen in the cellar has
all the old fittings. The gardens
were laid out during restoration work in the 18th century.
The Schathuis (treasury), formerly used to store the food
brought by the townspeople
to the castle, currently houses
a café and restaurant.

🏰 Menkemaborg
Menkemaweg 2. 🚌 *61.* 📞 *0595-
431970.* 🕐 *Mar–Apr & Oct–early
Jun: 10am–noon & 1–4pm Tue–Sun;
May–Sep: 10am–5pm daily.*
⚫ *mid-Jan–Feb.* 🅿️

Recovering seal in one of the ponds at Pieterburen

Wedding in traditional dress in the gardens of the 14th-century Menkemaborg in Uithuizen

Appingedam ❽

Road map E1. 🏃 12,400. 🚌
140, 155. ℹ️ Prof. Cleveringaplein
1a (0596-620300). 🚋 Sat.

THIS TOWN, a member of
the Hanseatic League in
the Middle Ages, was granted
its charter in 1327. Standing
at a junction of waterways as
it once did and with a sea-
port, it quickly grew into a
major international trading
city. The medieval layout of
the city has remained largely
unchanged. The **hanging
kitchens**, visible from the
Vlinterbrug bridge, were built
this way to create more space
in the houses. Directly over
the water are doors from
which people drew water for
their household needs.

In the 18th century, the
town again prospered, as the
Ebenhaëzerhuis well illustrates. Appingedam, with
over 65 listed buildings, has a
preservation order as a town
of historical interest.

Slochteren ❾

Road map E1. 🏃 2,600. 🚌 78,
178. ℹ️ Noorderweg 1 (0598-
422970). 🚋 Thu.

WHEN A NATURAL GAS field
was discovered here
in 1959, Slochteren gained
overnight national renown.
The "Slochteren Dome"
appeared to be the largest in
the world when it was first
discovered, and the revenue it
brought in made Holland rich.

The past of this historic town
is closely associated with the
lords of the Fraeylemaborg.
The Reformed Church in
Slochteren consists of the
remnants of a 13th-century

Steam pumping station (1878) at the Winschoten polder, now a museum

Romanesque-Gothic cross-
naved church. The environs
are excellent for walking or
cycling, particularly around
places like nearby Schildmeer.

Fraeylemaborg ❿

Road map E1. 🚌 78, 178. ℹ️ Noorderweg 1, Slochteren (0598-422907).

FRAEYLEMABORG IS ONE of the
most imposing castles of
Groningen. It dates back to
the Middle Ages. Three embra-
sures in the kitchen and the
hall above it bear silent witness to the defensive functions the castle once had. In
the 17th century, two side
wings were added, and in the
18th century it was given its
present form with the addition
of the monumental main wing.
The castle is surrounded by a
double moat.

The extensive wooded park
just beyond the castle is an
interesting combination of
the 18th-century Baroque
garden style and the 19th-
century English landscape
gardens.

🏛 **Fraeylemaborg**
Hoofdweg 30–32, Slochteren.
📞 0598-421568. 🕐 1 Mar–31 Dec:
10am–5pm Tue–Fri; 1–5pm Sat,
Sun & public hols. 📷

Winschoten ⓫

Road map E2. 🏃 18,500. 🚌 17,
29. ℹ️ Stationsweg 21a (0597-
412255). 🚋 Sat.

THIS LITTLE TOWN in Oost-
Groningen is known
primarily for its three mills:
Berg, a corn and hulling mill
from 1854; Dijkstra, which
is 25 m (82 ft) in height and
dates from 1862; and Edens,
a corn and hulling mill from
1761. The interesting **Museum
Stoomgemaal** contains a
steam-powered pump from
1878 which was used to
drain the flooded polderland.

🏛 **Museum Stoomgemaal**
Oostereinde 4. 📞 0597-425070.
🕐 Jun–Sep: 1–5pm Mon–Fri; Jul &
Aug also 11am–5pm Sun. 📷

ENVIRONS: In Heiligerlee
stands a monument to the
Battle of Heiligerlee in 1568.
This battle is famous for being
over in just two hours and
for the death of Count Adolf
of Nassau. In the **Museum
"Slag bij Heiligerlee"** there
is an exhibition dedicated to
the bloody battle.

🏛 **Museum "Slag bij
Heiligerlee"**
Provincialeweg 55. 📞 0597-418199.
🕐 Apr: 1–5pm Tue–Sun; May–mid-
Sep: 10am–5pm Tue–Sat, 1–5pm Sun;
mid-Sep–Oct: 1–5pm Tue–Fri & Sun.
⚫ public holidays. 📷

The historical castle of Fraeylemaborg at Slochteren

Veendam

Road map E2. 28,500.
71, 73. *Veenlustpassage 8
(0598-626255).* Mon.

Pᴀʀᴋsᴛᴀᴅ Veendam
(Veendam Garden City) is
so called for the lush greenery in the town, which for
centuries was the industrial
heart of the peat colonies.
However, at the end of the
19th century, peat-cutting
fell into decline. Although
shipping grew in importance
– Veendam even had its own
maritime school – the town
retained its character as a
peat-cutting town.

The **Veenkoloniaal
Museum** (peat colony museum) offers a permanent exhibition illustrating the history
of peat-cutting, navigation,
agriculture and industry in
the Groningen peatlands.

The most renowned inhabi-
tant of Veendam was Anthony
Winkler Prins (1807–1908),
who wrote the famous encyclopaedia which is still associated with his name.

🏛 **Veenkoloniaal Museum**
Winkler Prinsstraat 5.
0598-616393. *11am–5pm
Tue–Fri, 1–5pm Sat & Sun.*
public holidays.

Bourtange

Road map E2. 600. 171, 71
at Alteveer and lijntaxi at Vlagtwedde.
*Willem Lodewijkstraat 33
(0599-354600).*

Rɪɢʜᴛ ᴀᴛ the German border
is the magnificent fortified
town of Bourtange, whose
history dates back to 1580,
when William of Orange
ordered that a fortress with
five bastions be built in the
swampland at the German
border. The defence works
were continuously upgraded,
until the fort gradually lost its
defensive functions. It has
now been painstakingly
restored to its 18th-century
appearance. **Museum "De
Baracquen"** exhibits artefacts
excavated in the fort.

The charming town itself
lies within a star-shaped
labyrinth of moats.

Aerial view of the impressive fortress of Bourtange

🏛 **Museum "De Baracquen"**
Meestraat 3. 0599-354600.
*Apr–Oct: 10am–5pm Mon–Fri, 12:30–
5pm Sat & Sun; Nov–Mar: 1:30–5pm
Sat & Sun.* 25 & 26 Dec.

Oude en Nieuwe Pekela

Road map E2. 13,500. 75.
*Stationsweg 21a, Winschoten
(0597-412255).* Wed, Thu.

Tʜᴇ "ᴏʟᴅ" ᴀɴᴅ "ɴᴇw" villages
of Pekela are typical ribbon
developments with a marked
rural, peatland character. In
the 18th century, potato flour
and straw-board manufacture
grew in importance in the
region. The footpaths along
the main canal running
through the villages are
pleasant places for walking.

Ter Apel

Road map E2. 7,800. 26, 73.
Molenplein 1 (0599-581277).
Thu.

Iɴ ᴛᴇʀ ᴀᴘᴇʟ, situated in the
Westerwolde region between
Drenthe and Germany, is a
1465 **monastery** of the same
name. In 1933, the monastery
was thoroughly restored and
now functions as a museum
devoted to ecclesiastic art and
religious history. The fragrant
herb garden located in the
cloisters contains a collection
of nutrient-rich herbs such as
birthwort and common rue.

🏛 **Museum-klooster
Ter Apel**
Boslaan 3. 0599-581370.
*10am–5pm Mon–Sat, 1–5pm
Sun & public hols.* 1 Jan, Mon
(Nov–Mar).

The beautifully restored cloisters at the Ter Apel monastery

FRIESLAND

RIESLAND, OR FRYSLÂN AS IT IS OFFICIALLY CALLED, *is a remarkable province perhaps best known outside the Netherlands for its distinctive Frisian cows. Parts of it are below sea level, and its size has increased since historic times as a result of land reclamation schemes on the former Zuiderzee.*

Much of the province is fenland, a feature which no doubt helped the freedom-loving Frisians fight off invaders. The 1345 battle of Warns, when the Frisians beat the Dutch army, is still commemorated every year. In the 7th century, the Frisians under their king Radboud inhabited an independent territory that stretched all the way to Flanders and Cologne *(see pp44–5)*, and they have preserved their distinctive language to this day. Other features peculiar to this province are unique sports and recreations like sailing and racing in *skûtjes* (traditional Frisian boats), hunting for plovers' eggs, *fierljeppen* (pole-vaulting), *keatsen* (a ball game), and the famous *Elfstedentocht*, a winter ice-skating marathon around 11 Frisian towns.

The provincial capital of Leeuwarden has some interesting and unique museums, while elsewhere in the province visitors can enjoy collections consisting of items as diverse as historic costumes and hats, ceramics, letters, ice skates and sledges, vernacular paintings, bells, model boats and human mummies. Outside the towns, the landscape is interesting too, from the mud flats on the Waddenzee to the forests and heathland of the Drents-Friese Woud National Park, away to the east. Tourism is becoming increasingly important in Friesland nowadays and its inhabitants less insular. Visitors are greeted with open arms and *Jo binne tige welcom* – "You are heartily welcome."

Bartlehiem, the junction of the *Elfsteden* (11 towns) – a favourite summer destination for day-trippers

◁ The famous Waterpoort van Sneek (Sneek Gateway), dating from 1613

Exploring Friesland

Frisian flag

FRIESLAND IS FAMOUS for its vast meadows and its distinctive farmhouses of the *kopp-hals-romp* and *stelp* types. It also boasts a varied landscape. In the southwest are the popular *Friese meren* (Frisian lakes), while the north is typified by undulating dykes, *terp* villages and church steeples with pitched roofs. Gaasterland in the south has rolling woodlands and cliffs, whereas the *Friese wouden* (Frisian woods) in the province's southeastern corner, with their forests, heathland and drifting sands, are more reminiscent of Drenthe.

The sea dyke at Wierum

SIGHTS AT A GLANCE

Appelscha **14**
Beetsterzwaag **13**
Bolsward **5**
Dokkum **2**
Franeker **3**
Gaasterland **8**
Harlingen **4**
Hindeloopen **7**
Leeuwarden **1**
Oude Venen **12**
Sloten **9**
Sneek **10**
Thialfstadion **11**
Workum **6**

0 kilometres   10

0 miles   10

The Noorderhaven in Harlingen

GETTING AROUND

Friesland is convenient and easy to get to. It is crossed by the A7 (east-west) and the A32 (north-south) motorways. Rail and bus links are unproblematic. Most of the larger villages and towns have a railway station; those which don't can be reached by bus. From Harlingen, Holwerd or Lauwersoog, the islands are only a short boat ride away. The province also has a good network of minor roads, walking routes and cycle tracks.

FRANEKER **3**

HARLINGEN **4**

A31

N359

A7

5 BOLSWARD

N359

10 SNEEK

N354

WORKUM **6**

Fluessen

7 HINDELOOPEN

Sloter-meer

STAVOREN

8 GAASTERLAND

N359

9 SLOTEN

LEMMER

Gabled houses along Het Diep in Sloten

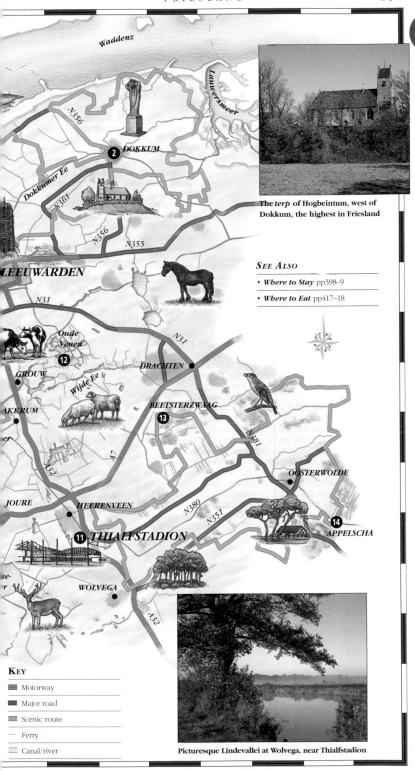

The _terp_ of Hogbeintum, west of Dokkum, the highest in Friesland

SEE ALSO

- **_Where to Stay_** pp398–9
- **_Where to Eat_** pp417–18

Picturesque Lindevallei at Wolvega, near Thialfstadion

KEY

- ▬ Motorway
- ▬ Major road
- ▬ Scenic route
- — Ferry
- ▭ Canal/river

The Elfstedentocht

THE ELFSTEDENTOCHT, or 11-town race, is a 200-km (124-mile) ice-skating marathon which passes through Leeuwarden, Skeen, IJlst, Sloten, Stavoren, Hindeloopen, Workum, Bolsward, Harlingen, Franeker, Dokkum and back to Leeuwarden. Participants are awarded the famous Elfstedenkruisje only when they have collected all the stamps on their starter's card and provided they get back to Leeuwarden before midnight. The winner of the race is guaranteed eternal fame.

1909: the first official *tocht*

The "Elfstedenkruisje" (Elfsteden cross) is in the shape of a Maltese cross. In the middle i. an enamel coat arms of Friesla. and the inscrip tion "De Friesch Elf Steden" – "The 11 Frisian towns".

THE TOCHT DER TOCHTEN

The Tocht der Tochten (literally, "Race of Races"), as the Elfstedentocht is known, is a combination of race and touring marathon and has acquired almost mythical status in Holland. The race is a real media event, keeping millions glued to their television screens. Although the marathon has been held only 15 times in the last century, the entire country falls under the spell of the event as soon as the mercury falls even slightly below zero. If there is a lasting frost, the area supervisors measure daily the thickness of the ice, as it has to be at least 15 cm (6 in) thick for the race to be held. When the magic words *It sil heve* (It shall happen) are uttered by the supervisors, Friesland is transformed, overflowing with excited

Franeker in a festive mood

crowds. Trains are packed, the roads are jammed with cars and entire villages are mobilized to provide hot tea and oranges for the skaters. Wandering musicians whip the crowd into a frenzy of enthusiasm. The Dutch language has been enriched with the Frisian word *klúnen*, which means to walk overland on skates past places where the ice is impassable.

HARNS ⑨
(HARLINGEN)

FRJENTS
(FRANEKE

⑩

Harlingervaart

BOALSERT
(BOLSWARD)

⑧

S
(

Workumer Trekvaart

WARKUM ⑦
(WORKUM)

DRYLTS
(IJLST)

HYLPEN
(HINDELOOPEN) ⑥

STARUM ⑤
(STAVOREN)

SLE
(SLOT

Dropping out is a common occurrence during the race. Despite being affected by snow blindness and symptoms of frostbite, many participants in the race attempt to complete the course. Some break down in tears when they realize that they will be unable to collect the much-coveted Elfstedenkruisje (Elfsteden cross).

0 kilometres   10

0 miles

The hamlet of Bartlehiem is famous for its foot-bridge over the Finkumervaart. Bartlehiem is the best-known skating area in all of Holland and is a psychological milestone for the skaters. Those who still must get to Dokkum may pass skaters travelling in the opposite direction, having already won their stamp from the northernmost point on the route. Many skaters have to take the Bartlehiem-Dokkum section in the dark. The Northern Lights seen at this time of year also attract thousands of spectators.

Two-time winner
Evert van Benthem

All winners of the Elfstedentocht are national heroes, but Evert van Benthem even more so. A farmer from Sint-Jansklooster, he managed to cross the finishing line at the Bonkevaart in Leeuwarden in first place twice in a row (1985 and 1986). Van Benthem's double victory gave him a legendary status throughout the Netherlands. The prize itself is a laurel wreath, both for men and for women. The names of the winners are engraved on the Elfstedenrijder monument in Leeuwarden.

DOKKUM
⑪

Dokkumer Ee

BARTLEHIEM

FINISH

LJOUWERT
(LEEUWARDEN)
①

A32

Long before sunrise, tens of thousands of skaters start off from the FEC (Frisian Exhibition Centre) in Leeuwarden.

THE EERSTE FRIESE SCHAATSMUSEUM

The Eerste Friese Schaatsmuseum (first Frisian skating museum) in Hindeloopen (see p296) has among its exhibits such items as antique skates, original workshops, sleds and historical documents covering the 90 or so years that the Elfstedentocht has been held. Displays on innumerable winners, including Reinier Paping, Jeen van den Berg and Henk Angenet, are also featured here. Among the highlights of the museum's collection are the skating packs of various skating heroes of the event, the skates of two-time winner Evert van Benthem and the starter's card of WA van Buren. One of the most moving exhibits in the collection is the right big toe of Tinus Udding, which he lost to frostbite during the harsh race in the cold winter of 1963.

Willem-Alexander, alias WA van Buren, in the arms of his mother, Queen Beatrix, after the 1985 race

KEY

▬ Route of the Elfstedentocht

═ Road

Leeuwarden ●

Road map D1. 🏛 *89,000*. 🚉 🚊
🛈 *Achmeatoren, Sophialaan 4
(0900-2024060).* 🚢 *Mon, Fri & Sat.*

Atmospheric Dokkum, a major port in the 8th century

F RISIAN CAPITAL and home to
Mata Hari, Peter Jelles Troel-
stra and Jan Jacob Slauerhoff,
Leeuwarden was also the residence of the Frisian Nassaus
(1584–1747). The town park
and gardens of the Prinsentuin
and Stadhouderlijk Hof date
back to this period.

Characteristic of Leeuwarden
is the statue of **Us Mem** (our
mother), honouring the
famous Frisian cattle. The
Fries Museum, situated
in an 18th-century patri-
cian house, has a large
collection of items exca-
vated from *terps,* as well
as collections of clothes,
art and applied arts. The
museum **Het Princesse-
hof**, housed in a palace
which was formerly the
residence of Maria Louise van
Hessen-Kassel (also known
as Marijke Meu), contains a
unique collection of ceramics
of international importance.
The holdings include Asian,
European and contemporary
ceramics and tiles.

**Frisian
coat of arms**

The old municipal orphanage
now is home to the **Fries
Natuurmuseum** (natural history museum), whose exhibition of "Friesland underwater"
is well worth a visit.

🏛 **Fries Museum**
Turfmarkt 11. 📞 *058-2555500.*
⏰ *11am–5pm Tue–Sun.* 🚫 🚻 🎧
🏛 **Het Princessehof**
Grote Kerkstraat 11. 📞 *058-2948958.*
⏰ *11am–5pm Tue–Sun (also Mon
May–Aug).* 🚫
🏛 **Fries Natuurmuseum**
Schoenmakersperk 2. 📞 *058-
2129085.* ⏰ *10am–5pm Tue–Sat,
1–5pm Sun.* 🚫

Dokkum ●

Road map D1. 🏛 *13,000.* 🚉
🛈 *Op de Fetze 13 (0519-293800).*
🚢 *Wed.*

T HE TRADING and garrison
town of Dokkum was the
headquarters of the Frisian
Admiralty between 1596 and
1645, though it owes its fame
above all to the killing here of
St Boniface by pagan Frisians
in AD 754 *(see pp44–5).* The
local history museum, the
Admiraliteitshuis, has an
exhibition on the life of the
saint. Other exhibits include

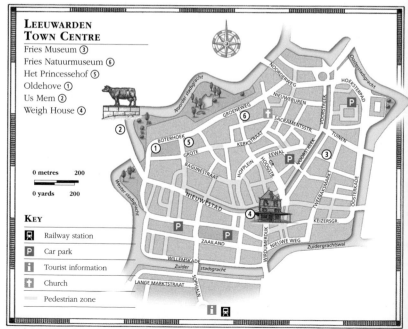

LEEUWARDEN TOWN CENTRE

Fries Museum ③
Fries Natuurmuseum ⑥
Het Princessehof ⑤
Oldehove ①
Us Mem ②
Weigh House ④

0 metres   200
0 yards   200

KEY

🚉 Railway station
P Car park
🛈 Tourist information
✚ Church
▬ Pedestrian zone

artefacts excavated from *terps*, costumes, silverware, handicrafts and folk art. In addition to the **Bonifatiuskerk**, Dokkum has a park for religious processions with the stations of the cross and a chapel. Water drawn from the well of **Bonifatiusbron** is believed to have therapeutic qualities. On the former **town walls**, now a park, are two 19th-century **stellingmolen**-type mills known as *De Hoop* and *Zeldenrust (see p21)*.

Admiraliteitshuis
Diepswal 27. 0519–293134.
Apr–Oct: 10am–5pm Tue–Sat.
Nov–Mar: 2–5pm Tue–Sat.

Franeker ❸

Road map C1. 13,000.
Voorstraat 51 (0900-5900001).
Wed & Sat.

FRANEKER WAS a university town from 1585 to 1811. Today, it is regarded as the centre of skating in Friesland. In and around the Voorstraat are a variety of monumental buildings, including the 15th-century Martenahuis and the 16th-century Botniahuis. The Cammingahuis, which dates from the 14th century, now houses the **Kaatsmuseum** (skating museum). The museum **'t Coopmanshûs**, in a fine 18th-century building, has a collection about the former university and an unusual wood collection in book form, as well as fine art and applied arts. The Renaissance **Stadhuis**

Eise Eisinga Planetarium

(town hall) has an ornate façade. Directly opposite is the famous **Planetarium** (1781) built by wool industrialist Eise Eisinga. For two centuries now, the planets have rotated around its ceiling with great accuracy. Beside the Sjûkelân, a sacred place for Frisian skating, is the Bogt fen Guné (16th century), Holland's oldest student residence.

🏛 **Kaatsmuseum**
Voorstraat 2. 0517-393910.
May–Sep: 1–5pm Tue–Sat.
🏛 **'t Coopmanshûs**
Voorstraat 49. 0517-392192.
10am–5pm Tue–Sat;
Apr–Sep: also 1–5pm Sun.
🏛 **Planetarium**
Eise Eisingastraat 3. 0517-393070.
10am–5pm Tue–Sat; May–mid Sep:
also 1–5pm Sun & Mon.

Harlingen ❹

Road map C2. 14,500.
Voorstraat 34 (0900-5400001).
Wed, Sat.

THE PORT TOWN of Harlingen retains much of its old charm. The **Zoutsloot** and **Noorderhaven** have been painstakingly restored. A statue of **Hans Brinker** *(see p19)* stands at the ferry port. South of Harlingen is **Pingjum**. Menno Simons (1496–1561), the evangelical preacher after whom many of the Dutch Anabaptists named themselves, started his religious life here. It is now visited by Mennonites from all over the world.

Bolsward town hall

Bolsward ❺

Road map C2. 10,000.
Marktplein 1 (0515-572727). Thu.

MODEST BOLSWARD first arose in the 11th century as a trading post, enjoying the height of its development in the 15th century. **Martinikerk**, a pseudo-basilica whose tower features a saddleback roof, was built during this period. The **Stadhuis** (town hall), with its local history museum, the **Oudheidkamer**, is the town's centrepiece. **Sonnema Distillery** (Stoombootkade 12), where local tipple *berenburg* is distilled, runs a tour finishing with a tasting session.

🏛 **Oudheidkamer**
Jongemastraat 2. 0515-578787.
2–4pm Mon; 9am–noon & 2–4pm
Tue–Fri.

MATA HARI

Margaretha Geertruida Zelle (1876–1917), who became known to all the world as Mata Hari (Malaysian for "eye of the day"), grew up in Leeuwarden. Her life came to a tragic end in Vincennes outside Paris, where she was executed by firing squad after a French tribunal found her guilty of espionage. The Fries Museum tells you more about this legendary woman, who has gained international notoriety through all the films and books made about her life. The house where she lived with her parents from 1883 to 1890 on Grote Kerkstraat 212 now houses the Frysk Letterkundlich Museum (Frisian museum of letters).

Workum ❻

Road map C2. 🚶 *4,000*. 🚌 🚉
ℹ️ *Noard 5 (0900-540001).*

THE ELONGATED Zuiderzee town of Workum flourished around 1300. Workum is known for the fine façades of its houses and its unfinished 16th-century church, the **Grote of Gertrudiskerk**. Beside the lock is the centuries-old wharf of **de Hoop**, where traditional boats are still built. The most popular attraction in Workum is **Jopie Huisman Museum**, which is the most-visited

The Football Boots of Abe Lenstra by Jopie Huisman

museum in Friesland. It features the autodidactic art of painter and scrap metal merchant Jopie Huisman (1922–2000). His drawings and paintings tell the stories of the daily grind and poverty, the drudgery and toil of the tradesman, the housewife and the ordinary person.

The picturesque 17th-century weigh house contains the **Museum Warkums Erfskip**. This museum delves into the history of Workum, and, principally, that of its shipping and pottery industries.

🏛️ **Jopie Huisman Museum**
Noard 6. 📞 *0515-543131*. 🕐 *Apr–Oct: 10am–5pm Mon–Sat, 1–5pm Sun; Mar & Nov: 1–5pm daily.* 🅿️ ♿
🏛️ **Museum Warkums Erfskip**
Waaggebouw. 📞 *0515-543155*. 🕐 *Apr–Oct: 11am–5pm Tue–Fri, 1–5pm Mon, Sat, Sun.* 🅿️

Hindeloopen ❼

Road map C2. 🚶 *850*. 🚌 🚉
ℹ️ *Nieuwstad 26 (0900-540001).*

HINDELOOPEN PLAYS a special role in Friesland. This picturesque old town of seafarers and fishermen has its

Lockkeeper's house with its inviting bench, in Hindeloopen

own dialect, its own costume and its own style of painting. The town is full of little canals with wooden bridges and a variety of pretty captains' houses, with their characteristic façades. One of the most distinctive spots is the picturesque 17th-century lockkeeper's house by the port, with its wooden bell-tower.

In the **Museum Hidde Nijland Stichting** (museum of the Hidde Nijland foundation), the life of the wealthy citizens of Hindeloopen during the 18th century is showcased. Well-appointed period rooms show the colourful clothes and the now-famous painted furniture of the time. A substantial exhibition of paintings vividly illustrates the development of painting in Hindeloopen.

The **Eerste Friese Schaatsmuseum** (first Frisian skating museum) *(see p293)* offers a unique collection of old skates. It also has a fine exhibition dedicated to the Elfstedentocht and various traditional workshops (such as a smithy and a carpenter's), as well as a comprehensive collection of sledges and historical material such as old tiles and prints.

🏛️ **Museum Hidde Nijland Stichting**
Dijkweg 1. 📞 *0514-521420*. 🕐 *Mar–Oct: 10am–5pm Mon–Sat, 1:30–5pm Sun & public hols.* 🅿️
🏛️ **Eerste Friese Schaatsmuseum**
Kleine Weide 1–3.
📞 *0514-521683*. 🕐 *10am–6pm Mon–Sat, 1–5pm Sun.* 🅿️

Gaasterland ❽

Road map C2. 🚌 ℹ️ *De Brink 4, Oudemirdum (0900-540001).*

THIS AREA OF fine, rolling woodlands in the southwestern corner of Friesland offers many opportunities for walking and cycling. The region's name comes from the word "gaast", which refers to the sandy heights formed during the last two Ice Ages.

At the edge of Gaasterland are a number of steep cliffs, such as the **Rode Klif** and the **Oudemirdumerklif**, formed when the Zuiderzee eroded the coastline. On the Rode Klif at Laaxum is an enormous boulder bearing the inscription *Leaver dea as slaef*, or, *Rather dead than a slave*, a memento of the 1345 Frisian victory over the Dutch.

A cyclist in Gaasterland

The **Rijsterbos** wood, with its abundant bracken, dates from the 17th century and once consisted mainly of oak. The little river of Luts, which is now known because of the Elfstedentocht, was used for the transport of oak logs and oak bark for tanneries. In the village of **Oudemirdum** is a hostel, shops and an old pump. **Informatiecentrum Mar en Klif** (Sea and Cliff Information Centre) has information about how the landscape was formed and about local flora and fauna. Special attention is paid to badgers, and in the wild garden, a bat tower has been built.

The Luts river in **Balk**, flanked by linden trees, inspired the poem *Mei* by Herman Gorter (1864–1927).

⁂ Informatiecentrum Mar en Klif
De Brink 4. **📞** *0514-571777.*
◯ *Apr–Oct: 10am–5pm Mon–Sat.*

Sloten ❾

Road map C2. **👤** *650.* 🚌
ℹ *Knestraat 44 (0900-540001).*

THE SMALLEST TOWN in Friesland, replete with picturesque canals, embankments and water-gates, was designed by famous Frisian fortifications engineer Menno van Coehoorn. Built at a junction of roads and waterways, it was at the height of its development in the 17th and 18th centuries. On either side of the town are old cannons. The old fortress mill at the Lemsterpoort is an octagonal *bovenkruier*-type mill from 1755. The **Museum Stedhûs Sleat** houses the **Laterna Magica**, a museum of magic lanterns, an antique museum and a special collection of old costumes, hats, fans and bells.

🏛 Museum Stedhûs Sleat
Heerenwal 48. **📞** *0514-531541.*
◯ *10am–noon & 2–5pm Tue–Fri.* 📷

Sneek ❿

Road map C2. **👤** *31,600.* 🚌 🚊
ℹ *Marktstraat18 (0515-414096).*
🅿 *Tue, Sat.*

SNEEK'S centrepiece is the Waterpoort (water-gate) dating from 1613. Sneekweek is the name of a popular sailing event that in early August brings together amateur sailors and partygoers from all over

Typical stepped gables in Sloten

Mummy in Wieuwerd

the country. **Fries Scheepvaart Museum** focuses on the history of navigation and shipbuilding. Its exhibits include a *skûtje* deckhouse, the cabin of a *boeier* yacht and approximately 200 model ships. The *zilverzaal* (silver room) houses one of the richest collections of Frisian silver.

🏛 Fries Scheepvaart Museum
Kleinzand 14. **📞** *0515-414057.*
◯ *10am–5pm Mon–Sat, noon–5pm Sun.* 📷

ENVIRONS: The village of **Wieuwerd**, north of Sneek, is known for the human mummies in its 13th-century St Nicholas church (open in summer). They were discovered by chance in 1765 and the reason for their mummification is not known.

SCHUITJE SAILING

Schuitje sailing, *or skûtsjesilen,* is a sport which has gained great popularity in the lakes of Friesland, *skûtje* being the name of the typical local spritsail barges. Originally used for the carriage of goods and as ferries, these boats are raced by representatives of various towns and villages. The result is a series of spectacular events held in July and August in various places, each time on a different lake and from a different base. Every day certain prizes are won, and on the last day, in Sneek, the champion of the year is announced and fêted. The races are held over the course of 11 racing days and three rest days.

The Thialfstadion ⓫

THE THIALFSTADION IN HEERENVEEN, completely renovated in 2001, is regarded as the temple of Dutch ice-skating and has international renown. The exuberant crowds that converge on the stadium for international events create a unique atmosphere. Skating heroes such as Marianne Timmer, Gunda Niemann and Rintje Ritsma have all experienced emotional highlights in their sporting careers here.

THE ART OF ICE-MAKING

Making a good ice surface is an art. The Thialf ice-makers strive to strike a balance between deformation – the extent to which the ice breaks down under the pressure of the skate – and the smoothness of the ice.

Thialf Spectators
The fans here are famous for their colourful garb and their imaginative banners.

Underneath the ice are 70 km (43 miles) of cooling elements.

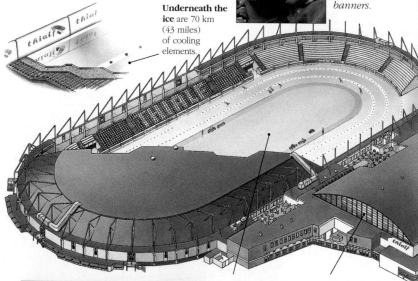

The great hall covers an area of 15,000 m² (17,950 sq yd) and can accommodate 13,000 spectators.

The ice hockey hall is 1,800 m² (2,150 sq yd) and has room for 4,000 spectators.

Hinged Skates
Skates which have a hinge between the shoe and the blade give significantly better results. All new world records have been achieved with the help of klap-schaatsen *(hinged skates).*

Triumph
The climax of every major skating event in the Thialfstadion is the procession of winners through the stadium on a special sleigh drawn by a Frisian horse.

Stately Lauswolt, now a luxury hotel with a restaurant

Oude Venen ⑫

Road map D2. 🚌 ℹ️ *P Miedema-weg 9, Earnewâld (0511-539500).*

THIS REGION, whose name literally means "the old fens", is a fine area of peat-marshes with reedlands, swampy woodlands and sunken polders between

The Oude Venen

Earnewâld and Grou. The lakes were formed in the 17th and 18th centuries by peat-cutting and now offer a home to over 100 species of birds and approximately 400 plant species. There is a large colony of great cormorants and various rare birds such as the spotted crake, the purple heron, the white-fronted goose, the barna-cle goose, the Eurasian wigeon and the ruff, all of which are best watched in spring.

In and around the water are water lilies, yellow water lily, marsh lousewort and cotton-grass. The area's hayfields are yellow with marsh marigold in spring.

Reidplûm visitors' centre of *It Fryske Gea* at Earnewâld provides information on the surrounding area and is a good starting point for hiking and sailing expeditions. Beside the centre is the Eibertshiem, a breeding centre for storks.

A great deal of attention has been paid to water cleanliness in the region, and now otters have returned to breed. In winter, the area hosts many skating tours.

🦩 Bezoekerscentrum De Reidplûm
Ds v.d. Veenweg 7, Earnewald.
📞 *0511-539410.* ⬜ *mid-Apr–Sep: 1–5pm daily.*

Beetsterzwaag ⑬

Road map D2. 🏛️ *3,700.* 🚌
ℹ️ *Hoofdstraat 59, Gorredijk (0513-461875).*

THIS VILLAGE was once one of the seats of the Frisian landed gentry and so has a number of stately homes and gardens. Fine examples of these are **Lauswolt,** the **Lycklamahuis** and the

Harinxmastate. Beetster-zwaag is surrounded by a varied countryside, with coniferous and deciduous forests, heath and fens offering ample opportunities for a leisurely afternoon of rambling and cycling.

Appelscha ⑭

Road map D2. 🏛️ *4,500.* 🚌
ℹ️ *Boerestreek 23 (0516-431760).*

THE VAST CONIFEROUS forests, drifting sands and colour-ful heath and fen areas around Appelscha form stunning sur-roundings. The village was created in the 19th century when the main industry was peat-cutting and is now on the edge of the **Nationaal Park Drents-Friese Woud**.

A favourite place with visi-tors is the **Kale Duinen** area of drifting sands. On the Bos-berg – at 26 m (85 ft) above sea level, the highest spot in the area – is a viewing tower and information centre run by the forestry service.

A distinctive phenomenon in southeast Friesland is the **Klokkenstoel** (bell stool). This "poor men's church tower" was a provisional church tower built when funds were low; it was usually situated in the churchyard. In Appelscha you will find a *klokkenstoel* dating from 1453. Langedijke is home to what is presumed to be the oldest bell in the Netherlands, dating from 1300.
ENVIRONS: At Ravenswoud, 5 km (3 miles) northeast of Appelsche, an 18-m (59-ft) observation tower provides outstanding views.

Drifting sand dune near the small town of Appelscha

DRENTHE

O NCE, DRENTHE WAS A FREE REPUBLIC *of farmers, and its inhabitants have always lived close to the land. Although the region has no cities and few towns, the rural poverty that once prevailed is no more, and tourists, especially those interested in archaeology and nature, are arriving in increasing numbers.*

Drenthe, whose landscape is a product of the last Ice Age, has managed to keep time at bay by holding on to its character, reputed by the rest of the country to have been born of peat, gin and suspicion. Moraines and megaliths dot the countryside. The extensive woodland, heathland and peat bogs have a primeval atmosphere, although this does not mean that there has been no human intervention. The top level of peat has been largely removed, while the traditional *esdorps,* the local hamlets, have modern outskirts. However, peat moors and forests, ancient burial mounds, canals, flocks of sheep and green fields are the principal features here.

There are more than 50 megaliths in Drenthe, the remains of tombs dating from the Neolithic era; information about this period, with archaeological finds, is displayed in the museum at Borger. Other museums in the region feature glass blowing, artworks, natural history and paper-cutting. Orvelte boasts a fine open-air museum with Saxon farmhouses and traditional crafts, while Dwingeloo looks to the future at the Planetron observatory and planetarium.

Visitors come to Drenthe for peace and quiet after the rigours of city life. But this does not mean there are no facilities – local centres such as Assen, Emmen and Hoogeveen are urbanized areas that grew out of villages, and there is a variety of hotels, guesthouses and restaurants throughout the region.

The largest horse market in western Europe, at Zuidlaren

◁ **Keystone in the 13th-century Romanesque church near the village of Norg**

Exploring Drenthe

THE FINEST NATURAL AREAS of Drenthe are the Hondsrug ridge, between Zuidlaren and Emmen, and the Ellertsveld region between Assen and Emmen. The areas around Diever, Dwingeloo and Norg are a resplendent green (or purple, when the heather is in bloom). The eastern part of the region, with its endless excavated peatlands and the wilderness of the Amsterdamsche Veld, is relatively unknown. The provincial capital of Assen is also a regional centre, as is Emmen, where Noorder Dierenpark Zoo, in the middle of the town, has become one of the most-visited attractions in Holland. The megaliths are concentrated around Emmen, along the Hondsrug and at Havelte.

SIGHTS AT A GLANCE

Assen ②
Borger ⑧
Coevorden ⑬
Diever ⑫
Dwingeloo ⑪
Eelde-Paterswolde ④
Emmen ⑭
Hondsrug ⑥
Norg ③
Orvelte ⑨
Rolde ⑦
Westerbork ⑩
Zuidlaren ⑤

Tour
The Megalith Route pp304–5 ①

The 14th-century Siepelkerk at Dwingeloo

The broad and silent heath

0 kilometres   10

0 miles   10

Thatcher at work in Havelte

KEY

▬ Motorway

▬ Major road

═ Minor road

▬ Scenic route

▭ Canal/river

The landscape reserve of the Drentse Aa river, an exceptionally peaceful hiking area near Hondsrug

SEE ALSO

- *Where to Stay* p399
- *Where to Eat* p418

5 ZUIDLAREN

ANLOO

1 THE MEGALITH ROUTE

GIETEN

7

ROLDE

6 HONDSRUG

BORGER **8**

10

RBORK **9** ORVELTE

Ellertsveld

EXLOO

ODOORN

Historical wooden walkway through the peatland (Valthe)

N381

SLEEN

EMMEN **14**

KLAZIENAVEEN

N37

LANDSCHE VELD

SCHOONEBEEK

COEVORDEN **13**

GETTING AROUND

Every year, Drenthe is the venue of the *Rijwielvierdaagse*, a four-day cycle tour which attracts more than 25,000 participants. There are 500 km (310 miles) of marked cycle routes in the region. The A28 motorway crosses the province through Meppel, Hoogeveen and Assen, and the railway follows the same route. Other motorways include the N371 from Meppel to Assen along the Drentse Hoofdvaart, the N37 Hoogeveen-Emmen and the N34 Emmen-Zuidlaren. Emmen is also the last stop on the railway to Zwolle via Coevorden. Bus service is limited, particularly in the evenings.

The Megalith Route ❶

O F THE 54 MEGALITHS in Holland, 52 are in Drenthe and the remaining two are in Groningen. These megaliths, or *hunebedden*, are the remains of ancient tombs built of boulders some 5,000 years ago by the Neolithic Beaker Folk. What can be seen today are only the frameworks of the tombs, which were all hidden underneath sandhills. It is still not known whether these were common graves or the tombs of prominent individuals.

Witte Wieven ① are ghosts that inhabit the tumuli, such as the Negen Bergen at Norg. They come out at midnight – particularly when it is misty – to dance.

At Diever and Havelte are three megaliths which are not on the route described here. The largest consists of 23 upright stones, 9 top stones, 2 keystones and a gate of 4 uprights and 2 top stones. At least 665 ancient pots have been found here. In World War II, the megalith was demolished to make way for an airfield. It was reconstructed in 1950.

The Great Megalith ⑧ of Balloo is at the end of a sandy path in the Tumulibos woods, an area which abounds with tumuli.

```
0 kilometres        5
0 miles             5
```

KEY

▬	Tour route
═	Other road
─	Railway
🛏	Megalith
🏛	Museum

Megalith at Loon ⑨ One of the best-preserved megaliths in Holland is at Loon, northeast of Assen. Before 1870 it was in even better condition, when the original top stone was still in place.

De Zeven Marken ⑦ the open-air museum o Schoonoord, tells you about such things as th legend of the giants El and Brammert.

BUILDING THE MEGALITHS

Until the 19th century, it was believed that the megaliths were built by the *huynen*, giants of great strength and after whom the *hunebedden* are named. Modern historians believe that the boulders were placed with their flat edges on rollers, which thus allowed them to be moved to the site of the tomb. The upright stones were placed in pits dug beforehand. A gentle slope of earth was then made to allow the top stones to be dragged up. There is, however, no explanation of how the people of the Stone Age managed to organize such large-scale projects.

Seventeenth-century depiction of megalith builders

Typical beakers *after which the Beaker Folk are named. Pottery shards of these containers are the most common finds in the megaliths.*

Beaker

Pitcher

Anloo ② *is one of the most picturesque Drenthe villages.*

Collared flask

The largest megalith in Holland ③ *measures 22.5 m (74 ft), has 9 top stones and 26 upright stones. Excavations were carried out in Borger in 1685, but none of the finds has been preserved.*

Het Flint'n Hoes, the Nationaal Hunebedden Informatiecentrum ④, *(National Megalith Information Centre), has been set up beside Holland's largest megalith.*

TIPS FOR DRIVERS

Length: 95 km (60 miles)
Stopping-off places: All villages on the route offer refreshments and meals. To see most megaliths you will need to leave your car and walk, as only a few are by the road-side. They are almost invariably well sign-posted and make excellent picnic spots.

The Exloo Necklace ⑤ *was found in the peat in 1881. It is made of beads of tin, faience, bronze and amber, which is evidence of trading links between prehistoric Drenthe and the Baltic countries, Cornwall and even Egypt.*

(map of Drenthe region with places: Annen, Anloo, OOËRVELD, Eext, oërkuil, Gieten, lloo, DROUWENERZAND, Drouwen, HONDSRUG, N857, N374, Borger, Buinen, Schoonloo, Uitzichttoren, Exloo, ERTSVELD, boonoord, Open-air museum, Odoorn, Valthe, N376, 't Haantje, SLEENERZAND, N381)

Flint *was the main material used by the hunter-gatherers of prehistoric Drenthe to make such items as knives, axes, scrapers and arrowheads.*

MEGALITHS (HUNEBEDDEN)

There are no longer any complete megaliths. Until 1734, when trading in boulders was forbidden, thousands of megaliths were hacked up to be used as building material. There are definite traces of 88 megaliths, 82 of them in Drenthe. The 54 surviving megaliths are all restorations. The most common finds from excavations are pottery shards. Scrapers, axes, arrowheads, and amber and copper jewellery – all extremely valuable trading goods in Drenthe in 3000 BC – are much rarer finds.

De Papeloze Kerk *(the Popeless Church)* ⑥ *This megalith is so called because of the Calvinist sermons that were held here in the 16th century against the "popish" (Catholic) faith. In 1959, the megalith was restored to its original state, to the extent of covering half of the tomb with sand.*

The Yde girl, a reconstructed peat-bog corpse

Assen ❷

Road map D2. 🏛 *61,500.* 🚊 ℹ
Marktstraat 8 (0900-2022393). 🛒 *Wed.*

A SSEN IS the capital of Drenthe, although it was only upgraded from village to a town in 1809. The **cloister** of the abbey church of Maria in Campis (1258–1600) now forms part of the Rijksarchief (national archive) of the Brink. Also on the

Bartje

Brink is the **Drents Museum** of local history, which is housed in the abbey church, the Ontvangershuis (1698), the Drostenhuis (1778) and Provinciehuis (1885). The museum contains a wealth of exhibits on prehistoric times and the history of the town, as well as collections of local art and a "discovery room" for the children.

The controversial finds of **Tjerk Vermaning** (1929–87), who in the 1960s single-handedly extended the history of human habitation in Holland by tens of thousands of years, are in a separate display case: disputes on the genuineness of the flint tools he found have not yet been resolved.

Outside the formal gardens of the Drostenhuis is the town's trademark **Bartje**, a statue of the little peasant boy from Dutch author Anne de Vries' book (1935) who did not want to pray before his daily meals of brown beans. The Vaart and the Markt have the characteristic stately white houses of Assen, built

in the late 18th to the early 19th century.

Between Markt and Brink is the commercial centre with its pedestrian precinct and excellent facilities. Modern-day Assen comes to life when the **circuit van Assen** TT motor racing event is held here. Children can race all the year round on the go-kart track of the Verkeerspark Assen *(see p448).*

🏛 **Drents Museum**
Brink 1–5. 📞 *0592-37773.* ◯
Tue–Sun. ⬤ *Mon, 25 Dec, 1 Jan.* 🖼
♿ 🖥 🎫 🅦 www.drentsmuseum.nl

Sacrificial victim from the peat bogs, at the Drents Museum

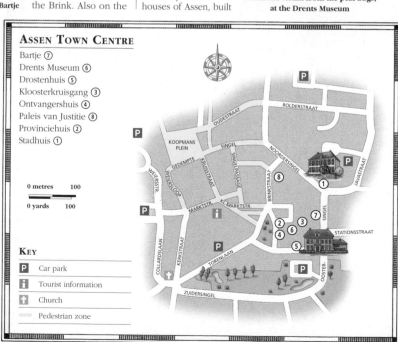

ASSEN TOWN CENTRE

Bartje ⑦
Drents Museum ⑥
Drostenhuis ⑤
Kloosterkruisgang ③
Ontvangershuis ④
Paleis van Justitie ⑧
Provinciehuis ②
Stadhuis ①

0 metres   100
0 yards   100

KEY

🅿   Car park

ℹ   Tourist information

🛉   Church

▬   Pedestrian zone

The 13th-century Romanesque church on the Brink of Norg

Norg ③

Road map D2. 🚶 *3,500.* 🚌 **ℹ**
Brink 1 (0592-613128). 🏪 *Wed.*

THE ROMANESQUE CHURCH on the Brink dates from the 13th century. The unique frescoes in the choir have barely survived through the centuries and are in very poor condition.

ENVIRONS: The area around Norg is steeped in prehistory. Three megalithic tombs are to be found there, while in the Noorderveld are Bronze Age tumuli (the **Negen Bergen**). Norgerholt is the name given to the oak woods where the local people used to assemble during the Middle Ages.

Eelde-Paterswolde ④

Road map D2. 🚶 *10,500.*
🚌 *52, 53.* **ℹ** *B Boermalaan 4 (050-3092136).* 🏪 *Wed.*

THE VILLAGE OF Eelde-Paterswolde is squeezed between the **Paterswoldse Meer** lake and **Groningen Airport**, which despite its name is in Drenthe rather than Groningen. The lake is popular among water sports enthusiasts. The airport serves primarily domestic flights (it is a half-hour flight to Schiphol) and flying enthusiasts.

The distinctive modern brick building housing the **Museum voor figuratieve kunst De Buitenplaats**

(De Buitenplaats museum of figurative art), was designed by the architects Alberts and Van Huut. It is a fine example of their organic architecture. In addition to hosting changing exhibitions, the museum is used as a concert hall. There are also formal and landscape gardens, the former fronting the 17th century curator's residence, the **Nijsinghuis**. Since 1983 the house has been painted by figurative artists and is periodically opened to visitors by arrangement.

🏛 **Museum voor figuratieve kunst De Buitenplaats**
Hoofdweg 76. **ℹ** *050-3095818.*
⏱ *Tue–Sun, Easter Sun & Easter Mon.*
⬛ *25 Dec, 1 Jan.* ♿▯

Zuidlaren ⑤

Road map E2. 🚶 *10,000.* 🚌
ℹ *Stationsweg 69 (050-4092333).*
🏪 *Fri.*

THE colourful Zuidlaren **horse market**, now the largest in Western Europe, predates even the 13th-century church which stands on the Brink. The market is held every spring and autumn (April and October). The 17th-century **havezathe Laarwoud** was built on the remnants of the fortified residence of the counts of Heiden, who ruled the region in the 14th century. Today it is the town hall. The **Zuidlaardermeer** lake offers everything that watersports enthusiasts may require. Children will especially enjoy the subtropical swimming complex of Aqualaren as well as De Sprookjeshof recreation centre with playpark; they can be combined on one round tour.

The Hondsrug area

Hondsrug ⑥

Road map E2. 🚌 **ℹ** *VVVs in Zuidlaren, Rolde, Gieten (0592-267791), Exloo (0591-549182), Borger, SchoonoOrd (0591-381242) or Emmen.*

BETWEEN THE DRENTSE sand plateau in the west and the Drents-Groningen peat moors in the east lies the Hondsrug ridge. Prehistoric people found it a safe place to settle, and it is the area where the megaliths now stand *(see pp304–5)*.

The Drentse Aa river basin, the old villages of Gieten, Gasselte, Exloo and Odoorn, the drifting sand areas of the Drouwenerzand and the heathland of Ellertsveld are particularly attractive hiking areas, with plenty of streams in which to cool off.

Children Bathing in a Stream (c.1935) by
Von Dülmen-Krumpelmann, Drents Museum

Rolde 7

Road map E2. 🏛 *6,200.* 🚌
ℹ *Gieterstraat 1a (0592-241375).*

ROLDE WAS important for a considerable time. There are prehistoric tumuli (in the **Tumulibos** woods), and three megaliths, two of which are on the mound directly behind the church. During the Middle Ages, people were tried at the **Ballooërkuil**; if guilty they were held prisoner in the 15th-century church, a magnificent Gothic edifice. Forests, peatland and drifting sands surround the village. Flocks of sheep graze on the Ballooëveld.

Borger 8

Road map E2. 🏛 *4,700.* 🚌 *59.* ℹ
Grote Brink 2a (0599-234855). 🛍 *Tue.*

BORGER IS THE CAPITAL of the *hunebeddengebied*, or megalith region. There are eight megaliths in and around the town, including the largest in Holland. Nearby is the **Nationaal Hunebedden Informatiecentrum** (´t Flint'n Hoes), with a fine exhibition about the Beaker Folk and a stone casket from the most recently excavated megalith, which was discovered in 1982 in Groningen.

🏛 **Nationaal Hunebedden Informatiecentrum**
Bronnegerstraat 12. 🕿 *0599-236374.*
🔲 *daily.* ⬤ *1 Jan, 31 Dec.* 🎫 ♿ ⬛

ENVIRONS: Drents Boomkroonpad (tree-top walk), 2 km (1 mile) down the "Staatsbossen" turnoff on the Rolde-Borger road, is an

Boomkroonpad's tree-top walkway

interesting attraction. The walk starts at the roots, with a 23-m (75-ft) tunnel where you can see all aspects of tree roots. This leads into a 125-m (410-ft) ascent to a height of 22.5 m (74 ft), affording a fascinating view of the forest.

🌳 **Drents Boomkroonpad**
Paviljoen de Woudstee, Boswachterij
Gieten/Borger. 🕿 *0592-241693.*
🔲 *daily.* ⬤ *1 Jan.* 🎫 ⬛

Orvelte 9

Road map E2. 🏛 *90.* 🚌 *122.*
ℹ *Dorpsstraat 1a (0593-322335).*

THE WHOLE OF ORVELTE is in effect an open-air museum. In the restored Saxon farmhouses from the early 19th century, there are exhibits on agriculture and displays of traditional crafts. Cars are banned from the area, but tours in horse-drawn trams or covered waggons are offered. The more interesting attractions of the town include a tinsmith's shop.

🏛 **Openluchtmuseum**
Dorpsstraat 3. 🕿 *0593-322335.*
🔲 *Apr–Oct daily.* 🎫 🎟 ♿ 🍴 ⬛

Farmers at work in the Orvelte open-air museum

Westerbork 10

Road map E2. 🏛 *8,000.* 🚌
ℹ *Hoofdstraat 16 (0593-331381).*

THE HOOFDSTRAAT (main street) features a Late Gothic 14th-century church, which now houses the **Museum voor Papierknipkunst** (paper-cutting museum) and Saxon farmhouses which bear witness to a prosperous past. However, Westerbork is visited primarily for its more recent history. In World War II, the Westerbork Transit Camp stood here. It was from this camp that 107,000 Jews, Gypsies and resistance fighters were held before deportation to the Nazi extermination camps. Anne Frank *(see pp108–9)* was one of its inmates.

🏛 **Herinneringscentrum Kamp Westerbork**
Oosthalen 8, Hooghalen. 🕿 *0593-592600.* 🔲 *Feb–Nov daily.* 🎫 ♿

Dwingeloo 11

Road map D2. 🏛 *1,800.* 🚌 *20.*
ℹ *Brink 46 (0521-591331).* 🛍 *Tue.*

THE FIRST THING that strikes visitors about Dwingeloo is the deformed dome of the 14th-century church tower (the **Siepelkerk**). You can read about the legend behind this oddity on the information board located nearby.

There is some impressive countryside around the town. The **Dwingelderveld** is a national park and the **krentenbossen** (currant plantations) which flower in April and May – the fruit ripening in July or August – are delightful in every respect: they are pleasant to the eye and to the taste buds. At the edge of the Dwingelose Heide heath is a radio-telescope.

The interesting and child-friendly **Planetron** nearby is an observatory where there is a planetarium as well as an electronic games area.

📷 **Planetron**
Drift 11b. 🕿 *0521-593535.* 🔲 *daily during school hols.* ⬤ *1 Jan, Mon outside school hols.* 🎫 🍴 ⬛

Diever ⑫

Road map D2. 🏘 3,700. 🚌 117.
ℹ Bosweg 2a (0521-591748).

DIEVER WAS an important centre from prehistoric times to the Middle Ages. Tumuli, megaliths and remains of the 9th-century wooden foundations of the village church lend it historical importance. The church features a 12th-century Romanesque tower of tufa stone. Diever is in the middle of the **Nationaal Park Het Drents-Friese Woud**: the town is now synonymous with cycling and rambling.

In the summer months, the **Shakespeare-markten** (Shakespeare fair) is held during performances of the playwright's works in the open-air theatre, **Openluchttheater**.

ENVIRONS: In **Vledder**, 10 km (6 miles) west of Diever, is a **museum** of graphic art, glassblowing and art forgery.

Lime kilns at Diever

🏛 **Museum voor Valse Kunst/Museum voor Hedendaagse Grafiek en Glaskunst**
Brink 1, Vledder. 📞 0521-383352.
⬜ Apr–beg Jan: Wed–Mon. 🎦 🎟

Coevorden ⑬

Road map E3. 🏘 34,000. 🚌 🚆
ℹ Haven 2 (0524-525150).
🅿 Mon.

THE CASTLE here dates fromaround 1200. The star-shaped moat and surviving bastions and town walls define the look of the town, while the façades of the Friesestraat and Weeshuisstraat are telling of past centuries. **Stedelijk Museum**

Brown bears in the popular Noorder Dierenpark in Emmen

Drenthe's Veste highlights the town's history.

🏛 **Stedelijk Museum Drenthe's Veste**
Haven 4. 📞 0524-516225.
⬜ Tues–Fri. 🎦 🖼

Emmen ⑭

Road map E2. 🏘 105,000. 🚌 🚆
ℹ Hoofdstraat 22 (0591-613000).
🅿 Fri.

DRENTHE'S LARGEST district has grown only since World War II. Eleven megaliths, including **Langgraf op de Schimmer Es** or long barrow on the Schimmer Es, the urn-fields (see p43) and prehistoric farmland (the **Celtic Fields**) in the vicinity and the 12th-century tower on the Hoofdstraat reflect the district's history. At **Noorder Dierenpark**, animals roam freely. The Biochron museum and Vlindertuin butterfly gardens are also here.

🐾 **Noorder Dierenpark**
Hoofdstraat 18. 📞 0591-642040.
⬜ daily. 🎦 🚻 🖼 🍴
🌐 www.noorderdierenpark.nl

ENVIRONS: 10 km (6 miles) east of Emmen are the **Amsterdamsche Veld** upland peat marshes, perhaps the loneliest place in Holland. In Barger-Compascuum, **Veenpark** re-creates the times when the people of Drenthe lived in poverty, cutting peat. In 1883, Vincent van Gogh stayed at the Scholte ferryhouse in Veenoord (Nieuw-Amsterdam). At the **Van Gogh House**, his room on the first floor has been restored to the way it was in 1883, as has the café-restaurant below, including its menu.

🏛 **Veenpark**
Berkenrode 4, Barger-Compascuum.
📞 0591-324444. ⬜ Apr–Nov daily.
🎦 🚻 🖼
🏛 **Van Gogh Huis**
Van Goghstraat 1, Nieuw-Amsterdam.
📞 0591-555600. ⬜ 1–5pm
Tue–Sun. 🖼 🍴 🎟

Van Gogh's *Peat Boat with Two Figures* (1883) in Drents Museum, Assen

OVERIJSSEL

O VERIJSSEL, A PROVINCE IN THE EAST *of Holland, has many areas of natural beauty and lovely old towns. In a sense it is a province of two halves, divided by the heathland and woods of the Sallandse Heuvelrug near Nijverdal, which separate the eastern district of Twente from the rest of the province.*

This division is noticeable in many ways. The two halves differ in their spoken dialect, and they each have their own cultural traditions. There are also religious differences, with Twente being mainly Catholic while the rest of the province is strictly Protestant. Twente, with its larger towns, has a more modern appearance, and Enschede, for example, is livelier than western towns like Zwolle and Deventer.

Zwolle, however, is the capital of the province, a charming town dating back to the 13th century, when its port at a busy river junction led it to join the powerful Hanseatic League, growing rich from trade with England and the Baltic. Kampen and Deventer, on the IJssel river, were later members of the same league.

Overijssel's numerous unique museums and attractions highlight local history and printing, tobacco, salt and farmhouses, as well as traditional costumes, tin soldiers, Dutch painting and modern art. For children, the Hellendoorn adventure park, the Los Hoes open-air museum and Ecodrome Park *(see p447)* are always popular.

Apart from these activities, however, the principal attraction in Overijssel is the countryside, which is ideal for walking, hiking and touring by bicycle. In places like Giethoorn you can tour the rivers, lakes and canals by boat, while the Weerribben wetlands in the northwest offer opportunities for nature rambles and watersports.

Cigar-maker at work at the Tabaksmuseum (tobacco museum) in Kampen

◁ **Weerribben wetlands nature reserve in the northwest of Overijssel**

Exploring Overijssel

THE IMPRESSIVE HISTORICAL monuments of Deventer and Kampen recall their prosperous pasts as Hanseatic cities. However, Overijssel has plenty to offer those who are interested in more than splendid old buildings. Those who enjoy peace and natural surroundings will find some of the finest spots in Holland. The peaceful countryside of the Sallandse Heuvelrug is ideal for rambling walks, while De Weerribben is suitable for yachting. There are many picturesque spots, such as Ootmarsum, Delden and Giethoorn. There is plenty for children to do at Slagharen and Hellendoorn. In addition to this, Overijssel also has many interesting museums, such as the national tin figure museum in Ommen.

The quiet port of Blokzijl near Vollenhove

KEY

▣	Motorway
▣	Major road
▭	Secondary roads
▣	Scenic route
▭	Canal/river

0 kilometres   10

0 miles   10

OVERIJSSEL AT A GLANCE

The IJssel north of the old Hanseatic city of Deventer

GETTING AROUND

Overijssel can be explored easily by car, bicycle or on foot. Large parts of the region are also well connected by public transport. Note, however, that bus timetables are different on weekends than on weekdays. Areas of natural beauty such as De Weerribben, for example, are not easy to reach by public transport on weekends. In some places, too, buses operate only during the daytime.

Farmhouse by the river Reest, separating Drenthe from Overijssel

The old Twente tradition of horn-blowing in winter

Kasteel Rechteren by Dalfsen, near Zwolle

SEE ALSO

• *Where to Stay* pp399–400

• *Where to Eat* pp418–19

Zwolle ❶

Road map D3. 🏰 *107,000*. 🚉
ℹ *Grote Kerkplein 14 (0900-
1122375).* 🐄 *Fri (cattle market), Sat.*

IN THE MIDDLE AGES, Zwolle,
capital of the province of
Overijssel, was, along with
towns such as Deventer, Kampen and Zutphen, a city of the
Hanseatic League, a network
of trading cities. Its past is
evident in the relatively large
historical centre. The finest
buildings in Zwolle, which
was granted its city charter in
1230, are largely to be found in
the area that used to fall within the city fortifications, which
can still be seen in the form of
a moat. However, only a few
dozen metres of these ancient
fortifications are left standing,
along with the fine Sassenpoort gate, dating from 1406,
and the Late Gothic 15th-cen-
tury Pelsertoren tower.

On one side of the Grote
Kerkplein is a sculpture by
Rodin entitled *Adam,* while
on the Grote Markt stands the
magnificent building of the
Hoofdwacht (guard house),
which dates from 1614. Today
it houses, quite appropriately,
a police station.

The **Grote Kerk,** also
known as **St Michaelskerk,**
is worth a visit as well. The

View of Zwolle during the Hanseatic Period (anonymous, c.14th century)

original Romanesque church,
built in 1040, was enlarged in
1370 and again in 1452 to
become the present-day
three-naved Gothic church.

The **Stedelijk Museum
Zwolle** (Zwolle local history
museum) features, among its
other interesting exhibits on
local history, an 18th-century
kitchen, a Renaissance room
from Blokzijl and an
Overijssel print room. The
fine façade of the old part of
the building, which dates
from 1741, is impressive.

The town is also home to
the **Ecodrome Park** *(see
p447),* which is dedicated to

the natural environment in the
past, present and future and
features finds from the Ice Age.

🏛 **Stedelijk Museum Zwolle**
Melkmarkt 41. 📞 *038-4214650.*
🕐 *10am–5pm Tue–Sat, 1–5pm Sun
& hols.* ● *1 Jan, Easter Day, Whitsun,
25 Dec.* 🔲 🎦 🅿 ✏
Ecodrome Park
Willemsvaart 19. 📞 *038-4215050.*
🕐 *Nov–Mar: 10am–5pm Wed, Sat &
Sun; Apr–Oct: 10am–5pm daily.* 🔲

ENVIRONS: The **Kunstwegen**
(Art Paths) are outdoor sculp-
ture installations between
Nordhorn and Zwolle, and
Emmen and Zwolle.

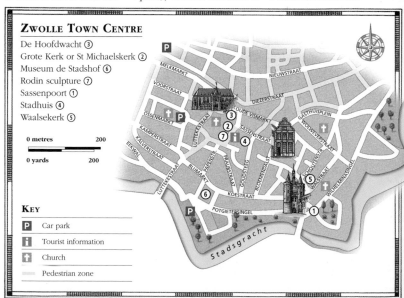

ZWOLLE TOWN CENTRE

De Hoofdwacht ③
Grote Kerk or St Michaelskerk ②
Museum de Stadshof ⑥
Rodin sculpture ⑦
Sassenpoort ①
Stadhuis ④
Waalsekerk ⑤

0 metres   200
0 yards   200

KEY

🅿 Car park
ℹ Tourist information
✝ Church
  Pedestrian zone

The waterfront of the magnificent, well-preserved Hanseatic city of Kampen on the river IJssel

Kampen ❷

Road map D3. 🏛 *48,000.* 🚉
ℹ️ *Oudestraat 151 (038-3313500).*
🛍 *Mon morning.*

KAMPEN, KNOWN FOR its theological university where Protestant theologians are educated, is a pleasant and lively town containing 500 monuments. The beauty of this former Hanseatic city is immediately apparent from the IJssel riverfront. The fact that the town used to be well fortified is evident from the three remaining town gates: the Koornmarspoort, the Broederpoort and the Cellebroederspoort. The area inside the old fortifications features the magnificent Dutch Reformed church St Nicolaaskerk, and the Gotische Huis, which now houses the **Stedelijk Museum Kampen,** the town's local history museum. Particularly noteworthy is the old town hall, or Oude Raadhuis, with a façade decorated with fine sculptures.

Kampen, which is first mentioned in documents in 1227, is also famed for its cigars, which explains why the **Kamper Tabaksmuseum** (Kampen tobacco museum) is located here.

Kampen was at the height of its development between 1330 and 1450. It revived its fortunes only when the Flevoland and Noordoostpolder regions were reclaimed and it acquired the function of regional centre. However, it was never a mighty city because it did not have any powerful ruler. Kampen did not apply to join the Hanseatic League until relatively late – 1440. At that time, Holland was at war with the Hanseatic League, and Kampen joined the powerful league for the sake of security.

🏛 **Stedelijk Museum Kampen**
Oude Straat 158. 📞 *038-3317361.*
⏱ *1 Feb–mid Jun, 19 Sep–30 Dec: 11am–12:30pm & 1:30–5pm Tue–Sat; mid Jun–mid Sep: 11am–5pm Tue–Sat, 1–5pm Sun.* ⚫ *Whitsun, 25, 26 & 31 Dec.* ♿

🏛 **Kamper Tabaksmuseum**
Botermarkt 3. 📞 *038-3315868.*
⏱ *by appointment only.* ♿

Vollenhove ❸

Road map D2. 🚉 *71.*
ℹ️ *Aan Zee 2–4 (0527-241700).* 🛍 *Tue.*

VOLLENHOVE IS a picturesque place which was once known as the town of palaces because of the many nobles who lived here. The aristocratic residences are known as *havezaten,* or manors. This otherwise small town has a relatively large church,

known variously as the **Grote Kerk**, **St Nicolaaskerk** or **Bovenkerk**, which dates from the late 15th century. Another popular attraction in the town is the **Tuin van Marnixveld** (Marnixveld Garden).

The largest employer in Vollenhove is the **Royal Huysman Shipyard**, where today luxurious yachts for the world's rich and famous (including American internet millionaire Jim Clark) are built.

De Weerribben ❹

Road map D3. 🚉 *81.*

DE WEERRIBBEN IS an unspoiled area of wetlands at the northwestern end of Overijssel. There is plenty for cyclists, walkers and also canoeists to do in this beautiful nature reserve.

🏞 **Natuuractiviteiten-centrum De Weerribben**
Hoogewerf 27, Ossenzijl. 📞 *0561-477272.* ⏱ *Apr–Oct: 10am–5pm daily.* 🍴 🅿️

Water lilies in the nature reserve of De Weerribben

Street-by-Street: Giethoorn ❺

IF ANY VILLAGE were to be given the title "prettiest village in Holland", quaint Giethoorn would be the one. This well-deserved accolade is due to the village's picturesque canals which are flanked by numerous farmhouse-style buildings. Many of these buildings now contain interesting, if small, museums. The village of Giethoorn can be easily explored both by boat and by bicycle. Founded in 1230 by religious refugees, the village's distinctive form came about from peat-cutting, eventually resulting in the formation of ponds and lakes. The small canals were used for transporting peat.

Giethoorn is also known a the Green Venice because c its abundant natural beauty. Several ponds and lakes surround this charming town. The best way to enjoy the area is by hiring a small boat.

★ **Tjaskermolen**
This windmill, which turns an Archimedes' screw, is located in Giethoorn-Noord. Another one can be seen in the Olde Maat Uus museum.

★ **Olde Maat Uus**
This pleasant farmhouse which has been converted into a museum should definitely not be missed. It illustrates life in Giethoorn as it used to be.

BINNENPAD

STAR SIGHTS

★ **Olde Maat Uus**

★ **Punts**

★ **Tjaskermolen**

The delightful houses of Giethoorn contain numerous and varied tourist attractions, giving visitors plenty to do on each visit.

| 0 metres | | 50 |
| 0 yards | | 50 |

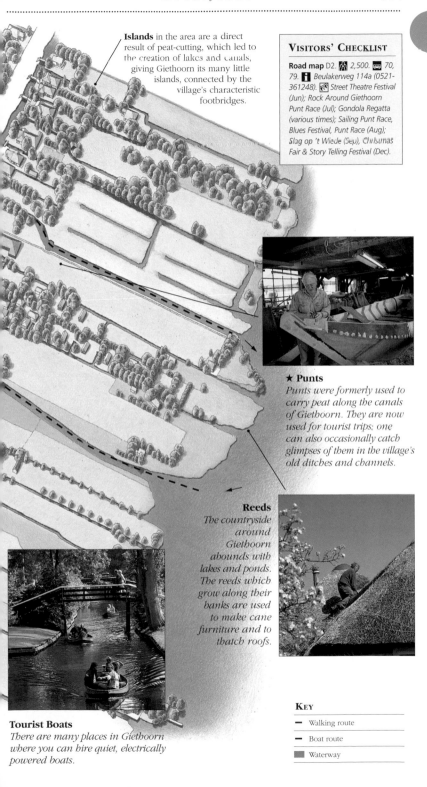

Islands in the area are a direct result of peat-cutting, which led to the creation of lakes and canals, giving Giethoorn its many little islands, connected by the village's characteristic footbridges.

VISITORS' CHECKLIST

Road map D2. 2,500. 70, 79. Beulakerweg 114a (0521-361248). Street Theatre Festival (Jun); Rock Around Giethoorn Punt Race (Jul); Gondola Regatta (various times); Sailing Punt Race, Blues Festival, Punt Race (Aug); Slag op 't Wiede (Sep); Christmas Fair & Story Telling Festival (Dec).

★ Punts
Punts were formerly used to carry peat along the canals of Giethoorn. They are now used for tourist trips; one can also occasionally catch glimpses of them in the village's old ditches and channels.

Reeds
The countryside around Giethoorn abounds with lakes and ponds. The reeds which grow along their banks are used to make cane furniture and to thatch roofs.

Tourist Boats
There are many places in Giethoorn where you can hire quiet, electrically powered boats.

KEY

— Walking route

— Boat route

Waterway

Deventer, larger than Amsterdam in its heyday

Staphorst ❻

Road map D3. 🏚 *15,000.* 🚌 *40.* 🚫
Sun. 🏛 *Wed morning.*

STAPHORST IS KNOWN throughout Holland as a stronghold of strict Christian beliefs. It was where the Gereformeerde Bond (reformed union), one of the strictest embodiments of Protestantism, ruled within the Dutch Reformed Church. The lovely old farmhouses, painted in a characteristic green and blue, are often monumental buildings. To get an idea of what these farmhouses once looked like, it is worth visiting the **Museumboerderij** (farmhouse museum).

The townspeople continue to wear traditional dress, a custom which has practically vanished elsewhere in the country. Throughout Staphorst you will see women, especially elderly women, wearing the blue and black outfits.

🏛 Museumboerderij
Gemeenteweg 67. 📞 *0522-462526.*
🕐 *1 Apr–31 Oct: 10am–5pm*
Mon–Sat. ● *Sun & hols.* 🏛

Ommen ❼

Road map D3. 🏚 *17,000.* 🚉
ℹ *Kruisstraat 6 (0529-451638).*
🏛 *Tue morning.*

THE DISTRICT OF Ommen lies in stunningly beautiful countryside extending from the town to nearby villages and hamlets. One-third of its total area of 18,000 ha (44,500 acres) is covered by nature reserves and forests. A former Hanseatic city, Ommen itself

is home to a few interesting museums, including the **Nationaal Tinnen Figuren Museum** (national tin models museum).

🏛 Nationaal Tinnen Figuren Museum
Markt 1. 📞 *0529-454500.*
🕐 *Apr–Oct: 10am–5pm
Tue–Sat, 1–5pm Sun & hols;
Nov–Mar: 11am–5pm Sat, 1–5pm
Sun & hols.* ● *1 Jan, 25 Dec.* 🏛

ENVIRONS: To find out more about the nature reserves in Ommen, visit the **Natuurinformatiecentrum Ommen**, which houses a permanent exhibition illustrating the cultural history of the surrounding countryside. Particularly worth seeing are the typical Saxon farmhouses at Beerze, Junne, Stegeren, Besthem and Giethmen.

🌾 Natuurinformatiecentrum Ommen
Hammerweg 59a. 📞 *0529-450702.*
🕐 *May–Oct: 1–5pm Wed–Sun;
Nov–Apr: 1:30–4pm Wed, Sat & Sun.*

Deventer ❽

Road map D3. 🏚 *86,000.* 🚉
ℹ *Keizerstraat 22 (0900-3535355).*
🏛 *Fri morning & Sat.*

THE LIVELY CENTRE of the old Hanseatic city of Deventer features numerous medieval houses, including the oldest stone house in Holland today. Buildings worth seeing in particular are those situated on the pleasant Brink (green) and the Bergkerk. In the middle of the Brink stands the impressive Waag (weigh house) from 1528, which now contains the **Historisch Museum de Waag**, with interesting exhibits that illustrate the town's history. On the first Sunday of August, the town holds the **Deventer Boekenmarkt** (book fair), the largest in Europe. It is preceded by a poetry festival.

A tin soldier

🏛 Historisch Museum de Waag
Brink 56. 📞 *0570-693780.*
🕐 *10am–5pm Tue–Sat, 1–5pm
Sun.* ● *Closed for restoration until 2004.* 🏛

Nijverdal ❾

Road map D3. 🏚 *23,500.* 🚉 ℹ
Grotestraat 59 (0548-612729). 🏛 *Sat.*

THE IMPRESSIVE BEAUTY of the Sallandse Heuvelrug, with its fine heathland and woodland, is especially apparent at Nijverdaal, where there is plenty of scenic countryside to enjoy. This is the last remaining breeding ground in the Netherlands for black grouse.

Flock of sheep in the Bezoekerscentrum Sallandse Heuvelrug

An interesting exhibition on the Heuvelrug region can be seen at the **Bezoekerscentrum Sallandse Heuvelrug** (Sallandse Heuvelrug visitors' centre), with its clever and unusual "Forester's Corner".

Bezoekerscentrum Sallandse Heuvelrug

Grotestraat 281. 0548-612711. Mar–Oct, Dec & spring hols: 10am–5pm Tue–Sun; Nov, Jan & Feb: 10am–4pm Sat & Sun. Mon, 1 Jan, Easter Sun, 30 Apr, 5 May, Whitsun, 25 & 31 Dec.

ENVIRONS: Avonturenpark Hellendoorn (Hellendoorn adventure park) *(see p446)* is a paradise for children.

Delden ⓾

Road map E3. 7,000. Langestraat 29 (074-3761300). Fri afternoon.

Delden is a pretty residential village, ideal for rambling walks. This Twente hamlet has a number of attractions, including the **Zoutmuseum** (salt museum) and the 12th-century **Oude Blasiuskerk.**

Zoutmuseum

Langestraat 30. 074-3764546. May–Sep: 11am–5pm Mon–Fri, 2–5pm Sat & Sun; Oct–Apr: 2–5pm Tue–Fri & Sun.

ENVIRONS: Some 2 km (1.2 miles) northeast of Delden are the lovely, picturesque gardens of **Kasteel Twickel**.

Tuinen Kasteel Twickel (Kassteel Twickel Gardens)

Twickelerlaan 1a, Ambt Delden. May–Oct: 11am–4:30pm Mon–Fri.

Enschede ⓫

Road map E3. 150,000. Oude Markt 31 (053-4323200). Tue & Sat.

Enschede is regarded as the capital of Twente, as it is the largest town in Overijssel. It was devastated in 1862 by a fire – little of the old town survived. One of the few historical buildings that can still be seen in the otherwise pleasant centre is the **Grote Kerk** on the Oude Markt.

In addition to this centre, with its theatres, concert halls and cinemas, Enschede has a number of museums, of which the **Rijksmuseum Twenthe** should not be missed. The permanent exhibits here range from manuscripts, paintings and portraits to modern, primarily Dutch, art.

Miracle Planet Boulevard, just outside town, offers non-stop entertainment in three mega-complexes.

Rijksmuseum Twenthe

Lasondersingel 129–131. 053-4358675. 11am–5pm Tue–Sun & hols. 1 Jan.

Ootmarsum ⓬

Road map E3. 4,000. 64 (Oostnet) from Almelo. Markt 1 (0900-2021987). Thu morning.

The village of Ootmarsum is one of the prettiest places in all of Holland. On the map since 900, Ootmarsum was granted its town charter in 1300. It has grown little since then; indeed, not much has changed here at all, making it

Stained glass in the 13th-century Catholic church at Ootmarsum

quite suitable for an open-air museum. Places of interest not to be missed are the Roman Catholic church, the only Westphalian hall-type church in Holland, built between 1200 and 1300. Here you can see the burial vaults and some impressive works of art. The rococo former town hall dates from 1778 and is now the VVV (tourist) office. There are also some interesting old draw-wells.

The **Openluchtmuseum Los Hoes** (Los Hoes open-air museum) showing what life was once like in Twente is also worth a visit.

Openluchtmuseum Los Hoes

Smithuisstraat 2. 0541-293099. 10am–5pm daily. Jan.

ENVIRONS: Nature lovers will find plenty to do in the countryside surrounding Ootmarsum, which is located in one of the finest parts of Twente. The landscape offers an ever-changing scenery, with its rushing brooks, old watermills, winding woodland paths, prehistoric tumuli and Saxon farmhouses.

The viewing point on the Kuiperberg affords a stunning vista over the entire Twente region and provides visitors with the place names of the various sights.

The half-timbered Stiepelhoes in Ootmarsum, dating from 1658

FLEVOLAND

FLEVOLAND IS HOLLAND'S YOUNGEST PROVINCE, *created by the Dutch entirely out of water, sandbanks and mud flats, thanks to massive reclamation schemes which created dykes and polders (reclaimed land, sometimes below sea level) from the turbulent Zuiderzee following an Act of Parliament in 1918.*

This act provided funds for damming the northeastern part of the Zuiderzee and reclaiming the land behind the dykes. When the Afsluitdijk was completed in 1932, drainage works on the Noordostpolder began and, with the seawater pumped out, the islands of Urk and Schokland and the town of Emmeloord became by 1942 a part of the mainland. Further schemes to the south and southwest were completed in 1957 and 1968 respectively, and since 1986 these three new polders have officially constituted the Netherlands' newest province, named Flevoland after "Flevo Lacus", the original name given to the Zuiderzee by the Roman historian Pliny nearly 2,000 years ago.

Initially, the idea had been to use the polders as farmland only, with the occasional village here and there.

However, as the built-up areas around Amsterdam and Utrecht became increasingly congested, new towns have grown up. The conurbation around Almere, with its highly impressive modern architecture, is among these. Other towns include Lelystad, with its several modern museums, and Dronten, where the Six Flags amusement park proves an irresistible magnet for younger visitors. Lelystad, whose name honours Cornelius Lely, the genius behind the massive land creation project *(see p324)*, is the provincial capital. There are many other attractions for visitors to this compact and attractive region, including a number of fascinating museums featuring subjects as varied as archaeology and World War II.

The exotic spoonbill, an icon of the new wildlife in Flevoland

◁ **Beekeepers at work in the rape fields of Flevoland, which are gradually disappearing**

Exploring Flevoland

Urk villager

THE NOORDOOSTPOLDER, which is the northern-most part of Flevoland, is distinguished by its polder landscape and its rich farmland, fruit orchards and bulb fields. There are also many young forests, including Emmelerbos, which is recommended for walkers. Apart from the main town of Emmeloord, there are a number of small new villages, as well as the old fishing village of Urk. Oostelijk (eastern) and Zuidelijk (southern) Flevoland are relatively sparsely populated and have a lot of greenery. Between Almere, the largest town of Flevoland, characterized by modern architecture, and Lelystad, the provincial capital, there stretches a fine nature reserve known as the Oostvaardersplassen, or Oostvaarder lakes. The coastal lakes have inviting sand beaches and marinas.

The picturesque harbour of the fishing village of Urk

SIGHTS AT A GLANCE

Almere **12**
Bataviawerf **8**
Dronten **6**
Emmeloord **1**
Knardijk **10**
Lelystad **7**
Nagele **3**

Oostvaardersplassen **9**
Schokland **4**
Swifterbant **5**
Urk **2**
Zeewolde **11**

The replica of the *Batavia* at Lelystad

A fine view of Almere harbour

KEY

▬ Motorway

▬ Major road

▬ Minor road

▬ Walking route

– Ferry

▬ Canal/river

Markerwaarddijk

N30

Markermeer

LELYS

BATAVIAWERF 8

**OOSTVAARDERS-
EN LEPELAARSPLASSEN 9**

ALMERE-BUITEN

A6

*Zuide
Flevol*

12

ALMERE

ALMERE-HAVEN

A27

Gooimeer

N305

0 kilometres   10

0 miles   10

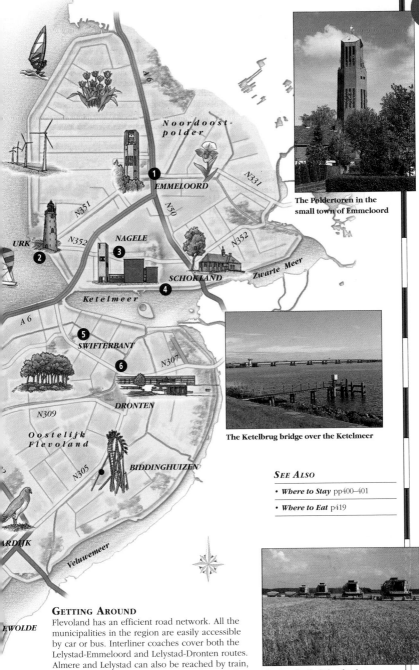

The Poldertoren in the
small town of Emmeloord

The Ketelbrug bridge over the Ketelmeer

SEE ALSO

• *Where to Stay* pp400–401

• *Where to Eat* p419

Flat farmland of Flevoland

GETTING AROUND

Flevoland has an efficient road network. All the
municipalities in the region are easily accessible
by car or bus. Interliner coaches cover both the
Lelystad-Emmeloord and Lelystad-Dronten routes.
Almere and Lelystad can also be reached by train,
and a ferry links Urk and Enkhuizen during July
and August. The flat expansive landscape of
Flevoland also makes exploration by bicycle ideal.
Numerous excellent cycling and hiking routes
have been laid out throughout the province.

Emmeloord ❶

Road map D2. Noordoostpolder.
🏚 *24,800.* 🚌 **ℹ** *De Deel 21a
(0527-612000).* 🛒 *Thu eve.*

W HEN THE OLDEST polder in
Flevoland was drained,
Emmeloord sprang up like a
pioneer settlement. Over the
years it has developed into a
pleasant town. It is the main
town of the municipality of
Noordoostpolder, encompass-
ing *groendorps* (green villages).
Emmeloord is known mainly
for its octagonal **Poldertoren**
built in 1959, a 65-m (214-ft)
water tower topped by a 5-m
(16-ft) wind vane in the shape
of an old merchant ship. The
carillon, one of Holland's biggest, has 48 chimes. The viewing platform (open in summer)
offers a view of the polder.

Urk ❷

Road map C3. 🏚 *16,500.* 🚢 *from
Enkhuizen, summer only.* 🚌 **ℹ** *Wijk
2–2 (0527-684040).* 🛒 *Sat am.*

T HE FISHING VILLAGE of Urk
attracts many tourists with
its sloping alleys and charming
fishermen's cottages. Until its
land was reclaimed, Urk was
an island. Some 1,000 years
ago, the island was much larger
and had five villages; flooding
gradually reduced its size. The
townspeople moved to the
highest point on the island,

a hill of boulder clay. Even
after the polder was drained,
Urk managed to retain its
character in the middle of the
new land surrounding it. Some
of the older residents wear
the traditional dress, though
this is increasingly rare.
Beside the old village centre
the fishing quay, the lighthouse (1844) and the little
church (1786) are worth a
look. In the **Museum Het
Oude Raadhuis**, situated in
the old town hall, you can
find out about the history of
Urk and the fishing industry.

**🏛 Museum Het Oude
Raadhuis**
Wijk 2–2. **【** *0527-683262.*
◯ *Apr–Sep: 10am–5pm Mon–Sat;
spring & autumn hols: 2–5pm.*
🚫 **&** 🅿 **☞** *by appointment.*

Nagele ❸

Road map D3. 🏚 *1,900.* 🚌
ℹ *0527-612000.*

T HIS VILLAGE was built in the
1950s to designs by the
De Acht en de Opbouw, a
group of architects which
included the famous Rietveld,
Van Eyck and van Eesteren,
who represented the Nieuwe
Bouwen movement. The
flat-roofed residential buildings surround a park-like
centre with shops, schools
and churches. The village
is surrounded by a belt of

Schokland before land reclamation

Schokland after reclamation

woodland. **Museum Nagele**
provides information about
the village's architecture.

🏛 Museum Nagele
Ring 23. **【** *0527-653077.*
◯ *1–5pm Thu–Sun.* **●** *1 Jan,
25, 26 & 31 Dec.* 🚫 **&** 🅿 **🔢**

Schokland ❹

Road map C3. 🚌 **ℹ** *see museum.*

L IKE URK, Schokland was
once an island. Archaeo-
logical finds show that the site
was inhabited in prehistoric
times. In 1859, the population
had to abandon the island
because it was disappearing
into the sea. Today the "island"
is a hill on the landscape.
Museum Schokland, consisting of the restored church
and reconstructions of fishermen's cottages, is dedicated
to geology and local history
from the Ice Age up until the
land was reclaimed. At the
south end of the village are
the ruins of a medieval
church. In the Schokkerbos
forest to the west is the
Gesteentetuin, gardens
featuring Ice Age boulders.

🏛 Museum Schokland
Middelbuurt 3, Ens. **【** *0527-251396.*
◯ *Apr–Oct: 11am–5pm Tue–Sun;
Jul–Aug: daily; Nov–Mar: Fri–Sun.*
● *1 Jan, 25 Dec.* 🚫 **&** 🔢

CORNELIS LELY (1854–1929)

Flevoland has come into existence thanks largely to the
plans and ambitions of civil engineer Cornelis Lely. From
1885 to 1891, as a member of the Zuiderzee-
vereniging (Zuiderzee Society), he was
responsible for studying the possibility of
closing off and draining the Zuiderzee.
His appointment as minister for trade and
industry in 1891 gave him the chance to
convince the government and parliament
how necessary it was to tame the unpredictable Zuiderzee, though it was not
until his third term in office (1913–18) that
the law for retaining and draining the
Zuiderzee was finally passed. Apart from
the Zuiderzee projects, Lely worked to
improve the Noorzeekanaal. From 1902
to 1905 he was governor of Suriname.
He died in 1929, but his name lives on
in that of Flevoland's capital, Lelystad.

Statue of Lely

Swifterbant ⑤

Road map C3. 🚶 *6,500.* 🚌
ℹ️ *0321-318687.* 🛒 *Tue aft.*

THIS YOUNG VILLAGE is known primarily to archaeologists for the flint tools and earthenware of the **Swifterbant culture** that were unearthed here. The Swifterbant culture inhabited the region in the 4th millennium BC.

In spring, flower enthusiasts can enjoy the nearby bulbfields, which burst into a riot of vivid colour.

ENVIRONS: The Swifterbos forest nearby is an excellent spot for recreation. The Ketelbos is a resting place for bird species.

Dronten ⑥

Road map D3. 🚶 *22,500.* 🚌 ℹ️
De Rede 149 (0321-318687). 🛒 *Wed.*

DRONTEN IS well-endowed with greenery and recreation facilities. The Meerpaal Complex here combines a theatre, cinema and events venue. Outside the town hall stands the Airgunnersmonument, a propeller in honour of the airmen who lost their lives in World War II.

ENVIRONS: Around Dronten are many pretty woods and recreation areas. At Biddinghuizen, a district of Dronten, is the **Six Flags Holland** amusement park *(see p448).*

Lelystad ⑦

Road map C3. 🚶 *67,000.* 🚌 🚉
ℹ️ *Stationsplein 186 (0320-243444).*
🛒 *Sat (Gordiaan), Tue (Lelycentre).*

LELYSTAD, a provincial capital, has a modern centre with a number of outstanding buildings. The cylindrical **Nieuw Land Poldermuseum** has models and audio-visual materials illustrating the history of the fight against the sea, of the land reclamation and of the culture of the Zuiderzee.

On the Airship Plaza is the **Zep/allon** museum of balloon and airship flight. East of the town is **Natuurpark Lelystad**, where there are animals such as bison and Przewalski horses. As well as cycling and pedestrian paths, the park boasts a shipwreck and a reconstructed prehistoric village. The new **Nationaal Luchtvaartthemapark Aviodrome**, at Lelystad airport, has historic aircraft, a cinema and a reconstruction of Schiphol Station from 1928.

🏛 **Nieuw Land Poldermuseum**
Oostvaardersdijk 01–13. 🕻 *0320-260799.* 🕙 *10am–5pm Mon–Fri; 11:30am–5pm Sat & Sun.* ● *1 Jan, 25 Dec.* 🎟 🚹 🖥 🍴 ♿
🐾 **Natuurpark Lelystad**
Vlotgrasweg 11. 🕻 *0320-286111.* 🕙 *sunrise–sunset daily.* 🎟 *by appt.* 🚹 🅿
🐾 **Nationaal Luchtvaart themapark Aviodrome**
Dakotaweg 11a, Luchthaven Lelystad.
🕻 *0320-289840.* 🕙 *Apr–Oct: 9:30am–5:30pm daily; Nov–Mar: 10am–5pm daily.* ● *25 Dec.*
🎟 🚹 🅿 ♿

Bataviawerf ⑧

Road map C3. Oostvaardersdijk 01–09, Lelystad. 🕻 *0320-261409.* 🕙 *10am–5pm Mon–Fri; 11:30am–5pm Sat & Sun.* ● *1 Jan, 25 Dec.* 🎟 🚹 🅿 🍴
🌐 *www.bataviawerf.nl*

FROM 1985 TO 1995, a replica of the Dutch East India Company ship *Batavia (see p256)* was built at the Bataviawerf on the Oostvaardersdiep. The shipyard's current project is a replica of the 17th-century *De Zeven Provinciën.* Visit the sailmaking and woodcarving workshops. The entry ticket is also valid for **NISA**, the Netherlands Institute for Submarine Archaeology, with its fascinating display on shipwrecks.

The *Batavia,* which went down off the Australian coast in 1629 with 341 people on board

Observation huts on the Oostvaardersplassen lakes, situated amidst abundant bird populations

Oostvaarders-plassen 9

Road map C3. **ℹ** *Staatsbosbeheer, informatiecentrum, Kitsweg 1, Lelystad (0320-254585).*

BETWEEN LELYSTAD and Almere is internationally renowned marshland covering 6,000 ha (14,825 acres). The land was originally earmarked as an industrial area. When Zuidelijk Flevoland was drained, the low-lying area beyond the Oostvaardersdijk remained a wetland. Plans to drain this area were put forward but were ultimately dismissed because the place had by this time become an area of unique natural interest.

The nature reserve includes lakes, mud flats, marshes, willow thickets and grasslands and serves as a port of call for hundreds of species of birds that come here to forage and feed. Indeed, some birds which have been unable to settle elsewhere have found their place here, including the hen harrier (the symbol of Flevoland) and the great cormorant. Other birds seen here include the great bittern, the Eurasian spoonbill, heron, rail and, more recently, the sacred ibis. The many grey geese that forage here, along with the wild cattle, wild horses and red deer that occur here, have helped the region's vegetation to proliferate.

The marshland is largely off-limits to visitors, but some fine views are to be had from the edge of the swamp, the Oost-vaardersdijk and the Knardijk.

Additionally, the region of **De Driehoek** has a 5-km (3-mile) walking route, open sunrise to sunset. The route starts at the information centre and passes by natural woodland, lakes and observation huts.

Knardijk 10

Road map C3. **ℹ** *Staatsbosbeheer (0320-254585).*

THE KNARDIJK MARKS the border between Oostelijk and Zuidelijk Flevoland (eastern and southern Flevoland). It was built in the 1950s between the island of Lelystad-Haven and Harderwijk to enable the entire area to be placed within a polder at one time. After Oostelijk Flevoland had been dried out, it formed the southwestern ring dyke of this

polder. The Knardijk is of great interest to nature lovers, as it offers a fine view of the Oostvaardersplassen lakes. A great many birds live at the foot of the dyke, including hen harriers and marsh harriers. Two bird-watching huts can also be reached along the dyke. The dyke leads in a southeasterly direction along the nature reserve known as the **Wilgenreservaat**, which has evolved naturally into a mixture of woodland and clearings. Many songbirds, woodland birds, and birds of prey are to be found here, as are deer, foxes, polecats and ermines. Part of the reserve can be seen via a circular path. Nearby is the Knarbos forest, also boasting a variety of flora and fauna. A 6-km (4-mile) hiking route has been marked out.

Hen harrier

The Knardijk, looking out over a variegated natural landscape

Zeewolde ⓫

Road map C3. 🎿 *19,400.* 🚌
🛈 *Raadhuisstraat 15 (036-5221405).*
🗓 *Fri.*

WITH ITS picturesque marina, this village on the Wolderwijd coastal lake is a popular recreational spot. Zeewolde is the youngest village in Flevoland, having officially become a municipality in 1984. Its youth is evident from the imaginative architecture, particularly that of the town hall, library and church. An enjoyable 7-km (4-mile) walking route has been laid out in and around Zeewolde, with landscape art along the way (for information, call De Verbeelding, 036-5227037).

ENVIRONS: South of Zeewolde is the **Horsterwold**, which at 4,000 ha (9,900 acres) is the largest deciduous forest in Western Europe.

Almere ⓬

Road map C3. 🎿 *165,000.* 🚌 🚉
🛈 *Spoordreef 20, Almere-Stad (036-5334600).* 🗓 *Wed, Sat (Almere-Stad), Thu (Almere-Buiten), Fri (Almere-Haven).*

ALMERE IS Holland's fastest-growing town. Its name recalls the 8th-century name for the Zuiderzee. The earliest

Almere, a laboratory for modern architects

signs of habitation date from 65 centuries earlier. Almere today consists of three centres: Almere-Stad, which is undergoing major renovation and is where all the facilities are; Almere-Buiten, which is a green suburb; and Almere-Haven, with its lovely marina. If you are interested in modern and unusual architecture, the districts to visit are Muziewijk, Filmwijk and Stedenwijk in Almere-Stad, and the colourful Regenboogbuurt (rainbow neighbourhood) in Almere-Buiten. Also worth a visit are the town hall, the Almeers Centrum Hedendaagse Kunst **ACHK – De Paviljoens** (Almeren centre for modern

art), with works by late 20th-century Dutch and foreign artists.

ENVIRONS: Near Almere are many recreation areas and nature reserves: the Weerwater; the Leegwaterplas lake; the Beginbos forest, with walking, cycling and bridleways; the Buitenhout; the Kromslootpark, with its polder vegetation; the lakes of Noorderplassen; **Lepelaarsplassen**, where rare wading birds occur; and the Oostvaardersplassen.

ACHK – De Paviljoens
Odeonstraat 3–5. 📞 *036-5450400.*
⏰ *noon–5pm Wed–Sun (to 9pm Thu & Fri).* ⬤ *1 Jan, 25 Dec.* 📷 📶

LANDSCAPE ART

In the countryside around Flevoland you will come across the odd works of "landscape art". These are associated with various features of the landscape. East of Almere-Haven, for instance, is the *Groene Kathedraal (Green Cathedral)* (top photo), designed by Marinus Boezem and consisting of 178 Lombardy poplars planted to re-create the outline and pillars of Reims Cathedral. The *Observatorium Robert Morris* (bottom photo) consists of two round earth embankments, with three notches in them from which the sunrise can be observed when the seasons change. On the Ketelmeerdijk, you will find Cyriel Lixenberg's *Wachters op de Dijk (Watchmen on the Dike),* consisting of a circle, a triangle and a square. Piet Slegers' *Aardzee (Earth Sea),* situated between Zeewolde and Lelystad, consists of a series of elongated artificial ridges resembling waves.

GELDERLAND

GELDERLAND IS HOLLAND'S LARGEST PROVINCE. *Its name derives from the 11th-century county of Gelre, which was linked with the town of Geldern, just over the border in Germany. The town was the fiefdom of Gerard de Rossige, whose grandson Gerard II of Wassenberg pronounced himself Count of Gelre in 1104.*

Succeeding counts skilfully expanded their territory to include the Veluwe region to the north, the Betuwe in the southwest and the county of Zutphen *(see p339)*. When in 1248 the imperial town of Nijmegen was annexed, Gelre became a power to be reckoned with. A number of its towns joined the Hanseatic League, and in 1339 the county was promoted to a duchy by the German emperor. The increasing power of the Burgundians threatened the independence of the Gelders, eventually leading to the duke having to cede the territory in 1543 to Charles V. Gelderland thus became part of the Netherlands.

This colourful history is manifest today in the number of medieval buildings, churches, castles and fortified towns that welcome visitors throughout the province. In more recent times, the region, and especially the strategically located towns of Arnhem and Nijmegen, saw heavy fighting towards the end of World War II. The heroic action at Arnhem is remembered in the town's Airborne Museum, while museum in Nijmegen recalls this town's long history from pre-Roman times to the tyranny of the Holy Roman Empire.

While visitors can enjoy many modern attractions, perhaps Gelderland's greatest asset is its contrasting natural scenery, which ranges from heaths and woodlands in the north to the beautiful Betuwe river valley and the pretty agricultural region of the Achterhoek.

A 17th-century granary near Winterswijk

◁ **The mighty Waal, one of Holland's primary waterways**

Exploring Gelderland

GELDERLAND IS MADE UP OF three distinct regions. In the north is the Veluwe, an extensive natural area of woodland, heaths and large tracts of drifting sand, where those looking for peaceful natural surroundings can find exactly that. To the east is the Achterhoek. This region, too, is rich in natural beauty but has a completely different character: it consists of small fields with wooden fences, old farms, stately homes and castles. In the southwest of the province, between the Rhine, the Maas and the Waal rivers, is the river-valley region with the Betuwe. This area is distinguished by its many small dykes and river banks, which offer ample opportunities for cycling and walking.

The dolphinarium in Harderwijk

SIGHTS AT A GLANCE

Apeldoorn **2**
Arnhem **12**
Barneveld **8**
Bronkhorst **14**
Buren **26**
Culemborg **25**
Doesburg **20**
Elburg **4**
Gelderse Poort **22**
Groesbeek **23**
Harderwijk **6**
Hattem **3**
's-Heerenberg **18**
Nationaal Park De Hoge Veluwe **11**

Kröller-Müller Museum pp336–7 **10**
Lochem **16**
Montferland **19**
Nijkerk **7**
Nijmegen pp340–41 **21**
Nunspeet **5**
Paleis Het Loo pp332–3 **1**
Tiel **24**
Vorden **15**
Wageningen **9**
Winterswijk **17**
Zaltbommel **27**
Zutphen **13**

KEY

▬ Motorway
▬ Major road
▬ Minor road
▬ Scenic route
▬ Canal/river

0 kilometres   10
0 miles   10

The majestic red deer – king of the Veluwe

GETTING AROUND

Gelderland has an excellent road network. A number of major
motorways pass through the province, including the A2 and the
A50. Public transport is also good. Many towns have rail links, and
the bus will even take you deep into the Nationaal Park De Hoge
Veluwe. The numerous bicycle tracks and footpaths allow the
province to be conveniently explored either on foot or by bicycle.
Cycling routes of varying lengths are well marked, and there are
several walking routes across the province, including the very
scenic Maarten van Rossum route.

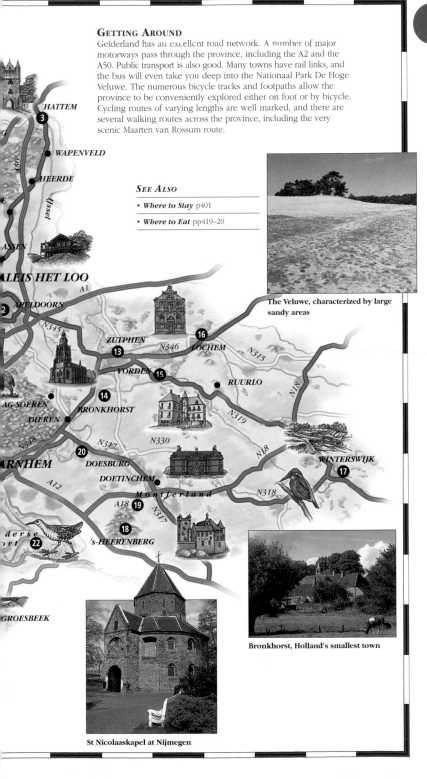

SEE ALSO

* **Where to Stay** p401

* **Where to Eat** pp419–20

The Veluwe, characterized by large
sandy areas

Bronkhorst, Holland's smallest town

St Nicolaaskapel at Nijmegen

Paleis Het Loo ❶

THE STADHOLDER WILLIAM III built the elegant palace of Het Loo in 1692 as a hunting lodge. For generations, the Orange family used it as a summer residence. Its pomp and splendour have led to its being dubbed the "Versailles of the Netherlands". Its main architect was Jacob Roman (1640–1716); the interior and the gardens were designed by Daniel Marot (1661–1752). The severe Classical façade belies the ornate interior. After intensive restoration work was carried out, the palace is now open as a museum.

Coat of Arms *(1690) of William and Mary, future king and queen of England.*

★ **Bedroom of the Stadholder William III** *(1713)*
The wall coverings and draperies in this bedroom are of rich orange damask and purple silk.

King's Garden

William III's bedroom

Closet of the Stadholder William III *(1690)*
The walls of William's private chamber are covered in scarlet damask. His paintings and Delftware are on display here.

Vintage Cars
This 1925 Bentley, nicknamed Minerva, was owned by Prince Hendrik, husband of Queen Wilhelmina. It is one of the royal family's many old cars and carriages on display in the stables.

STAR FEATURES

★ **Dining Hall**

★ **The Formal Gardens**

★ **William III's Bedroom**

VISITORS' CHECKLIST

Koninklijk Park 1
(Amersfoortseweg), Apeldoorn.
📞 055-5772400.
🚆 Apeldoorn, then bus.
Palace and gardens 🕙 10am–
5pm Tue–Sun & hols. ● 25 Dec.
📷 🅾 gardens only. 🅿 🍴 ♿
✉ W www.paleishetloo.nl

★ **Dining Hall** *(1686)*
*The marble-clad walls are
hung with tapestries depicting
scenes from Ovid's poems.*

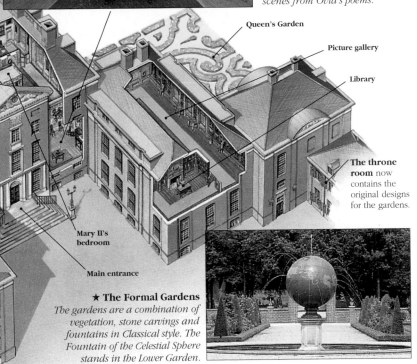

Queen's Garden

Picture gallery

Library

**The throne
room** now
contains the
original designs
for the gardens.

Mary II's
bedroom

Main entrance

★ **The Formal Gardens**
*The gardens are a combination of
vegetation, stone carvings and
fountains in Classical style. The
Fountain of the Celestial Sphere
stands in the Lower Garden.*

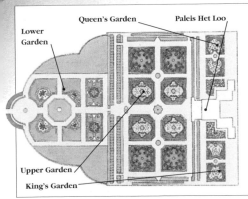

Queen's Garden Paleis Het Loo

Lower
Garden

Upper Garden

King's Garden

THE FORMAL GARDENS

When the formal gardens on the land
behind the palace were reconstructed, garden designers based their
designs on old illustrations, prints,
documents and plans. In the 18th
century, the original ornamental
gardens had been grassed over. In
1983, the intricate patterns of the
original gardens were restored and
planting began. The Het Loo gardens
are typical of a formal garden in the
17th century in which the ideal was
the harmonization of art and nature.

Plan of the formal gardens

Stroking monkeys in Apenheul

Apeldoorn ➋

Road map D3. 🏛 152,000. 🚇 🚌.
ℹ Stationstraat 72 (0900-1681636).

A PELDOORN IS first mentioned as Appoldro in 793, and for centuries it was a small rural town in the Veluwe. This was changed by William III in 1692 when he built his hunting lodge Het Loo *(see pp332–3)* here. Many wealthy burghers followed William's example and set themselves up in Apeldoorn. The engaging **Historisch Museum Apeldoorn** gives a good overview of the area's history.

The **Apenheul** is a special zoo situated in the Berg en Bos nature park, where more than 30 species of monkeys run free among the visitors.

🏛 Historisch Museum Apeldoorn
Raadhuisplein 8. 📞 055-5788429.
◯ 10am–5pm Tue–Sat, 1–5pm Sun & Tue. ● public hols. 🎦 🔓
✗ Apenheul
JC Wilslaan 31. 📞 055-3575757.
◯ Apr–Oct: 9:30am–5pm; Jun–Aug: 9:30am–6pm. 🎦 🔓 🏛

Hattem ➌

Road map D3. 🏛 12,000. 🚌 ℹ
Kerkhofstr. 2 (038-4443014). ● Wed.

T HE PICTURESQUE TOWN of Hattem (first mentioned in 891), was granted its town charter as early as 1299, joining the Hanseatic League in the 15th century. Its monumental buildings, such as the house of Herman Willem Daendals, later the governor-general of the Dutch Indies,

bear witness to Hattem's eventful and prosperous past. St Andreaskerk (St Andrew's Church) is particularly remarkable, its oldest part dating from 1176. The **Anton Pieck Museum** is dedicated to the Dutch painter and graphic artist Anton Pieck (1895–1987); it has been merged with the **Voerman Museum**, which showcases the IJssel painter Jan Voerman and his son, who illustrated the famous Verkade card albums.

🏛 Anton Pieck Museum/ Voerman Museum
Achterstraat 46–48. 📞 038-4442192 & 038-4442897. ◯ 10am–5pm Mon–Sat (Jul & Aug also open 1–5pm Sun); ● 1 Jan, 9–31 Jan, 30 Apr, 25 Dec; Nov–Apr: Mon. 🎦 🔓

Elburg ➍

Road map D3. 🏛 21,500. 🚌 ℹ
Ledigestede 31 (0525-681520). ● Tue.

E LBURG IS the best-preserved fortified town on the former Zuiderzee. The prosperity of this old town is illustrated in the 14th-century St Nicolaaskerk, with its imposing 38-m (125-ft) tower you can clearly make out the medieval rectangular street pattern.

Beside the **Vischpoort** (fish gate), once a former defence tower, is the oldest ropemaker's workshop in Holland. In early times, Elburg was much nearer to the coast, but in the late 14th century the flood-plagued town was moved well away from the sea. The interesting local history museum,

the **Gemeentemuseum**, is housed in a 15th-century monastery. Also well worth a visit is the herb garden designed by Alfred Vogel.

🏛 Gemeentemuseum Elburg
Jufferenstraat 6–8. 📞 0525-681341.
◯ 10am–5pm Tue–Fri, 2–5pm Mon. ● Oct–Mar: Mon. 🎦 🔓

Nunspeet ➎

Road map D3. 🏛 26,000. 🚇 🚌.
ℹ Stationsplein 1 (0900-2530411). ● Thu.

The Oudheidkamer at Nunspeet

N UNSPEET IS a good starting point from which to explore the nearby wooded countryside. Nunspeet's history comes to life in the **Oudheidkamer**. The nearby **Veluwemeer** lake is a popular water-sports centre.

ENVIRONS: Some 15 km (9 miles) south of Nonspeet is the idyllic **Uddelermeer** lake, a remnant from the last ice age.

The pleasant market square of Hattem, with its 17th-century town hall

Harderwijk 6

Road map C3. 38,500.
Havendam 58 (0341-426666).

THE EEL-SMOKING frames may have disappeared from the streets, but the Zuiderzee town of Harderwijk is still a pleasant place to wander around. The town has an interesting history. In the 13th century it had become so important through fishing and the trade in dyes that in 1221 Count Otto II of Gelre granted it a town charter and ordered fortifications to be built. Remnants of the old fortifications are still intact in places, including the **Vischpoort** gate. Between 1647 and 1811 Harderwijk even had a university, from which the Swedish scholar Linnaeus graduated in 1735. For years now Harderwijk's main attraction has been the **Dolphinarium** *(see p447)*, Europe's largest zoo for marine animals. Here visitors can stroke a ray or even a hound fish. The **Veluws Museum** of local history in the Donkerstraat is also worth visiting.

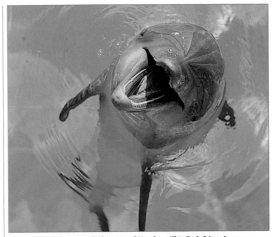
One of the favourite inhabitants of Harderwijk's Dolphinarium

Ray

Nijkerk 7

Road map C3. 27,000.
Plein 2 (0900-2021065). Fri.

NIJKERK IS A PLEASANT old town with many shops, restaurants and open-air cafés. The tobacco industry made the town rich in the 18th century. The Grote Kerk features the tomb of Kiliaen van Renselaer, one of the founders of New York. Just outside Nijkerk, on the Arkemheem polder, is the **Hertog Reijnout** *stoomgemaal*, a paddle-wheeled steam pumping-station, the last functioning one of its kind in Europe. Even today it is used to pump water out at times of flooding.

ENVIRONS: On the road to Putten is the **Oldenaller** estate with a castle from 1655. The picturesque cycling and walking area is open to the public.

In **Putten** itself you can visit **De Gedachenisruimte** (hall of remembrance) in honour of the 600 men of the town who in October 1944 were taken from the village to the Neuengamme concentration camp, from where only 50 returned alive.

🚂 Stoomgemaal Hertog Reijnout
Zeedijk 6. 033-2457757. 13 Apr–1 Oct: 10am–4pm Tue–Fri; 10am–1pm Sat. Sun & Mon.

Barneveld 8

Road map D4. 47,000.
Kapteijnstraat 26 (0342-420555). Fri.

BARNEVELD OWES its place in history books to one individual: **Jan van Schaffelaar**, commander-in-chief of the armed forces who on 16 July 1482 chose suicide rather than surrender and leapt from the tower of today's Nederlands Hervormde kerk (Reformed church). The **Nairac** museum of local history devotes considerable attention to this event. Today Barneveld is known as a poultry centre. The local **Pluimveemuseum** (poultry museum) shows how this industry has developed here.

🏛 Pluimveemuseum
Hessenweg 2a. 0342-400073. Apr–Oct: 10am–5pm Tue–Sat.

Wageningen 9

Road map C4. 33,000.
Stadsbrink 1 (0317-410777). Wed.

WAGENINGEN, situated at the southwestern edge of the Veluwe, is a pleasant town because of the local Landbouw Universiteit (agricultural university). The university's botanical gardens are open to the public. Wageningen played an important role at the end of World War II; on 5 May 1945 the Germans signed the official surrender in the **Hotel de Wereld**.

🚂 Hotel De Wereld
5 mei Plein. 0317-482030. 5 May–20 Aug & telephone bookings.

The leap of Jan van Schaffelaar

Kröller-Müller Museum ⑩

THIS MUSEUM OWES ITS EXISTENCE above all to one person: Hélène Kröller-Müller (1869–1939). In 1908, with the support of her industrialist husband Anton Kröller, Hélène Kröller-Müller started to collect modern art. In 1935, she donated her entire collection to the state, and a special museum was built to house it. As well as its large collection of modern art, which includes 278 works by Vincent van Gogh, the museum is renowned for its unique sculpture garden, the Beeldenpark.

★ Beeldenpark
Jardin d'Email *by Jean Dubuffet is one of the most distinctive sculptures in the 21-ha (52-acre) sculpture garden. The garden provides a natural backdrop for works by sculptors such as Auguste Rodin, Henry Moore, Barbara Hepworth and Richard Serra.*

Mondriaan
In addition to old Flemish masters, the Kröller-Müller also has a major collection of 19th- and 20th-century French paintings and a dozen abstract paintings by Piet Mondriaan.

Entrance to the Beeldenpark

STAR FEATURES
★ **Beeldenpark**
★ **Van Gogh Collection**

Shop

Main entrance

St Hubertus was a fun-loving person, until the day he repented for his lax life while out hunting, when he saw a stag with a glowing cross between its antlers.

Jachthuis St Hubertus
This hunting lodge, from 1914 to 1920 by the architect HP Berlage, was commissioned by the Kröller-Müller family.

The Studio Boat
Claude Monet's 1874 painting is in the 19th- and 20th-century French collection.

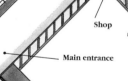

VISITORS' CHECKLIST

Kröller-Müller Museum
Houtkampweg 6, Otterlo.
📞 *0318-591041.* ⏰ *10am–5pm Tue–Sun & public hols.; sculpture garden 10am–4:30pm.* ⬤ *1 Jan.*
♿ 🎫
Jachthuis St Hubertus
🎫 *daily (Jan: open Sat & Sun only). Reserve tickets at the visitors' centre (see column at right).*

★ **Van Gogh Collection**
Café Terrace at Night *(1888). Van Gogh's huge collection of drawings, paintings and prints are the heart of the museum.*

MUSEUM GUIDE

The museum, together with the sculpture garden, gives expression to the notion that nature, architecture and art should be combined to form a whole.

KEY TO FLOORPLAN

☐ Exhibition rooms

Restaurant

Exhibition rooms

Nationaal Park De Hoge Veluwe ⑪

Hautkampweg, Otterlo. 📞 *0318-591627 (visitors' centre).* 🚂 *Ede, Apeldoorn.* ⏰ *daily.*

LIKE THE Kröller-Müller Museum, De Hoge Veluwe is also the result of a collector's ambition. The Kröller-Müllers collected plots of unused land in the Veluwe until they possessed one single tract of natural land. They even bought, in 1914, the public road between Otterlo and Hoenderlo. The 5,500 ha (13,600 acres) of woodland, marshland, heath and drifting sand now make up the largest nature reserve in Holland. The park is a treasure trove for all kinds of wildlife: rare birds, butterflies, plants and fungi. Red deer, roe deer and mouf-flon sheep still live freely here. If you are lucky, you may be able to catch a glimpse of a wild boar or a stag (they are very shy animals). Bicycle and pedestrian paths have been laid out everywhere, and at the visitors' centre you can borrow a white bicycle free of charge.

Underneath the visitors' centre is the world's first underground museum, the **Museonder**, giving visitors an idea of what life is like below the earth's surface. You can see the roots of a 140-year-old beech tree, experience a re-created earthquake and drink ancient Veluwe groundwater. The park has two restaurants: the Rijzenburg at the Schaarsbergen entrance and the De Koperen Kop café-restaurant located in the visitors' centre.

Underground museum

Arnhem ⑫

Road map D3. 🏛 *136,500.* 🚉 🚌
ℹ️ *Willemsplein 8 (0900-2024075).*
🛒 *Fri & Sat (Kerkplein).*

A RNHEM, the capital of the province of Gelderland, was declared the centre of the regional government back in 1544 by Charles V. In September 1944, the town suffered serious damage in the Battle of Arnhem, one of the most notorious battles of World War II. All the townspeople were forced to abandon their homes and were not able to return until 1945, when the peace treaty was signed. Arnhem rose again from the ashes and is now sprucing itself up rapidly. The monuments that have been restored include the

Traditional houses in the Openluchtmuseum

Allied troops landing in Arnhem on 17 September 1944

Eusebiuskerk from 1560, which was almost totally destroyed during the war. The tower, at 93 m (305 ft), is now taller than it ever was and has a glass lift which affords visitors a stunning view of the Rhine valley. The **Duivelshuis**, built in 1545 by Maarten van Rossum *(see p343)*, is an outstanding example of Dutch Renaissance architecture. Arnhem is also known for its monumental parks, such as the **Sonsbeek**, a romantic landscape park, and **Zypendaal**. In **Bronbeek**, a home for exservicemen, there is an exhibition dedicated to the former Dutch Indies. It is also worth allowing time for a visit to the **Burgers' Zoo** *(see p447)* and **Openluchtmuseum** (openair museum), where the staff, dressed up in traditional costume, illustrate the rural way of life, handicrafts and industry in the Netherlands of the 19th century.

🏛 **Openluchtmuseum**
Schelmseweg 89. 📞 *026-3576100.*
⏰ *Apr–Oct: 10am–5pm daily.* 📷

Environs: The much-visited **Posbank** at Rheden is an example of the lateral moraine landscape of Veluwe.

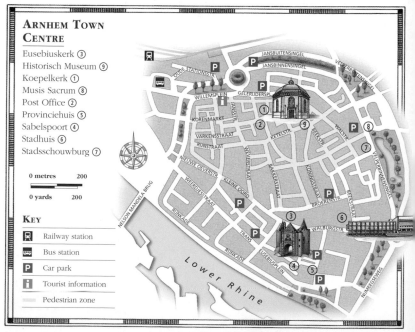

ARNHEM TOWN CENTRE

Eusebiuskerk ③
Historisch Museum ⑨
Koepelkerk ①
Musis Sacrum ⑧
Post Office ②
Provinciehuis ⑤
Sabelspoort ④
Stadhuis ⑥
Stadsschouwburg ⑦

| 0 metres | 200 |
| 0 yards | 200 |

KEY

🚉 Railway station
🚌 Bus station
🅿 Car park
ℹ️ Tourist information
⬜ Pedestrian zone

Old book at St Walburgskerk library

Zutphen ⑬

Road map D4. 🚶 36,000. 🚆
ℹ️ *Stationsplein 39 (0900-2692888).*
🚢 *Thu morning, Sat.*

T HE HANSEATIC town of Zutphen is one of Holland's
first historical towns. One of
the most distinctive features
of the town, which is first
mentioned in 1030, is the preserved medieval street layout.
The main sights of Zutphen
are the **St Walburgskerk**, the
church square and the remains
of the fortifications. They
include the **Drogenapstoren**
tower, which dates from 1444.
   Zutphen has a number
of interesting museums,
including the informative
Stedelijk Museum (local
history museum) and the
Grafisch Museum (graphic
art museum), which is
highly recommended.
   Definitely worth visiting is
the reading room of the unique
Librije (library) of the St
Walburgskerk. All of the 750
books in it date from before
1750 and include 80 incunab-
ula printed before 1500. The
books in the library, which
was built in 1564, are chained
to the desks. This is because
it was a public library which

was unsupervised at the time.
There are only four other
libraries of this kind in the
world: two are in England
and two are in northern Italy.

ℹ️ **St Walburgskerk and
Librije**
Kerkhof 3. ☎ *0575-514178.*
🕐 *usually 1:30–4:30pm in spring
and summer, but call first.* 🎫

Bronkhorst ⑭

Road map D4. 🚶 160. 🚌 *GVM 52
& ferry from Brummen (station &
GVM 36).*

B RONKHORST'S 160 inhabi-
tants make it the smallest
town in Holland. The lords
of Bronkhorst were granted
a town charter in 1482. This
very rural town, which once
stood in the shadow of a
castle (the castle no longer
exists), never really flourished
and has remained a village of
farmsteads. It has many
restored farmhouses, has no
new buildings and prohibits
motor vehicles, which means
cars must be left in a car
park outside the town. All
that remains of the once-
mighty castle of the Lords
of Bronkhorst, which had
fallen into disrepair by the
17th century, is the *kasteel-
heuvel* (castle hill).
   The Lords of Bronkhorst,
together with the noble
Bergh, Baer and Wisch
families, belonged to the
Baanderheren, nobles who
were allowed to wage war
under their own flag, which
was an old hereditary right.

Vorden ⑮

Road map D4. 🚶 *8,400.* 🚆
ℹ️ *Kerkstraat 1 (0575-553222).*
🚢 *Fri morning.*

T HERE IS mention of a Huis
Vorden (Vorden house)
as early as 1208, whereas the
first mention of the family
dates from 1315. The **Neder-
lands-herformde kerk**,
which dates from around
1300, is well worth a visit.
   The best-known figure to
come from Vorden is the poet
of Achterhoek **ACW Staring**
(1767–1840), who lived in
the De Wildenborch castle
from 1791 until his death.

ENVIRONS: Around Vorden are
eight castles in very picturesque surroundings. A bicycle trip of the area, passing
farms and country estates, is
definitely worth the effort.

A water mill at Vorden

Lochem ⑯

Road map D3. 🚶 *19,000.* 🚆
ℹ️ *Tramstraat 4 (0573-251898).*
🚢 *Wed morning.*

L OCHEM, one of the oldest
villages in the Achterhoek
to have its own parish church,
was granted its town charter
in 1233. During the 80 Years
War, the town was often besieged. It was razed to the
ground in 1615. Only the
Grote kerk, also known as
St Gudulakerk, with its 56-m
(185-ft) steeple, was spared.
This 14th-century hall-type
church has fine murals from
Catholic times (it is now a
Reformed Church). The **Stadhuis** (town hall) across from
the church dates from 1615.

Bronkhorst, a tiny picturesque village of farmsteads

A charming old farmhouse near Winterswijk

Winterswijk ⑰

Road map E4. 👥 *28,000.* 🚃
ℹ️ *Markt 17a (0543-512303).*
🅿️ *Wed morning, Sat.*

THE 20TH CENTURY has not
been kind to the town of
Winterswijk. The grand railway
station bears witness to better
times. There is now only a
single railway track, although it
is evident that in the past the
rail traffic was much heavier.
The **Museum Freriks** is pleasant with its exhibits relating to
the textile industry that flourished here after World War II.
The museum also has prints by
Pieter Mondriaan Sr, whose
famous painter son Piet spent
his childhood in Winterswijk.

🏛 **Museum Freriks**
Groenloseweg 86.
📞 *0543-533533.* ⏰ *9am–5pm
Tue–Fri, 2–5pm Sat & Sun.* 📷

ENVIRONS: The picturesque
countryside around Winterswijk has numerous large
farmhouses and an interesting
quarry. The **Erve Kots** open-
air museum in Lievelde has
several farmhouses, including
a *los boes* farmhouse from
1500, as well as craftsmen's
shops, such as a charcoal-
burner's hut.

🏛 **Erve Kots**
Eimersweg 4, Lievelde.
📞 *0544-371691.* ⏰ *10am–5pm
daily (1 Nov–Easter: Tue–Sun only).*
🔴 *1 Jan, 25 Dec.* 📷

's-Heerenberg ⑱

Road map D4. 👥 *18,000.*
🚃 *24.* ℹ️ *VVV Informatiecentrum
Montferland, Kilderseweg 1,
Zeddam (0900-6663131).*
🅿️ *Thu afternoon.*

THE OLD CASTLE town of
's-Heerenberg and its
surroundings are among
the prettiest corners of
Achterhoek. The little
town, which was granted
its charter in 1379, retains
its historical centre, with
buildings from the 15th and
16th centuries. **Huis Bergh**
is one of Holland's finest
castles and houses the
art collection of the textile
magnate JH van Heek.

🏛 **Huis Bergh**
Information:
📞 *0314-661281.* 📷

Montferland ⑲

Road map D4. ℹ️ *Kildersweg 1,
Zeddam (0900-6663131).*

MONTFERLAND, one of the
few hilly areas in the
Netherlands, is exceptionally
attractive. Apart from **'s-
Heerenberg** (*see above*),
there is a number of other
attractions, such as Zeddam,
Beek and nature reserves
where you can walk, cycle,
swim or even dive. The
natural spring in Beek,

"het Peeske", and the historic
farmhouses along the
Langeboomseweg in
Velthuizen are worth seeing.

Doesburg ⑳

Road map D4. 👥 *11,000.* 🚃
27/29 Arnhem & 26/28 Dieren.
ℹ️ *Kerkstraat 16 (0313-479088).*
🅿️ *Wed, Sat.*

DOESBURG is a snug
Hanseatic town on the
IJssel. Granted its town charter in 1237, this small town's
well-preserved old town centre has had listed status since
1974. Doesburg contains at
least 150 national monuments,
including a Late Gothic town
hall, one of the earliest in
Holland. The **Grote** or
Martinuskerk, a Late Gothic
basilica with a 97-m (320-ft)
tower, is another of the
town's noteworthy buildings,
along with the local museum
De Roode Toren.

🏛 **De Roode Toren**
Roggestraat 9–11–13.
📞 *0313-474265.* ⏰ *10am–noon,
1:30–4:30pm Tue–Fri, 1:30–4:30pm
Sat (Nov–Mar: pm only).*

Nijmegen ㉑

Road map D4. 👥 *152,000.*
🚃 ℹ️ *Keizer Karelplein 2
(0900-1122344).* 🅿️ *Mon, Sat.*

NIJMEGEN IS ONE of the
oldest towns in Holland.
Archaeological remains show
that the Batavians were settled
here even before the first
millennium, while the Romans

Huis Bergh, one of Holland's finest castles

had a fort here from 12 BC. In AD 104, the emperor Trajan granted trading rights to a new settlement west of present-day Valkhof. The town's ancient name of Ulpia Noviomagus Batavorum is presumably also from this time.

Nijmegen owes its existence to its strategic position on the river Waal. A fort has stood here since early times, and even in World War II, the town was an important battle scene. The most important sights include the **Valkhof**, with its new **museum**, which

Nijmegen's Waag, dating from 1612

stands on the spot where the fort of the Batavians, Roman engineering works and, later, one of Charlemagne's palaces stood. All that remains of the palace which was rebuilt by Frederick Barbarossa is the **St Maartenskapel** from 1155 and the **St Nicolaaskapel**, one of the earliest stone buildings in all of Holland. This chapel (part of which dates back to 1030) is a rare example of Byzantine architecture in northern Europe. Other noteworthy buildings include the St Stevenskerk, the construction of which began in 1254, the **Waag** (weigh house) and the **Kronenburgerpark**, with the remnants of fortifications (the Kruittoren tower).

Nijmegen is perhaps best known for its annual four-day rambling meet, the Wandelvierdaagse, in which tens of thousands of ramblers take part. With its many cafés, the town also has a vibrant nightlife.

Ruins of the Valkhof in Nijmegen

🏛 **Museum Valkhof**
Kelfkensbos 59, Nijmegen.
📞 *024-3608805.* ⏱ *10am–5pm Tue–Fri, noon–5pm Sat, Sun & public hols.* ♿

ENVIRONS: Close to Nijmegen is the Ooypolder, a beautiful, relaxing oasis for nature lovers. Here you can cycle and walk.

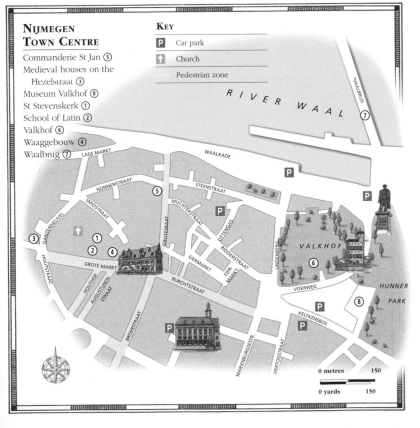

NIJMEGEN TOWN CENTRE

Commanderie St Jan ⑤
Medieval houses on the Hezelstraat ③
Museum Valkhof ⑧
St Stevenskerk ①
School of Latin ②
Valkhof ⑥
Waaggebouw ④
Waalbrug ⑦

KEY

🅿 Car park

✝ Church

Pedestrian zone

RIVER WAAL

LAGE MARKT
NONNENSTRAAT
SMIDSTRAAT
GANZEHEUVEL
WAALKADE
STEENSTRAAT
MUCHTERSTRAAT
GROTESTRAAT
HOUTSTRAAT
GROTE MARKT
HOUTHOF
AUGUSTIJNEN STRAAT
EIERMARKT
EIER MARKT
RIDDERSTRAAT
OTTENGAS
BURCHTSTRAAT
BROERSTRAAT
MARIENBURGSESTR.
HERTOGSTRAAT
KELFKENSBOS
VOERWEG
LINDENBERG
VALKHOF
HUNNER PARK

0 metres   150
0 yards   150

Beavers introduced to the Gelderse Poort now thrive

Gelderse Poort ②

Road map D4. ℹ *Arnhem (026-4426767).*

At the point where the Rhine enters the Waal, the IJssel and the Neder-Rijn (Lower Rhine) is the Gelderse Poort. This is a protected area where the flora and fauna have been allowed to grow freely. At the heart of it is the Millingerwaard, where the currents are particularly strong and where, at high water, the surrounding area regularly floods. The river banks, woodlands and marshes provide ideal breeding grounds for endangered species of birds such as the corncrake and the penduline tit.

🐾 Gelderse Poort Visitors' Centre
Molenhoek 2, Herwen. ℹ *0900-202 4075.* ⊙ *Apr–Oct: 9am–5pm daily.*

Groesbeek ②

Road map D4. 🏃 *19,000.* 🚌
ℹ *Dorpsplein 1a (024-3977118).*

Its hilly woodland surroundings make Groesbeek an attractive place for cyclists and hikers. The route of the four-day annual hike *(Wandelvierdaagse)* follows the Zevenheuvelenweg from Groesbeek to Berg and Dal, past the Canadian war cemetery. Groesbeek was subjected to heavy bombardment at the

end of World War II. The **Bevrijdingsmuseum** (liberation museum) illustrates the development of Operation Market Garden (1944) and Operation Veritable (1945), which brought about the final liberation of Holland. Groesbeek has two other popular museums: the **Bijbels Openluchtmuseum** and the **Afrika Museum**.

🏛 Bevrijdingsmuseum 1944
Wylerbaan 4. ℹ *024-3974404.* ⊙ *10am–5pm Mon–Sat, noon–5pm Sun.* 📷 ♿ 🎁

Tiel ②

Road map C4. 🏃 *36,500.* 🚉 🚌
ℹ *Tolhuisstraat 22–26 (0344-677060).* 🕑 *Mon, Sat.*

Tiel, situated on the Waal, is an ancient town that flourished during the Middle Ages because of its strategic location on the trading routes to and from Cologne. One of the best-preserved monuments from this time is the **Ambtmanshuis**, dating back to 1525. The town also has the oldest elm tree in the country. The local history museum, **De Groote Sociëteit** on the Plein, is also worth a visit. Tiel has, since time immemorial, been the centre of fruit farming in the Betuwe region. On the second Saturday in September of each

THE GREAT RIVERS

The great rivers have made an important mark on the history and landscape of Gelderland. The fortified trading towns that grew on the banks of the rivers brought prosperity to the region; dykes were built to protect the land from flooding.

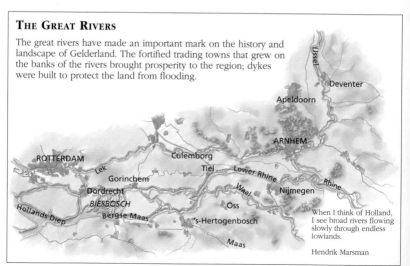

When I think of Holland, I see broad rivers flowing slowly through endless lowlands.

Hendrik Marsman

Dyke house on the Linge

year, it also becomes the centre of the **Fruitcorso** *(see p34)*, as a procession of floats decorated with fruit winds through the streets of the town. Tiel is also renowned for its tinsmith industry.

Environs: Asperen is a peaceful little town on the River Linge. On the Lingedijk is **Fort Asperen**, which is part of the Nieuwe Hollandse Waterlinie. A little farther upstream is the little town of **Acquoy,** with its crooked 15th-century tower. A Lady Pisa is buried in the town's churchyard, but there is no connection to the Leaning Tower in Italy.

Culemborg ㉕

Road map C4. 🏘 24,000. 🚊 🚌
🛈 't Jach 32 (0345-531252). 🚢 Tue.

THE OLD "DRIESTADJE" (triple town) of Culemborg, formerly consisting of three walled towns, is picturesquely situated on the River Lek. It is a great place to wander around and discover interesting corners. If you enter the former fortress through the old Binnenpoort gate, you'll reach the Markt. Here is the Late Gothic Stadhuis (town hall), built by Flemish master-builder Rombout Keldermans for Vrouwe Elisabeth van Culemborg (1475–1555). Her estate was sufficient to finance the Elisabeth Weeshuis (1560), which is now operated as a historical museum.

Other well-preserved buildings in Culemborg are the Huize de Fonteyn in the Achterstraat and the house where Jan van Riebeeck, who founded Cape Town,

South Africa, was born. The large clock in the Grote Kerk was a gift from South Africa. Even today, the "papklok" bell, which is used to announce the closing of the town gates, is tolled each and every evening at 10 o'clock.

🏛 **Museum Elisabeth Weeshuis**
Herenstraat 29. 📞 0345-513912. ◻ 1–5pm Tue–Fri, 2–5pm Sat & Sun. 🖏

Buren ㉖

Road map C4. 🏘 1,800. 🚌 🛈
Lingewaal (0345-634000). 🚢 Fri.

ON THE MAIN ROAD between Tiel and Culemborg is Buren. This little town is known for its historic links with the House of Orange, and the entire town has been listed. One of the most beautiful houses is the **Koninklijk Weeshuis** (Royal Orphanage), which was built in 1613 by Maria of Orange. The late Gothic **Lambertuskerk** is also worth seeing.

Zaltbommel ㉗

Road map C4. 🏘 11,000. 🚊 🚌
🛈 Markt 15 (0418-518177). 🚢 Tue.

BOMMEL, AS ITS inhabitants say, is more than 1,000 years old. During the 80 Years War *(see p49)*, it was an important mainstay of the Republiek der Zeven Verenigde Nederlanden (Republic of the Seven United Netherlands). The town is surrounded by two well-preserved sets of walls, which have now been laid out as a park. Within the town walls, the first building worth mentioning is the 15th-century **St Maartenskerk**, whose low towers give the town its distinctive skyline. The interior of the church is worth a look.

Another worthwhile stop is at the house of the Gelderland commander-in-chief **Maarten van Rossum** (1478–1555), who is known for plundering The Hague in 1528. The house is now an intimate museum with a large collection of drawings and prints from the region; it also hosts visiting exhibitions.

🏛 **Maarten van Rossummuseum**
Nonnenstraat 5. 📞 0418-512617. ◻ 10am–12:30pm & 1:30–4:30pm Tue–Fri, 2–4:30pm Sun. 🖏

The house of Maarten van Rossum in Nonnenstraat, Zaltbommel

SOUTHERN
NETHERLANDS

Southern Netherlands at a Glance

Sprovinces of North Brabant and Limburg, whose ambience is quite different from that of the northern provinces. The atmosphere here is more easygoing, more sociable. Both eating and drinking well are held in high regard here. Visitors to the Southern Netherlands will also find cities with historical centres, such as Den Bosch, Breda, Thorn and Maastricht; the beautiful countryside of Kempen, Peel and the hills of Zuid Limburg; thriving modern towns; and peaceful rural villages.

The Gothic Church of Sint Ja (see pp358–9) *in Den Bosch wa started in the late 14th century and completed in the 1500s.*

's-Hertogenbosch

Eindho

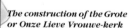

The construction of the Grote or Onze Lieve Vrouwe-kerk *(Church of Our Lady)* (see p360–61) *in Breda began in 1410. The church, which is finished in the Brabant Gothic style, has a 97-m (318-ft) tower, offering a stunning view over the town and the surrounding countryside.*

0 kilometres   20

0 miles   20

The Van Abbemuseum (see p362) *in Eindhoven has undergone extensive renovation. Architect Abel Cahen has preserved the old building while creating light-filled spaces in the angular, slanting new wing. A large collection of modern art, including video and other installations, is on display.*

The Kasteeltuinen, the gardens of the 17th-century Castle Arcen (see p368) in the town of the same name on the river Maas, have a lovely rose garden, as well as subtropical gardens, a forest of Scots pines and a golf course.

ORTH BRABANT
(pp 352–363)

LIMBURG
(pp 364–379)

Maastricht

The Bonnefantenmuseum (see pp372–3) in Maastricht is housed in a striking building designed by the Italian architect Aldo Rossi. The collections of old works of art and contemporary international art are impressive.

The route through the Heuvelland (see pp378–9) passes among hills and dales and by meandering rivers, their banks dotted with old castles. Outstanding examples of these are the 17th-century Kasteel Eijsden and Kasteel Schaloen in Valkenburg.

Catholicism and Devotion

ONE OF THE MAIN REASONS for the differences between Holland's southern and northern provinces is the marked presence of Catholicism in the south, even in these secular times. Religious imagery is a common sight here. The churches in the Brabant Gothic or Neo-Gothic style are decorated flamboyantly and many hold traditional processions throughout the year.

Crucifix

SANCTA MARIA ORA PRO NOBIS
MDCCCLIII J.J. BOSTEN PASTOR

Religious images, usually of the Madonna and Child, are a common roadside sight in Limburg. This one is set into the façade of a house in Mechelen.

The Maria Magdalena Chapel *(1695) in Gemert is also known as the Spijkerkapelleke ("nail chapel") because people made offerings of nails here in the hopes of having their skin disorders cured. Every 22 July, which is the day of Mary Magdalene, an open-air mass is held here.*

Decorative carving

Candles abound around images of St Mary.

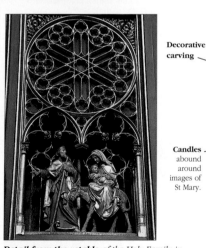

Detail from the retable *of the Holy Family in the Basilica of the Holy Sacrament in Meerssen, Limburg. It depicts Mary, Joseph and the infant Jesus fleeing from Egypt. This fine altar is richly decorated with scenes from the life of the Holy Family. The Holy Sacrament is honoured in the church. The hosts are kept in the Unique Sacramentstoren (sacrament tower) in the choir. The church itself is an example of Maasland Gothic and part of it (the nave and the choir) dates from as far back as the 14th century.*

This tomb *in the Late Romanesque/Early Gothic Onze-Lieve-Vrouwemunsterkerk (Minster Church of Our Lady) in Roermond dates from the 13th century. Inside the tomb lies Count Gerard van Gelre and his wife Margaretha van Brabant. At the time, Roermond was part of the duchy of Gelre.*

Anna-te-Drieën – the trinity of *nna, ber daugh- er Mary and the fant Jesus – is a miliar image in ligious art. This statue from chelen incorpo- rates the town's coat of arms.*

Statue of St Mary in the Onder de Linden Chapel in Thorn (Limburg).

*The **Basiliek van de HH Agatba en Barbara** (Basilica of SS Agatha and Barbara) in Oudenbosch is a copy of St Peter and St John of the Laterans in Rome. The picture on the right shows the façade, based on St John of the Laterans. The church is richly decorated in the interior, though appear- ances are deceiving: what appears to be marble is actually painted wood.*

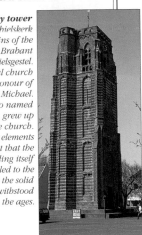

ONDER DE LINDEN CHAPEL IN THORN

The Onder de Linden Chapel, located just outside the town of Thorn in Limburg, was founded in 1673 by Clara Elisabeth van Manderscheidt-Blankenheim, who lies buried in the parish church of Thorn. This chapel, dedicated to St Mary, is opulently decorated with carvings and Baroque paintings depicting scenes of the life of the Mother of God. Shown in the picture on the left is the Onze-Lieve-Vrouwebeeld (statue of Our Lady). St Mary's Chapel is also called the Loretokapel, after the Holy House of Nazareth in the Italian town of Loreto, on which the earlier 17th-century part of the chapel is based.

*The **15th-century tower** of the Michielskerk is all that remains of the North Brabant Sint-Michielsgestel. The medieval church was built in honour of the archangel Michael. The village, also named after the saint, grew up around the church. Neglect and the elements have meant that the church building itself has been levelled to the ground, but the solid tower has withstood the ages.*

*The **church of Rolduc**, a former canon's abbey at Kerkrade which today houses a Catholic middle school and a training school for priests, has a fine altar depicting the Lamb of God. The Lamb of God represents Christ, who was sacrificed in the same way as a lamb, in order to take away the sins of the world.*

Carnival

Carnival-goers

Eʌery year in February, in the week before Ash Wednesday, carnival breaks out along the great rivers. While life goes on as usual in the north of the country, people in the south celebrate this old tradition, which is also honoured in other parts of the Catholic world. A festive mood abounds everywhere, with the best-known celebrations being held in Den Bosch, Bergen op Zoom and Maastricht. For days on end, there is drinking, singing and dancing all over Brabant and Limburg.

Carnavalsstokken (carnival rods) are brightly decorated. They are carr... by the Prince of the Carnival when h passes through the streets on his floa...

Music plays an important role at carnival time. Every year, the associations choose the official carnival anthem that will be played over and over again. The Zaate Herremienekes of Maastricht (pictured left) are among the better-known bands. Dozens of its members march through the streets blaring out enthusiastically; what their music may lack in elegance is made up for by their verve. On Shrove Tuesday they compete in the Herremienekes competition.

Although in high spirits, his question is profound (the sign on the pram reads "where are we going?")

CARNIVAL – PUTTING YOUR WORRIES ASID

The carnival season officially starts on 11 November – the eleventh of the eleventh – or "day of fools", when the Council of Eleven names the Prince of the Carnival. From then on, the municipalities are busy with preparations, and on the Sunday (in many places now on the Friday) before Ash Wednesday, the festivities begin. Wild celebrations are held throughout North Brabant and Limburg, and most public institutions are closed. Long processions with floats parade through the towns. People dress up festively: the more colourfu and exuberant the costume, the better. "Dansmarietjes" (dancing girls) accompany the floats in their colourful costumes, and the mood everywhere is upbeat. All the merriment comes to an end after Shrove Tuesday, the climax of the carnival.

Refreshments both indoors and outdoors at carnival time

CARNIVAL FLOATS

At carnival time, long processions with extravagantly decorated floats wind their way through the main streets of towns and villages. Months of preparation often go into creating the floats, and secrecy prevails during their preparation. The decoration of the float is usually on an upbeat and amusing theme, but current events are sometimes illustrated in imaginative ways. When leading politicians are featured, they are more often than not caricatured mercilessly, and social ills are exposed, often using costumed participants in *tableaux vivants*.

A festive float

The Raad van Elf (Council of Eleven) is the central office of the local carnival organization. Every year, the council appoints a Prince of the Carnival, who holds power in a municipality on the days of the carnival. The council's ritual number is 11, which is considered the number of fools. From 11 November onwards, the Raad van Elf is busy preparing carnival events. At the lively meetings, many a beer is drunk to a call of "Alaaf!" ("Eleven!").

Prince Carnival's adjutant

Characteristic carnival cap with feather

Prince Carnival

Colourful fool

Silly clothes are mandatory at carnival time. In earlier times it was customary to put on masks, whereas today the trend is to dress up in as unusual a way as possible. The northerners' belief that it is enough to put on a peasant's smock to be properly dressed is a misconception.

NORTH BRABANT

HOLLAND'S SECOND LARGEST PROVINCE *is distinguished primarily by its natural beauty. In the south and south-east are the relatively high elevations of Kempen and the Peel; in the northwest, the watery Biesbosch. Here, arms of the Waal and Maas rivers converge through a wilderness of sandbanks.*

North Brabant has been inhabited by humans since the earliest times. The Celts settled here in the 7th century BC and stayed for many centuries. They were defeated by Julius Caesar *(see p43)*, who describes them as the "Belgae" in his writings. The Rhine became the northern frontier of the Roman Empire and Roman remains have been found in the area. When the Romans left, the Franks took charge of Toxandria, as the region was known in those days. Under Charlemagne *(see p45)*, this region grew in importance as new towns expanded at points along trade routes, and in the 12th century became part of the Duchy of Brabant. The Dukes of Brabant, among them Godfried III and Henry I, expanded their territory and founded towns such as Breda and 's-Hertogenbosch. The Duchy flourished until the 16th century, when the 80 Years War left the south of Brabant under Spanish rule and the north under the rule of the Netherlands.

Although North Brabant has its fair share of commerce and industry, and Eindhoven is a major manufacturing centre, tourism has become increasingly important. The region's colourful history is evident from the medieval buildings and bastions in many of the towns, and the castles dotted around the countryside, with a range of fine exhibits in churches and museums. For younger visitors the highlight is the fairytale theme park De Efteling at Kaatsheuvel, northeast of Breda.

Het Grote Peel, an area of outstanding natural beauty in North Brabant

◁ **The Binnen-Dieze in 's-Hertogenbosch, now fully restored and here straddled by houses**

Exploring North Brabant

NORTH BRABANT'S RICH HISTORIC PAST and unspoiled
countryside have given the province its unique
character. The centres of 's-Hertogenbosch and Breda
and the picturesque fortified towns of Heusden and
Willemstad are of great historical interest. The beautiful
natural areas of the Loonse and Drunense dunes, Peel,
Kempen and Biesbosch areas provide opportunities
for various tours. Van Abbemuseum in Eindhoven,
De Wieber in Deurne and the many other museums
in the region offer a great deal of cultural interest. De
Efteling is one of Europe's best-known theme parks.

Shipping locks at the historical
fortress town of Willemstad

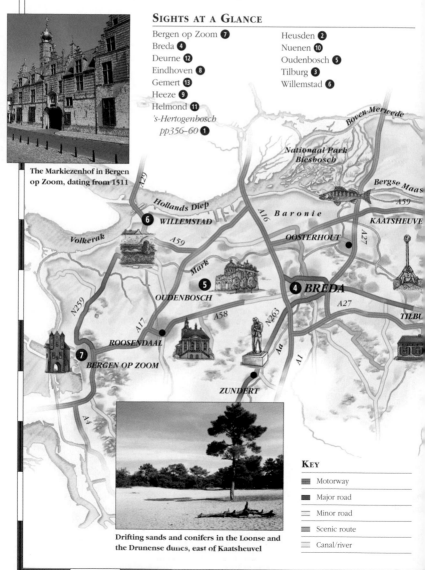

The Markiezenhof in Bergen
op Zoom, dating from 1511

SIGHTS AT A GLANCE

Bergen op Zoom **7**   Heusden **2**
Breda **4**   Nuenen **10**
Deurne **12**   Oudenbosch **5**
Eindhoven **8**   Tilburg **3**
Gemert **13**   Willemstad **6**
Heeze **9**
Helmond **11**
's-Hertogenbosch
pp356–60 **1**

Drifting sands and conifers in the Loonse and
the Drunense dunes, east of Kaatsheuvel

KEY

■ Motorway

■ Major road

— Minor road

▬ Scenic route

═ Canal/river

GETTING AROUND

North Brabant has an excellent transport infrastructure. All the larger towns, as well as many smaller towns and villages, can be reached easily by train. There is an extensive network of long-distance coaches which will take you to even the smallest village. The province can be explored by car with great ease thanks to its dense motorway network, which includes the A2, the A58 and the A65, as well as to its many good major roads. Areas of natural beauty such as the Peel and Kempen are ideal countryside for cycling.

The 14th-century Kasteel Heeswijk, rebuilt numerous times during its lifetime

SEE ALSO

- *Where to Stay* pp401–2
- *Where to Eat* pp420–21

Sheep on the Strabrechtse Heide, near Heeze

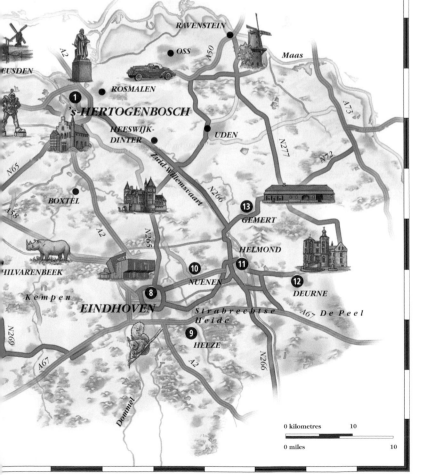

Street-by-Street: 's-Hertogenbosch ❶

IN 1185, HENRY I OF BRABANT founded the town of 's-Hertogenbosch. The strategically positioned town – usually called Den Bosch – grew rapidly. From the 16th century its prosperity waned, when the States General *(see p50)* ignored Brabant and chose to favour other regions. Its prestige rose again after 1815, when it became the capital of North Brabant. Today, it is a vibrant, lively town.

Carved figure of St Lucia

Stone Plaque with Swan
Such plaques are a commo[n] sight in the city centre.

Moriaan
The medieval building known as De Moriaan, with its stepped gable, is the town's oldest building. It now houses the town's tourist office.

★ Binnen-Dieze
The Binnen-Dieze, the city's inner canal, runs partly underground. It is possible to make a spectacular round trip along the recently restored town walls.

STAR SIGHTS

★ Binnen-Dieze

★ Noordbrabants Museum

★ Sint Jan

★ Sint Jan
The flying buttresses of the Sint Jan Church (see pp358–9) are decorated with a variety of figures.

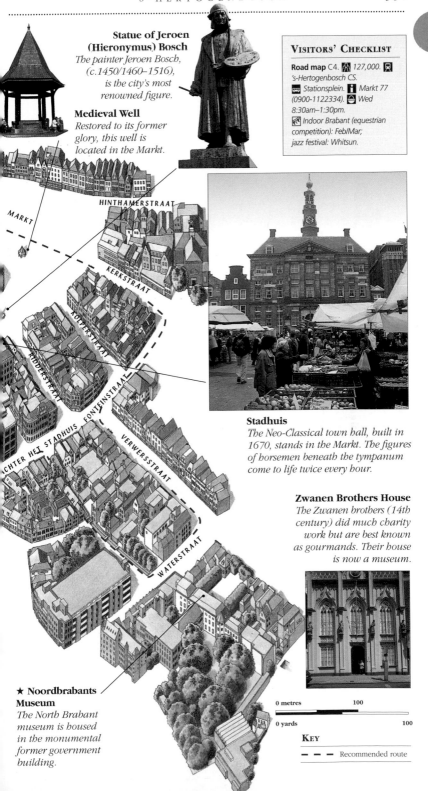

Statue of Jeroen (Hieronymus) Bosch
The painter Jeroen Bosch, (c.1450/1460–1516), is the city's most renowned figure.

Medieval Well
Restored to its former glory, this well is located in the Markt.

MARKT

HINTHAMERSTRAAT

KERKSTRAAT

KOLPERSTRAAT

RIDDERSTRAAT

ACHTER HET STADHUIS

FONTEINSTRAAT

VERWERSSTRAAT

WATERSTRAAT

VISITORS' CHECKLIST

Road map C4. 127,000. 's-Hertogenbosch CS. Stationsplein. Markt 77 (0900-1122334). Wed 8:30am–1:30pm. Indoor Brabant (equestrian competition): Feb/Mar; jazz festival: Whitsun.

Stadhuis
The Neo-Classical town hall, built in 1670, stands in the Markt. The figures of horsemen beneath the tympanum come to life twice every hour.

Zwanen Brothers House
The Zwanen brothers (14th century) did much charity work but are best known as gourmands. Their house is now a museum.

★ **Noordbrabants Museum**
The North Brabant museum is housed in the monumental former government building.

| 0 metres | 100 |
| 0 yards | 100 |

KEY

– – – Recommended route

Sint Jan

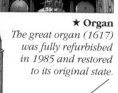

THERE WAS A CHURCH OF SINT JAN (St John) in Den Bosch as early as the beginning of the 13th century, although nothing of the original Romanesque church exists today. The present-day Gothic church was built from the late 14th to the 16th century. The majestic cathedral survived the iconoclastic riots of 1566 *(see p52)* and a devastating fire in 1584. The damaged building is undergoing continuous restoration.

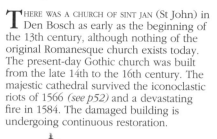

Statue of St Mary
The 13th-century miracle-working figure of the Zoete Lieve Vrouw of Den Bosch (Our Good Lady of Den Bosch) was for centuries kept in Brussels but was returned to Sint Jan in 1853.

★ Organ
The great organ (1617) was fully refurbished in 1985 and restored to its original state.

Gargoyles
The gargoyles are designed to channel rainwater pouring off the roof. Here, the drain pipes are encased by the head of mythical animals.

Baptistery
The baptismal font in the baptistery dates from 1492. The figures on the cover depict the baptism of Jesus by St John.

Flying buttresses
are designed to strengthen the structure of the building. They are richly ornamented with saints, angels and other figures.

The ornamental south portal is dedicated to Saint John the Evangelist.

STAR SIGHTS
★ Organ
★ Sanctuary
★ Stained-Glass Windows

Antoniuskapel
The Chapel of St Anthony contains a spectacular Passion altar made by a studio in Antwerp. The Church of Sint Jan managed to buy the retable in 1901 for one guilder.

VISITORS' CHECKLIST

Choorstraat 1. ☎ 073-6130314.
○ 8am–5pm daily.
✝ 9am & 12:30pm Mon–Fri,
9am & noon Sat,
10:15am & noon Sun.
☛ by request at V V V or
☎ 0900-1122334.
W www.sint-jan.nl

Baldachin
The revolving baldachin in the middle of the cathedral is ascribed to Alart Duhameel. The all-seeing eye looks down from the vaults.

The stained-glass window frame depicts the woman and the dragon from *The Book of Revelation.*

★ Stained-Glass Windows
The Church of Sint Jan was restored in Neo-Gothic style during the 19th century. A great deal was changed, including the lively and colourful stained-glass windows.

★ Sanctuary
The sanctuary was built from 1380 to 1425 by Willem van Kessel. The vaults are painted with a variety of biblical scenes, among them the coronation of St Mary.

The seven radiating chapels around the choir form an elegant crown.

Exploring 's-Hertogenbosch

ALONG WITH A LARGE NUMBER of historical buildings and interesting museums, the town of 's-Hertogenbosch offers a wide choice of fine restaurants. The excellent Noordbrabants Museum has an excellent exhibition of art from the Southern Netherlands from 1500 to the present. The most striking building in 's-Hertogenbosch is the majestic Gothic church of Sint Jan. The historic district of Uilenburg offers ample opportunities to while away the time with a drink or a bite to eat in a café.

Four putti (1731) by Walter Pompe, Noordbrabants Museum

THE SPLENDID CHURCH of Sint Jan *(see pp358–9)* is Den Bosch's crowning glory. In the Markt stand historical buildings such as **De Moriaan** (parts of which date back to the 12th century) and the town hall, dating from 1670. A statue of the great painter Hieronymus Bosch (c.1453–1516) stands between the two grand buildings. Born in 's-Hertogenbosch, Bosch spent most of his life here. In the town's historical district of Uilenburg, beyond the Markt, are plenty of good cafés and restaurants. The **Binnen-Dieze**, the city's inner canal, surfaces at this point; houses here stand directly in its water. Right by Sint Jan is the majestic **Zwanenbroedershuis** *(see p357)*, as well as the Museum Slager, which showcases paintings by the Slager family.

🏛 Noordbrabants Museum

Verwersstraat 41. ☎ 073-6877877.
🕐 10am–5pm Tue–Fri, noon–5pm Sat, Sun & public hols. 🎫 ♿ 🖵

The excellent Noordbrabants Museum displays art by renowned artists such as Pieter Brueghel and Teniers, as well as modern artists such as van Gogh, Mondriaan and Sluyters. The museum also features exhibits on the history of the province of North Brabant, from prehistoric times to the present.

Heusden ❷

Road map C4. 🏚 *42,000.* 🚍 🚺 *Pelsestraat 17 (0416-662100).* 🍴 *Thu.*

AFTER A THOROUGH refurbishment that started in 1968 and lasted for decades, the picturesque ancient fortified town of Heusden on the river Maas has been restored to its former glory. That Heusden fell victim to the redevelopment craze of the 1960s matters little. Walls, houses, moats, the **Veerpoort** (ferry gate) and the **Waterpoort** have all been restored in the old style. As advertising is banned in Heusden, it is easy to imagine that time has stood still here, save for the fact that motor vehicles are allowed into the fortress.

Tilburg ❸

Road map C5. 🏚 *190,000.* 🚉 🚍 🚺 *Spoorlaan 364 (0900-2020815).* 🍴 *Tue, Fri, Sat.*

TILBURG, THE SIXTH largest town in Holland, once had a flourishing textile industry. The interesting **Nederlands Textielmuseum**, which is housed in a former textile mill, illustrates the history of the country's textile industry and explains how textiles were produced.

The **kermis van Tilburg** (Tilburg fair), held each year at the end of July, is the biggest fair in Holland. The entire town puts all its energy into the event, and people come from far and near to attend the event.

🏛 Nederlands Textielmuseum

Goirkestraat 96. ☎ 013-5367475.
🕐 10am–5pm Tue–Fri, noon–5pm Sat & Sun. 🎫 ♿ 🖵 by appointment. 🖵 🍴

ENVIRONS: Kaatsheuvel is home to **De Efteling**, the famous theme park, where all kinds of fairytale personalities come to life *(see pp448–9).*

Breda ❹

Road map B5. 🏚 *157,000.* 🚉 🚍 🚺 *Willemstraat 17–19 (0900-5222444).* 🍴 *Tue & Fri.*

THE OLD BASTION of Breda was built at the confluence of the rivers Aa and Mark around the **Kasteel van Breda**, where the Koninklijke Militaire Academie (royal military academy) is now established. Breda was granted its town charter in 1252.

A walk through the old centre will take you to the **Grote kerk**, also known as the Onze Lieve Vrouwe Kerk (Church of Our Lady). It is prominent on the Grote Markt and cannot be missed. Construction of this magnificent Brabant Gothic-style church began in 1410; in 1995–8 it underwent restoration.

Mills on the bastion of the old fortified town of Heusden

It was at the Spanjaardsgat water-gate, near the castle, that the Spaniards, in 1590, tricked their way in with a peat barge and subsequently conquered the town.

Breda's Museum is housed in the old barracks of the Chassékazerne. The museum displays interesting exhibits which illustrate the history of the town.

🏛 **Breda's Museum**
Parade 12–14. 📞 076-5299300.
🕐 10am–5pm Tue–Sun. 🖼 ♿ 🖳

Oudenbosch ❺

Road map B5. 🏛 29,400 (municipality of Halderberge). 🚉 🚌 🛈 St Anna-plein 1 (0165-390555). 🔺 Tue.

Between 1860 and 1870, Oudenbosch was the point from which the Zouaves set out on their journey to Rome to defend the pope against Garibaldi. Upon their return, they had the architect PJH Cuypers (see p369) build a replica of St Peter's basilica in Rome, the **Basiliek van de HH Agatha en Barbara** (Basilica of SS Agatha and Barbara).

The basilica of Oudenbosch, a miniature copy of St Peter's in Rome

Willemstad ❻

Road map B4. 🏛 36,500 (municipality of Zevenbergen). 🚌 🛈 Hofstraat 1 (0168-476055). 🔺 Mon.

The bastions of Willemstad, were built in 1583 by William of Orange. The Mauritshuis (1623), the former hunting lodge of Maurice, Prince of Orange, is today a museum. The influence of the Oranges can also been seen in the white Oranjemolen mill (1734).

Bergen op Zoom ❼

Road map B5. 🏛 64,000. 🚉 🚌
🛈 Grote Markt 1 (0164-277482).
🔺 Thu & Sat.

The old town of Bergen op Zoom grew around a chapel that was dedicated to St Gertrude. In 1260, Bergen op Zoom was granted its town charter, after which it enjoyed a period of prosperity. The 15th-century **St Geertruids-kerk**, with its striking tower, stands on the site of the original chapel. The lords of Bergen op Zoom built the **Markiezenhof**, which was finally completed in 1511. The castle is today a museum, with period rooms and an unusual collection of fairground items.

🏛 **Markiezenhof**
Steenbergsestraat 8. 📞 0164-242930.
🕐 Oct–Mar: 2–5pm Tue–Sun; Apr–Sep: 11am–5pm Tue–Sun. 🖼 ♿ 🖳

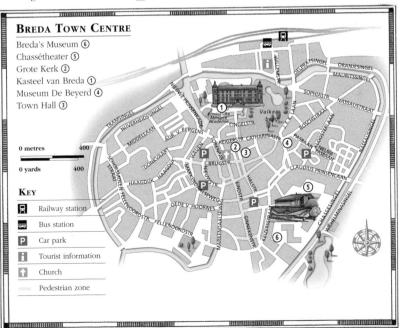

BREDA TOWN CENTRE

Breda's Museum ⑥
Chassétheater ⑤
Grote Kerk ②
Kasteel van Breda ①
Museum De Beyerd ④
Town Hall ③

0 metres   400
0 yards   400

KEY

🚉 Railway station
🚌 Bus station
🅿 Car park
🛈 Tourist information
✚ Church
  Pedestrian zone

Woman in Green (1909) by Picasso,
Van Abbemuseum (Eindhoven)

Eindhoven ❽

Road map C5. 🏛 *198,000.*
🚆 🚌 **ℹ** *Stationsplein 17 (0900-
1122363).* 🏪 *Wed, Fri & Sat.*

THE OLD MARKET town of
Eindhoven was merged
with the villages of Strijp,
Woensel, Tongelre, Stratum
and Gestel in the 19th
century. The municipality
of Eindhoven grew enor-
mously in the last century
when Philips, the electronics
company, sited its factory
there. Philips's best-known
building, the distinctive
Witte Dame (white lady)

was built in 1922 by architect
L Scheffer; it has now been
sold and converted into a
design college, library and
centre for artists. The former
Philips area in Strijp is also
being developed into a
residential area with shops,
restaurants and theatres.

Another major local
employer was the car-maker
DAF. In the **DAF-museum**
there are hundreds of cars,
buses and trucks on display,
and the original 1928 workshop of the founders, Hub
and Wim van Doorne.

Kruysen's *Brabantse Hut* (1923),
Museum Kempenland (Eindhoven)

The most important sight,
however, is the **Van
Abbemuseum**, which is
devoted to modern art.
The original building was
designed in 1936 by AJ
Kropholler and has been
described as a "brick castle".
In the 1990s, architect Abel
Cahen was commissioned
to expand the museum.
Cleverly integrating the
existing building into a
large new wing, he quadru-
pled the exhibition space
and added a restaurant and
multimedia centre. Queen
Beatrix opened the museum
in January 2003. The collection contains works by
Chagall, Lissitzky and
Beuys, and is particularly
known for Picasso's
Woman in Green (1909).

🏛 **DAF-museum**
Tongelresestraat 27.
☎ *040-2444364.*
🕐 *11am–5pm Tue–Sun.*
♿ 🛍 💻

🏛 **Van Abbemuseum**
Bilderdijklaan 10.
☎ *040-2381000.*
🕐 *11am–5pm Tue–Sun.*
♿ 🛍 💻
🌐 *www.vanabbemuseum.nl*

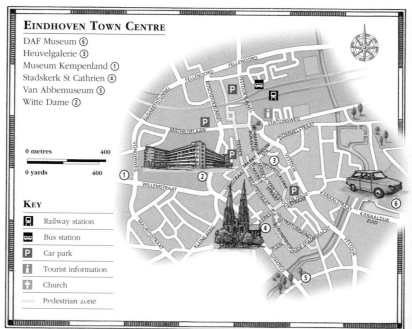

EINDHOVEN TOWN CENTRE

DAF Museum ⑥
Heuvelgalerie ③
Museum Kempenland ①
Stadskerk St Cathrien ④
Van Abbemuseum ⑤
Witte Dame ②

0 metres	400
0 yards	400

KEY

🚆 Railway station

🚌 Bus station

P Car park

ℹ Tourist information

✝ Church

▬ Pedestrian zone

Heeze ⑨

Road map C5. 🧍 15,300.
🚗 🚌 ℹ️ *Jan Deckersstraat 2, Leende (040-2241400).* 🛒 *Thu.*

THE 17TH-CENTURY castle of **Kasteel Heeze** is the centrepiece of this small Brabant town just outside Eindhoven. Designed by Pieter Post, it stands amidst lovely streams, woods and meadows. Among the many exhibits set out in the castle's 30 halls are valuable Gobelin tapestries.

🏰 **Kasteel Heeze**
Kapelstraat 25. ☎️ *040-2261431.* ◻️ *Mar–Oct.* 📷 📷 *Mar–Oct: 2pm Wed, 2 & 3pm Sun (Jul–Aug: also at 2pm Wed).*

Nuenen ⑩

Road map C5. 🧍 23,000. 🚌
ℹ️ *Berg 17 (040-2844868).* 🛒 *Mon.*

NUENEN, northeast of Eindhoven, is the village where van Gogh lived from 1883 to 1885. **Van Gogh Documentatiecentrum** deals comprehensively with his time in Nuenen.

The magnificent Kasteel Heeze

The vast Strabrechtse Heide at Heeze and Geldrop

🏛 **Van Gogh Documentatiecentrum**
Papenvoort 15. ☎️ *040-2631668.* ◻️ *9am–noon, 2–4pm Mon–Fri.*

Helmond ⑪

Road map C5. 🧍 77,600. 🚗 🚌
ℹ️ *Markt 213 (0492-543155).* 🛒 *Wed & Sat.*

THE MOST outstanding feature of Helmond is the **castle** dating from 1402, today the **Gemeentemuseum** (local history museum). The museum has many historical artefacts as well as a fine collection of modern art including works by Breitner and Charley Toorop.

🏛 **Gemeentemuseum**
Kasteelplein 1. ☎️ *0492-547475.* ◻️ *10am–5pm Tue–Fri, 2–5pm Sat & Sun.* 📷 ♿ 📷 📷

Deurne ⑫

Road map D5. 🧍 32,000. 🚗 🚌
ℹ️ *Markt 2 (0493-323655).* 🛒 *Fri.*

THE RELAXING TOWN of Deurne is an artistic centre. The house (1922) of the extravagant doctor and painter Henrik Wiedersma, who used to make house calls on his motorcycle, is now a **museum** of expressionist works by the doctor and his avant-garde friends, including Ossip Zadkine, who often stayed with him. Poets such as Roland Holst, Nijhoff and Bloem were also regular visitors to the house.

🏛 **Museum De Wieger**
Oude Liesselseweg 29. ☎️ *0493-322930.* ◻️ *noon–5pm Tue–Sun.* ⚫ *Mon & public hols.* 📷 📷

Gemert ⑬

Road map C5. 🧍 27,300 ity of Gemert-Bakel). 🚌 plein 49 (0492-3666

GEMERT IS imp was o Ge

LIMBURG

L IMBURG IS HOLLAND'S SOUTHERNMOST PROVINCE, *squeezed by the course of history into its present unusual shape bounded partly by Belgium to the west and to the south and by Germany on the eastern flank. Yet its outline is not the only remarkable thing about this delightful multilingual province.*

From a geological point of view, Limburg is much older than the rest of Holland, sitting on coal deposits that are around 270 million years old. In the mining museum at Kerkrade, east of Maastricht, you can see how coal used to be mined in this region. The caves that can be seen in many places in South Limburg are also mines, albeit for the local limestone laid down between 60 and 70 million years ago. The best-known cave systems, parts of which date from the Roman era, are at Valkenburg and at St Pietersberg near Maastricht.

The Maas river valley has been attractive to settlers since the last Ice Age. There is evidence of early nomads, followed by sedentary society like the "Bandkeramikers" and the Beaker Folk (see p42). The Romans were here for around 400 years and Maastricht, which they founded, has much evidence of their impressive buildings. Heerlen was also an important Roman crossroads and the bathhouse museum here makes an excellent and informative visit. In the Middle Ages, Limburg was split up and fought over at various times by the German Empire, Gelder, Liège, Brabant and the Spanish. It acquired its present borders in the 19th century. Nowadays it has plenty to offer visitors, from historic towns with fine architecture, shops and nightlife to countryside dotted with half-timbered houses, farms, water mills in the rivers, and countless castles and country houses.

Half-timbered houses in the South Limburg town of Cottessen

◁ The countryside of Limburg with its rolling hills, unique in Holland

Exploring Limburg

Noord Limburg is made up of the Peel and the Maas regions. Between the river Maas and the German border are nature reserves with fens, woodland, heathland and river dunes. The former wilderness known as the Peelgebied is on the border with North Brabant. Middle Limburg is the section from the Maasplassen lakes, which were created by the digging of gravel pits. It is now one of the most important watersports areas in the country. Zuid Limburg consists of Maastricht, the Mijnstreek (mining country) and the pretty chalk-hill landscape to the south.

Picking asparagus in Noord Limburg

Key

▬	Motorway
▬	Major road
═	Minor road
▬	Scenic route
═	Canal/river

National park of De Grote Peel

Getting Around

Limburg is easily reached by rail and by road, which are also the best ways to explore it. The motorways and railways invariably follow the same routes, that is to say: Nijmegen-Venlo-Roermond-Geleen-Maastricht, Weert-(Roermond)-Geleen-Maastricht and, finally, the triangle Maastricht-Geleen-Heerlen. For cyclists there are long sections of cycle paths along the Julianakanaal and the Zuid-Willemsvaart. The south of Zuid Limburg in particular is simply ideal for cycling (including racing) and rambling. The tourist railway or "environmental line" from Schin near Geul to Kerkrade via Wijlre, Eys and Simpelveld operates from April to October on Sundays and Wednesdays, with two steam-trains and a "rail-bus".

The St.-Martinuskerk in Weert

WEERT

TH

EC

A2

SITTARI
GELEEN
ELSLOO
A2

Maas

MAASTRICHT

VALKENB
A278

EIJSDEN

...one quarry with old passageways

M

Sights at a Glance

Field chapel in Heuvelland

0 kilometres   10

0 miles   10

Mining, once the mainstay of Limburg's industry

Kasteel Schaloen at Valkenburg (13th century), rebuilt in the 17th century

Mook ●

Road map D4. 🏛 *825*. �autobus *83*.
ℹ *Raadhuisplein 2 (024-6961762)*.

THE VILLAGE of Mook is
on the river Maas in the
very north of Limburg. On
14 April 1574, the Prince of
Orange's army was routed
on the nearby **Mookerhei**
by the Spanish. The star-
shaped fortifications of the
Heumense Schans from the
80 Years War stand atop a
43-m (141-ft) ridge from the
Saalian Ice Age. It offers a
fantastic vantage point from
which to view the Maas valley.
   South of Mook is the recreation area of the Mookerplas
lake and the fine estate of **Sint
Jansberg**, where the Bovenste
Plasmolen, an ancient watermill, has been restored and is
now fully functioning.

Venray ●

Road map D5. 🏛 *37,000*. 🚍 *29,
Interliner 415*. �autobus ℹ *Henseniusplein
13 (0478-510505)*. 🔄 *Mon*.

DURING WORLD WAR II, Noord
Limburg was the scene of
heavy fighting. An English
and a German (at Ysselsteyn)
military cemetery lies near the
town. Nearby Overloon is
home to the Oorlogs-en Verzetsmuseum (war museum).
In 1944, Venray was largely
destroyed. The 15th-century
basilica of **St Petrus Banden**,
with its magnificent interior,
was given a new 80-m (262-ft)
tower in restoration works. The
Geijsteren estate on the Maas,
where old Maas terraces are
visible in the terrain, is an
outstanding rambling area.

Arcen ●

Road map D5. 🏛 *9,000*. 🚌 *83*.
ℹ *Wal 26 (077-4731247)*.

THE MAIN ATTRACTION of Arcen,
picturesquely located on
the Maas, is the finely restored
17th-century Arcen castle with
its **Kasteeltuinen** (castle gardens). They incorporate a rose
garden, subtropical gardens,
Eastern gardens, a pine forest
and a golf course. You can

The magnificent 16th-century Venlo town hall in the Markt

also take the waters at the
Thermaalbad Arcen spa; its
mineral-rich water is extracted
from 900 m (2,955 ft) underground. Other local delights
include the special Arcen beer,
asparagus (complete with an
asparagus market on Ascension
Day), and the drink distilled
by the Branderij De IJsvogel,
housed in the 17th-century
Wijmarsche water mill.
Outside Arcen is the 1,500 ha
(3,705 acre) **Nationaal Park
Landgoed de Hamert**.

🌿 **Kasteeltuinen**
Lingsforterweg 26. 🕻 *077-4731882*. ◯
*29 Mar–27 Oct: 10am–6pm; Nov week-
ends 10am–5pm.* ● *23 Dec–7 Jan.* 🖼

The exquisite gardens of Arcen

Venlo ●

Road map D5. 🏛 *60,000*. 🚍 ℹ
Koninginneplein 2 (077-3543800).
🔄 *Sat*.

THE COMBINED city of Venlo/
Blerick began as a Roman
settlement. In the Middle Ages
it grew rich on trade. The
15th-century St Martinuskerk,
a Gothic hall-type church, and
Ald Weishoes, a Latin school
dating from 1611 built in the
Gelderland Renaissance style,
are among the few historical
buildings to survive World War
II. The town hall was designed
between 1597 and 1600 by
Willem van Bommel. The local
**Museum Van Bommel-Van
Dam** features modern art; the
Limburgs Museum, archaeological finds.

🏛 **Museum Van Bommel-
Van Dam**
Deken van Oppensingel 6.
🕻 *077-3513457*. ◯ *11am–5pm
Tue–Sun.* ● *Mon, 1 Jan, Carnival,
25 Dec*.
🏛 **Limburgs Museum**
Keulsepoort 5. 🕻 *077-3522112*. ◯
11am–5pm Tue–Sun. ● *1 Jan, Carnival,
25 Dec.* 🖳 *www.limburgsmuseum.nl*

Weert ❺

Road map C5. 🏛 *47,700*. 🚗 🚌 *31*.
ℹ *Maasstraat 18 (0495-536800)*.
📅 *Sat*.

Tʜᴇ ᴊᴇᴡᴇʟ ᴏꜰ ᴡᴇᴇʀᴛ is the **St Martinuskerk**, one of the few Late Gothic hall-type churches in Holland (in hall-type churches, the side aisles are equal in height and width to the nave). When restoration works were carried out around 1975, paintings from the 15th and 16th centuries were discovered beneath the layers of whitewash on the vaulted ceilings. Before the high altar (1790) by Italians Moretti and Spinetti lies the tomb of the lord of Weert, beheaded in 1568 on the order of Alva in Brussels. Not far from the church is the **Ursulinenhof**, an example of a new building successfully integrated into a historical centre.

Surrounding areas such as Weerterbos forest and the **Nationaal Park De Grote Peel** are remnants of a region of peat moors.

Roermond ❻

Road map D5. 🏛 *43,000*. 🚗 🚌 *30, 77*. ℹ *Kraanpoort 1 (0900-2025588)*. 📅 *Sat*.

Tʜᴇ ᴏʟᴅᴇsᴛ ᴄʜᴜʀᴄʜ in the see of Roermond is the 13th-century Late Romanesque, Early Gothic **Onze-Lieve-**

Interior of the Onze-Lieve-Vrouwemunsterkerk in Roermond

Vrouwemunsterkerk (minster church of Our Lady), which was originally the church of a Cistercian abbey. The interior of the church is worth a visit. The **St Christoffel-kathedraal**, a Gothic cruciform basilica with a gilded statue of St Christopher on the tower, dates from the early 15th century. The church's stained-glass windows are by the local glazier Joep Nicolas.

Roermond is by the Maasplassen lakes, one of the country's largest areas for watersports. The lakes cover more than 300 ha (740 acres) and have a length of approximately 25 km (15 miles). The **Maasplassen** were created through large-scale gravel quarrying in the Maas valley, which went on as far as Maaseik in Belgium.

Limburg asparagus

De Meinweg ❼

Road map D6. 🏛 *none*. 🚌 *78, 79*.
ℹ *Bezoekerscentrum, Meinweg 2, Herkenbosch (0475-528500)*.

Tʜᴇ ᴇxᴘᴀɴsɪᴠᴇ ɴᴀᴛɪᴏɴᴀʟ park of De Meinweg in the east of the province possesses a unique natural beauty. Six hiking routes have been laid out here. You can also tour the park by horse-drawn cart, accompanied by expert guides.

Dʀ PJH Cᴜʏᴘᴇʀs

Architect Pierre Cuypers was born in Roermond in 1827. He lived and worked both in his hometown and in Amsterdam. One of Cuypers' sons and one of his nephews also became renowned architects. Considered one of the prime representatives of the Netherlands Neo-Gothic, Cuypers designed the Central Station and the Rijksmuseum in Amsterdam, and De Haar castle in Haarzuilens. He was also the architect and restorer of countless churches, including the *munsterkerk* (minster church) in Roermond.

Munsterkerk in Roermond

The 1,600-ha (3,955-acre) De Meinweg national park

Street-by-Street: Maastricht ❽

Gevelsteen

Maastricht emerged in Roman times at a point along the river Maas which could be crossed on foot (Mosae Traiectum), on the Roman road that led from Colonia Agrippina (Cologne) to Bononia (Boulogne). The founder of Christian Maastricht was St Serviatus, bishop of Tongeren, who died in AD 384 in Maastricht and was buried in the cemetery then located outside the town walls. The magnificent basilica of St Servaas was built over his tomb. In addition to the basilica, another fine church is the Romanesque Onze-Lieve-Vrouwebasiliek.

Sculpture of Pieke
This sculpture in Stok-straat is of Pieke and his dog, from a book by Ber Hollewijn.

KEY

– – – Recommended route

The Generaalshuis
Now the Theater an het Vrijhof, this Neo-Classical palace was built in 1809. General Dibbets, who succeeded in keeping Maastricht part of the Netherlands, lived here around 1830.

GROTE GRACHT

STATENSTRAAT

HELMSTRAAT

VRIJTHOF

STAR SIGHTS

★ **Cemetery**

★ **Onze-Lieve-Vrouwebasiliek**

★ **Stadhuis**

★ **Cemetery**
Now one of the city's main squares, the cemetery was located outside the town walls when the construction of St Servaas began.

In den Ouden Vogelstruys
One of the many street cafés flanking the Vrijthof, this lively, popular spot serves a small selection of meals.

★ Stadhuis
The town hall on the Markt was built from 1559–1664 and is a masterpiece by Pieter Post of the Northern Netherlands. The lobby is open to visitors.

VISITORS' CHECKLIST

Road map C6. ⚄ 121,500. ☒
Stationsplein. 🚌 Stationsplein. ℹ
Kleine Staat 1 (043-3252121). ⛴
Wed, Fri, Sat. 🎌 Apr: Amstel Gold
Race (cycling classic); May: Vrijthof
Fair; St Servaas procession; end of
Aug: Preuvenemint culinary festival.

St Servaasbrug
This bridge is a solid yet elegant structure of seven semicircular arches dating from 1280. Ships can reach the Wyck side through a modern section.

GROTE STAAT

KLEINE STAAT

M BRUGSTRAAT

M SMEDEN STRAAT

MAASBOULEVARD

WOLFSTRAAT

...TIELSTRAAT

MINCKELERSTRAAT

PLANKSTRAAT

STOKSTRAAT

100

100

★ Onze-Lieve-Vrouwebasiliek
In one of the chapels of this Romanesque cruciform basilica is the votive statue of Our Lady "Sterre der Zee".

The Wall Lizard
This animal can be seen in parts of Maastricht, the only Dutch town it occurs in.

Bonnefantenmuseum

Bounds of Sense

THE BONNEFANTENMUSEUM (also known as the Limburg Provincial Museum) is situated on the right bank of the Maas in a distinctive new building designed by the Italian architect Aldo Rossi. The museum's exhibits range from early art (sculpture and painting from the period 1300–1650) to a celebrated international collection of modern art.

★ Cupola by Aldo Rossi
The tower houses a restaurant and an exhibition hall.

La Natura è l'Arte del Numero
This installation designed by Mario Merz consists of tables covered with glass, branches, stones, vegetables and numbers fashioned out of fluorescent tubes.

Domed hall

Terrace

Madonna with St John the Baptist
Here, German painter Lucas Cranach the Younger (1515–86) shows Mary holding the infant Jesus, while John the Baptist looks on in veneration.

★ Wood Carvings
The fine collection of medieval wood carvings includes St Anna-te-Drieën, a walnut sculpture by Jan van Steffeswert (1470–1525).

STAR FEATURES

★ **Staircase**

★ **Cupola by Aldo Rossi**

★ **Wood Carvings**

Plattegronden
by René Daniels (b. 1950) is a simplified re-creation of a museum hall. Daniels painted yellow rectangles over the red flat paintings, which are out of sync with the perspective of the hall, thus creating a disorienting effect.

The Census at Bethlehem

This scene was painted by Pieter Brueghel the Younger (1565–38). The painting is a copy of one by his father, Brueghel the Elder.

Christ Blessing the Children

by Ambrosius Francken II (c.1590–1632).

Print room

Models

Staircase
The monumental staircase runs through the middle of the museum and leads into the different wings and floors of the museum.

Entrance

Inner tower

MUSEUM GUIDE

The Bonnefantenmuseum was designed by Aldo Rossi. It has a permanent collection of early and contemporary art; in addition, a range of temporary exhibitions are organized. The highlight of the museum is its magnificent collection of medieval wood carvings.

St Stephen
Giovanni del Biondo (1356–99) painted this work, thought to be part of a triptych, as the panel has signs of being cut with a saw.

Exploring Maastricht

MAASTRICHT IS CONSIDERED to be one of the oldest towns in Holland. It was the country's first bishopric and an impressive fortress. It has some outstanding historical monuments, including the Romanesque Onze-Lieve-Vrouwebasiliek (Basilica of Our Lady); the Romanesque St Servaas Basilica, with a very old crypt and a carved Gothic portal (early 13th century); six Gothic churches; a Baroque church formerly belonging to the Augustine order (1661); and a Walloon church from 1733. A great deal remains of the fortifications, including Roman foundations, part of the medieval wall system, a 17th-century bastion, and 18th- and 19th-century fortification works.

Maastreechter Gees

The medieval Helpoort gate, the oldest city gate in the country

🏛 Natuurhistorisch Museum

De Bosquetplein 7. ☎ 043-3505490. ⏰ 10am–5pm Mon–Fri, 2–5pm Sat & Sun. ⬤ public hols. 📷

This attractive natural history museum showcases the natural history of the south of Limburg through the ages. Highlights of the museum include the remains of the enormous mosasaur and giant tortoises found in the limestone strata of St Pietersberg.

⚏ Roman Foundations of the Tower

OL Vrouweplein. ☎ 043-3251851. ⏰ Easter Day–autumn hols: 11am–5pm Mon–Sat, 1–5pm Sun.

In the courtyard of the Onze-Lieve-Vrouwebasiliek you can see the foundations of a Roman tower which was once part of the Roman *castellum*. The *castellum* stood on the banks of the river Maas, just south of the St Servaasbrug

bridge, where the Romans settled in 50 BC and where the district of Stokstraat, with its medieval and Golden Age buildings, now lies. The pavement of Op de Thermen, a small and peaceful square in this district where the original Roman fort once was, has been marked with the outlines of the old Roman baths. The first medieval wall around Maastricht dates from around 1229. Of these, the Onze-Lieve-Vrouwewal – which has cannons standing in front of it – and the Jekertoren tower can still be seen.

⚏ Helpoort

St Bernardusstraat 1. ☎ 043-3257833. ⏰ Easter Day–autumn hols, 2–5pm daily. 📷 voluntary donation.

Mosasaurus hofmanni in the natural history museum, known locally as the terrible Maas lizard

The Helpoort gate, dating from the early 13th century, also forms part of the early medieval town fortifications. It stood at the southern end of the town and is the oldest surviving town gate in Holland, and the only one still standing in Maastricht.

Other structures from this period can be seen across the river Maas in Wyck: the Waterpoortje gate, the Stenen Wal (wall) along the river, and the Maaspunttoren. The second medieval fortifications, made necessary by the rapid growth of the city, were built around 1350. Of these, the Pater Vinktoren near the Helpoort gate, and the romantic embankment wall and the semicircular towers known as De Vijf Koppen and Haet ende Nijt continue to survive to this day.

The impressive Pater Vink tower

🏛 Museum Spaans Gouvernement

Vrijthof 18. 📞 043-3217878.
🕐 1–5pm Tue–Sun. ● public hols. 📷
This museum, housed in a 16th-century chapterhouse, features period rooms from the 17th and 18th centuries, and Dutch paintings from that era.

🏛 Centre Céramique

Avenue Céramique 50. 📞 043-350 5600. 🕐 call ahead. ● public hols. 📷 🌐 www.centreceramique.nl
This information centre has a library, archive, cafés and the European Journalism Centre.

⋂ Grotten St-Pietersberg

Luikerweg. 📷 phone for details (043-3217878). 📷
The famous St Peter's caves were created when limestone was quarried through the centuries. Eventually a maze of over 20,000 passageways came into being. Some of the inscriptions on the walls are very old indeed, and some of the miners reveal considerable artistic skills.

The Gothic Bergportaal (15th century) of the St Servaasbasiliek

🏛 St-Servaasbasiliek

Keizer Karelplein. **Treasury**
📞 043-3210490. 🕐 10am–5pm daily (Jul & Aug: 10am–6pm, Nov–Apr: 12:30–5pm on Sun).
● 1 Jan, Carnival, 25 Dec.
Construction on St Servatius Basilica began around the year 1000 on the spot where the saint was buried (upon which stood an earlier church). The nave, the crypt, the transept and the chancel are the oldest parts of the basilica, dating back to the 11th century. The apse and the two chancel towers were built in the following century. The western end also dates from the 12th century. The southern Bergportaal gate dates from the early 13th century, and is one of the earliest Gothic buildings in the Maasland

region. This portal is dedicated to St Mary, with representations of her life, death and Assumption in the arch. The side chapels and the Gothic transept date from approximately 1475.

Highlights of the basilica's treasury are the 12th-century reliquary containing the relics of St Servatius and St Martin of Tongeren, and the golden bust of St Servatius. The latter was donated to the town by the Duke of Parma when Maastricht was taken over by the Spaniards in 1579.

During the 19th century, thorough restoration works were undertaken by Pierre Cuypers. He restored the western end to its original Romanesque splendour, as well as commissioning new

Crypt in the eastern part of the Onze-Lieve-Vrouwebasiliek

murals and ceiling paintings. These were repainted during a subsequent restoration which was completed in 1990.

🏛 Onze-Lieve-Vrouwebasiliek

O-L-Vrouweplein. **Treasury** 📞 043-3251851. 🕐 Easter Day–autumn hols: 11am–5pm Mon–Sat, 1–5pm Sun. **Church** ● during services.
Construction of Onze-Lieve-Vrouwebasiliek began around 1000. The oldest part of the basilica is the imposing west façade. Once this was completed, work began on the nave and transept. The chancel followed in the 12th century, built over an 11th-century crypt. The apse pillars, made from limestone, are crowned with lavishly sculpted capitals, such as the renowned Heimokapiteel.

THE RELIQUARY OF ST SERVATIUS

The magnificent restored reliquary is a monumental shrine containing the relics of St Servatius and St Martin of Tongeren. It is made of wood covered with embossed gilded copper plate in the shape of a house. It dates from about 1160 and was built by artists from the Maasland region. The front of the reliquary depicts Christ, with the 12 apostles along the sides, and St Servatius surrounded by angels on the back. The "roof" of the "house" is decorated with scenes from the Last Judgement.

The 12th-century reliquary

The impressive medieval Kasteel Hoensbroek

Thorn ❾

Road map D5. 🏠 *2,600.* 🚌 *73.*
ℹ️ *Wijngaard 14 (0475-562761).*

Southeast of Weert on the A2 is the little town of Thorn, which with its picturesque narrow streets and houses, historical farm buildings and monumental **Abbey Church** looks like an open-air museum. For some 800 years, until 1794, Thorn was the capital of an autonomous secular foundation headed by an abbess. The Wijngaard, the village square, is surrounded by whitewashed houses where the noble ladies of the foundation once lived. The 14th-century abbey church with its 18th-century interior

A whitewashed house of Thorn

was thoroughly restored at the end of the 19th century by renowned architect Pierre Cuypers, who also added a splendid Gothic tower. Clara Elisabeth van Manderscheidt-Blankenheim, a canoness of the foundation, founded the **Kapel van O-L- Vrouwe onder de Linden** (Chapel of Our Lady under the Linden) north of the town in 1673.

Sittard ❿

Road map D6. 🏠 *46,500.* 🚍 🚌
31, 33, 61, 63. ℹ️ *Rosmolenstraat 2 (0900-9798).* 🛒 *Thu & Sat.*

In the 13th century, Sittard was granted its town charter and built its defensive walls, of which considerable sections remain intact, including **Fort Sanderbout**. The Grote Kerk, or St Petruskerk, built around 1300, is worth a visit. The 80-m (262-ft) tower is built of layers of alternating brick and limestone blocks, or "speklagen" (bacon layers). In the Markt is the 17th-century Baroque **St Michielskerk**; Our Lady of the Sacred Heart basilica stands in the Oude Markt. The oldest house in Sittard is the half-timber house built in 1530 on the corner of the Markt and the Gats and containing the De Gats coffee house. The Jacob Kritszraedthuis, a patrician house, was built in 1620 in Maasland Renaissance style.

Hoensbroek ⓫

Road map D6. 🏠 *25,500.* 🚍 🚌
33, 36, 39. ℹ️ *Bongerd 22, Heerlen (0900-9798).* 🛒 *Fri morning.*

Before the state-run Emma mine was opened here in 1908, Hoensbroek was a sleepy farming town. It subsequently grew into the centre of the Dutch coal mining industry. Its industrial importance waned with the closing of the mines.
   Kasteel Hoensbroek was built in the Middle Ages. All that remains of the original castle is the round corner-tower. The wings and towers around the rectangular inner courtyard date from the 17th and 18th centuries. The castle is moated and today functions as a cultural centre.

***Thermae* at the Thermenmuseum**

Heerlen ⓬

Road map D6. 🏠 *95,000.* 🚍 🚌
25, 26, 31, 36, 52, 57. ℹ️ *Bongerd 22 (0900-9798).* 🛒 *Tue, Thu & Fri.*

The roman town of Coriovallum has been discovered beneath Heerlen. **Thermenmuseum** contains the foundations of the ancient *thermae* and many everyday items from Roman times. Romanesque **St Pancratiuskerk** dates back to the 12th century. In the 20th century, until 1974, Heerlen was the centre of coal mining in Limburg. FPJ Peutz, an architect who remained in obscurity for some time, built the town hall and Schunck department store (known as the *Glaspaleis,* or crystal palace) in the 1930s.

🏛 **Thermenmuseum**
Coriovallumstraat 9. 📞 045-5605100.
🕙 *10am–5pm daily.* 🔴 *1 Jan, Carnival, 24 & 25 Dec.* 🎫

Valkenburg ⑬

Road map D6. 🏛 *5,500.* 🚗 🚌
36, 63, 47. 🛈 *Th. Dorrenplein 5
(0900-9798).* 🛒 *Mon morning.*

THE OLD FORTIFIED town of
Valkenburg, situated in an
area dotted with castles, is popular with visitors. In addition to
sights such as the old gates of
Berkelpoort and Grendelpoort,
a 13th-century Romanesque
church and the ruins of a 12th-
century castle, there are many
new attractions, such as a
casino, catacombs, the Flu-
weelen cave, **Gemeentegrot**
(a Roman quarry), a cable car,
the Prehistorische Monstergrot
and the **Steenkolenmijn**
(coal mine).

⋔ Gemeentegrot
Cauberg 4. 📞 *043-6012271.* ⬜ *Palm
Sun–31 Oct: 9am–5pm Mon–Sat,
10am–5pm Sun; 31 Oct–Palm Sun:
10am–4pm Sat & Sun.* ⬛ *1 Jan,
carnival, 25 Dec.* 🎫 🚫 📷 🏛

Gulpen ⑭

Road map D6. 🏛 *7,500.* 🚌 *54, 56,
57.* 🛈 *Dorpsstraat 27 (0900-9798).*
🛒 *Thu morning.*

GULPEN LIES ON the confluence of the Geul and Gulp
streams. The town's surrounding countryside, with its half-
timbered houses, water mills
and orchards, is probably the
prettiest in Limburg. Hiking

The picturesque sloping streets of the Maasland village of Elsloo

routes are marked. The 17th-
century Kastell Neubourg, built
on the site of a Roman temple
from 2,000 years ago, is now a
hotel and restaurant. Beside the
castle is the Neubourgermolen
mill with a fish ladder for trout.
The Gulpen brewery is worth a
visit. The common kingfisher,
a rare bird, can be seen here.

Elsloo ⑮

Road map D6. 🏛 *8,650.* 🚗 🚌 *31.* 🛈
Rosmolenstraat 2, Sittard (0900-9798).

ARTEFACTS BELONGING to the
banded pottery culture
found at Elsloo are on display
in the Maasland Renaissance-
style local history museum,
De Schippersbeurs. In the
Waterstaatskerk, dating from

1848, is the 16th-century **St-
Anna-te-Drieën** by the Master
of Elsloo. Remnants of Elsloo's
earliest castle can be seen in
the middle of the river at
low water. Of the
later Kasteel
Elsloo, only one
tower survives.

Eijsden ⑯

Road map C6. 🏛 *4,800.*
🚗 🚌 *58, 59.* 🛈 *Julianastraat
15, Epen (0900-9798).*
🛒 *Thu afternoon.* **Kingfisher**

EIJSDEN, the southernmost
municipality in the Netherlands, is a protected rural area.
There is a pleasant walk to be
had along the Maas quay. Kasteel Eijsden was built in 1636
in the Maasland Renaissance
style on the foundations of an
earlier stronghold. The castle
is not open to the public, but
the park makes for a nice stroll.

Vaals ⑰

Road map D6. 🏛 *5,500.* 🛈
Maastrichterlaan 73 a (0900-9798).
🛒 *Tue morning.*

VAALS' WOODED countryside
is known for the Drielan-
denpunt, from which three
countries are visible. At 322 ▮
(1,058 ft), it is also the high▮
point in Holland. Worth visi▮
are Kasteel Vaalsbroek an▮
the Von Clermonthuis; b▮
date from the 18th cent▮
De Kopermolen, once ▮
church, is now a mus▮

Limburg's picturesque countryside, with the meandering Jeker river

Heuvelland ⑱

IN THE ZUID LIMBURG REGION of Heuvelland, the hills, and the valleys cut through them by the river, are covered with fertile loess soil, which occurs nowhere else in Holland. In the peaceful rolling countryside, with its stunning views, is a region of wooded banks, orchards and fields, dotted with picturesque villages and castles, and criss-crossed by narrow roads passing through cuttings with roadside shrines and field chapels. Heuvelland just may be one of the prettiest parts of Holland.

The orchid garden ③ *in the traffic-free Gerendal, a dry valley between Schin op Geul and Scheulder, is the pride of the region. The garden was laid out by the national forestry commission and is situated behind the forester's lodge. Twenty varieties of wild orchid grow here.*

The Basilica of the Holy Sacrament ② *in Meerssen, built in the late 14th century of limestone in Maasland Gothic style, is one of the most elegant churches in all of Holland. The chancel features a lavishly decorated tabernacle.*

Kasteel Eijsden ⑧ *was built in the Maasland Renaissance style in 1636. This style is easily distinguished by its combined use of brick and stone masonry, with stone being used to frame doors and windows.*

BUNDE

MEERS

ROTHEM

MAASTRICHT

CADIE KEER

SINT-GEERTRUID

EIJSDEN

TIPS FOR DRIVERS

Length: 80 km (50 miles). Part of the route passes through hilly areas with narrow roads.
Stopping-off points: especially good viewing points are to be found at Noorbeek, Slenaken and Epen.

GRAPE-GROWING IN ZUID LIMBURG ①

In the past, grape-growing and wine-making was more widely practised in Zuid Limburg than it is today. For example, in the 18th century, there were at least 200 ha (495 acres) of vineyards on and around St-Pietersberg. Today, a few small professional vineyards can still be found in the region, the most famous being the Apostelhoeve. On this vine-growing estate situated to the south of Maastricht on the Louwberg above the de Jeker valley, white wine is made from Müller-Thürgau, Riesling, Auxerrois and Pinot Gris grapes.

Grapes from Limburg

The American War Cemetery ④ at Margraten contains the graves of 8,300 American soldiers who died in World War II, marked by plain white crosses.

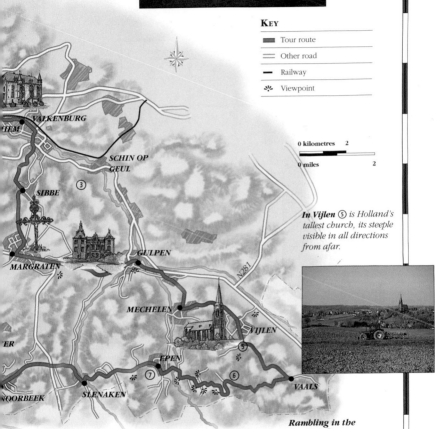

KEY

━━ Tour route

══ Other road

━ Railway

⚜ Viewpoint

VALKENBURG

SCHIN OP GEUL

SIBBE

③

MARGRATEN

GULPEN

MECHELEN

VIJLEN

⑤

EPEN

⑦

⑥

VAALS

SLENAKEN

NOORBEEK

0 kilometres   2

0 miles   2

N281

In Vijlen ⑤ is Holland's tallest church, its steeple visible in all directions from afar.

Large stretches of forest ⑥ are rare in Zuid Limburg, which is otherwise very densely wooded. Exceptions are the Boswachterij Vaals with the Vijlenerbos forest, and the forests by the Brunsummerheide (Brunsummer heath). The wooded slopes of Zuid Limburg with their many springs are well known.

Rambling in the Geuldal ⑦

At Epen, turn off towards Plaat and take the road to the fulling mill in Geul. Carry on after the bridge. A path on the opposite side follows the river upstream into Belgium. Along the Geul are poplars with mistletoe growing in the branches, which can be seen particularly well in winter. The path leads past the Heimansgroeve, a quarry for rock from the Carboniferous perio

TRAVELLERS' NEEDS

WHERE TO STAY

HOLLAND OFFERS a variety of accommodation to suit every traveller's taste and needs, ranging from cheap budget accommodation to expensive luxury. You can stay in one of the luxury hotels of international chains, although there is also good accommodation to be had in old castles, farms, historical buildings and houses that have been converted into hotels, *pensions,* youth hostels or B&Bs. Campers, too, will be spoiled for choice in Holland, with numerous campsites and

Hotel porter

caravan parks, which are often situated in stunning locations. Camping is an especially economical way to stay in a particular area over a longer period of time. If you need more spacious or convenient accommodation over a longer period, you can book into one of the 350-odd bungalow parks in the country, or rent an apartment in one of the many coastal towns. The hotels in the review section *(see pp390–403)* vary in both class and price, and are considered either the best or the most pleasant hotels in that particular area or town.

HOTEL TYPES

THERE IS A HUGE difference in the price, quality and facilities offered by different hotels. The choice is greatest in Amsterdam and the larger cities, where there is something to suit every traveller's pocket. But even further afield there is also plenty of choice. After hotels, bed-and-breakfast (B&B) accommodation is becoming increasingly plentiful in Holland. This type of accommodation varies greatly, as these lodgings are provided by individuals rather than by chains. One night you might be staying in an ordinary family home, and the next you might be staying in an old historical building. **Bed & Breakfast Holland** can help with reservations at specific B&Bs. Traditional *pensions* are now fewer in Holland than they were some decades ago. The main difference between a *pension* and a bed-and-breakfast is that in a *pension* everybody eats the same meal and guests tend to stay slightly longer. You will find *pensions* mainly in the south of the country. You can also stay in a farmhouse. Farmhouses offering accommodation are usually members of **Hoeve-Logies Nederland**, and they often provide stabling for horses, or you can help with the farm work. For slightly more upmarket farm accommodation, you can visit the **Hotel de Boerenkamer** in North

The hotel Groot Warnsborn in Arnhem, a country manor until 1950

Holland. The least expensive form of overnight accommodation is the youth hostel *(jeugdherberg).* **Stayokay** runs no fewer than 30 youth hostels throughout the country. They are no longer exclusively reserved for young people. Accommodation is usually in dormitories of four to six people, and you have to bring your own bed linen, or you can rent it for the night.

HOTEL CHAINS

JUST ABOUT ALL major hotel chains are represented in Holland. You will find most of them, such as the **Hilton**, **Mercure**, **Golden Tulip**, Marriott, Best Western, **Holiday Inn** and Ramada in the big cities, although some like the **Bilderberg** are situated in country areas. The hotels range from good to luxury, both for tourists

Châteauhotel Havesathe De Havixhorst in De Wijk

◁ **The restaurant d'Vijff Vlieghen in Amsterdam dating back to 1627**

The hotel Het Schimmelpenninck Huys in Groningen

and for business travellers.

The scale of these hotels and the often internationally recognized style means that they are less personal than small hotels, but when you spend the night in one of them you get what you pay for and are assured of excellent service and a high level of comfort.

CATEGORIES

HOTELS ARE CLASSED by a variety of systems. Some hotels, for instance, are recognized by the ANWB. ANWB sets store by the management of the hotel and the quality of the facilities. Regular checks are carried out on these hotels. You can recognize them by the blue ANWB sign, and they are listed in a guide which is available from the ANWB office and bookshops. After ANWB-recommended hotels, there are those listed by Holland Hotels Hartverwarmend which are characterized by the personal atmosphere they offer. Lists of these hotels are available for a small charge from places such as the VVV offices. All hotels in Holland have to be categorized under the Benelux Hotel Classification system, which awards each hotel with between one and five stars. The number of stars given depends on the minimum facilities on offer.

The more stars a hotel has, the more luxurious it is. A one-star hotel is simple and may or may not offer breakfast. In two-star hotels, at least 25 per cent of the rooms will have their own bathroom or shower and WC. These hotels will also have a guest lounge, and it will have a lift if it is more than three storeys high. A three-star hotel is considered middle of the range. Their rooms have central heating and at least half have their own bathrooms. Four-star hotels will have a night bar, 80 per cent of the rooms will have en-suite bathrooms, and all of them will have telephones. A five-star hotel will be of deluxe category, having 24-hour service, large rooms with ensuite facilities, a restaurant and so on. One slight drawback of this classification, which looks mainly at the facilities provided and ignores both the hotel's location and atmosphere,

erkend
hotel
ANWB

is that many simple but pleasant little hotels do not score well.

The hotel's star rating is displayed on a blue and white sign by its main entrance.

APARTMENTS

THE NUMBER of self-catering apartments in the cities is limited, and you will usually have to pay a considerable deposit. VVV will inform you of organizations which rent out apartments, or you can look in the Visitors' Guide section of the Yellow Pages *(Gouden Gids)*. If you hire an apartment through an agency, you will generally be required to stay for at least one week. It is also possible to hire apartments through some hotels, for example, the Renaissance Amsterdam Hotel.

Along the Dutch coast, in Zeeland and on the West Frisian Islands, there are many "apartment-hotels", which are apartment buildings with hotel facilities, such as bars, swimming pools and reception areas.

PRICES

ROOM PRICES generally include the *toeristenbelasting* (tourist tax) as well as breakfast. In the larger and more expensive hotels, breakfast is usually charged separately. Obviously, a hotel which provides more than the average facilities will be pricier than a basic hotel. Hotels in larger cities, particularly in Amsterdam, are relatively more pricey than those further afield, although in large towns it is easier to find hotels in wider-ranging price categories.

People travelling alone usually end up paying only 20 per cent less than the same accommodation would cost two people sharing. People travelling in larger groups can stay more cheaply by sharing a *meerpersoonskamer* (multiple room).

The hotel Oortjeshekken, situated in Ooij

The bar of the Hotel Van der Werff on Schiermonnikoog

BOOKING ACCOMMODATION

THE SPRINGTIME, when the tulips are in bloom, is the busiest time for tourists in Holland. If you wish to book a hotel room at this time, you should do so several weeks in advance, particularly when booking in the major cities and along the coastline. For popular hotels along Amsterdam's canals, book well in advance all year round.

Bookings can be made by telephoning the hotel directly. It is a good idea to ask for written confirmation of your booking in order to avoid problems upon your arrival.

You can also select and book hotels online over the internet. There is a wide range of hotel booking websites both in Dutch and in English. As well as general websites featuring a variety of hotels, many hotels and hotel chains also have their own websites where you can find information about them and online booking forms. Some useful websites are www.hotels-holland.com, www.hotelnet.nl, www.bookings.nl, **www.anwb.nl** (hotels listed by ANWB) and ase.net (a search engine which allows you to search for hotels all over the world). The best way of searching for individual hotels or major hotel chains is by name. Stayokay hostels can be found through www.stayokay.com. Another way of booking hotel rooms anywhere in Holland is through the **Amsterdam Tourist Board Offices (VVV)**, which also arranges bed and breakfast in private homes, for which it charges a small commission. You will have to pay the VVV for the first night's accommodation, the hotel for the remaining nights. The **Netherlands Reservations Centre** will help you book just about any form of accommodation by phone or via the internet, at **www.hotelres.nl**. At Schiphol airport KLM runs a counter where travellers can book hotels; of course, most agents can also help you to book hotel accommodation.

PAYMENT

MAJOR CREDIT CARDS are accepted at most hotels. When you give your credit card number when booking a hotel, payment is often required in advance. Smaller hotels, *pensions*, B&Bs and youth hostels do not generally accept credit cards, and usually require cash payment.

DISCOUNTS

DISCOUNTS ARE OFTEN available with many hotels for accommodation booked well in advance. This applies particularly to the major US hotel chains. Many hotels which cater to business travellers during the week often offer reductions at the weekends in order to attract more customers. Conversely, hotels which are usually full with tourists at the weekends may offer reductions on weekdays.

Children under the age of 12 can usually stay free of charge if they share their parents' room (sometimes this means sharing a bed with their parents) or can in any case stay at a greatly reduced rate. Parents who are members of the Stayokay usually get a free membership card for children under the age of 15.

PACKAGES

IN ADDITION TO overnight accommodation, many of the hotels in Holland, including the major chains, offer special packages of one or two nights, with breakfast and dinner included. These packages are often based on a particular theme; for example, a cycling or rambling package may include cycle hire, or a beauty package may include treatment by beauty experts. More detailed information is available from the hotels themselves or from the VVV.

Amstel Hotel (right) in Amsterdam, with its picturesque riverside location

TRAVELLERS WITH DISABILITIES

THE HOTEL LISTINGS in this book state whether a hotel has wheelchair access, has other facilities for disabled travellers and whether it has a lift. This information is based on the information provided by the hotels themselves. Some hotels which have wheelchair access but no lifts will have some bedrooms on the ground floor. It is best to check when making your reservation.

Some hotels post the international disabled access symbol (a pictogram of a person in a wheelchair), which is recognized by the provincial disabled department. These hotels provide independent disabled access.

NIZW/Infolijn Ziekten en Handicaps provides information on accommodation with access for travellers with disabilities. **AccessWise** provides information on holiday opportunities. The ANWB has many publications available specifically for disabled travellers, and the VVV's hotels folder also shows which hotels have access and facilities for people with disabilities.

Holland's smallest hotel, De Kromme Raake in Eenrum, featuring an authentic "bedstede" or traditional in-built bed

GAY HOTELS

MOST GAY-ORIENTED hotels are in Amsterdam; indeed, a gay couple is unlikely to produce a raised eyebrow in this tolerant city. One advantage of gay-oriented hotels, which include the **Black Tulip** and **The Golden Bear**, is that they provide a great deal of information on gay hangouts and events. Then there are hotels which are not specifically gay-oriented but make special provision for gay clients, or are gay-friendly. One of these is the **Quentin**, which is popular with women,

and the Waterfront (see p391) which attracts mainly male guests. The Pulitzer and the Grand, among others, have been classed as "gay-friendly" by the International Gay and Lesbian Travel Association. This organization can provide information on gay-friendly accommodation over the internet (www.iglta.com). The **Gay & Lesbian Switchboard** (also accessible over the internet) provides further information about hotels.

English-language publications offering comprehensive listings are available and can be found in some bookshops,

---

DIRECTORY

TYPES OF HOTEL

Bed & Breakfast Holland
Theophile de Bockstraat 3
1058 TV Amsterdam.
[020-6157527.
[w] www.bbholland.com

Hoeve-Logies Nederland
Guide with addresses can be ordered on the internet:
[w] www.dutch-farm holidays.com

Hotel de Boerenkamer
[0299-655726. (9am–5pm daily). [w] www.hotel-boerenkamer.nl

Stayokay
[010-264064.
[w] www.stayokay.com

HOTEL CHAINS

Bilderberg
[0317-318319.
[w] www.bilderberg.nl

Golden Tulip
[020-5174717.
[w] www.goldentulip.nl

Hilton
[0800-0223346.
[w] www.hilton.nl

Holiday Inn
[0800-0221155.
[w] http://beneluxsix continentshotels.com

Mercure
[020-6545727.
[w] www.mercure.nl

RESERVATIONS

Amsterdam Tourist Board (VVV) Offices
See p435.
[w] www.vvv.nl

Netherlands Reservations Centre
Nieuwe Gouw 1, 1442 LE
Purmerend. [0299-689 144. [w] www.hotelres.nl

[w] **www.anwb.nl/ hotels/index.jsp**

TRAVELLERS WITH DISABILITIES

AccessWise
Postbus 532
6800 AM Arnhem.
[026-3706161.
[w] www.accesswise.org

NIZW/Infolijn Ziekten en Handicaps
[030-2306603
(9am–5pm Mon–Fri).

GAY HOTELS AND INFORMATION

Black Tulip
Geldersekade 16
1012 BH Amsterdam.
[020-4270933.
[fax] 020-6244281.

The Golden Bear
Kerkstraat 37
1017 GB Amsterdam.
[020-6244785.
[fax] 020-6270164.

Quentin
Leidsekade 89
1017 PN Amsterdam.
[020-6262187.
[fax] 020-6220121.

Gay & Lesbian Switchboard
[020-6236565
(2pm–10pm daily).
[w] www.switchboard.nl

Bungalow Parks

HOLLAND HAS AT LEAST 350 "bungalow parks", which is not surprising considering that they provide an excellent way of enjoying the country in all types of weather. These parks are holiday villages with dozens to hundreds of bungalows or cabins, many designed for four to eight persons, together with numerous facilities such as supermarkets and restaurants. They also provide many recreation facilities, some open-air and others indoors for days when the weather is not at its best. Rental is usually by the week. The parks are often situated in areas of natural beauty and offer plenty to do in the surrounding area. A selection of the best parks in the country is given here.

KEY AND BOOKING NUMBERS

⬤	Euroase-parken (033-4600800)
◯	Zilverberk (0900-8810)
⬤	CenterParcs (0800-0300)
⬤	Landal GreenParks (0900-8842)
⬤	Overheemparken (0572-3392798)
⬤	RCN-recreatiecentra (0343-513547)
⬤	Hogenboom Vakantieparken (0297-381650)
◯	Other parks

TERSCHE
WEST FRIS
ISLANDS
VLIELAND
SLUFTERVALLEI
KRIM
PARC TEXEL TEXEL
CALIFORNIE CREATIEF BEA
PARK TEXEL

NORTH
HOLL

AMSTERDA
ZANDVOORT
Haarlem

SOLASSI

'T EEKHOORN
UTREC
Utre

Den Haag
KIJKDUINPARK

SOUTH
HOLLAND
Rotterdam

TOPPERSHOEDJE
PORT ZÉLANDE
DUINOORD PARK PORT GREVE
PARC
BURGH-HAAMSTEDE
DE SCHOTSMAN

EFTELING
DROOMRIJK
NOO

DE RO

Middelburg

HOF VAN ZEELAND DE FLAASBLOEM
BRAE
BOERDERI
ZWAF

ZEEBAD
PANNENSCHUUR ZEELAND
HET VENNENI

B
E
L
G
I

Port Zélande
The CenterParcs Park in a south-of-France style at Lake Grevelingenmeer features numerous recreation facilities and comfortable bungalows.

Fun for the Children
All recreation parks pay special attention to giving children plenty to do. Illustrated here is RCN's De Flaasbloem Park in Chaam.

0 kilometres 20

0 miles 20

SCHIERMONNIKOOG

PARK
LIEKE **AMELAND**
BOOMHIEMKE
CREATIEF NATUURDORP
SUYDEROOGH

GRONINGEN
Groningen

Leeuwarden
IT WIID

FRIESLAND

E POTTEN

WITTERZOMER
PARC STADSKANAAL
DE ROGGEBERG
Assen
PARC BORGER
BOSMEER
AELDERHOLT
DE NOORDSTER
DRENTHE HET ZUIDERVELD
VAKANTIEPARK
DE WILTZANGH
DE HUTTENHEUGTE

HET STOETENSLAGH

Lelystad
OVERIJSSEL
Zwolle
CREATIEF VILLAPARK
DE VLEGGE
VOLAND
GERNER
HOOGWOLDE
HOGE HEXEL
DE JAGERSTEE
B.C. HELLENDOORN
PARC EPE
ZILVERBERK HELLENDOORN
EMHOF
SALLANDSHOEVE
LANDGOED
ZEEWOLDE 'T LOO
VAKANTIEPARK
AS
DE PRINS
RABBIT HILL
TWENHAARSVELD
ELDORADO
RUIGHENRODE
GGELENBERG
PARC
BEEKBERGEN
HEIDEHEUVEL
'T STIEN 'N BOER
ROTE BOS
COLDENHOVE
GELDERLAND
Arnhem
'T ZONNETJE
KELDUIN

SCHUTTERSOORD

rtogenbosch
HET HEIJDERBOS
BANT

ARCEN
LOOHORST
HET MEERDAL
PARC
VLIERDEN
EMPERVENNEN
DE LOMMERBERGEN
WEERTERBERGEN
LIMBURG

HOMMELHEIDE

tricht
SIMPELVELD
DE MECHELERHOF
HOOG VAALS

GERMANY

RCN
*RCN recreation parks offer
bungalows at relatively
inexpensive prices.*

Aqua Mundo
*These spectacular subtropical
paradises which belong to
CenterParcs offer a wonderful
time for all.*

Landal GreenPark Hoog Vaals
*In the rolling landscape of Limburg,
Landal combines beautiful countryside
with a variety of activities.*

Camping

MANY PEOPLE REGARD CAMPING as the ideal way to take a holiday. It's cheap, you are in the open air and generally in beautiful natural locations. Camping can take many different forms: moving from one location to another, or settling on one site for the whole holiday; you can camp in a tent, a caravan, a tent-trailer or a camper van; you can camp in natural surroundings, on a farm or on a campsite. Holland, with its many different types of campsites, has something to offer everyone.

TYPES OF CAMPSITE

CAMPSITES IN HOLLAND fall into two main categories. There are *natuurterreinen*, (nature sites), which are small or medium-sized campsites with basic facilities, often situated in the most spectacular

Camping at one of Holland's many nature sites

countryside that Holland has to offer. The other group consists of larger campsites with a good range of facilities, often near recreation areas or other attractions. Both types of campsite are to be found throughout Holland. On both types of campsite you can either set up your own tent or caravan or you can rent

accommodation. The advantage of renting accommodation, of course, is that you can travel lighter.

NATURE CAMPING

CAMPING off designated campsites is prohibited by law. However, there are plenty of campsites which give you the feeling that you are camping in nature. These campsites are known as *natuur-kampeerterreinen*. They are situated in breathtaking locations with plenty of countryside around for exploring on foot or by bicycle. You can pitch a tent or park your caravan, tent-trailer, camper or motorhome here. There are no fixed pitches. Sanitary arrangements are fairly basic but good. The campsites are usually equipped with children's playgrounds. Using these facilities requires having a Natuurkampeerkaart membership card, which is

De Roos campsite at Beerze, located on the river Vecht

available from the **Stichting Natuurkampeerterreinen**. This organization will also provide you with a booklet containing the addresses of more than 100 campsites.

The campsites of the Vereniging Gastvrije Nederlandse Landgoederen en Kastelen (**LKC**) combine the attraction of natural surroundings with that of cultural history. These sites are privately owned and are situated on private estates, usually by forests or a castle or stately home. The association's 16 sites are distinguished by their peace, atmosphere and wide spaces. Camping on a farm means you will be assured of a tranquil rural atmosphere. LKC campsites are almost invariably near areas of natural beauty which provide abundant opportunities for rambling,

Camping in Zeeland, popular among Dutch and foreign holidaymakers alike

cycling or horse-riding. Farms offer a variety of experiences. For example, you will often be able to help the farmers feed the animals or harvest the crops.

Another excellent way of experiencing the countryside is by using *trekkershutten*, or hikers' huts. These huts are designed for use by walkers on hiking-trips. They offer very basic accommodation for up to four people at a time. They are often situated at campsites whose facilities are available to the hikers. It is necessary to bring your own bedding.

Hanging the laundry to dry among the fragrant blossoming trees

LARGE FAMILY CAMPSITES

L ARGE *gezinscampings* (family campsites) are popular among Dutch holidaymakers taking a break in their own country. The most important aspect of these camping sites is the social life. The management of the sites, be they individually owned or part of a chain of sites, organizes various events, such as barbecue evenings, karaoke, games and competitions and sports events. In this way people quickly get to know their fellow campers.

This form of camping is also ideal for the children, as they can meet others of their age and there is plenty of room for running around and playing. The largest campsites have extensive sanitary facilities and hot water. They also provide electrical hook-ups for caravans, as well as running water and sewage connections. Campsite shops mean that you can do most of your shopping on-site, and if you don't feel like cooking your own food, there is frequently a restaurant or snackbar where you can get something to eat. Launderettes and dry-cleaning services are also often available. Many of these campsites have a swimming pool and other recreation facilities such as tennis courts, mini-golf and so on.

The ANWB has classed the best campsites in Europe as "Eurotopcampings". These offer excellent sanitary facilities and have large pitches. Their other facilities are also top of the range. Thirteen of these campsites are located in Holland. You will find these in the organization's camping guides or on the internet at www.anwb.nl/campings/index.jsp.

Choosing a Hotel

THE FOLLOWING PAGES contain a selection of the finest and most interesting hotels in the Netherlands. Between them they offer a broad range of prices and facilities to suit all needs and pockets. Each hotel is described in brief, with symbols to indicate what facilities are available. The colour-coding at the top edge of the page will help you to find the right province quickly.

AMSTERDAM

Hotel	Credit Cards	Number of Rooms	Restaurant	Free for Under-12s	Swimming Pool/Gym/Sauna
OUDE ZIJDE: *Amstel Botel.* W www.intercontinental.com €€€ Oosterdokskade 2–4. **Map** 2 F4. 020-6264247. FAX 6391952. A stay aboard the only remaining floating hotel in Amsterdam is a unique experience.	AE DC MC V	176			
OUDE ZIJDE: *Doelen Hotel.* W www.dedoelen.com €€€€ Nieuwe Doelenstraat 24. **Map** 2 D5. 020-5540600. FAX 6221084. One of Amsterdam's oldest hotels, located in a historic building, with well-appointed rooms. There is even a private landing-stage for sightseeing trips.	AE DC MC V	85			
OUDE ZIJDE: *The Grand Westin Demeure.* €€€€€ Oudezijds Voorburgwal 197. **Map** 2 D5. 020-5553111. FAX 5553222. This exclusive hotel occupies the former city hall. It has been furnished in the style of an English country house.	AE DC MC V	182	■		■
OUDE ZIJDE: *Radisson SAS Hotel.* W www.radisson.com €€€€€ Rusland 17. **Map** 2 D5. 020-6231231. FAX 5208200. Right in the heart of historic Amsterdam, this hotel boasts very comfortable rooms furnished in a variety of styles.	AE DC MC V	241	■		■
NIEUWE ZIJDE: *Winston Art Hotel.* W www.winston.nl €€ Warmoesstraat 129. **Map** 2 D4. 020-5309530. FAX 5309599. Each room is a work of art, from the Bridal Suite to the Guest Room. Many arts events are held here, which often go on late into the night.	AE DC MC V	67			
NIEUWE ZIJDE: *Avenue.* W www.dutchhotels.nl/avenue.hotel €€€€ Nieuwezijds Voorburgwal 33. **Map** 2 D4. 020-5309530. FAX 5309599. Situated in a former Dutch East India Company warehouse, the Avenue has attractive rooms with exposed beams and wicker furniture.	AE DC MC V	77			
NIEUWE ZIJDE: *Singel.* W www.lempereur-hotels.nl €€€€ Singel 15. **Map** 2 D5. 020-6263108. FAX 6203777. This small hotel covers three 17th-century canalside houses. Though small, the rooms are brightly decorated.	AE DC MC V	32			
NIEUWE ZIJDE: *Crowne Plaza Amsterdam City Centre* €€€€€ Nieuwezijds Voorburgwal 5. **Map** 2 D3. 020-6200500. FAX 6201173. Although most of the rooms are small, they are well appointed. The hotel has its own swimming pool.	AE DC MC V	270	■	●	■
NIEUWE ZIJDE: *Die Port van Cleve.* W www.portvancleve.com €€€€€ Nieuwezijds Voorburgwal 176–180. **Map** 1 C4. 020-6244860. FAX 6220240. This is a convivial hotel with modern rooms behind the royal palace. It is famous for the numbered steaks served in its brasserie.	AE DC MC V	120	■		
NIEUWE ZIJDE: *Hotel de l'Europe.* W www.leurope.nl €€€€€ Nieuwe Doelenstraat 2–8. **Map** 5 A2. 020-5311777. FAX 5311778. This magnificent hotel's location by the Amstel in the heart of the city and at a junction of public transport links means that all of the major sights of Amsterdam are within easy reach.	AE DC MC V	100	■	●	
NIEUWE ZIJDE: *NH Grand Hotel Krasnapolsky* €€€€€ Dam 9. **Map** 2 D5. 020-5548080. W www.nhhotels.nl/gtghkrasnapolsky.htm This famous hotel is known for its renowned guests. It has several outstanding restaurants.	AE DC MC V	468	■	●	
NIEUWE ZIJDE: *NH Hotel Barbizon Palace.* W www.nh-hotels.com €€€€€ Prins Hendrikkade 59–72. **Map** 2 E4. 020-5564564. FAX 6243353. This hotel comprises 19 historic buildings. The rooms are luxurious and well appointed.	AE DC MC V	275	■	●	■

<table>
<tr><td colspan="2">

Price categories are for a standard double room per night, including breakfast.

€ under €45
€€ €45–€70
€€€ €70–€115
€€€€ €115–€180
€€€€€ over €180

</td><td>

CREDIT CARDS
Credit cards accepted: *AE* American Express; *DC* Diners Club; *MC* MasterCard/Access; *V* Visa.
RESTAURANT
Hotel with restaurants serving lunch and dinner. Sometimes reserved for hotel guests only.
FREE FOR UNDER-12s
Children under the age of 12 free if sharing a room with their parents.
SWIMMING POOL/GYM/SAUNA
Hotel has a swimming pool, fitness centre or sauna.

</td></tr>
</table>

	CREDIT CARDS	NUMBER OF ROOMS	RESTAURANT	FREE FOR UNDER-12s	SWIMMING POOL/GYM/SAUNA
NIEUWE ZIJDE: *Renaissance Amsterdam Hotel* €€€€€ Kattengat 1. **Map** 2 D3. 020-6212223. www.renaissancehotels.com/AMSRD Reasonably priced hotel right by the Centraal Station. The hotel can also arrange the rental of nearby apartments.	AE DC MC V	405	■	●	■
NIEUWE ZIJDE: *Victoria Hotel Amsterdam* €€€€€ Damrak 1–5. **Map** 2 D4. 020-6234255. FAX 6274259. This Neo-Classical hotel opposite the Centraal Station is an oasis of peace thanks to its double-glazed windows.	AE DC MC V	305	■	●	■
CANAL RING: *Hans Brinker.* www.hans-brinker.com € Kerkstraat 136–138. **Map** 5 A3. 020-6220687. FAX 6382060. This large, youth-oriented hotel has small bedrooms and its own nightclub. A "media lab" is one of the hotel's most recent additions.	AE DC MC V	120	■	●	
CANAL RING: *Asterisk.* www.asteriskhotel.nl €€ Den Texstraat 16. **Map** 5 A4. 020-6262396. FAX 6382790. Comfortable hotel in a quiet part of the centre. All rooms are now ensuite.	MC V	40			
CANAL RING: *Prinsenhof.* www.hotelprinsenhof.com €€ Prinsengracht 810. **Map** 5 A3. 020-6231772. FAX 6383368. Attractive rooms in a canalside hotel, but reasonably priced nevertheless. Only two rooms have their own bathrooms, and these are more pricey.	AE MC V	11			
CANAL RING: *De Admiraal.* www.deadmiraal.nl €€€ Herengracht 563. **Map** 4 E1. 020-6262150. FAX 6234625. The nearby nightlife means that this hotel is not always peaceful. Most rooms are on the large side.	AE DC MC V	9			
CANAL RING: *Fantasia.* www.fantasia-hotel.com €€€ Nieuwe Keizersgracht 16. **Map** 5 B3. 020-6238259. FAX 6223913. Well-appointed family hotel in a canalside house c.1733. Located in peaceful area near Stopera (opera house) and Artis. ● *16–27 Dec & 5 Jan–28 Feb.*	AE MC V	19			
CANAL RING: *Orlando.* @ www.hotelorlando@zonnet.nl €€€ Prinsengracht 1099. **Map** 5 B3. 020-6386915. FAX 6252123. An attractive little canalside hotel with personal service. Stylishly appointed but with an informal atmosphere.	AE DC MC V	5			
CANAL RING: *Van Onna.* www.netcentrum.nl/onna €€€ Bloemgracht 102–108. **Map** 1 A4. 020-6265801. Simple hotel in three restored canalside houses in the heart of Amsterdam's lively Jordaan district.		41			
CANAL RING: *Canal House.* www.canalhouse.nl €€€€ Keizersgracht 148. **Map** 4 E1. 020-6225182. FAX 6241317. Comfortable rooms in two historic buildings, with a breakfast room overlooking the pleasant garden.	AE DC MC V	26			
CANAL RING: *Mercure Arthur Frommer.* www.mercure.nl €€€€ Noorderstraat 46. **Map** 5 A4. 020-6220328. FAX 6203208. Conveniently situated in a quiet part of the centre, within walking distance of the Rijksmuseum.	AE DC MC V	90			
CANAL RING: *Seven Bridges* €€€€ Reguliersgracht 31. **Map** 5 A3. 020-6231329. A busy hotel with pleasant rooms in a 200-year-old building. Attractively situated between two canals.	AE MC V	8			
CANAL RING: *Ambassade.* www.ambassade-hotel.nl €€€€€ Herengracht 335–353. **Map** 4 F1. 020-6262333. FAX 5550277. Pleasant rooms in ten 17th-century canalside houses. The lounges and breakfast rooms are decorated with antiques.	AE DC MC V	59			

Price categories are for a standard double room per night, including breakfast.

€ under €45
€€ €45–€70
€€€ €70–€115
€€€€ €115–€180
€€€€€ over €180

CREDIT CARDS
Credit cards accepted: *AE* American Express; *DC* Diners Club; *MC* MasterCard/Access; *V* Visa.

RESTAURANT
Hotel with restaurants serving lunch and dinner. Sometimes reserved for hotel guests only.

FREE FOR UNDER-12s
Children under the age of 12 free if sharing a room with their parents.

SWIMMING POOL/GYM/SAUNA
Hotel has a swimming pool, fitness centre or sauna.

	CREDIT CARDS	NUMBER OF ROOMS	RESTAURANT	FREE FOR UNDER-12s	SWIMMING POOL/GYM/SAUNA
CANAL RING: *American Hotel.* W www.bc.com €€€€€ Leidsekade 97. **Map** 4 E2. 020-5563000. FAX 5563222. This Art Deco hotel faces the Leidseplein square. The renowned Café Americain has been a favourite watering hole for years.	AE DC MC V	174	■		■
CANAL RING: *Blakes.* W www.blakes-amsterdam.com €€€€€ Keizersgracht 384. **Map** 4 F2. 020-5302010. FAX 5302030. New luxury hotel with sylish décor, on one of the city's most picturesque canals. Tremendous restaurant.	AE DC MC V	41	■		
CANAL RING: *Dikker & Thijs Fenice Hotel.* W www.dtfh.nl €€€€€ Prinsengracht 444. **Map** 4 E2. 020-6201212. FAX 6258986. Small luxury hotel which has been recently thoroughly refurbished. The quietest rooms are on the canal side.	AE DC MC V	42	■	●	
CANAL RING: *Pulitzer.* W www.pulitzer.nl €€€€€ Prinsengracht 315–331. **Map** 4 E1. 020-5235235. FAX 6276753. Consisting of at least 25 17th- and 18th-century canalside buildings, this hotel has a wonderful garden, where you can eat and drink in summer. Numerous pleasant bars and lounges, and a good art collection.	AE DC MC V	230	■	●	
CANAL RING: *Schiller* €€€€€ Rembrandtplein 26–36. **Map** 5 A2. 020-5540700. FAX 6240098. The public rooms are hung with paintings by Frits Schiller. The rooms at the back are quietest.	AE DC MC V	92	■		
MUSEUM QUARTER: *Stayokay Hostel Amsterdam Vondelpark* € Zandpad 5. **Map** 4 D2. 020-5898996. FAX 5898955. W www.stayokay.nl Situated on the edge of the Vondelpark, by the Leidseplein.	MC V	57	■		
MUSEUM QUARTER: *AMS Atlas Hotel.* W www.ams.nl €€€ Van Eeghenstraat 64. **Map** 4 D3. 020-6766336. FAX 6717633. This picturesque Art Nouveau hotel overlooks the Vondelpark. The dining room offers various Dutch dishes.	AE DC MC V	23	■		
MUSEUM QUARTER: *De Filosoof.* W www.hotelfilosoof.nl €€€ Anna van den Vondelstraat 6. **Map** 3 C3. 020-6833013. FAX 6853750. The rooms in this hotel have been designed on a variety of philosophical themes. It is a favourite meeting place for intellectuals.	AE MC V	38			
MUSEUM QUARTER: *Blaines B&B at the Park* €€€€ Gerard Brandstraat 14. **Map** 3 C3. 06-41305852. W www.blainesamsterdam.com This tasteful B&B doesn't have many rooms, but a stay here is a real pleasure. A garden, internet access and a good breakfast are provided.	AE MC V	3			
MUSEUM QUARTER: *Owl.* W www.owl-hotel.nl €€€€ Roemer Visscherstraat 1. **Map** 4 D2. 020-6189484. FAX 6189441. A hospitable establishment with comfortable rooms. The lovely garden is reached through the dining room.	AE DC MC V	34			
MUSEUM QUARTER: *Amsterdam Marriott Hotel* €€€€€ Stadhouderskade 12. **Map** 4 D2. 020-6075555. FAX 6075511. W www.marriott.com The Marriott provides all the facilities you would expect from a major international hotel chain. A pleasant bar.	AE DC MC V	392	■	●	■
MUSEUM QUARTER: *Jan Luyken Hotel & Résidence.* €€€€€ Jan Luykenstraat 58. **Map** 4 E3. 020-5730730. W www.janluyken.nl Comfortable rooms with a sofa-bed in the family rooms. A sumptuous breakfast is served in the pleasant basement.	AE DC MC V	62			
MUSEUM QUARTER: *Vondel.* W www.hotelvondel.nl €€€€€ Vondelstraat 28–30. **Map** 4 D2. 020-6120170. FAX 6854321. Named after the poet Joost van den Vondel, this hotel is within walking distance of three major museums and the city centre.	AE DC MC V	70			

OUTSIDE THE CENTRE: *Hotel Kitty Muijzers* €€ | 10
Plantage Middenlaan 40. **Map** 6 D3. 020-6226819.
A simple *pension* full of religious and classical imagery. Near Artis zoo.

OUTSIDE THE CENTRE: *Bed & Breakfast Flores & Puck* €€€ | 1
Rietwijkerstraat 51. 020-4080755. **FAX** 4080770. info@amsterdambedandbreakfast.org
This small pavilion, which sleeps two, stands in a large garden and comes
with its own bath and fridge – and bicycles. Breakfast is included.

OUTSIDE THE CENTRE: *Best Western AMS Hotel Beethoven* €€€€ | AE | 55
Beethovenstraat 43–51. **Map** 4 D5. 020-6644816. **FAX** 8502415. www.bestwestern.nl | DC
Located on a smart shopping street, this hotel is within easy reach of the | MC
WTC (train station). The centre is just a short tram ride away. | V

OUTSIDE THE CENTRE: *Bilderberg Garden Hotel.* €€€€ | AE | 124
Dijsselhofplantsoen 7. **Map** 4 D5. 020-5705600/0800-1400. www.gardenhotel.nl | DC
A pleasant hotel with colourful rooms, all with Jacuzzis. The Mangerie | MC
de Kersentuin serves excellent food. | V

OUTSIDE THE CENTRE: *Hotel Arena BV.* www.hotelarena.nl €€€€ | AE | 121
's-Gravezandestraat 51. **Map** 6 D4. 020-6947444. **FAX** 8502415. | DC
This trendy hotel has a theatre hall, featuring on weekends theme discos | MC
aimed at people in their thirties. | V

OUTSIDE THE CENTRE: *Villa Borgmann* €€€€ | AE | 15
Koningslaan 48. **Map** 3 B4. 020-6735252. **FAX** 6762580. | DC
A peacefully situated hotel with some extremely large rooms, | MC
it is within easy reach of the big museums. | V

OUTSIDE THE CENTRE: *Amstel Inter-Continental* €€€€€ | AE | 79
Prof. Tulpplein 1. **Map** 5 B4. 020-6226060. www.interconti.com | DC
One of the best and most luxurious hotels in the city; guests have | MC
included countless international stars. | V

OUTSIDE THE CENTRE: *Amsterdam Hilton.* www.hilton.com €€€€€ | AE | 275
Apollolaan 138. **Map** 3 C5. 020-7106000. **FAX** 7106080. cb_@hilton.com | DC
The Amsterdam Hilton gained world fame when John Lennon and Yoko | MC
Ono held their "bed-in" for world peace here. | V

OUTSIDE THE CENTRE: *Okura Amsterdam.* www.okura.nl €€€€€ | AE | 370
Ferdinand Bolstraat 333. **Map** 4 F5. 020-6787111. **FAX** 6712344. | DC
A quintessential business person's hotel, near the RAI Congress Centre. The | MC
top floor affords a breathtaking view of the city. | V

OUTSIDE THE CENTRE: *Toro* €€€€€ | AE | 22
Koningslaan 64. **Map** 3 B4. 020-6737223. **FAX** 6750031. toro@ams.nl | DC
The mansion occupied by this hotel is in a peaceful and | MC
fashionable district at the edge of the Vondelpark. | V

NORTH HOLLAND

ALKMAAR: *Stad & Land* €€ | MC | 26
Stationsweg 92–94. **Road Map** C3. 072-5123911. **FAX** 5118440. | V
Lively, modern hotel near the centre of Alkmaar;
it is an excellent base for tours of the region.

BERGEN: *Het Witte Huis.* www.hotel-hetwittehuis.nl €€€ | AE | 31
Ruïnelaan 15. **Road Map** C3. 072-5812530. **FAX** 5813957. | DC
Pleasant family hotel at the edge of woodland and within walking distance | MC
of the centre. It has a large sun terrace. | V

BUSSUM: *NH Jan Tabak Hotel* €€€€€ | AE | 87
Amersfoortsestraatweg 27. **Road Map** C4. 035-6959911. **FAX** 6959416. | DC
Centrally located hotel with large, comfortable rooms. Friendly restaurant | MC
with international cuisine. | V

DE RIJP: *Watergemaal* €€ | 2
Oostdijkje 14. **Road Map** C3. & **FAX** 0299-673072.
Have a relaxing, exclusive stay surrounded by works of art in this former
pumping station in the majestic natural area of de Eilandspolder.

ENKHUIZEN: *Die Port van Cleve.* www.dieportvancleve.com €€€ | AE | 26
Dijk 74–78. **Road Map** C3. 0228-312510. **FAX** 318765. | DC
A pleasant hotel by the harbour in the old centre. Centuries ago, it was a | MC
hostelry where foreign merchants spent the night. | V

For key to symbols see back flap

				CREDIT CARDS	NUMBER OF ROOMS	RESTAURANT	FREE FOR UNDER-12S	SWIMMING POOL/GYM/SAUNA

Price categories are for a standard double room per night, including breakfast.

€ under €45
€€ €45–€70
€€€ €70–€115
€€€€ €115–€180
€€€€€ over €180

CREDIT CARDS
Credit cards accepted: *AE* American Express; *DC* Diners Club; *MC* MasterCard/Access; *V* Visa.
RESTAURANT
Hotel with restaurants serving lunch and dinner. Sometimes reserved for hotel guests only.
FREE FOR UNDER-12S
Children under the age of 12 free if sharing a room with their parents.
SWIMMING POOL/GYM/SAUNA
Hotel has a swimming pool, fitness centre or sauna.

	Credit Cards	Number of Rooms	Restaurant	Free for Under-12s	Swimming Pool/Gym/Sauna
HAARLEM: *die Raeckse* €€ Raaks 1–3. **Road Map** C3. (023-5326629. ℻ 5317927. Pretty hotel a five-minute walk from the city centre. All rooms have ensuite bathrooms. Pleasant brasserie. **P 🛏 ♨ 🔒**	AE MC V	23	■		
HEEMSKERK: *Slot Assumburg* € Tolweg 9. **Road Map** C3. (0251-232288. ℻ 251024. Simple B&B occupying an impressive castle. Both the interior and the exterior are steeped in history. **♨ 🔒**	AE DC MC V	31			
HILVERSUM: *Ravel.* W www.ravel.nl €€€ Emmastraat 35. **Road Map** C4. (035-6210685. ℻ 6243777. Authentic Gooi villa in Art Deco style. Within walking distance of the centre and the station. **🛏 ♨**	AE DC MC V	19			
HOORN: *De Keizerskroon.* W www.keizerskroon.nl €€ Breed 31. **Road Map** C3. (0229-212717. ℻ 211022. Cheerful, centrally located hotel with well-appointed rooms. Dinner in the restaurant is accompanied by piano music. **P 🛏 ♨ 🔒 ♿**	AE DC MC V	25	■		
VOLENDAM: *Best Western Hotel Spaander.* W www.bestwestern.nl €€€ Haven 15–19. **Road Map** C3. (0299-363595. ℻ 369615. This hotel on the IJsselmeer has a typical Dutch late 19th-century atmosphere. Rooms vary from standard to deluxe. **P 🛏 ♨ 🔒 🛏 ♿ 🏊**	AE DC MC V	80	■		
WESTZAAN: *De Prins.* W www.hotel-prinshendrik.nl €€ Kerkbuurt 31. **Road Map** C3. (075-6281972. ℻ 6289136. Originally a 16th-century inn, this hotel is situated among windmills and old houses, some ten minutes drive from the Zaanse Schans. The rooms are modern and well appointed. **P 🛏 ♨ 🔒 🏊**	AE DC MC V	14	■		

UTRECHT

	Credit Cards	Number of Rooms	Restaurant	Free for Under-12s	Swimming Pool/Gym/Sauna
AMERSFOORT: *Best Western Berghotel Amersfoort.* W www.berghotel.nl €€€ Utrechtseweg 225. **Road Map** D4. (033-4620444. ℻ 4650505. Tasteful rooms in a hotel which has everything you need to relax. Close to the town centre, with halls for hire. **P 🛏 ♨ 🔒 🏊 ♿ 🏊**	AE DC MC V	90	■		■
BAARN: *Kasteel de Hooge Vuursche* €€€€ Hilversumsestraatweg 14. **Road Map** C4. (035-5412541. ℻ 5423288. A unique hotel where history has been cleverly combined with modern comforts. Facilities include conference space and a large garden. **P 🛏 ♨ 🔒 🏊**	AE DC MC V	25	■		
BUNNIK: *Ridderhofstad Rhijnauwen.* W www.stayokay.nl/bunnik €€ Rhijnauwenselaan 14. **Road Map** C4. (030-6561277. ℻ 6571065. Youth hostel in a stately home on the Amelisweerd Estate, just to the south of Utrecht, and situated on a manor farm which was rebuilt in 1830. **P 🛏 ♨ 🏊 ♿**	AE DC MC V	23	■		
DRIEBERGEN: *De Koperen Ketel* €€€ Welgelegenlaan 26–28. **Road Map** D4. (0343-516174. ℻ 532465. Peacefully situated hotel ideal both for business travellers and for tourists. Some rooms have balconies. **P 🛏 🔒 🏊**	AE DC MC V	15			
LAGE VUURSCHE: *De Kastanjehof.* W www.dekastanjehof.nl €€€ Kloosterlaan 1. **Road Map** D2. (035-6668248. ℻ 6668444. Fine, spacious rooms in a small hotel with an extensive garden. Has an excellent restaurant. **P 🛏 🔒 🏊**	AE DC MC V	10	■		
RHENEN: *'t Paviljoen Hotel.* W www.paviljoen.nl €€€€ Grebbeweg 103–105. **Road Map** D4. (0317-619003. ℻ 617213. Atmospheric hotel on the Grebbelberg hill. Spacious rooms and a lounge with an open fireplace. **🛏 ♨ 🔒 ♿ 🏊**	AE DC MC V	32	■		

UTRECHT: *Parkhotel* €€
Tolsteegsingel 34. **Road Map** C4. 030-2516712. FAX 2540401.
Comfortable hotel offering personal attention to guests.
Situated not far from the town centre.
AE MC V · 8

UTRECHT: *Maliehotel*. www.maliehotel.nl €€€€
Maliestraat 2. **Road Map** C4. 030-2316424. FAX 2340661.
Situated in a 19th-century building on the elegant Maliebaan
right by the centre. Modern, comfortable rooms.
AE DC MC V · 45

UTRECHT: *NH Utrecht* €€€€
Jaarbeursplein 24. **Road Map** C4. 030-2977977. FAX 2977999.
A large hotel near the station and the trade fair. Extremely well-appointed
rooms, ideally suited for business travellers.
AE DC MC V · 276

UTRECHT: *Tulip Inn Utrecht Centre* €€€€
Janskerkhof 10. **Road Map** C4. 030-2313169. FAX 2310148.
Modern hotel in a monumental building in the centre of Utrecht.
Comfortable rooms.
AE DC MC V · 45

VREELAND: *De Nederlanden* €€€€
Duinkerken 3. **Road Map** C1. 0294-232326. FAX 231407.
Spectacularly located 17th-century inn on the river Vecht.
Fresh fruit and flowers in every room.
AE MC V · 7

WIJK BIJ DUURSTEDE: *De Oude Lantaarn* €€€
Markt 2. **Road Map** D4. 0343-571372. FAX 573796.
Situated in a historic building in central Wijk, near Duurstede. All rooms
have ensuite bathrooms and the majority have balconies.
AE MC V · 20

ZEIST: *Bilderberg Kasteel 't Kerckebosch*. www.bilderberg.nl €€€€
Arnhemse Bovenweg 31. **Road Map** C4. 030-6926666. FAX 6926600.
The woodland situation of this hotel gives it its atmosphere.
The castle has a pretty garden and a good restaurant.
AE DC MC V · 30

SOUTH HOLLAND

DELFT: *De Ark*. www.delfthotels.nl/ark €€€€
Koornmarkt 65. **Road Map** B4. 015-2157999. FAX 2144997.
Modern comforts by a picturesque canal in the centre of town. The
17th-century breakfast room has an open fire in winter.
AE DC MC V · 38

DORDRECHT: *Bellevue Dordrecht* www.bellevueDordrecht.nl €€€
Boomstraat 37. **Road Map** B4. 078-6137900. FAX 6137921.
Pleasantly located at the point where the Oude Maas, Noord and
Merwede converge. Attractive weekend offers.
AE DC MC V · 39

GOEDEREEDE: *De Gouden Leeuw*. www.goudenLeeuw.nl €
Markt 11. **Road Map** B5. 0187-491371. FAX 493941.
Located in a fine 15th-century Gothic building by the quay.
Simple but spacious rooms.
AE MC · 9

THE HAGUE: *Parkhotel Den Haag*. www.parkhoteldenhaag.nl €€€€
Molenstraat 53. **Road Map** B4. 070-3624371. FAX 3614525.
Exclusive hotel bordering the gardens of the Noordeinde palace.
Comfortable rooms.
AE DC MC V · 114

THE HAGUE: *Des Indes Inter-Continental Den Haag* €€€€€
Lange Voorhout 54–56. **Road Map** B4. 070-3612345. www.intercontinental.com
This stylish hotel exuding the atmosphere of the 19th century epitomizes
this fashionable city.
AE DC MC V · 76

THE HAGUE/SCHEVENINGEN: *Corel*. www.hotelcorel.nl €€€
Badhuisweg 54–56. **Road Map** B4. 070-3559939. FAX 3504853.
Close to the beach, the casino and the Circustheater.
AE MC V · 15

THE HAGUE/SCHEVENINGEN: *Steigenberger Kurhaus*. €€€€€
G Deynootplein 30. **Road Map** C3. 070-4162636. www.kurhaus.nl
This hotel on the main boulevard was built in 1885; rooms were renovated
100 years later. The hotel hosts musical events.
AE DC MC V · 255

LEIDEN: *Hotel De Doelen*. www.dedoelen.com €€€
Rapenburg 2. **Road Map** B4. 071-5120527. FAX 5128453.
Hotel situated in an old patrician residence near the centre. Some of
the rooms are substantial in size and have open fireplaces.
AE DC MC V · 16

For key to symbols see back flap

		Price categories		

Price categories are for a standard double room per night, including breakfast.

€ under €45
€€ €45–€70
€€€ €70–€115
€€€€ €115–€180
€€€€€ over €180

CREDIT CARDS
Credit cards accepted: *AE* American Express; *DC* Diners Club; *MC* MasterCard/Access; *V* Visa.
RESTAURANT
Hotel with restaurants serving lunch and dinner. Sometimes reserved for hotel guests only.
FREE FOR UNDER-12s
Children under the age of 12 free if sharing a room with their parents.
SWIMMING POOL/GYM/SAUNA
Hotel has a swimming pool, fitness centre or sauna.

	CREDIT CARDS	NUMBER OF ROOMS	RESTAURANT	FREE FOR UNDER-12s	SWIMMING POOL/GYM/SAUNA
LEIDEN: *Nieuw Minerva.* W www.nieuwminerva.nl €€€ Boommarkt 23. **Road Map** B4. 071-5126358. **FAX** 5142674. Snug hotel arranged over several old canal-houses right by the centre. Simple rooms with traditional furnishings.	AE DC MC V	39	■		
ROTTERDAM: *Breitner.* W www.hotelbreitner.nl €€€ Breitnerstraat 23. **Road Map** B5. 010-4360262. **FAX** 4364091. An oasis of peace in the bustling centre, this hotel is within walking distance of the Euromast and Spido.	AE DC MC V	36			
ROTTERDAM: *New York.* W www.hotelnewyork.nl €€€ Koninginnenhoofd 1. **Road Map** B5. 010-4390500. **FAX** 4842701. In the old offices of the Holland-America shipping line on the river Maas. A water taxi takes you to the other side of the river.	AE DC MC V	72	■		
ROTTERDAM: *Best Western Savoy.* W www.edenhotelgroup.com €€€€ Hoogstraat 81. **Road Map** B5. 010-4139280. **FAX** 4045712. Comfortable hotel situated right by the Oude Haven. Some of the rooms have a large terrace.	AE DC MC V	94	■		
ROTTERDAM: *Bilderberg Parkhotel.* W www.bilderberg.nl €€€€€ Westersingel 70. **Road Map** B5. 010-4363611. **FAX** 4364212. Right by the Museumpark, the harbour and the Coolsingel; some of the rooms afford a spectacular view of the city.	AE DC MC V	189	■		■
VOORBURG: *Savelberg.* W www.slh.com/pages/e/ergneta.html €€€€ Oosteinde 14. **Road Map** B4. 070-3872081. **FAX** 3877715. Exclusive restaurant and hotel in a stately 17th-century country house. The rooms are nicely furnished in various styles.	AE DC MC V	14	■		
WASSENAAR: *Holland Hotel Duinoord.* W www.hotelduinoord.nl €€€ Wassenaarseslag 26. **Road Map** B4. 070-5119332. **FAX** 5112210. Peacefully situated in the nature reserve of Berkheide, right on the beach. The pleasant rooms overlook the dunes.	AE MC V	20	■		
ZEELAND					
BRESKENS: *De Schelde* €€ Dorpsstraat 74. **Road Map** A6. 0117-381923. **FAX** 381923. This family hotel in the centre of Breskens is near the beach. It has tidy rooms, swings and a sandbox for children.		12	■		
CADZAND: *Badhotel de Wielingen* €€€ Kanaalweg 1. **Road Map** A6. 0117-391511. **FAX** 391630. Situated atop a sand dune by the beach, the hotel has comfortable rooms, including 14 suites, with balconies and sea views.	MC V	17	■		■
DOMBURG: *De Burg.* W www.hoteldeburg.nl €€ Ooststraat 5. **Road Map** A5. 0118-581337. **FAX** 582072. Family hotel on a lively shopping street within walking distance of the beach, woods, golf-course, spa and bowling alley.	AE MC V	22	■		
DOMBURG: *Zonneduin.* W www.hotelzonneduin.nl €€€ Nehalenniaweg 1. **Road Map** A5. 0118-581329. **FAX** 582267. Hotel situated right on the beach with a relaxed atmosphere and modern appointments. Cosy rooms with ensuite bath or shower, some with a balcony or terrace.	MC V	24			
DREISCHOR: *In d'n Aoren Waereld* €€ Ring 5. **Road Map** A4. 0111-401801. **FAX** 406730. A four-century-old building on the Oude Ring, right by the beach and forests. Non-smoking only. Rooms must be booked in advance.		3			

GOES: *Terminus.* W www.terminus.nl
Stationsplein 1. **Road Map** A6. (0113-230085. FAX 232579.
Modern hotel in a renovated old building, near the railway station.
The windows of the new rooms have double-glazing. P 🛏 🔓 ⤴

€€€ | AE DC MC V | 24 | ▨

MIDDELBURG: *Fletcher Hotel du Commerce*
Loskade 1. **Road Map** A5. (0118-636051. FAX 626400.
A sound hotel in the historic centre of Middelburg.
Offers a sumptuous breakfast buffet. 🛏 🏢 🔓 ⤴

€€€ | AE MC V | 46 | ▨

ST ANNALAND: *De Gouden Leeuw*
Voorstraat 50. **Road Map** B5. (0166-652305. FAX 653122.
Comfortable hotel with modern rooms, adjoining a pleasant café.
Situated not far from the marina. 🛏 🔓 🔒

€ | AE MC V | 9

VEERE: *De Campveerse Toren.* W www.campveersetoren.nl
Kaai 2. **Road Map** A5. (0118-501291. FAX 501695.
Tasteful hotel in a tower which was once part of the town defences.
Some of the rooms overlook Lake Veere. P 🛏 🏢 🔓 🔒

€€€€ | AE DC MC V | 12 | ▨

WESTENSCHOUWEN: *De Zilvermeeuw.* W www.hoteldezilvermeeuw.nl
Lageweg 21. **Road Map** A5. (0111-652272. FAX 658255.
Peacefully located family hotel near the beach. All rooms have
ensuite showers, and five have ensuite WCs. P 🛏 🔒

€€ | | 9 | ▨

ZOUTELANDE: *Beach Hotel Zoutelande.* W www.beachhotel.nl
Duinweg 97. **Road Map** A5. (0118-561255. FAX 561269.
Peacefully situated behind the dunes in wooded countryside.
All the rooms are well equipped. P 🛏 🏢 🔒

€€ | | 40 | ▨

WEST FRISIAN ISLANDS

AMELAND/HOLLUM: *Resort hotel d'Amelander Kaap*
Oosterhiemweg 1. **Road Map** D1. (0519-554646. W www.amelander-kaap.nl
Ideal location by the lighthouse. Forty modern, well-lit rooms and
136 suites. Numerous facilities. P 🛏 🏢 🔓 ♿ ⤴

€€ | AE DC MC V | 40 | ▨

AMELAND/NES: *Hofker.* W www.hotelhofker.nl
J Hofkerweg 1. **Road Map** D1. (0519-542002. FAX 542865.
Well-appointed rooms and suites in a peacefully located hotel.
Well suited for families with children. P 🛏 🏢 🔓 ⤴

€€€ | | 40 | ▨ | ▨

SCHIERMONNIKOOG: *Van der Werff.* W www.vanderwerff.net
Reeweg 2. **Road Map** E1. (0519-531203. FAX 531748.
This hotel, which has been in existence since 1726, has become an
institution on the island. It offers comfortable rooms. 🛏 🏢 🔓 🔒 ♿ ⤴

€€€ | DC MC V | 50 | ▨

SCHIERMONNIKOOG: *Graaf Bernstorff*
Reeweg 1. **Road Map** E1. (0519-532000. FAX 532050.
This hotel, located in the centre of this listed village, offers
17 luxurious rooms and 29 opulent suites. 🛏 🏢 🔓 🎴 ⤴

€€€€ | AE DC MC V | 46 | ▨ | ▨

TERSCHELLING/LIES: *De Walvisvaarder.* W www.walvisvaarder.nl
Lies 23. **Road Map** C1. (0562-449000. FAX 448677.
Restored farmhouse in the middle of the island, situated
on the edge of a nature reserve. Many facilities. P 🛏 🏢

€€€ | | 70 | ▨

TERSCHELLING/WEST: *Golden Tulip Resort Hotel Schylge*
Burg. van Heusdenweg 37. **Road Map** C1. (0562-442111. W www.goldentulip.nl
Modern luxury hotel on a picturesque bay. Comfortable rooms
and a romantic bridal suite. P 🛏 🏢 🔓 ♿ ⤴

€€ | AE DC MC | 98 | ▨ | ▨

TEXEL/DE KOOG: *Opduin.* W www.opduin.nl
Ruyslaan 22. **Road Map** C2. (0222-317445. FAX 317777.
Modernized hotel amongst the dunes. Opulent rooms fitted
with all facilities and conveniences. P 🛏 🏢 🔓 🎴 🔒 ♿ ⤴

€€€ | AE DC MC V | 90 | ▨ | ▨

TEXEL/DEN BURG: *De Lindeboom.* W www.lindeboomtexel.nl
Groeneplaats 14. **Road Map** C2. (0222-312041. FAX 310517.
Situated in a historic building in the town centre, 5 km (3 miles) from
the beach and forest. Terrace and restaurant. P 🛏 🏢 ▤ 🔓 🔒 ⤴

€€€ | | 17 | ▨ | ▨

VLIELAND: *Golden Tulip Strandhotel Seeduyn*
Badweg 3. **Road Map** C1. (0562-451560. W www.goldentulip.nl
Right on the North Sea, by a beach. Very comfortable rooms and
suites. Luxurious indoor swimming facilities. 🛏 🏢 🔓 ♿ ⤴

€€€ | AE DC MC V | 90 | ▨ | ▨

<table>
<tr><td colspan="2">Price categories are for a standard double room per night, including breakfast.

€ under €45
€€ €45–€70
€€€ €70–€115
€€€€ €115–€180
€€€€€ over €180</td><td>CREDIT CARDS
Credit cards accepted: AE American Express; DC Diners Club; MC MasterCard/Access; V Visa.
RESTAURANT
Hotel with restaurants serving lunch and dinner. Sometimes reserved for hotel guests only.
FREE FOR UNDER-12s
Children under the age of 12 free if sharing a room with their parents.
SWIMMING POOL/GYM/SAUNA
Hotel has a swimming pool, fitness centre or sauna.</td></tr>
</table>

	CREDIT CARDS	NUMBER OF ROOMS	RESTAURANT	FREE FOR UNDER-12s	SWIMMING POOL/GYM/SAUNA
GRONINGEN					
APPINGEDAM: *Landgoed Ekenstein.* w www.ekenstein.com €€€ Alberdaweg 70. **Road Map** E2. (*0596-628528.* FAX *620621.* Stately country home from 1648 situated in an old park. Some of the comfortable rooms are located in an additional wing. P ⊟ ⊞ ▮ ⌁ ⛫	AE DC MC V	28	■		
DELFZIJL: *Eemshotel.* w www.eemshotel.nl €€€ Zeebadweg 2. **Road Map** E2. (*0596-612636.* FAX *619654.* This unique hotel is built on piles driven into the sea and is reached via a bridge. The rooms are well equipped. P ⊟ ⊞ ▮ ⛫	AE DC MC V	20	■		■
EENRUM: *De Kromme Raake.* w www.eenrum.com €€€€ p/a Molenstraat 5. **Road Map** E1. (*0595-491600.* FAX *491400.* One of Holland's few one-room hotels, situated in an old herbalist's shop. It is in fact a suite with a bedstead. P ⊟	AE DC MC V	1			
GRONINGEN: *Auberge Corps de Garde.* w www.corpsdegarde.nl €€€ Oude Boteringestraat 74. **Road Map** E2. (*050-3145437.* FAX *3136320.* This former watch-house built in 1634 was once used to guard the Boteringerpoort. The rooms are stylishly decorated. P ⊟ ⊞ ⛫	AE DC MC V	24			
GRONINGEN: *Hotel de Ville.* w www.deville.nl €€€€ Oude Boteringestraat 43. **Road Map** E2. (*050-3181222.* FAX *3181777.* A stylish hotel furnished with a combination of antique and modern furniture. Most rooms have a view of the Martinitoren. P ⊟ ⊞ ▮ ⌁ ⛫ ⛭	AE DC MC V	45	■		
GRONINGEN: *Schimmelpenninck Huys.* w www.schimmelpenninckhuys.nl €€€€ Oosterstraat 53. **Road Map** E2. (*050-3189502.* FAX *3183164.* Historic patrician house in the centre of town. The Grand Café is a popular meeting place for the locals. P ⊟ ⊞ ⛫	AE DC MC V	46	■		
TER APEL: *Boschhuis.* w www.hotelboschhuis.nl €€ Boslaan 6. **Road Map** E2. (*0599-581208.* FAX *581906.* A rurally located hotel in the old brewery of the 15th-century monastery opposite. Simple but comfortable rooms. P ⊟ ⊞ ▮ ⛫ ⛭	AE DC MC V	10	■		
VEENDAM: *Holland Hotel Parkzicht.* w www.parkzicht.com €€ W Prinsstraat 3. **Road Map** E2. (*0598-626464.* FAX *619037.* Hospitable family hotel in the town centre. The contemporary rooms offer all comforts. P ⊟ ⊞ ▮ ⌁ ⛫ ⛰ ⛭	AE MC V	50	■		
ZOUTKAMP: *'t Reitdiep* €€ Dorpsplein 1. **Road Map** E1. (*0595-402426.* FAX *401827.* Hospitable village hotel by the ferry from Lauwersoog to Schiermonnikoog. Each room has a coffee maker. P ▮ ⛫		5	■		
FRIESLAND					
BEETSTERZWAAG: *Landgoed Lauswolt.* w www.bilderberg.nl €€€€ Van Harinxmaweg 10. **Road Map** D2. (*0512-381245.* FAX *381496.* A welcoming luxury hotel belonging to the Bilderberg group. Impeccable service and good restaurants. P ⊟ ⊞ ▮ ⛫ ⛭ ⛰	AE DC MC V	58	■		■
BOLSWARD: *Stadsherberg Heeremastate.* w www.publiciteit.nl/heeremastate €€ Heeremastraat 8. **Road Map** D2. (*0515-573063.* FAX *573974.* A fine town inn where you can spend the night in an atmosphere of olden times, albeit with modern luxuries. P ⊟ ⊞ ⌁	AE DC MC V	4			
DOKKUM: *De Abdij van Dockum.* w www.abdij.nl € Markt 30–32. **Road Map** D1. (*0519-220422.* FAX *220414.* Located in a fine historic abbey, with a tap room, a cultural information centre and a pleasant patio. P ⊟ ⊞ ▮ ⛫	AE DC MC V	15	■		

EERNEWOUDE: *Princenhof.* w www.princenhof.nl €€€
P Miedemaweg 15. **Road Map** D2. 0511-539206. FAX 539319.
Peaceful location by the Frisian lakes. Excellent accommodation
and great hospitality. P 🚶 🎱 🔟 🛏 🕭 🔼

AE	43	■	
DC			
MC			
V			

FRANEKER: *De Stadshersberg.* w www.stadshersbergfraneker.nl €€€
Oude Kaatsveld 8. **Road Map** D2. 0517-392686. FAX 398095.
This small hotel has a rich history. You can dine in either of the two
conservatories or sun yourself on the roof terrace. Jacuzzi. P 🚶 🛏 🔟

AE	7	■	
MC			
V			

LEEUWARDEN: *Hotel Paleis Het Stadhouderlijk Hof* €€€€
Hofplein 29. **Road Map** D2. 058-2162180. w www.stadhouderlijkhof.nl
This hotel is located in a former 18th-century palace in the town centre.
Pleasant apartments and suites. 🚶 🎱 🔟 🛏 🕭 🔼

AE	28	■	
DC			
MC			
V			

ORANJEWOUD: *Golden Tulip Tjaarda Oranjewoud* €€€€
Kon. Julianaweg 98. **Road Map** D2. 0513-433533. FAX 433599. w www.tjaarda.nl
Luxury hotel in woodland. Beauty and spa centre. P 🚶 🎱 🔟 🛏 🕭 🔼

AE	70	■	■
DC			

OUDKERK: *Landgoed De Klinze.* w www.klinze.nl €€€
Van Sminiaweg 32–36. **Road Map** D2. 058-2561050. FAX 2561060.
Accommodation in a magnificent country house in the middle of a park.
Tasteful, modern rooms. P 🚶 🎱 🔟 🛏 🕭 🔼

AE	27	■	■
DC			
MC			
V			

ST NICOLAASGA: *De Oorsprong.* w www.hoteldeoorsprong.nl €€€
Huisterheide 7. **Road Map** D2. 0513-432662. FAX 432786.
Former stud-farm which also has stabling facilities. Rooms are
equipped with all conveniences. P 🚶 🎱 🔟 🛏 🕭

AE	35	■	
MC			
V			

DRENTHE

DE WIJK: *Châteauhotel de Havixhorst.* w www.dehavixhorst.nl €€€€
Schiphorsterweg 34–36. **Road Map** E3. 0522-441487. FAX 441489.
Peacefully located 18th-century castle with magnificent rooms
in English country-house style. Excellent restaurant. P 🚶 🎱

AE	8	■	
DC			
MC			
V			

DWINGELOO: *Wesseling.* w www.hotelwesseling.nl €€€
Brink 26. **Road Map** E3. 0521-591544. FAX 592587.
Comfortable family hotel with special offers, particularly for public holidays.
The hotel has both a café and a restaurant. P 🚶 🔟 🛏 🕭 🔼

AE	23	■	
DC			
MC			
V			

EEN: *Plaggenhut Nijdams Erf.* w www.nijdamserf.nl €
Hoofdstraat 49. **Road Map** E2. 0592-656453.
Experience how people in Drenthe lived 70 years ago, in this authentic turf
hut. Bring your own bedding. 🎱

	1

EEXT: *Pension-theeschenkerij Abrahams-hofke* €€
Gieterstraat 20. **Road Map** E2. 0592-263376. FAX 553222.
Five small houses and two studios in an idyllic parkland setting. Pets are very
welcome. In the winter, high tea is served in the tea rooms. P 🚶 🎱 🛏

	7

GIETEN: *Braams.* w www.hotelbraams.nl €€
Brink 9. **Road Map** E2. 0592-261241. FAX 262028.
Comfortable hotel with a fabulous garden, as well as a swimming pool,
sauna and squash court. P 🚶 🎱 🔟 🛏 🔼

AE	50	■	■
DC			
MC			
V			

NIJENSLEEK: *De Nijenshof.* w www.denijenshof.nl €€€
Dwarsweg 15. **Road Map** D2. 0521-380022. FAX 380603.
This converted farmhouse has atmospheric *chambres d'hôtes* and two
apartments. Enjoy the *table d'hôte* four-course dinner. P 🚶 🎱 🔟 🛏 🕭

AE	8		
DC			
MC			
V			

ODOORN: *Lubbelinkhof* €€€€
Hoofdstraat 19. **Road Map** E2. 0591-535115.
Luxurious, modern hotel and restaurant in an old farmhouse. Fine atmosphere
and good service. Some rooms have a private terrace. P 🚶 🔟 🛏 🕭

MC	32	■	
V			

WESTERBORK: *Boshotel Ruyghe Venne.* w www.ruyghevenne.nl €€
Beilerstraat 24a. **Road Map** E3. 0593-331444. FAX 332888.
Cosy hotel with well-appointed rooms. The restaurant serves tasty local
Drenthe specialities. P 🚶 🎱 🔟 🛏 🕭

AE	14	■	
MC			
V			

OVERIJSSEL

BLOKZIJL: *Kaatje bij de Sluis.* w www.kaatje.nl €€€€
Zuiderstraat 1. **Road Map** D3. 0527-291833. FAX 291836.
In addition to good food, this establishment offers fine accommodation.
Rooms provide every comfort and modern furnishings. P 🚶 📋 🎱 🛏

AE	8	■	
DC			
MC			
V			

Price categories are for a standard double room per night, including breakfast.

€ under €45
€€ €45–€70
€€€ €70–€115
€€€€ €115–€180
€€€€€ over €180

CREDIT CARDS
Credit cards accepted: *AE* American Express; *DC* Diners Club; *MC* MasterCard/Access; *V* Visa.

RESTAURANT
Hotel with restaurants serving lunch and dinner. Sometimes reserved for hotel guests only.

FREE FOR UNDER-12s
Children under the age of 12 free if sharing a room with their parents.

SWIMMING POOL/GYM/SAUNA
Hotel has a swimming pool, fitness centre or sauna.

		CREDIT CARDS	NUMBER OF ROOMS	RESTAURANT	FREE FOR UNDER-12s	SWIMMING POOL/GYM/SAUNA
DELDEN: *Carelshaven.* W www.carelshaven.nl €€€ Hengelosestraat 30. **Road Map** E4. 074-3761305. FAX 3761291. Stylish country house in the Twente region on the Twickel estate. Spacious and comfortable rooms, all featuring terraces or balconies offering a lovely view of the surrounding pastures.		AE DC MC V	21	■		
DEVENTER: *Gilde Hotel.* W www.gildehotel.nl €€ Nieuwstraat 41. **Road Map** E4. 0570-641846. FAX 641819. Located in a cosy historic building but providing modern-day comforts. Lively café sports a garden terrace.		AE DC MC V	22	■		
ENSCHEDE: *De Hölterhof.* W www.holterhof.nl €€ Hölterhofweg 325. **Road Map** E4. 053-4611306. FAX 4613875. Romantic English-style country house near a nature reserve. The rooms are distributed over three buildings in the park and gardens.			34	■		
GIETHOORN: *De Pergola* € Ds. TO Hylkemaweg 7. **Road Map** D3. 0521-361321. FAX 362408. Convivial family-run hotel situated by the waterside. Pleasant rooms with modern facilities.			23	■		
HENGELO: *'t Lansink.* W www.lansinkhotel.nl €€€ CT Storkstraat 18. **Road Map** F4. 074-2910066. FAX 2435891. Situated in Tuindorp 't Lansink. Well-appointed rooms and a comfortable lounge with an open fireplace.		AE DC MC V	16	■		
KAMPEN: *Hotel van Dijk* €€ IJsselkade 30. **Road Map** D3. 038-3319925. FAX 3316508. @ wessels@worldonline.nl Rooms on the front of this family hotel offer fine views of the river IJssel.		MC V	18			
NIJVERDAL: *Dalzicht.* W www.dalzicht.nl €€ Grotestraat 285. **Road Map** E4. 0548-612413. FAX 614465. Convivial hotel with comfortable rooms. Pretty countryside and plenty to do in the surrounding area.		AE DC MC V	22	■		
ZWOLLE: *Bilderberg Grand Hotel Wientjes.* W www.bilderberg.nl €€€ Stationsweg 7. **Road Map** E3. 038-4254254. FAX 4254260. Luxury hotel with well-appointed rooms in a 19th-century mayoral residence. There are five special theme rooms. Various break offers are available.		AE DC MC V	58	■		
FLEVOLAND						
ALMERE: *Bastion Deluxe Hotel Almere.* W www.bastionhotels.nl €€€ Audioweg 1. **Road Map** C4. 036-5367755. FAX 5367009. This modern hotel near the centre offers all amenities, especially in the deluxe rooms. Bar and library.		AE DC MC V	100	■		
BIDDINGHUIZEN: *Dorhout Mees.* W www.dorhoutmees.nl €€€€ Strandgaperweg 30. **Road Map** D3. 0321-331138. FAX 331057. Situated in woodlands. The rooms have all modern comforts, and the hotel has its own hunting, shooting and golf grounds.		DC MC V	42	■		■
DRONTEN: *Het Galjoen.* W www.hotelhetgaljoen.nl €€€ De Rede 50. **Road Map** D3. 0321-317030. FAX 315822. Centrally situated hotel with a cosy atmosphere. You can enjoy a drink by the open fire.		AE DC MC V	18	■		
EMMELOORD: *'t Voorhuys.* W www.voorhuys.nl €€€ De Deel 20. **Road Map** D3. 0527-612870. FAX 617903. Hotel conveniently located in the town centre. Luxurious rooms, a fine restaurant and Grand Café.		AE DC MC V	25	■		

KRAGGENBURG: *Van Saaze.* W www.hotelvansaaze.nl €€ AE MC V 16
Dam 16. **Road Map** D3. 📞 *0527-252353.* FAX *252559.*
Spacious, comprehensively appointed rooms with all conveniences in a modern hotel. Will arrange cycling tours on request. P ☐ ☐ ☐ ☐

LELYSTAD: *Mercure Lelystad Congrescentrum.* W www.mercure.nl €€€ AE DC MC V 86
Agoraweg 11. **Road Map** D3. 📞 *0320-242444.* FAX *227569.*
Large modern hotel designed for business travellers, situated in the heart of the town. Restaurant, bar, and casino. P ☐ ☐ ☐ ☐ ☐ ☐

URK: *Pension De Kroon* €€ AE MC V 6
Wijk 7 54. **Road Map** D3. 📞 *0527-681216.* FAX *681216.*
Simple *pension* on the outskirts of the village, by the waterside. P ☐ ☐

GELDERLAND

ARNHEM: *Landgoed Hotel & Restaurant Groot Warnsborn* €€€€ AE DC MC V 30
Bakenbergseweg 277. **Road Map** D4. 📞 *026-4455751.* W www.grootwarnsborn.nl
This oasis of peace is in the middle of woodlands. The surrounding countryside is excellent for walking, cycling, golfing and riding. P ☐ ☐ ☐ ☐

BUURMALSEN: *De Lingehoeve.* W www.lingehoeve.nl € 4
Rijksstraatweg 41. **Road Map** D5. 📞 *0345-574721.*
Small, rustic *pension* in an old farmhouse right by the river De Linge. Simply furnished rooms. P ☐ ☐

ECHTELD: *Het Wapen van Balveren.* W www.wapenvanbalveren.nl €€ DC V 8
Voorstraat 8. **Road Map** D4. 📞 *0344-643270.* FAX *643590.*
Cosy new hotel in a picturesque village in the pretty countryside of Betuwe. Outstanding restaurant. P ☐ ☐ ☐ ☐

ERMELO: *Het Roode Koper.* W www.roodekoper.nl €€€€ AE DC MC V 28
Jhr Dr JC Sandbergweg 82. **Road Map** C3. 📞 *0577-407393.* FAX *407561.*
English-style country house from the early 20th century. Spacious, well-lit rooms, some of them in annexes amongst the woods. P ☐ ☐ ☐ ☐

HOOG SOEREN: *Hotel Oranjeoord.* W www.oranjeoord.nl €€€ AE DC MC V 35
Hoog Soeren 134–138. **Road Map** D3. 📞 *055-5191227.* FAX *5191451.*
This hotel from 1898 is set among wooded areas and farm estates. Each room is individually decorated in traditional English style. P ☐ ☐ ☐ ☐

OOIJ: *Oortjeshekken.* W www.oortjeshekken.nl €€ 11
Erlecomsedam 4. **Road Map** D4. 📞 *024-6631288.* FAX *6633004.*
Fine riverside location, just outside Nijmegen. ☐ ☐ ☐ ☐

OTTERLO: *Carnegie's Cottage.* W www.carnegiecottage.nl €€ 12
Onderlangs 35. **Road Map** D4. 📞 *0318-591220.*
Small, peacefully located hotel in the middle of the Hoge Veluwe. Furnishings contribute to the warm cosiness. P ☐ ☐ ☐

VORDEN: *Bloemendaal.* W www.bloemendaal.nl €€ MC V 15
Stationsweg 24. **Road Map** D4. 📞 *0575-551227.* FAX *553855.*
Convivial village hotel in the Achterhoek. Substantial rooms with ensuite bathrooms. Lounge with open fireplace. P ☐ ☐ ☐

ZUTPHEN: *Best Western Zutphen Museumhotel.* €€€ AE DC MC V 74
's Gravenhof 6. **Road Map** D4. 📞 *0575-546111.* W www.bestwestern.nl
Hotel in a listed 17th-century building. The atmosphere and the furnishings are a successful combination of old and new. P ☐ ☐ ☐ ☐ ☐ ☐ ☐

NORTH BRABANT

BERGEN OP ZOOM: *Mercure De Draak.* W www.hoteldedraak.com €€€€ AE DC MC V 68
Grote Markt 36–38. **Road Map** B6. 📞 *0164-252050.* FAX *257001.*
This late 14th-century hotel is the oldest in the country. The rooms are spacious and comfortable. P ☐ ☐ ☐ ☐ ☐ ☐ ☐

BREDA: *Stadshotel De Klok.* W www.hotel-de-klok.nl €€€ AE DC MC V 21
Grote Markt 26–28. **Road Map** C5. 📞 *076-5214082.* FAX *5143463.*
Family-run hotel in the centre of Breda. The terrace is a nice spot for an evening drink. ☐ ☐ ☐ ☐ ☐

BREDA: *Tulip-Inn Keyser Breda.* W www.hotel-keyser.nl €€€ AE DC MC V 79
Keizerstraat 5. **Road Map** D5. 📞 *076-5205173.* FAX *5205225*
Recently renovated, this hotel is right in the heart of the town, opposite ample parking facilities. ☐ ☐ ☐ ☐ ☐ ☐ ☐

Price categories are for a standard double room per night, including breakfast.

€ under €45
€€ €45–€70
€€€ €70–€115
€€€€ €115–€180
€€€€€ over €180

CREDIT CARDS
Credit cards accepted: *AE* American Express; *DC* Diners Club; *MC* MasterCard/Access; *V* Visa.
RESTAURANT
Hotel with restaurants serving lunch and dinner. Sometimes reserved for hotel guests only.
FREE FOR UNDER-12s
Children under the age of 12 free if sharing a room with their parents.
SWIMMING POOL/GYM/SAUNA
Hotel has a swimming pool, fitness centre or sauna.

	CREDIT CARDS	NUMBER OF ROOMS	RESTAURANT	FREE FOR UNDER-12s	SWIMMING POOL/GYM/SAUNA
DEURNE: *Goossens.* w www.hotelgoossens.nl €€ Stationsplein 30. **Road Map** D6. 0493-312530. FAX 312578. Pleasant little hotel by the station. Wooded location, with plenty of recreation opportunities.	AE MC V	8	■		
DRUNEN: *Hotel Royal.* w www.hotelroyal.nl €€€ Raadhuisplein 13. **Road Map** C5. 0416-372381. FAX 373772. This hotel in the centre dates back around 100 years and is a good base for those who want to explore the nearby dunes. Tasteful, comfortable rooms and an excellent restaurant.	AE DC MC V	12	■		
EINDHOVEN: *Parkhotel.* w www.parkzicht.nl €€€ A Thijmlaan 18. **Road Map** D6. 040-2114100. FAX 2114100. Situated on the edge of the town centre opposite the park. Good restaurant and a lively, cheerful bar.	AE DC MC V	44	■		
GEMERT: *De Hoefpoort.* w www.hoefpoort.nl €€€ Binderseind 1. **Road Map** D5. 0492-392008. FAX 392489. A small, hospitable hotel across from Gemert's castle. The comfortable rooms are individually decorated.	MC V	8			
HEEZE: *Hostellerie Van Gaalen.* w www.hostellerie.nl €€€ Kapelstraat 48. **Road Map** D6. 040-2263515. FAX 2263876. Hotel with an informal atmosphere and comfortable rooms. Member of the Alliance Gastronomique Néerlandaise.	AE DC MC V	14	■		
HELMOND: *West Ende.* w www.westende.nl €€€ Steenweg 1. **Road Map** D6. 0492-524151. FAX 543295. Majestic hotel with an atmosphere of comfort on the edge of the town centre. Modern, tasteful rooms.	AE DC MC V	28	■		
's-HERTOGENBOSCH: *Marktzicht.* w www.marktzicht.nl € Oude Engelenseweg 22a. **Road Map** C5. 073-6218277. FAX 6218306. Opposite the Brabanthallen and therefore often booked up during events. Simply appointed rooms.	MC V	14	■		
's-HERTOGENBOSCH: *Best Western Eurohotel.* €€€€ Hinthamerstraat 63. **Road Map** C5. 073-6137777. w www.eurotel-denbosch.com Lively hotel in the town centre, right by the cathedral and shopping streets. Comfortable rooms.	AE DC MC V	42	■		
HEUSDEN: *In den Verdwaalden Koogel* €€€ Vismarkt 1. **Road Map** C5. 0416-661933. FAX 661295. Charming hotel in a 17th-century building with a stepped gable. The cannonball in the gable is from the 80 Years War. The comfortable rooms are decorated in Bordeaux red and green-blue.	MC V	12	■		
KAATSHEUVEL: *Golden Tulip Efteling Hotel.* w www.efteling.nl €€€€ Horst 31. **Road Map** D5. 0416-282000. FAX 281515. Steps from Efteling Theme Park, this hotel offers various theme suites, such as the Hansel & Gretel Room and the Fifties Room. The regular rooms are just as comfortable. Abundant recreation opportunities.	AE DC MC V	120	■		
OUDENBOSCH: *Tivoli.* w www.hotel-tivoli.nl €€€ Markt 68. **Road Map** C5. 0165-312412. FAX 320444. This hotel and congress centre is housed in an abbey built by Jesuits during the 19th century. They added a picturesque park. The rooms are comfortably furnished in English style.	AE DC MC V	43	■		
ZUNDERT: *De Roskam.* w www.hotel-de-roskam.nl €€ Molenstraat 1. **Road Map** C6. 076-5972357. FAX 5975215. Easily accessible hotel situated in the village centre. Well-maintained rooms and a relaxing lounge.	AE DC MC V	25	■		

LIMBURG

ARCEN: *De Maasparel.* W www.maasparel.nl €€€ MC V 12
Schans 3–5. **Road Map** E6. 077-4731296. **FAX** 4731335.
A pleasant modern hotel in the village centre right on the river Maas.
Nice rooms and cosy restaurant with terrace. **P**

BERG EN TERBLIJT: *Kasteel Geulzicht.* W www.kasteelgeulzicht.nl €€€€ AE DC MC V 9
Vogelzangweg 2. **Road Map** D7. 043-6040432. **FAX** 6042011.
Magnificent 18th-century castle with tastefully furnished and comfortable
rooms. The restaurant offers Limburger specialities. **P**

ELSLOO: *Kasteel Elsloo.* W www.kasteelelsloo.nl €€€€ AE DC MC V 24
Maasberg 1. **Road Map** D7. 046-4377666. **FAX** 4377570.
Pleasant and spacious rooms provided with every comfort.
The restaurant is fashionable among connoisseurs. **P**

EPEN: *NH Zuid-Limburg* €€€€ AE DC MC V 47
Julianastraat 23a. **Road Map** D7. 043-4551818. **FAX** 4552415.
In the Geuldal valley near Maastricht, Aken and Luik. Pleasant apartments
and bedrooms. Numerous opportunities for relaxation. **P**

HEERLEN: *Best Western Grand Hotel Heerlen.* W www.bestwestern.nl €€€ AE DC MC V 108
Groene Boord 23. **Road Map** D7. 045-5713846. **FAX** 5741099.
Modern hotel with good accessibility. The rooms are provided with all
conveniences. Pleasant lounge. **P**

KERKRADE: *Brughof.* W www.brughof.nl €€€€€ AE DC MC V 44
Oud Erensteinerweg 6. **Road Map** D7. 045-5461333. **FAX** 5460748.
Hotel situated on the edge of the unspoiled Anstelvallei. Luxurious rooms and
suites. Stylish restaurant in Kasteel Erenstein next door. **P**

LANDGRAAF: *Winselerhof.* W www.winselerhof.nl €€€€€ AE DC MC V 49
Tunnelweg 99. **Road Map** D7. 045-5464343. **FAX** 5352711.
Luxuriously appointed rooms in a monumental 16th-century manor farm.
Intimate atmosphere. Various culinary events. **P**

MAASTRICHT: *Best Western Grand Hotel de l'Empereur* €€€ AE DC MC V 80
Stationsstraat 2. **Road Map** D7. 043-3213838. W www.bestwestern.nl
Cosy luxury hotel with an excellent restaurant. The rooms have been
adapted to modern-day requirements. **P**

MAASTRICHT: *Golden Tulip Hotel Derlon* €€€€ AE DC MC V 42
O-L-Vrouweplein 6. **Road Map** D7. 043-3216770. **FAX** 3251933.
Situated in the Stokstraat quarter on a pleasant square. Modern rooms and an
excellent brasserie. Museum with Roman finds in the cellar. **P**

SWALMEN: *'t Graeterhof* €€€ AE DC MC V 10
Graeterweg 23. **Road Map** D6. 0475-501340. **FAX** 504588.
This former hunting lodge is situated in the magnificent Swalmdal valley,
with a grand staircase and mosaic floors. Cosy rooms. **P**

TEGELEN: *Bilderberg Château Holtmühle.* W www.bilderberg.nl €€€€ AE DC MC V 66
Kasteellaan 10. **Road Map** E6. 077-3738800. **FAX** 3740500.
Magnificent restored 14th-century castle. Excellent restaurant.
The rooms are furnished in English style. **P**

VAALS: *Dolce Kasteel Vaalsbroek.* W www.dolce.com/vaalsbroek €€€€ AE DC MC V 130
Vaalsbroek 1. **Road Map** D7. 043-3089308. **FAX** 3089333.
Rurally located hotel in a magnificent park. Luxurious rooms. The restaurant
offers international cuisine. **P**

VALKENBURG: *Château St Gerlach.* W www.stgerlach.com €€€ AE DC MC V 58
J Corneli Allée 1. **Road Map** D7. 043-6088888. **FAX** 6042883.
Luxury hotel in a historic monastery complex. Rooms as well as 39
apartments and suites on offer. Kneipp spa centre. **P**

WEERT: *Hostellerie Munten.* W www.hostelleriemunten.nl €€€ AE MC V 14
Wilhelminasingel 276. **Road Map** D6. 0495-531057. **FAX** 544596.
Romantic and luxurious rooms. **P**

WITTEM: *Kasteel Wittem.* W www.kasteelwittem.nl €€€€ AE DC MC V 12
Wittemer Allée 3. **Road Map** D7. 043-4501208. **FAX** 4501260.
In a medieval knight's castle. Comfortable rooms of various dimensions.
The lounge is in Louis XVI style. **P**

For key to symbols see back flap

WHERE TO EAT

THE DUTCH ARE innovative people, and this quality comes out in their cooking. There is a growing number of chefs who are demonstrating an artistic approach to their profession; in recent years the number of ethnic restaurants has been growing, particularly in larger towns. Whereas previously you would find only one Chinese, one Italian and one Indonesian restaurant in these towns, now you can also enjoy dishes from countries as varied as Spain, Turkey, Greece, Morocco, Israel, Lebanon, Ethiopia, India, Thailand, Japan, Korea and Vietnam.

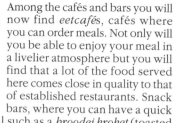

Chef

Among the cafés and bars you will now find *eetcafés*, cafés where you can order meals. Not only will you be able to enjoy your meal in a livelier atmosphere but you will find that a lot of the food served here comes close in quality to that of established restaurants. Snack bars, where you can have a quick meal such as a *broodej kroket* (toasted sandwich with meat) are now an established feature of the Dutch culinary scene. The restaurants listed on pages 408–21 have been selected on the basis not only of the quality of food served but also of the atmosphere and service.

Eating out, a pastime growing rapidly in popularity in Holland

TYPES OF RESTAURANT

HOLLAND BOASTS a wide variety of restaurants, and as the Dutch are eating out with increasing frequency, this means that the range of restaurants they can choose from is increasing as well. Because of the historical ties with Indonesia, Indonesian ("Indisch") restaurants are numerous in Holland. Amsterdam is one of the best places in Europe to sample the diverse flavours of that country. For purists, much of the cooking may lean too heavily towards the Chinese style, but it is still possible to sample genuine Indonesian recipes. Chinese restaurants and pizzerias have also spread far and wide throughout the country.

Traditional Dutch cooking is best described as frugal. As a maritime nation, Holland docs have large numbers of fish restaurants, particularly

along the coast. There is an overwhelming number of restaurants serving French cuisine. Their numbers are increasing steadily, and quality is also improving constantly. The chefs frequently add some local ingredients to the French recipes, such as fennel or asparagus. This means that in Holland you can eat wild duck on endive *stamppot* (mashed potato and cabbage), a combination which is as yet unheard of in France. Nobody looks askance at tuna tartare, deep-fried celeriac or green asparagus and guacamole. It is in areas such as these that Dutch chefs are showing increasing inventiveness.

In recent years there has also been an increase in the number of ethnic restaurants in Holland. The quality varies,

and the range of foods on offer is vast, from Vietnamese to Lebanese, Thai to Greek, Indian to Turkish, Moroccan to Japanese. Indeed, one would be hard-pressed to find a country in the world whose cuisine is not represented by some restaurant in Holland. There is also an infinite variety in the range of food, decoration, contents, presentation and price. The majority of ethnic restaurants are situated in larger towns and cities, but even in the countryside their numbers are steadily increasing.

EETCAFÉS

EETCAFÉS (eating cafés) are a relatively recent phenomenon in Dutch eating. Initially, some cafés and bars

Inter Sclades in Kruiningen, one of the best restaurants in the country

An *eetcafé*, one of the many in Holland serving increasingly refined meals

sold snacks to go with their drinks, such as an appetizer, a sandwich or a meatball. These snacks have since been refined to a growing extent. Coffee shops have gradually evolved into *eetcafés* where you can enjoy sandwiches at lunch time and cheap, often very decent, meals in the evenings. They vary from very simple dishes such as soups, sandwiches, salads, omelettes and French fries to exceptionally good three-course menus. Many such cafés are now concentrating increasingly on the food aspect. The prices charged at these cafés are in many cases much lower than those in traditional restaurants.

VEGETARIAN RESTAURANTS

MOST RESTAURANTS have a number of vegetarian dishes on their menus. This applies both to Dutch/French restaurants and to ethnic restaurants. There are also an increasing number of restaurants which cater exclusively to vegetarian diners.

OPENING HOURS

HOLLAND HAS NOT had a tradition of lunching, but this is also gradually changing, with increasing numbers of restaurants now opening at lunch time. In the evenings the majority of restaurants open at 6pm; the kitchens usually stop serving food at 10pm or 10:30pm. Also – and in particular in the large

towns and cities – there is a growing number of night restaurants, with the kitchens staying open until after midnight. This allows you to round off a visit to the theatre, movies or café with a late dinner.

Traditionally, many restaurants do not open on Mondays, though this is also changing.

A snack bar, ideal for a quick but satisfying bite to eat

RESERVATIONS

ANYBODY WISHING to eat in one of the country's more renowned restaurants would do well to book, and sometimes booking a few days in advance is advisable. It can get crowded in cafés and other informal restaurants in the evenings, but reservations are usually accepted only for large groups if at all.

TIPPING

A SERVICE CHARGE of 15 per cent is included on the bill at most Dutch bars, cafés, and restaurants. However, it is customary to round up the amount. The tip should be left as change rather than included on a credit-card payslip.

ETIQUETTE

THE ATMOSPHERE at most Dutch restaurants is fairly informal, and when going out to dine you can generally wear what you like; smart casual or semi-formal dress is suitable almost everywhere. There are some exceptions, however: in some very upmarket restaurants dressing smartly is considered very important.

PRICES

MOST DUTCH restaurants display a menu giving the prices of various dishes or set meals on the wall or the front door so that you can get an idea of whether the prices suit you or not before going in. The prices are given inclusive of VAT (BTW) and service. Prices can vary markedly, and a restaurant can be found in each price class: you can find many establishments where you can eat for less than €22.50; in top restaurants, however, you should not be surprised if your bill comes to €70, excluding wine. The cost of drinks is invariably extra and the mark-up levied by a restaurant, especially on cheap wine, can be high.

TRAVELLERS WITH DISABILITIES

MOST RESTAURANTS at ground floor level are accessible for wheelchairs. Toilet facilities, however, tend to pose a problem, with many of them reached via steep stairs and therefore not easily accessible by wheelchair.

DRINKS

IN RECENT TIMES a growing number of restaurants has been paying more attention to the wine list: in many of them, you can choose from a range of outstanding, often French, wines to accompany your meal. The list of often exotic aperitifs available is also growing in many establishments. However, beer is the drink of preference in most Dutch cafés and bars, and all have a wide selection of local and imported brews.

What to Eat in Holland

Fresh peas

TRADITIONAL DUTCH FOOD is hearty and wholesome and prepared with simple ingredients. Fresh herring, sole, mussels and salted lamb are among the best that the country offers. Holland's potatoes are world famous, as are its dairy products such as milk, cream, butter and, of course, cheese. Fruit and vegetables thrive in the Dutch climate, with the harvest of the creamy white asparagus being the high point of the year.

Mussels *are eaten when an "r" appears in the name of the month.*

Paling in 't groen *(stewed eel with vegetables) is one version of stewed eel. Smoked eel is another tasty delicacy.*

Hollandse garnalen, *or Dutch prawns, often come with bread and sauce.*

Fresh herring, *the best the sea has to offer, is typically served raw with onions or herbs and accompanied by chilled koren- wijn (purified malt wine).*

Zeetong *(sole) grows to its largest size in the North Sea. It is best baked in butter, served with a slice of lemon.*

Zeekraal *(glasswort) is a plant from the mud flats and salt marshes that goes very well with fish.*

Wholemeal bread *is the pride of Dutch bakers.*

CHEESE

Dutch cheese is exported to all corners of the world. Gouda, Edam and Leiden cheese are the best known, but every part of the country where cows outnumber humans makes its own cheese, from mild to extra-mature, from seasonal cheese to mass-produced cheese, plain or flavoured with nettle, cumin, chives, cloves or garlic. Sheep's and goat's cheese extend the range. Cheese is often served on a cheese board with traditional *rogge-brood* (rye bread).

Cheese platter: Oude Beemster, Leerdammer, Leiden and Limburg goat's cheese with rye bread

Pancakes *are eaten with all kinds of fillings: bacon (and syrup), cheese or fruit.*

Eendenborst *(breast of duck) is a highlight of the menu in Dutch restaurants.*

Texel lamb *is salty. The potato served with it is the famous* Opperdoezer Ronde.

Zure zult (brawn) and *metworst* **sausage** *are typical Dutch cold meats.*

Salad *with tomatoes and radishes.*

Apple tart *is a favourite Dutch dessert. This one has a central filling of raisins in brandy.*

White asparagus *with ham and egg is a speciality of both Limburg and East Brabant.*

Dutch straw-berries *are a real treat, especially with whipped cream.*

INDONESIAN CUISINE

Indonesian cooking is a colonial legacy that has become common property. The best way to start off with Indonesian food is to order a *rijsttafel*. Together with a large bowl of rice, you will be given some 25 bowls of snacks. Look out for the word *pedis* (hot!).

Stir-fried noodles

Bami goreng (fried noodles, chicken, prawns, garlic, pepper, vegetables)

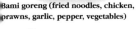

Satay daging (marinated beef)

Satay ajam (chicken in peanut sauce)

Ajam panike (chicken in mild sauce)

Sambal goreng (red chilli sauce)

Peanut sauce

Soy sauce with chillies

Babi asam pedis (spicy pork)

Udang bakar (grilled tiger prawns)

Gado gado (mixed vege-tables with peanut sauce)

Nasi goreng (fried rice with meat, prawns, mushrooms and soy sauce)

Choosing a Restaurant

THE RESTAURANTS IN THIS SECTION have been chosen
for their exceptional food or their good value. The
chart on the right shows which credit cards are accepted
for payment, whether the restaurant opens until late,
whether it has a terrace and whether it has a wide
range of wines on offer.

		CREDIT CARDS	**LATE OPENING**	**OUTSIDE TABLES**	**SPECIAL WINE LIST**

AMSTERDAM

OUDE ZIJDE: *Café Bern*   €
Nieuwmarkt 9. **Map** 5 B1. 📞 *020-6220034.*
An *eetcafé* with simple but wholesome fare, including cheese fondue, on
the menu. Frequented by journalists and Amsterdam bohemians. 🔲 🚻

| | | | ● | | |

OUDE ZIJDE: *Centra*   €
Lange Niezel 29. **Map** 2 E4. 📞 *020-6223050.*
Simple Spanish restaurant in the middle of the red-light district, serving
good down-to-earth food; guests are seated at small formica tables. The
atmosphere is relaxing. Reservations are recommended. 🚻

| | | | ● | | |

OUDE ZIJDE: *Kinderkookcafé*   €
Oudezijds Achterburgwal 193. **Map** 2 D5. 📞 *020-6253257.*
On Wednesday afternoons, children prepare their own meals here. Adults
are admitted only if accompanied by a child. ● *every day except Wed.* 🚻

OUDE ZIJDE: *Nam Kee*   €
Zeedijk 111. **Map** 2 E4. 📞 *020-6243470.*
Cantonese cooking in one of Amsterdam's most popular and best-loved
Chinese restaurants. ● *Mon.* 🔲 🚻

OUDE ZIJDE: *Wau*   €
Zeedijk 35. **Map** 2 E4. 📞 *020-4212487.*
Malaysian restaurant with an emphasis on satay dishes, meat being grilled
continuously on charcoal. The dishes largely resemble Indonesian cuisine,
but with the odd Thai influence here and there. ● *Tue.* 🔲 🚻

| | | AE DC MC V | ● | | |

OUDE ZIJDE: *De Verdwenen Minnaar*   €€
Zeedijk 32. **Map** 2 E4. 📞 *020-3309809.*
While the food here is good, the main emphasis is on live music,
especially jazz. In fine weather you can sit outside by the water. 🎵

| | | AE V | ● | ■ | |

OUDE ZIJDE: *Raap & Peper*   €€
Peperstraat 23–25. **Map** 2 F5. 📞 *020-3301716.*
Old-fashioned décor and classical French menus of superb quality.
Service is very attentive. ● *Sun, Mon.*

| | | AE DC MC V | | | |

OUDE ZIJDE: *Blauw aan de Wal*   €€€
Oudezijds Achterburgwal 99. **Map** 1 D5. 📞 *020-3302257.*
Modern ambience in a building from the Golden Age. Contemporary
Mediterranean cuisine. Outside terrace; reservations necessary. ● *Sun.* 🔲 ♿

| | | AE DC MC V | | ■ | ● |

OUDE ZIJDE: *Hemelse Modder*   €€€
Oude Waal 11. **Map** 2 E4. 📞 *020-6243203.*
Located along one of the calmest and most picturesque canals of
Amsterdam. You can enjoy a well-prepared meal in this modern
social space. Very busy on the weekends, so reserve in advance.
● *Mon.* 🔲 ♿

| | | AE DC MC V | | | ● |

OUDE ZIJDE: *Krua Thai Classic*   €€€€
Staalstraat 22. **Map** 5 A2. 📞 *020-6229533.*
A new Thai restaurant with fantastic food served
by charming, attentive staff. ● *Mon.* 🔲

| | | MC V | | | |

OUDE ZIJDE: *Vermeer*   €€€€
Prins Hendrikkade 59–72. **Map** 2 E3. 📞 *020-5564885.*
Vermeer is one of Holland's top contemporary restaurants, with
creativity and finesse being the bywords of the kitchen, which
always has a surprise in store. Varied wine list, outstanding service.
● *Sat, Sun (lunch).* 🔲 🚻 ♿

| | | AE DC MC V | ● | | ● |

<table>
<tr><td colspan="2">

Price categories are for a three-course meal for one with half a bottle of house wine, including tax and service.

€ under €30
€€ €30–€45
€€€ €45–€60
€€€€ over €60

</td><td>

CREDIT CARDS
Credit cards accepted: *AE* American Express; *DC* Diners Club; *MC* MasterCard/Access; *V* Visa.
LATE OPENING
Kitchen is open after 10pm, and you can usually dine until at least 11pm.
OUTSIDE TABLES
Seating available on a terrace or garden.
SPECIAL WINE LIST
The restaurant offers a wide range of good wines.

</td></tr>
</table>

		CREDIT CARDS	LATE OPENING	OUTSIDE TABLES	SPECIAL WINE LIST
NIEUWE ZIJDE: *Brasserie De Poort* Nieuwezijds Voorburgwal 176–180. **Map** 1 C5. 020-6240047. This restaurant, located in the Hotel Die Port van Cleve, offers typical Dutch dishes: De Poort's steaks are renowned and are individually numbered. Reservations are a good idea. ● *Mon.* V ⚡ &	€€	AE DC MC V	●		
NIEUWE ZIJDE: *Club Inez IPSC* Amstel 2. **Map** 5 A2. 020-6392899. The idiosyncratic interior was furnished by artist Peter Giele (now deceased) in his unique style. Equally idiosyncratic cuisine. V	€€	AE DC MC V	●		
NIEUWE ZIJDE: *De Jaren* Nieuwe Doelenstraat 20–22. **Map** 5 A2. 020-6255771. Spacious *eetcafé* serving international (primarily South European) dishes. Large terrace with a view of the Amstel. V ⚡	€€		●	■	
NIEUWE ZIJDE: *Vasso* Rozenboomsteeg 10–14. **Map** 1 C5. 020-6260158. Modern Italian restaurant serving regional cuisine. Good quality food and a pleasant atmosphere. V ⚡	€€	AE DC MC V	●	■	
NIEUWE ZIJDE: *Excelsior* Nieuwe Doelenstraat 2–8. **Map** 5 A2. 020-5311705. The restaurant of the Hotel de l'Europe offers culinary masterpieces by chef Jean-Jacques Menanteau. Attentive service. Pricey, but worth a visit. Smart dress required! V ⚡ & ♫	€€€€	AE DC MC V	●	■	●
NIEUWE ZIJDE: *Supperclub* Jonge Roelensteeg 21. **Map** 1 C5. 020-3446400. Customers don't sit at tables here, but recline to enjoy the dishes from the "love kitchen", as the owner calls it. This is a place for people who want to try something seriously different. ● *Sun–Tue.* V ♫	€€€€	AE DC MC V			
CANAL RING: *Café Cox* Marnixstraat 429. **Map** 4 D1. 020-6207222. On the ground floor, Cox is a trendy theatre café, while the restaurant on the first floor serves mainly French meals. Often very crowded. V ⚡	€	AE DC MC V	●		
CANAL RING: *De Prins* Prinsengracht 124. **Map** 4 F2. 020-6249382. Here, amidst the lively throng of a crowded café, you can enjoy simple but delicious food from a wide-ranging menu. ⚡	€	MC V	●	■	●
CANAL RING: *Piet de Leeuw* Noorderstraat 11. **Map** 4 F2. 020-6237181. Piet van Leeuw's *eetcafé* serves delicious steaks, which are the house speciality. ● *Sun, Mon.* V ⚡ &	€		●		
CANAL RING: *Burger's Patio* 2de Tuindwarsstraat 12. **Map** 1 B3. 020-6236854. An attempt to compete with more exclusive competition using simple means. Specializes in vegetarian dishes. V ⚡	€€	AE DC MC V	●	■	
CANAL RING: *Chez Georges* Herenstraat 3. **Map** 1 C3. 020-6263332. The Belgian chef Georges François Roorda prepares superior dishes, from salad with paté de foie gras to tricolour chocolate mousse. Friendly, professional service. ● *Sun, Wed.* V	€€	AE DC MC V	●		●
CANAL RING: *Garlic Queen* Reguliersdwarsstraat 27. **Map** 4 F1. 020-4226426. In this restaurant, as its name implies, the emphasis is on garlic; however, it is possible to order dishes without garlic. ● *Mon, Tue.* V ⚡	€€	AE DC MC V	●	■	●

For key to symbols see back flap

Price categories are for a three-course meal for one with half a bottle of house wine, including tax and service.

€ under €30
€€ €30–€45
€€€ €45–€60
€€€€ over €60

CREDIT CARDS
Credit cards accepted: *AE* American Express; *DC* Diners Club; *MC* MasterCard/Access; *V* Visa.
LATE OPENING
Kitchen is open after 10pm, and you can usually dine until at least 11pm.
OUTSIDE TABLES
Seating available on a terrace or garden.
SPECIAL WINE LIST
The restaurant offers a wide range of good wines.

	Price	CREDIT CARDS	LATE OPENING	OUTSIDE TABLES	SPECIAL WINE LIST
CANAL RING: *Le Zinc... et les Autres* Prinsengracht 999. **Map** 1 C3. ☎ *020-6229044.* At Le Zinc... et les Autres, you can enjoy French regional cooking. Good service and a nice atmosphere. ● *Sun.* 🆅 👤 🎵	€€	MC V	●		●
CANAL RING: *Pasta e Basta* Nieuwe Spiegelstraat 8. **Map** 4 F2. ☎ *020-4222229.* Eccentric Italian restaurant with plenty of atmosphere and good-quality dishes. Live music. Reservations required. 🆅 👤 🎵	€€		●	▪	●
CANAL RING: *Pata Negra* Utrechtsestraat 124. **Map** 5 A3. ☎ *020-4226250.* A tapas bar with pleasant décor, Pata Negra exudes an authentic atmosphere. Delectable snacks. 🆅 👤	€€		●		
CANAL RING: *Sichuan Food* Reguliersdwarsstraat 35. **Map** 4 F1. ☎ *020-6258775.* Chinese restaurant with one star in the Michelin guide. Formal atmosphere and extremely polite service. 👤	€€	AE DC MC V	●		●
CANAL RING: *Tempo Doeloe* Utrechtsestraat 75. **Map** 5 A3. ☎ *020-6256718.* One of the city's finest Indonesian restaurants. Hot food (clearly indicated on menu) but extremely tasty and authentic; milder dishes also available. 🆅 👤	€€	AE DC MC V	●		
CANAL RING: *Toscanini Ristorante* Lindengracht 75. **Map** 1 B3. ☎ *020-6232813.* Some regard this as the best Italian restaurant in town, and so reservations are necessary. Surprising, but delicious, dishes. ● *Sun.* 🆅 👤	€€	AE DC MC V	●	▪	●
CANAL RING: *Van Harte* Hartenstraat 24. **Map** 1 C5. ☎ *020-6258500.* Situated in a charming long and narrow room, and serving magnificent French dishes. There is a comprehensive wine list. ● *Tue.* 🆅 👤	€€	AE DC MC V	●	▪	●
CANAL RING: *Van Vlaanderen* Weteringschans 175. **Map** 4 E2. ☎ *020-6228292.* This Michelin-starred restaurant offers creative variations on French culinary traditions. Interesting wine list, too. ● *Sun, Mon.* 🆅 👤	€€	AE MC V	●	▪	●
CANAL RING: *Bordewijk* Noordermarkt 7. **Map** 1 C3. ☎ *020-6243899.* Creative, daring and experimental: chef Ben van Geelen treats his visitors to some exquisite creations. Bordewijk is without doubt among Amsterdam's finest restaurants. ● *Mon.* 🆅 👤	€€€	AE MC V	●	▪	●
CANAL RING: *De Prinsenkelder* Prinsengracht 438. **Map** 4 E1. ☎ *020-4222777.* Stylish restaurant in the basement of a building on the Leidseplein: outstanding food, professional and friendly service. ● *Sun, Mon.* 🆅 👤 🎵	€€€	AE DC MC V	●	▪	●
CANAL RING: *Dining Eleven* Reesstraat 11. **Map** 1 B5. ☎ *020-6207968.* Sleek, modern restaurant with adventurous food and professional service. 🆅	€€€		●		
CANAL RING: *Het Tuynhuys* Reguliersdwarsstraat 28. **Map** 4 F1. ☎ *020-6276603.* This former coach house serves French-Dutch dishes, always prepared with fresh ingredients. Garden. ● *Sat, Sun (lunch).* 🆅 👤	€€€	AE DC MC V	●	▪	●

CANAL RING: *Le Pêcheur* €€€
Reguliersdwarsstraat 32. **Map** 4 F1. **☎** *020-6243121.*
Cosy restaurant with terrace garden in the middle of a major entertainment
centre. Here you can enjoy the finest freshly caught fish. **●** *Sun.* **V &**
AE DC MC V

CANAL RING: *Les Quatre Canetons* €€€
Prinsengracht 1111. **Map** 1 C3. **☎** *020-6246307.*
Les Quatre Canetons serves French-Dutch dishes, such as mullet salad with
foie gras and truffles vinaigrette, and pasta dessert with red fruit. Duck is the
house speciality. **●** *Sat (lunch), Sun.* **V ♣**
AE DC MC V

CANAL RING: *Lof* €€€
Haarlemmerstraat 62. **Map** 2 D3. **☎** *020-6202997.*
Down-to-earth fresh fare – most of the ingredients have been bought from
the market that day. A fine and adventurous wine list. **●** *Mon.* **V ♣**

CANAL RING: *Zuid Zeeland* €€€
Herengracht 413. **Map** 4 F1. **☎** *020-6243154.*
Straightforward food (fish and French dishes) in a restaurant frequented by
those in Amsterdam's bohemian circles. **V ♣ ♫**
AE DC MC V

CANAL RING: *Christophe* €€€€
Leliegracht 46. **Map** 1 B4. **☎** *020-6250807.*
Chef-owner Jean-Christophe Royer serves up terrific food for his guests –
and you can even arrive by boat, if you choose. Extensive menu.
● *Sun, Mon.* **V**
AE DC MC V

MUSEUM QUARTER: *Loetje* €
Johannes Vermeerstraat 52. **Map** 4 E4. **☎** *020-6628173.*
Loetje, an *eetcafé* in a peaceful part of Amsterdam-Zuid, serves simple but
wholesome dishes. **●** *Sat (lunch), Sun.*
AE DC MC V

MUSEUM QUARTER: *De Knijp* €€
Van Baerlestraat 134. **Map** 4 E4. **☎** *020-6714248.*
De Knijp is good for eating in a sociable, café-like atmosphere
after midnight: useful if you're feeling peckish after a concert.
● *Sat, Sun (lunch).* **V ♣**
AE DC MC V

MUSEUM QUARTER: *Sama Sebo* €€
PC Hooftstraat 27. **Map** 4 E2. **☎** *020-6628146.*
At Sama Sebo you can enjoy some wonderful traditional Indonesian dishes,
including *rijsttafel*, in a Malay-style setting. **●** *Sun.* **V &**
AE DC MC V

MUSEUM QUARTER: *Brasserie van Baerle* €€€
Van Baerlestraat 158. **Map** 4 E4. **☎** *020-6791532.*
Classy establishment run by Floor van Ede and Wilmar te Winkel.
It's best known as a chic lunch spot and has a good wine list. **V**
AE DC MC V

MUSEUM QUARTER: *Le Garage* €€€
Ruysdaelstraat 54–56. **Map** 4 E4. **☎** *020-6797176.*
TV celebrity chef Joop Braakhekke serves classical yet quirky French
dishes. Busy with prominent Dutch figures. Reservations required.
● *Sat, Sun (lunch).* **V ♫ &**
AE DC MC V

OUTSIDE THE CENTRE: *Amsterdam* €
Watertorenplein 6. **Map** off map. **☎** *020-6822666.*
An enormous restaurant (seating 260) where modest, well-presented French
dishes are served at a reasonable price. **V ♣ &**
AE DC MC V

OUTSIDE THE CENTRE: *Boerderij Meerzicht* €
Koenenkade 56. **Map** off map. **☎** *020-6792744.*
Pancakes in the Amsterdamse Bos in a convivial ambience. It is also
possible to have a barbecue inside. **V ♣ &**
AE DC MC V

OUTSIDE THE CENTRE: *Cambodja City* €
Albert Cuypstraat 58. **Map** 4 F4. **☎** *020-6714930.*
Enjoy some delightful and good value Thai, Cambodian and Vietnamese
specialities in a very laid-back atmosphere. **●** *Mon.* **V &**
MC V

OUTSIDE THE CENTRE: *De Waaghals* €
Frans Halsstraat 29. **Map** 4 F4. **☎** *020-6799609.*
Situated in a part of De Pijp where an increasing number of hotels and cater-
ing establishments are springing up, you can enjoy some deliciously cooked
vegetarian dishes. A cluttered, convivial atmosphere. **●** *Mon.* **V ♣ &**

For key to symbols see back flap

		CREDIT CARDS	**LATE OPENING**	**OUTSIDE TABLES**	**SPECIAL WINE LIST**
Price categories are for a three-course meal for one with half a bottle of house wine, including tax and service. € under €30 €€ €30–€45 €€€ €45–€60 €€€€ over €60	**CREDIT CARDS** Credit cards accepted: *AE* American Express; *DC* Diners Club; *MC* Master Card/Access; *V* Visa. **LATE OPENING** Kitchen is open after 10pm, and you can usually dine until at least 11pm. **OUTSIDE TABLES** Seating available on a terrace or garden. **SPECIAL WINE LIST** The restaurant offers a wide range of good wines.				
OUTSIDE THE CENTRE: *Mamak Den* Olympiaplein 150. **Map** 3 B5. **☎** 020-6791165. Delicious Indonesian (Sumatran) cuisine in a simple restaurant. The fish dishes and the *rendang* (curry) in particular are worth tasting. ● *Mon.* Ⓥ ♿ €		●		
OUTSIDE THE CENTRE: *Oud Zuid* Johannes Verhulststraat 64. **Map** 3 C4. **☎** 020-6766058. Oud Zuid has been reinvigorated with a new owner and staff. Ⓥ ♿ €	AE DC MC V	●		●
OUTSIDE THE CENTRE: *Soeterijn* Linnaeusstraat 2. **Map** 6 E3. **☎** 020-5688392. This restaurant belonging to the Tropenmuseum gives you the chance to try dishes from all over the world. ● *Sun.* Ⓥ ♿ €		●	■	
OUTSIDE THE CENTRE: *Amstelhaven* Mauritskade 1. **Map** 5 C4. **☎** 020-6652672. The former River Café has a new name – and a new signature dish: the Amstelburger. Disco on Fridays. ● *Sun (lunch).* Ⓥ €€		●	■	
OUTSIDE THE CENTRE: *De Berkhof* Wibautstraat 220. **Map** 5 C5. **☎** 020-6651313. The odd blemish can be overlooked in this restaurant: it is where trainees for the hotel management show their culinary arts. Food is served from 12:15pm; reservations are required. The menu changes regularly. ● *Sat, Sun.* ♿ €€		●		
OUTSIDE THE CENTRE: *De Wereldbol* Piraeusplein 59. **Map** off map. **☎** 020-3628725. In this restaurant on KNSM Island, delicious light meals with an Italian flavour are served. During the summer you can dine on the sunny harbour-side terrace and watch the ships sail past. ● *Mon, Tue.* Ⓥ ♿ €€			■	
OUTSIDE THE CENTRE: *La Vallade* Ringdijk 23. **Map** 6 F5. **☎** 020-6652025. In the Vallade *eetcafé* you get what they give you: usually French cuisine, but Indonesian on the first Saturday in the month. ♿ €€		●	■	
OUTSIDE THE CENTRE: *Mamouche* Quellijnstraat 104. **Map** 4 F4. **☎** 020-6736361. Authentic mint tea and delicious couscous are on offer at this North African teahouse. The combination of goldleaf decoration and candlelight creates an enchanting ambience. ● *Mon.* Ⓥ €€	AE DC MC V	●		
OUTSIDE THE CENTRE: *Panama* Oostelijke Handelskade 4. **Map** off map. **☎** 020-6652672. Panama is located in a well-renovated old building on the harbour to the east of the city centre. Here, one can eat dinner or enjoy a dance performance in the theatre/nightclub. Trendy crowd. Ⓥ ♫ €€	AE MC V	●	■	●
OUTSIDE THE CENTRE: *Puyck* Ceintuurbaan 147. **Map** 4 F4. **☎** 020-6767677. French-Asiatic cuisine is served in this starkly decorated restaurant. Reservations are recommended on the weekend. ● *Sun, Mon.* Ⓥ ♿ €€	MC V			●
OUTSIDE THE CENTRE: *Trèz* Saenredamstraat 39. **Map** 4 F4. **☎** 020-6762495. A restaurant where you can enjoy delightful original dishes from the Mediterranean. The menu changes regularly. Ⓥ ♿ €€		●	■	
OUTSIDE THE CENTRE: *Visaandeschelde* Scheldeplein 4. **Map** off map. **☎** 020-6751583. This is the place for fish. Try the fresh lobster or the grilled *dorade* (bream). The service is professional. ● *Sat, Sun (lunch).* €€	AE DC MC V	●	■	●

OUTSIDE THE CENTRE: *Aujourd'hui* €€€
Cornelis Krusemanstraat 15. **Map** 3 B5. **(** 020-6790877.
In this historical corner building, you can enjoy the culinary
highlights created by master chef Henk Tuin. ● *Sat (lunch), Sun.* **V** &

	AE	●	■	●
	DC			
	MC			
	V			

OUTSIDE THE CENTRE: *Kaiko* €€€
Jekerstraat 114. **Map** off map. **(** 020-6625641.
Sushi bar that is much visited by Japanese locals. Fresh ingredients
are used for all of the dishes. ● *Sun, Thu.* **V** &

	AE	●		●
	DC			
	MC			
	V			

OUTSIDE THE CENTRE: *Le Hollandais* €€€
Amsteldijk 41. **Map** off map. **(** 020-6791248.
Laid-back atmosphere in a rather nonchalant ambience and daring recipes
from an inspired chef. ● *Sun, Mon.* &

| | MC | ● | ■ | |
| | V | | | |

OUTSIDE THE CENTRE: *Restaurant en Kwekerij De Kas* €€€
Kamerlingh Onneslaan 3. **Map** off map. **(** 020-4624562.
Distinctive location in the greenhouse ("kas") of the former Amsterdam
park authorities. Freshly picked vegetables grown by the restaurant itself.
● *Sun.* **V** **Ħ** &

	AE		■	
	DC			
	MC			
	V			

OUTSIDE THE CENTRE: *Halvemaan* €€€€
Van Leijenberghlaan 20. **Map** off map. **(** 0800-022447.
Chef John Halvemaan works wonders with local ingredients,
making this an oasis in the culinary desert of Amsterdam-Buitenveldert.
● *Sat, Sun.* **V**

	AE		■	●
	DC			
	MC			
	V			

OUTSIDE THE CENTRE: *La Rive* €€€€
Prof. Tulpplein 1. **Map** 5 B4. **(** 020-5203273.
This is the Amstel Hotel restaurant. Edwin Kats is considered the best cook
in the Netherlands: the dishes he prepares are in a class of their own.
However, the prices are unusually high. Formal clothing required;
reservations are an absolute necessity. **V** **Ħ** &

	AE	●	■	●
	DC			
	MC			
	V			

OUTSIDE THE CENTRE: *Okura Hotel* €€€€
Ferdinand Bolstraat 333. **Map** 4 F5. **(** 020-6787111.
The Okura has a number of outstanding restaurants, including
Ciel Bleu (French, adventurous, with a view from the 23rd floor),
Sazanka (Japanese, unusual, *teppanyaki*) and Yamazato
(Japanese, top-quality). **V** &

	AE	●		●
	DC			
	MC			
	V			

NORTH HOLLAND

ALKMAAR: *Bios Food & Wines* €€
Gedempte Nieuwesloot 54a. **Road map** B3. **(** 072-5124422.
Arranged in a former cinema, tables are set in galleries around the old
cinema hall. The food is French cuisine. ● *Mon.*

	AE		■	●
	DC			
	MC			
	V			

DE RIJP: *Het Rijper Wapen* €€
Oosteinde 31–33. **Road map** B3. **(** 0299-671523.
The Mediterranean fish and meat dishes served in this former theatre are
truly a delight. ● *Sun, Mon.* **V** **Ħ** &

	AE		■	●
	DC			
	MC			
	V			

HAARLEM: *De Lachende Javaan* €
Frankestraat 27. **Road map** B3. **(** 023-5328792.
Feast on the finest Javan dishes, both mild and hot, in a relaxing
atmosphere. ● *Mon.* **V** **Ħ** &

	AE			
	DC			
	MC			
	V			

HAARLEM: *De Componist* €€€
Korte Veerstraat 1. **Road map** B3. **(** 023-5328853.
Here you can enjoy the Mediterranean dishes of master-chef Cor van
Dusschoten. Live piano music. **V** **Ħ** & ♫

	AE		■	●
	DC			
	MC			
	V			

HOORN: *Oasis de la Digue* €€
De Hulk 16. **Road map** C3. **(** 0229-553344.
In this former polder pumping station, you can try local dishes
such as braised duck from Beemster and pike perch from the IJsselmeer.
● *Sat (lunch), Sun.* **V** **Ħ**

	AE		■	●
	DC			
	MC			
	V			

IJMUIDEN: *Imko's* €€€
Halkade 9c. **Road map** B3. **(** 0255-517526.
Michelin-recognized fish restaurant, which gives as much
thought to the wine as to the fish. Low-key ambience.
● *Sat (lunch).* **V** **Ħ** &

	AE		■	●
	DC			
	MC			
	V			

For key to symbols see back flap

<table>
<tr><td colspan="2"></td><th>CREDIT CARDS</th><th>LATE OPENING</th><th>OUTSIDE TABLES</th><th>SPECIAL WINE LIST</th></tr>
</table>

Price categories are for a three-course meal for one with half a bottle of house wine, including tax and service.

€ under €30
€€ €30–€45
€€€ €45–€60
€€€€ over €60

CREDIT CARDS
Credit cards accepted: *AE* American Express; *DC* Diners Club; *MC* MasterCard/Access; *V* Visa.
LATE OPENING
Kitchen is open after 10pm, and you can usually dine until at least 11pm.
OUTSIDE TABLES
Seating available on a terrace or garden.
SPECIAL WINE LIST
The restaurant offers a wide range of good wines.

	CREDIT CARDS	LATE OPENING	OUTSIDE TABLES	SPECIAL WINE LIST
MUIDEN: *De Doelen* €€ Sluis 1. **Road map** C3. *0294-263200.* Here you can enjoy the finest French dishes in a relaxed atmosphere in a lovely village on the Vecht. ● *Sat, Sun (lunch).* V ᚻ &	AE DC MC V			●
NAARDEN-VESTING: *Het Arsenaal* €€€ Kooltjesbuurt 1. **Road map** C3. *035-6949148.* Master-chef Paul Fagel displays his culinary skills in a restaurant designed by Jan des Bouvrie. ● *Mon.* V ᚻ &	AE DC MC V		▨	●
OUDERKERK AAN DE AMSTEL: *Restaurant Ron Blaauw* €€€€ Kerkstraat 56. **Road map** C3. *020-4961943.* Much sought-after restaurant run by chef Ron Blaauw. Pricey, but wonderful experiments with the taste buds. ● *Sat (lunch), Sun.* V ᚻ &	AE DC MC V			●
OVERVEEN: *De Bokkedoorns* €€€€ Zeeweg 53. **Road map** B3. *023-5263600.* Top restaurant with two stars from Michelin, where chef Lucas Rive gives vent to his culinary skills; the menu includes, among other things, rouleau of home-made venison ham with lobster and salad of oxheart cabbage. ● *Mon.* V	AE DC MC V		▨	●
SCHOORL: *Restaurant Hotel Merlet* €€€ Duinweg 15. **Road map** B3. *072-5093644.* Provence-style establishment behind the Hondsbossche Zeewering; perfect fish, relaxing atmosphere. 18 hotel rooms. ● *Sat (lunch).* V ᚻ &	AE DC MC V		▨	●
WIJDEWORMER: *Mario Uva* €€€ Neck 15. **Road map** B3. *0299-423949.* A seven-course menu of north Italian specialities changing on a daily basis. Chef Mario, his son Rafaele and mother Tini are there to pamper you. There are four hotel rooms for dinner guests. ● *Mon.* V ᚻ &	AE DC MC V		▨	●
ZAANDAM: *De Hoop op d'Swarte Walvis* €€€ Kalverringdijk 15. **Road map** B3. *075-6165629.* Situated in a pleasant historical building, where you can taste the finest French-Dutch dishes in a relaxing atmosphere. ● *Sat (lunch), Sun.* V & ♫	AE DC MC V		▨	●

UTRECHT

	CREDIT CARDS	LATE OPENING	OUTSIDE TABLES	SPECIAL WINE LIST
AMERONGEN: *Den Rooden Leeuw* €€€ Drostestraat 35. **Road map** C4. *0343-454055.* Located in a period building where on Sundays from 12–9:30pm a limited menu is served at long dining tables. ● *Tue, Wed.* V ᚻ &	AE DC MC V		▨	
AMERSFOORT: *De Raadspensionaris* €€ Krommestraat 2. **Road map** C4. *033-4623006.* This is a tiny restaurant with a fixed menu, but of surprisingly good quality. Despite its small size, there is a non-smoking area. ● *Sun, Mon.* V	AE DC MC V	●	▨	●
BOSCH EN DUIN: *De Hoefslag* €€€€ Vossenlaan 28. **Road map** C4. *030-2251051.* Renowned restaurant where chef Niels van Halen will surprise you with some amazing culinary creations. ● *Sun (bistro remains open).* V ᚻ &	AE DC MC V	●	▨	●
DRIEBERGEN: *Lai Sin's* €€€€ Arnhemsebovenweg 46. **Road map** C3. *0343-516858.* Original Chinese dishes of excellent quality make Lai Sin's a popular restaurant. Reservations are a necessity. ● *Sat (lunch), Sun, Mon.* V &	AE DC MC V		▨	●
HOUTEN: *Kasteel Heemstede* €€€ Heemsteedseweg 20. **Road map** C3. *030-2722207.* This refined restaurant is set in the basement of a restored castle and looks out over the gardens. A non-smoking area is available. ● *Sun.* V &	AE DC MC V	●	▨	●

LOENE AAN DE VECHT: *De Proeverij*	€€€	AE	●	■	
Kerkstraat 5a. **Road map** C4. **[** *0294-234774.*		DC			
Fine dinners are served here in a relaxed, traditional setting.		MC			
If you can't get in here, Tante Koosje is nearby and also excellent.		V			
● *lunchtime; Mon, Tue.* **V** **↟**					

MAARSSEN: *Auguste*	€€€	AE	●	■	●
Straatweg 144. **Road map** C4. **[** *0346-565666.*		DC			
French-Italian restaurant with a modern ambience. Top-notch welcome		MC			
and service. ● *Sat (lunch), Sun.* **V** **&**		V			

UTRECHT: *Goesting*	€€€	AE	●	■	●
Veeartsenijpad 150. **Road map** C4. **[** *030-2733346.*		DC			
This pretty, luxurious restaurant set in a park serves stylish dishes.		MC			
● *Sun; Christmas Day, New Year's Eve, New Year's Day.* **V** **↟**		V			

UTRECHT: *Jean d'Hubert*	€€€€	AE	●		●
Vleutenseweg 228. **Road map** C4. **[** *030-2945952.*		DC			
Two young brothers offer innovative dishes here. Great atmosphere too.		MC			
● *Sun, Mon.* **V**		V			

UTRECHT: *Wilhelminapark*	€€€€	AE		■	●
Wilhelminapark 65. **Road map** C4. **[** *030-2510693.*		DC			
Classy restaurant in stunningly peaceful park location. Pleasant atmosphere		MC			
and attentive service. Reservations are recommended. ● *Sat, Sun.* **V** **&**		V			

SOUTH HOLLAND

DELFT: *Le Vieux Jean*	€€€	AE	●	■	●
Heilige Geestkerkhof 3. **Road map** B4. **[** *015-2130433.*		DC			
Original French cooking in a homely restaurant. Fine French wines,		MC			
friendly and attentive service. ● *Sat (lunch), Sun, Mon.* **V** **&**		V			

DELFT: *De Zwethheul*	€€€€	AE		■	●
Rotterdamseweg 480. **Road map** B4. **[** *010-4704166.*		DC			
Up-and-coming chef Erik van Loo takes a fascinating approach here:		MC			
sumptuous menus with a wine arrangement. Excellent service.		V			
One Michelin star. ● *Sat & Sun (lunch), Mon.* **V** **&**					

DORDRECHT: *De Stroper*	€€	AE	●	■	
Wijnbrug 1. **Road map** B4. **[** *078-6130094.*		DC			
Very sociable, crowded canalside restaurant. Known for its many fish		MC			
specialities. ● *Sat, Sun (lunch).* ▤		V			

GORINCHEM: *Solo*	€€	AE			
Zusterhuis 1–2. **Road map** C4. **[** *0183-637791.*		DC			
Inventive international food in a café setting; excellent house wine.		MC			
● *Sat (lunch), Sun (lunch).* **V** **↟** **&**		V			

GOUDA: *De Mallemolen*	€€	AE		■	●
Oosthaven 72. **Road map** B4. **[** *0182-515430.*		DC			
A modest little eatery located in a splendid old building, serving traditional		MC			
French food. ● *Mon.* **V** **↟**		V			

THE HAGUE: *Aubergerie*	€€	AE		■	
Nieuwe Schoolstraat 19. **Road map** B4. **[** *070-3648070.*		DC			
Near the theatre Pepijn you can dine on subtle French dishes. Both the		MC			
duck's liver and *crème brûlée* are very popular. ● *Sat (lunch), Sun & Mon.*		V			

THE HAGUE: *Julien*	€€€	AE		■	
Vos in Tuinstraat 2a. **Road map** B4. **[** *070-3658602.*		DC			
Traditional French offerings in the stylish atmosphere of The Hague.		MC			
Impeccable service. ● *Sun.* **V** **↟**		V			

THE HAGUE: *Le Bistroquet*	€€€	AE	●	■	●
Lange Voorhout 98. **Road map** B4. **[** *070-3601170.*		DC			
This restaurant, located on the Voorhout, offers classic dishes, fine		MC			
wines and an intimate atmosphere. Regulars include prominent politicians.		V			
● *Sat (lunch), Sun.* **↟** **&**					

THE HAGUE: *The Raffles*	€€€	AE		■	●
Javastraat 63. **Road map** B4. **[** *070-3458587.*		DC			
Enjoy delicious Indonesian specialities in a relaxed atmosphere. Friendly		MC			
and attentive service; some astonishing wines on the wine list. ● *Sun.* **V** **&**		V			

<table>
<tr><td colspan="2">

Price categories are for a three-course meal for one with half a bottle of house wine, including tax and service.

€ under €30
€€ €30–€45
€€€ €45–€60
€€€€ over €60

</td><td colspan="4">

CREDIT CARDS
Credit cards accepted: *AE* American Express; *DC* Diners Club; *MC* MasterCard/Access; *V* Visa.
LATE OPENING
Kitchen is open after 10pm, and you can usually dine until at least 11pm.
OUTSIDE TABLES
Seating available on a terrace or garden.
SPECIAL WINE LIST
The restaurant offers a wide range of good wines.

</td></tr>
</table>

	CREDIT CARDS	LATE OPENING	OUTSIDE TABLES	SPECIAL WINE LIST
LEIDEN: *De Jonge Koekop* €€ Lange Mare 60. **Road map** B3. (071-5141937. Innovative food – from France and much further afield – is served here in a 19th-century warehouse. ● *Sun (lunch).* 🟦 🔴 ⛎	MC V			
LEIDEN: *Engelbertha Hoeve* €€€ Hoge Morsweg 140. **Road map** B3. (071-5765000. Classic French dishes served in an attractive setting: an old farmstead on the water, just outside the city centre. ● *Sat, Sun (lunch), Mon.* 🟦 🔴 ⛎	AE DC MC V		■	●
ROTTERDAM: *La Vilette* €€ Westblaak 160. **Road map** B4. (010-4148692. Fred Mustert's fusion creations result in an astonishing combination of dishes with balanced flavours. Original menu at affordable prices. Professional service. ● *Sat (lunch), Sun.*	AE DC MC V			
ROTTERDAM: *De Engel* €€€ Eendrachtsweg 19. **Road map** B4. (010-4138256. Busy renowned restaurant with a Mediterranean menu. Only the finest ingredients are used. ● *Sun.* 🟦	AE DC MC V	●		
ROTTERDAM: *Parkheuvel* €€€€ Heuvellaan 21. **Road map** B4. (010-4360766. One of the best restaurants in South Holland and the country's only Michelin three-starred restaurant. Informal but proper service. ● *Sat (lunch), Sun.* 🔴 ⛎	AE DC MC V		■	●
SCHEVENINGEN: *Seinpost* €€€ Zeekant 60. **Road map** B4. (070-3555250. Fantastically good fish dishes in a restaurant with a view of the sea. Exemplary service. ● *Sat (lunch), Sun & hols.* 🟦 🔴 ⛎	AE DC MC V			●
VOORBURG: *Savelberg* €€€€ Oosteinde 14. **Road map** B4. (070-3872081. Top restaurant in a pleasant country house. Terrific wines and menus. Overnight accommodation is also available. ● *Sat (lunch), Sun & Mon.* 🟦 🔴 ⛎	AE DC V		■	●
ZEELAND				
GOES: *La Dolce Vita* € Piet Heinstraat 3a. **Road map** A5. (0113-221339. Italian-inspired cooking full of surprises. A lavish meal can be had at a decidedly low price. ● *Mon, Tue.* 🔴	DC MC V			
KRUININGEN: *Inter Scaldes* €€€€ Zandweg 2. **Road map** A5. (0113-381753. This is Zeeland's top restaurant. Everything is perfect: exquisite dishes, good service, fine wine list. Overnight accommodation available. ● *Mon, Tue.* 🟦 🔴 ⛎ 🎵	AE DC MC V	●	■	●
MIDDELBURG: *Het Groot Paradijs* €€€ Damplein 13. **Road map** A5. (0118-651200. Elegant restaurant in the provincial capital of Zeeland offering excellent fish and meat dishes with a local touch. ● *Sat (lunch), Sun & Mon (lunch).* 🟦 🔴	AE DC MC V	●	■	
SLUIS: *Oud Sluis* €€€ Beestenmarkt 2. **Road map** A5. (0117-461269. Down-to-earth meals in a restaurant with a fine view of the Oosterschelde. Excellent Zeeland lobster. ● *Mon, Tue.* 🟦 🔴 ⛎	AE DC MC V	●	■	
VLISSINGEN: *Grand Hotel Arion* €€ Boulevard Bankert 266. **Road map** A5. (0118-410502. Spacious restaurant with a pleasant atmosphere offering excellent fish dishes. Friendly service. 🟦 🔴 ⛎ 🎵		●	■	

YERSEKE: *Nolet 'Het Reymerswale'* €€€€
Jachthaven 5. **Road map** A5. **(** *0113-571642*.
This intriguing restaurant in Yerseke serves typical dishes of Zeeland such as
mussels, lobster and oysters, as well as game. ● *Mon, Tue, Wed.* **V ⚥ &**
DC MC V

WEST FRISIAN ISLANDS

SCHIERMONNIKOOG: *Van der Werff* €€
Reeweg 2. **Road map** D1. **(** *0519-531203*.
The restaurant of the renowned hotel of the same name on
Schiermonnikoog serves good, hearty fare. **V ⚥ & ♫**
DC MC V

TERSCHELLING (TERSCHELLING-WEST): *Zeezicht* €
Willem Barentszkade 20. **Road map** C1. **(** *0562-442268*.
Eat well in the convivial atmosphere of a restaurant with a spectacular view
of the sea. Very affordable prices. **V ⚥ &**

TEXEL (DEN BURG): *Het Vierspan* €€€
Gravenstraat 3. **Road map** B2. **(** *0222-313176*.
Het Vierspan serves some very good fish dishes; however, Texel lamb is the
restaurant's speciality. ● *Mon, Tue.* **V ⚥**
AE MC V

GRONINGEN

ADUARD: *Onder de Linden* €€€€
Burgemeester van Barneveldweg 3. **Road map** D1. **(** *050-4031406*.
Superb restaurant in a restored inn from 1733. Traditional dishes,
an exceptional wine list and attentive service. ● *Sun, Mon.* **V &**
AE DC MC V

GRONINGEN: *De Parelvisser* €€€
Gelkingestraat 58–60. **Road map** D1. **(** *050-3686044*.
Refined, imaginative fish dishes are served in this new restaurant in the
Schimmelpennick Huys (*see p398*). ● *Sat (lunch), Sun, Mon.* **V &**
AE DC MC V

GRONINGEN: *Muller* €€€€
Grote Kromme Elleboog 13. **Road map** D1. **(** *050-3183208*.
Delicious food in a lively restaurant where Alsatian chef Jean-Michel Hengge
demonstrates his culinary skills. ● *lunchtime; Sun, Mon.* **V ⚥**
AE DC MC V

LEENS: *Schathoes Verhildersum* €€€
Wierde 42. **Road map** D1. **(** *0595-572204*.
Fine food in the picturesque Verhildersum castle, with good service and low
prices. The chef uses local ingredients in the menu. ● *Mon, Tue.* **V ⚥ &**
AE DC MC V

MOLENRIJ: *'t Korensant* €€
H van Cappenbergweg 34. **Road map** E2. **(** *0595-481134*.
Chef Wicher Werk doesn't shy away from daring combinations of flavours,
and the results are unfailingly good. ● *Mon, Tue.* **V ⚥ &**
MC V

FRIESLAND

BEETSTERZWAAG: *De Heeren van Harinxma* €€€€
Van Harinxmaweg 10. **Road map** D2. **(** *0512-381245*.
The restaurant on the attractive Lauswolt estate serves imaginative dishes,
at a pace suited to *bon vivants*. ● *Sat (lunch), Sun.* **V ⚥ &**
AE DC MC V

BOLSWARD: *De Lavendelhof* €€
Nieuwmarkt 24. **Road map** C2. **(** *0515-577988*.
Good food in a magnificent building in Bolsward: oven-baked scampi, veal
loin with duck's liver rolls and fillet of guinea fowl are favourites. ● *Sun.* **V &**
AE DC MC V

DRACHTEN: *Koriander* €€€
Burg. Wuiteweg 18. **Road map** D2. **(** *0512-548850*.
Very popular establishment on two floors run by chef Gaastra.
Fantastic desserts. One Michelin star. ● *Mon, Tue.* **V ⚥ &**
AE DC MC V

HARLINGEN: *De Gastronoom* €€
Voorstraat 38. **Road map** C2. **(** *0517-412172*.
Wonderfully delectable creations in an outstanding restaurant run by
Marco Poldervaart. ● *Mon.* **V ⚥ &**
AE DC MC V

LEEUWARDEN: *Eindeloos* €€
Korfmakersstraat 17. **Road map** D1. **(** *058-2130835*.
Chef Marcel Haven, with Nynke Jansma at front of house, provides
high-quality dinners. ● *lunchtime; Mon, Tue.* **V ⚥**
MC V

		CREDIT CARDS	LATE OPENING	OUTSIDE TABLES	SPECIAL WINE LIST

Price categories are for a three-course meal for one with half a bottle of house wine, including tax and service.

€ under €30
€€ €30–€45
€€€ €45–€60
€€€€ over €60

CREDIT CARDS
Credit cards accepted: *AE* American Express; *DC* Diners Club; *MC* MasterCard/Access; *V* Visa.
LATE OPENING
Kitchen is open after 10pm, and you can usually dine until at least 11pm.
OUTSIDE TABLES
Seating available on a terrace or garden.
SPECIAL WINE LIST
The restaurant offers a wide range of good wines.

MAKKUM: *It Posthûs*   €€

	CREDIT CARDS	LATE OPENING	OUTSIDE TABLES	SPECIAL WINE LIST
	MC V	●	■	

Plein 15. **Road map** D1. 📞 0515-231153.
Séan O'Connor cooks some good Irish meals, as well as dishes with some
French influences. Convivial atmosphere, good service. ● *Mon.* **V** 🏃

DRENTHE

ASSEN: *De Gulle Gans*   €€

MC V	●		■	

Markt 18. **Road map** D2. 📞 0592-302427.
This busy restaurant is open only at dinnertime. The food and the service
get top marks. ● *lunchtime; Mon.* **V** 🏃 ♿

COEVORDEN: *Gasterie Het Kasteel*   €€

AE DC MC V	●	■		●

Kasteel 29. **Road map** E3. 📞 0524-512170.
First-class food in the vaulted cellar and garden of Coevorden castle.
A non-smoking area is available. ● *Sat (lunch), Sun & Mon.* **V** 🏃

DE SCHIPHORST: *De Havixborst*   €€€

AE DC MC V	●	■		

Schiphorsterweg 34–36. **Road map** D3. 📞 0522-441487.
Jos Wijnland's restaurant, in an imposing historic building, is known for its
excellent food. Accommodation also available. ● *Sat (lunch), Sun & Mon.* **V** 🏃

EMMEN: *La Couronne*   €€

AE MC	●	■		

Zuidbargerstraat 108. **Road map** E2. 📞 0591-630813.
Delicious food offered at a restaurant where they don't shun
experimentation. Attentive service. The challenge is finding this establishment, as it is located some way outside the town. ● *Sat (lunch), Sun.* **V**

ZUIDLAREN: *De Vlindertuin*   €€€

AE DC MC V	●	■		

Stationsweg 41. **Road map** E2. 📞 050-4094531.
Pleasantly appointed establishment serving high-quality dishes.
Both traditional and tasty. ● *Sun, Mon.* **V** ♿ ♫

ZWEELOO: *Idylle*   €€€

AE DC MC V	●	■		

Kruisstraat 21. **Road map** E2. 📞 0591-371857.
Exceptionally good food in Drenthe's finest restaurant, which is situated
in an old thatched farmhouse. Peaceful atmosphere, beautiful garden.
● *Sat (lunch), Mon.* **V** 🏃 ♿

OVERIJSSEL

BLOKZIJL: *Kaatje bij de Sluis*   €€€€

AE DC MC V	●	■		●

Brouwerstraat 20. **Road map** D2. 📞 0527-291833.
Fantastic food from the kitchen of André Mol, with his sublime culinary
creations. Accommodation available. Not cheap, but very special.
● *Sat (lunch), Mon & Tue.* **V** 🏃

DELDEN: *In den Drost van Twenthe*   €€€

AE DC MC V	●	■		●

Hengelosestraat 8. **Road map** E3. 📞 074-3764055.
An outstanding restaurant which offers classical dishes. Has a very good
wine list. ● *Sat (lunch), Sun.* **V** 🏃 ♿

ENSCHEDE: *Het Koetshuis Schuttersveld*   €€€€

AE DC MC V	●	■		

Hengelosestraat 111. **Road map** E3. 📞 053-4322866.
Convivial and pleasantly designed restaurant where you can try traditional
dishes such as pheasant with sauerkraut and truffles. Attentive service, nice
relaxed atmosphere. ● *Sat (lunch), Sun & Mon.* **V** 🏃

GIETHOORN: *De Lindenhof*   €€€€

AE DC MC V	●	■		●

Beulakerweg 4. **Road map** D2. 📞 0521-361444.
De Lindenhof is housed in a cosy little building with a reed-thatched roof.
Top-class culinary performances, with pleasant service bordering on the
nonchalant. ● *Thu.* **V** 🏃 ♿

HAAKSBERGEN: *Villa De Blanckenborgh* €€€
Enschedesetraat 65. **Road map** E4. ☎ 053-5741155.
This convivial restaurant in a converted villa serves specialities such as
Veluwe venison with fried aubergine. ● *Sat (lunch), Mon.* 🔽 🔆 ₺
| AE | DC | MC | V |

HARDENBERG: *De Bokkepruik* €€€
Hessenweg 7. **Road map** E3. ☎ 0523-261504.
De Bokkepruik serves delicious classical fare. Good service.
Overnight accommodation available. ● *Sat (lunch), Sun.* 🔽 🔆
| AE | DC | MC | V |

HENGELO: *Le Rossignol* €€€
CT Storksstraat 18. **Road map** E3. ☎ 074-2910066.
The restaurant of the Hotel 't Lansink will surprise you, and for a very
reasonable price. ● *Sat (lunch), Sun.* 🔽 🔆 ₺
| AE | DC | MC | V |

ZWOLLE: *De Librije* €€€€
Broerenkerkplein 13. **Road map** D3. ☎ 038-4212083.
De Librije is housed in a pleasant period building with a classical dining
room: the food is top-class and the service superb. Chef Jonnie Boer is
an artist. Overnight accommodation available. ● *Sun, Mon.* 🔽 🔆
| AE | DC | MC | V |

FLEVOLAND

ALMERE: *Bakboord* €€
Veerkade 10. **Road map** C3. ☎ 036-5404040.
Nice restaurant with a good French kitchen and an attractive view over the
harbour. Attentive service and pleasant terrace. 🔽 🔆 ₺
| AE | MC | V |

EMMELOORD: *Le Mirage* €€
Beursstraat 2. **Road map** D2. ☎ 0527-699104.
Terrific French fish and meat dishes are served in this pleasant eatery with
first-class service. 🔽 🔆 ₺
| AE | DC | MC | V |

URK: *Mes Amis* €€
Wijkstraat 1–65. **Road map** C3. ☎ 0527-688736.
This cosy restaurant overlooks the busy harbour. Fish dishes are the high
point of the menu. Good value for money. ● *Sat (lunch), Sun.* 🔽 🔆
| AE | DC | MC | V |

GELDERLAND

AALST: *De Fuik* €€€€
Maasdijk 1. **Road map** C4. ☎ 0418-552247.
In De Fuik you can dine well on French-oriented meals – as well as have
a nice view of the river Maas. ● *Mon.* 🔽 🔆 ₺
| AE | DC | MC | V |

BUREN: *Proeverijen De Gravin* €€€
Kerkstraat 4–5. **Road map** C4. ☎ 0344-571663.
An Austrian chef serves superb French cuisine in this tasteful restaurant in
the Betuwse Buren. Rather pricey. ● *Sat, Sun, Mon (lunch).* 🔽 🔆 ₺
| AE | DC | MC | V |

HARDERWIJK: *Olivio* €€€
Vischmarkt 57a. **Road map** C3. ☎ 0341-415290.
French-oriented cuisine in a lively restaurant on a charming little square in
the middle of the town. ● *Sun, Mon.* 🔽 🔆
| AE | MC | V |

HOOG-SOEREN: *De Echoput* €€€€
Amersfoortseweg 86. **Road map** D3. ☎ 055-5191248.
Refined, delicious meals from the kitchen of Theus de Kok. Magnificent
wines to accompany your meal. ● *Sat (lunch), Mon.* 🔽 🔆
| AE | DC | MC | V |

HOOG-SOEREN: *Het Jachthuis* €€€
Hoog Soeren 55. **Road map** D3. ☎ 055-5191397.
Good food is served in this picturesquely located restaurant.
🔲 *from 5pm (Sun from 1pm).* 🔽 🔆
| AE | DC | MC | V |

NIJKERK: *De Salentein* €€€
Putterstraatweg 7–9. **Road map** C3. ☎ 033-2454114.
This lively, well-run family restaurant serves exquisite food such as smoked
breast of pigeon with pineapple vinaigrette. ● *Sun, Mon.* 🔽 🔆 ₺
| AE | MC | V |

NIJMEGEN: *De Fusie* €€€
Waalkade 1. **Road map** D4. ☎ 024-3606264.
Fusion cuisine in this restaurant on the Waal: decent prices, with outdoor
seating in fine weather. Reservations are essential. ● *Mon.* 🔽 🔆 ₺
| AE | DC | MC | V |

<table>
<tr><td colspan="2">
Price categories are for a three-course meal for one with half a bottle of house wine, including tax and service.

€ under €30
€€ €30–€45
€€€ €45–€60
€€€€ over €60
</td><td colspan="5">
CREDIT CARDS
Credit cards accepted: *AE* American Express; *DC* Diners Club; *MC* MasterCard/Access; *V* Visa.
LATE OPENING
Kitchen is open after 10pm, and you can usually dine until at least 11pm.
OUTSIDE TABLES
Seating available on a terrace or garden.
SPECIAL WINE LIST
The restaurant offers a wide range of good wines.
</td></tr>
</table>

	CREDIT CARDS	LATE OPENING	OUTSIDE TABLES	SPECIAL WINE LIST
ZALTBOMMEL: *La Provence* €€ Gamersestraat 81. **Road map** C4. ☎ 0418-514070. This restaurant serves good, hearty traditional French food. Quality fare, reasonably priced. ● *Sat (lunch), Sun & Mon.* V 👥 ♿	AE DC MC V		■	
ZUTPHEN: *Bij d'n open haard* €€ Houtmarkt 60. **Road map** D4. ☎ 0575-512165. Intriguing medieval dishes are served in this restaurant, located in this Hanseatic city in a listed building dating from 1400. Friendly service. ● *Mon–Wed.* V 👥	V	●		

NORTH BRABANT

	CREDIT CARDS	LATE OPENING	OUTSIDE TABLES	SPECIAL WINE LIST
BREDA: *De Sinjoor* € Nieuwe Ginnekenstraat 3. **Road map** B5. ☎ 076-5211199. *Eetcafé*-style atmosphere in this lively restaurant; good, original food at low prices. V 👥 ♿	AE DC MC V		■	
BREDA: *Wolfslaar Restaurant* €€ Wolfslaardreef 100. **Road map** B5. ☎ 076-5608080. Stylish restaurant in the former coach-house of the Wolfslaar estate, with beautifully presented food and good service. Terrace tables look out over the park. ● *Sat (lunch), Sun, Mon.* V 👥 ♿	AE DC MC V		■	●
EINDHOVEN: *De Karpendonkse Hoeve* €€€€ Sumatralaan 3. **Road map** C5. ☎ 040-2813663. Renowned and welcoming restaurant where the chef provides guests with simple but delicious meals. ● *Sun.* V 👥	AE DC MC V	●	■	●
EINDHOVEN: *De Luytervelde* €€ Jo Goudkuillaan 11. **Road map** C5. ☎ 040-2622090. Pretty restaurant in a huge farmhouse from 1912, where chef Leon Bogers offers French and international food. Garden. ● *Sat (lunch), Sun.* V 👥 ♿	AE DC MC V		■	
GEERTRUIDENBERG: *'t Weeshuis* €€€ Markt 52–56. **Road map** C4. ☎ 0162-516002. Cosy restaurant set in a lovely building from 1436. Good French food and reliable service. ● *Sat, Sun (lunch).* V	AE MC V		■	
HEEZE: *Hostellerie Van Gaalen* €€ Kapelstraat 48. **Road map** C5. ☎ 040-2263515. The Mediterranean décor and cooking is of high quality in this restaurant on the edge of the Strabrechtse Heide. Pleasant atmosphere, punctilious service. Accommodation available. ● *Sat (lunch), Sun & Mon (lunch).* V 👥	AE DC MC V			
HEEZE: *Boreas* €€€ Jan Deckersstraat 7. **Road map** C5. ☎ 040-2263232. This new restaurant puts its own spin on French dishes, such as *grietpotje* with truffles. The lovely terrace is ringed with plane trees. ● *Sun, Mon.* V 👥 ♿	AE DC MC V		■	
'S-HERTOGENBOSCH: *Indonesia* € Kruisstraat 35. **Road map** C4. ☎ 073-6147772. Strikingly friendly restaurant, serving speciality dishes from central Java. Friendly service and decent prices. A real treat after a long day of sightseeing. V 👥 ♿	AE DC MC V	●		●
'S-HERTOGENBOSCH: *Châlet Royal* €€€ Wilhelminaplein 1. **Road map** C4. ☎ 073-6135771. Outstanding French cuisine is served in this former villa. Pleasant atmosphere, good service. Reservations recommended but not always necessary. ● *Sun, Mon.* V 👥	AE DC MC V		■	●

HOOGERHEIDE: *La Castelière* €€€ | MC ▪ ●
Nijverheidsstraat 28. **Road map** B5. ☎ 0164-612612. | V
A welcoming and very good restaurant in a picturesque setting. Attentive
service. Magnificent wines. Accommodation available. ● *Sun–Tue.* **V**

OISTERWIJK: *De Swaen* €€€€ | AE ● ▪ ●
De Lind 47. **Road map** C5. ☎ 013-5233233. | DC
Renowned restaurant run by celebrity chef Cas Spijkers. Refined, strong | MC
tastes, albeit slightly on the dear side. ● *Sun, Mon.* **V** ⚡ & | V

OVERLOON: *De Heeren van Overloon* €€€ | AE ● ▪
Irenestraat 1. **Road map** D5. ☎ 0478-642227. | MC
Excellent food is served in a cosy atmosphere in this Overloon restaurant.
Friendly and attentive service. Fresh ingredients. ● *Mon.* **V** ⚡

LIMBURG

GULPEN: *Le Sapiche* €€€ | AE ▪ ●
Rijksweg 12. **Road map** D6. ☎ 043-4503833. | MC
"French, young and fresh rolled into one", as chef Sascha Cremers puts it. | V
Imaginative food. Excellent service. ● *Tue, Wed.* **V** ⚡

HEERLEN: *De Boterbloem* €€€ | AE ▪ ●
Laanderstraat 27. **Road map** D6. ☎ 045-5714241. | DC
A small restaurant offering some fine dishes such as *zwezerik* (sweetbreads) | MC
on a sauerkraut stew with stewed apple. Friendly service. ● *Sat (lunch), Sun.* | V

KERKRADE: *Kasteel Erenstein* €€€ | AE ▪ ●
Oud Erensteinerweg 6. **Road map** D6. ☎ 045-5461333. | DC
In the middle of the Limburg hills is the medieval castle Erenstein, | MC
where excellent food is served. Accommodation is also available. | V
● *lunchtime; Sun.* **V** ⚡

MAASBRACHT: *Da Vinci* €€ | AE ●
Havenstraat 27. **Road map** D6. ☎ 0475-465979. | DC
This restaurant has an enjoyable combination of architecture, atmosphere and | MC
food. The meat dishes are especially good. ● *Sat (lunch), Mon & Tue.* **V** ⚡ | V

MAASTRICHT: *Beluga* €€€€ | AE ▪ ●
Plein 1992, No.12. **Road map** D6. ☎ 043-3213364. | DC
Beluga serves Mediterranean dishes in a lively restaurant. The fish dishes | MC
in particular are commendable. ● *Sat, Sun (lunch), Mon.* | V

MAASTRICHT: *Château Neercanne* €€€€ | AE ▪ ●
Cannerweg 800. **Road map** D6. ☎ 043-3251359. | DC
Stylish restaurant in a magnificent castle. Excellent dining, on the terrace | MC
in summer, while enjoying a view of the surrounding countryside. | V
Delicious wines. ● *Sat (lunch), Mon.* **V** ⚡ &

MAASTRICHT: *Toine Hermsen* €€€€ | AE ●
Sint Bernardusstraat 2–4. **Road map** D6. ☎ 043-3258400. | DC
Culinary expert and proprietor Toine Hermsen treats his guests to | MC
sumptuous meals in this tastefully appointed top restaurant. Relaxed | V
service, reasonable prices. ● *Sat (lunch), Sun, Mon.* **V** ⚡

UBACHSBERG: *De Leuf* €€€ | AE ▪ ●
Dalstraat 2. **Road map** D6. ☎ 045-5750226. | DC
This pleasantly furnished farmhouse serves delicious food in a friendly | MC
atmosphere. Accommodation available. ● *Sat (lunch), Sun & Mon.* **V** ⚡ & | V

VALKENBURG: *Château St Gerlach* €€€€ | AE ▪ ●
Joseph Corneli Allée 1. **Road map** D6. ☎ 043-6088888. | DC
Enjoy local dishes in Les Trois Corbeaux restaurant, situated in this | MC
magnificent castle. Accommodation available. ● *Sat (lunch), Mon.* **V** ⚡ & | V

VALKENBURG: *Prinses Juliana* €€€€ | AE ▪ ●
Broekhem 11. **Road map** D6. ☎ 043-6012244. | DC
The fish dishes are especially commendable in this pleasant, stylish | MC
restaurant with its tasteful furnishing. French cuisine. Accommodation | V
available. ● *Sat (lunch).* ⚡ &

WITTEM: *Kasteel Wittem* €€€ | AE ▪ ●
Wittemer Allée 3. **Road map** D6. ☎ 043-4501208. | DC
This beautiful castle belonging to Peter and Marc Ritzen has a stylish restaurant | MC
serving magnificent food. Accommodation available. ● *Mon–Thu (lunch).* **V** | V

For key to symbols see back flap

SHOPPING IN HOLLAND

Children's clothes

THROUGHOUT HOLLAND you will find a huge range of shops and markets. Many towns have shops and department stores belonging to large retail chains, but you will also find unique independent shops selling clothes, everyday goods and knick-knacks. Large specialized shops such as furniture stores, factory outlets and garden centres are usually on the outskirts of towns and sometimes grouped together in retail parks with parking facilities, child-care facilities and a cafeteria. Most are open on public holidays, which is usually when they are the busiest. Recent fashion items and worn leather jackets can often be picked up cheaply at street markets and second-hand shops.

Shop selling antiques and engrossing curios

MARKETS

PRACTICALLY EVERY town and village holds a general market at least once a week. There are also specialized markets, for example, the farmers' markets, where you can buy fresh farm produce, as well as antique markets and book fairs. Famous specialized markets include the cheese markets of Alkmaar, Edam and Gouda. Then there are also flea markets, where traders and individuals alike sell second-hand goods.

Holland's biggest flea market takes place on Koninginnedag (Queen's Day) *(see p32)*, when practically half of the country tries to get rid of unwanted goods on the street. Fairs are also popular events and are held twice a year. Most markets start at 9:30am and shut at 4pm or 5pm, while some are open either in the mornings or the afternoons only.

ANTIQUES

ANTIQUE COLLECTORS will find plenty to occupy themselves with in Holland. If you are fortunate, you may strike it lucky in second-hand shops or at flea markets, but likely your best bet is to go to an authentic antique dealer. Many antique dealers specialize in a particular period or a particular field – prints or clocks, for instance. If you prefer buying antiques at auctions, you would probably do best to visit the branches of the international auctioneers **Sotheby's** or **Christie's**. In smaller auction houses too, interesting pieces often go under the hammer. Another way of buying antiques is to visit the antique markets and fairs that are held regularly throughout the country.

Amsterdam's Nieuwe Spiegelstraat is the place for antique collectors. Vendors include antique dealers specializing in ceramics, glass, antique prints, paintings and nautical memorabilia.

Haarlem, Middelburg and 's-Hertogenbosch have particularly large numbers of antique shops; these are often located in old farmhouses. The most common pieces on sale are pine or oak furniture. The **MECC** in Maastricht and the **Brabant-hallen** in 's-Hertogenbosch are the venues of annual antique fairs, such as the renowned TFFAF, the world's biggest art and antique fair. Antique dealers from around the world come here to trade.

FASHION

Antique dealer's shop sign

THE DUTCH are spending more and more of their incomes on good-quality fashionable clothing. Besides internationally renowned couturiers, many up-and-coming fashion designers set up their own boutiques. Their clothes are often hand-made and fairly pricey. More affordable clothes are available at the larger fashion retailers, both home-grown and international. A typical Dutch way of being fashionable is to combine a new and expensive garment with second-hand clothes. To see the designs of the most famous couturiers, it is best to go to Amsterdam. On the PC Hooftstraat you will find clothes by Hugo Boss, Armani and Yves Saint-Laurent, among others. Classical English clothing and shoes are to be found in the shops on the Haagse Noordeinde in The Hague. Chains such as Burberry's and K-Shoes sell plain, everyday and durable clothing.

One of the many antique and second-hand shops in Holland

A trendy clothing boutique featuring the very latest in Dutch fashion

RETAIL STORES AND SHOPPING CENTRES

THE MOST UPMARKET retail store in Holland is the **Bijenkorf**, which offers contemporary furniture, the latest names in fashion, a huge book department and all major cosmetics brands. The Vroom & Dreesmann department stores are slightly smaller and offer lower prices than the Bijenkorf. One step lower on the prices scale is Hema, which offers a wide range of things such as lighting accessories and household goods. At most shopping centres you will find the same names, although some centres are reserved for more exclusive shops. One of these is the **Magna Plaza** in Amsterdam, where you will find upmarket boutiques and jewellers' shops. De Groene Passage in Rotterdam is a covered shopping centre dedicated to the environment, selling items ranging from organic meat to New Age books. **La Vie** in Utrecht contains numerous disparate shops; while **De Passage** in The Hague is that town's prime shopping centre. Batavia Stad Outlet Shopping centre in Lelystad is a shopping village built to resemble a 17th-century town. Here manufacturers of expensive brands sell end-of-line products, in particular clothes, at heavy discounts. The designer outlet park in Roermond is a similar place to find bargains.

FURNITURE

HOLLAND'S TOP furniture designer, Jan des Bouvrie, has his own shop in a converted arsenal in Naarden called Studio het Arsenaal. At Van Til Interior in Alkmaar you can buy designer furniture. In Amsterdam-Zuidoost, you can spend a day viewing furniture in the 75 shops of the Villa Arena. Woonthemacentrum De Havenaer in Nijkerk and Palazzo Lelystad also offer interesting collections. You will find "meubelboulevards", shopping streets of furniture stores, throughout the country.

AUCTION AND SALES HOUSES

THE FAMOUS British auction houses **Sotheby's** and **Christie's** have branches in Amsterdam, where international collections in particular are auctioned. The **Eland De Zon** **Loth Gijselman** in Diemen, as well as antiquities and art, also auctions furniture and estates. **Holbein** in Rijssen sells art and antiques, the **Postzegel, Munt en Veilinghuis** in Zwolle specializes in stamps and coins.

GARDEN CENTRES

PRODUCTS ON SALE at garden centres are not confined to plants, seeds and bulbs, but also include plant pots and containers, soil, compost and garden furniture. For more unusual plants it is best to go to special growers, of which there are many in Holland. Garden centres are usually on the edge of towns or just outside them. They are usually open for business on Sundays and public holidays.

An abundance of flowers at a Dutch garden centre

CHOCOLATE

VERKADE AND DROSTE are Holland's best-known chocolate makers, and you can find their products everywhere. Many towns now have specialized confectioners' shops. The renowned Belgian confectioner **Leonidas** has numerous outlets in the country. **Puccini Bomboni** produce exceptional chocolates, sold individually.

TEA AND COFFEE

HOLLAND HAS BEEN a tea and coffee importer for centuries, and you can find specialist tea and coffee shops everywhere; many still roast their own coffee. **Simon Levelt** always has at least 25 varieties of coffee and 100 tea blends on sale. **Geels & Co**, an old family business, has a roasting house and museum.

Magna Plaza *(see p90)*, open for Sunday shopping

What to Buy in Holland

IN THE CITIES AND TOURIST RESORTS, souvenir shops are not difficult to find. But if you are looking for something out of the ordinary, either for yourself or as gifts, you can often find something in more specialized shops, or even in a supermarket. Flowers and Delftware never fail to delight. For other things worth taking home, for example, local delicacies such as Dutch cheese and *speculaas* or drinks such as *jenever* gin, see page 426.

Souvenir Dolls
Dutch national costume is hardly worn in Holland any more, except by souvenir dolls such as this trio from Volendam.

Miniature Houses
Painted miniature pottery houses (often Delft blue) are a popular souvenir. Some are designed to be filled with jenever *gin, while others are purely ornamental.*

Painted Wooden Clogs
The traditional wooden clog has come to symbolize Holland. They can be bought in all colours and sizes. They can also be ordered via the internet at http://www.woodenshoes.com

Dutch
bulbs

Red Coral
Necklaces of red coral are often part of traditional costume in places such as Volendam. However, they also add a nice touch when worn with modern clothing.

Gouda Pipes
Long-necked clay pipes from Gouda known as Grouwenaars *(see p237), have been made here since the beginning of the 17th century and make a nice gift for smokers and non-smokers alike*

Flowers
Bulbs and cut flowers are available all the year round in the innumerable flower shops, flower stalls and garden centres to be easily found throughout Holland.

Prints of Dutch windmills

Old Maps and Prints

Amsterdam in particular has made its mark in the field of cartography. Many antique shops sell atlases and books of prints.

Reproductions of maps of Amsterdam and Russia

Inlaid diamond necklace

Diamonds

Diamonds were cut in Amsterdam as early as the 16th century, and the town continues to be one of the main diamond centres of the world. Many jewellers sell uncut diamonds and second-hand diamond rings.

Diamond brooch

Diamonds of different colours

Modern Delftware

Modern blue Delftware items decorated with windmills or other images of Holland are available in the form of tea sets, sculptures, vases and even royal Delft ashtrays. When buying, make sure that there is a certificate of authenticity (see p26) to go with it.

Delftware mugs

Makkum Pottery

This colourful earthenware, primarily tiles, plates and bowls, is still produced by the Tichelaar factory (see p27) at Makkum in Friesland.

Speculaas
These biscuits, flavoured with cinnamon, cloves and ginger, are eaten mainly around St Nicholas' day.

Speculaas

A distinctive Edam cheese

Edam Cheese
The world-famous Edam cheese (see p172) has an excellent taste and makes a good souvenir.

Speculaas Board
Mould your own speculaas *biscuits in these biscuit moulds, or use them for attractive wall ornaments.*

Haagse Hopjes
These coffee-flavoured sweets were first made at the end of the 18th century at the inspiration of a Baron Hop of The Hague.

Zeeland Butter Candies
These butter-flavoured sweets from Zeeland, made of glucose sugar syrup and butter, are delicious.

Butter candies

Hopjes

Dutch Beer
The Dutch are renowned beer-drinkers. In addition to the three brands depicted here, there are countless other varieties available.

Jonge grain jenever

Sonnema herenburg

Zwarte Kip advocaat

Zaans Mustard
This coarse mustard is made at De Huisman mustard plant on the Zaanse Schans (see p173).

Spirits
Renowned Dutch spirits include jenever, *a kind of gin sold in glass or stoneware bottles (there is* jonge *and* oude *clear* jenever, *as well as that with herbs),* berenburg *(see p295), the Frisian distilled herbal drink and* advocaat, *made of brandy and eggs.*

Gingerbread

Gingerbread
This scrumptious bread comes in a variety of regional variations, and is excellent at breakfast or even as a snack – especially with a thick layer of butter.

Liquorice Drops
The ubiquitous liquorice drops are sold either salted or sweet.

DIRECTORY

ANTIQUES

Amsterdam Antiques Gallery
Nieuwe Spiegelstraat 34,
Amstordam.
℡ 020-6253371.

A Votre Servies
Vughtstraat 231,
's-Hertogenbosch.
℡ 073-6135989.

Brabanthallen
Diezekade 2,
's-Hertogenbosch.
℡ 073-6293911.
Spring antique fairs.

De Tijdspiegel
Nieuwstraat 17,
Middelburg.
℡ 0118-627799.

EH Ariëns Kappers
Nieuwe Spiegelstraat 32,
Amsterdam.
℡ 020-6235356.

Emmakade 2 Antiek
Emmakade 2,
Leeuwarden.
℡ 058-2153464.

Jan de Raad Antiquiteiten
Postelstraat 28–30,
's-Hertogenbosch.
℡ 073-6144979.

Le Collectionneur
Damplein 5,
Middelburg.
℡ 0118-638595.

Le Magasin Antiek & Curiosa
Klein Heiligland 58,
Haarlem.
℡ 023-5321383.

MECC
Forum 100,
Maastricht.
℡ 043-3838383.
TEFAF in March.

Paul Berlijn Antiques
Amsterdamse Vaart 134,
Haarlem.
℡ 023-5337369.

RETAIL STORES AND SHOPPING CENTRES

De Bijenkorf
Rembrandtshof 3,
Amstelveen.
℡ 020-4567700.
Dam 1,
Amsterdam.
℡ 020-6218080.
Ketelstraat 45,
Arnhem.
℡ 026-3715700.
Wagenstraat 32,
The Hague.
℡ 070-4262700.
Piazza 1,
Eindhoven.
℡ 040-2604700.
Coolsingel 105,
Rotterdam.
℡ 010-2823700.
Sint-Jacobsstraat 1a,
Utrecht.
℡ 030-2346700.
🖳 www.bijenkorf.nl

Magna Plaza
Nieuwez. Voorburgwal 182,
Amsterdam.
℡ 020-6269199.

De Passage
Passage,
The Hague.
℡ 070-3463830.

La Vie Shoppingcentre
Lange Viestraat 669,
Utrecht.
℡ 030-2341414.

FURNITURE

Studio het Arsenaal
Kooltjesbuurt 1,
Naarden-Vesting.
℡ 035-6941144.

Van Til Interieur
Noorderkade 1038,
Alkmaar.
℡ 072-5112760.

Villa Arena
Arena Boulevard,
Amsterdam-Zuidoost.
℡ 0800-8455227.
🖳 www.villaarena.nl

Woonthema-centrum De Havenaer
Ampèrestraat,
Nijkerk.
℡ 033-2462622.

AUCTION AND SALES HOUSES

Christie's
Cornelis Schuytstraat 57,
Amsterdam.
℡ 020-5755255.

De Eland De Zon Loth Gijselman
Industrieterrein Verrijn
Stuart,
Weesperstraat 110–112,
Diemen.
℡ 020-6243205.

Holbein Kunst- en Antiekveilingen
Jutestraat 31,
Rijssen.
℡ 0548-541577.

Postzegel, Munt en Veilinghuis
Voorstraat 23,
Zwolle.
℡ 038-4211045.

Sotheby's
De Boelelaan 30,
Amsterdam.
℡ 020-5502200.

CHOCOLATES

Huize van Wely
Beethovenstraat 72,
Amsterdam.
℡ 020-6622009.
Hoofdstraat 88,
Noordwijk (ZH).
℡ 071-3612228.

Leonidas
Damstraat 15,
Amsterdam.
℡ 020-6253497.
Bakkerstraat 2,
Arnhem.
℡ 026-4422157.
Passage 26,
The Hague.
℡ 070-3649608.
Fonteinstraat 3,
's-Hertogenbosch.
℡ 073-6143626.
OL Vrouweplein 17a,
Maastricht.
℡ 043-3255320.
Pottenbakkersingel 2,
Middelburg.
℡ 0118-634750.

Beurstraverse 69,
Rotterdam.
℡ 010-4136034.
Oude Gracht 136,
Utrecht.
℡ 030-2317738.

Puccini Bomboni
Staalstraat 17,
Amsterdam.
℡ 020-6265474.
Singel 184,
Amsterdam.
℡ 020-4278341.

TEA AND COFFEE

Abraham Mostert
Schoutenstraat 11,
Utrecht.
℡ 030-2316934.

Geels & Co
Warmoesstraat 67,
Amsterdam.
℡ 020-6240683.

In de drij swarte mollen
Hinthamerstraat 190,
's-Hertogenbosch.
℡ 073-6871411.

Het Klaverblad
Hogewoerd 15,
Leiden.
℡ 071-5133655.

Koffiebrander Blanche Dael
Wolfstraat 28,
Maastricht.
℡ 043-3213475.

Simon Levelt koffie- en theehandel
Prinsengracht 180,
Amsterdam.
℡ 020-6240823.
Veerstraat 15,
Bussum.
℡ 035-6939459.
Zwanestraat 38,
Groningen.
℡ 050-3114333.
Gierstraat 65,
Haarlem.
℡ 023-5311861.
Botermarkt 1–2,
Leiden.
℡ 071-5131159.
Vismarkt 15,
Utrecht.
℡ 030-2342226.

ENTERTAINMENT IN HOLLAND

CULTURAL LIFE IN HOLLAND is not confined to the Randstad. Outside the big cities there is also plenty to do. There is a theatre or a cultural centre in just about every town, where theatre groups, cabaret artists, orchestras and rock bands perform. There is also a growing number of entertainment complexes, such as the Miracle Planet Boulevard centre in Enschede. You can find out what's on in terms of entertainment either by contacting the relevant venue or through the local VVV (tourist)

Engelenbak theatre logo

offices; another possibility is the AUB Ticketshop *(see p147)* in Amsterdam. Here more often than not you can book tickets centrally, or obtain more information about the performance in which you are interested. You can also get tickets and information via the Uitlijn (0900-0191). The major national dailies publish a list of events every week. Most cities publish their own weekly *uitkrant*, or entertainment guide, while the internet offers another convenient way of getting an idea of the wide-ranging cultural events that are on offer.

THEATRE

HOLLAND BOASTS a large number of theatres, the majority of them located in Amsterdam. That city's top theatre is the Stadsschouwburg *(see p147)*, where many touring theatre companies put on performances. The Netherlands' largest theatre company, Amsterdam Theatre Group, is based here and is now directed by Ivo van Hove.

The annual highlight for opera, theatre and dance is the Holland Festival. The best in international cultural offerings is to be had during the Amsterdam Festival. During the International Theatre School Festival in June, experimental drama is performed at venues such as **De Brakke Grond** *(see p147)* and **Frascati**. The **Soeterijn**, on the other hand, specializes in theatre from developing countries. The theatre company frequently wins prizes under the inspired leadership of Theu Boermans. De Dogtroep is a company that stages spectacular street theatre, while the Theatergroup Hollandia has also won great acclaim with its performances in large halls and aircraft hangars. The musical dramas of Orkater can be seen in various parts of the country at different times of the year, but mainly at the Stadsschouwburg and **Bellevue/Nieuwe de la Mar**. Youth-focused theatre is

put on in **De Krakeling**. For years now the performances by the **Toneelschuur** in Haarlem have won critical acclaim. The De Appel group stages both experimental and repertory theatre at the **Appeltheater** in The Hague. Throughout Holland there are numerous excellent theatre groups. Het Zuidelijk Toneel of Eindhoven in the south always packs theatre halls, as do the Theater van het Oosten from Arnhem in the east of the country and the Noord Nederlands Toneel from Groningen in the north.

Every year in May, the Festival aan de Werf in

Utrecht presents an appealing smorgasbord of theatre and cabaret performances.

MUSICALS AND CABARET

HOLLAND'S MOST outstanding musical theatres are the **VSB Circustheater** of The Hague, the **Beatrix Theater** in Utrecht and the Koninklijk Theater Carré *(see p147)* in Amsterdam. These stage big box-office hits such as *Les Misérables* and *Miss Saigon*. De Kleine Komedie *(see p147)*, a magnificent 17th-century building on the Amstel river opposite the Muziektheater, is a favourite venue for cabaret groups.

Scene from the musical *Oliver!* at the Theater Carré

Muziektheater, is a favourite venue for cabaret groups. In recent years, stand-up comedy has gained popularity mainly through this venue. Other comedy venues in Amsterdam are **Comedy Café**, **Toomler** and **Boom Chicago**.

DANCE

HOLLAND IS the proud home of two world-famous ballet troupes: the Nationale Ballet and the Nederlands Dans Theater (NDT). The Nationale Ballet is based in the Musiektheater *(see p147)*, which is commonly known among Amsterdam theatre-goers as the "Stopera". This contemporary building can accommodate 1,600 people and is a significant centre both for dance and for opera. The foyer affords a spectacular view of the river Amstel.

The Nederlands Dans Theater, which is based in the **Lucent Danstheater** in The Hague, puts on works

De Dogtroep performing lively and spectacular street theatre

Noord Nederlands Toneel staging Anton Chekhov's *The Seagull*

primarily by its former artistic director Jiří Kylián, who was succeeded by Marianne Sarstadt in 1999. Under the direction of the company's present choreographer Ed Wubbe it has staged sold-out performances with live music. Introdans of Arnhem performs an exciting combination of jazz, flamenco and ethnic dance. Holland's biggest choreographers use the Holland Festival as a platform to present their new creations to the public. During the Internationale

Theaterschool Festival, which also takes place in June, the proportion of dance performed is growing. The festival venue is the Nes, one of Amsterdam's oldest streets. Julidans is the name given to a summer dance festival in Amsterdam in which contemporary dance by various international dance companies is performed.

FILM

GOING TO THE MOVIES continues to be a popular pastime in Holland, and you will find at least one or more cinemas in almost every town. Amsterdam alone has more than 45 cinemas. Foreign-language films are shown in the original language with subtitles. The most magnificent cinema in Amsterdam is Tuschinski, an Art Deco masterpiece built from 1918–21, with a stylish foyer and generous seating *(see p115)*. The major premieres are held here: if you want to see famous faces, the best time is Wednesday evenings at the cinema entrance. There is a list of all films that are showing at the box office of every cinema, and such lists are also displayed in cafés and restaurants. Cinema programmes change every Thursday, so you will find a list of films that are on in Wednesday's evening papers and in Thursday's morning papers. *De Filmkrant* is a

much-respected movie magazine that is published every Monday, which in addition to the week's film listings also provides background information on major films. Major film events in Holland are the Nederlands Film Festival, which is held in Utrecht in September and October, where Dutch films are premiered and where the *Gouden Kalf* (Golden Calf) Dutch film awards are handed out in 12 categories (including those for TV), and the renowned International Film Festival in Rotterdam which takes place every year in January.

ORCHESTRAL, CHAMBER AND CHOIR MUSIC

THE CONCERTGEBOUW *(see p147)* in Amsterdam is traditionally the most important venue for concert music. The Grote Zaal hall is famous for its acoustics, and its resident musicians are the Koninklijk Concertgebouworkest. During summer the orchestra puts on special concerts. The Beurs van Berlage *(see p147)*, formerly the stock exchange, has for some time now been the home of the Nederlands Philharmonisch Orkest. Many of the country's better orchestras and choirs perform here.

De Ijsbreker is situated in a magnificent building on the Amstel, and has for 20 years been the prime venue in Amsterdam for modern classical music.

The Golden Calf

The Amsterdamse Koninklijk Concertgebouworkest performing

An outstanding orchestra is the Rotterdams Philharmonisch Orkest, which for the last few years has been conducted by the Russian conductor Valeri Gergjev. The orchestra is based in **De Doelen** in Rotterdam. The Residentie Orkest, whose history goes back almost 100 years, performs regularly at the **Anton Philipszaal** in The Hague and is not to be confused with the **Muziekcentrum Frits Philips** in Eindhoven, where the Brabants Orkest is based.

The Gelders Orkest makes regular appearances in the **Musis Sacrum** concert hall in Arnhem. Another venue offering a rich programme of music is the **Muziekcentrum Vredenburg**.

CHURCH MUSIC

O F THE MANY ORGANS in Holland *(see pp28–9),* that of the **Grote Kerk** in Elburg is probably the best known. Every year it is used in the national amateur organist competition. The instruments in the **Oude Kerk** and the **Nieuwe Kerk** are the most famous of Amsterdam's 42 church organs. Organ concerts can also be heard at the **Waalse Kerk** and also on Tuesdays at lunch time in the **Westerkerk**.

The programme of the 17th-century **Engelse Kerk** contains a wide variety of music, ranging from Baroque to modern. In the **Domkerk** in Utrecht, concerts are performed on a regular basis.

OPERA

E STABLISHED IN 1988 in Amsterdam, the **Muziektheater** is the home of the Nederlandse Opera. One of Europe's most modern opera theatres, its stage has been graced by many established international companies, although it is also used for experimental works. The Stadsschouwburg *(see p147)* on the Leidseplein is also host to a great deal of opera, although if experimental opera is your thing, the Westergasfabriek is probably the best venue. The **Twentse Schouwburg** in Enschede, in conjunction with the Nationale Reis-opera, organizes the Twents Opera Festival each year in July and August.

ROCK AND POP

T WO VENUES in particular have established themselves as the most important rock venues in Holland: **Ahoy'** in Rotterdam and Vredenburg in Utrecht, although international rock stars now perform in many parts of Holland. With a capacity of over 5,000, the easily accessible **Heineken Music Hall** is Amsterdam's prime rock venue. It has been used for concerts by megastars such as Michael Jackson and the Rolling Stones. However, for locals, there are only two real rock venues: **Paradiso**

and **De Melkweg**. Paradiso, in a former church on the Leidseplein, enjoys the greatest respect. The Melkweg (Milky Way), which is also on the Leidseplein, owes its name to the fact that the building in which it is located used to be a dairy. The programme in both of these respected venues changes constantly, and all rock and pop enthusiasts will eventually find something to their taste.

Every Sunday in summer there are free open-air concerts in the Vondelpark, often with renowned bands on the line-up. Programmes are displayed at the entrances to the park. In June the world's largest free pop festival, the Haagse Zuiderpark Parkpop, is held in The Hague. Another annual festival which attracts visitors from near and far is the Pinkpopfestival in Landgraaf (Limburg).

JAZZ

T HE FOREMOST VENUE of the jazz scene in Amsterdam is the **Bimhuis**. Although the casual visitor might find the atmosphere a tad pretentious, the music here is of top quality, and the Bimhuis enjoys a reputation that goes far beyond the country's borders. There are good jazz cafés to be found all over Amsterdam, most of them featuring local **Hans Dulfer** jazz bands. Around the Leidseplein are the **Alto Jazz Café** and **Bourbon Street**, which is open until 4am on weekdays and until 5am on weekends. Alto is best on Wednesdays, when the "godfather" of Amsterdam jazz, Hans Dulfer, performs. His daughter Candy, who has gained international renown, sometimes plays in **De Heeren van Aemstel**. **De Engelbewaarder** is a venue for Sunday jazz. Meanwhile, in The Hague, the annual North Sea Jazz Festival takes place in the Congresgebouw. **Dizzy** jazz café has become a household name among jazz-lovers in Rotterdam, hosting over 100 jazz concerts every year.

DIRECTORY

THEATRES

Appeltheater
Duinstraat 6–8,
The Hague.
[070-3502200.

Arsenaaltheater
Arsenaalplein 7, Vlissingen.
[0118-415244.

**Bellevue/Nieuwe
de la Mar**
Leidsekade 90,
Amsterdam.
[020-5305301/02.

Chassé Theater
Claudius Prinsenlaan 8,
Breda.
[076-5303132.

Compagnietheater
Kloveniersburgwal 50,
Amsterdam.
[020-5205320.

Concordia
Oude Markt 26, Enschede.
[053-4311089.

De Flint
Conickstraat 60,
Amersfoort.
[033-4229229.

De Harmonie
Ruiterskwartier 4,
Leeuwarden.
[058-2330233.

De Krakeling
Nwe Passeerdersstraat 1,
Amsterdam.
[020-6169655.

Frascati
Nes 63, Amsterdam.
[020-6235723.

Orpheus
Churchillplein 1,
Apeldoorn.
[0900-1230123.

Soeterijn
Linnaeusstraat 2,
Amsterdam.
[020-5688500.

Stadsschouwburg
Leidseplein 26, Amsterdam.
[020-6242311.

't Spant
Kuyperlaan 3, Bussum.
[035-6913949.

**Theater aan het
Vrijhof**
Vrijthof 47, Maastricht.
[043-3505555.

Toneelschuur
Lange Begijnestr 9,
Haarlem. [023-517390.

Transformatorhuis
Haarlemmerweg 8–10,
Amsterdam.
[020-6279070.

MUSICALS AND CABARET

Beatrix Theater
Jaarbeursplein 6, Utrecht.
[030-2447044.

Boom Chicago
Leidseplein 12, Amsterdam.
[020-5307300.

Comedy Café
Max Euweplein 43–45,
Amsterdam.
[020-6383971.

Toomler
Breitnerstr. 2, Amsterdam.
[020-6707400.

VSB Circustheater
Circusstraat 4, The Hague.
[070-3511212.

DANCE

Lucent Danstheater
Spuiplein 152, The Hague.
[070-3604930.

**Rotterdamse
Schouwburg**
Schouwburgplein 25,
Rotterdam.
[010-4118110.

**Schouwburg
Arnhem**
Koningsplein 12, Arnhem.
[026-4437343.

ORCHESTRA, CHAMBER AND CHOIR MUSIC

Anton Philipszaal
Spuiplein 150, The Hague.
[070-3609810.

**Concertgebouw
De Vereeniging**
Keizer Karelplein,
Nijmegen.
[024-3228344.

De Doelen
Schouwburgplein 50,
Rotterdam.
[010-2171717.

De IJsbreker
Weesperzijde 23,
Amsterdam.
[020-6939093.

Musis Sacrum
Velperbuitensingel 25,
Arnhem.
[026-4437343.

**Muziekcentrum
Frits Philips**
Heuvelgalerie, Eindhoven.
[040-2655600.

**Muziekcentrum
Vredenburg**
Vredenburgpassage 77,
Utrecht.
[030-2314544.

CHURCH MUSIC

Domkerk
Domplein, Utrecht.
[030-2310403.

Engelse Kerk
Begijnhof 48,
Amsterdam.
[020-6211211.

Grote Kerk
Van Kinsbergenstraat,
Elburg.
[0525-681520.

Nieuwe Kerk
Dam, Amsterdam.
[020-6268168.

Oude Kerk
Oudekerksplein 23,
Amsterdam.
[020-6249183

Waalse Kerk
Walenplein 157,
Amsterdam.
[020-6232074.

Westerkerk
Prinsengracht 281,
Amsterdam.
[020-2513413.

OPERA

**Muziektheater
Amsterdam**
see p147.

**Twentse
Schouwburg**
Langestraat 49, Enschede.
[053-4858500.

ROCK AND POP

Ahoy'
Zuiderparkweg 20–30,
Rotterdam.
[010-4104304.

**Heineken Music
Hall**
Arena Boulevard 1,
Amsterdam.
[0900-3001250.

Melkweg
Lijnbaansgracht 234 a,
Amsterdam.
[020-6241777.

Paradiso
Weteringschans 6-8,
Amsterdam.
[020-6264521.

JAZZ

Alto Jazz Café
Korte Leidedwarsstraat
115, Amsterdam.
[020-6263249.

Bimhuis
Oude Schans 73–77,
Amsterdam.
[020-6231361.

Bourbon Street
Leidsekruisstraat 6–8,
Amsterdam.
[020-6233440.

De Engelbewaarder
Kloveniersburgwal 59,
Amsterdam.
[020-6253772.

**De Heeren van
Aemstel**
Thorbeckeplein 5,
Amsterdam.
[020-6202173.

Dizzy
's-Gravendijkwal 129,
Rotterdam.
[010-4773014.

SURVIVAL
GUIDE

PRACTICAL INFORMATION

Because HOLLAND is relatively small and has a dense road and motorway network with good public transport, getting around does not take up a lot of time. Whether you are going to Amsterdam, the Veluwe, Maastricht or Zandvoort, you can get there from anywhere in the country very quickly by car or by train. The flat landscape

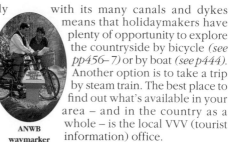

ANWB
waymarker

with its many canals and dykes means that holidaymakers have plenty of opportunity to explore the countryside by bicycle *(see pp456–7)* or by boat *(see p444)*. Another option is to take a trip by steam train. The best place to find out what's available in your area – and in the country as a whole – is the local VVV (tourist information) office.

VVV and ANWB offices, which often share the same premises

TOURIST INFORMATION

THE BEST SOURCE of information for tourists is the local or regional **VVV** office. Many towns and places of interest have VVV offices where you can drop in and ask for advice and brochures about places of interest, local events, walks, cycle routes and excursions in the town or region. In addition, they can provide maps and books about other parts of Holland. The VVV-*gidsen* series in Dutch is very practical, with information and facts about individual provinces and regions.

At VVVs you can also book domestic excursions, hotels, short breaks and theatre tickets anywhere in the country. Annual museum cards and CJPs *(see p147)* are also on sale here. Smaller VVV outlets, although providing comprehensive information about the local area, do not provide other services.

ANWB offices in the Netherlands also have a selection of cycling, rambling and motoring guides, tickets, camping guides and road atlases. ANWB members have access to specialized membership information about various subjects and holiday offers. In many cases the VVV and the ANWB share the same premises. If you are travelling to Holland from abroad you can obtain information in advance from the **Netherlands Board of Tourism (NBT)** in your own country.

ANWB

ENTERTAINMENT

MANY VVV-*gidsen* guides have an annual review of events in a particular region or province. For up-to-date information on events, exhibitions, performances and films, it is worth looking in the entertainment supplements issued by daily papers *(see p146)*, or ask at the local VVV office. Plays, concerts, special events and festivals are usually advertised on billboards or in cafés.

Special regional and local entertainment guides are also a good source of information; for example, the monthly *Uitkrant* tells you what's on in Amsterdam in the way of theatre, while the weekly *Uitloper* is Utrecht's entertainment guide. These guides are distributed at many sites free of charge.

Tickets for concerts and events are available not only at the box office of the venue itself but also via the national **Ticket Service** and at VVV offices. Some towns also have their own booking bureau; for instance, in Amsterdam you can book your tickets at the AUB *(see pp146–7)*, and in The Hague you can get your tickets at the Bespreekbureau Haagsche Courant (tel. 070-3656806).

MUSEUM CARD

THE ANNUAL Museum Card *(Museumjaarkaart)* has quickly risen to huge popularity. It costs €29.95 for people over the age of 25, and €12.50 for under-25s. It gives the holder free entry to over 440 museums in the country. However, you usually have to pay a supplement for

Signpost pointing to tourist sights

◁ **The hard-working Dutch taking time out to relax**

special exhibitions. The card is available at all participating museums and at VVVs, and requires a passport photograph. It can also be ordered from the **Stichting Museumjaarkaart** (also available over the internet).

Museum Card

TRAVELLERS WITH DISABILITIES

Most public buildings have good facilities for travellers with disabilities. Museums, art galleries, cinemas and theatres generally are wheelchair-accessible. Only some establishments in very old buildings are less accessible, but there are always staff who are able to lend a hand. It's best to phone in advance. Accessibility information for hotels is given on page 385.

For disabled people travelling by train, the NS has issued a pack entitled *Gehandicapten*. This contains information on Dutch railway stations and what facilities they have, and also lists the stations (there are approximately 150 of them) where people in wheelchairs can get assistance when boarding and alighting from trains. If you require assistance, it's a good idea to contact the **Bureau Assistentieverlening Gehandicapten** three hours before travelling.

OPENING HOURS

Although until recently just about every shop was open from 9am to 6pm, today there is an increasing variety in shop opening hours. Smaller shops still usually close at 6pm, but many retail stores and supermarkets are open until 7pm or later. In the cities, shops tend to stay open longer, but opening hours vary greatly from one

business to another. Many towns have a "shopping evening" *(koopavond)* once a week, when most shops remain open until 9pm. This is usually on Thursday (Amsterdam and The Hague), or Friday (Utrecht). In an increasing number of towns there are shops which open on Sundays at least once in the month. Many shops have half-day closing, either in the morning or the afternoon, once during the week. The half-day is usually Monday, but varies from one region to another.

Banks are usually open on weekdays from 9am to 5pm, and VVVs are also open on Mondays to Fridays from 9am or 10am to 5pm (sometimes on *koopavond* until 9pm). On Saturdays they close early or even all day, and most are closed on Sundays. Some VVVs are closed during the winter.

Many museums are shut on Mondays, and open from 10am to 5pm for the rest of the week. On Sundays and public holidays they tend to open later. Practically all museums are closed on New Year's Day, and many are closed on Christmas Day. Open-air museums and small museums tend to close for the winter.

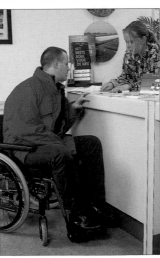

Wheelchair-accessible tourist office

DIRECTORY

TOURIST INFORMATION

Amsterdam Tourist Board
Argonautenstraat 98, Leidseplein 1 and Stationsplein 10.
📞 0900-4004040.

ANWB Main Office
Wassenaarseweg 220, 2596 EC The Hague.
📞 070-3147147.
information line: 0800-0503.
🖥 www.anwb.nl

VVV
🖥 www.vvv.nl

VVV The Hague
Koningin Julianaplein 30.
📞 0900-3403505.

VVV Maastricht
Kleine Staat 1.
📞 043-3252121.

VVV Rotterdam
Coolsingel 67.
📞 0900-4034065.

VVV Utrecht
Vinkenburgstraat 19.
📞 0900-12UTRECHT/0900-128873248.

NETHERLANDS BOARD OF TOURISM (NBT)

Vlietweg 15, 2266 KA Leidschendam.
📞 070-3705705.
🖥 www.holland.com

In the UK:
Imperial House, 7th Floor, 15–19 Kingsway, London WC2B 6UN.
📞 020-7539 7950.

DISABLED TRAVELLERS

Bureau Assistentieverlening Gehandicapten
Postbus 2429, 3500 GK Utrecht.
📞 030-2305522 (Mon–Fri).

OTHER USEFUL ADDRESSES

Stichting Museumjaarkaart
Postbus 5020, 2900 EA Capelle a/d IJssel.
📞 0900-4040910.
🖥 www.museumjaarkaart.nl

Ticket Service
📞 0900-3001250.
🖥 www.ticketservice.nl

Flower seeds and bulbs, freely exported items (with certificate)

VISAS AND CUSTOMS

TRAVELLERS FROM other EU countries can travel freely in and out of Holland provided they have a valid passport or European identity card. For a stay lasting up to three months, travellers from Australia, New Zealand and North America need only a valid passport.

EU residents may bring an unlimited quantity of goods into the country provided they are for their personal use. For tobacco and alcohol, the following quantities are considered limits for personal use: 800 cigarettes, 400 cigars, 1 kg of tobacco, 10 litres of spirits, 20 litres of liqueurs, 90 litres of wine (or 60 litres of fortified wine) and 110 litres of beer. Duty will be charged on quantities exceeding these specified limits.

For travellers from outside the EU, the limits are 200 cigarettes, 100 cigarillos, 50 cigarettes or 250 g of tobacco, 2 litres of unfortified wine plus 1 litre of spirits or 2 litres of fortified wine or liqueur wine or spirits, 50 g of perfume, 0.25l of eau de toilette and other items up to a value of 175. Since 1 July 1999, residents of other EU countries may no longer import goods on which VAT has not been paid. If you are entering or leaving the EU, you can take non-VAT paid goods with you.

More details are available from the **Customs Helpline** *(Douanetelefoon),* which gives precise information on customs regulations. Travellers from outside the Netherlands may be able to obtain information at the local embassy.

TIME

LIKE ALL ITS neighbouring countries, the Netherlands is on Central European Time, 1 hour ahead of Greenwich Mean Time in winter and 2 hours ahead in the summer. Summer time starts on the first weekend in April and continues until the last week of October.

Sydney is 9 hours ahead in winter (8 hours in summer), Johannesburg 1 hour (the same as Holland in summer), New York is 6 hours behind, Los Angeles 9 hours behind.

TIPPING

TAXI DRIVERS expect a tip of around 10 per cent, except on longer journeys. Although service charge is

Customers showing their appreciation with a tip

included on restaurant bills, it is customary to round the bill up slightly *(see p405).*

In hotels you may if you like leave something for the chambermaid after a longer stay, even though it is not generally the rule.

PUBLIC TOILETS

THERE IS A limited number of public conveniences in Holland. In some cities you will find toilets where you have to insert money into a slot to open the door. Popping into a café to use the toilets there is accepted practice in Holland; some establishments have an attendant who should be paid a small amount. Large retail stores and stations also have toilets, and you generally need to pay a small fee to use these. The latter also have nappy-changing facilities for babies. On motorways you will find toilets at all service stations.

ELECTRICITY

IN HOLLAND the electrical voltage is 220/230 volts. Dutch plugs are of the two-pin type,

Standard continental plug

and adapters are available for visitors from countries with different plugs (for example, Great Britain).

TELEVISION AND RADIO

THE TELEVISION programmes on offer in Holland are undergoing a great deal of development at the moment. The traditional system was to have a large number of broadcasting networks, each with their own political or religious leanings, being given a certain amount of air-time on each of the three public TV stations (Nederland 1, 2 and 3). More recently, however, commercial television stations have emerged to compete with Hilversum (the town where Holland's main networks are based, *see pp188–9*).

As well as national TV networks, Holland has a number of regional and local providers, such as Omrop Fryslân, Omroep Flevoland, Omroep Gelderland and the Amsterdam local network AT5. In addition, large numbers of foreign programmes can be received on cable TV, the range varying depending on the local cable company.

Holland has five national radio stations, each of them with their own "personality": Radio 1 deals mainly with current affairs and sport, Radio 2 broadcasts light music and various information programmes, Radio 3 rock and pop and Radio 4 classical music. 747 AM is a news channel.

NEWSPAPERS AND MAGAZINES

Holland has four national morning newspapers (*De Telegraaf, de Volkskrant, Algemeen Dagblad* and *Trouw*) and two national evening papers

(*Het Parool* and *NRC Handel-sblad*). These tend to focus on the west of the country. Regionally the more popular papers are the *Nieuwsblad van het Noorden, Friesch Dagblad, Tubantia, De Gelderlander, Utrechts Nieuwsblad, Provinciale Zeeuwsche Courant, Brabants Dagblad* and *Dagblad De Limburger*, which contain information on local holiday activities and events. The more famous Dutch weekly news magazines include *HP/De Tijd, Elsevier* and *Vrij Nederland*.

The major bookshops in the large cities (as well as the main railway stations) sell many major international newspapers and magazines.

PETS

If you bring your dog or cat to Holland from abroad, you need to be able to prove that your pet has been immunized against rabies. This is shown by a valid pet's passport provided by your veterinarian which indicates when the animal was last vaccinated. The hotel

A selection of newspapers available

listings on pages 390–403 show which of the hotels reviewed in this book welcome dogs.

EMBASSIES AND CONSULATES

If you are visiting from abroad and your passport is lost or stolen, you should report the loss to your consulate or embassy. Most embassies are situated in the administrative capital, The Hague. A number of countries also have consulates, which tend to be in Amsterdam.

Cat in a travel basket

DIRECTORY

EMBASSIES AND CONSULATES

Australia
Embassy:
Carnegielaan 4,
2517 KH The Hague.
070-3108200.
www.australian-embassy.nl

Belgium
Embassy:
Lange Vijverberg 12,
2513 AC The Hague.
070-3123456.
FAX 070-3645579.

Canada
Embassy:
Sophialaan 7,
2514 JP The Hague.
070-3111600.
www.dfait-maeci.gc.
ca/~thehague

hague@dfait-maeci.
gc.ca

France
Embassy:
Smidsplein 1,
2514 BT The Hague.
070-3125800.
FAX 070-3125824.

Germany
Embassy:
Groot Hertoginne-laan
18–20,
2517 EG The Hague.
070-3420600.
FAX 070-3651957.

Consulate:
Honthorststraat 36–38,
1071 DG Amsterdam.
020-5747700.
FAX 020-6766951.

Great Britain
Embassy:
Lange Voorhout 10,

2514 ED The Hague.
070-4270427.
FAX 070-4270345.

Consulate General:
Koningslaan 44,
1075 AE Amsterdam.
020-6764343.
FAX 020-6761069.

Ireland
Embassy:
Dr Kuyperstraat 9,
2514 BA The Hague.
070-3630993/4.
FAX 070-3617604.

New Zealand
Embassy:
Carnegielaan 10,
2517 KH The Hague.
070-3469324.
FAX 070-3632983.
nzemb@bart.nl

South Africa
Embassy:

Wassenaarseweg 40,
2596 CJ The Hague.
070-3924501.
www.zuidafrika.nl

United States
Embassy:
Lange Voorhout 102,
2514 EJ The Hague.
070-3109209.
FAX 070-3104688.
www.usemb.nl

Consulate:
Museumplein 19,
1017 DJ Amsterdam.
020-5755309.
FAX 020-5755310.
www.usemb.nl

CUSTOMS HELPLINE

0800-0143.
8am–10pm Mon–Thu,
8am–5pm Fri.

Personal Security and Health

I F YOU KEEP to a few basic safety rules, you should have a trouble-free stay in Holland. Obviously it is better not to carry large amounts of cash or valuables around, and not to keep passports, cheques and credit cards together in one place. Visitors from abroad can always insure themselves against losses of money and personal items from theft. It is also a good idea to insure

yourself against medical expenses when travelling abroad. For those who do find themselves in trouble on holiday, the country has efficient emergency services and facilities.

The police logo

EMERGENCIES

T HE NATIONAL **emergency number** for the police, fire brigade and ambulance is 112. This number must only be dialled in emergencies. For less urgent help, it is best to contact the nearest police station, hospital or a local doctor. If your car breaks down, members of the ANWB can call out the roadside assistance service of the **ANWB Wegenwacht** 24 hours a day, 7 days a week, using the roadside emergency phones or by dialling a toll-free phone number. The same also applies to members of associated organizations, such as the **AA** and **RAC**, as long as you have a letter showing you are entitled to compensation for the costs of repair and recovery (up to a certain limit).

PERSONAL BELONGINGS AND SAFETY

I T IS AS TRUE of Holland as elsewhere in Europe that opportunity makes the thief. When in busy shopping streets or on public transport, do not leave your wallet in your back pocket, and if you need to go to the lavatory on the train or when in a restaurant, take your handbag or wallet with you. Do not leave any valuables in your car, and always make sure it has been properly locked. Large cities, particularly Amsterdam, have a big

problem with bicycle theft, so a decent lock is a good investment. Muggings are rare, but at night it is better to avoid unlit areas and parks. Women can visit cafés in the evening without risk.

REPORTING CRIME

I F YOU HAVE been the victim of theft or a mugging, report it to the nearest police station (some smaller municipalities do not have their own police station). You will need to make a verbal report describing any loss and, if necessary, injury. Many insurance companies require you to report within 24 hours of the incident taking place. If your passport is stolen, you should report this to your embassy *(see p437)* as well as to the police.

Dutch police officers

MEDICAL TREATMENT AND INSURANCE

M INOR MEDICAL problems can usually be dealt with at a pharmacy, though the prescription of drugs is very strict. The majority of drugs are available only on prescription. Pharmacies – which are recognizable by their snake symbol – are open on weekdays from 8:30 or 9am to 5:30 or 6pm.

If the pharmacy is closed, you will find on the door a list of the nearest pharmacies that are open. Local newspapers also give details of duty doctors, pharmacies and other health services in the town or region. In an emergency you can get treatment in hospitals, which are open 24 hours a day.

Visitors from abroad who will be carrying prescription drugs with them should ask their doctor for a medical passport. This is a document stating your condition and the medication you require for it. The passport can be shown at the customs as evidence that you are bringing the medication in for your personal use.

Travellers from Belgium and other EU countries can generally have low-cost dental and medical treatment in Holland reimbursed through their basic medical insurance packages. As, however, the costs of medical treatment can become quite high, it is

Fire engine

Police car

Ambulance

a good idea to purchase comprehensive medical insurance if it is not included in your travel insurance.

MOSQUITOES

Aᴛᴛʀᴀᴄᴛᴇᴅ ʙʏ the canals, mosquitoes can be a real irritant. Residents and regular summer visitors deal with them in various ways. Burning coils, ultra-violet tubes, mosquito nets, repellent sprays and anti-histamine creams and tablets are available from large pharmacies and supermarkets.

LOST PROPERTY

Iꜰ ʏᴏᴜ ʟᴏsᴇ any valuables, you can check at the police station to see whether anyone has handed them in. Local police stations usually keep articles that have been handed in before passing them on to the central police station for the district. If you lose your passport you must also inform your consulate *(see p437)*. If you lose something on a train, inform the station first. Small stations keep lost

A crowded street festival: a place to be wary of pickpockets

SPOED-EISENDE HULP OPNAME

Oprijden tot de slagboom
Blijf in uw auto zitten
Druk uw raam open
U wordt aangesproken via de intercom

Emergency room sign

property for one day. After that they are taken to the nearest main station, and finally to the **Central Lost Property Office** *(Centraal Bureau Gevonden Voorwerpen)* in Utrecht. By filling in a search form (available at railway stations), you can describe the items you have lost. If you lose something on a bus, tram or metro, you should contact the office of the local or regional transport organization (look for "openbaar

vervoer" (public transport) in the Yellow Pages). **Schiphol** Airport has a special lost property number.

DRUGS

Aʟᴛʜᴏᴜɢʜ ᴛʜᴇ ᴜsᴇ of soft drugs is officially illegal in Holland, the police will not take action if you have a small quantity of hashish or marijuana in your possession. It is worth remembering that not every restaurant or café owner will take kindly to tourists lighting up on the premises. People caught with hard drugs will be prosecuted.

DIRECTOR

EMERGENCY NUMBERS

Ambulance, Fire Brigade, Police
Ⓒ *112.*
For the deaf and hard of hearing Ⓒ *0800-8112.*

SAFETY

Police
Non-urgent matters:
Ⓒ *0900-8844 (you will be connected to the nearest police station).*
For the deaf and hard of hearing Ⓒ *0900-1844.*

Police Amsterdam-Amstelland
Head office:
Elandsgracht 117,
1016 TT Amsterdam.
Ⓒ *0900-8844.*

HOSPITALS IN MAJOR CITIES

Amsterdam:

Academisch Medisch Centrum
Meibergdreef 9.
Ⓒ *020-5669111.*

Onze Lieve Vrouwe Gasthuis
1ste Oosterparkstraat 297.
Ⓒ *020-5999111.*

Sint Lucas Andreas Ziekenhuis
Andreas location:
Theophile de Bockstraat 8.
Ⓒ *020-5111115.*
Lucas location:
Jan Tooropstraat 164.
Ⓒ *020-5108911.*

Slotervaart Hospital
Louwesweg 6.
Ⓒ *020-5129333.*

VU Medisch Centrum
De Boelelaan 1117.
Ⓒ *020-4444444.*

The Hague:

Bronovo Hospital
Bronovolaan 5.
Ⓒ *070-3124141.*

MCH Hospital Westeinde
Lijnbaan 32.
Ⓒ *070-3302000.*

Rotterdam:

Erasmus Medisch Centrum
Dr Molewaterplein 40.
Ⓒ *010-4639222.*

Utrecht:

Academisch Hospital Utrecht
Heidelberglaan 100.
Ⓒ *030-2509111.*

LOST PROPERTY

Central Lost Property Office
2de Daalsedijk 4,
3551 EJ Utrecht.
Ⓒ *030-2353923
(8am–8pm Mon–Fri,
9am–5pm Sat).*

Schiphol – Lost Property
Ⓒ *0900-SCHIPHOL /
0900-72447465.*

ROADSIDE ASSISTANCE

ANWB Wegenwacht
Ⓒ *0800-0888
(toll-free).*

AA
Ⓒ *00–800–88776655.*

RAC
Ⓒ *00–33–472435255.*

Banking and Local Currency

C ASH IS STILL THE MOST POPULAR form of payment in Holland, though cash cards and other forms of plastic money are becoming increasingly common. Many hotels, shops and restaurants accept major credit cards in payment. Other means of payment are traveller's cheques (with identification), and, occasionally, US dollars (particularly at antique and souvenir shops). In 2002, Holland began to use the euro. The best place to change money is at a bank. You can take an unlimited amount of currency into Holland, and you can withdraw limited amounts of cash at an ATM.

Cash machine with logos

BANK OPENING HOURS

B ANKS ARE generally open from Mondays to Fridays from 9am to 4 or 5pm. Some banks remain open longer on *koopavond,* or shopping evening, often a Thursday.

These bureaux can still be found at the now unguarded border crossing points, at Amsterdam Schiphol Airport and at major railway stations. Most GWK bureaux are open daily and have extended opening hours.

chipknip/chipper (which are top-up cards available from Dutch banks or the Postbank). Most payphones *(see pp442–3)* accept credit cards for calls.

Whether you are shopping or taking a taxi, eating out or seeing a movie, credit cards are increasingly becoming the accepted means of payment in Holland.

GWK *(grenswisselkantoor),* **Holland's official exchange bureau**

CHEQUES

T HE ADVANTAGE of traveller's cheques is that you are protected against loss and theft. You can also use traveller's cheques to pay at hotels and restaurants, although often you will not be given change from them if the value of the cheque is greater than that of the bill.

It is usually best as well as more convenient to obtain traveller's cheques in euros before you leave home.

CHANGING MONEY

F OREIGN CURRENCY can be changed at banks, post offices and American Express offices. A small commission is charged on these transactions.

In small bureaux de change (often open outside business hours), located throughout the major cities and in larger towns, you can exchange money from non-Euro–zone countries, though often at unfavourable rates.

The Netherland's official bureaux de change, GWK *(grenswisselkantoor),* is a privatized state enterprise, which gives reasonable rates of exchange and charges relatively low commissions, as well as providing various other services for travellers.

BANK AND CREDIT CARDS

Y OU CAN USE your bank card to withdraw money at any Dutch bank displaying your card's logo, but usually there is a substantial commission charge. You can also use bank cards to withdraw cash at cash machines 24 hours a day. These machines usually also accept Eurocard/ MasterCard, American Express, Diner's Club and Visa cards. An ATM belonging to the Postbank is known as a *Giromaat.*

Shops, restaurants and hotels post signs stating whether you can pay by credit card, switch card or

The ING Bank logo

THE HISTORY OF DUTCH CURRENCY

B EFORE THE INTRODUCTION of the guilder, the Dutch national currency unit before the euro, duiten, stuivers, rijders, schellings and ducats made out of various metals were used. Until 1847 there was a double standard where the value of the coin was equal to the value of the gold or silver in it. Silver coins were minted until 1967, when nickel or bronze coins were minted. Gold and silver coins from earlier centuries are now valuable collector's items.

THE EURO

THE NETHERLANDS, together with 11 other countries, has replaced its traditional currency, the guilder, with the euro. Austria, Finland, France, Germany, Greece, Ireland, Italy, Luxembourg, the Netherlands, Portugal and Spain all chose to join the new currency. The euro came into circulation in the Netherlands on 1 January 2002. Each country using the euro produces their own coins, which have one common European side and one country-specific side. These, like the notes, which are all unified in design, can be used inside any participating member state. Be aware, though, that in the Netherlands some shops will not accept notes larger than 100 euros.

Bank Notes

Euro bank notes have seven denominations. The 5-euro note (grey in colour) is the smallest, followed by the 10-euro note (pink), 20-euro note (blue), 50-euro note (orange), 100-euro note (green), 200-euro note (yellow) and 500-euro note (purple). All notes show the 12 stars of the European Union.

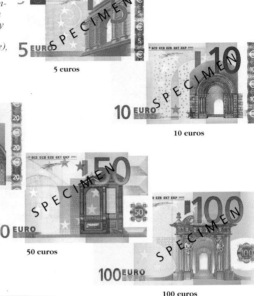

5 euros

10 euros

20 euros

50 euros

100 euros

200 euros

500 euros

2 euros

1 euro

50 cents

20 cents

10 cents

Coins

The euro has eight coin denominations: 1 euro and 2 euros; 50 cents, 20 cents, 10 cents, 5 cents, 2 cents and 1 cent. The 2- and 1-euro coins are both silver and gold in colour. The 50-, 20- and 10-cent coins are gold. The 5-, 2- and 1-cent coins are bronze.

5 cents

2 cents

1 cent

Communications

BEFORE 1989, TELEPHONE AND POSTAL SERVICES in Holland were part of the same state-run company, PTT. This has now been separated into two companies – KPN Telecom and PTT Post. Both services are among the most forward-looking and efficient in Europe. For some years, Telfort public telephones have also been appearing beside the KPN boxes. The Telfort telephones are mostly found at train stations.

KPN kiosk

Storefront of a telephone shop

USING THE TELEPHONE

YOU WILL FIND the green KPN telephone kiosks in the streets, in post offices and outside many railway stations. Most KPN telephone kiosks take both phonecards and most major credit cards (the logo on the telephone will tell you which credit cards are accepted). If you use a credit card, you need to remove it from the slot before speaking (phonecards are only removed when you have finished your call), and you have to pay a surcharge of €1.15. In KPN booths, locals can also use their bank or giro card to make phone calls, if these are fitted with a "chipper" or "chipknip" (which means you can top them up). ANWB members can also use

KPN Telecom logo

KPN telephone kiosks to call the roadside assistance patrol (*see p439*).

There are no longer any solely coin-operated payphones. KPN phone boxes accept only KPN phonecards or special kiosk-cards, available at some train stations. KPN phonecards can be purchased at post offices, tobacconists, train stations and department stores, as well as at the GWK, and come in various denominations.

At train stations you will often find Telfort phone boxes, painted blue and orange. These accept Telfort phonecards, available at ticket windows and in the Wizzl station shops and also at the GWK. Telfort phones also accept coins (10, 20 and 50 cent, €1 and €2) but do not give

change, credit cards (with a €1.15 surcharge) and special kiosk-cards.

Instructions on how to use KPN and Telfort telephones can be found in the booths in Dutch, English and other west European languages.

PHONING ABROAD

FROM HOLLAND you can direct-dial almost all destinations abroad. First you need to dial the international number 00, followed by the country number, and then the local number without the first digit (usually a 0), and finally the individual number. Many country codes are listed in telephone booths. Telephone directories have more detailed lists. Directories for the whole of the country are available. Telephone calls made from your hotel room are usually fairly expensive.

USING A PAYPHONE

KPN payphone

1 Lift the receiver

2 Insert your card or (Telfort phones only) coins. Wait for the dialling tone (a low hum).

3 Dial the number. The display panel tells you how much time you have left.

4 Replace the receiver at the end of your conversation and remove your card.

Prepaid plastic cards for mobile telephones

ELECTRONIC COMMUNICATIONS

Faster than a letter and cheaper than a phone call, sending and receiving electronic mail has never been easier or more convenient. There are many internet cafés in Amsterdam and they are becoming increasingly popular in other cities as well. At these cafés you can, for a modest fee, check your email account in comfort. They offer a variety of refreshments ranging from alcohol and coffee to light snacks. Opening hours vary, but often the cafés are open late into the night. With the arrival of easyInternetCafé in Amsterdam (it now has three locations: Damrak, Reguliersbreestraat and Leidsestraat), and with others now open in Rotterdam (Stadhuisplein), Maastricht (Wolfstraat) and Hertogenbosch (Pensmarkt), it is now possible to go online at any time of the day or night.

Visitors to Amsterdam will find *www.amsterdam.nl* worth a look. Financed by Amsterdam city council, it offers information about the city in Dutch and English, as well as access to commercial services and hundreds of local home pages.

FINDING THE RIGHT NUMBER

- Directory enquiries for phone and fax numbers in Holland dial 0900-8008 or 118 (only one number per call on either service).
- Directory enquiries for phone and fax numbers abroad dial 0900-8418, or visit www.detelefoongids.nl.
- National or international calls through the operator dial 0800-0410.
- Collect calls in Holland or abroad dial 0800-0101.
- National dialling codes are: Australia 61, New Zealand 64, South Africa 27, the United Kingdom 44, and the USA and Canada 1.

Post Offices

Post offices in Holland can be recognized by the TPG logo. In addition to buying stamps, sending telegrams and sending mail, you can also change money and traveller's cheques, make phone calls and send faxes. Larger post offices also have photocopy services and sell stationery. Smaller municipalities sometimes have only a sub post office (in a supermarket, for example) providing only basic services.

Dutch TPG postbox

New postage stamps

SENDING MAIL

Most TPG postboxes have two slots. The right slot is for local mail (post codes are given above the slot), the left one is for other destinations. A sign on the box indicates when the mail is collected (a red sign means 5pm or 6pm, a blue board means 7pm). There is no Saturday mail collection.

Postcards and letters weighing less than 20 g cost €0.39 to send to destinations within Holland; European destinations cost €0.59. To other parts of the world, the cost is higher.

Postcards and letters weighing less than 20 g to destinations within Europe are sent by priority mail. For other international mail which you

want to send with priority over standard mail, you will need to obtain a priority sticker at the post office. The cost is extra.

It is a good idea to send important documents by insured or registered mail. Urgent mail can be sent by TNT, the courier service used by TPG Post.

Shops selling postcards often sell stamps as well. This is a distinct advantage, as there are often queues at post offices. Most post offices are open from 9am to 5pm weekdays; some also open on Saturdays until 1pm. There are no longer post offices in most villages or small towns.

POSTE RESTANTE

If you do not know where you'll be staying, you can have mail sent to *Poste Restante,* addressed to the Central Post Office. You will need some sort of identification with a photograph, such as a passport or a driving licence, to pick up your mail.

Sports Holidays

WITH ITS ABUNDANCE OF WATER, Holland lends itself to all kinds of watersports such as boating, sailing and canoeing; however, there are also plenty of opportunities for sporting activities on dry land, whether you want to kick a ball about or play golf or tennis, or even go riding. Most *VVV-gidsen (see p434)* tell you where there are golf courses and tennis courts in the locality, and they give the addresses of angling clubs, stables, boatyards, sailing schools and so on.

Ramblers in the Heuvelrug of Utrecht

Holland offers much in the way of water sports, such as canoeing

WATERSPORTS

THE FAVOURITE places in the Netherlands for watersports are the Frisian seas, the coastal lakes, the Plassengebied (lakelands), the southwest river delta, and the lakes of the Vechtplassen, the Maasplassen, the IJsselmeer and, of course, the North Sea. Everywhere there are abundant marinas and water-sports centres, often with equipment for hire. The ANWB publishes the *Wateralmanakken,* available at ANWB and VVV offices and in bookshops, which give details of sailing regulations, bridge and lock opening times,

port information and so on. The *ANWB/ VVV waterkaarten* (navigation charts) are also used by many people. You can obtain information on sailing and surfing organizations at institutions such as the **Commissie Watersport Opleidingen** (water-sports training commission) and the ANWB. Surfers will find plenty to do on the North Sea and IJsselmeer coast (surfing beaches, equipment hire), and it is also possible to surf on many inland waters, including the Reenwijkse Plassen, the Randmeren and the Frisian lakes. For further information on sailing, boating and windsurfing, ask at the **Koninklijk Nederlands Watersport Verbond** (royal water-sports association) for diving include the Oosterschelde and Grevelingenmeer; for more information apply to the Dutch underwater-sports association, the **Nederlandse Onderwatersport Bond**.

For canoeing, your first port of call should be the **Nederlandse Kano Bond** (canoeing association). Dozens of round trips in various craft organized in lakes, rivers and the sea are also available. The local VVV tourist office will be able to direct you further.

RAMBLING AND CYCLING

RAMBLERS' GUIDES and maps can be obtained in many places, including the VVV, ANWB and bookshops. The VVV also provides information on walking tours and local events. The *ER op Uit!* booklet published by the Dutch Railways contains numerous rambling routes from one station to another. The majority of them are 15 to 20 km (9 to 12 miles), though some two-day hikes are also described. You will find route maps at the station where the hike begins. Around 30 long-distance hiking trails have been marked out in Holland. These routes,

SAILING

Sailing courses suitable for all ages and experience levels are widely available along the Dutch coast for practically all types of vessel. Taking lessons at a CWO registered sailing school will give you an internationally recognized CWO sailing certificate. More experienced sailors can explore the North Sea, the IJsselmeer (watch out for strong winds), the Waddenzee (where you have to watch the shallows) or the

Yachting on the Oosterschelde

Westerschelde (which has strong tidal currents). However, you can also go for a more relaxing experience on the Vinkeveense Plassen lakes. Cruises are also widely available. Hollands Glorie (tel. 010-4156600) offers cruises on traditional sailing craft on waterways such as the IJsselmeer, the Waddenzee and the Frisian lakes.

Sailing dinghy

Golfers on the Lauswolt Estate *(see p398)* in Friesland

which are at least 100 km (62 miles) in length, follow mainly unmetalled tracks. A popular hiking trail is the Pieterpad (LAW 9), stretching 480 km (300 miles) from Pieterburen in Groningen to the Sint-Pietersberg at Maastricht.

Wandelplatform-LAW publishes guides to the routes, with and without accommodation details. Many natural areas are criss-crossed by footpaths and cycle tracks, among them the Nationaal Park Hoge Veluwe *(see p337)*. You can find out about accessibility of various areas and about enjoyable routes or excursions at VVV or ANWB tourist information offices, at the Staatsbosbeheer (forestry commission) (tel. 030-692 6213) or the Vereniging Natuurmonumenten *(see p269)*. For details on cycling, see pages 456–7.

GOLF AND TENNIS

HOLLAND HAS some 160 golfing clubs, all members of the Nederlandse Golf Federatie (**NGF**). Many clubs also provide opportunities for non-members to play, although some may require some proof of golfing proficiency. Many of them also offer training courses. Golf courses in Holland are in dunelands, woodland and polderland.

In many areas you will find tennis clubs with outdoor and indoor courts. Most bungalow parks have tennis courts for the use of residents.

FISHING

FISHING IS a popular sport in Holland. In the inland waterways you can angle for bream, carp and pike, while flatfish and mackerel can be caught along the coast and in the sea. Local angling associations will give you information on when and where to fish. Don't forget to obtain a fishing permit (which is compulsory for inland waters). The permits are available at post offices, VVVs or angling associations. Sometimes you also need a permit for a particular lake or river. Along the coast, angling trips are organized on the North Sea and in the Waddenzee.

HORSE RIDING

THERE ARE many stables where you can hire horses for pony-trekking. Some stables hire out horses only if you have a riding permit or if you are on a guided tour (information is available from the **SRR**). For some nature reserves which allow riding you will need to get a riding permit from the organization managing the area, and you will have to keep to the bridleways. Beach riding is an unforgettable experience, but keep an eye on the signs, because some sections of beach – especially in summer – are closed to horses.

Riding on Ameland

DIRECTORY

WATERSPORTS

Commissie Watersport Opleidingen (CWO)
Postbus 87, 3980 CB Bunnik.
📞 030-6566599.

Koninklijk Nederlands Watersport Verbond
Postbus 87, 3980 CB Bunnik.
📞 030-6566550.

Nederlandse Kano Bond
Postbus 1160, 3800 BD Amersfoort. 📞 033-4622341.

Nederlandse Onderwatersport Bond
Nassaustraat 12, 3583 XG Utrecht. 📞 030-2517014.

WALKING AND CYCLING

Cycletours
Buiksloterweg 7a, 1031 CC Amsterdam. 📞 020-6274098.

Fietsvakantiewinkel
Spoorlaan 19, 3445 AE Woerden
📞 0348-421844.

Nederlandse Wandelsport Bond
Pieterskerkhof 22, 3512 JS Utrecht. 📞 030-2319458.

NTFU
Postbus 326, 3900 AH Veenendaal. 📞 0318-581300.

Stichting Landelijk Fietsplatform
Postbus 846, 3800 AV Amersfoort. 📞 033-4653656.

Wandelplatform-LAW
Postbus 846, 3800 AV Amersfoort. 📞 033-4653660.

GOLF

NGF
Postbus 221,
3454 ZL De Meern.
📞 030-2426370.

FISHING

Nederlandse Vereniging van Sportvissersfederaties
Postbus 288, 3800 AG Amersfoort. 📞 033-4634924.

HORSE RIDING

SRR
Postbus 456, 3740 AL Baarn.
📞 035-5483650.

Amusement and Theme Parks

Holland offers a great variety of theme parks and amusement parks. Whether you want to see dolphins, take a white-knuckle ride, admire vintage cars or spend the day splashing in a swimming pool, there is something for everyone. And because the Dutch weather doesn't always do its best to help, most parks have a considerable proportion of their attractions indoors. Listed below is a small sample of the amusement and theme parks to be found in the country.

Hellendoorn adventure park

ARCHEON

This archaeological theme park brings the past to life in an interesting way. It's an open-air museum where visitors wander through prehistoric times, the Roman period and the Middle Ages: all the re-creations are brought to life by actors. First you are able to see for yourself how the prehistoric hunter-gatherers lived, and how farmers tilled their fields. Further on, you enter a Roman town complete with bath-house, temple and theatre. After that you come to the centre of a medieval city, where you can watch craftsmen at work and visit a monastery. The park offers many activities in which you can participate, including a trip in a prehistoric canoe.

HET ARSENAAL

A large attraction with a maritime theme has been set up at Het Arsenaal in Vlissingen. First visitors watch a naval review with models of famous ocean liners, including the *Titanic*. And, for those looking for a more palpable experience, you can go into a shipwreck simulator, and – especially exciting for the children – a scary pirate cave on a treasure island. In Onderwaterwereld you can observe sharks, lobsters and other inhabitants of the deep. A highlight for many visitors is the shallow pool with rays and the impressive skeleton of a sperm whale.

The 64-m (210-ft) tower of Het Arsenaal gives a fine view of Walcheren and the

Westerschelde. In addition, the complex features the Carousel Centre where there are family restaurants and other facilities, a snooker centre, a theatre and a restaurant.

AUTOTRON ROSMALEN

Model "T" Fords, Spykers and vintage fire engines are just some of the collection of old vehicles on display at AutoDome, the new museum building of Autotron. In addition to an exhibition covering almost one century of motoring history, it looks into the future as well as at innovation, traffic management and the environment. The amusement park outside has a variety of car-related attractions. Children can get behind the wheel on the 4 x 4 track, a vintage car track and a Ferrari track, and can get an Autotron driving licence in the traffic gardens. An enjoyable experience for young and old alike are the *trapkarretjes,* carts with huge wheels. In addition, there is a go-kart track, pedalo hire and various children's playgrounds, including the covered SpeeloDome, with its numerous games for children.

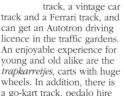

Vintage car in Autotron, Rosmalen

AVONTURENPARK HELLENDOORN

This adventure park offers much more than can be described here. A small selection includes: the Canadian River log-ride (with a 12-m (39-ft) drop in a tree trunk), the Sungai Kalimantan rafting-ride, the Tornado and Rioolrat (underground) rat ride, a monorail over a dinosaur park, a boat ride, a jungle journey,

Montezuma's Revenge (you'll definitely get wet on this one) and the mysterious villa of an eccentric explorer who gives his visitors a gruesome experience they won't forget.

You can also have a look at a Western town with its stores and a pretty French town square. In addition, there are various presentations, such as a parrot show and the Magical Monkey Show. Younger children can have fun in Dreamesland (Dreamland), where there are old mail-coaches, a play castle and much more.

The park is picturesquely located on the Sallandse Heuvelrug hills.

ATTRACTIEPARK SLAGHAREN

This extensive recreation park offers visitors some 40 attractions, including a monorail, a 50-m (165-ft) big wheel, the Looping Star roller coaster, a boat ride and the Zwunka flying carpet. You can relive the colourful Wild West in the OK Corral City, where Western shows are put on, as well as in the 19th-century Wild West City. If you like swimming, you can choose between the indoor Bergbad

Enjoying the breathtaking slide at Slagharen theme park

Suspension bridge through the tropical rainforest in Burgers' Bush

and an outdoor pool with a sun terrace and a fantastic water playground. Young children can ride Shetland ponies and amuse themselves with the attractions offered by Kid's Country. There is also a special theatre for children.

BURGERS' ZOO

Burgers' zoo is more than just a zoo: it gives you the chance to see animals from many parts of the world in their natural environments, which have been carefully recreated here.

In Burgers' Desert, in a hall that soars to 20 m (65 ft), you can wander through a rocky cactus desert with birds, fish and an oasis with fish.

Burgers' Bush for its part is a dense tropical jungle covering 1.5 ha (4 acres) inhabited by caimans, tortoises and hundreds of birds. There is also a suspension bridge by which you can cross a safari park with giraffes, rhinoceroses, lions and other animals of the savannah.

In Burgers' Ocean, the zoo's latest addition, you can stand on a tropical coral beach and see, through glass windows, what goes on in the sea.

DOLFINARIUM

Entertaining dolphin displays and performances by seals and walruses always draw large crowds. But in addition to this, the Lagune, a large bay in which dolphins, seals, sea lions and fish live, makes a captivating show in itself. On the Roggenrif you can walk among seals and stroke rays and sharks, while in Fort Heerewich you can learn about how stranded dolphins are cared for. An underwater show and three-dimensional film are guaranteed to provide additional excitement. There is also a play park for children.

The splash ride in Duinrell

DUINRELL

The picturesque woodland and dune region of Wassenaar is home to the Duinrell theme park. Its rides include the Waterspin, toboggan runs, a frog roller coaster, a splash-ride and a monorail. These and a host of other attractions guarantee an eventful day out for young and old alike. In summer, the park hosts spectacular shows, including the *Music Laser Light Show*. For the little ones there is a fairytale wonderland, a large playground and numerous kids' shows. A big attraction is the **Tikibad**, an indoor pool with spectacular slides, a surf pool, a water ballet show and a wide variety of other water attractions. The picturesque countryside surrounding the park offers good opportunities for rambling, cycling, riding, squash and golf. You can also camp or rent a bungalow here.

ECODROME

The natural environment is the central theme of this park in Zwolle. The Natuurmuseum contains archaeological finds dating back to the Ice Age as well as fossils and stuffed birds. The tropical and subtropical greenhouse features a dinosaur skeleton and a pavilion which hosts temporary exhibitions and a display showing how the earth was created. Outside are a number of themed gardens and a bee garden.

Numerous hands-on activities both inside and outside are enjoyable and educational for children. For example, they can dig up mammoth bones and generate power in the Edon energy square. The playgrounds, the water playgrounds and the swan pedaloes are also a hit with the younger visitors.

ECOMARE

Ecomare, on the island of Texel, is an information centre for the tidal flats of the Waddeneilanden and the North Sea. There is a fascinating exhibition about the creation of Texel, the island's nature and the inhabitants of the North Sea and the Waddenzee. The Waterzaal is full of aquariums and exhibitions on the ecology of the Waddenzee and the North Sea. There is also a large aquarium with small-spotted dogfish and a basin where you can stroke rays. The complex includes a reception centre for stranded seals and seabirds which is open to the public. The attached 70-ha (173-acre) dune park offers exhilarating walks.

Stranded seals recovering their health in EcoMare on Texel

Dwarfs watch Snow White's coffin at De Efteling theme park

De Efteling

DE EFTELING theme park in Kaatsheuvel is based on the world of fantasy. In the fairytale forest you can meet a variety of fairytale characters, including Little Red Riding Hood, Sleeping Beauty and Snow White. In the village of 't Lavenlaar, the miraculous Laaf people bake their pies. In Fata Morgana you can discover the world of the Arabian Nights and view the entire park from a 45-m (148-ft) Flying Temple.

For those seeking more extreme fun, there are the Python, the Pegasus and the underground Vogel Rok roller coasters, as well as a haunted house, wild water ride, bobsleigh ride and the mysterious Villa Volta. For a more laid-back approach, boat past the islands full of flowers.

If a day here isn't enough, accommodation is available in the Efteling Hotel.

Linnaeushof

THIS IS EUROPE'S largest playground, with at least 350 different pieces of equipment, including a super slide, cable rides, a skate-rail, trampolines, a climbing wall, 360-degree swings, pedaloes, a mini-golf course and a "spider's web", where you risk falling into the water as you clamber along nets to the pirates' crow's nest.

Toddlers enjoy themselves most in their own special playground, which has a huge sandpit and a road village where they can ride around on tricycles and toy aeroplanes.

If it's raining, there is still plenty to do in the indoor playground with air-karts and miniature cars in an aerial castle. A water playground is open in hot weather.

Het Land van Ooit

HET LAND VAN OOIT (Never-Never Land) is in Drunen. This is a special theme park where past, present and future come together and children are in charge. The "Governor's old estate" is inhabited by knights in shining armour,

A giant towers over all visitors to the Land van Ooit

maidens, giants and other unusual characters. Kloontje the Giant's Child, Dame Grandeur, Knight Granite and other characters make sure that your children will have an unforgettable day out. In indoor and open-air theatres they can watch plays and listen to songs and storytellers. There are also jousting tournaments, as well as adventures in which they can take part themselves, such as the Reuzenland

playground, which is a giant bouncy castle presided over by the 15-m (50-ft) Durfslurf. The Laser Castle and the Iron Horse Paradise, along with a playground for children in wheelchairs, are further attractions of the park.

Noordwijk Space Expo

THIS IS EUROPE'S largest permanent exhibition dedicated to outer space and is very informative for all ages. It has genuine as well as reconstructions of rockets and satellites, a piece of moon rock 4 billion years old, the motor unit of a launcher rocket, a model lunar module and much more. You can walk around a space station, and watch spectacular multimedia and video presentations. Children can take part in an enjoyable treasure-hunt and experience weightlessness in a simulator.

Aqua Zoo Friesland

IN ADDITION TO OTTERS, this park near Leeuwarden allows beavers, minks, polecats, storks and other animals to live in their natural surroundings. Otters have disappeared in Holland because the freshwater environment which forms their habitat is too polluted. Aqua Zoo is striving to restore this environment. A route has been marked out which you can follow, gathering interesting information along the way. A glass tunnel also allows you to watch the behaviour of otters under water. The exhibition building provides further information about the otters' habitat.

Six Flags Holland

FORMERLY the Walibi Flevo, the Six Flags Holland theme park features, in addition to crowd-pullers such as the El Condor roller coaster, the Rio Grande white-water course and the Space Shot, which shoots you 60 m (200 ft) into "space", 30 new attractions and shows. The Giant Wheel towers 45 m (148 ft) into the air, and there are four brand-new roller coasters. Superman The Ride shoots

Rides at Six Flags Holland

you from 0 to 90 km/h (60 mph) in just three seconds, while the Boomerang Coaster loops the loop at least six times. The park's American theme is immediately evident the minute you step into Main Street. You will also meet various characters from *Looney Tunes* such as Bugs Bunny.

VERKEERSPARK ASSEN

ASSEN HAS the largest road theme park in Europe. In the middle of the park is a circuit with roads, roundabouts, traffic lights and traffic signs where children aged between 6 and 12 can drive around and learn to deal with various traffic situations. There is a traffic control tower from which someone keeps an eye on the participants.

For younger children there is a partly indoor children's corner, a roundabout and other rides such as mini-scooters and pedal locomotives. Older children can try to negotiate an obstacle course in motorized jeeps. However, there is far more to the park than this, such as radio-controlled boats, amusing "bouncy bikes", minigolf, a climbing tower, a boating lake and a karting track (for over-fours).

The Verkeerspark Assen, a paradise for budding motorists

DIRECTORY

Aqua Zoo Friesland
De Groene Ster 2, 8926 XE Leeuwarden. **[** 0511-431214. **]** 9:30am–5:30pm daily.

Archeon
Archeonlaan 2, 2408 ZB Alphen a/d Rijn. **[** 0172-447744. **]** mid Apr–beg Oct: 10am–5pm Tue–Sun.

Het Arsenaal
Arsenaalplein 1, 4380 KA Vlissingen. **[** 0118-415400. **]** 10am–7pm daily (to 8pm Jul & Aug). **]** 1 Jan, 25 Dec, 31 Dec.

Attractiepark Slagharen
Zwartedijk 37, 7776 PB Slagharen. **[** 0523-683000. **]** Apr–Oct: 10am–5:30pm Mon–Fri, 10am–6pm Sat & Sun.

Autotron Rosmalen
Graafsebaan 133, 5248 NL Rosmalen. **[** 073-5233300. **] Automuseum**: mid Apr–May: 10am–5pm Sat, Sun & school holidays; Jun–Aug: 10am–5pm daily.

Avonturenpark Hellendoorn
Luttenbergerweg 22, 7447 PB Hellendoorn. **[** 0548-659159. **]** mid-Apr–Aug: 10am–5pm daily; Nov–Dec: 10am–5pm Sat & Sun.

Burgers' Zoo
Schelmseweg 85, 6816 SH Arnhem. **[** 026-4424534/4450373. **]** Apr–Oct: 9am–7pm daily; Nov–Mar: 9am–sunset.

Dolfinarium Harderwijk
Strandboulevard oost 1, 3841 AB Harderwijk. **[** 0341-467467/0900-DOLFIJN/464767. **]** late Feb–Oct: 10am–6pm daily; Nov–Dec: 10am–5pm Sat & Sun.

Duinrell
Duinrell 1, 2242 JP Wassenaar. **[** 070-5155258. **] Theme park**: Apr–end Oct: 10am–5pm (Jul–Aug to 6pm). **Tikibad**: Apr–end Oct: 10am–10pm daily; Oct–Mar: 2–10pm Mon–Fri, 10am–10pm Sat & Sun. **Tikisauna**: 2–11pm Mon–Fri, noon–11pm Sat & Sun.

Ecodrome
Willemsvaart 19, 8019 AB Zwolle. **[** 038-4215050. **]** Apr–Oct: 10am–5pm daily; Nov–Mar: 10am–5pm Wed, Sat & Sun; daily during school hols. **]** 1 Jan, 25 Dec, 31 Dec.

EcoMare
Ruyslaan 92, 1796 AZ De Koog, Texel. **[** 0222-317741. **]** Jan–Dec: 9am–5pm daily (seals are fed at 11am and 3pm). **]** 1 Jan, 25 Dec.

De Efteling
Europalaan 1, 5171 KW Kaatsheuvel. **[** 0416-288111 (for information on how to get to Efteling and the best time to visit). **]** Apr–mid-Jul, Sep, Oct: 10am–6pm daily; mid-Jul–Aug: 10am–9pm Sun–Fri, 10am–midnight Sat. **Winter Efteling**: open around Christmas.

Het Land van Ooit
Parklaan 40, Drunen. **[** 0416-377775. **]** mid-Apr–Oct: 10am–5pm daily (only Sat & Sun in Sep).

Linnaeushof
Rijksstraatweg 4, 2121 AE Bennebroek. **[** 023-5847624. **]** Apr–Sep: 10am–6pm daily.

Noordwijk Space Expo
Keplerlaan 3, 2201 AZ Noordwijk. **[** 0900-87654321. **]** Jan–Dec: 10am–5pm Tue–Sun, also open Mon during school hols. **]** 1 Jan, 25 Dec.

Six Flags Holland
Spijkweg 30, 8256 RJ Biddinghuizen. **[** 0321-329999. **]** Apr–Jun: 10am–5pm Mon–Fri, 10am–6pm Sat & Sun; beg Jul–mid Jul: 10am–7pm daily; mid Jul–Aug: 10am–9pm daily; Sep: 10am–5pm Fri, 10am–6pm Sat & Sun; autumn hols: 10am–6pm daily.

Verkeerspark Assen
De Haar 1–1a, 9405 TE Assen. **[** 0592-350005. **]** Apr–Aug (and late Oct): 9:30am–5pm daily (to 6pm Jul–mid-Aug); Sep: 9:30am–5pm Wed, Sat, Sun; Nov–Mar: 11am–5:30pm Wed, Sat, Sun. **]** during Assen TT races (Jun).

TRAVEL INFORMATION

ALMOST EVERY MAJOR European airport has direct flights to Schiphol, but this modern international airport southwest of Amsterdam also has direct connections with other airports around the world, including many in the United States. Holland also has efficient rail links with neighbouring coun-

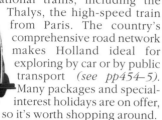

The Parking Hopper at Schiphol

tries. Major stations are served by international trains, including the Thalys, the high-speed train from Paris. The country's comprehensive road network makes Holland ideal for exploring by car or by public transport *(see pp454–5)*. Many packages and special-interest holidays are on offer, so it's worth shopping around.

Car-hire counter at Schiphol

BY AIR

SCHIPHOL AIRPORT handles some 175,000 flights a year by many international carriers. To increase this volume further, there are serious plans to expand the airport. KLM (Royal Dutch Airlines) and its airline partners have flights to Amsterdam from over 350 cities worldwide. Northwest Airlines offers non-stop flights from Boston, Detroit and Washington, Delta Air Lines from Atlanta and New York (JFK) and Continental Airlines from Newark. There are many flights a day from the UK and the Irish Republic. Low-cost airline easyJet serves Amsterdam from Luton, and bmi british midland from East Midlands and London Heathrow. To get the lowest fare, generally you must book well in advance.

SCHIPHOL AIRPORT

Schiphol has only one terminal. The airport signs are colour-coded, with yellow signs indicating transfer desks and gates, green ones amenities such as coffee bars, restaurants and shops. Lounge South is designated for passengers travelling to countries in the Schengen agreement. At Schiphol Plaza you can find shops, book hotels, hire a car or buy a railway ticket. Beneath it are the platforms of Schiphol railway station. From the car park there are transfer buses to take you to the terminal. The long-stay car park is served by an automatic bus, the Parking Hopper, that takes you to the transfer bus.

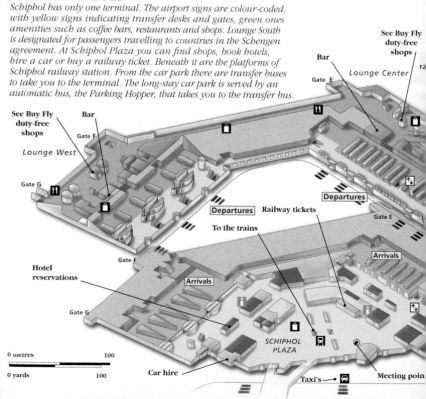

Planes at Amsterdam Schiphol Airport

SHOPPING

IF YOU ARE LEAVING Holland by plane, you will find the large See Buy Fly shopping centre when you leave customs control. Although travellers to other EU member states are not permitted to buy duty-free goods at the airport *(see p436)*, it is still possible to find some bargains with the low See Buy Fly prices; only alcohol and tobacco is sold here at the same price as in local shops. Passengers to destinations outside the EU can still purchase duty-free alcohol and tobacco. The centrally located Schiphol Plaza is open to everyone, but the goods stocked here are not sold at See Buy Fly prices.

GETTING TO AND FROM SCHIPHOL

EVERY MAJOR CITY in Holland can be reached by train from Schiphol Station. The journey to Amsterdam Centraal Station takes 20 minutes. Schiphol is also on the night-train network of the Western Netherlands *(see p454)*. In addition, the airport has good bus connections with many towns. KLM runs a bus service (the KLM Hotel Shuttle), linking the airport with some 20 hotels in central and south Amsterdam. There are also abundant taxis waiting at the

Watch shop at Schiphol

airport to take you wherever you need to go, although you may find they are not the cheapest way to travel.

REGIONAL AIRPORTS

EINDHOVEN, Maastricht, Rotterdam and Groningen are all served by domestic flights, with flights between Eindhoven and Schiphol, Maastricht and Schiphol, Groningen and Rotterdam and Eindhoven and Rotterdam. There are direct international flights between Rotterdam and Eindhoven and Manchester and London, and between Maastricht and Munich, Berlin and London.

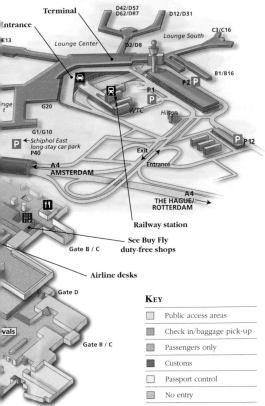

Terminal

Entrance

E13

Lounge Center

D42/D57
D62/D7

D2/D8

D12/D31

Lounge South

C3/C16

B1/B16

P2

P1

G20

WTC

Hilton

G1/G10

Schiphol East
long-stay car park
P40

Exit

Entrance

A4
AMSTERDAM

P12

A4
THE HAGUE/
ROTTERDAM

Railway station

**See Buy Fly
duty-free shops**

Gate B / C

Airline desks

Gate D

vals

Gate B / C

KEY

☐	Public access areas
☐	Check in/baggage pick-up
☐	Passengers only
■	Customs
☐	Passport control
☐	No entry

Information screens at Schiphol

By Rail

H OLLAND CAN easily be reached by train from most European countries, although visitors from further afield may have to change trains several times en route. Eurostar runs from London via the Channel Tunnel; passengers for Amsterdam must change at Brussels.

There are direct trains from a number of European stations. For example, Brussels, Paris, Berlin, Zurich, Vienna and (seasonally) Milan have direct rail links to Amsterdam Centraal Station (CS) and Utrecht CS. From Brussels and from Antwerp there are trains to Amsterdam all day, stopping at Roosendaal, Rotterdam, The Hague and Schiphol, including five journeys daily by the Thalys high-speed train from Paris.

Many other towns, particularly those which are in the border regions of Belgium and Holland, can easily be reached by train. Hook of Holland is connected by trains which connect with ferries from the UK port of Harwich.

Special Tickets

T OURISTS FROM other EU countries can purchase cards in their countries that will entitle them to special reductions. An Interrail card for people aged 26 and under, along with a slightly dearer version for the over-26s, allows travellers to use the entire European rail network at a

The Thalys high-speed train

Ferries serve Rotterdam, Hook of Holland and IJmuiden

discount. A Eurodomino card allows 3, 5 or 8 days of unlimited travel in the country of your choice and is available at a reduction for under-26s. Eurail Selectpass offers unlimited travel on the national rail networks of any three to five bordering countries out of 18 European nations, including Holland.

By Coach

F OR TRAVELLERS from many European countries the cheapest way to reach Holland is by coach. Most long-distance coaches have toilets and make regular stops. In summer in particular there are large numbers of coaches from other countries serving a whole range of towns in Holland. **Eurolines** offers a very extensive network of coach connections. It has coaches running from many European cities to Holland at least once per week. Dozens of points in Holland (depending on the point of departure and route) are served by them. From Brussels and Antwerp there are coaches to places such as Breda, Rotterdam, The Hague, Utrecht and Amsterdam.

Ferries

A NUMBER OF FERRY companies serve routes between Britain and Holland. **P&O North Sea Ferries** sails

A Eurolines coach

between Hull and Rotterdam/ Europoort, while **Stena Line** sails between Harwich and Hook of Holland (by seacat). **DFDS Seaways** serves Newcastle and IJmuiden. Other convenient ferry ports for visitors from Great Britain are Zeebrugge (from Hull) and Oostende (from Dover) in Belgium, and Calais and Boulogne (from Folkestone and Dover) in France. Crossing times range from 16 hours (Newcastle–IJmuiden) to 35 minutes (Dover–Calais by **Hoverspeed** hovercraft).

Ticket prices depend on the speed of crossing. In summer it is a good idea to book.

Motoring in Holland

H OLLAND'S GOOD system of roads makes all parts of the country easy to reach by car. Beware, however, in the Randstad region: you may have to put up with traffic jams during the rush hour.

To drive in Holland you need to have a valid national driving licence, though many car-hire firms prefer to see an international driving licence. In addition, if in your own car, you will need to have your vehicle log book and your insurance papers with you.

Roads in Holland are divided into three categories. Provincial roads are designated with the letter "N" before the road number, national motorways are designated with an "A" before the number and international highways have the letter "E" before the number. All Dutch motorways are equipped with emergency telephones from which motorists can call the **ANWB** road assistance service *(see p438)* if their car breaks down. A non-member can pay for the ANWB's services, or become a temporary ANWB member. Unless otherwise signposted, the maximum speed for cars in Holland is 120 km/h (75 mph) on motorways, 100 km/h (62 mph) on major roads, 80 km/h (50 mph) on secondary roads and 50 km/h (30 mph) in built-up areas. At unmarked junctions, give way to traffic coming from the left, except for trams, which always have right of way (except when you are driving along a

Emergency phone

road which has right of way). In built-up areas motorists must give way to buses that are leaving bus stops.

Finding somewhere to park is often a problem in the cities. As clamping is prevalent and theft rife, it is often best to look for a car park rather than to try to find street parking. When you enter a car park, take a ticket from the machine at the barrier, and pay at the payment machine before leaving. Avoid out-of-order street meters as you could get fined or your car clamped. You may not park on yellow lines, and on yellow broken lines you may not park even to load or unload. If you stop on a blue line, you will need to have a parking disc.

CAR HIRE

To HIRE A CAR you need to be at least 21 years old and have a valid driving licence. Some hire companies also require at least one year's driving experience. The main international car-hire companies such as Avis, Budget, Europcar and Hertz have offices at Schiphol and in all major cities. Local car-hire firms are often substantially cheaper. When hiring a car without a credit card, you may have to pay a hefty deposit.

One way of taking your bike along

DIRECTORY

SCHIPHOL AIRPORT

Information and services
📞 0900-SCHIPHOL /
0900-72447465.
🌐 www.schiphol.nl

REGIONAL AIRPORTS

Eindhoven Airport
📞 040-2919818.

Groningen Airport Eelde
📞 050-3097070.

Maastricht Aachen Airport
📞 043-3589999/
3589898.

Rotterdam Airport
📞 010-4463444/
4463454.

AIRLINES

Aer Lingus
📞 020-6238620.
📞 1-8868888 (Eire).
🌐 www.aerlingus.ie

bmi british midland
📞 020-3469211.
📞 0870-6070555 (UK).
🌐 www.flybmi.com

British Airways
📞 020-3469559.
📞 0845-7733377 (UK).
🌐 www.ba.com

Continental Airlines
📞 1-800-5233273 (US).
🌐 www.continental.com

Delta Air Lines
📞 1-800-2414141 (US).
🌐 www.delta-air.com

easyJet
📞 0870-6000000 (UK).
🌐 www.easyjet.com

KLM & KLM Cityhopper
📞 020-4747747.
📞 0870-5074074 (UK).
🌐 www.klm.nl

Martinair
📞 020-6011444/
020-6011767.

Northwest Airlines
📞 1-800-2252525 (US).
🌐 www.nwa.com

Transavia
📞 020-4060406.

RAILWAYS

Public transport travel information
📞 0900-9292.
🌐 www.ov9292.nl

International public transport information
📞 0900-9296
(Netherlands).

In the UK:
European Rail Ltd.
📞 020-73870444.
🌐 www.europeanrail.com

BUS COMPANIES

Eurolines Nederland
Amstelbusstation
Julianaplein 5,
1097 DN Amsterdam.
📞 020-5608788.
🌐 www.eurolines.nl

Rokin 10,
1012 KR Amsterdam.
📞 020-5608788.

Eurolines (UK)
📞 01582-456654 (UK).
🌐 www.go-by-coach.com

FERRIES

DFDS Seaways
📞 0800-0227880.
🌐 www.dfdsseaways.co.uk

Hoverspeed/ Seacat
📞 0800-12111211.
🌐 www.hoverspeed.co.uk

P&O North Sea Ferries
📞 0181-255555.
🌐 www.ponsf.com

Stena Line
📞 0900-8123/0174-
315800.
🌐 www.stenaline.co.uk

BY CAR

ANWB
📞 0800-0503 (Head office).

CAR HIRE FIRMS AT SCHIPHOL

AVIS
📞 020-6556050.

Budget Rent a Car
📞 020-6041349.

Europcar
📞 020-3164190.

Hertz
📞 0800-23543789.

Public Transport

Holland has a comprehensive and efficient public transport system. Major cities can be easily reached by train, while towns and villages are served by local buses. The Randstad in particular gets fairly snarled up in the morning and evening rush hour. If you need to travel at that time, the best thing to do is to leave the car and take the train. The luxury Interliner long-distance coaches connect destinations without fast rail links.

Dutch Railways logo

By Bus

Holland has a good network of local buses and inter-city coaches. Booklets are available giving detailed information on routes, timetables and fares, although it is also possible to get information from **Openbaar Vervoer Reisinformatie** (0900-9292). Ticket strips are available from the driver, but it is cheaper to buy them in advance. They are available from GVB offices, post offices, railway stations and shops which display the sign in the window. Give the ticket to the driver for stamping. Every used strip above the base strip allows you to travel in a certain zone. In June, July and August you can buy a *Zomerzwerfkaart* (summer rover), which allows you to travel all day by bus, tram and metro anywhere in Holland.

Interliners are luxury long-distance coaches. They usually follow direct routes between places and stop less frequently than local buses *(streekbussen)*. In the evenings they do not operate as late as the local buses. The timetables for buses are based on the railway timetable. Tickets are available from the driver or in advance at Interlinerverkooppunten (Interliner sales offices) and at many railway and bus stations. They can also be ordered by telephone from **Interliner Services** at 0900-8998998. Interliner stops are green and have an information display.

Interliners cover an expanding number of routes

By Train

The trains of the Dutch Railways (Nederlandse Spoorwegen, or NS) generally run on time. Timetables are displayed on yellow boards in stations. Rail tickets are available at ticket offices, Wizzl station shops and from ticket machines in stations, or, with a substantial supplement,

Steam Trains

There are many places in Holland where you can take a nostalgic ride in a steam train. There is, for example, the 22-km (14-mile) Dieren–Apeldoorn line, the 16-km (10-mile) Kerkrade–Schin op Geul, (the "million line", *see p366*), the 15.5-km (9.5-mile) Goes–Oudelande, around the Valkenburgse Meer lake and through the Hoogoventerrein at IJmuiden (21 km/13miles), departing from Beverwijk Station, *see p186*). A steam train runs the 20 km (12 miles) between Hoorn and Medemblik in summer *(see p176)*. Check with the VVV, as schedules vary.

Dieren-Apeldoorn steam train

from the conductor aboard the train. Dutch Railways has a wide variety of fare discounts on offer, including *Railrunner* tickets for children, and other offers for people regularly using the same route. Combined season tickets for the train and local or urban transport are also available. For information it is best to ask at ticket offices, or telephone 0900-9292.

Many railways in Friesland, Groningen and the Achterhoek are run by NordNed and Syntus. NS cards are also valid on these lines. Night trains run on the Utrecht CS-Amsterdam CS-Schiphol-Leiden Centraal-The Hague CS-Delft-Rotterdam CS lines.

By Tram

There are trams in Amsterdam, Rotterdam, Utrecht and The Hague. They generally run from 6am to midnight. On Sundays they start one or one and a half hours later. Tram stops display the name of the stop, the tram numbers that stop there and show the other stops on the

An NS double-decker train speeding past tulip fields

RAIL TICKETS, TICKET STRIPS AND SEASON TICKETS

In addition to ordinary train tickets, there are a variety of discount tickets giving reductions for travelling off-peak, for example. *Strippenkaart* (ticket strips) are valid on buses, trams, metros and some rail routes. Instructions on using the ticket are on the back. Daily, weekly, monthly and annual tickets for urban and local travel are also available.

Discount card

Railway ticket

Strippenkaart

route. Tram shelters display maps of the tram network.

You can board or alight from any door, unless there is a conductor on the tram, when the rear door is for boarding only. Ticket strips can be bought aboard trams from the drivers or the conductor, if there is one, or at a machine. However, it will be less expensive to buy your ticket strip or a rover ticket in advance.

Tram stops are normally announced, but if you aren't sure where to get off, you can always ask the driver to call out the stop.

METRO

A MSTERDAM and Rotterdam are the only towns in Holland with a metro. Both networks are fairly extensive. Amsterdam's metro has three lines, two of which begin at the Centraal Station, and the third at Station Sloterdijk. They go as far as Gaasperplas and Gein. From Centraal Station there is also a suburban tram to Amstelveen. The Rotterdam metro system comprises two lines which cross one another, the north-south line going from the Centraal Station to Spijkenisse, and the west-east line from Marconiplein to Capelle, with a branch to Ommoord-Zevenkamp.

Buying and franking tickets involves the same procedure as for buses and trams. The first metro leaves the terminus at around 6am (around 7:45am on Sundays), and the last train arrives at its destination at approximately 0:15 or 0:30am.

TAXIS

I F YOU NEED a taxi, the best thing is to either go to a taxi-stand or phone a Taxicentrale: telephone numbers can be found in the telephone directory and in the Yellow Pages. It is less common to hail a taxi in the street, although it

A treintaxi

can be done. Taxis have a meter showing the cost of the ride so far. The price depends on the distance travelled and the time. In addition, there is also an initial charge. Taxis cost more at night.

RAIL TAXIS

A ROUND 100 Dutch railway stations operate a rail taxi, or *treintaxi*, service which enables you to travel cheaply to a destination in the same or nearby district. A ticket costs €3.80 at the station or €4.80 from the driver and is valid whatever the length of the journey. The taxi will also take other passengers to their destinations, and so will usually take a roundabout route.

Rail taxis operate from 7am (8am on Sundays and public holidays) until just after the arrival of the last train. You can book the service by phoning the national number 0900-TREINTAXI/8734682. At the station, book it by pressing the button on the blue-yellow column. Information on places covered by the service is given in the NS leaflet *Treintaxi-stations op en rijtje.*

SPECIAL OUTINGS

The *Museumboot* in Amsterdam is a river boat that stops near almost all the main sights of the capital (tel. 020-5309010). In the summer it departs every half hour from opposite the Centraal Station from 10am to 5pm, and in other seasons operates every 55 minutes. Tickets are available at the Centraal Station VVV office, or at one of the boat stops. An all-day *Museumboot-dagkaart* (day ticket) gives you reductions of 10 to 50 per cent on admission to most museums. Another boat, the *Artis Express*, takes you from the Centraal Station to Artis zoo. This boat also runs every half hour (tel. 020-5309010). A boat tour of the canals of places like Amsterdam, Utrecht, Leiden and Delft gives you an entirely different view of the inner cities. Almost all the boats have transparent roofs which are opened in fine weather. Tours in horse-drawn trams are available in some towns in Holland, such as Delft (April to September, departing from the Markt). In Gouda you can take a sightseeing tour in a horse-drawn carriage from late June to August (departing at the Agnietenkapel, behind the Waag). Details are available from the local VVV office.

The *Museumboot* in Amsterdam

Cycling

THE FLAT LANDSCAPE of Holland makes it a boon for cyclists. At least 85 per cent of the population have a bicycle. However, there is no shortage of maps and guidebooks with interesting cycling routes. You can use the LF-routes (see p457) to plan your own daytrip or cycling holiday. Another possibility is to take part in an organized cycle tour, where you are awarded a souvenir medal at the end.

Guides showing cycling routes

ROAD SAFETY

THE LARGE NUMBER of cycle paths and cycle lanes, often equipped with traffic lights for cyclists, make cycling in Holland a safe and enjoyable activity. However, it's worth keeping a look-out for the occasional moped that may make use of a cycle path. Cycling in the peaceful countryside and cycling in the busy city are two quite separate experiences. In Amsterdam particularly, the traffic is fairly chaotic – mostly because of the large number of cyclists, who tend to ignore the traffic regulations. If you are unaccustomed to this, it's worth taking extra care. Front and rear lights, a rear reflector and reflective strips or reflective circles are compulsory at night. Many cyclists ride without this equipment, often leaving them almost invisible.

CYCLE HIRE

THERE ARE plenty of cycle hire shops in Holland. You can either go to private cycle hire places or hire a

bike from some 100 railway stations with a *Rijwielshop* or *Fietspoint*. Cycle hire usually costs around €5.40 per day. Cycle hire shops also offer weekly tariffs that work out relatively cheaper. Many of them require a deposit, which can range from €30 to €145, and often

Sign for the Rijwiel cycle hire shop, found at nearly 100 railway stations

want proof of identity. Tandems are also sometimes available, though they cost more, and their lack of manoeuvrability does not make them very suitable for use in city traffic.

If you are planning to make a train journey and hire a cycle from your destination, it is worth buying a *huurfietskaartje* (cycle hire ticket) when setting out. It is a good idea to reserve the bicycle by telephone in advance.

The NS publishes a special pamphlet, *Fiets en Trein*, which lists stations where you can hire bicycles. The VVV and ANWB can also direct you to cycle hire shops.

SECURITY

EVEN IF your bicycle is equipped with a rear-wheel lock, it's a good idea – particularly in the big cities – to secure your bicycle to a post or a bicycle rack by the front wheel. Cycle hire shops will often provide you with a lock for the bike, especially in cities where bicycle theft is a problem. At many railway stations you can leave your bicycle in a secure bicycle-park for around €1.00. Do not leave any luggage on your bicycle if you park it somewhere, not even in a guarded bicycle park.

BICYCLES AND PUBLIC TRANSPORT

FOR AN ADDITIONAL payment you can take your bicycle on the train, except during rush hours (Sep–Jun: 6:30–9am and 4:30–6pm Mon–Fri). To do this, you need to buy a *Dagkaart fiets* in addition to your ordinary train ticket. These tickets cost €6.00 and are valid for the whole day regardless of the length of your journey. Places for bicycles on trains are marked with stickers on the carriage. Folding cycles, when folded, may be taken on trains free of charge. Bicycles may be taken on metros and suburban (fast) trams, for which you need to stamp a section on a pink *strippenkaart*, but they are not allowed on buses and city trams.

An organized cycling tour on the Zaanse Schans

CYCLING TOURS

If you want to get from point A to point B by the quickest possible route, just follow the white-and-red ANWB cycle route signposts. Maps and guides for cyclists describing routes of various lengths are available from the VVV, the ANWB and many bookstores. They often contain a variety of local background information, as well as the addresses of cycle hire shops and places to stay, such as *pensions*, camping sites and hiking huts *(see also p389)*. Useful examples are the regional *ANWB/VVV Toeristenkaarten*, which suggest some particularly enjoyable routes, and the *Dwarsstap-fiets-mappen*, which give descriptions of cycle routes, often in the area surrounding big cities, and also contain topographical maps. The regional *ANWB/VVV-fietsgiden* have maps and provide descriptions of hundreds of enjoyable cycling trips of around 25 km (15 miles), from the *Amelandroute* to the *Maasdalroute* in Limburg. Many of these routes are marked with hexagonal signs. Around 45 railway-based routes are also offered under the name *NS-Fietstocht*. Maps of the route are on sale at the relevant railway stations. NS publishes a booklet, entitled *Er op Uit!*, describing these routes. Long-distance tours of at least

Cyclists on tour stopping to enjoy an ice cream

200 km (125 miles) in length (for example, the 230-km/143-mile *Elfstedenroute* in Friesland) are described in guides such as the *ANWB/VVV Lange Fiestronde*. These routes are also signposted. Another organization, the **Stichting Landelijk Fiets-platform**, or national cycling association *(see p445)*, has a network of some 6,000 km (3,730 miles) of numbered National Cycle Routes (*Landelijke Fiestroutes*, or *"LF"*). These often follow quiet byroads and cycle tracks and are described in two of the *LF-busisgidsen*. Some are marked with square signs, such as LF-15, which is the *Boerenlandroute* (farmland route) from Alkmaar to Enschede. Guides to individual routes are also available. The *Fietsideeënkaart,* a map available from the VVV and ANWB, also provides brief descriptions of LF and other

Cycle lane sign

marked cycling routes around the country. To take part in an organized cycle tour, contact organizations such as **Cycletours** or the **Fiets-vakantiewinkel** *(see p445)*, some of the main VVV offices and the ANWB (members only). These organizations can arrange cycle tour packages, including accommodation and luggage transfer. For information on cycling in nature reserve areas, see page 445.

CYCLING EVENTS

National cycling Day (Landelijke Fiestdag) is held in Holland every year on the second Saturday in May. It is estimated that approximately 200,000 cyclists cover fixed routes of around 35 km (22 miles). Again, descriptions of the routes are available from the VVV or ANWB, and on the day itself at the starting points of the route. Local cycle touring clubs organize regular non-competitive tours through picturesque or interesting areas, although you have to pay a fee to join. For further information, apply at the Dutch cycle tour society (Nederlandse Toer Fiets Unie, or **NFTU**, *see p445*). Dozens of local tours lasting several days are organized locally, such as the *Drense Reijwiel-vierdaagse* in July. Participants can often choose between routes of lengths varying from 25 to 100 km (15 to 60 miles) per day. You will find an overview of these in the NFTU pamphlet *Fiestmeerdaagsen* which is available from the VVV.

The ferry at Wijk near Duurstede, which carries bicycles

Index

Acknowledgments

DORLING KINDERSLEY would like to thank the following people for their help in preparing this guide:

FOR DORLING KINDERSLEY
TRANSLATION FROM DUTCH Mark Cole (Linguists for Business)
DESIGN AND EDITORIAL ASSISTANCE Jo Cowen, Jacky Jackson, Ian Midson, Conrad van Dyke, Stewart Wild
DTP DESIGNERS Jason Little, Conrad van Dyke
MANAGING EDITOR Helen Townsend
PUBLISHING MANAGER Jane Ewart

FOR INTERNATIONAL BOOK PRODUCTIONS
PROOFREADER Maraya Radhua

MAIN AUTHOR
Gerard ML Harmans graduated in biology and philosophy at the Vrije Universiteit (Amsterdam), and then chose to work in publishing. He edited an encyclopaedia for Het Spectrum before setting up an independent business with Paul Krijnen in 1989 called *de Redactie*, boekverzorgers.

OTHER CONTRIBUTORS
All contributors were selected from *de Redactie*, boekverzorgers in Amsterdam. The team of authors, translators and editors share a broad field of expertise. Every member of the team made an invaluable contribution.

Anneliet Bannier graduated in translation studies from Amsterdam University. She works as a translator and sub-editor on travel guides. She lives in Zaanstreek.

Hanneke Bos is an editor and translator in the fields of linguistics, cultural history and travel literature.

Jaap Deinema, from Eindhoven, is an expert in the field of the Netherlands. He has made numerous contributions to travel guides. He was responsible for the ATO/VVV edition *Infopocket Amsterdam*.

Jérôme Gommers, born in Paris, is a freelance author and lover of the Dutch landscape and its poetry. Among other things, he has conducted a comprehensive study of the construction and development of the Noordoostpolder.

Ron de Heer studied philosophy in Amsterdam. For ten years he has been working as a translator/editor, primarily of travel guides, novels and culinary publications.

Marten van de Kraats writes and translates texts in the fields of travel and automation. Every year he edits the Dutch edition of the Rough Guide Travels on the internet, the best-selling internet book on Holland and Belgium.

Paul Krijnen is a social geographer who has specialized in medieval mark organizations of the Netherlands, such as the Erfgooiers. His great passion is the Dutch borderlands.

Frans Reusink studied Dutch language. After working as a copywriter, he has been active as a photographer, written travel reports for magazines, and edited travel guides.

Theo Scholten is a Dutch scholar. He has worked on many literary publications but is currently active in non-fiction as an editor and translator. He has made previous contributions to travel guides on Belgium and France.

Ernst Schreuder, a Frisian editor, won the Elfsteden Cross for completing the Tocht der Tochten in 1986 and 1997. Travel and travel guides are his occupation and his hobby.

Catherine Smit studied Dutch language and letters at Utrecht and has contributed as editor and translator to many books, including travel guides.

Jacqueline Toscani graduated in European Studies from Amsterdam University. Since 1992 she has been working as an editor and translator of travel guides, including many titles from the Capitool and Marco Polo series. In the latest series she was co-author of the *Vakantieplanner (holiday planner)*.

Willemien Werkman is a historian and, after studying the history of the Vecht estates, has devoted herself to translation and editing.

ADDITIONAL CONTRIBUTORS
Paul Andrews, Hedda Archbold, Christopher Catling, Jaap Deinema, Marlene Edmunds, Adam Hopkins, Marten van de Kraats, David Lindsey, Fred Mawer, Alison Melvin, Robin Pascoe, Catherine Stebbings, Richard Widdows, Stewart Wild. Other contributions were taken from the *Eyewitness Travel Guide Amsterdam* by Robin Pascoe and Christopher Catling, which previously appeared in a translated and revised edition *(Capitool Reisgids Amsterdam)* published by *de Redactie*, boekverzorgers.

ADDITIONAL ILLUSTRATIONS
Peter de Vries, Mark Jurriëns, Hilbert Bolland, Gieb van Enckevort, Armand Haye and Stuart Commercial Artists: Jan Egas and Khoobie Verwer.

EDITORIAL AND DESIGN ASSISTANCE
Ron Putto, Erna de Voos, Willeke Vrij, Martine Hauwert, Peter Koomen, Pascal Veeger, Willem Gerritze, Martine Wiedemeijer, Inge Tijsmans, Frank Bontekoning, Lucinda Cooke, Sylvia Tombesi-Walton, Sadie Smith.

PICTURE RESEARCH
Harry Bunk; Corine Koolstra; Dick Polman; *de Redactie*, boekverzorgers.

SPECIAL ASSISTANCE
John Bekker; Wim ten Brinke; Bert Erwich; Niek Harmans; Frits Gommers; Hans Hoogendoorn; Cathelijne Hornstra; Petra van Hulsen; Frank Jacobs; Chris de Jong; Nina Krijnen; Mies Kuiper; Louise Lang; Frank van Lier; Bas de Melker; Miek Reusink; Dick Rog; Joske Siemons; Erika Teeuwisse; Wout Vuyk, Douglas Amrine.

PICTURE CREDITS
t = top; tl = top left; tlc = top left centre; tc = top centre; tr = top right; trc = top right centre; c = centre; cl = centre left; cla = centre left above; clb = centre left below; ca = centre above; cr = centre right; cra = centre right above; crb = centre right below; bc = bottom centre; b = bottom; bl = bottom left; br = bottom right.

Every effort has been made to trace the copyright holders. Dorling Kindersley apologizes for any unintentional omissions and would be pleased, in such cases, to add an acknowledgment in future editions.

B&U International Picture Service: 101bl, 105br, 161bl, 210cl; Aart de Bakker: 347t, 347br, 368tr, 371t, 371cr, 374tr, 422cla; Bonnefantenmuseum, Maastricht: 372tl, 372tr, 372cl, 372bl, © Rene Daniels *Platte Gronden*, 1986, 1999 c/o Beeldrecht Amstelveen 372br; 373tl, 373cra, 373bl, 373br; Boijmans-van Beuningen Museum, Rotterdam: 232cl; Henk Bransden: 45bc, 304cla, 305tl, 305tr, 305ca; Bridgeman Art Library: Christie's London, *Grote Markt, Haarlem*, Gerrit Berkheyde 182l; Stapleton Collection 19th-century Delft tile 224tl; Private collection *Self-portrait* © Kazimir Malevitch 129br; Quinta Buma: 34t; Harry Bunk: 22bl, 33cl, 69tr, 138clb, 139rb, 139cr, 143tl, 146t, 200b, © Ossip Zadkine *De verwoeste stad* 1947, 1999 c/o Beeldrecht Amstelveen 228cl; 229cra, 229crb, 229bc, 230tl, 235cr, © Mari Andriessen *Cornelius Lely*, 1983, 1999 c/o Beeldrecht Amstelveen 324bc; 405lb, 422t, 423bl, 440c, 442c; Cees Buys: 19tl, 47ca, 188c, 242bc, 278clb, 281c, 285b, 297c, 300, 302cla, 307tl, 313cr, 315t, 318tl, 319tr, 319bl, 323tr, 323cr, 337br, 365b, 379ca, 379crb, 386clb, 435tl; George Burggraaff: 1, 14t, 17bl, 26tr, 32cr, 32clb, 42cl, 164tr, 166tr, 166cla, 187tl, 195ca, 198cla, 214tr, 235tl, 244tr, 244br, 247crb, 252tr, 253tr, 253br, 256cr, 258clb, 259cra, 259br, 276br, 279tr, 295cr, 299cl, 312cl, 315br, 316ca, 316cl, 317cr, 317crb, 323br, 331bl, 334br, 341cl, 341tr, 343br, 351tl, 351tr, 356br, 359ca, 434bl, 443bl.

Catharijneconvent, Utrecht: 45cra, 46tl, 50bl, 52tr, 199cra, 349tl; Centraal Museum, Utrecht: 202tl, 202cla, 203tl, 203tr, 203br; Cleveland Museum, Cleveland: 50/51c; Cobra Museum, Amstelveen: © Karel Appel Foundation, Karel Appel *Questioning Children* 1949, 1999 c/o Beeldrecht Amstelveen 187br.

DAF Museum, Eindhoven: 23c; Jan Derwig: 99tr, 141b; Jurjen Drenth: 2/3, 12, 26cla, 28/29c, 30lb, 30/31c, 32ca, 35bl, 43crb, 53bl, 60/61, 67tr, 68tr, 68cla, 68bl, 68br, 69cra, 69cr, 74b, 79bl, 86tr, 108tr, 116, 118tr, 118tr, 384br, 405c, 136clb, © Hildo Krop *Berlage*, 1999 c/o Beeldrecht Amstelveen 142bl; 144cl, 145cr, 146cr, 147tr, 158/159, 161 tr, 164cl, 164/165c, 167br, 168, 169b, 171cr, 172bl, 190, 191b, 192clb, 194bl, 195b, 196cl, 196br, 197br, 198bc, 199bc, 201tl, 201br, 206, 207b, 208cla, 208clb, 209bl, 212clb, 217crb, © Peter Struycken *Lichtkunstwerk NAi* 1994, 1999 c/o Beeldrecht Amstelveen 231t; 234tr, 235tr, 235br, 238ca, 241b, 242tl, 244bc, 245bc, 247tl, 250tl, 250cr, 254/255, 257crb, 261bl, 262, 264tr, 264br, 265tl, 265br, 268/269c, 270cra, 273br, 274/275, 275b, 280b, 282tr, 282clb, 284tr, 285tr, 288, 290tr, 290br, 295ca, 297tr, 302b, 303cr, 305cra, 308bl, 310, 311b, 318br, 321b, 322tl, 322clb, 328, 336cla, 339tl, 343tl, 346tr, 350tl, 350cl, 350bl, 351cr, 351ca, 352, 353b, 356tl, 356c, 360tr, 361tr, 362c, 363bc, 367cr, 369c, 370bl, 374cr, 378br, 380/381, 384tl, 385tr, 388tr, 404cl, 430/431, 438tl, 440cra, 440bl, 442tr; Drents Museum, Assen: 42br, 306tl, 306cr, *Badende kinderen bij stroompje* c.1935 © von Duelman-Krumpelmann 307br, 309br; DRO-VORM: Mirande Phernambucq 142cla, 143br.

Robert Eckhardt: 286bl, 366c; Joop van de Ende Producties: 426br; Escher in Het Paleis, The Hague: 216cla; Mary Evans Picture Library: 40bc.

Gert Fopma: 269br, 271bl; Foto Natura: 162bl (B van Biezen), 289b (J Vermeer), 307tr and 308t (F de Nooyer), 326t (J Sleurink); Frans Hals Museum, Haarlem: 65tc, 184t, 184cl, 184br, 185tl, 185tr, 185br, 185bl; Fries Museum, Leeuwarden: 44tl.

Gemeentearchief Amsterdam: 99tl, 99cl, 100clb, 101br, 102bl, 103tr, 103cr, 104tr, 105tr, 105cr; Gemeentemuseum, The Hague: © Piet Mondrian/Holtzman Trust *Victory Boogie-Woogie* (unfinished), 1942-44, 1999 c/o Beeldrecht Amstelveen 222cl; Carel van Gestel: 28tl, 28cl, 28bl, 28br,

29ca, 29tr, 29bl; Groninger Museum, Groningen: 257tr, 282tl, 282cla, 282bc, 282br, 283tl, 283tr, 283bl.

Tom Haartsen, J Holtkamp collection: 26br, 26/27c; Vanessa Hamilton: 101c; Robert Harding Picture Library: 10bl; Martine Hauwert: 441tl; Jan den Hengst: 3c, 91br; Hollandse Hoogte: 301b, 426t, 427tr, 427b; P. Babeliowsky 293tl, 293cra; B. van Flymen 32br, 298cra, 298bl; M. Kooren 14bl, 16tl, 33c, 34cr, 35tr, 41cro, 41br, 59bc; M. Pellanders 59br, G. Wortel 277tl, 292c, 293br; Hortus Botanicus, Leiden: 212cla; Hulton Getty Collection: 66t.

Iconografisch Bureau: 103tl; Internationaal Bloembollencentrum: 31cr, 210br, 211tl, 211clb, 211cl, 211clo, 211bl; Internationaal Instituut voor Sociale Geschiedenis, Amsterdam: 55crb.

Wim Janszen: 256cl, 260cl, 264cl; Wubbe de Jong: 59clb, 109tl; Joods Historisch Museum, Amsterdam: 67br; Jopie Huisman Museum, Workum: 296cla.

Hugo Kaagman: © Hugo Kaagman *Delft blue plane-tail decoration* 1996-1997, 1999 c/o Beeldrecht Amstelveen 27tr; Anne Kalkhoven: 281bl, 309tr, 342tl; Jan van de Kam: 15b, 37tr, 37cra, 37crb, 37br, 167tr, 167cra, 167crb, 258tl, 258cl, 258bc, 259tr, 259cr, 260tl, 260cla, 260cra, 260br, 260bl, 261tl, 261tlc, 261trc, 261tr, 261crb, 261cro, 261br, 266tl, 266tr, 267tl, 267tc, 267tr, 267cra, 267crb, 267bc, 267clb, 267bl, 267br, 268tl, 268tr, 268bl, 268br, 269ca, 269cra, 271tr, 272br, 276cl, 291tr, 312b, 321, 326c, 326br, 330br, 331crb, 340tl, 344/345, 346br, 348tr, 348cla, 348clb, 348br, 348/349c, 349tr, 349cr, 349bl, 355ca, 356tr, 356cla, 357ca, 357cr, 358clb, 363cl, 366cla, 367tr, 369bl, 370tl, © Joep Nicolas, *Pieke* 1995-1996, 1999 c/o Beeldrecht Amstelveen 370tr; 370cla, 370br, 371br, © Mari Andriessen *Maastreechter Gees* 1961-1962, 1999 c/o Beeldrecht Amstelveen 374tl; 374bl, 375cl, 376bl, 377cr, 378tr, 378cla, 378crb, 379bc; Koninklijke Bibliotheek, The Hague: 52cl; Koninklijk Concertgebouworkest/Marco Borggreve: 147c; Koninklijk Instituut voor de Tropen, Amsterdam: 56tr, 56/57c; Koninklijk Paleis, Amsterdam/RVD: 65cr, 88cla, 88clb, 89tr, 89crb; Corine Koolstra: © Suze Boschma-Berkhout *Bartje*, 1999 c/o Beeldrecht Amstelveen 306cl; Peter Koomen: 176tr; René Krekels, Nijmegen: 19crb; Kröller-Müller Museum, Otterlo: © Jean Dubuffet *Jardin d'Émail* 1973-4, 1999 c/o Beeldrecht Amstelveen 336tr; 336br, 337c.

Andries de la Lande Cremer: 263b, 276tr; Leeuwarder Courant: Niels Westra 292bl; Frans Lemmens: 30c, 320, 389tr; Claude Lévesque: 350/351c.

Mauritshuis, The Hague: 8/9, 220tr, 220c, 220bl, 221tc, 221crb, 221cro, 221co, 225tl; Arnold Meine Jansen: 240, 406br, 407ca; Multatuli Museum, Amsterdam: 57tr; Musée de la Chartreuse, Douai: 50clb; Museum Boerhaave, Leiden: 50bc, 51tl, 51clb; Museum Boijmans-van Beuningen, Rotterdam: © Aristide Maillol *La Méditerranée* 1905, 1999 c/o Beeldrecht Amstelveen 232tr; 232cl, 232br, © Constant *Mother and Child*, 1951, 1999 c/o Beeldrecht Amstelveen 233tl; 233ca, 233cr, 233br; Museum Bredius, The Hague: 218bl; Museum Lambert van Meerten, Delft: 227tr; Museum Kempenland, Eindhoven: 362c; Museum Nairac, Barneveld: 335br; Museum Het Rembrandthuis, Amsterdam: 73bc, 78br; Museum Schokland: 324tr, 324cra.

National Gallery, London: 239tr; Wick Natzijl: 406/407; Nederlands Architectuur Instituut: 105cl, 142/143c; Nederlands Scheepvaartmuseum, Amsterdam: 48tl, 65bc, 132tl; Niedersächsische Staats- und Universitätsbibliothek, Göttingen: 44/45c; Flip de Nooyer: 266/267c; North Sea Jazz Festival/Rob Drexhage: 33br.

Onze-Lieve-Vrouwebasiliek, Maastricht: 375tr.

PALEIS HET LOO, NATIONAAL MUSEUM, APELDOORN: E. Boeijinga 332tr; A. Meine Jansen 332cla, 333tl, 332bl; R. Mulder 332cla; DE PAVILJOENS, ALMERE: © Robert Morris *Observatorium*, 1977, 1999 c/o Beeldrecht Amstelveen 327br; PAUL PARIS: 20tr, 22cl, 23tr, 66br, 67bl, 70, 166/167c, 167tl, 188br, 192tr, 243br, 251br, 261cl, 266cla, 277cra, 280tr, 284clb, 286tr, 291br, 297br, 299br, 303tr, 304clb, 305br, 313tr, 329b, 346bl, 366tr; DICK POLMAN: 264tl, 272c; ROBERT POUTSMA: 16bl, 67tl, 142tr, 142br, 143tr, 143cr, 144cr, 144br, 160cl, 173tl, 274, 338ccr, 382ca, 422br, 423tl, 424c; PROJECTBUREAU IJBURG: 165t; PTT MUSEUM, THE HAGUE: 50tl.

RANGE PICTURES: 48cla; HERMAN REIS: 15c, 16c, 17tr, 21cl, 23crb, 52bl, 209br, 234b, 235tr, 268cla, 270br, 309cl, 317bl, 435bc; RIJKSMUSEUM, AMSTERDAM: 24tr, 24cl, 24bl, 24/25c, 25tr, 25cr, 25bl, 38, 40tr, 53t, 53crb, 57tl, 64cla, 66c, 122cl, 122bc, 123t, 123c, 123br, 124tr, 124bl, 125tr, 125b, 193bl; RIJKSMUSEUM MUIDERSLOT, MUIDEN: 51cr; RIJKSMUSEUM VAN OUDHEDEN, LEIDEN: 42tl, 42clb, 43t, 43bc, 44bc, 44crb, 212ca; RIJKSMUSEUM VOOR VOLKENKUNDE, LEIDEN: 56bl, 57crb; RIJKSWATERSTAAT: 244clb, 245tl, 245cr, 270tl; MARNIX RUEB: 218tl.

HERMAN SCHOLTEN: 21bl, 170l, 173bl, 176tl, 178ca, 188tl, 193t, 197tr, 200cla, 204tr, 219b, 229tc, 238b, 244cla, 246tl, 246tr, 246cl, 247cra, 252c, 252bl, 256b, 278cla, 278b, 279br, 281tr, 290cl, 294tr, 294cl, 322tr, 322c, 331br, 354cla, 355tr, 371bc, 376tl; SCHOOLMUSEUM, ROTTERDAM/WOLTERS-NOORDHOFF, GRONINGEN: 46/47c, 49tl, 54/55c; SINGER MUSEUM: Particuliere Collection 189bl; SINT-JAN, DEN BOSCH: E Van Mackelenbergh 358cla, 358bc, 359tl; SPAARNESTAD FOTOARCHIEF: 55tr, 57b, 58clb, 58br, 59cla, 99bc, 143bl; SPOORWEGMUSEUM, UTRECHT: 199crb; SPL: Earth Satellite Corporation 10cl; STEDELIJK MUSEUM, AMSTERDAM: © Gerrit Rietveld *Steltman chair* 1963, 1999 c/o Beeldrecht Amstelveen 66bl; 128tr, © Marc Chagall *Portrait of the Artist with Seven Fingers* 1912, 1999 c/o Beeldrecht Amstelveen 128cla; © Gerrit Rietveld *Red Blue Chair* c.1918, 1999 c/o Beeldrecht Amstelveen 128bl; © Piet Mondrian/Holtzman Trust *Composition in Red, Black, Blue, Yellow and Grey* 1920, 1999 c/o Beeldrecht Amstelveen 128br; 129tl, © Karel Appel Foundation *Man and Animals* 1949, 1999 c/o Beeldrecht Amstelveen 129ca; © Jasper Johns *Untitled* 1965, 1999 c/o Beeldrecht Amstelveen 129bc; 129br, *Tanzende* 1911 © Ernst Ludwig Kirchner 129tl; STEDELIJK MUSEUM DE LAKENHAL, LEIDEN: 46cl,

104br, 214b; STEDELIJK MUSEUM, ZWOLLE: 314tr; STICHTING LEIDENS ONTZET: 35tl; STICHTING PAARDENREDDINGBOOT AMELAND: 273t; STICHTING VESTING BOURTANGE: 287tr; STICHTING4-STROMENLAND, TIEL: 34bl; STICHTING DE KOEPEL, UTRECHT: 23tl; STUDIO PUTTO, DERIJP: 14bl, 16c, 22tl, 23bl, 30/31b, 33tr, 41bl, 41crb, 44br, 84tr, 113bl, 171tr, 171cr; RONALD SWEERING, AMSTERDAM: 23br; STUDIOPRESS: Guy van Grinsven 172tr; 442tr; 442br.

TELFORT: 442bc; TONY STONE IMAGES: 100tr, 177cla, 211tl; SVEN TORFINN: 357tl, 357br; TPG NEDERLAND: 442crb, 443cra, 443c; HANS TULLENERS: 99cr, 100cr, 102c.

VAN GOGH MUSEUM, AMSTERDAM: 126cla, 126clb, 127t, 127tr, 127cr; GERARD OP HET VELD: 30tr, 142c, 296tr, 334cr, 339bl, 340br, 354bc, 363tr, 366bl, 367br, 369tr, 377tr, 377bl; 383b; VERENIGING DE FRIESCHE ELF STEDEN 292rb; GOVERT VETTEN: 15tr, 56tl, 68cl, 69bl, 81br, 120clb, 142/143c, 193br, 194t, 258cla, 383b, 422c, 434br; VOLKSKRANT: Wim Ruigrok 18tr; SIETSKE DE VRIES, AMSTERDAM: 30cl; WILLEKE VRIJ: 31tr.

WACON-IMAGES/RONALD DENDEKKER: 147cl; PIM WESTERWEEL: 160cr, 161cr, 162crb, 193cra, 257cra, 257b, 260clb, 327tr, 339cr, 347cr, 360bl; WEST-FRIES MUSEUM, HOORN: 56cla; WL/DELFT HYDRAULICS: 162br.

ZEEUWS MUSEUM, MIDDELBURG: 248tl, 248bc, 248crb; ZUIDERZEEMUSEUM, ENKHUIZEN: 163tr.

FRONT ENDPAPER LEFT: JURJEN DRENTH tl, tc, tr, cl, bl, br; JAN VAN DER KAM cr; ARNOLD MEINE JANSEN bc.

FRONT ENDPAPER RIGHT: ANWB AUDIOVISUELE DIENST bc; CEES BUYS cra; JURJEN DRENTH c, br; ROBERT POUTSMA tr.

JACKET
FRONT - DK PICTURE LIBRARY: cl, b; Steve Gorton cr; GETTY IMAGES: Ken Ross main image. BACK - DK PICTURE LIBRARY: b, t. SPINE - GETTY IMAGES: Ken Ross.

All other images © Dorling Kindersley. For further information see: www.dkimages.com

DORLING KINDERSLEY SPECIAL EDITIONS

Dorling Kindersley books can be purchased in bulk quantities at discounted prices for use in promotions or as premiums. We are also able to offer special editions and personalized jackets, corporate imprints, and excerpts from all of our books, tailored specifically to meet your own needs.

To find out more, please contact: (in the United Kingdom) – Sarah.Burgess@dk.com or SPECIAL SALES, DORLING KINDERSLEY, 80 STRAND, LONDON WC2R 0RL;

(in the United States) – SPECIAL MARKETS DEPARTMENT, DK PUBLISHING, INC., 375 HUDSON STREET, NEW YORK, NY 10014.

Phrase Book

In Emergency

Help!	**Help!**	Help
Stop!	**Stop!**	Stop
Call a doctor	**Haal een dokter**	Haal uhn **dok**-tur
Call an ambulance	**Bel een ambulance**	Bell uhn ahm-bew-**luhns**-uh
Call the police	**Roep de politie**	Roop duh poe-**leet**-see
Call the fire brigade	**Roep de brandweer**	Roop duh **brahnt**-vheer
Where is the nearest telephone?	**Waar is de dichtstbijzijnde telefoon?**	Vhaar iss duh **dikhst**-baiy-zaiyn-duh tay-luh-**foan**
Where is the nearest hospital?	**Waar is het dichtstbijzijnde ziekenhuis?**	Vhaar iss het **dikhst**-baiy-zaiyn-duh **zee**-kuh-houws

Communication Essentials

Yes	**Ja**	Yaa
No	**Nee**	Nay
Please	**Alstublieft**	Ahls-tew-**bleeft**
Thank you	**Dank u**	Dahnk-ew
Excuse me	**Pardon**	Pahr-**don**
Hello	**Hallo**	Hallo
Goodbye	**Dag**	Dahgh
Good night	**Slaap lekker**	Slaap **lek**-kah
morning	**Morgen**	**Mor**-ghuh
afternoon	**Middag**	**Mid**-dahgh
evening	**Avond**	**Ah**-vohnd
yesterday	**Gisteren**	**Ghis**-tern
today	**Vandaag**	Vahn-**daagh**
tomorrow	**Morgen**	**Mor**-ghuh
here	**Hier**	Heer
there	**Daar**	Daar
What?	**Wat?**	Vhat
When?	**Wanneer?**	Vhan-**eer**
Why?	**Waarom?**	Vhaar-**om**
Where?	**Waar?**	Vhaar
How?	**Hoe?**	Hoo

Useful Phrases

How are you?	**Hoe gaat het ermee?**	Hoo ghaat het er-**may**
Very well, thank you	**Heel goed, dank u**	Hayl ghoot, dahnk ew
How do you do?	**Hoe maakt u het?**	Hoo maakt ew het
See you soon	**Tot ziens**	Tot zeens
That's fine	**Prima**	**Pree**-mah
Where is/are?	**Waar is/zijn?**	Vhaar iss/zayn...
How far is it to...?	**Hoe ver is het naar...?**	Hoo vehr iss het naar...
How do I get to...?	**Hoe kom ik naar...?**	Hoo kom ik naar...
Do you speak English?	**Spreekt u engels?**	Spraykt ew **eng**-uhls
I don't understand	**Ik snap het niet**	Ik snahp het neet
Could you speak slowly?	**Kunt u langzamer praten?**	Kuhnt ew **lahng**-zahmer praa-tuh
I'm sorry	**Sorry**	Sorry

Useful Words

big	**groot**	ghroaht
small	**klein**	klaiyn
hot	**warm**	vharm
cold	**koud**	khowt
good	**goed**	ghoot
bad	**slecht**	slekht
enough	**genoeg**	ghuh-**noohkh**
well	**goed**	ghoot
open	**open**	open
closed	**gesloten**	ghuh-**slow**-tuh
left	**links**	links
right	**rechts**	rekhts
straight on	**rechtdoor**	rehkht dohr
near	**dichtbij**	dikht baiy
far	**ver weg**	vehr vhekh
up	**omhoog**	om-**hoakh**
down	**naar beneden**	naar buh-**nay**-duh
early	**vroeg**	vrookh
late	**laat**	laat
entrance	**ingang**	**in**-ghahng
exit	**uitgang**	**ouht**-ghang
toilet	**wc**	vhay say
occupied	**bezet**	buh-**zett**
free (unoccupied)	**vrij**	vraiy
free (no charge)	**gratis**	**ghraah**-tiss

Making a Telephone Call

I'd like to place a long-distance call	**Ik wil graag interlokaal telefoneren**	Ik vhil ghraakh **inter**-loh-kaahl tay-luh-foe-**neh**-ruh
I'd like to call collect	**Ik wil "collect call" bellen**	Ik vhil "collect call" **bel**-luh
I'll try again later	**Ik probeer het later nog wel eens**	Ik pro-**beer** het laater nokh vhel ayns
Can I leave a message?	**Kunt u een boodschap doorgeven?**	Kuhnt ew uhn **boat**-skhahp **dohr**-ghay-vuh
Could you speak up a little please?	**Wilt u wat harder praten?**	Vhilt ew vhat **hahr**-der **praah**-tuh
Local call	**Lokaal gesprek**	Low-**kaahl** ghuh-**sprek**

Shopping

How much does this cost?	**Hoeveel kost dit?**	Hoo-**vayl** kost dit
I would like	**Ik wil graag**	Ik vhil ghraakh
Do you have...?	**Heeft u...?**	Hayft ew...
I'm just looking	**Ik kijk alleen even**	Ik kaiyk alleyn **ay**-vuh
Do you take credit cards?	**Neemt u credit cards?**	Naymt ew credit cards aan
Do you take traveller's cheques?	**Neemt u reischeques aan?**	Naymt ew **raiys**-sheks aan
What time do you open?	**Hoe laat gaat u open?**	Hoo laat ghaat ew opuh
What time do you close?	**Hoe laat gaat u dicht?**	Hoo laat ghaat ew dikht
This one	**Deze**	**Day**-zuh
That one	**Die**	Dee
expensive	**duur**	dewr
cheap	**goedkoop**	ghoot-**koap**
size	**maat**	maat
white	**wit**	vhit
black	**zwart**	zvhahrt
red	**rood**	roat
yellow	**geel**	ghayl
green	**groen**	ghroon
blue	**blauw**	blah-ew

Types of Shops

antique shop	**antiekwinkel**	ahn-**teek**-vhin-kul
bakery	**bakker**	**bah**-ker
bank	**bank**	bahnk
bookshop	**boekwinkel**	**book**-vhin-kul
butcher	**slager**	slaakh-er
cake shop	**banketbakkerij**	bahnk-**et**-bahk-er-aiy
cheese shop	**kaaswinkel**	**kaas**-vhin-kul
chip shop	**patatzaak**	pah-**taht**-zaak
chemist (dispensing)	**apotheek**	ah-poe-**taiyk**
delicatessen	**delicatessen**	daylee-kah-**tes**-suh
department store	**warenhuis**	**vhaar**-uh-houws
fishmonger	**viswinkel**	**viss**-vhin-kul
greengrocer	**groenteboer**	**ghroon**-tuh-boor
hairdresser	**kapper**	**kah**-per
market	**markt**	mahrkt
newsagent	**krantenwinkel**	**krahn**-tuh-vhin-kul
post office	**postkantoor**	**pohst**-kahn-toar
shoe shop	**schoenenwinkel**	**sghoo**-nuh-vhin-kul
supermarket	**supermarkt**	**sew**-per-mahrkt
tobacconist	**sigarenwinkel**	see-**ghaa**-ruh-vhin-kul
travel agent	**reisburo**	**raiys**-bew-roa

Sightseeing

art gallery	**gallerie**	ghaller-ee
bus station	**busstation**	**buhs**-stah-shown
bus ticket	**strippenkaart**	**strip**-puh-kaahrt
cathedral	**kathedraal**	kah-tuh-**draal**
church	**kerk**	kehrk
closed on public holidays	**op feestdagen gesloten**	op **fayst**-daa-ghuh ghuh-**slow**-tuh
day return	**dagretour**	**dahgh**-ruh-tour
garden	**tuin**	touwn
library	**bibliotheek**	bee-bee-yo-**tayk**
museum	**museum**	mew-**zay**-uhm
railway station	**station**	stah-**shown**
return ticket	**retourtje**	ruh-**tour**-tyuh
single journey	**enkeltje**	**eng**-kuhl-tyuh
tourist information	**VVV**	fay fay fay
town hall	**stadhuis**	staht-**houws**
train	**trein**	traiyn

STAYING IN A HOTEL

Do you have a vacant room?	**Zijn er nog kamers vrij?**	Zaïyn er nokh **kaamers** vray
double room with double bed	**een twees persoonskamer met een twee persoonsbed**	uhn **tvhay**-per soans-kaa-mer met uhn **tvhay**-per-soans beht
twin room	**een kamer met een lits-jumeaux**	uhn **kaa-mer** met uhn lee-zjoo-**moh**
single room	**eenpersoonskamer**	ayn-per-**soans-kaamer**
room with a bath	**kamer met bad**	**kaa-mer** met baht
shower	**douche**	doosh
porter	**kruier**	**krouw**-yuh
I have a reservation	**Ik heb gereserveerd**	Ik hehp ghuh-ray-sehr-**veert**

EATING OUT

Have you got a table?	**Is er een tafel vrij?**	Iss ehr uhn **tah-fuhl** vraiy
I want to reserve a table	**Ik wil een tafel reserveren**	Ik vhil uhn **tah-fuhl** ray-sehr-**veer**-uh
The bill, please	**Mag ik afrekenen**	Mukh ik **ahf**-ray-kuh-nuh
I am a vegetarian	**Ik ben vegetariër**	Ik ben fay-ghuh-**taahr**-ee-er
waitress/waiter	**serveerster/ober**	Sehr-**veer**-ster/**oh**-ber
menu	**de kaart**	duh kaahrt
cover charge	**het couvert**	het koo-**vehr**
wine list	**de wijnkaart**	duh **vhaiyn**-kaart
glass	**het glas**	het ghlahss
bottle	**de fles**	duh fless
knife	**het mes**	het mess
fork	**de vork**	duh fork
spoon	**de lepel**	duh **lay**-pul
breakfast	**het ontbijt**	het ont-**baiyt**
lunch	**de lunch**	duh lernsh
dinner	**het diner**	het dee-**nay**
main course	**het hoofdgerecht**	het **hoaft**-ghuh-rekht
starter, first course	**het voorgerecht**	het **vohr**-ghuh-rekht
dessert	**het nagerecht**	het **naa**-ghuh-rekht
dish of the day	**het dagmenu**	het **dahgh**-munh-ew
bar	**het cafe**	het kaa-**fay**
café	**het eetcafe**	het **ayt**-kaa-**fay**
rare	**rare**	'rare'
medium	**medium**	'medium'
well done	**doorbakken**	dohr-**bah**-kuh

MENU DECODER

aardappels	**aard**-uppuhls	potatoes
azijn	aah-**zaiyn**	vinegar
biefstuk	**beef**-stuhk	steak
bier, pils	beer, pilss	beer
boter	boater	butter
brood/broodje	broat/**broat**-yuh	bread/roll
cake, taart, gebak	"cake", taahrt, ghuh-**bahk**	cake, pastry
carbonade	kahr-bow-**naa**-duh	pork chop
chocola	show-coa-**laa**	chocolate
citroen	see-**troon**	lemon
cocktail	cocktail	cocktail
droog	droakh	dry
eend	aynt	duck
ei	aiy	egg
garnalen	ghahr-**naah**-luh	prawns
gebakken	ghuh-**bah**-ken	fried
gegrild	ghuh-**ghrillt**	grilled
gekookt	ghuh-**koakt**	boiled
gepocheerd	ghuh-posh-**eert**	poached
gerookt	ghuh-**roakt**	smoked
geroosterd brood	ghuh-**roas**-tert broat	toast
groenten	**ghroon**-tuh	vegetables
ham	hahm	ham
haring	**haa**-ring	herring
hutspot	huht-spot	hot pot
ijs	aiyss	ice, ice cream
jenever	yuh-**nay**-vhur	gin
kaas	kaas	cheese
kabeljauw	kah-buhl-**youw**	cod
kip	kip	chicken
knoflook	**knoff**-loak	garlic
koffie	coffee	coffee
kool, rode of witte	coal, **roe**-duh off **vhit**-uh	cabbage, red or white
kreeft	krayft	lobster
kroket	crow-**ket**	ragout in bread-crumbs, deep fried
lamsvlees	**lahms**-flayss	lamb

lekkerbekje	lek-kah-bek-yuh	fried fillet of haddock
mineraalwater	meener-**aahl**-vhaater	mineral water
mosterd	**moss**-tehrt	mustard
niet scherp	neet skehrp	mild
olie	**oh**-lee	oil
paling	**paa**-ling	eel
pannekoek	**pah**-nuh-kook	pancake
patat frites	pah-**taht** freet	chips
peper	**pay**-per	pepper
poffertjes	**poffer**-tyuhs	tiny buckwheat pancakes
rijst	raiyst	rice
rijsttafel	**raiys**-tah-ful	Indonesian meal
rode wijn	roe-duh vhaiyn	red wine
rookworst	**roak**-vhorst	smoked sausage
rundvlees	**ruhnt**-flayss	beef
saus	souwss	sauce
schaaldieren	**skaahl**-deeh-ruh	shellfish
scherp	skehrp	hot (spicy)
schol	sghol	plaice
soep	soup	soup
stamppot	**stahm**-pot	sausage stew
suiker	**souw**-ker	sugar
thee	tay	tea
tosti	**toss**-tee	cheese on toast
uien	**ouw**-yuh	onions
uitsmijter	**ouht**-smaiy-ter	fried egg on bread with ham
varkensvlees	**vahr**-kuhns-flayss	pork
vers fruit	fehrss frouwt	fresh fruit
verse jus	**vehr**-suh zjhew	fresh orange juice
vis	fiss	fish/seafood
vlees	flayss	meat
water	**vhaa**-ter	water
witte wijn	**vhih**-tuh vhaiyn	white wine
worst	vhorst	sausage
zout	zouwt	salt

NUMBERS

1	**een**	ayn
2	**twee**	tvhay
3	**drie**	dree
4	**vier**	feer
5	**vijf**	faiyf
6	**zes**	zess
7	**zeven**	**zay**-vuh
8	**acht**	ahkht
9	**negen**	**nay**-guh
10	**tien**	teen
11	**elf**	elf
12	**twaalf**	tvhaalf
13	**dertien**	**dehr**-teen
14	**veertien**	**feer**-teen
15	**vijftien**	**faiyf**-teen
16	**zestien**	**zess**-teen
17	**zeventien**	**zayvuh**-teen
18	**achtien**	**ahkh**-teen
19	**negentien**	**nay-ghuh**-teen
20	**twintig**	**tvhin**-tukh
21	**eenentwintig**	**aynuh**-tvhin-tukh
30	**dertig**	**dehr**-tukh
40	**veertig**	**feer**-tukh
50	**vijftig**	**faiyf**-tukh
60	**zestig**	**zess**-tukh
70	**zeventig**	**zay**-vuh-tukh
80	**tachtig**	**tahkh**-tukh
90	**negentig**	**nayguh**-tukh
100	**honderd**	**hohn**-durt
1000	**duizend**	**douw**-zuhnt
1,000,000	**miljoen**	mill-**yoon**

TIME

one minute	**een minuut**	uhn meen-**ewt**
one hour	**een uur**	uhn ewr
half an hour	**een half uur**	uhn hahlf ewr
half past one	**half twee**	hahlf tvhay
a day	**een dag**	uhn dahgh
a week	**een week**	uhn vhayk
a month	**een maand**	uhn maant
a year	**een jaar**	uhn jaar
Monday	**maandag**	**maan**-dahgh
Tuesday	**dinsdag**	**dins**-dahgh
Wednesday	**woensdag**	**vhoons**-dahgh
Thursday	**donderdag**	**donder**-dahgh
Friday	**vrijdag**	**vraiy**-dahgh
Saturday	**zaterdag**	**zaater**-dahgh
Sunday	**zondag**	**zon**-dahgh

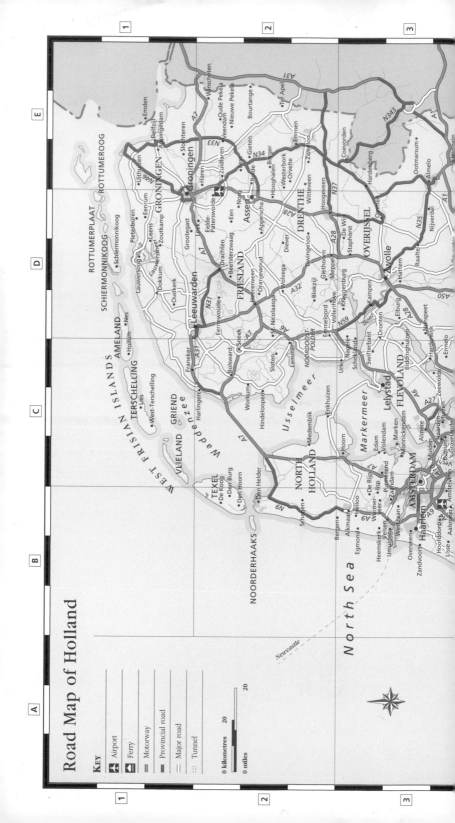